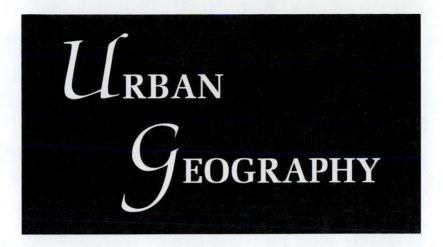

URBAN GEOGRAPHY

SECOND EDITION

DAVID KAPLAN

JAMES WHEELER

STEVEN HOLLOWAY

WILEY

JOHN WILEY & SONS, INC.

PUBLISHER	Jay O'Callaghan
EXECUTIVE EDITOR	Ryan Flahive
MARKETING MANAGER	Danielle Torio
CREATIVE DIRECTOR	Harry Nolan
ART DIRECTOR	Jeof Vita
SENIOR ILLUSTRATION EDITOR	Sandra Rigby
ASSOCIATE PHOTO EDITOR	Sheena Goldstein
SENIOR MEDIA EDITOR	Lynn Pearlman
SENIOR PRODUCTION EDITOR	Trish McFadden
ASSISTANT EDITOR	Courtney Nelson
PRODUCTION MANAGEMENT SERVICES	Katie Boilard/Pine Tree Composition, Inc.
COVER PHOTO	Ian Cumming/Getty Images

This book was set in 10/12 Times by Laserwords Private Limited, Chennai and printed and bound by RRD Crawfordsville. The cover was printed by Phoenix Color.

This book is printed on acid-free paper. ∞

To order books or for customer service please, call 1-800-CALL WILEY (225-5945).

ISBN-13: 978-0-471-79815-6

Printed in the United States of America.

10 9 8 7 6 5 4 3 2 1

PREFACE

This text is designed, organized, and written to serve students of Urban Geography, ranging from introductory students, including those at the junior and senior undergraduate level, to beginning graduate students. The book is self-contained.

Our objective has been to write a textbook that would uncover all of the excitement and richness found in cities, while tackling the wide variety of urban challenges. We offer a comprehensive treatment of urban geography, to include the most current research in urban studies, to introduce elements of urban theory and methodology, and to address the urban experience as a global one. This book is consciously oriented around particular topics, and it introduces some subjects not typically found within existing urban geography texts. We hope that the student reader will discover just how much cities matter—to urbanites and nonurbanites alike.

David H. Kaplan of Kent State University in Kent, Ohio, was primarily responsible for writing Chapters 2, 11, 12, 13, 14, 15, and 16. James O. Wheeler, University of Georgia in Athens, Georgia, drafted Chapters 1, 3, 4, 5, 6, and a part of Chapter 7. Steven R. Holloway, also at the University of Georgia, focused on Chapters 8, 9, and 10, as well as part of Chapter 7. We endeavored throughout this joint effort to make this a textbook that reflected our vision as a whole, so that the entire book is a product of all three authors.

The second edition of *Urban Geography* has benefited from comments from several outside reviewers, comments we have received from colleagues who have used the first edition, as well as our own evaluations. We thank all who have provided those many helpful suggestions.

We have undertaken both general and specific changes in this edition. First, data have been updated to include the most recent available. As much of the material is based on the U.S. urban experience, we utilized the 2000 Bureau of the Census figures or subsequent Census estimates, rather than the 1990 data used in the first edition. Statistics for other countries also rely on the most recent sources available. Second, the figures (maps, graphs, and photographs) are improved in quality, rendered sharper, more consistent, and with more distinct categories. Third, each chapter includes an additional textbox or in-text material showing how modern computer techniques—Geographic Information Systems, statistical modeling, remote sensing, and global positioning—are used either to reshape our cities or to enhance our understanding of urbanism.

Many of the additions to this edition incorporate research published since the final draft of the earlier edition was submitted to the publisher in 2003. For example, Chapter 1 incorporates the new 2003 Census definition of micropolitan areas and textbox 1.1 provides an example. Chapter 2 includes information on how scientists use remote sensing techniques to uncover lost cities. Chapter 3 reviews recent publications that update Jean Gottmann's concept of megalopolis, and Chapter 4 introduces John Short's treatment of world cities in the global urban network. Chapter 5 now includes new figures and accompanying text on global telecommunications flows, and Chapter 6 introduces Larry Ford's six-stage model of downtown revitalization and reinvention. Chapter 7 offers recent data on U.S. manufacturing decline, a decades-long issue. Chapter 8 expands the discussion of social diversity in cities with attention drawn to issues surrounding women in cities and sexuality in cities. Chapter 9 expands the discussion of using GIS techniques to examine urban sprawl. Chapter 10 introduces a discussion of Participatory GIS in the context of addressing issues of urban poverty.

Chapter 11 adds new data specifically from the 2000 census that tracks ethnicity in U.S. cities far more closely. Chapters 12 and 13 present an updated look at the governance and planning aspects of cities. In addition to making certain that the graphics were clearer and incorporating information on high technology and the global digital divide, Chapters 14, 15, and 16 include more current data where this is available.

Dave Kaplan is grateful for the input of several individuals. James M. Smith helped edit several chapters, Leena Woodhouse examined the chapter proofs and helped with some of the figures, and Samantha Hoover helped prepare some of the additional material for the second edition. Najat Al-Thaibani inspired the idea for the cover of this new edition. Brian Forn offered some good advice based on his usage of the text. Dave's knowledge of different aspects of urban geography was greatly enhanced by the research of several of his students, most recently Christina Nichols, Steve Oluic, Matt Stewart, and Rajrani Kalra. Veronica Jurgena has added greatly to Dave's perception of the urban scene, pointing out features of the urban landscape that would have otherwise been missed. Dave is grateful to Jim Wheeler for having brought him into this project, and to Steve Holloway, for years of fruitful collaboration, of which this book is but the latest example.

Jim Wheeler much appreciates and wishes to thank several people who assisted him in various ways in the preparation of this book. They are, alphabetically, M. Victoria Berry, Stanley D. Brunn, Kim Daniels, Mark Dotson, Emily Duggar, Jodie Traylor Guy, Audrey Hawkins, Tommy Jordan, James B. Kenyons, C. P. Lo, Deb Martin, Heather Reed, Loretta Scott, Selima Sultana, Lynn Usery, and my wife, Emily. Special thanks go to Emily Coffee, Kim Hawkins, and Benjamin Prewitt, who expertly and expeditiously prepared the final chapters, as well as ushering in the chapters through their several iterations.

Steve Holloway is grateful to students in his urban geography courses over the years: much of what makes sense in his chapters derives from attempting to make the geography of cities comprehensible, interesting, and relevant for students! Dorothy Holloway and our children (Zach, Ben and Lily) have been exceedingly patient with the time demands associated with this project. Finally, many thanks to Jim Wheeler for initiating and providing ongoing energy for this effort, and Dave Kaplan for his willingness to join in as lead author.

In addition, we thank the many people at John Wiley & Sons, Inc., who performed their essential, behind-the-scenes activities in producing and marketing the second edition of this book. Particular thanks go to Denise Powell, who prodded us through the first edition, Deepa Chungi, who worked diligently with us in launching this second edition, Laura Spence Kelleher, who guided us during the process, and Courtney Nelson, who expertly directed the book to completion. And we would like to offer especially strong thanks to Ryan A. Flahive, Executive Editor for Geography, Geology and Anthropology. We congratulate Ryan on his being named John Wiley & Sons, Inc. Editor of the Year, for 2006, and for having receiving this award for two of the last three years!

David H. Kaplan
Kent, Ohio
James O. Wheeler
Steven R. Holloway
Athens, Georgia
March 15, 2007

ACKNOWLEDGMENTS

We would also like to thank the following reviewers for their input:

Robert Amey, *Bridgewater State College*; Alison Bain, *Trent University*; Sanjoy Chakravorty, *Temple University*; Brian L Crawford, *West Liberty State College*; Steve Driever, *University of Missouri—Kansas City*; Jay D. Gatrell, *Indiana State University*; Dennis Grammenos, *Northeastern Illinois University*; Stephen Higley, *University of Montevallo*; Tulashi Joshi, *Fairmont State University*; Dave Lanegran, *Macalester College*; Unna I. Lassiter, *Stephen F. Austin State University*; David Lewis, *University of Albany*; Johanna W. Looye, *University of Cincinnati*; Kenji Oshiro, *Wright State University*; Keith Ratner, *Salem State College*; Gundars Rudzitis, *University of Idaho*; Narushige Shiode, *SUNY Buffalo*; Peter Siska, *Austin Peay State University*; Selima Sultana, *University of North Carolina—Greensboro*; Ray Sumner, *California State University Long Beach*; H. R. Trendell, *Kennesaw State University*; Mila Zlatic, *University of Maryland*.

CONTENTS

AN INTRODUCTION TO THE CHANGING FIELD OF URBAN GEOGRAPHY

It takes a great deal of history to produce a little history.

—HENRY JAMES

The purpose of this chapter is, first, to introduce you to the field of urban geography within its historical and contemporary context. We begin with the origin and evolution of urban geography, especially in North America, over the past 100 years or so, focusing on four traditions: (1) the physical geography tradition, (2) the human-environmental tradition, (3) the regional tradition, and (4) the spatial tradition. We place special emphasis on the spatial tradition and on critiques of that tradition over the past 55 years (Berry and Wheeler, 2005). In addition, we examine the role of Geographic Information Science (GIS) in urban geography and several major substative trends in the field. This chapter also provides an overview of the traditional Chicago School of urban geography in contrast with the contemporary Los Angeles School (Dear, 2005). At the end of the chapter we introduce you to the contents and approach of this book, to capture the excitement and dynamics of modern urban geography, a field of growing educational importance as more and more people live in cities, both in the industrial and nonindustrial countries of the world (Figures 1.1 and 1.2).

INTRODUCTION

Although it was unnoticed by most journalist and scholars, the mid-1990s marked the first time that more than 50 percent of the world's then 5.8 billion people were living in urban areas. Today, the world's urban population numbers over 3.4 billion of the 6.6 billion people on the earth, more people than in all the planet's vast stretches of rural and agricultural land combined, along with numerous small scattered villages and hamlets. The urban population percentages are of course much greater in the advanced capitalist economies of the world, such as the United States and Canada, Western Europe, Japan, Australia and New Zealand, and the rapidly emerging economies of Korea, Singapore, and Taiwan. In the United States and Canada, over 80 percent of the population is classified as urban by census definitions and virtually everyone is dependent on urban connections in everyday life. The world has become urban, and the advanced capitalist countries—themselves strongly linked—are almost totally locked into the urban way of life. Nonurban (nonmetropolitan)

1

Figure 1.1 An elementary school teacher instructs a third-grade class on the geography of the state of Georgia, now with a population of 8.7 million people, with more than 80 percent living in Georgia's 15 metropolitan areas.

Figure 1.2 The Higginbotham home school. It is estimated that more than 1.7 million children were home schooled in the United States in 2004, a 17 percent increase since 2000. From left to right are Wade, Caitlin, Dian (teacher/mother) and Dude, the white cat.

areas in North America are utterly dependent upon large metropolitan centers for their life sources, such as information, economic viability, social ties, entertainment and leisure activities, political expressions and attitudes, cultural attributes, and popular-cultural manifestations of behavior. We are all part of the city, whether we physically live there or not.

Different countries of the world have varied definitions of city, urban area or regions, and metropolitan areas. The U.S. Bureau of the Census has carefully defined designations for the United States. The **central city** is the politically defined city, and a **suburb** is the remainder of the metropolitan area. Metropolitan areas are defined based on county boundaries. In the media, the terms city, urban, urban center, and metropolitan area are used more

or less interchangeably. Sometimes we follow this general usage in this book if a precise definition is not called for.

In 2006, approximately 80 percent of Americans lived in metropolitan areas, concentrated into less than one-quarter of the U.S. land area. The New York metropolitan area is by far the largest with 18.8 million people compared to second-ranked Los Angeles with 12.9 million and third-ranked Chicago with 9.5 million (Table 1.1). Eleven other metropolitan areas have between 4 and 6 million population: Dallas-Fort Worth, Philadelphia, Houston, Miami, Washington, Atlanta, Detroit, Boston, San Francisco, Phoenix, and Riverside. A total of 38 U.S. metropolitan areas have between 1 million and 4 million people. The top 50 metropolitan areas are homes to more than half of the total U.S. population.

Table 1.1   20 Largest U.S. Metropolitan Areas in Population, 2006, and Percentage Change, 2000–2006

Rank	Metropolitan Area	2006* Population (in millions)	Percentage Change, 2000–2006
1	New York, NY	18.8	2.7
2	Los Angeles, CA	12.9	4.7
3	Chicago, IL	9.5	4.5
4	Dallas-Fort Worth, TX	6.0	16.3
5	Philadelphia, PA	5.8	2.5
6	Houston, TX	5.5	17.5
7	Miami, FL	5.4	9.1
8	Washington, D.C.	5.3	10.3
9	Atlanta, GA	5.1	21.0
10	Detroit, MI	4.5	0.4
11	Boston, MA	4.4	1.4
12	San Francisco, CA	4.2	1.4
13	Phoenix, AZ	4.0	24.2
14	Riverside, CA	4.0	23.7
15	Seattle, WA	3.3	7.2
16	Minneapolis, MN	3.2	6.9
17	San Diego, CA	2.9	4.5
18	St. Louis, MO	2.8	3.6
19	Tampa, FL	2.7	12.6
20	Denver, CO	2.4	10.5

Source: U.S. Bureau of the Census, 2000.
*Census estimates.

Among the 20 largest U.S. metropolitan areas between 2000 and 2006 are Phoenix (24.2%), Riverside (23.7%), and Atlanta (21.0%) (Table 1.1). Overall, Las Vegas grew at 29.2 percent. The slowest-growing centers during this period are Detroit (0.4%) and Boston and San Francisco, each at 1.4 percent.

In 2000 the Office of Management and Budget (OMB) announced new guidelines for defining metropolitan areas based on the 2000 census. The new system defined areas denoted as "Core Based Statistical Areas." Metropolitan areas are centered around a core of at least 50,000 inhabitants and typically include a number of contiguous counties based on economic ties as measured by volume of commuting. OMB defined a new type of area—**micropolitan areas**. In 2003, the U.S. Bureau of the Census provided data for the U.S. micropolitan areas (Box 1.1). A micropolitan area has a core (city) of at least 10,000 but fewer than 50,000 people. Micropolitan areas may also include more than the core county depending on the degree

of social and economic integration as measured through commuting ties with other counties.

What is it that brings human beings together in such concentrated agglomerations that we call cities, urban areas or metropolitan centers? Why do humans, who throughout almost all of their history lived in small, often migratory groups of kinship tribes at low population densities, have only in the past eight or nine millennia come to cluster in large settlements? Why was it only around 1900 that the total U.S. urban population first exceeded 30 million, a figure easily surpassed today by metropolitan New York and Los Angeles combined? And why is it that in 1920 the percentage of urban Americans first came to exceed 50 percent of the total U.S. population? And finally, why is it that more than 50 metropolitan areas in the United States and Canada with populations of more than 1 million people have emerged? What are these powerful, seemingly inexorable forces pulling human beings increasingly together in our metropolitan regions and at the same time pushing us apart in the suburbs? The purpose

BOX 1.1 MICROPOLITAN AREAS

In 2000, the U.S. Office of Management and Budget created new guidelines for defining a Metropolitan Statistical Area (MSA). At the heart of the new definition is the concept of a Core-Based Statistical Area (CBSA). MSAs are centered on a core of at least 50,000 population, plus adjacent counties that are strongly linked with the core by an employment interchange (commuting).

In 2003, the U.S. Bureau of the Census created a new geographic designation called **micropolitan areas**. Micropolitan areas are centered on a CBSA (city) of at least 10,000 population and less than 50,000, including the county in which the city is located and surrounding counties if the employment interchange (commuting) is at least 25 percent with the core county.

Dublin, Georgia, in central Georgia, with a 2000 population of 22,000, qualifies as a micropolitan

core. Located in Laurens County, Dublin is connected with Macon and Savannah via Interstate 16. Not only is Laurens County a micropolitan area, but so also is adjacent Johnson County, just to the northeast because a community interchange of over 25 percent exists between the two counties. The principal city in Johnson County is Wrightsville, with a 2000 population of 2,200. Wheeler County, also located adjacent to Laurens County, however, is not part of the micropolitan area. Whereas there are relatively few jobs in Johnson County and the highway commute to Dublin is only approximately 15 miles over a good quality two-lane road, the trip from McRae, county seat in Wheeler County, is more than 30 miles over a fair quality two-lane road.

of this book, in large part, is to provide insight and answers to these fundamental questions of human settlement concentrations and diffusions.

THE FIELD OF URBAN GEOGRAPHY

Geographers study both the world's physical and human environments. They explore how humans have altered and are currently altering our natural landscapes, our atmosphere, our water, and our soils. Whereas physical geographers examine landforms (geomorphology), long-term weather trends and patterns (climatology), and the natural and human-modified spatial distributions of plant and animals (biogeography), human geographers focus their attention on the location of people and their activities over geographic space. This locational focus may emphasize economic activities and behaviors, social and cultural features of human society, and political and power relations as expressed in places or over spaces (regions). Urban geography is thus a subfield of human geography, a subfield that studies cities or urban areas.

Urban geographers have centered their attention on the study of cities and metropolitan areas in two ways: (1) by stressing relationships *among* a system or group of cities at the regional, national, or international (or global) level, that is, by adopting an intermetropolitan approach, and (2) by highlighting the internal locational arrangements of humans, activities, and institutions *within* metropolitan areas known as an intrametropolitan approach (Figure 1.3). At the same time, urban geographers may organize their analyses—whether following the intermetropolitan or intrametropolitan approach—by studying cities in different regions of the world (Russian cities, Arabic cities) or by examining particular topical issues (poverty, ethnicity).

In this book, Part II (Metropolitan Systems—Chapters 3–6) follows the intermetropolitan, topical approach (lower left quadrant of Figure 1.3), Parts III, IV, and V (Chapters 7–13) adopt the intrametropolitan, topical perspective (lower right quadrant of Figure 1.3), and Part VI (Cities Around

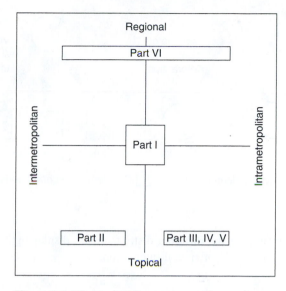

Figure 1.3 The vertical line represents the continuum between the *regional* (a study of a limited number of places over a large range of topics or attributes) and the *topical* (a study of one or a few characteristics over a wide range of places) approaches to urban geography. The horizontal line displays the continuum between *intermetropolitan* (system of centers) and *intrametropolitan* (activities located within a center) studies of urban geography.

the World—Chapters 14–16) pursues the regional tradition, utilizing both intermetropolitan and intrametropolitan viewpoints.

An important additional way urban geographers study urban centers—whether at the intermetropolitan or the intrametropolitan scale—is by understanding the varying levels of interaction or linkages among places, either among cities or among places within cities (Figure 1.4). For example, consider a group of urban areas within a region that are connected via volume of truck traffic. Some centers, because of their size and proximity (interstate highways) to other centers, will experience a greater volume of traffic flows between themselves and the other centers. The volume of these flows is a measure of the **spatial interaction,** defined as linkages over space among the centers. Likewise, at the intrametropolitan level, traffic volume will

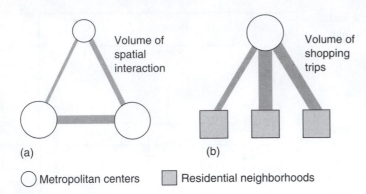

Figure 1.4 Schematic diagram illustrating hypothetical levels of spatial interaction or linkage intensity (a) among metropolitan centers and (b) among distribution points (warehouses or manufacturing plants) and an urban market. An example of Figure 1.4a is the number of airline passengers moving among the three urban centers in a given year, and an example of Figure 1.4b is motor truck volumes among places.

vary among the different districts, again displaying various levels of spatial interaction.

THE ORIGIN AND EVOLUTION OF URBAN GEOGRAPHY

Urban geography as a subdiscipline of the field of geography is a twentieth century development. In 1900, when only 40 percent of the U.S. population lived in cities, geographers were primarily interested in issues in physical geography, especially the study of landforms or geomorphology (then termed physiography). To the more limited extent that geographers carried out research in human geography, the subdiscipline of agricultural geography and the geographies of resource extraction were at the forefront because of their greater economic significance at the time. The first half of the twentieth century saw the gradual emergence of urban geography based around several fundamental concepts developed by a limited number of scholars. The first courses in urban geography were not taught until the late 1940s (by Chauncy Harris, the father of urban geography, at Indiana University and by Edward Ullman at Harvard University). It was the second half of the twentieth century that witnessed the development of urban geography as a major substantive subdiscipline in geography (Berry and Wheeler, 2005). At the dawn of the twenty-first century, only the technical field of Geographic

Information Science (GIS) had more members in the leading and largest professional geography society, the Association of American Geographers (AAG), than did the urban geography group.

THE FOUR TRADITIONS, 1900–1970

As we have already noted, four overarching traditions or research themes were evident within urban geography: (1) the physical geography tradition, (2) the human-environment tradition, (3) the regional tradition, and (4) the spatial tradition. In some ways, the transitions between these traditions may be compared to a sudden change in TV channels. The old was quickly discarded for the new, as if we switched from the CBS Nightly News to CNN News. It was still news (urban geography), but it was different. These four traditions, originally set forth by Pattison (1964) as "The Four Traditions in Geography," describe the changes in urban geography until approximately 1970. Figure 1.5 shows the relative importance of these traditions from 1900 through 1970.

The Physical Tradition
At the beginning of the twentieth century, most geographers were interested in the earth's physical environment, especially landforms and climate. At that time, urban geography was a little-studied subfield. It was not until urban geography had emerged as

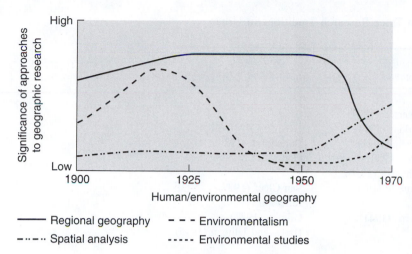

Figure 1.5 The relative significance of the three traditions in U.S. urban geography from 1900 to 1970, showing the early interest in the physical traditions; the overwhelming dominance of the regional tradition; the rise and fall of the environmentalism point of view; the minor role of the spatial analysis approach until the mid-1950s and its subsequent rise in importance; and the renewed interest in the human-environmental impact studies, starting in the late 1960s.

a well-developed area of geography in the 1960s and the 1970s that it took interest in the physical environment of the city. Studies found, for instance, that high-income residential districts tended to be located in areas of high elevations, places with a view. Studies also showed that Manhattan could support skyscrapers because of its strong bedrock foundation. Some geographers concentrated on natural hazards, such as floods, mudslides, and hurricanes. A particularly notable topic of research was on heat islands within cities, a feature now common among the nightly local weather forecasts, whereby downtown areas register higher temperatures than outlying rural areas, the result of so many concrete structures and streets in the downtown area reflecting solar heating. The physical tradition, however, continues to be neglected by many urban geographers.

The Human-Environment Tradition

Tracing back at least as far as Aristotle in Western culture is the somewhat vague but pervasive concept that the physical environment, especially climate, determines or "controls" the development of human civilization, a concept that became known in geography as **environmental determinism.** Environmental determinism held, for example, that civilization could not develop in the monotonous climate of the tropics, where humans were seen as "primitive,"

but would instead flourish in the variable climates of the midlatitudes of Western Europe and the United States—ignoring the civilizations and large city settlements in West Africa, in the Yucatán (the Mayas), the Andes (the Incas), and central Mexico (the Aztecs). After 1925, few geographers pursued the racist-based notions of environmental determinism, the best-known proponents being Elsworth Huntington and Griffith Taylor (Table 1.2).

Geographers who felt that environmental determinism took a too-rigid and causal position, instead embraced the philosophy of **possibilism.** According to this approach nature sets limits or possibilities for human activities, but human behaviors are expressed through their cultural traditions that create a given way of life. Whereas determinism would hold that humans could not survive in northern Siberia, possiblism would suggest that the probability of human existence, though low, in such an environment would not be impossible.

The human-environmental tradition in urban geography brought about an interest in the sites of cities, that is, locations of cities at deep harbors for ocean-going vessels, on rivers for navigation, at the base of mountain ranges for gateway positions and at mining locales for mineral and resource extraction. The interpretation is that the site of a city determines the city's future economic and population

Table 1.2 Prominent Milestones in Three Research Traditions in Urban Geography to 1953

Human-Environment (Environmental Determinism)	Regional	Spatial Analysis
Semple (1897)		
Tower (1905)	Emerson (1907)	
Semple (1911)	Parkins (1914)	
	Strong (1921)	Hartshorne (1924)
	Platt (1928)	Platt (1928)
	Whitaker (1930)	
	Johnson (1936)	Van Cleef (1937)
		Jefferson (1939)
	Harris (1941)	Ullman (1941)
		Harris and Ullman (1945)
Huntington (1945)		
Taylor (1949)	Dickinson (1947)	
		Hägerstrand (1952)
		Schaefer (1953)
		Smailes (1953)
		Ullman (1953)

Source: Compiled by J. O. Wheeler.

growth. The determinist would say, "Show me the site of New York City or Charleston, South Carolina, and I will tell you the future of the city to develop there." This approach led one geographer (Tower, 1905, p. 588) to study "the chief geographic controls in the growth of the larger centres of population," focusing on the "natural conditions" that favored growth of large U.S. cities. Ellen Churchill Semple argued that a mountainous environment discourages the growth of large cities. In her words, "Mountain tribes are always like a pack of hounds on the leash, each straining in a different direction. The broken relief of ancient Greece produced the small city-state...the geography of the land instilled in them [the people] the principle of political aloofness" (Semple, 1911, p. 591). She clearly could not anticipate a modern, high-elevation metropolis such as Zürich, Switzerland, or Bogotá, Colombia.

The Regional Tradition
The third great tradition in urban geography was the **regional studies** viewpoint, which was in its

ascendancy from approximately 1920 to 1960. Regional or area studies of cities typically focused on a single city as a case study. The studies were routinely descriptive rather than analytical—they simply described the geography of the city. The case studies usually had a historical approach, emphasizing how the city grew and evolved. In addition, the investigation was characteristically regional, that is, all important features (physical and human) of the city were described. Finally, given the paucity of published data in the early- to mid-twentieth century, regional studies commonly utilized field surveys and interviews. The regional studies approach led to an accumulation of specific geographies of many cities, but did not develop generalization. A few examples suffice: F. V. Emerson (1907), Almon Parkins (1914), Helen Strong (1921), and Chauncy Harris (1940). The regional research theme was long dominant in American urban geography, and its preoccupation with description rather than analytical interpretations of the urban landscape kept urban geography out of the mainstream social sciences.

The Spatial Tradition

Gradually replacing the regional tradition in urban geography during the late 1950s was the **spatial analysis** approach, which remains an important research thrust in the twenty-first century. Spatial analysis involves an emphasis on developing theory, hypotheses, quantitative methods, and mathematical model building. The overriding concern in spatial analysis is location theory, where cities are located. In examining the spatial analysis tradition, we will first provide a brief overview of precursors to this analytic approach extending back several decades from its recognized inception in the mid- to late-1950s (Table 1.3). Second, we will explore European influences on the development of urban geography that paved the way for spatial analysis. Third, we highlight interdisciplinary forces and technological developments that encouraged quantitative research. We end this section with one example of how the spatial analysis tradition differs from the regional tradition that it replaced, and we examine the strengths and weaknesses of both traditions.

Precursors of Spatial Analysis in Urban Geography

As Figure 1.5 reminds us, spatial analysis as a way of doing research in urban geography was not widely practiced until the mid- to late-1950s. At that time the spatial analysis approach displaced the regional tradition, giving rise to the misnamed but popular term "**quantitative revolution.**" Only a handful of urban geographers conducted research in the spatial analytic tradition from the 1920s through the mid-1950s; instead, the regional theme was dominant. Perhaps the earliest substantial precursor to the spatial analysis tradition was Robert Platt's (1928) **microgeography.** Platt's study of an extremely small area (microgeography) of Ellison Bay, Wisconsin, started out as another regional study. To explain how such a small community functioned, however, Platt had to examine the spatial or geographic linkages of that tiny place with many other places. It turned out that Ellison Bay did not exist independently of other places but was, in fact, fundamentally and geographically linked with many areas, some surprisingly far away. Thus,

Table 1.3   Prominent Milestones in Spatial Analysis, 1954–1970

Years	Authors	Publications
1954	Lösch	*The Economics of Location* (translated into English)
1954	Mayer et al.	"Urban Geography," in *American Geography: Inventory and Prospect*
1956	Walter Isard	*Location and Space-Economy*
1958	Berry and Garrison	Two articles on central-place theory in *Economic Geography*
1959	Mayer and Kohn	*Readings in Urban Geography*
1960	Walter Isard	*Methods of Regional Science*
1961	Berry and Pred	*Central Place Studies*
1963	Berry	*Commercial Structure and Commercial Blight*
1964	Wolpert*	"The Decision Process in a Spatial Context," in *Annals, AAG*
1966	Christaller	*Central Places in Southern Germany* (translated into English)
1966	Murphy	*The American City*
1967	Berry	*Market Centers and Retail Distribution*
1967	Garner	"Models of Urban Geography and Settlement Location," in *Models in Geography*
1967	Golledge and Brown*	"Search, Learning and the Market Decision Process," in *Geofrafiska Annaler B*
1969	Rushton*	"Spatial Behavior by Revealed Space Preference," in *Annals, AAG*
1969	Harvey	*Explanation in Geography*
1970	Berry and Horton	*Geographic Perspectives on Urban Systems*

Source: Compiled by J. O. Wheeler.
*Behavioral spatial analysis.

Platt's spatial links provided a conceptual framework for later research in spatial analysis.

In addition to Platt, Mark Jefferson's research made him probably the best-known early urban geographer based on his conceptual structure of the geography of cities. He is remembered most for his "Law of the Primate City" (Jefferson, 1939), which foreshadowed a large body of research in the late 1950s and 1960s on city-size distributions (see Chapter 3). A later precursor of spatial analysis was the introduction in 1945 by Chauncy Harris and Edward Ullman of the three most-reproduced models of intraurban spatial structure (see Chapter 10), which continue to appear in contemporary textbooks in urban geography and sociology (see Harris, 1997).

European Influences on Spatial Analysis in Urban Geography

Three German scholars, Walter Christaller (1933), geographer, and economists August Lösch (1938) and Alfred Weber (1929, originally published in German in 1909), published books that were to have major impacts on urban geography, although not until many years after their original writings. Christaller's analysis of central place systems in southern Germany was not fully available in English until 1966. Similarly, Lösch's economic locational analysis was not translated into English until 1954. Weber devised a simple but insightful theory of industrial location based on three principles: transport cost, labor cost, and cost saving from agglomerative location (proximity to other firms). These writings had enormous consequences for the direction of urban geography in the late 1950s, throughout the 1960s, and beyond.

Originally published in Swedish, Torsten Hägerstrand's (1953) *Innovation Diffusion as a Spatial Process* was translated into English in 1967 and generated a firestorm of research activity in urban geography. Like central place theory, Hägerstrand's concept of spatial diffusion had wide applications and was amenable to theoretical, analytic, and quantitative interpretation.

It remained for the British geographer Peter Haggett (1966) to first make sense of all of the outpouring of articles in spatial analysis, most of which were written in the United States, in his insightful synthesis entitled *Locational Analysis in Human Geography*. Not only did his book give a more solid and confident foundation to the "new" quantitative and analytic research of the past decade (1958–1966), but it also introduced British and indeed all European geographers to new concepts and methodologies. The book was also eagerly read by American geographers.

Extradisciplinary Influences on Spatial Analysis in Urban Geography

By far the most pronounced external force affecting the direction and nature of research in urban geography was use of statistical and mathematical models, a methodology that had already been adopted in other social, biological, and physical sciences, as well as certain other social sciences. Indeed, urban geography was the leader in following the new paths within geography. Taaffe (1974) characterized the introduction of these techniques into geography, a change we referred to earlier as the "quantitative revolution" of the late 1950s and early 1960s, as a three-part revolution: (1) technical (statistical and mathematical), (2) theoretical, and (3) definitional. Basic statistical techniques were applied to urban data to establish relationships and generalizations; theoretical models were advanced by setting forth hypotheses; and geography became defined as a generalizing, rather than a descriptive, field. These changes in ideas led to a rejection of the traditional regional study, with its emphasis on describing unique places. The then-new spatial analysis approach placed priority on reaching generalizations via hypothesis testing and scientific replication of results.

A major factor that assisted urban geographers in conducting quantitative studies was the growing availability of computer resources in major research universities in the 1960s. Statistical algorithms (software packages)—at first reproduced on a sequence of punch cards—became easy to copy, and enabled geographers to utilize larger and larger data sets. Although extremely primitive by today's standards, computer-assisted research had enormous consequences not only for urban geography but also for all of the social, behavioral, and natural sciences. Toward the end of the 1960s computer graphics (including maps) became possible, though exceeding ugly by current standards.

One individual, Walter Isard, played an especially important role in the evolution of urban geography. In 1954, Isard formed the Regional Science Association, a professional society that now has a worldwide presence and that publishes a number of scholarly journals. Isard, trained as an economist, was interested in inserting spatial analysis into the general economic models of his day. The development and expansion of this society, comprised largely of economists, geographers, and other quantitatively inclined scholars, helped create a strong interest in statistical research among urban geographers in the late 1950s and 1960s which in turn helped to shape theoretical and methodological thinking about urban areas. The Regional Science Association continues to influence the subdiscipline of urban geography to this day.

Critiques of Spatial Analysis in Urban Geography

Behavioral Urban Geography   Ironically, almost as soon as the spatial analysis forces in urban geography began to gain a respectable foothold in the mid-1960s—though not universal acclaim—concerted efforts at modifying this approach were proposed and pursued by others (Figure 1.6). The first of these efforts involved the behavioral group led initially by Julian Wolpert, Reginald Golledge, Larry Brown, and Gerald Rushton and primarily associated with the University of Iowa and Michigan State University. The behavioralists began their work in the mid-1960s, not so much by attacking spatial analysis as by modifying its intent. The behavioral group in urban geography followed the analytical approach but were concerned with how individuals made spatial decisions, that is, where to buy a house or how to select the best route to work. The emphasis was a person's attitudes and expectations of places, how one learns about different parts

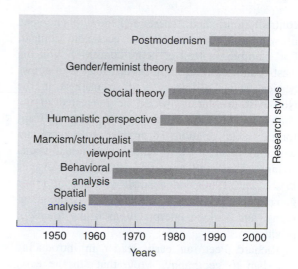

Figure 1.6 Research styles in urban geography, 1960–2005. Although here presented as distinctive research approaches, these research streams in fact merge into one another, are derivative, and/or are critiques of earlier research styles.

of the city, makes geographic choices and decisions, assesses risk and uncertainty, and one's daily spatial behavior. The behavioral researchers believed that the aggregate-level analysis (examining large groups of people) that was used by most of the spatial analysts was too broad to explain how actual individuals and groups of people selected, say, an apartment, an industrial site, or a public library location.

Marxist Interpretations   Beginning in 1969 with the publication of *Antipode: A Radical Journal of Geography* at Clark University, Marxist interpretations of the geographic landscape became increasingly common. Just as behavioralists saw spatial analysis as too preoccupied with geometric arrangements of locations, so too did Marxists, who emphasized capitalist production and labor relations in studying the underlying causes of urban poverty, discrimination against women and minorities, unequal access to urban social services, and Third World underdevelopment. Marxist urban geographers studied these phenomena in terms of their contradictions, and where and how phenomena fit within a wider social and economic context. For example, instead of being concerned with the least-cost or optimal shipment distribution of strawberries from California to urban markets in the Northeast, a Marxist would be interested in the "hidden" cost of low-paid migrant pickers in California. Social relations of production (owners and workers) created the potential for violent social change. Thus, the concern with social relevance in the late 1960s led a small minority of urban geographers to embrace radical approaches to geography, and Marxist interpretations of the forces of production.

Richard Peet, an early leader in introducing Marxism to geography, wrote that "In the early 1970s...the new [Marxist] criticism centered on geography's pervasive distinction between the spatial dimension of human activity and...socioeconomic problems with spatial magnifications" (Peet, 1998, p. 74). For example, the theory of industrial location focuses on the profits of industrialists rather than concerns of the working class (Massey, 1973). David Harvey, a widely quoted Marxist geographer, emphasized the contrast and conflicts between the capitalists and the workers: "Labor power has to go home every night and reproduce itself before coming back to work the next morning" (Harvey, 1989, p. 19). The daily commuting physical limit is interpreted, not as a maximum distance constraint, but rather as a factor based on the buying and selling of labor power by the capitalists.

Humanistic Urban Geography   The term humanistic geography may be traced to Yi-Fu Tuan (1976), who reflected on its meaning (p. 266):

> Humanistic geography achieves an understanding of the human world by studying people's relations with nature, their geographical behavior as well as their feelings and ideas in regard to space and place.

Humanistic geography did not so much criticize spatial analysis as offer a benign alternative to number crunching. It was not concerned with a theoretical perspective and hypothesis testing as it was with attitudes, perceptions, and values toward the landscape—**topophilia,** the love of the land.

Humanistic geography relates not only to urban geography but also to rural scenes. An example of a humanistic urban geographer would be a geographer walking through downtown St. Louis. The geographer is not interested in numerical data or generalized models of downtown land use. No, this geographer wants to soak up the surrounding smells and sounds and enjoy the nearby sights and longer views, feeling and experiencing downtown St. Louis. Later, these perceptions and personal interpretations may be placed on paper.

Social Theory   The late 1970s and the 1980s witnessed the development and incorporation of social theory into human geography in general and urban geography in particular. Social theorists view urban geography "as social and cultural in origin and political in intent...influenced by nonlogical beliefs and cultural meanings, and by body and emotion as well as mind" (Peet, 1998, p. 6). In opposition to spatial analysis with its inductively derived "facts" and mathematical equations, social theory takes on a critical political perspective, "dedicated to changing the world in some way for the better. Social theory is almost always leftist in style, character, and intent—that is, dedicated to human emancipation.... Social theory is different from other types of theory not only in terms of levels of generality and politics but also in that it specifically theorizes human beings in social groups" (Peet, 1998, p. 7). Social theorists rejected the notion that spatial relations—distance, rate of diffusion, intervening places—determined such social activities as commuting and migration; rather, they argued that social relations explained the observed spatial or geographic distributions or patterns identified on maps. The social theorist came to refer to those following the spatial analysis, scientific approach by the prejorative term "positivist." The spatial analysts considered the social theorists' use of "theory" as mere assertions, not testable propositions.

Thus the "human agency" or social context and power relationships must be uncovered and understood before spatial attributes can be comprehended. All human reality is "socially constructed," that is, created by humans.

Postmodernism The introduction of postmodernism in geography can be traced to writings by Michael Dear (1988) and Ed Soja (1989). The concepts of postmodernism in geography evolved through an awareness stemming from debates on social theory. At its core, postmodern thinking is antimodern, that is, antiscientific. Since the Enlightenment of the eightieth century, modern Western thought has been based on logic, reason, and scientific understanding. Modernity espouses the rational individual sharing agreed-upon moral norms of society based on reason and knowledge, rather than on some divine authority. Science, considered modernist thinking, leads to an egalitarian, fair, impartial, and technologically superior society.

In contrast, postmodernity—with its rejection of modern science, rationality, and grand schemes of understanding—celebrates a sensitivity to differences. In fact, given its spurning of categories, as well as its many and varied interpretations, postmodernism virtually repudiates any simple definition. Table 1.4, however, directs our attention to the essential philosophy and fundamental attributes of postmodernism, with its rejoicing in complexity and plurality, the subjective and indefinable, and disorder and contradictions. Postmodern thought also has a fundamental political viewpoint, associating modern society with a system of power that abuses and ignores socially marginalized people. Postmodernism wishes to unleash repression and inhibitions created by the forces of modernism, and eliminate such socially based power relationships as racism and sexism.

Most urban geographers embrace postmodern thought as one of several valued perspectives to understanding the city in all of its diversity and inequality. Because different individuals have varied urban experiences as they undergo their life cycle, each person's involvement with city life is

Table 1.4 Attributes of Postmodernism

Postmodern Perspectives

Revolt against rationality of modernism
Complexity celebrated
Disorder and chaos
Diversity
Paradigms renounced
Heterogeneity
Subjective and indefinable
Multiple voices
Ephemeral and ad hoc
Plurality and contradictions
Disjointed and incomplete
Tolerates the incommensurable
Eclectic kaleidoscope

Source: Compiled by J. O. Wheeler.

seen as equally valid with everyone else's. All viewpoints and expressions, according to postmodernists, are coequally accurate and correct. For example, Michael Dear, in his preface to *The Postmodern Urban Condition* (2000), declared that "The tenets of modernist thought have been undermined, discredited; in their place, a multiplicity of new ways of knowing have been substituted." Dear continued: "As these geographies of the twenty-first century are being born, the rise of postmodern thought has encouraged, even insisted on new ways of seeing. Founded on a sensitivity to difference and radical undecidability, postmodernism has brought into question the ways we need, represent, and make choices" (p. 1).

At the same time that advocates of postmodern thinking reject much of the modern world as essentially obsolete, postmodern thought has stimulated its critics, who see it as merely "pondering" geography in an idiosyncratic, self-gratifying, meandering, dangerous, and nonserious vein. For example, in a 1998 article Michael Dear and Steve Flusty proposed an initial step toward deriving a concept of "postmodern urbanism." They highlighted the "Los Angeles School" which is fundamentally characterized by "a global-local connection, a social polarization, and urban process in which hinterland organizes the center." Their essay generated criticism, including comments from Sui (1999), who, taking an avowedly modernist stance, declared that "postmodern discourse has permeated certain subfields of geography like a [deadly] virus" and that "postmodern geography has increasingly become irrelevant both socially and intellectually" (p. 408).

Berry (1999, p. 589), though critical of postmodern urbanism, provides an understanding of how postmodern ideas have evolved:

> To postmoderns, newborn minds are blank slates that fill with individualized experience, resulting in unique worldviews. Collective understanding supported by repeated scientific observation cannot, in this view, exist. As a result reason is replaced by rhetoric and the common good by what feels good.

The great majority of urban geographers today, although familiar with postmodernism, do not embrace it in their everyday teaching and research. It is primarily a younger generation of urban geographers who are most intellectually comfortable with postmodernism. This text does not follow a postmodern perspective, although we deal with many of the concepts and topics listed in Table 1.4 as attributes of postmodernism.

Geographic Information Science and Urban Geography

Geographic Information Science (GIS) is one of the most recent and fastest growing areas of geography. It was only in 1986 that members of the Association of American Geographers (AAG) established a specialty group in GIS. Within a year, however, the GIS group was the largest of all the AAG specialty groups and remains so today, with the urban geography group ranking second.

GIS evolved out of traditional subareas of geography such as cartography, remote sensing and image processing of satellite data, as well as computer science and geodata coding. Following the wording adopted by the United States Geological Survey, GIS is defined as "a system of hardware, software, and procedures designed to support the capture, management, manipulation, analysis, modeling, and display of spatially referenced data for solving complex planning and management problems." Although GIS did not become crystallized as a distinct subfield until the mid-1980s, by the late 1980s, it had become a common offering in the North American college and university curriculum. GIS continues as the leading growth area in geography in the twenty first century as reflected in job creation, papers presented at professional meetings, and in the publication of books and especially articles in academic journals (Box 1.2).

GIS has natural appeal to urban geographers, who make routine use of GIS in planning, research, and teaching. With the coalescence of urban analysis with computer systems and information technology (IT), it is not surprising that "GIS has become an important field of academic study, one of the fastest growing sectors of the computer industry and, most importantly, an essential component of information technology infrastructure in modern society" (Lo and Yeung, 2000, p. 1). Government agencies, including those involved in urban and regional planning, and academic researchers in urban studies have greatly expanded the scope and possibilities for applications of GIS to urban issues and problems.

GIS utilizes geographic data, which are characterized by **geographic space** and **geographic scale.** Geographic space requires that the data be registered in terms of coordinate space, commonly x-y axes such as longitude and latitude so that point, linear, and area data from different sources can be cross-referenced. Geographic scale implies that data recorded for small areas may need to be displayed or analyzed at different and more specialized or generalized scales, especially in highly complex urban areas.

Figure 1.7 shows several typical data layers of an urban GIS. Some of the data, such as retail sales per establishment, may be represented by coordinate points. Other data, for example administrative or political units, may be measured with polygons, that is, a series of lines enclosing an area. Still other data such as roads, streams, or utilities can be rendered in

BOX 1.2 TECHNOLOGY AND URBAN GEOGRAPHY

GLOBAL POSITIONING SYSTEMS (GPS)

Developed originally by the U.S. Department of Defense for military navigation, the Global Positioning System (GPS) now has a large and growing number of urban applications. GPS is simply a technology that allows the accurate determination of precise locations on the Earth.

The principles behind GPS are fairly basic, but the implementation of GPS has involved a high-tech multibillion dollar investment by the U.S. government. The system involves a constellation of 24 satellites grouped in precisely spaced orbital planes approximately 12,500 miles above the Earth. Each satellite broadcasts radio signals to Earth, where a person with a GPS receiver can intercept the signals. The satellites and the Earth receivers operate with synchronized electronic clocks, allowing unerring accuracy in the calculation of the time it takes the radio signals, traveling at the speed of light, to reach a particular spot on the Earth (Figure B1.1). Through a triangular process involving three (sometimes four) satellite signals, the location of the GPS receiver is given to an accuracy of 15 to 30 feet. A moving GPS receiver may give somewhat less exact measures.

A major urban application of GPS involves the installation of satellite-receiving devices on automobiles to track stolen cars. Another urban application is surgically implanting rice-sized microchips in pets to help reunite them with their owners. Similarly, positioning devices can be placed on cellular phones to aid in finding lost hikers, and, as the price of GPS receivers continues to decline, to retrieve tourists and conventioneers lost in our modern urban labyrinths.

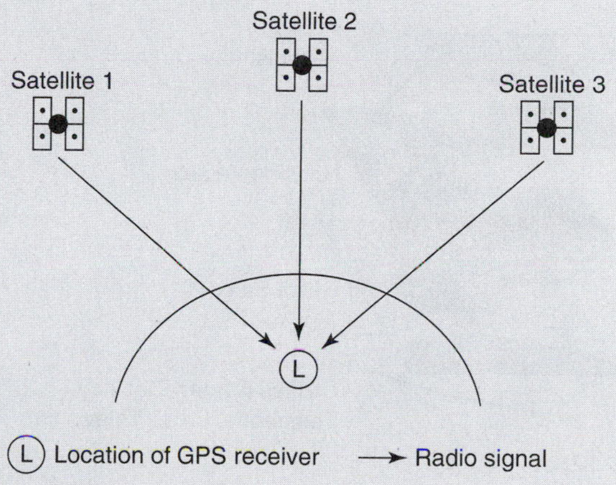

Figure B1.1 Triangulation from satellites sending radio signals, traveling at the speed of light, allows the exact location (L) of any place on Earth to be determined, based on the time it takes for the three radio signals to reach a GPS receiver having an electronic clock on Earth synchronized exactly with clocks in the satellites.

How far should the application of GPS go in urban social space? For example, should society permit the implantation of microchip GPS receivers in Alzheimer's patients in the event these patients should wander off? Should the technology be used to track paroled prisoners, including child molesters, or shadowy drug dealers, or suspected unfaithful spouses? In neighborhoods that fingerprint children, why not insist on inserting a helpful GPS microchip in each child? Clearly, as with other technologies, there are many possibilities, and then there are the moral issues.

a linear format. GIS allows these data to be integrated for display, modeling, analysis, and management, despite the different formats of the original data.

Businesses in urban areas use GIS to integrate data from a variety of sources to plan for market area change, to analyze sales performance, and to select locations for new businesses or identify existing locations where performance is unsatisfactory. Data may be derived from U.S. Census and other governmental sources, from consulting firms, and from company records. The data may be based on census tracts, local planning districts,

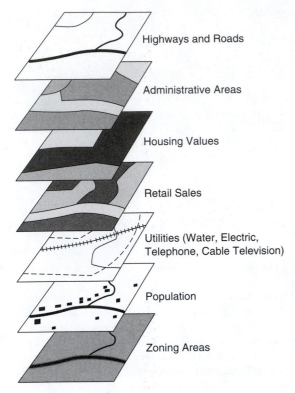

Highways and Roads

Administrative Areas

Housing Values

Retail Sales

Utilities (Water, Electric, Telephone, Cable Television)

Population

Zoning Areas

Figure 1.7 An example of data layers of an urban GIS.

traffic activity zones, ZIP codes, retail market areas, or individual household interviews. GIS will allow these data sources to be combined to analyze various business growth scenarios; to project the likely impact of firm expansion, added competition, or new technologies; and to determine needed shipments among supply and demand points. In general, the spatial models developed and applied in the 1960s are increasingly being utilized in GIS in urban business enterprises, in urban planning, and in academic urban research and teaching (Sui, 1994).

SUBSTANTIVE TRENDS IN URBAN GEOGRAPHY

Next we examine five major trends or themes in urban geography, all of which make substantive contributions to the field. The first three, global cities, feminist themes, and urban cultural issues, have seen

major surges of interest in the late 1990s and the 2000s. The last two, historical studies of cities and spatial analysis, continue to generate strong interest but have not enjoyed the same dynamics of the former three.

Urbanization and Global Cities

Urbanization can be defined and measured as the percentage of the population classified as urban as opposed to rural (nonmetropolitan) within an area, region, country, or other meaningful area unit. In other words, urbanization is the number of urban dwellers divided by the total population. Urbanization is a process through which countries evolve from agrarian to industrial and postindustrial economies. In fact, the percentage of a country's urban population has long been used as a measure of that country's level of economic development, with the technologically more advanced countries having the largest share of their populations classified as urban. Increased urbanization has occurred primarily through the shift in population from rural to urban locations (migration) and secondarily through natural increase (births minus deaths). As Figure 1.8 indicates, since 1800 human populations have been moving from a dispersed rural settlement pattern to one in which larger numbers of people are concentrating in urban areas. Whereas in 1800 only 4 percent of the world's population lived in urban

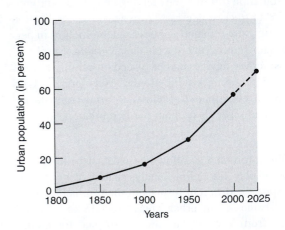

Figure 1.8 World urbanization trends, 1800–2025.

areas, by 2006 that number had increased to 54 percent. Not only are more people living in cities, but the cities themselves are becoming larger.

Today, a growing number of geographers study **global cities,** defined as cities whose functions extend throughout the capitalist world (see Chapter 4). These functions include capital transfer and accumulation, management and corporate control, information and communications activities, and tourist and cultural activities. These global cities may be examined as a group in a comparative sense (Clark, 1996) or individually as with "Minneapolis-St. Paul in the Global Economy" (Kaplan and Schwartz, 1996). The three major global cities are New York, London, and Tokyo (Sassen, 1991, 2002). Global cities need to be distinguished from **megacities,** defined here as cities with more than 8 million people. Megacities are a recent phenomenon in human history. Megacities are not necessarily global cities, because the latter implies worldwide influence. For example, Tokyo is a global megacity but Calcutta and Jakarta are not. Only New York and London qualified as megacities 60 years ago. By 1990, 20 megacities existed, 15 of which were in less economically developed regions of the world (Table 1.5). By 2005, the number of megacities had increased to 26, again all except six located in the less-developed world regions. These numbers offer clear indications that most of the rapidly growing large world cities are located in the lesser developed regions. Megacities in the developed world are growing much more slowly, as are populations in general in these more economically developed regions (North America, Western Europe, Japan, Australia and New Zealand). The slightly slower projected percentage growth in world urbanization after 2010 reflects the correspondingly minor decrease in the rate of world population growth in general (Figure 1.8).

Feminist Urban Geography

It was not until the late 1970s that gender and feminist theory entered meaningfully into geographic research. Hanson and Hanson (1980), for example, studied journey-to-work patterns of males and females in Uppsala, Sweden, and found that "a

Table 1.5 Megacities of the World

1950	1990	2005
More Developed Economies		
New York	Tokyo	Tokyo
	New York	New York
London	London	London
	Los Angeles	Los Angeles
	Osaka	Osaka
	Paris	Paris
		Seoul
Less Developed Economies		
	Mexico City	Mexico City
	São Paulo	São Paulo
	Shanghai	Shanghai
	Calcutta (Kolhata)	Mumbai
	Buenos Aires	Beijing
	Mumbai	Jakarta
	Seoul	Delhi
	Beijing	Buenos Aires
	Rio de Janeiro	Logos
	Moscow	Moscow
	Tianjin	Tianjin
	Jakarta	Lima
	Cairo	Rio de Janeiro
	Delhi	Tehran
	Manila	Dhaka
		Cairo
		Manila
		Karachi
		Bangkok
		Istanbul
		Bangalore (Bengaluru)

Source: United Nations, *World Urbanization Prospects*.

significantly lower level of mobility existed for working women than for working men" (p. 294). Throughout the 1980s and to the present, interest in feminist geography greatly accelerated, due in part to the increased numbers and proportions of females gaining advanced degrees (MAs and PhDs) and faculty positions in geography. By 2006, more than 36 percent of membership in the major professional geographic society in the United States and Canada (the AAG) were women.

As Melissa Gilbert (1997, p. 166) has observed, "Feminist research on urban processes and daily life is flourishing, as evidence by the proliferation of conference papers, journal articles, and books on these topics." She also noted that "many feminist urban geographers have begun to examine the diversity of women's experiences in cities, and the ways in which different structures of inequality shape urban processes" (p. 167). Women in cities typically experience different habits of daily behavior compared to men. Advertising is heavily slanted to women shoppers, women often have greater domestic responsibilities, and women are more likely to head single-parent families.

Feminist theory and feminist urban geography were initially closely associated with Marxism and social theory in general and focused on women's experiences of oppression and exclusion from positions of power. Feminist theory has its background in the history of women's movements. "Feminist theory argues that gender, like class and race, is a basic building block of social organization. To this extent gender relations sustain a system of power capable of shaping . . . capacities of individuals. Gender . . . is not a . . . given of biology but is a product of male and female actions that is institutionalized through families, schools, the workplace, and the state" (Pickles and Watts, 1992, pp. 312–313). Gender is thus socially constructed and determined. These understandings have helped bring a feminist consciousness to the study of urban geography, in contrast to earlier studies that assumed a "masculine" city, for example, that the "head of house" was male. Gilbert succinctly summarized the current status of feminist urban geography: "Feminist urban geographers, while maintaining the significance of gender as an analytic category, are now examining at a concrete level how different structures and relations of inequality are mutually and spatially constituted. The exploration of differences in women's experiences of this city often requires reconceptualizing feminist urban theory" (p. 168).

Many traditional models and concepts in urban geography are implicitly based on masculinist assumptions. Feminist theorists, as well as empirical analysis that take feminist perspectives, have questioned these traditional concepts and have sought to make research in urban geography more gender inclusive.

Blake and Hanson (2005), for example, rethink the concept of innovation to encompass gender considerations. Whereas innovation is typically viewed as a technological change and "overly masculinist," particularly in manufacuturing, their research found that many of the entrepreneurs they interviewed, largely but not exclusively women, "saw their businesses as innovative in the sense that they brought economically viable, new ideas to a place and created significant positive change in that place" (p. 682). Technologically based definitions of innovation would exclude businesses often female-owned and operated that serve primarily local markets. Blake and Hanson concluded that the concept of innovation should be expanded beyond "technologically defined and growth-oriented originality" and "be more gender inclusive" (p. 681).

Urban Culture Geography

Cultural geography, in which humanistic and social geography become linked, with emphasis on the power of culture, the role of style, consumption, and ideology, expanded its scope rapidly in the 1980s, especially in the United Kingdom. Mitchell (2000, p. 63) wrote that the constructs and themes of the "new cultural geography" has infused all of human geography, "from economic to political, from urban to regional, from feminist to Marxist." The conventional rural-based cultural geography stressed temporal relationships passed down over generations. The new urban cultural geography focuses on place, understanding culture to be revealed in places and over space. Traditionally, the subfield of cultural geography studied the rural landscape (Figure 1.9). In the Midwest, for example, cultural geographers such as Fraser Hart, Cotton Mather, and Wilber Zelinsky wrote about such cultural elements as farms and fences, barn styles, food habits, and place names. In California, Carl Sauer and his students were interested in a cultural geography that was fashioned from the natural environment, and

Figure 1.9 Regional cultural features such as barbeque eateries dot the U.S. rural Southern landscape, each establishment attempting to create a distinctive image. Here Fresh Air Bar-B-Que features a black-and-white pig, tail raised, as its air-fresh logo and declares itself as "Georgia's Best" tasty hog meat cooked over hardwood fires.

emphasized aboriginal American rural landscapes, historical evolution, and the spread and origin of cultural practices within human societies. Until the 1990s, cultural geography was antiurban in outlook. Urban cultural geography has flourished with the recent emphasis on the "selling" of culture in urban society as tied to both mass and niche consumption.

Leitner (1992, p. 110) precisely captures the key difference between traditional rural cultural geography and contemporary urban cultured geography: "Instead of treating the landscape as an object to be described, classified, and interpreted as a reflection of the impact of cultural groups, this new cultural geography . . . concentrates on interpreting the symbolic nature of landscapes, paying particular attention to how the meanings enshrined in the landscape are used to advance or retard the attainment of social and political goals." The naming of schools and streets for Dr. Martin Luther King, Jr., is one instance of symbolic landscape features (Alderman, 2002). The academic journal

Urban Geography has published numerous research articles in urban cultural studies (Wheeler, 1998). These topics include retail (regional mall) culture, cultures of racism and ethnicity, corporate culture, public versus private spaces, and popular culture. The rise of urban cultural geography is providing us a great deal of weight into how city landscapes are constructed (created by society), reconstructed, and deconstructed over time. As Trevor Barnes (2005) put it, "Culture had finally left the farm and hit the streets" (p. 312).

Urban Historical Geography

A long tradition in urban geography and one vigorously pursued in contemporary research as well is urban historical geography. Although a great many geographers are interested in the modern urban environment, changing land use, and the impact of rapid technological changes on urban lifestyles, many other students of the city wish to understand cities of the past. Two basic approaches to urban historical geography have been followed: (1) studying a city or group of cities at one point in time, for example, Boston in 1850; and (2) examining a city or group of cities throughout a given time period, for example, the evolution of cities in the U.S. South from the end of the Civil War (1865) until 1880, the Reconstruction era. The former approach provides a detailed inspection of a particular place at a particular time, lending comprehensive insight into the local area's geography. The latter offers a generalized conception of the chief geographic changes that have occurred over time.

Urban historical analyses are by no means limited to geographies of antiquity. Studies on the "restless" or rapidly changing urban landscape are a case in point. Our cities are constantly changing, and contemporary urban historical geographies are of much interest and relevance. New technologies, new societal attitudes and norms, and political and legal changes all modify the urban landscape and urban lifestyles. Urban areas become restructured economically, change through immigration flows, and are impacted by information technology. New York, Los Angeles, Miami—and even smaller centers such as Kalamazoo, Omaha, Wichita, and especially Las Vegas—are by no means the same places they were just 10 years ago, to say nothing of 30 or 50 years or more in the past. Urban historical geographers are interested in understanding the urban past, be it the ancient or the recent past.

Locational Analysis in Urban Geography

As a core of the spatial analysis that blossomed in the 1960s, locational analysis continues to play an important role in contemporary geography. Locational analysis takes a distributional view of urban geography, that is, what are the mappable patterns or the geometry of the objects geographers study? Are they random or do they reveal some order, some recurrence, even some predictability? "*Where* are things?" has long been a fundamental interest of geography. Of even more interest, however, is *why* are geographic features distributed as they are? For example, what factors are responsible for the distribution of manufacturing plants or the location of

banks within an urban area? Locational analysis, then, is concerned with abstracting geographical space into (1) **nodes** (places conceived as points), (2) **networks** (connections among nodes), (3) **movements** (flows on nodal networks), (4) **hierarchies** (sequential ordering of nodes and networks), and (5) **surfaces** (three-dimensional representations). Geographical equivalents of these abstract geometric concepts are a city (node), a road system (network), airline passenger volumes among a group of urban areas (movement), the arrangement of cities from largest to smallest in population size (the urban hierarchy), and the population distribution within a city viewed in three dimensions (surface) (Haggett, 1966).

Locational analysis promotes an abstract way of thinking about urban geography, both within and among cities. Abstract thinking is an aid to generalization. It generates new questions to be asked on which to design case studies or empirical analysis. Abstraction for its own sake may rightly be seen as an idle exercise, but, when combined with comparison with real world geographies, abstracting and theorizing can offer satisfying understandings of how an otherwise hopelessly convoluted reality actually operates.

A few basic abstract spatial concepts may be briefly noted, demonstrating that these concepts are not vague, meaningless philosophic constructs detached from reality but rather are concepts that we ourselves use (consciously or not) in our everyday lives. Examples here are (1) *distance*, (2) *direction*, (3) *diffusion* (**the three Ds**), and (4) *position*. Distance may be thought of in different ways: physical distance measured in feet, miles, or kilometers; economic distance based on the cost or time for movement to occur between places; and social distance or societal barriers that exist or that are perceived to exist between two or more groups derived from differences among a combination of culture, ethnicity, and race. Direction implies an orientation with respect to north (measured in degrees) or movement bias along certain paths or sectors in the urban area rather than others. Diffusion implies a spread across geographic space, such as the spread of suburbanization. Position is simply the location of an object in geographic space, often measured with respect to a coordinate system (longitude and latitude, or x and y).

From the three Ds, we can derive the notions of *accessibility* and *connectivity*. Accessibility refers to proximity, that is relative nearness or isolation in space. Connectivity is defined as the level of connections between or among places, usually thought of as based on a network, such as a highway network. By adding the concept of position to the three Ds, we can derive the abstract idea of **site** and **situation.** Site can be the equivalent of position or location, and in urban geography it usually refers to the characteristics of the physical location of a city. Thus, a city may be located on a coast, in the interior, on a river, at the foothills of a mountain range, on a bay, and so on. For example, San Francisco is perched on a hilly peninsula, which explains why it developed its now-famous cable cars instead of the more common trolley cars that were characteristic of other cities located on flatter sites. Situation refers to relative location, or the location of a city with respect to other cities or places. Many cities play important economic functions because they are accessible to other important places. For example, Chicago, though located in an area that was formerly a swampy lowland relic of the now smaller Lake Michigan (its site), became a major city because it developed extensive rail connections with other places in growing Midwest. Thus, Chicago owes its prominence to its situation (relative location), not to its original site. Situation helps explain, for example, why the busiest Amtrak stations in 2004 were in New York (4.4 million boardings), Washington D.C. (1.9 million), Philadelphia (1.8 million), Chicago (1.2 million), and Newark (0.7 million). All of these stations, except for the rail center of Chicago, are located in the high-density east coast corridor.

THE CHICAGO AND LOS ANGELES SCHOOLS OF URBAN GEOGRAPHY

Historically, urban geography as a field of study may be usefully viewed as constituting two "schools" of thought, emphasizing different themes, methods, and conclusions: the Chicago School and the Los Angeles School. Chicago and Los Angeles, two very different kinds of metropolitan areas, served as the primary prototypes and study areas for these schools.

The Chicago School

Not to be confused with the 1920s Chicago School of Human Ecology or Urban Sociology, the Chicago School of Urban Geography developed and reached its apex in the 1960s (Yeates, 2005). This axis of the Chicago School stretched between the University of Chicago and Northwestern University. The foremost leader of the Chicago School was Brian J. L. Berry at the University of Chicago, along with his many PhD students, who carried Berry's ideas throughout North America. Other leading urban geographers at Chicago were Chauncy Harris and Harold Mayer. At Northwestern, Edward J. Taaffe, himself a Chicago PhD, led the urban geography program. The Chicago School became known for developing several major themes in urban research: cities as systems within systems of cities, a classification of commercial land uses, central place theory, residential patterns within cities, and housing location and racial composition. In the mid-1960s the Chicago School was asked to review the 1960 definition of metropolitan areas. The result was a new (1970) definition that recognized a nucleus or core central city but also a surrounding functional set of counties demarcated by commuting flows, an approach still in use in 2000. Throughout the 1960s and well into the 1970s and 1980s, the Chicago School formed the core of urban geography.

The Los Angeles School

Whereas the Chicago School was concerned with the application of logic, rationality, and the scientific method, the Los Angeles School is more associated with postmodern thinking (Dear, 2005, p. 328). Michael Dear wrote that "The Los Angeles School of urbanism emerged as a coherent challenge to established urban theory during the mid-1980s. For example, instead of the traditional monocentric model of the city based on research on the city of Chicago, with the central business district organizing employment, retailing, and social, cultural, and political activities, the Los Angeles School celebrates the hinterland or suburbs organizing the entire metropolitan area." Charles Jencks (1993, p.7) summarized the most important characteristics of Los Angeles:

> Los Angeles, like all cities, is unique, but in one way it may typify the world city of the future: there are only minorities. No single ethnic group, nor way of life, nor industrial sector dominates the scene. Pluralism has gone further here than in any other city in the world and for this reason it may well characterize the global metropolis of the future.

Whereas some urban scholars are critical of the notion of a "new" Los Angeles School of Urban Geography, Dear (2005) is quick to acknowledge that it is not the intent of the LA School to replace the traditional Chicago School:

> The LA School justifies a presentation of LA not as *the* model of contemporary urbanism... but as one of a number of space-time geographical prisms through which current [urban] processes...may be advantageously viewed... It is but one component in an emerging new comparative urban studies working out of Los Angeles.

So we have traveled in this chapter, according to Michael Dear, from Chicago to Los Angeles, and many places elsewhere and in between.

THE NEW URBANISM

New Urbanism "is a complex planning paradigm and social movement that has recently become influential in planning, residential development, and government housing" (Al-Hindi and Till, 2001, p. 189). The concept emerged in the 1980s as a feature of architecture using unusual colors and whimsical styles. The new urbanism as pursued

by planners emphasizes a pedestrian scale, clearly defined centers, mixed-use spaces, accessible open space, and high-density land use. New urbanism remains controversial as it is antisprawl, pedestrian oriented, and anti–automobile dependent. New urbanism seeks more environmentally, ecologically, economically, and socially sustainable communities, family-oriented lifestyles, livable neighborhoods— really an urban and suburban utopia (Al-Hindi and Till, 2001). Despite its widespread appeal in principle, new urbanism has been limited to only a relatively few neighborhoods, primarily in the South (Florida and the Washington, D.C. area of Maryland and Virginia) and West (California).

INTRODUCTION TO THIS TEXTBOOK

As we have discussed, urban geography has evolved into one of the leading teaching and research subareas of geography over the past few decades. Urban geography has been taught to tens of thousands of undergraduates in recent years, many of whom have gone on to pursue graduate degrees and careers in urban geography, urban and regional planning, public administration, and related fields, as well as in teaching. To a great many students, the study of urban geography has proved to be a fascinating and stimulating field with high relevance to everyday life. Having provided a contemporary overview of this field, we conclude this chapter with a brief summary of this textbook.

Following this introductory chapter, we turn to the origins and historical developments of cities. Why did early cities arise when they did and why did they prosper in certain locations and not in others? These first two chapters constitute Part I of the book. Part II, which constitutes Chapters 3 through 5, focuses on metropolitan systems. Chapter 3 introduces theories and issues associated with the evolution of the American urban systems, including the American urban hierarchy, during the years 1630–2006. It addresses the concepts of metropolitan dominance, urbanization processes, and contemporary urban-economic restructuring. Chapter 4 treats the world urban system from a globalization perspective, examining world cities and the role of capitalism, linkages among world cities, and the role of multinational corporations. A unique feature of this book is Chapter 5, which explores the role of telecommunications and the city at both the intraurban and interurban levels. The chapter presents evidence that telecommunications normally leads to greater concentration of human activities rather than dispersal, despite the fact that it enables people to communicate instantaneously over great distances. How can that be?

Part III—Chapters 6 and 7—turn to the economic landscape within metropolitan areas. Chapter 6 explores the changing role of the downtown or the central business district and the rise and development of suburbanization of people, retailing, and manufacturing during the twentieth century. This study of the economic landscape is followed by an examination of landscapes of production, that is, manufacturing, in Chapter 7. Not only has industrial employment undergone a drastic decline in absolute and relative numbers in recent decades but the location of industrial land use within metropolitan areas has also manifested fundamental locational changes.

Part IV, which consists of Chapters 8 through 11, treats the social landscapes of the metropolitan area. Here the focus is on people and how and where they live. Chapter 8 presents traditional models of urban social space but also examines new factors that organize intraurban space—globalization and postmodernism. Chapter 9 focuses on urban housing, particularly the role of government, the debate over discrimination in the housing market, housing "blight," neighborhood revitalization (gentrification), and urban sprawl. Chapter 10 relates the topics of residential segregation, race, and poverty, with careful attention to the North American inner city. This chapter deals with all of the difficult and controversial issues of discrimination, welfare reform, and the "underclass." Chapter 11 analyzes the relationships among the issues of immigration, ethnicity, and urbanism, with special emphasis on the geographic patterns of Latino and Asian immigration. This chapter will be of utmost interest to those of you who lived in a rapidly changing social and ethnic environment.

Part V introduces the political landscapes of metropolitan areas, with Chapter 12 presenting major issues of metropolitan governance and geographical and political fragmentation. Chapter 13 explains how urban planning works and how it can help create a better city. Those of you who wish to make a career in planning will find this chapter especially informative.

The final section of the book, Part VI, first examines cities in the developed or industrial parts of the world other than the United States and Canada (Chapter 14) and in the less developed nonindustrial areas of the world (Chapter 15). These are fascinating reviews of where and how people live such different lives in the world cities. Finally, Chapter 16 details the geographic layout of cities in Latin America, Sub-Saharan Africa, South Asia, and Southeastern Asia.

WRAPPING UP

Urban geography today is the leading substantive area of geography and the one in which GIS technology, the leading growth segment in contemporary geography, is most often applied. As with other social and behavioral sciences, urban geography is a product of the past century, with most of its accomplishments occurring only within the past few decades. Urban geography has taken advantage of the opportunities of using multiple perspectives on how to conduct research to better understand our changing urban regions in the United States and Canada and around the world. Given the rich academic and pedagogic traditions built by multiple generations of geographers interested in the city, contemporary urban geographic education, training, and research offer challenging employment opportunities in private industry, government, planning, and education.

READINGS

Alderman, Derek H. 2002. "School Naming as Cultural Arenas: The Naming of U.S. Public Schools after Martin Luther King, Jr.," *Urban Geography*, Vol. 23, pp. 601–626.

Al-Hindi, Karen Falconer and Karen E. Till. 2001. "(Re)Placing the New Urbanism Debates: Toward an Interdisciplinary Research Agenda," *Urban Geography*, Vol. 22, pp. 189–201.

Barnes, Trevor. 2005. "The 1990s Show: Culture Leaves the Farm and Hits the Streets," in B. J. L. Berry and James O. Wheeler, eds. *Urban Geography in America, 1950–2000: Paradigms and Personalities*. New York: Routledge, pp. 311–326.

Berry, Brian J. L. 1999. "Beyond Postmodernism," *Urban Geography*, Vol. 20, pp. 289–590.

Berry, Brian. J. L., and Allan Pred. 1961. *Central Place Studies: A Bibliography of Theory and Applications*. Philadelphia: Regional Science Research Institute.

Berry, Brian J. L. and James O. Wheeler, eds. 2005. *Urban Geography in America, 1950–2000: Paradigms and Personalities*. New York: Routledge.

Blake, Megan K. and Susan Hanson. 2005. "Rethinking Innovation: Context and Gender," *Environment and Planning A*, Vol. 37, pp. 681–701.

Christaller, Walter. 1933. *Die Zentralen Orte in Süddeutschland*. Translated by C. W. Baskin, 1966, as *Central Places in Southern Germany*. Englewood Cliffs, NJ: Prentice-Hall.

Clark, David. 1996. *Urban World/Global City*. New York: Routledge.

Dear, Michael. 1988. "The Postmodern Challenge: Reconstructing Human Geography," *Transactions, Institute of British Geographers*, Vol. 13, pp. 262–274.

Dear, Michael. 2000. *The Postmodern Urban Condition*. Madden; MA: Blackwell.

Dear, Michael, ed. 2002. *From Chicago to L.A.* Thousand Oaks, CA: Sage Publications.

Dear, Michael. 2005. "The Los Angeles School of Urbanism: An Intellectual History." In B. J. L. Berry and J. O. Wheeler, eds., *Urban Geography in America, 1950–2000: Paradigms and Personalities*. New York: Routledge, pp. 327–348.

Dear, Micheal, and Steve Flusty. 1998. "Postmodern Urbanism," *Annals of the Association of American Geographers* Vol. 88, pp. 50–72.

Emerson, F. V. 1907. *A Geographical Interpretation of New York*. Chicago: University of Chicago.

Gilbert, Melissa R., 1997. "Feminism and Differences in Urban Geography," *Urban Geography*, Vol. 18, pp. 166–179.

Gottmann, Jean. 1961. *Megaopolis: Urbanization of the Northeastern Seaboard of the United States*. New York: The Twentieth Century Fund.

Haggett, Peter. 1966. *Locational Analysis in Human Geography*. New York: St. Martin's Press.

Hägerstrand, Torsten. 1952. *Innovationsförloppet ur korologisk Synpunkt*. Translated by A. Pred, 1967, as *Innovation Diffusion as a Spatial Process*. Chicago: University of Chicago Press.

Hanson, Susan, and Perry Hanson. 1980. "Gender and Urban Activity Patterns in Uppsala, Sweden," *Geographical Review*, Vol. 70, pp. 291–299.

Harris, Chauncy D. 1940. *Salt Lake City: A Regional Capital*. Chicago: University of Chicago Press.

Harris, Chauncy. 1997. "The Nature of Cities and Urban Geography in the Last Half Century," *Urban Geography*, Vol. 18, pp. 15–35.

Harris, Chauncy D., and Edward L. Ullman. 1945. "The Nature of Cities," *Annals of the American Academy of Political and Social Science*, Vol. 242, pp. 7–17.

Hartshorne, Richard. 1939. *The Nature of Geography*. Lancaster, PA: Association of American Geographers.

Harvey, David. 1989. *The Urban Experience*. Baltimore, MD: Johns Hopkins University Press.

Jefferson, Mark. 1939. "The Law of the Primate City," *Geographical Review*, Vol. 29, pp. 226–232.

Jencks, Charles. 1993. *Heteropolis: Los Angeles, the Riots, and the Strange Beauty of Hetero-architecture*. New York: St. Martins.

Kaplan, David H., and Alex Schwartz. 1996. "Minneapolis-St. Paul in the Global Economy," *Urban Geography*, Vol. 17, pp. 44–59.

Leitner, Helga. 1992. "Urban Geography: Responding to New Challenges," *Progress in Human Geography*, Vol. 16, pp. 105–118.

Lo, C. P., and A. K. W. Yeung. 2000 *Concepts and Techniques of Geographic Information Systems*. Upper Saddle River, NJ: Prentice Hall.

Lösch, August. 1938. *Die Räumliche Ordnung der Wirtscraft*. Translated by W. H. Woglom and W. F. Stolper, 1954, as *The Economics of Location*. New Haven, NJ: Yale University Press.

Massey, Doreen. 1973. "Towards a Critique of Industrial Location Theory," *Antipode*, Vol. 5, pp. 33–39.

Mitchell, Don. 2000. *Cultural Geography*. Madden, MA: Blackwell Publishers.

Nelson, Howard. 1949. *The Livehood Structure of Des Moines, Iowa*. Chicago: University of Chicago.

Parkins, A. 1914. *The Historical Geography of Detroit*. Chicago: University of Chicago Press.

Pattison, William. 1964. "The Four Traditions in Geography," *Journal of Geography*, Vol. 63, pp. 211–216.

Peet, Richard. 1998. *Modern Geographic Thought*. Malden, MA: Blackwell.

Pickles, John, and M. J. Watts. 1992. "Paradigms for Inquiry." In Ron F. Abler, Melvin G. Marcus, and Judy M. Olson, eds., *Geography's Inner Worlds*. New Brunswick, NJ: Rutgers University Press.

Platt, Robert S. 1928. "A Detail of Regional Geography: Ellison Bay Community as an Industrial Organism," *Annals of the Association of American Geographers*, Vol. 18, pp. 81–126.

Sassen, Saskia. 1991. *The Global City: New York, London, Tokyo*. Princeton, NJ: Princeton University Press.

Sassen, Saskia. 2002. *Global Networks, Linked Cities*. New York: Routledge.

Semple, Ellen C. 1911. *Influences of the Geographic Environment*. New York: Henry Holt and Company.

Soja, Ed J. 1989. *Postmodern Geographies: The Reassertation of Space in Critical Social Theory*. London: Verso.

Strong, Helen. 1921. *The Geography of Cleveland*. Chicago: University of Chicago Press.

Sui, Daniel Z. 1994. "GIS and Urban Studies: Positivism, Post-Positivism, and Beyond," *Urban geography*, Vol. 15, pp. 258–278.

Sui, Daniel Z. 1999. "Postmodern Urbanism Disrobed: Or Why Postmodern Urbanism Is a Dead End for Urban Geography," *Urban Geography*, Vol. 20, pp. 403–411.

Taaffe, Edward J. 1974. "The Spatial View in Context," *Annals of the Association of American Geographers*, Vol. 64, pp. 1–16.

Taylor, Griffith. 1949. *Urban Geography: A Study of Site, Evolution, Pattern and Town Classification in Villages, Towns and Cities*. London: Methuen.

Tower, Walter S. 1905. "The Geography of American Cities," *Bulletin of the American Geographical Society*, Vol. 37, pp. 577–588.

Tuan, Yi-Fu. 1976. "Humanistic Geography," *Annals of the Association of American Geographers*, Vol. 66, pp. 266–276.

Weber, Alfred. 1929. *Theory of the Location of Industry*. Chicago: University of Chicago Press.

Wheeler, James O. 1998. "Urban Cultural Geography: Country Cousin Comes to the City," *Urban Geography*, Vol. 19, pp. 585–590.

Yeates, Maurice. 2005. "Yesterday as Tomorrow's Song: The Contribution of the 1960s 'Chicago School to Urban Geography'." In B. J. L. Berry and J. O. Wheeler, eds., *Urban Geography in America, 1950–2000: Paradigms and Personalities*. New York: Routledge, pp. 73–92.

CHAPTER 2

THE ORIGINS AND DEVELOPMENT OF CITIES

Between the rail and the river there is sparse cultivation and little villages of mud huts or reed-mat shelters are dotted here and there; but westwards of the line is desert blank and

unredeemed. Out of this waste rise the mounds which were Ur, called by Arabs the highest of them all, the Ziggurat hill, "Tell al Muqayyar," the Mound of Pitch.

—WOOLLEY, 1930, P. 17 (FIGURE 2.1)

Only in the most recent period of human history has a significant proportion of people lived in cities. Yet, cities have existed for as long as history itself, and, although they accommodated only a few people, they stored and nurtured most of the principal features of human civilization: organized religion, complex political systems, writing and learning, crafts and technology. Perhaps cities loom so large in our narratives because the people who wrote about history and most of the subjects of history lived in cities. Ur, Athens, Xian, Mohenjo Daro, Timbuktu, Rome, Tenochtitlán, Baghdad, Venice, Hangchow, London—by modern standards these cities were never of enormous size; only a few even surpassed a million inhabitants. But these and hundreds of other cities anchored human society and even became agents of societal change.

WHAT ARE CITIES?

Cities have been defined in various ways. Historically, cities were distinguished from other forms of settlement by their larger population size, occupations in that they included populations of people not directly involved in agriculture, and position as

centers of political, economic, and social power. The elite resided within the city. Cities were also generally marked by high densities, a crowding of people who functioned together as a social unit, which distinguished the city from the area surrounding it (Figure 2.2).

The well known public intellectual, Lewis Mumford, divided the city between its *physical aspects*, which included a "fixed site, the durable shelter, the permanent facilities for assembly, interchange, and storage" and its *social aspects*, in which the city functioned as "a geographic plexus, an economic organization, an institutional process, a theater of social action, and an aesthetic symbol of collective unity" (Mumford 1937, in LeGates and Stout 2003). It was the social functions of the city—the fact of its centrality in various fields of human interaction—that was key to its existence.

We might add that the city throughout its development has been marked by all forms of social functions, and that it has witnessed both stability and transformation in regard to the nature of these functions. The primary engine of change has been *economic*, as cities have developed as central points within various economic systems: agrarian, merchant capitalist, industrial. But there have also

Figure 2.1 The Ziggurat of Ur, one of the world's most ancient cities.

Figure 2.2 This photo of the ancient city of Arbela highlights high density levels. One of the aspects of early cities was that they have a dense concentration of people.

been major *political* changes too, as cities have centralized power at ever-expanding scales and have served as capitals for different types of political regimes. And there have been major changes in *culture*. In some situations, cities have thrived as centers of orthodoxy, as reaffirmations of the status quo. At other times, cities have served as agents of profound cultural change.

Preconditions to Urban Formation

We know that cities are a relatively recent phenomenon, going back only about 6,000 years at the earliest and not globally common until 300 years ago. We also know that cities emerged in agricultural areas and, thus, that they developed only

after agriculture had been introduced and adopted by the population (Box 2.1). The emergence of cities seems to have required something beyond more than just the adoption of agriculture, however, because many agricultural regions—Amerindian cultures in southeast North America and in Amazonia, for example—did not develop cities.

One fundamental precondition for the emergence of cities is the existence of a civilization. The words *cities* and *civilization* share the same Latin root, and their connection is evident in the historical record. Although the definition of a **civilization** is even more problematic than the definition of a city, we might consider it to be *a complex sociocultural organization that contains formal institutions and*

BOX 2.1 CITIES WITHOUT AGRICULTURE?

Most researchers assume that cities could only arise in places that already had an agricultural economy, but might it have worked the other way around? Such a view is based largely on the evidence of two settlements that may have existed before agriculture had been introduced: Çatal Hüyük (in modern-day Turkey) and Jericho (on the West Bank of Jordan) (Figure B2.1).

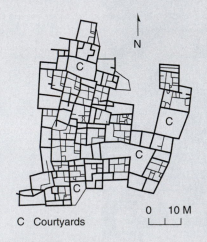

C Courtyards

0   10 M

Figure B2.1 Diagram of Çatal Hüyük.

These places reproduced many of the attributes of cities. Jericho, for example, dates back to 8000 B.C. and appears to have been a densely developed settlement of people who had just turned to agriculture. Its immense stone wall has been made famous by the Biblical story and song. Çatal Hüyük appears to have had a large concentration of people, with dwellings that people entered through the roof covering some 32 acres. The settlement dates back to 7500 B.C. That these settlements predate Sumerian cities is unquestioned, but there is a great deal of dispute as to whether these settlements can be called cities. They may have been overgrown agricultural villages, composed principally of farmers, although the discoverer of Çatal Hüyük described it as filled with a variety of workers and industries.

Using this information, Jane Jacobs 1969 has gone so far as to claim that Çatal Hüyük emerged in a preagricultural milieu—an idea spurned by most mainstream archaeologists. Its basis for existence would have been trade in important commodities like obsidian. The food was initially gathered from the immediate area or through trade. Later, the city's very existence as a trading entrepôt would have spurred intensified agriculture.

that organizes strangers into a cohesive community under the control of a centralized authority. That *civilization* has become a culturally loaded term should not detract from the need to distinguish the organization, order, and complexity that it represents from simpler forms of human association.

Certainly, cities cannot exist independently of civilization. The ability to establish a fixed settlement of several hundreds or several thousands of people who did not produce their own food required the organization, order, and complexity associated with a civilization's attributes. Conversely, most civilizations in world history developed cities, although these were of varying magnitudes. For example, the records for ancient Egyptian civilization suggest that Egyptian cities were small and temporary. In contrast, the Aztec Empire at the time of Montezuma spawned the enormous central city of Tenochtitlán. Most cities became the focal point for their civilizations; the place where the highest aspects of that civilization might be found.

Ecology, Technology, and Power   In addition to the existence of a civilization, three preconditions need to be in place in order for cities to form: proper ecological settings, technology, and social power.

1. *Ecological settings.* Cities required food, so they were located in relatively fertile areas. Most of the earliest cities seem to have developed in subtropical regions, where frost was not as great a problem. Moreover, these early cities were often established on river banks, near a fixed source of water and where the soils were easily worked. Beyond that, cities benefited from the proximity of other physical resources: natural transportation features (such as a river or a harbor), some types of mineral resources (such as a useful metal), building materials, and often militarily defensive attributes (elevation, for example). The earliest cities in Egypt and China were located near the Nile and Yellow (Huang He) rivers, respectively, where fresh water and fertile soils were available.
2. *Technology.* Certain advances in agricultural and nonagricultural areas were necessary before cities could develop. Because cities required enough food to be able to support a population of nonagricultural specialists, they could not emerge until agricultural

production had increased sufficiently to provide for sustained surpluses. In many cases, cities arose in areas where irrigation was required. Also essential to the emergence of cities were technological improvements related to the transportation and storage of food. Finally, cities themselves required substantial advances in building technology in order to accommodate the population, fortify the settlement, and build the incredibly elaborate ceremonial and monumental structures.

3. *Social organization and power.* Compared to agricultural villages, early cities were large and complex. They surpassed the point where all individuals could know one another and so required some other type of social organization to tie people together. In addition, cities required social coordination in order to (1) get food from the surrounding countryside, either through coercion or a trading relationship; (2) construct and maintain the physical aspects of the city and of its hinterland; and (3) regulate the activities of people who lived within the city. Social organization necessitated social power, which is defined as the degree to which one group was able to gain control over material and social resources and to marshal the activities of the population living inside and outside the city.

Cities could not have come into being unless all three of these preconditions were in place. Early cities also reflected these preconditions in that they served as places where agricultural surpluses were stored and distributed. Cities functioned economically as **centers of extraction and redistribution** from countryside to granaries to the urban population. One of the main functions of this central authority was to extract, store, and redistribute the grain. It is no accident that the granaries—storage areas for grain—were often found within the temples of early cities. The development of a writing system was critical to the growth of cities because it was the best method whereby a society could keep track of its grain surplus. The first types of writing seem to have been primitive ledger sheets that tracked the receipt and distribution of grain, as well as ration and wage lists. First and foremost, cities functioned politically as **seats of central power.** Cities also functioned as **centers of culture.** This is where the main hallmarks of the culture were codified and later disseminated and where power was legitimized.

Theories of Urban Origins

It is important to note how these preconditions related to one another. Favorable environments and improved agricultural technology, for example, probably increased populations, which in turn demanded even greater food production and may have necessitated a more complex social organization. The development of **social power** lies at the heart of most of the theories of urban origins. Arab historian and geographer Ibn Khaldun stated that "dynasties and royal authority are absolutely necessary for the building of cities and the planning of towns" (cited in Kostof, 1991, p. 33). Listing the preconditions for the emergence of cities, however, does not explain *why* cities developed. For decades scholars have searched for the reasons why cities appeared when and where they did. Early scholars sought a single reason for the emergence of cities. Because of the variety of urban origins, however, such monocausal explanations are too simple. Rather, it appears that cities emerged as a result of several interlinked factors. In his book *An Introduction to Urban Historical Geography*, Harold Carter 1983 summarizes four of the primary factors related to the emergence of towns and cities. These factors are agricultural surplus, religion, defensive needs, and trading requirements.

Agricultural Surplus   Over time, early farmers became better at producing enough food to feed themselves and their families, with a little extra left over. In a village environment, such an agricultural surplus would allow for a social surplus; that is, it freed up resources so that not every person had to farm. Within a small-scale society, this surplus might have been used to feed one or two people who were especially talented in creating certain objects, say, metal tools, and who could then devote more time to this occupation and get quite good at it. This early specialization involved a simple division of labor between farmers and nonagricultural specialists. As society grew larger and more complex, the surplus may have been collected to free up even more people to pursue nonagricultural work. Additionally, it might have been used so that farmers could allocate some of their time for other purposes.

There were several mechanisms whereby either a surplus was extracted directly or labor was used for a common purpose. **Tithing** involved voluntarily setting aside a fixed percentage of the harvest to be gathered collectively. **Taxation** was a system in which each farmer was compelled to pay a percentage of the harvest to the goverment. **Corvée labor** was a practice in which the government compelled individuals to work for a period of time on some grand public works. The building of the Egyptian tombs, for instance, was a product of slave labor and corvée labor.

A key question here is whether the existence of a surplus by itself necessitated the development of social power. According to early archaeologists such as Sir Leonard Woolley and V. Gordon Childe, producing and managing such a surplus required some organization, which in turn necessitated some form of social control. **Central authority** came about because it was needed to administer the surplus. This argument has been applied especially to the development of complicated irrigation systems, which required an elaborate organization of labor. But there were certainly civilizations and cities—such as early Sumerian society—that did not emerge as a result of extensive irrigation works. Moreover, it is just as likely that any large-scale public works came after the development of organized society. There is no definitive argument that surplus alone required mechanisms of social control.

Religious Causes   One of the common features of all early cities was the existence of a temple. In every case, the temple was far more prominent than any other element within the city. The great temple of Ur could be seen for miles over the flat Mesopotamian plain. Mohenjo Daro, in the Indus Valley in present-day Pakistan, included a religious citadel approximately 43 feet high (Figure 2.3). Even proto-cities, such as Çatal Hüyük in modern-day Turkey, show that much of the urban space was

Figure 2.3 This citadel was located at the edge of the Indus Valley city of Mohenjo Daro. This view shows the high western mound made up of a massive mud brick platform and brick houses of the Harappan period (2600–1900 B.C.). On top of the Harappan structures is a Buddhist period stupa made of mud brick that dates to the first century A.D.

given over to religious purposes. Certainly, religion was important enough in all preurban societies and religious structures so prominent in all early cities that it made sense for religion to be linked with the development of social power. This relationship was bolstered by the fact that early elites held both political and spiritual authority; king and high priest were one and the same.

Based on this history, it is easy to reconstruct a process by which a powerful priestly class emerged from the creation of agricultural surplus. Many of the early nonagricultural specialists were likely to be involved in producing tangible goods. But there were also a few especially charismatic individuals who explained the unknown tragedies—drought, flood, pests, disease—that were so much a part of the lives of the villagers. These individuals were given the status of specialists too, but with a twist: they were specialists in explaining and in codifying the necessary religious rituals that could help to appease the unknown. As these people became more powerful, they formed the prototype of a **priestly class**—a class of people concerned with explaining the supernatural and with mediating between the villagers and supernatural forces. Over generations, this priestly class became distinct from the rest of the population—

decreasing rules of membership and dictating how priestly status could be passed from parent to child—and in some cases claiming divine origins. Most important, they gained control over the surplus and were able to utilize it to serve their ends—all with the full acceptance of the overall population. This blending of religious and secular authority, a **theocracy,** was a hallmark of early civilizations.

Clearly, a priestly class was vitally important, but there is no proof that its emergence provided the sole impetus for complex social organization, and that by itself it transformed early village society into a concentrated, coordinated urban society.

Defensive Needs Another feature of early cities was the presence of some type of fortification. Most ancient cities had walls, and all of them displayed evidence of defensive works, a soldier class, and armaments production. The Egyptian hieroglyph for a town was a cross within a circle. The cross suggested a meeting place of sorts, perhaps in the form of a marketplace. The circle stood for the walls protecting this meeting place. Ironically, most ancient Egyptian cities did not have prominent walls, a point of distinction between these cities and the heavily fortified cities of ancient Sumeria (Figure 2.4).

Figure 2.4 Ancient walls and fortifications in a Sumerian city. Walls were an essential aspect of the early Sumerian city. They kept out attackers and also restricted access to outside villagers. The wall of Uruk stretched about 6 miles in circumference.

Early cities clearly needed some form of defense because of their storehouses of grain, their position as the seat of central authority, and their concentration of people. They probably made inviting and visible targets. We might imagine that, in the face of attack, cities would open up their gates to the inhabitants of the immediate hinterland, offering them shelter and providing them with a spear or a sling. As any soldier knows, a successful defense requires a tremendous amount of coordination, and such coordination requires a clear chain of command and a division of labor. The most successful armies were likely those that could afford to train full time, supplemented by additional, part-time soldiers when the demand was great. Much of the surplus would have been siphoned off to pay for the building of fortifications, the production of armaments, and the care and feeding of the soldiers. Once established, a military class would occupy a privileged position and be able to exert a degree of social control over the inhabitants of the city and the hinterland.

Trading Requirements The development of more complex cultures went hand in hand with the growth of a more complex economy. There is a fair amount of evidence that there was a brisk trade in particular commodities before cities had fully emerged. In the Near East, the trade seems to have been primarily in obsidian, a hard volcanic glass useful as bits for tools, but other items were traded as well. Many of the metal tools produced in Mesopotamia used copper, which would have had to come from the Anatolian plateau, a distance of more than 1,000 miles. Trade itself has been cited as a factor that sparked the emergence of marketplaces and that could have formed the basis of new cities. Preurban traders who traveled between settlements would have enabled early populations to barter items that were not universally available. Their trading of specialized goods promoted greater specialization and economic intensification as people sought to produce food surpluses to buy other agricultural and nonagricultural products. This trade also enabled skilled, nonagricultural craftsmen to thrive. Cities would have formed around the central focal point of trade, the marketplace.

Trade was certainly a significant component of many early cities, and it can be considered the principal factor in the reawakening of urban life during the Middle Ages (see later section). At the same time, there is less evidence that trade was *the* prime cause of development of the first cities. Marketplaces, while sometimes present, did not assume the grandeur and significance of temples and walls. The archaeological record does not indicate that merchants as a group were accorded a privileged status (in contrast to their status in the medieval trading cities). In fact, a capitalist economy beneficial to free trade did not exist until much later. Economic exchange was carefully regulated and subordinated to the rules and rituals of theocratic life.

It is clear from the preceding discussion that no single cause can be isolated as the key factor in the emergence of cities. Certain favorable social and ecological factors combined in specific places to allow for the evolution of the world's earliest urban centers and the birth of civilization.

PATTERNS OF EARLY URBANIZATION

The history of early cities takes place over broad stretches of time and space. At one time, scholars believed that cities developed in one place—early Mesopotamia—and from there diffused to all other places on earth. Although the earliest cities emerged in Mesopotamia, most scholars now propose that cities developed independently in several cultures and locations. And inasmuch as agriculture was a key requirement for supporting cities, urban settlement would have occurred only in places where a farming economy was first in place. From these initial hearths, urbanization then diffused.

Locations of Early Cities
The locations of early cities are indicated in Figure 2.5. (See Box 2.2, Uncovering Lost Cities.) Most researchers agree that the first true cities appeared in Sumeria (in southern Mesopotamia, now present-day Iraq) around 4750 B.C. Cities then appeared in Egypt around 3000 B.C., in the Indus Valley (in present-day Pakistan) about 2200 B.C., and in northern China, along the Huang He River, in 1500 B.C. There is also distinct evidence of independently developed cities in southern Mexico about A.D. 1, in Peru by about A.D. 1000, and possibly independent urban centers emerging in West Africa a bit later. All of these

cities show evidence of a powerful ruling class with a theocratic orientation, literacy, advanced means of redistributing surplus, and substantial records of irrigation works (except for Mesoamerica, which relied on maize). Cities may have also developed independently in other places, but the evidence for this is less clear.

It is important to point out that these early cities were all situated in regions of early agricultural production. Simply speaking, cities required a surplus and a sedentary population. Agriculture provided both of these elements. Successful agricultural production yielded a consistent surplus that could be planned for at harvest time. **Seed agriculture,** such as that practiced in all of the early urban sites, compelled the population to remain sedentary, focused around a plot of land. Agricultural production also increased the overall density of the population. Early hunting and gathering populations sported population densities of less than one person per square mile. The introduction of farming practices boosted these densities considerably, especially within the fertile valleys of Mesopotamia, the Indus, and the Huang He.

Diffusion of Urbanization
Cities diffused from the early hearths into many areas: from Mesopotamia and Egypt, throughout the eastern Mediterranean, and along the coasts of North Africa and southern Europe; from the Indus Valley through central Asia; from the Huang He region east to northern China; and throughout Mesoamerica. Archaeological expeditions continue to expand what is known about the number and scale of early cities (Figure 2.5). They also suggest points of contact among established civilizations, often in the form of settlements that developed along trading routes. There is also greater evidence that some cultures, such as ancient Egyptian culture and the Anasazi culture in what is now the southwestern United States, created temporary cities that were occupied for a period of time and then abandoned.

What made cities possible, necessary, or attractive to cultures, thus causing cities to diffuse? Certainly, advances in agricultural technology would have played an important role in creating the necessary

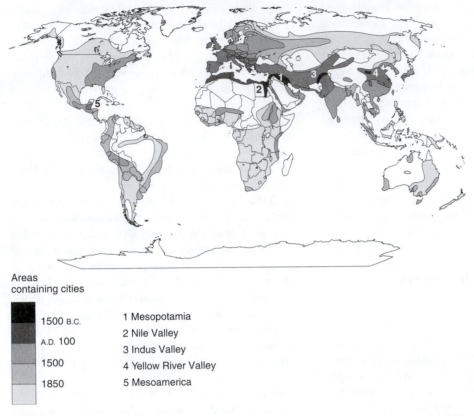

Areas
containing cities

1500 B.C.	1 Mesopotamia
A.D. 100	2 Nile Valley
1500	3 Indus Valley
1850	4 Yellow River Valley
	5 Mesoamerica

Figure 2.5 Urban diffusion. Cities diffused, slowly at first, from their original hearths. Diffusion occurred along with advances in agricultural technology, transportation improvements, and military conquest.

surpluses to support cities. Perhaps the most important of these advances was the transition from bronze to iron as a principal metal, beginning about 1200 B.C. Early agriculture was confined to river valleys with light, easily worked alluvial soil. Iron enabled people to build better axes so they could clear more land and to produce stronger plowshares that enabled them to dig up firmer, more fertile fields. All of this increased the amount of arable land. It is no accident that there was more urban growth in the first five centuries of the Iron Age than in the preceding 15 centuries of the Bronze Age.

Transportation improvements were also significant. Most cities emerged in places with good access to natural transportation routes such as rivers, but transportation advances allowed them to function within a broader area. Here too, iron was important in that it formed better wheels and faster ships. Transportation advances broadened the territory within which trade could occur. Traders, like the Phoenicians, established cities that helped them to extend their trade. The city of Carthage, in present-day Tunisia, was established this way. Minoan Crete likewise had a strong trading economy and established ports throughout Crete and on other Aegean islands. In addition, colonies were often established to accommodate surplus populations and to exploit new lands. In the case of the Greek colonies, found as far west as Sicily, these new settlements were autonomous.

BOX 2.2   TECHNOLOGY AND URBAN GEOGRAPHY

UNCOVERING LOST CITIES

Excavating ancient cities used to literally involve a great deal of spade work, as archaeologists used their own insights and shovels to unearth settlements buried beneath the ground. Now, the discovery of ancient cities has been aided immeasurably by orbiting satellites and remote sensing images. These images can "see" a landscape using different light spectrums, many invisible to the naked eye. Moreover, archaeologists can also use ground-penetrating radar that shows structures buried several feet underneath the surface. This is especially useful in landscapes buried under sandy deserts, as is true of many ancient settlements.

The lost city of Ubar, buried underneath the sands of present-day Oman, was discovered with a combination of painstaking research, intuition, and the utilization of remote sensing technology. Ubar grew as a center for the extraction and distribution of frankincense, an incense prepared from the sap of trees and used for medical and cosmetic purposes. It became prominent in the second century A.D. While myths had grown around the city, its existence was not known for sure. It was purportedly located in the midst of a vast sand desert and so was almost impossible to uncover in the traditional manner. But images from orbiting satellites (Figure B2.2) displayed features that were associated with the buried city, including ancient caravan tracks, and from that point on this important ancient city was uncovered again.

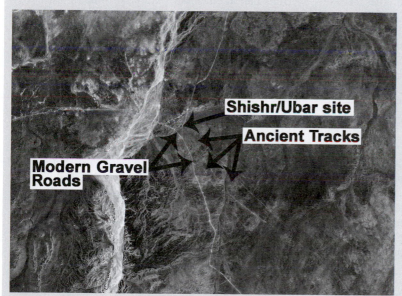

Figure B2.2 Landsat Image of Ubar. Arrows point out the incense trail leading to the Ubar site.

Military conquest consolidated smaller states into larger ones, as ambitious rulers compelled their people to take over adjoining areas. As the size of states grew larger, the number of independent political entities shrank. By 2300 B.C., all of the Sumerian city-states had been merged into a single state. Elsewhere, similar consolidations were taking place. Grand civilizations emerged from smaller civilizations, as conquests expanded the area under central control. Within these newly conquered territories, cities were established as centers of extraction and control.

URBAN EVOLUTION AND EARLY ECONOMIC IMPERATIVES: TRADITIONAL CITIES

Ancient cities varied enormously. The sizes of early cities ranged from about 2,000 to the million or so found in Xian (capital of Tang China), Rome, and Baghdad (as the center of the Islamic caliphate). The forms of cities were likewise varied: Some were more planned, whereas others appeared to emerge organically from a central focus. Similarly, some relied on heavy fortifications, but a few existed without walls. Yet cities also had a common function. This is even more true of traditional cities—those that existed prior to the onset of mercantile capitalism in the European Late Middle Ages. These traditional cities shared three key aspects:

1. *They depended for their existence on the (generally forced) extraction of goods from a hinterland.* The mechanism of this extraction might have been taxes or tribute, but it was by and large a compulsory relationship. Clearly trade existed, but it was less significant and did not form the economic basis of cities.
2. *They were focused around an elite group, usually but not always religious.* This group's establishment in the city demonstrated their central position and helped to elevate the city above the countryside. It was from this elite group that the city itself was established.
3. *They were centers of cultural orthodoxy.* Although they reflected the increased elaboration and sophistication of culture, politics, and economic relations, ancient cities mostly promoted the status quo and resisted change. They were at the centers of their civilizations, not at the margins of transformation. Cities were laid out spatially to promote this orthodoxy.

The Early City-States: Sumeria

As we have seen, the earliest identifiable cities were found in southern Mesopotamia, in Sumeria. Earlier settlements, like Jericho, are impressive and share many of the features of early cities, such as concentrated settlements and fortifications. But they stand isolated from any larger civilization and appear to have been populated with farmers. Along the valleys of the Tigris and Euphrates rivers we see the emergence of some of the first true cities within a broader civilization. Agriculture had flourished for a long time in this area, beginning in the mountains surrounding the river valley and then moving to the lowlands by approximately 5300 B.C. Beginning with Eridu in about 4750 B.C., by 3600 B.C. a number of cities were strung along the river banks: Uruk, Ur, Lagash, and Al'Ubaid (Figure 2.6). The populations of these early centers were enormous when we consider that most agricultural villages contained maybe 100 people. These cities contained as many as 10,000 people by 3100 B.C. and 50,000 people by 2600 B.C.

Sumerian civilization was organized around a dozen or so cities, initially politically separate from one another but culturally similar. Each city extracted a surplus from its **hinterland,** and it simply could not exist without the yields of the fertile area surrounding it. Because of this, the size of early cities was limited by the surplus gathered from the hinterland, and in the early urban period, agricultural surpluses were quite low. Even assuming a surplus of 20 percent (quite generous for this period), a city of 10,000 people would require a hinterland of 40,000 farmers, and a city of 50,000 would require a hinterland of 200,000 farmers. Only a very sophisticated political system could manage a hinterland of this size.

The relationship between city and hinterland was codified in the political form of the **city-state.** City-states are rare today, but they have been quite common throughout the history of cities. Each of the Sumerian cities was encased within a politically sovereign **state** (another term for *country*). It was a simple arrangement whereby the city politically and militarily controlled its surrounding countryside. The city itself was the tangible definition of central authority. Directives and policies flowed out to the hinterland just as surplus grain flowed into the city. Later, these city-states were consolidated into larger

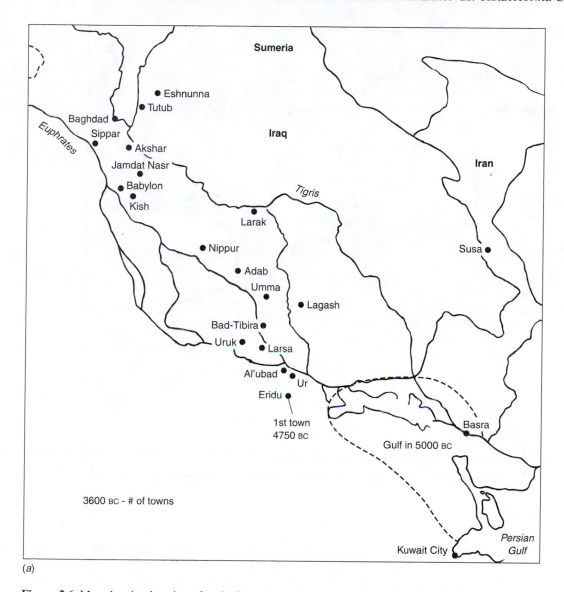

(a)

Figure 2.6 Map showing location of early Sumerian cities. Early Sumerian city-states stretched along the Tigris and Euphrates Rivers in what is now Iraq.

kingdoms. Other civilizations—most likely ancient Egypt and the Indus Valley—included several cities under one central authority.

The spatial arrangement of the early Sumerian city-states was best described by Gideon Sjoberg 1960 in his book *The Preindustrial City: Past and Present*. He meant this model to apply to all nonindustrial cities and, indeed, certain elements recur in cities throughout time and space. The model is most completely exemplified in the Sumerian city (Figure 2.7), as discussed next.

Each city was associated with a hinterland, the purpose of which was to provide food to the city. The city itself was almost always surrounded by

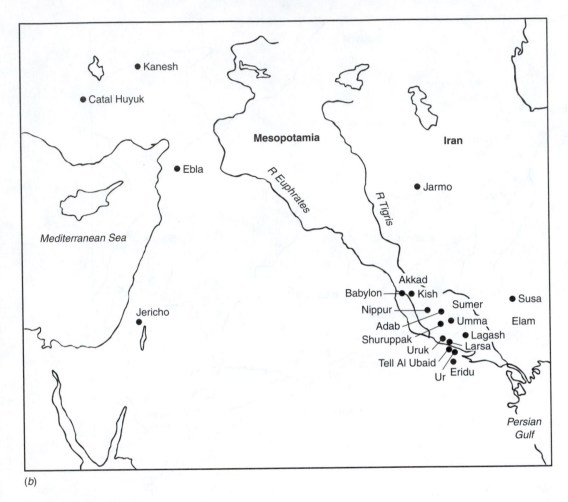

(b)

Figure 2.6 (*Continued*)

a wall. These were sometimes enormous. One of these early Sumerian cities, Uruk, had an area of close to 2 square miles and a surrounding wall about 6 miles long with 900 to 950 circular, defensive towers. The wall was between 10 and 20 yards thick and was built of mud brick. This obviously had defensive functions, but it also defined barriers between the more privileged urban dwellers and the less privileged rural folk. Access from the outside was limited to times when the gates were open.

In the center of the city, an elite compound or *temenos* was situated. Study of the very earliest cities show this compound to be largely composed of a temple and supporting structures. The temple rose some 40 feet above the ground and would have presented a formidable profile to those far away. The temple contained the priestly class, scribes, and record keepers, as well as granaries, schools, crafts—almost all nonagricultural aspects of society. One Sumerian temple employed more than 1,200 people.

The increasing complexity of early society was reflected in the emergence of separate structures within this elite compound. The first structure to emerge in very early cities was a palace. The existence of a palace suggests that secular authority may

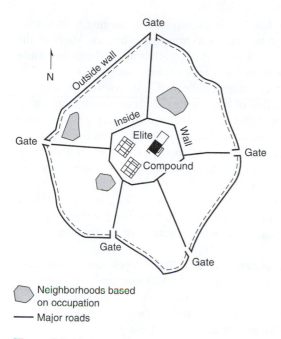

Neighborhoods based on occupation

—— Major roads

Figure 2.7 Model of a Sumerian city.

have existed apart from religious authority, although the same person likely held both offices. Another somewhat grisly finding, reported by Woolley 1930, were the kingly graves at Ur, which included the royal remains along with 74 sacrificed victims. Such sacrifices were common in many cultures and were probably entered into willingly, even gladly, as people looked forward to assisting their divine masters in the afterlife.

From the center of the city to the gates stretched the major roads of the city. Power and prestige were defined in terms of spatial access to the center, so these roads were often lined with the homes of the wealthier residents. In an **organic city,** such as the cities of ancient Sumeria, roads were not designed to fit in with some grand scheme or plan, but were developed in a more haphazard manner. Other ancient cities, like Mohenjo Daro in the Indus Valley, appear to have been developed as **planned cities,** with a regular street layout.

There was also a great deal of congestion in the ancient city. Tall buildings were impossible to build because everything was made of reeds or mud brick.

This put space at a premium as population densities within the city exceeded 25,000 people per square mile. In comparison, most modern American cities have densities of around 5,000 people per square mile, and this is with the extra floor space afforded by multistory buildings and skyscrapers.

Sanitation standards were poor. If a decent water supply existed, as it did in ancient Rome, it was usually found in the wealthy parts of the city. The streets themselves were poorly drained. In fact, excavations of a Sumerian city show that the street level was raised over time as the amount of human refuse piled up, and separate entrances had to be cut into buildings.

As urban society became more complex, non-religious specialists moved out of the temples and came to surround the elite compound. Neighborhoods in these early cities were organized around occupations. There would be a few blocks with just brewers and another with just metalworkers. By and large, distance from the center was a reflection of that occupation's status. Low-prestige occupations, like tanners and butchers, would be found near the edge of the city walls. As the complexity of society grew, the urban centers became more varied. Internal walls were developed to cordon off the elite areas from the sections for commoners and to define separate **occupational neighborhoods.** Later cities also contained different ethnic groups, who were also segregated by walls.

Other Ancient Cities

Cities developed from at least five distinct hearths, and even in diffusion, we would expect changes and adaptations to different social and ecological circumstances. The Sumerian city described above is an exemplar because of its age and because it enjoys a more complete historical record. Cities arising from other ancient cultures are shrouded in great mystery, rendering it more difficult to get a sense of what they were like.

Egypt   Urban development in Egypt was possibly influenced by Sumerian civilization, but it took a very different form. Primarily this was a result of the political structure. Whereas Sumerian civilization consisted of autonomous city-states, the entire Nile valley was controlled by a single pharaoh, so cities were subsumed to the Pharaoh's needs, primarily the need to construct a grand tomb. A city, complete with a government and servants, construction crews, skilled craftsworkers, and artisans, would be developed until the pharaoh was buried. After this, the city would be abandoned. Recent discoveries of a bakery in Giza have suggested that ancient Egyptian cities, although temporary, sometimes grew to an enormous size for their time.

Indus Valley The cities of the Indus Valley civilization spanned a Texas-sized area in what is now a contentious borderland straddling Pakistan and India. Archaeological excavations have revealed at least five major cities and a couple of dozen secondary settlements. The best known of these are Harappa, nearer the Himalayan foothills, and Mohenjo Daro, closer to the seas.

Each city was impressively sized at about a square mile and probably contained 20,000 people. In contrast to the Sumerian cities, which were unplanned **organic** cities, the Indus cities were **planned** cities. They were carefully laid out with broad straight streets, suggesting that they had been designed from the outset. The consistency of urban elements across all of the major cities suggests substantial coordination and possible political unification. Unlike the early Sumerians, the Indus civilization may have been a large kingdom. In addition, several elements from the Sumerian cities are missing from the Indus cities. There is little evidence of a wall containing the city; instead, some individual compounds within were walled. There is also no clear sign of a dominating temple; each city contained a citadel that likely held ceremonial significance, although it is difficult to determine exactly what was significant. This citadel was also located to the west of the main urban concentration and was itself heavily walled. The social structure appears to have been less theocratic and more oriented to artisans and trading; one archaeologist has described the Indus cities as an "elaborate middle-class society" (Edwards, 2000).

The housing stock was varied, ranging from single-room tenements to impressive houses. Many of the houses had working bathrooms, where the waste would flush out into a main sewer line.

Our understanding of this civilization and the structure of Indus urban life is clouded by our inability to decipher the language. We simply have no clue as to what the inscriptions say. Even the names we give the cities are modern creations. There is no historical continuity. Unlike every other early civilization, the cities of the Indus Valley civilization were annihilated about 1750 B.C., by light-skinned Indo-Europeans who had no use for their sophistication. There was no successor civilization.

Northern China The longest continuous civilization belongs to the Chinese, and the oldest evidence of this civilization rests along the Huang He River, in what is called the Shang culture. Urban development here dates from before 1500 B.C. or so. But our knowledge of these cities is vague. From what we have ascertained, they housed a literate society, rigidly stratified with a divine ruler at the top supported by a warrior elite. In addition, there was a fair degree of occupational specialization. Although cities clearly existed, they were limited in number. The cities themselves were probably walled, with a palace compound in the center. But the archaeological evidence is scant. Later periods of Chinese civilization, especially the Han period beginning in 200 B.C., yield a rich harvest of artifacts that show the flourishing and continuation of a grand imperial civilization.

Mesoamerican Cities The beginnings of civilization within the New World as a whole preceded substantial cities by several centuries. Instead, small ceremonial centers helped to anchor a more complex society. The first large city emerged in Teotihuacán before A.D. 1 and began to grow rapidly, probably under the auspices of a strong central authority. By about A.D. 500, Teotihuacán was at the height of its power, reigning over a large area that focused on the Valley of Mexico but whose influence extended into the Yucatan peninsula. The size of Teotihuacán was formidable. It occupied an area of 8 square miles, and contained a population of perhaps as many as 200,000 people, making it the largest city in the New World, although far smaller than Rome and Xian (the capital of China).

What is most fascinating about Teotihuacán is its elaborate design, established according to a cosmological plan. René Millon has mapped the entire city, and in so doing has uncovered a grid oriented toward enormous temples, one of which, the Pyramid of the Sun, equals at its base the greatest Egyptian pyramid. The regularity of Teotihuacán began with the main street, the "Street of the Dead," which stretched from the Great Compound and the Temple of Quetzacoatl to another great pyramid,

the Pyramid of the Moon (Figure 2.8). Every other major street, and even the river running through the city, was laid out either parallel or perpendicular to this grand avenue.

The city contained the religious and military elite, of course, but also a number of other nonagricultural workers. Teotihuacán's economic significance is underscored by several major markets, in which goods grown, mined, or manufactured throughout middle America would have been sold. Teotihuacán also appears to have been organized along the lines of some 2,000 apartment compounds, composed of several families that may have been linked occupationally or by kinship. Further, there are remains of what are clearly ethnic

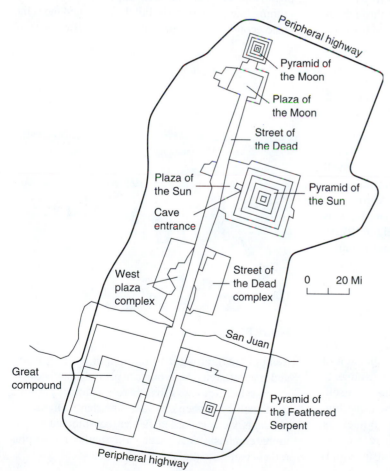

Figure 2.8 Urban plan for Teotihuacán. The ancient Mesoamerican city of Teotihuacán is an example of a planned city. The main "Street of the Dead" connected three great monuments and oriented each of the other streets.

neighborhoods, with different housing types and artifacts denoting distinct customs. The ethnic diversity in this city was echoed later in the Aztec capital of Tenochtitlán.

Imperial Cities

Toward the end of the first millennium B.C., the growth of large stable **empires** finally allowed for the development of truly huge cities of perhaps a million or more. Empires like the Roman Empire around the Mediterranean Sea, the Han and later Tang Empires in China, and the Islamic empire of the Middle East and North Africa contained upward of 50 million people and were controlled for part of their tenure by a single, dominating capital. In addition, such empires quickened the diffusion of urbanization, as cities were established throughout newly acquired lands in order to project imperial power and also as a base for colonists seeking new lands.

The scope of such cities is impressive, but these imperial cities were very similar to the older cities that had preceded them: They were based on an extractive economy, they were symbols of cultural orthodoxy, and they served as the headquarters for the elite. Of course, cities changed over the span of several millennia. Time improved building materials and architectural techniques, transportation networks, water supplies and plumbing, and defensive fortifications. Agriculture improved in efficiency and transportation advances meant that grains could come from farther afield. Social power expanded as small-scale polities merged into complex empires. The massive imperial cities looked nothing like Sumerian Ur, but they retained the same basic economic and cultural functions (Box 2.3).

BOX 2.3   THE COLLECTIVE ALTERNATIVE

In contrast to the model of a supreme ruler who arrogated all power to himself, there was also a countervailing tendency for some cities to be governed by a collective. Even in the cities of ancient Sumeria, some evidence suggests that they were governed by an assembly in the earliest period, one that was gradually supplanted by a single ruler (Figure B2.3). City-states in Greece offer the most famous example of cities that were governed by a group. The size of the enfranchised group was always small—maybe one-sixth of the overall population—but it still represented a more democratic approach to cities.

The appearance of collective power corresponds to a slightly different urban form. In general, there does not appear to have been as rigid a division of land use within the city between elite and nonelite groups or between the hinterland and the city itself. These cities often emerged in areas where the hinterland was small and where there was no need for large irrigation works. In addition, there was no clearly defined elite area. There was an **acropolis**

Figure B2.3 Athenian acropolis.

(temple area), an **agora** or common meeting place, and market areas. One other aspect of many collectively ruled cities was that there was a less parasitic relationship between city and hinterland. Hinterland residents were accorded full citizenship status, and more emphasis was placed on marketing surplus rather than on simply collecting taxes.

The size of all ancient cities was hindered by the amount of surplus that could be extracted. Over time cities became bigger for three reasons:

1. They gained a larger hinterland and, hence, a larger area from which they could extract surplus grain. Here, the important factor was the size of the state. Empires could support larger cities than small kingdoms. Because empires were so large, for the first time the sheer quantity of surplus became large enough to support a huge city. Not just crops were involved either; these vast hinterlands also made possible a large trade in luxury goods, metals, and often human slaves (Figure 2.9).
2. Agricultural technology improved, which meant that new lands were opened up and existing lands could feed more people. Many of these technologies, like the moldboard plow, allowed firm but fertile soils to be reworked. Other changes, like double-cropping of rice, meant that farmers could increase yields on the same plot of land.
3. The methods of transportation improved as ancient civilizations sought to take advantage of existing natural features or to create their own. For example, the building of the Grand Canal linking the Yangtze and Huang He rivers in Sung China was a milestone of hinterland expansion. It allowed the hungry cities in northern China to acquire rice grown in the south. Water access was crucial. Transport by land was five times as expensive as transport by river, and 20 times as expensive as transport by sea.

Imperial Rome   Rome has been called the eternal city, and in some respects it can lay claim to retaining its status as a true "world city" for an enormous length of time. It could also claim to be the single most influential city in history. Today, Rome is the capital of both Italy and of the Catholic church. In the past Rome's impact on Europe had no equal in conquest, language, administration, religion, and urbanization. Because of the Roman Empire, what had primarily been a wilderness landscape was transformed into a tableau of city, town, and farms connected by the legendary Roman roads.

Rome created an elaborate **urban system** (Figure 2.10). Roman colonies were organized as a means of securing Roman territory. The first thing that Romans did when they conquered new

territories was to establish cities. This practice reflected the Roman culture. Even rural Romans considered themselves to be urban people, and colonists (often loyal Roman legionnaires who were paid off in land) wanted to be assured that they could move to a settled community. Cities were important because they effectively projected Roman power and grandeur. Cities also facilitated the collection of taxes and made it easier for government and military officials, as well as traders, to get around. By some estimates, the Roman Empire contained about 1,200 cities, of which several exceeded 100,000 inhabitants. In the west, which had not previously been urbanized (the eastern Mediterranean lands having enjoyed a long pre-Roman period of civilization), even the smallest community was planned in accordance with the **grid pattern.** This pattern was of long duration, found in the Indus Valley many centuries prior and first postulated and consciously practiced by the Greek planner Hippodamus. The Romans, through sheer power and determination, managed to diffuse this pattern throughout the Mediterranean and Europe. The Roman grid began with two main streets constructed at right angles, paralleled by the secondary streets. A forum was then laid out at the crossing. Nearby were located a main temple, public baths, and theaters. A huge amphitheater, intended for gladiatorial and other exhibitions, was established on the outskirts of the community. Often there was a defensive wall, but sometimes it was not considered necessary for those cities situated well behind Roman lines. Through the establishment of cities, Roman control was enforced and Roman culture transmitted. The city of Rome itself was a sight to behold (Figure 2.11). It was the largest city of its time, a period that lasted from 100 B.C. until its conquest in A.D. 455 (although it suffered many decades of decline beforehand). In A.D. 300, the city contained at least 1 million people spread out over 8 square miles or more. This indicates a population density of about 200 people per acre at a time when apartments were limited to about half a dozen stories. Certainly we can see that ancient Rome was seriously **underbounded,** meaning that the official

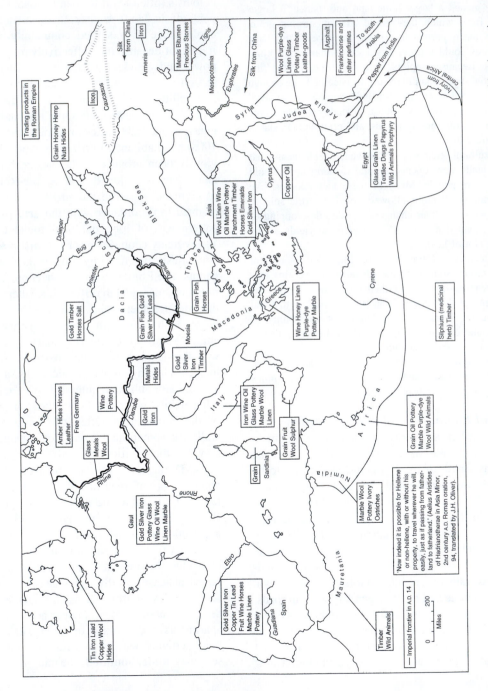

Figure 2.9 Map of Roman trade. Imperial cities, like Rome, benefited from an enormous area from which they could gain not just food, but luxury items, animals, metals, and even slaves.

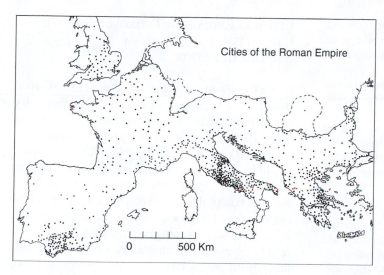

Figure 2.10 Map of Roman cities. Roman cities were primarily military and administrative, and were used to control the vast reaches of the Empire. These cities also served as magnets for Latin-speaking colonists and served to change the culture of the surrounding areas.

city limits could not contain the entire population. The Romans built seven walls, of which the largest, built in A.D. 272, stretched 11.5 miles in circumference. Rome contained eight bridges, two circuses, two amphitheaters, three theaters, 28 libraries, and 290 storehouses. The political organization of the city was likewise complex. Rome was subdivided into 14 regions and about 265 formal neighborhoods.

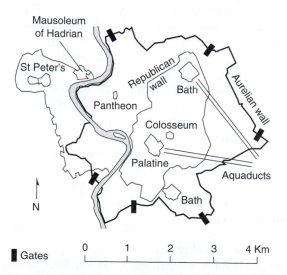

Figure 2.11 Map of ancient Rome. At its height, Rome was the biggest city in the world with about 1 million people spread out over 8 square miles.

Rome's Contribution to Urban Development

Rome synthesized a number of innovative urban elements, including mass housing, the forum, public monuments and buildings, and a more complex social geography:

- *Mass housing.* Housing was divided between the elite single-family units, called *domus*, and the popular three- to six-story tenements known as *insulae*, where the bulk of the population lived. The smallest insula contained five flats and maybe 30 or so people; larger insulae probably exceeded this number. In other cities, like the port city of Ostia, Romans built elaborate apartment complexes that contained between 40 and 100 apartments. Clearly, the Romans were well versed in developing urban housing for a growing population.
- *Roman forum.* The forum was the central area for political activity and commerce. Eventually this was lined with vast indoor halls, or *basilica*. The pressure on the forum grew so intense that, as the Roman population increased, the forum had to be repeatedly expanded.
- *Public monuments.* Each conquering general would come back and dedicate a monument to a god. The Roman state religion was **polytheistic,** which means that Romans worshipped several gods, and the number of gods continued to expand. Monuments to great leaders and especially emperors also proliferated.
- *Public buildings.* Members of the elite were expected to subsidize circuses and theaters for the population.

The Romans favored baths, enormous facilities that contained cool, warm, and hot pools along with other facilities for the hygiene and rejuvenation of the Roman citizen.

- *More complex social geography.* Rome contained a vast array of peoples, from all corners of the empire, who came to conduct business, to petition the government, or just to sightsee. Indeed, we can imagine that an inhabitant of the empire would have considered it the fulfillment of a lifelong wish to make a visit to such a luminous place. The cultural diversity of Rome led one Greek observer to write that

> he will not be far wrong who pronounces the city of the Romans an epitome of the whole earth, since you may see every other city organized collectively and many also separately … the days of an entire year would not suffice for a man who should attempt to count all the cities which are found in that uranopolis of Rome, so numerous are they. For indeed, some entire nations are settled there. (quoted in Piana, 1927, p. 206)

The size, density, and complexity of Rome created a need for greater planning. Rome was not a planned city by any means, and it had grown so large so fast that an organized design was impossible. Within the realm of the possible, though, there was a pressing need to regulate. The Romans responded to this need by categorizing their streets based on the volume of traffic and their urban function. One-way streets were imposed. Height limits, which were about 100 feet by A.D. 300, were enforced although sometimes flouted. Well known was Rome's creation of an underground city, 264 miles of aqueduct that moved away much of the city's sewage and supplied many of the inhabitants with fresh water. Despite its size, Rome was cleaner than most cities that came before or after. Of course, Rome is but one example of an imperial city. Contemporary cities like Xian and subsequent cities like Constantinople, Baghdad, and Tenochtitlán (the Aztec capital) were each at the centers of enormous empires that included several cities crowned by a big, complex capital. Other big cities into the modern era, including Paris, London, Beijing, Moscow, and Washington, D.C., would similarly rely on the surplus gathered from their hinterlands to allow them to grow and prosper.

CITIES AS ENGINES OF ECONOMIC GROWTH: CAPITALISM, INDUSTRIALISM, AND URBANIZATION

A brief assessment of the world around A.D. 1000 would have suggested that humanity's future lay in the East. Civilization at the time was vested in grand Eastern empires. The Byzantine Empire had become the successor to the fallen Roman Empire, but only in the eastern half of the Mediterranean. Its bejeweled capital was Constantinople, a city of some 500,000 that had become a kind of world emporium, with goods arriving from Europe and Asia. The Muslim religion, founded by Muhammad in the early seventh century A.D., had propelled the growth of an Islamic empire. By A.D. 1000, this empire had fragmented into several competing caliphates, but Islamic culture in its several variations, now stretched from South Asia through the Middle East, North Africa, and as far west as the Iberian Peninsula. Capitals like Córdoba and Cairo had populations of about 500,000; Baghdad probably had a population of more than 1 million. This urban heritage would continue despite the conquests of the Seljuk Turks and the later Crusades. China, the longest standing civilization, was in the midst of a golden age as the Tang dynasty gave way—after a short period of fragmentation—to the Song dynasty. This dynasty ruled two of the most impressive cities on the planet, Xian and Hangzhou.

In contrast, poor Western Europe had not recovered from the sacking of Rome and the collapse of the western half of the Roman Empire. For more than five centuries a steady process of **deurbanization**—whereby the population living in cities and the number of cities declined precipitously—had converted a prosperous landscape into a scary wilderness, overrun with bandits, warlords, and rude settlements (Box 2.4).

The New Trading Cities

The condition of Western Europe in A.D. 1000 made recovery seem laughable. Even more unbelievable was the prospect that this region would be the first to generate a new economy, one that would come

BOX 2.4   DEATH OF A CITY

In a precapitalist, imperial economy, the health and well-being of the cities depended on the empire remaining intact. This was especially true for the Roman Empire. Once the empire collapsed, marauding German tribes inherited much of the physical and human landscape, settling on estates, adopting the Latin language, and even becoming Christians. But they did not maintain the unity of the empire, dividing the spoils amongst themselves.

What were left were isolated populations living on far-flung estates ruled by German tribesmen. Roman cities were turned into wastelands, and deurbanization began in earnest. Rome itself is estimated to have lost 80 percent of its population in the first century after its collapse. By A.D. 1000, its population is estimated to have been at only 35,000. But at least Rome continued as the center of the Church, and it retained some urban functions. Other cities that depended on the Roman Empire for their economy declined even more precipitously.

Archaeological excavations of a city about 100 miles southeast of Rome, Minturnae, show what happened as the mantle of empire was stripped away. Minturnae once had 100,000 people; by A.D. 500 it had no more than 15,000. The city itself was a disaster area. Whole blocks of houses stood vacant. Fires would begin and wipe out a number of houses; earthquakes destroyed the aqueducts and people would just dig up their own wells; the street pavement fell into the underground sewers (Figure B2.4).

Individuals made do with what they could get. Abandoned houses and buildings were raided for materials. The papyrus scrolls in large libraries were used as a source of kindling, destroying centuries of knowledge. People were buried in abandoned porticos or theaters. In other cities in Europe, whole populations could be found living within the coliseum, which was large enough to contain the tiny population that remained. The few "cities" that remained were those focused around Church cathedrals and monasteries. In this way some of the trappings of urban life helped to preserve aspects of Roman civilization and also to pave the way toward a new urban revival.

Figure B2.4 Minturnae ruins.

to dominate the world and engender a new type of city far different in kind from the cities that had preceded it.

A Capitalist Economy   The impetus for renewed urbanization was the revival and primacy of a capitalist economy. Capitalism, as it was initially practiced by merchants, entailed the buying and selling of goods for profit (commercial capitalism). As practiced by artisans, capitalism entailed the creation of profit through the manufacture of finished goods (industrial capitalism). Capitalism in both forms was clearly a major force in the ancient world and continued to be important around the globe. But, with the possible exception of the Phoenicians, trade was dominated by the demands of a political structure that relied primarily on extraction. In China, for example, which had long enjoyed a strong trading economy, the merchant class was considered the lowest of the four traditional classes, whereas scholars were placed first. Throughout the world, merchants as a group were generally given very little status or autonomy. The economy, as well as the government, was primarily in the hands of the religious elite, soldiers, or great land owners. Even in Rome, many goods came into the city from the far corners of the empire, but few went out.

In Western Europe, trading had diminished so much that most people lived in self-sufficient estates, termed **autarky.** The feudal economy relied on the extraction of surplus from a peasant or serf class to the local lord or bishop, who demanded these as part of his hereditary right. Most of the surplus went to buy armor and to feed soldiers and horses. Often people starved to death because there was not enough food, much less an agricultural surplus that could be traded with someone else.

When the trading economy revived, it occurred independently of a large political empire. The new cities that grew up around trade tended to be located either outside or on the margins of feudal estates and kingdoms. There was a shift from the old traditional hinterland, based on political control and economic obligation, to a **commercial hinterland** from which the city could buy and sell its goods.

Unlike traditional cities, the new commercial cities could not rely on an agricultural hinterland from which to extract surplus. Rather they had to sustain themselves through buying and selling. Unlike traditional hinterlands, commercial hinterlands were not under anyone's singular control, although some powerful trading cities did later attempt to impose more exclusive relationships.

The Revival of Urbanization   The towns and cities that grew up in western Europe around this time were not very big. None came close to rivaling the size and splendor of eastern imperial capitals or of ancient Rome. Moreover, they emerged in the midst of political fragmentation. Earlier, the eighth-century empire of Charlemagne had succeeded in uniting a large swath of western continental Europe, but it was unable to outlast Charlemagne himself. True consolidation of many of these lands would not occur until the sixteenth century and later.

Despite this lack of centralizing authority, the population of Western Europe began to grow by A.D. 1000. Estimates suggest that Europe's population of 52 million grew to maybe 86 million between 1000 and 1350, a tiny increase by contemporary standards but a sharp contrast to the depopulation of the immediate post-Roman era. The exchange of goods, which had been much diminished but not completely extinguished, also began to accelerate. The cities that did exist began to increase the volume and variety of goods they imported and exported, and they enhanced the scope of their markets as well. In other places, a network of trading fairs (periodic markets that would attract vendors and buyers for a fixed period of time) emerged in the Champagne region of France and along the Rhine River. The manufacturing sector of the economy was rejuvenated. In the 500 years following Rome's fall, Western Europe served mainly as a source of raw materials—wood, furs, wool—for empires further east. Now, greater attention began to be paid to finished products. This was principally in textiles, but also in pewter and iron goods.

Finally, the number and size of cities began to expand. Although we know that the first three centuries following the turn of the millennium witnessed tremendous urban growth, the exact number of cities depends largely on definitions of what constitutes a city. Certainly a *town* was a legally defined entity in Medieval Europe, and many of these towns could also be considered small cities by the definitions given earlier. Norman Pounds (1990) estimates that about 6,000 new towns were established; at the peak, between 1250 and 1350, 75 to 200 new towns were established every decade just in central Europe. A small number of these were rebuilt from existing towns that had not completely collapsed during the Dark Ages. Some arose out of the needs of defense. Some developed around

monasteries and castles. A large number, however, appear to have originated as settlements of traders and craftsmen, often with permission of the neighborhood lord.

The cities of Europe—new and newly invigorated—were not large by the standards of the time. By A.D. 1250 or so, only a half dozen exceeded 50,000. In imperial China, such cities would have been smaller than provincial capitals. In A.D. 1000, when urban growth was first beginning, the only European city larger than 20,000 or so was probably Rome. The map of cities in Medieval Europe (Figure 2.12) shows where these cities were located. Many of the largest cities—Constantinople, Seville,

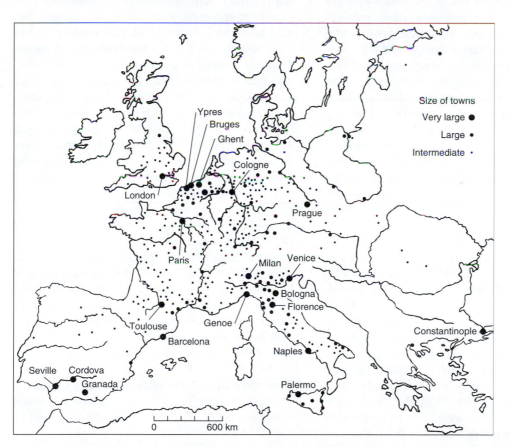

Figure 2.12 Cities in Medieval Europe. This map shows where cities and towns were located in the later Middle Ages. The largest cities were still attached to empires, but clusters of cities in northern Italy and northwest Europe attest to the revival of urbanism and the importance of trade.

Córdoba, Granada—were attached to empires, so people probably relied on the traditional means of sustenance. There were also several smaller cities in the interior regions of present-day France and Germany. Beyond these locations, the two areas of greatest urbanization were northern Italy and northwest Europe. These two areas were the fulcrums of a new capitalist, trading economy that was principally responsible for urban revival.

Northern Italy Foremost among the new capitalist cities were the towns of northern Italy, most famously Venice, Genoa, Milan, and Florence, but including several others. The cities are all now part of the country of Italy, but at the time they were independent city-states, jealous of their prerogatives. Although each city controlled a substantial amount of territory—Venice even carved out a seafaring empire—the territory was not the base of their economy. Rather, the economy was based on the activities of merchants and artisans. Merchants from these cities were involved in international trading across the Mediterranean. Many relied on intermediary groups to procure goods from the Far East. Trade was in a variety of **luxury** and **bulk commodities.** Venetian merchants, for example, traded timber, slaves, and iron from western and interior Europe in exchange for spices, silks, and porcelain from the East.

The success of these Italian cities was evident by their growing populations. By 1363 Venice had achieved a population of about 80,000, and Florence, Milan, and Genoa were not too far behind. (These population figures occurred after the Black Death of 1348–1350, so they represent a substantial decline.) These cities also became spectacularly wealthy. The success of these cities was also reflected in their growing political independence. They were initially under the control of a larger jurisdiction, but by 1300, they were completely sovereign. They were able to conduct an aggressive foreign policy and to establish elaborate defenses. Some cities even employed mercenaries to do their fighting for them. These cities became major political powerbrokers on the European stage.

The Venetian doge—a duke elected from the ranks of old merchant families—was one of the most powerful men in Europe. Despite their growing size and the political clout of these cities, the economic mission of the city was always given precedence.

Northern Europe In the north, along the Baltic and the North seas, trade began with a group of merchants based in small towns (Figure 2.13). Unlike the Italian traders to the south, merchants from these towns traded mainly in bulk commodities: salt from the North Sea coast, wool from England, flax from Belgium, herring from Norway, furs from the Russian interior, wine and grains from France, and oats and rye from German lands. These merchants were somewhat independent of the feudal system, but they relied on it for many of their products. From these towns was formed the **Hanseatic League.** This was a series of towns, mostly German speaking, that established special trading relationships with one another. At one time, the league probably included about 200 such towns. Importantly, the league was not a political union. These towns were geographically separated from one another and there was no unifying capital, but they agreed among themselves on a set of principles and standards.

Most Hansa towns were quite small, having fewer than 5,000 people. Later they would be overshadowed by some of the emerging trading and clothmaking cities to their west. These cities—Brugge, Ghent, Ieper—were heavily involved in woolen textiles. They would later be joined by cities like Amsterdam that used their position at the intersection of river and sea to become great trading centers and that were poised to take advantage of the shift in the main economy from the Mediterranean and the Baltic to the Atlantic and beyond.

Structure and Form of the Trading Cities
Changes in economic emphasis altered the social structure and form of these new trading cities, as discussed next.

Political and Economic Structure The notion of **citizenship** came to be highly regarded, reflecting

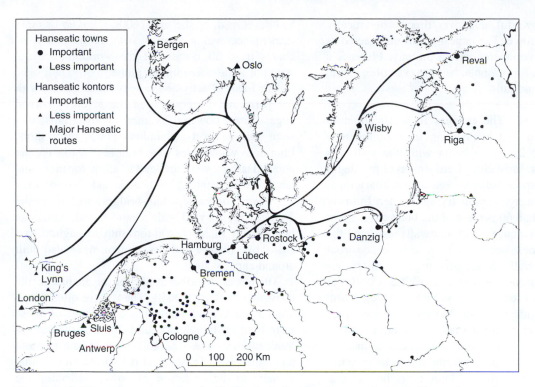

Figure 2.13 Hanseatic towns and trade. Unlike the Italian merchants to the south, Hanseatic merchants were more interested in trading bulk commodities: salt, wool, flax, fur, fish, and oats.

the separation of these cities from the feudal order that surrounded them. It was considered best to be a citizen of an independent or **chartered** city. The cities also contained many noncitizens: visitors from other cities and kingdoms, rural subjects, and even minority populations.

The social order in the city was headed by the **merchant class.** This group did not possess much real estate; rather they owned movable goods: merchandise, cargo ships, cash. In Florence around 1400, about 60 percent of the wealth was in the form of movable property, illustrating the tremendous shift away from the feudal and classical economy based mainly on land ownership. The power of the merchant class was politically recognized, and they were favored over the feudal aristocracy. Some cities passed laws meant to limit the intrusion of nobility in local affairs. It was not a democratic system in the modern sense. Some cities created a

new nobility of merchants that restricted entrance to merchants who came later, even the most successful ones. Higher councils and offices in Venice, for example, were reserved for the original families of the early merchant classes.

There was also an increased emphasis on production. Many wealthy merchants established their own workshops. They would often hire skilled craftsmen or artisans to produce various finished products, from cloth to metal products.

Merchants and artisans were both involved in the quintessential institution of this era: the **guild.** Guilds were occupational groupings, almost like a combination of a company and labor union today. Within a city, a guild would bring together similar workshops with a common interest in a particular craft. Initially, a distinction was made between merchant guilds and craft guilds, but the line between them was not closely drawn. The guilds became a politically powerful and, over time, economically conservative force. The largest guilds often acted as their own governments within the city. Florence's woolen guild, for example, had its own police force, magistrates, and jails.

Spatial Form   The changes in social structure were reflected in the changing form of the new cities (Figure 2.14). To begin with, the wall was still important. Most cities were jealous of privileges and worried about being sacked by a military invasion or by hungry peasants trying to enter. In many cities, more than 60 percent of the budget was spent on wall maintenance. Also, the walls restricted the growth of cities, occasionally leading to construction of new walls. Some growing and prosperous cities, like Brugge, had a moat as well as a wall. For growing cities especially, suburban development occurred outside the wall, but the wall continued to define the city until the late eighteenth century.

The new city was centered around a marketplace. The trading plaza became the focus of activity for these new cities. Major cities had several marketplaces—an often irregularly shaped central square, a spot near the town gates, even at a widening of the streets. In addition, there were spots near the marketplace where other sorts of business could be transacted. By the time Amsterdam

had developed, by the mid-1600s, the *dam* or main marketplace was a wonder with goods and merchants from all corners of the world. Nearby, a statue of Atlas lifted up his globe.

The focus of activity was very much tied up with the ports and waterways. Medieval cities owned huge cranes, powered by men on treadmills, that were built to load and unload goods from ships. Enormous warehouses were built nearby to store the goods. Harbors were dredged to allow for more and larger ships. Venice, built on islands, constructed a network of canals and bridges, including the 2-mile-long, 80-yard-wide Grand Canal. This was big enough to let a 200-ton ship through. Other cities, like Brugge and Amsterdam, were also built around canal systems.

There was a further reflection of change in the construction of guild halls. These were often found around the central marketplace. Sometimes these were built by individual guilds, as was the case in Venice; other times, the guilds would join to build a common hall. These guild halls were an essential element in the landscape of power, reflecting the guild influence in city government.

A more complex social geography also evolved at this time, leading to greater separation of different groups. Sometimes this separation was based on occupation or guild associations. Venice had distinct areas for linens, silks, and woolens. Separation also occurred on the basis of "nations," as different ethnic groups were referred to (Box 2.5). Venice was separated into zones where Greeks, Slavs, Albanians, and natives of other Italian city-states lived. Separation on the basis of family groupings also became more common as prosperous families built huge compounds within the cities and acted as if these places were sovereign. This sometimes prompted feuds and even open warfare between different sections of the city (Figure 2.15).

The street system of the Medieval trading city reflected its division into several districts. Most streets were not designed for access, rather they wound around the neighborhood core. Streets were set up for commerce and production, and street frontage was valuable land. Buildings were often

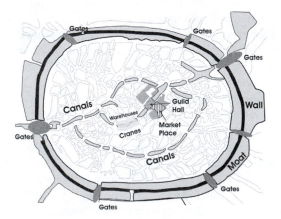

Figure 2.14 Map of Brugge as a model of a Medieval trading city.

BOX 2.5   THE FIRST GHETTOS

In the contemporary United States, a **ghetto** generally refers to a poor neighborhood inhabited primarily by members of a minority group. The term was first applied to a Jewish neighborhood in Venice, and likely comes from the Italian for little town, *borghetto*, or foundry, *gietto*. During the fourteenth and fifteenth centuries, Jews were allowed into Venice as moneylenders, functions proscribed to Christians. In 1516, the Venetian government decreed that a permanent Jewish quarter be established. A plaza area was enclosed by buildings and walls, which in turn were surrounded by a circular canal. Access was strictly controlled through two gates, and residents were not allowed outside the

ghetto after dark. In addition, residents were forced to pay the salaries of the guards that kept them confined. Escaping from the ghetto was severely punished by outside authorities and was also frowned on by most ghetto residents. Formal conversion to Christianity was the only legal method of escape (Figure B2.5).

The ghetto concept diffused to a number of cities—Frankfurt, Prague, Trieste, and Rome—and the prohibition of Jews from certain areas was widely applied across Europe. Long after the traditional European ghettos had vanished, the Nazis revived the concept with a hideous twist, using the ghetto as a waiting area before deporting Jews to the death camps.

Figure B2.5 Entrance to Venetian ghetto.

placed right on the street line, and the higher stories would protrude ever further into the street such that it was possible for someone on the third story to lean over and kiss someone across the street.

The cities that developed in the mid- to late-Middle Ages were entirely different from the cities that had existed before. At the same time, they came

to change the nature of the European economy as well. Specialization grew to be far more significant to the agricultural lands as land owners chose to grow crops that would bring them the most income. **Serfdom,** which had developed in an economy of self-sufficient manors, was less useful in this newly specialized economy. The nature of laws altered as the cities spearheaded a shift to a **secular law**

BOX 2.6   DESIGNING SPACES: BASTIDE CITIES AND THE GRAND MANNER

The early Medieval trading cities were largely organic in design, signifying their somewhat haphazard and disorganized economic development. Many were also separated from the structures and strictures of the feudal countryside and were in search of ever-greater freedoms from a fragmented feudal nobility. Later on, during the Renaissance and early modern periods, the ideals of urban design and planning took hold. This occurred alongside changing relationships between city and countryside, and between municipal and noble power. The consolidation of power under the authority of a prince or other grand nobleman signified the emergence of strong states and the decline of independent cities. In such an environment, cities developed under different conditions. Although they continued as centers of capitalist activity, cities existed now as places within a larger state. The ruler of that state could choose either to plant new cities on his domains, in the hopes of better securing the territory and of increasing his revenue stream, or to add a new addition to an existing city.

There is no single model for the designed cities, but there are a few principles. Many cities were constructed with fortifications, or *bastides*, in mind. These fortifications would often take the form of

a regular geometric shape, with towers laid out at regular intervals, and gates allowing entrance into the city itself. The streets within the **bastide city** were likewise regularly placed, intended to connect logically to each other, to the central market square, and to the town gates. The placement and pattern of streets was also intended to facilitate the movement of armaments and men to the city defenses. Building took place after the layout had been imposed, creating a more orderly landscape. Some of these cities were more geometrically curious than truly practical, as this picture of Palmanova, developed by Venetians in 1593, bears out (Figure B2.6).

Later, the expansion of even larger, more powerful kingdoms combined with baroque notions of design to form the ideal of the *Grand Manner*, a vision of city design. Here, the city was conceived of in its entirety, laid out ahead of time by an urban visionary as an assemblage of grand monuments, key buildings, terrain features, and parkland linked by a network of avenues and sightlines. Street landscaping, building architecture and cohesion, dramatic effects—all came together to produce a grand (and contrived) synthesis. Several important cities were laid out in this way, especially capitals

that was more independent of the Church, and to the territorial principle in law, in which one's place of residence determined which laws to obey.

The growth of states in Europe eventually put an end to the primacy of autonomous or independent trading cities. The new states that came of age beginning in the sixteenth century enjoyed advantages of size and unified markets, and several cities continued to fulfill more traditional roles, as centers of political or religious power. But the capitalist rationale that had guided the early trading cities carried over into the economies of many European states and became a force in the development of a single world economy.

Industrial Cities
The commercial cities abetted a new kind of economy and were clearly in the vanguard of change to a more capitalistic system throughout Europe. Still these cities did not get very large. Even the largest of them were limited in size and could not compare to imperial cities in other parts of the world. The political movement of some countries toward consolidated kingdoms—England and France among them—and more far-flung trading networks had increased the size of some cities in the early modern era. London is estimated to have had a population of about 200,000 in 1600, but that includes several suburban areas that may have been

Figure B2.6 View of Palmanova from the air.

that are now centers of substantial countries. Washington, D.C., is an example where the precepts of the Grand Manner were unencumbered by previous history. Planned by Pierre-Charles L'Enfant in 1791, for the first 100 years of its existence, the city's design outstripped the population. Charles Dickens wrote in 1842 that Washington was filled with "spacious avenues that begin in nothing and lead nowhere; streets a mile long that only want houses, roads, and inhabitants; public buildings that need only a public to be complete" (quoted in Mumford, 1961, p. 407).

predominantly rural. The population within the city proper was less than 100,000, as was also true of Paris, Amsterdam, and other major cities. The emergence of consolidated kingdoms may have had a greater influence in the creation of planned **bastide cities** (Box 2.6).

For society to urbanize extensively, and for some cities to get really large without requiring an enormous empire, meant that the economic basis of cities had to shift. The traditional cities had relied principally on extraction. The Medieval capitalist cities, despite a thriving handicraft industry, still relied primarily on the exchange of mostly rural goods. Cities initially accommodated the religious and political elite, along with the supporting population, and then a merchant and artisan class. However, these were not occupations that required huge numbers of people. Despite impressive gains in manufacturing during the Medieval period, there was still no way a group of artisans, no matter how well organized, could create the kind of supply and demand that was needed to sustain a large city. Most concerns were run out of a 6- by 20-foot front office that would subcontract work out to various specialists. Later, much of the textile production moved out of the cities into rural areas.

Figure 2.15 Due Torre in Bologna, Italy. Great and rivalrous families dominated many of the early trading cities, and they often constructed monuments to demonstrate their importance.

Industrial Revolution   What was required for cities to really take off was the creation of an entirely different economy, one based on the production and exchange of urban products that could sustain a large urban workforce. The creation of this new economy was bound up with the **Industrial Revolution,** a very loose term for a set of complementary processes:

- *Changes in the power supply*, largely through the introduction of the coal-burning steam engine;
- *Technical improvements in machinery*, through such inventions as the mechanical power loom and an iron puddling process to extract iron from iron ore; and

- *The shift from a production system based around small workshops to a **factory system*** that coordinated the activities of dozens and then hundreds of workers. Laborers could work under one roof, using machinery connected by a complicated series of belts to one steam engine.

As these various processes developed, true **mass production** became possible. But other ancillary developments had to take place beforehand. For one thing, the necessary capital needed to be available to take advantage of these technologies. This required some very wealthy merchants who were willing to invest in steam engines, machines, and factories. The increase in maritime trade to include much of Asia, Africa, and the Americas, as well as profits from the slave trade, greatly enriched many European merchants, but especially those in England, whose exports increased more than five times between 1700 and 1800. Secondly, agriculture had to advance to the point where it could feed all of the people who were working in the factories. Earlier agricultural productivity was, of course, quite low and could only allow for a small surplus. During the seventeenth and eighteenth centuries, greater agricultural efficiency (1) increased the surplus of farm products, allowing fewer farmers to support more people; (2) increased the demand for manufactured goods among the wealthier farm families; and (3) created a surplus labor force that was no longer needed in agriculture, but would now work in the urban factories of the Industrial Revolution. England was clearly at the center of these changes. London became the first truly global city by placing itself within the new global economy. English colonialism in North America, the Caribbean, South Asia, and later Africa and China helped to further fatten the wallets of many of its merchants. These colonies would later provide many of the raw materials for industrial production. England's hinterland was no longer confined to a portion of the world; it effectively became a global hinterland.

England had also been in the forefront of changes in the agricultural sector. Through better seed selection, animal breeding, forage crops, field rotations, and the shift toward fewer and larger farms, agricultural output during the eighteenth century increased far faster than the population, freeing more laborers to work in factories. Moreover, England enjoyed tremendous coal reserves (Figure 2.16). This was particularly important because coal power was used to run many of the new steam engines as well as the new instruments of transportation such as railroads and steamships.

The processes of the Industrial Revolution accelerated urbanization. Industrialization meant that large numbers of people could work in factories, producing goods that would be consumed by city and country dwellers alike. Further advances in transportation based on coal power, such as the railroad and the steamship, further extended the reach of industrial cities. Cities could get their food from a wider and wider area. London was able to get its grains from anywhere in the world: rice from India and wheat and beef from the United States and Canada. The sorts of raw materials needed for industrial goods could also be acquired from almost anywhere in the world. Products from North America, South America, and Asia found their way into the new factories. For example, the American South had become the major supplier of cotton by the mid-nineteenth century. Most of these changes resulted from people in rural areas moving to urban areas. Urbanization in nineteenth-century Europe was tremendous. While the population of Europe doubled in the 1800s, the urban population grew six times over. England was 20 percent urban in 1800, 40 percent in 1850, and more than 60 percent in 1890; it was the first urban country. By contrast, northern Italy in the heyday of the trading city was never more than about 20 percent urbanized.

Industrialization meant that many cities grew rapidly. The figures on population growth among British cities shows these effects: Manchester and Liverpool quadrupled in size. The largest cities finally were able to rival, and then exceed, the largest imperial cities. By 1800, London had a population of about 1 million; Paris about 550,000. By 1850, London was nearly 2.5 million and Paris 1 million. And by 1900, eight cities were larger than 1 million, headed by London at 6.5 million.

Changing Logic of City Location   Together, these events affected the logic of city location:

- The factory system required a concentration of labor in one place. The industrial system favored concentrated settlement in a few places as mass production in factories replaced small-scale production in workshops scattered in several locations.
- Steam engines required large amounts of coal, which was normally the bulkiest ingredient in the production process. Many of the new industrial cities sprang up around the coalfields, and increased their populations tremendously.
- Some cities, notably London, benefited by being at the center of industrial trade. Many smaller industries spun off by the Industrial Revolution also concentrated there.

Beyond the economic aspects, industrialization also changed the character of cities and their spatial arrangements. The popular image of nineteenth-century industrial cities is not a pretty one. Most images come from novels by Dickens and from various social commentators of that time. We think of black soot casting a pall over the city, of vast gaps between the rich and the poor, of mansions on the hills overlooking the city and the teeming slums near the factory gates. Friedrich Engels wrote of Manchester that "there is no town in the world where the distance between the rich and poor is so great, or the barrier between them so difficult to be crossed" and spoke of "the disgusting condition of that part of the town in which the factory workers lived." In response to these observations, a middle-class gentleman remarked, "and yet there is a great deal of money made here. Good morning, sir" (quoted in Briggs 1970, 106, 114).

They were both correct. Engels witnessed an urban environment that flaunted overwhelming disparities, in which the rich made more money, while the poor suffered. For rich and poor alike, Manchester was quite unhealthy. Like other industrial cities, it was a haven for disease. Contagious diseases like smallpox spread easily, bad hygiene led to typhus (spread by lice), and bad water supplies spread severe epidemics of cholera. In addition, there were inordinate numbers of industrial accidents, malnutrition among underfed workers, and

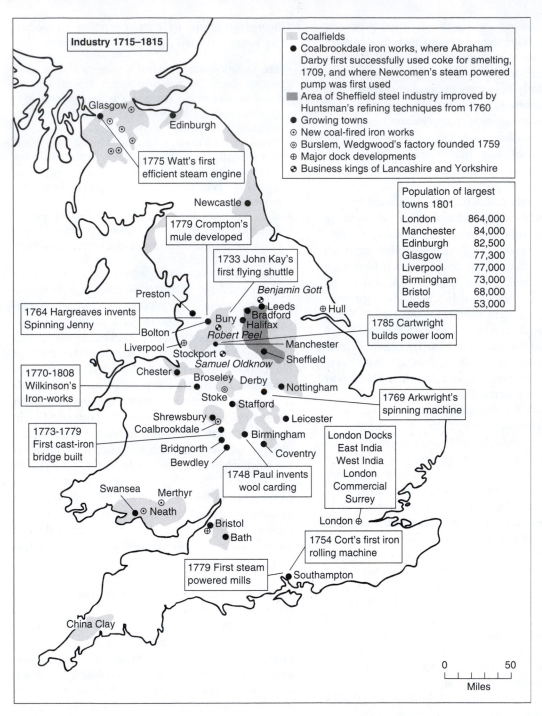

Figure 2.16 Map of coal deposits in Britain with manufacturing cities overlaid. Britain was particularly well supplied with coal and built most of its factories right next to the coal mines.

rickets from lack of sunlight. Until 1880, mortality rates were 50 percent higher in English cities than in the countryside. *A Report on the Sanitary Condition of the Labouring Population of Great Britain*, published in 1842, showed that the average age of death among Manchester's working class was a mere 17 years, less than half that of the rural town of Rutland. Even the professional classes suffered, dying at the age of 38 on average, as opposed to 52 in rural areas.

Elements of the Industrial City The major new elements of the industrial city were factories, railroads, and slums (Figure 2.17):

- The *factories* always took the best sites. In many cases, the founding of the factories led to the growth of the cities, so they were central to urban form. Of course, there were no pollution controls. The air was dirty, and the rivers were used for drainage and sewage.
- The *railroads* were the factories' connection to the main ports; in England these were London and Liverpool. Railroads were like factories on wheels and spread the pollution into all parts of the city and into the countryside.
- The *slums* were the last element. Mass production associated with the factory system required mass housing for the factory workers who worked there. Workers no longer lived in the same place they worked, as they had over the old workshops, but they needed to be close by. Housing also had to be constructed in a hurry, often by the factory owner, and was built on the cheap. Long rows of tenements were rapidly put up, often back to back, so as to minimize space (and ventilation).

The industrial city thrived on production, and it was able to employ large numbers of people in factories. Here, the spatial separation between social classes accelerated. The wealthy increasingly had the means to leave many of the urban problems behind (although as Manchester life expectancies suggest, they shared somewhat in the urban miseries in the early years). The workers found employment, but at an enormous cost to themselves and their families. They lived in the worst sections of the city. In bigger cities, like London, an additional class composed of clerks, storekeepers, and bureaucrats also expanded, often settling within separate areas

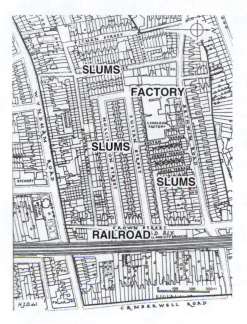

Figure 2.17 Map of Camberwell that illustrates elements of an industrial city.

of the city. In this manner, the social segregation of the modern-day city began to take shape. Changes in transportation technology and an expansion in the area of the city would further separate social classes.

WRAPPING UP

As our world fills up with more and more cities, it is easy to forget that urban centers are a relatively recent phenomenon. In order for cities to emerge, several preconditions had be in place. These included a sufficient agricultural surplus, a technology necessary to build and sustain cities, and the social power needed to marshal the resources of the population and to gather and redistribute the surplus. Exactly how cities came about is open to question. We do know that cities emerged independently in a number of hearths around the world. These early cities varied widely, but they shared a dependence on an extraction economy. Imperial cities, like ancient Rome, built on these early foundations and were able to grow as a result of control over a large area. It was only with the emergence of a capitalist economy between A.D. 1000 and 1200 that the basis for urban development changed, and cities became engines of economic growth. Industrialization allowed cities to grow even more, to the point where cities are now several times larger than was ever before possible, and they contain a greater percentage of people.

READINGS

Adams, Robert McC. 1966. *The Evolution of Urban Society: Early Mesopotamia and Prehispanic Mexico*. Chicago: Aldine Publishing Company.

Briggs, Asa. 1970. *Victorian Cities*. New York: Harper Colophon Books.

Calimani, R. 1987. *The Ghetto of Venice*. New York: M. Evans and Company.

Carter, Harold. 1983. *An Introduction to Urban Historical Geography*. London: Edward Arnold.

Davies, Norman. 1996. *Europe: A History*. New York: Oxford University Press.

Edwards, Mike. 2000. "Indus Civilization," *National Geographic*, Vol. 197, No. 6, pp. 108–131.

Girouard, Mark. 1985. *Cities and People*. New Haven, CT: Yale University Press.

Griffeth, Robert, and Carol Thomas, eds. 1981. *The City-State in Five Cultures*. Santa Barbara, CA: ABC-Clio.

Hammond, Mason. 1972. *The City in the Ancient World*. Cambridge, MA: Harvard University Press.

Hodge, Peter. 1972. *Roman Towns*. London: Longmans.

Jacobs, Jane. 1969. *The Economy of Cities*. New York: Random House.

Johnson, Jotham. 1973. "The Slow Death of a City." In Kingsley Davis, ed., *Cities: Their Origin, Growth and Human Impact*. San Francisco: W. H. Freeman Company, pp. 58–61.

Kenyon, Kathleen. 1994. "Ancient Jericho," *Scientific American Special Issue: Ancient Cities*, Vol. 5, No. 1, pp. 20–55.

Kostof, Spiro. 1991. *The City Shaped: Urban Patterns and Meanings Through History*. London: Bulfinch.

LeGates, Richard T. and Frederic Stout, eds. 2003. *The City Reader*. London and New York: Routledge.

Millon, René. 1994. "Teotihuacán." *Scientific American Special Issue: Ancient Cities*. Vol. 5, No. 1, pp. 138–148.

Morris, A. E. J. 1994. *History of Urban Form: Before the Industrial Revolution*. New York: Wiley.

Mumford, Lewis. 1961. *The City in History: Its Origins, Its Transformations, and Its Prospects*. New York: Harcourt Brace Jovanovich.

Palen, John. 1997. *The Urban World*. New York: McGraw-Hill.

Piana, G. 1927. "Foreign Groups in Rome," *Harvard Theological Review*, Vol. 20, pp. 183–403.

Pounds, Norman. 1990. *An Historical Geography of Europe*. New York: Cambridge University Press.

Rorig, Fritz. 1967. *The Medieval Town*. Berkeley: University of California Press.

Sjoberg, Gideon. 1960. *The Preindustrial City: Past and Present*. New York: The Free Press.

Sjoberg, Gideon. 1973. "The Origin and Evolution of Cities." In Kingsley Davis, ed., *Cities: Their Origin, Growth and Human Impact*. San Francisco: W. H. Freeman & Company, pp. 18–27.

Stambaugh, John E. 1988. *The Ancient Roman City*. Baltimore: Johns Hopkins University Press.

Stuart, George. 1995. "The Timeless Vision of Teotihuacán," *National Geographic*, Vol. 188, No. 6, pp. 2–35.

Vance, James. 1990. *The Continuing City: Urban Morphology in Western Civilization*. Baltimore: Johns Hopkins University Press.

Wheatley, Paul. 1971. *The Pivot of the Four Quarters*. Chicago: Aldine Publishing Company.

Woolley, C. Leonard. 1930. *Ur of the Chaldees: A Record of Seven Years of Excavation*. New York: Charles Scribners and Sons.

CHAPTER 3

THE EVOLUTION OF THE AMERICAN URBAN SYSTEM

Change is inevitable in a progressive country.
Change is constant.

—BENJAMIN DISRAELI

Why do some cities grow rapidly while others grow slowly and yet others either are stagnant or are experiencing population loss or economic decline? Why did boosterism in Atlanta in the civil rights decade of the 1960s declare it "A City Too Busy to Hate," while nearby Birmingham was referred to as "Bombingham"? Why did cities in the Dakotas and eastern Montana remain small while the midcontinent metropolises of Dallas-Fort Worth and Houston became huge? Why did Chicago's early loud-mouth boosterism give rise to the "Windy City" label, not its high-speed winds? Why did Detroit become the early center of the U.S. automotive industry, before the industry moved to the South? These are the kinds of questions we endeavor to answer in this chapter through an empirical examination of the North American urban system and through the introduction of several major conceptual models of urban change.

One of these models, **urban systems**, has to do with the ways that cities are related in interlinked, dependent ways, based on changing transportation and communications technologies. Cities exist within regional and national groups, larger and closer cities being more interdependent. The urban systems concept is derived from the basic notion of "situation" introduced in Chapter 1. The situation of a city or urban area relates to the cities' spatial relationships with other urban centers in the region or country. Cities do not exist in isolation and do not grow in population size or economic viability independent of other cities. Initially, it was primarily small cities located close to one another that competed for retail markets, industrial production, and rural-to-urban migrant workers. As the American economy grew and gradually matured and as transportation improved, more and more distant centers came into competition with each other. These urban struggles for economic, demographic and political influence involve a whole group or system of cities. Big cities try to get as far away from other big cities as they can, and small cities like to be as close as they can to other small cities. First it was New York and Chicago, and then after California became more populated, it is now New York and Los Angeles at the opposite ends of the continent.

Central to the concept of urban systems or a system of cities is the idea of the **urban hierarchy**. The urban hierarchy concept recognizes that urban centers are of different population sizes and have varying levels of economic leverage. One center may dominate another, and in turn may be dominated by a yet more powerful center. If we explore the ranks among centers, we can identify the largest and most dominant urban area down to the smallest and least economically important place.

61

By arraying these centers from top to bottom, or from bottom to top, an ordering or urban hierarchy can be established that is typically divided into a small number of arbitrary categories (perhaps four or five). Urban hierarchies, then, relate simply to the ranked order of cities based on different criteria, such as population size, economic power, retail sales, or number of industrial workers. By analyzing groups of urban centers, valuable insights may be gleaned into the processes whereby these centers interact in various ways with one another. By analyzing such an urban hierarchy over time, we can better understand how certain urban centers have come to change places with other centers within the urban hierarchy. It is thus the situation of these centers, as articulated through spatial interaction among them, that provides an understanding of the urban hierarchy.

THE AMERICAN URBAN HIERARCHY, 1630–2007

Colonial Imprints

There is evidence of Native American settlements throughout the present day United States and Canada. Native Americans, sometimes called First Americans, inhabited organized settlements, communities, and towns across the Americas. In fact, Native American settlements and their networks influenced the location and growth of the subsequent European towns and cities, as well as later roads and highways. The first relatively large human settlements, however, occurred as outposts of European economic exploration and exploitation and as military towns. The Spanish established the earliest settlements in Florida (St. Augustine) in 1565, and in what is now the U.S. Southwest (Los Angeles, San Antonio, San Diego, San Francisco, and Santa Fe). The colonial Dutch set up a fur trading post on New Amsterdam (Manhattan Island), later renamed New York, and the French pursued fur trading along the Great Lakes and Mississippi River, establishing the small settlements of Detroit, Montréal, New Orleans, Québec, and St. Louis.

It was the English colonists, however, who had the greatest and most lasting imprint on North American settlements and town and city development. Well known to American historians are the settlements at Jamestown (1607) and Williamsburg (1663), Virginia; Annapolis (1708), Maryland; Charleston (1672), South Carolina; Savannah, Georgia (1733); and Washington, D.C. (1791). The latter two cities were designed by James Oglethorpe and Pierre L'Enfant, respectively, using rectangular grids. William Penn laid out a street pattern for Philadelphia in 1682, and Boston, founded in 1630, quickly became an important center for European trade.

Although we think of New York today as the center of the U.S. economy and one of a very few global or world cities, in the colonial period and into the eighteenth century New York was no giant city. In fact, Philadelphia was the leading center of population from 1760 through 1790, the latter year marking the first U.S. Census of Population (Table 3.1). In 1760, even Boston was also larger than New York. In 1790 all settlements with populations exceeding 10,000 were port cities whose functions were tied with European ports, primarily the English ports of London and Liverpool. One of these ports, Charleston, South Carolina, in 1775 was the fourth largest city in North America. In contrast today it is only a modest-sized metropolitan area of some 265,000 people, reflecting a long tumble down the urban hierarchy. Baltimore got a late start as a port city but more than doubled its

Table 3.1 Population of Leading U.S. Port Cities, 1760–1790

Port Cities	1760	1775	1790
Baltimore	Not a city	6,734	13,503
Boston	15,631	16,000	18,038
Charleston	8,000	14,000	16,359
New Orleans	Not a city	Not a city	5,338
New York	14,000	22,000	32,305
Philadelphia	18,756	23,739	42,520

Source: Atlas of Early American History: The Revolutionary Era, 1760–1790.

population between 1775 and 1790, making it the fastest growing city during those 15 years and, by 1790, the fifth largest city on the East Coast.

The Early Development of the U.S. Urban Hierarchy

The urban population of the United States has grown steadily during each decade since 1790, as has the total population (Figure 3.1). Nevertheless, by contemporary standards it was relatively small until well into the twentieth century. In 1790 the total number of people living in U.S. cities was barely over 200,000, about the number living today in Naples, Florida. As late as 1850, as the railroad was gaining dominance as a transport mode for people and freight, the total U.S. urban population

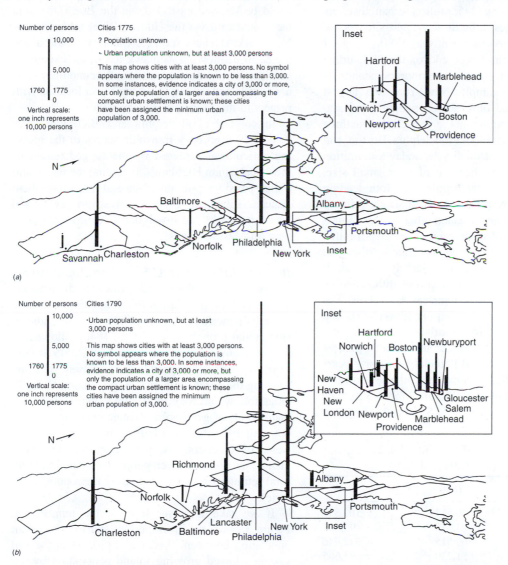

Figure 3.1 Population of major East Coast cities of North America, in (a) 1775 and (b) 1790. (*Source:* U.S. Census of Population.)

barely exceeded 3.5 million—a figure comparable with the population of the Miami-Fort Lauderdale metropolitan area today. By 1900 the U.S. urban population was only approximately 30 million, just slightly less than all of California's current population. The 1940 urban population of the United States, approximately 75 million, is similar to the current world's annual increase in population. We are now approaching 245 million urban dwellers in the United States, a figure that approximates the total U.S. population as recently as 1980.

In 1800 even the upper end of the U.S. urban hierarchy was tiny by contemporary standards (Table 3.2). For example, New York, the largest U.S. city, then had only 60,000 people, comparable to Casper, Wyoming, in the year 2005. The three other major cities in 1800, Philadelphia, Boston, and Baltimore, would not qualify by today's definition as metropolitan areas because of their small size, that is, less than 50,000 people. The four leading cities in 1800 were port cities with strong primary linkages to Britain and selected other Western European nations. All of these centers served a limited surrounding territory, called hinterlands (the land behind) to collect commodities (largely raw materials) for export and to distribute commodities (mainly manufactured items) from overseas as imports. The former were referred to as **export hinterlands** and the latter as **import hinterlands**.

In 1800 New York City was less than 50 percent larger than second-ranked Philadelphia. Forty years later, New York had become more than 3 times as large as second-ranked Baltimore (Table 3.2). The three second-tier cities in the U.S. urban hierarchy in

1840—Baltimore, Boston, and Philadelphia—were each of comparable size. The faster growth of New York during the first few decades of the 1800s was due principally to the center's ability to expand its import and export hinterlands into inland locations.

This expansion was due largely to the opening of the Erie Canal across upper New York State in 1825. Agricultural goods from the eastern Midwest could be shipped eastward via the Erie Canal and then southward via the Hudson River to the port of New York. Because the Erie Canal was built along the eastward-flowing Mohawk River, the expansion of New York's demographic and economic dominance reflected the city's strategic port location with respect to the Mohawk-Hudson valleys.

In contrast, Philadelphia and Baltimore were "blocked" from easy transport access to the growing agricultural Midwest by the rugged terrain of the Appalachian Highlands, including the Ridge and Valley physiographic province and the Appalachian Plateau. Likewise, Boston's westward hinterland was curtailed by the low-lying White Mountains of western Massachusetts.

Recent Shifts in the U.S. Urban Population

Figure 3.2 shows the overall growth in the percentage of the U.S. population living in cities, and more recently in metropolitan areas. The statistics indicate slow initial growth from 1790 to 1840, followed by rapidly increasing growth from 1840 to 1970, and then a tapering off of growth to the present. The line showing the percentage of U.S. population living in cities follows an **S-shaped curve**, which describes many kinds of geographic change over time. It was not until 1920 that over half of the U.S. population were city dwellers. The percentage today is more than 80 percent, and even people living in decidedly rural settings are daily affected by metropolitan life styles.

If we take a closer look at the numbers in Figure 3.2, we see an important spurt in the urban population between 1840 and 1850, when the rail system allowed growing inland penetration by the large East Coast cities and incipient centers on the

Table 3.2 Population of Leading U.S. East Coast Port Cities, 1800 and 1840

Cities	1800	1840
Baltimore	26,514	102,313
Boston	24,937	93,383
New York	60,515	312,710
Philadelphia	51,220	93,665

Source: U.S. Bureau of the Census.

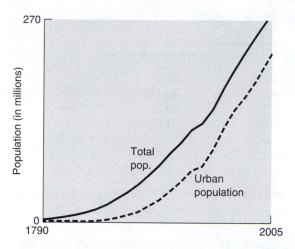

Figure 3.2 Absolute change in U.S. total and urban populations, 1790–2005. (*Source:* U.S. Bureau of the Census.)

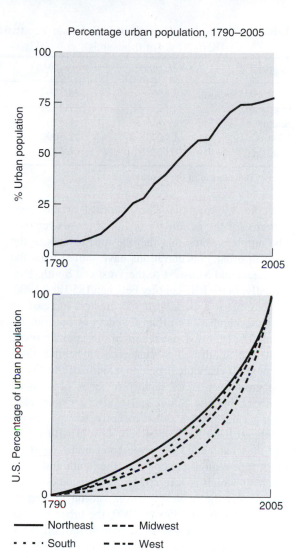

Figure 3.3 Percentage of U.S. urban population, 1790–2005. (*Source:* U.S. Bureau of the Census.)

eastern Great Lakes, such as Buffalo, Cleveland, and Detroit. The great expansion of the railroad, especially from the end of the Civil War in 1865 up to 1920, was of major importance in creating an interlocked system of cities and in generating an urban hierarchy based on economic prowess (manufacturing) and consequent population size. Strong growth continued until the 1930s, a decade marked by the Great Depression and a slowdown of rural-to-urban movement. Another jump in the urban population took place in the late 1940s, following World War II. Urban growth slowed somewhat after 1960, especially with **counterurbanization** (urban-to-rural migration) of the 1970s.

Not all regions of the United States shared equally in these urbanization trends. Because the United States and Canada were settled primarily from east to west, the U.S. Northeast urbanized most rapidly during the earliest decades (Figure 3.3). Urbanization in the West began much later. As late as 1850 the total population of the West consisted of only 180,000 people, over 6 percent of whom lived in cities. In contrast, today the West is the most urbanized part of the United States, with nearly 88 percent of the population classified as urban. The South was the most laggard region in urban growth.

It did not achieve a 50 percent urban population until the early 1950s, a figure achieved in the Northeast by 1880 and in the Midwest and West by 1920. Today, the South, despite its rapid recent growth, remains the least urbanized region of the United States, with 75 percent of its population living in urban areas, just behind the 73 percentage figure for the Midwest.

Table 3.3 Absolute Growth in U.S. Urban Population by Major Regions, 1850–2000 (in thousands)

Regions	1850–1900	1900–1950	1950–2000	1850–2000
Midwest	9,666	18,326	16,609	44,601
Northeast	11,622	17,462	10,927	40,012
South	3,677	18,535	46,044	68,256
West	1,707	12,309	40,823	54,839
U.S. total	26,672	66,632	114,403	207,707

Source: U.S. Bureau of the Census.

Table 3.3 examines the historical urbanization patterns for the nation's four major census regions. The numbers show that the one-time centers of the greatest urban concentrations have shifted from the Northeast and Midwest to the West and South. Historically, in the half-century between 1850 and 1900, the Northeast experienced the greatest increase in absolute numbers of urban dwellers of the four regions. The Midwest also recorded substantial growth, while the South and West lagged far behind. Over the next 50 years the urban population of the Northeast grew even more rapidly in terms of absolute numbers, but the South and Midwest experienced even greater growth. Most recently, since 1950 the Northeast has been a relatively slow-growth region and thus has added the fewest net urban residents of all four regions. In contrast, the South and West, much of which is referred to as the Sunbelt, have experienced the greatest urban expansion. During the half-century from 1950 to 2000, the urban population of the West grew by more than 40 million, while the South added 46 million urban dwellers. Of that 46 million, 63 percent were added after 1970 and 45 percent were added after 1980.

In 1961, the French urban geographer Jean Gottmann published *Megalopolis*. This seminal book focused on the continuously urbanized area of the Northeastern Seaboard of the United States, extending from north of Boston to south of Washington, D.C. The concept of **megalopolis** now refers to any of several continuously built-up urban areas, such as the San-San region of California (San Francisco to San Diego), the Detroit-Chicago-Milwaukee area (Mil-Chi-De), or the Charlotte-Atlanta-Birmingham region (the Atlanta X), which also stretches north to Chattanooga and south to Macon, forming a kind of cross. The multimetropolitan East Coast (also known as Bos-Wash) emerged in the late 1950s as the most powerfully urbanized concentration in the world in terms of political, economic, financial, and cultural influences (see Morrill, 2006).

A recent update of the U.S. urban population distribution some 45 years after Gottmann's *Megalopolis* is the **bathtub model** (Figure 3.4). In this rendering, not only is the Northeast coastal area a concentration of large metropolitan areas, economic dominance, and cultural influence—the first national core—but now a Pacific Coast core has emerged. As Figure 3.4 indicates, the U.S. large urban population is primarily bicoastal, representing a bathtub's front and back end. This figure was created by Henrie and Plane (2006) using Geographic Information Science techniques whereby successive 25-mile increments of population are mapped from each coast. In addition to the East and West Coast peaks (the bathtub), the 2000 U.S. population is much more concentrated in the eastern half of the country than in the "near-empty" western half. The greatest differences between the 1950 and 2000 urban population distribution is (1) the growth of the Pacific Coast, (2) the relatively unchanged densities from the East Coast, and (3) the somewhat less dense population with distance from the East Coast. For example, almost 18 percent of the U.S. population was along the Atlantic Coast in 1950 compared with just over 16 percent in 2000.

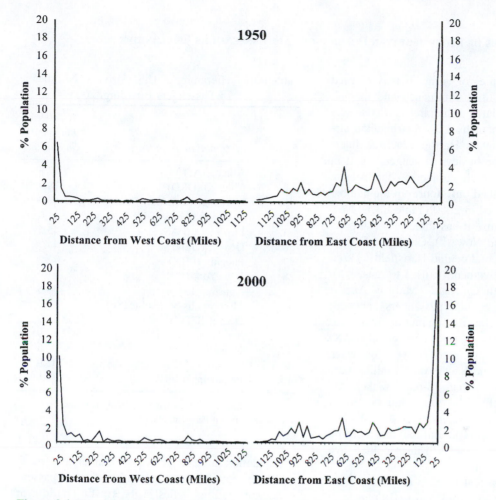

Figure 3.4 The "bathtub" view of the east-west U.S. population, showing the coastal concentrations along the Atlantic and Pacific oceans (*Source:* Used with permission of Henrie and Plane, 2006, p. 453).

METROPOLITAN DOMINANCE

Metropolitan or urban systems evolved over time, and their growth and economic maturity were typically gradual. No other single force was more important to their evolution and their particular spatial arrangement and regional development than transportation, initially the railroad, but today motor trucks and air transport (passengers and freight) (Box 3.1). The progress in transportation technology continues today to impact not only the growth of individual towns and cities, but also the degree of connectivity and the level of accessibility among urban groups or systems. We will discuss the effects of transportation on U.S. cities later in this chapter. However, long before modern metropolitan areas could become interconnected and interdependent, first through a series of improvements in freight and passenger transportation and now through telecommunications, the cities of the past somehow had to

BOX 3.1   Measures of Metropolitan Dominance: Air Passengers Emplaned

Many different measures or variables may be used to highlight metropolitan dominance and to rank metropolitan areas into a hierarchy. Let's take air passenger movement by U.S. metropolitan airports. Although Atlanta's Hartfield-Jackson International Airport is the busiest passenger airport in the world—perhaps in the universe—the Atlanta metropolitan area ranked only fourth in the number of passengers emplaned in 2000 (Table B3.1). New York ranks first because it has three major airports (La Guardia, JFK and Newark). Chicago's O'Hare airport now ranks second behind Hartsfield-Jackson in total passenger movement (it used to rank first). When combined with Chicago's Midway Airport with its modest 17 million passengers per year, Chicago still ranks second among metropolitan areas in air passengers. Los Angeles International (LAX) generates 63 million passengers per year, but when Burbank (5 million) and Santa Ana (8 million) are added, Los Angeles has a third-place rank in the air passenger hierarchy. The San Francisco airport generates 35 million passengers per year, but when combined with Oakland (10.6 million) and San Jose (13.1 million) the San Francisco metropolitan area achieves a rank of sixth.

Whereas we know that tourism accounts for the incredibly high rank of Las Vegas and Orlando in air passenger traffic, other metropolitan areas also rank higher than expected based on their population size because they serve a regional market. Examples include Atlanta, Denver, Phoenix, and Minneapolis-St. Paul, which rank first, sixth, seventh, and tenth respectively in passenger traffic but only ninth, twenty-second, fourteenth, and sixteenth

Table B3.1   Hierarchy of U.S. Airports: Number of Passengers Boarding, 2005

Rank	Metropolitan Area (Airport)	Number of Passengers (in millions)
1.	Atlanta (ATL)	87.8
2.	Chicago (ORD)	78.4
3.	Los Angeles (LAX)	63.0
4.	Dallas-Ft. Worth (DFW)	61.6
5.	Las Vegas (LAS)	45.6
6.	Denver (DEN)	44.7
7.	Phoenix (PHX)	42.2
8.	New York (JFK)	41.9
9.	Houston (IAH)	40.6
10.	Minneapolis-St. Paul (MSP)	40.0
11.	Detroit (DTW)	37.9
12.	San Francisco (SFO)	34.9
13.	Orlando (MCO)	34.8
14.	Newark (EWR)	33.9
15.	Philadelphia (PHL)	33.0

Source: Estimates based on data from Airports Council International-North America, 2005.

in population rank, respectively. Philadelphia, fourth ranked in population, is fifteenth ranked in passengers explained, as it lies in the **traffic shadow** of New York, Baltimore, and Washington D.C. By traffic shadow, we mean it faces stiff nearby airport competition. Other metropolitan areas rank nearly equally on passenger movement totals and population size. Houston and Detroit (eighth and tenth in population rank) are nineth and eleventh, respectively, in air passenger traffic.

sustain on their own a sufficient degree of economic growth by creating jobs and attracting a consuming population. How did that happen?

Geographers use the term **metropolitan dominance** to describe the process whereby a small settlement can grow into a village, a town, a city,

and even a great metropolis. Of course, not all early settlements became huge contemporary metropolitan areas. In fact, many settlements or hamlets died out and no longer exist. Others reached a certain population size and then grew extremely slowly or remained stable. Relatively few achieved large population size and economic viability. Again, we ask why did some human settlements expand dramatically while others experienced only intermediate or minimal growth, or even declined?

The urban geographer would respond by noting that, although site characteristics may play a part in the early establishment of a community, such as the confluence of two rivers, the foothills of a mountain range, or the oceanside, it is the situation (relative location) of a settlement that is ultimately responsible for its economic success and population growth. For example, Pittsburgh is located at a point where the Allegheny and Monongahela rivers converge to form the Ohio River. Pittsburgh's location also is affected by its situation, as it is linked to other places by its river location. Pittsburgh's fortunate site characteristics were translated into enormous situational advantages for steelmaking in the city's early growth and dominance. The three major ingredients needed to manufacture iron and steel were accessible: iron ore, coal to make coke, and limestone. Iron ore was transported on the nearby Great Lakes and then by rail to Pittsburgh. Coal fields and limestone rocks were located near Pittsburgh. Likewise, Pittsburgh was located near the East Coast markets and the growing industrial Midwest. Hence, Pittsburgh became, in its early and formative years, the "Steel City" due to its geographic situation. In contrast, Denver is located in the foothills of the Rocky Mountains and is both the city of the Great Plains and the Rocky Mountains. Santa Barbara is located on the mild Pacific coast, but the city grew slowly at first because it had no port function (site). It remained isolated from Los Angeles until the four-lane U.S. 101 highway was built (situation) in order to encourage migrants to live in Santa Barbara because of its climate amenities (site).

Pred's Model

If we take a hypothetical city that has at first only a small local market, we may identify the major forces leading to its economic and hence population expansion. Here we turn to **Pred's model of circular and cumulative causation** (Figure 3.5). We begin in the upper left-hand corner of the figure with

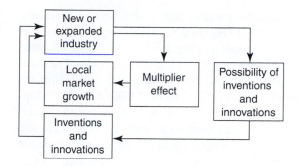

Figure 3.5 Pred's view of city and urban growth, the circular and cumulative causation model. (*Source:* Pred, 1966, p. 25.)

the establishment of a small manufacturing industry. The Pred model (1977) describes the growth of cities during the period of initial and rapid U.S. industrialization, from approximately 1865 to 1915. Imagine first a relatively small town serving a geographically limited surrounding area, which we have termed an *umland* from the German, or trade area. Agricultural products are grown in the surrounding area where they are consumed in a kind of self-sufficient economy, that is, what is produced on a farm is largely consumed there. Surplus products are sold in the nearby town, and the town serves itself and the surrounding area primarily as a service center for retailing (groceries, cloth, medicine) and services (doctor, pharmacist, blacksmith). The town has little interaction with other towns, even nearby ones, because of the slow speed and high cost of transportation. After morning farm chores, the farmer would hitch up the horse and wagon or buggy, travel a maximum of seven to ten miles into town once or twice a month, return home, do the evening chores, have a late dinner and retire to bed. There is no telegraph, and certainly no telephone. Human spatial interaction was by face-to-face contact, until postal services gradually became available to access increasingly remote farmsteads.

Now let us suppose a new manufacturing plant is located in our hypothetical small town. It will require workers, some of whom may migrate from the rural area to live in the small town. The workers may have families, who will increase the local demand for retailing and services, creating a **multiplier effect** (Figure 3.5). For example, the creation of 100 manufacturing jobs might create the need for 50 other jobs in retail and services. The multiplier effect will also increase the demand for the products of the manufacturing plant (buggy whips or even buggies), which will encourage the manufacturer to hire even more workers. Thus, a circular and cumulative process of economic and population growth is set in motion.

This process, however, is not the only process that operates. Take another look at Figure 3.5. The outer lines in the figure depict another kind of circular and cumulative process, this one having to do with invention and innovation. Once an industry or several industries have established themselves in a particular town or city, it becomes likely that improvements in the manufacturing process will take place, often gradually and incrementally. Sometimes, however, these improvements will represent "breakthroughs" or inventions that will give the company creating the inventions considerable market advantage through lowered production costs. This increased local market will lead to industrial expansion, that is, the need for more workers and therefore a growing city population. Larger urban areas are more likely to be centers of innovation and invention than smaller places, and a large industry or an industrial concentration has a greater probability of generating innovative inventions and patents than a smaller industry or industrial cluster. The net result is that larger urban areas will tend to grow larger and faster than smaller centers. Once an urban area has achieved a certain threshold size, that area has established an **initial advantage** at or near the top of the urban hierarchy. The momentum of large size, through Pred's multiplier effect and the innovation and invention process, tends to maintain a large urban center. The Pred model as depicted here describes the early economic and demographic growth of cities under the forces of industrialization.

Figure 3.6 illustrates the economic and demographic growth of a hypothetical city based on the Pred model. In Figure 3.6a, we observe a small settlement center, a village, that functions as an agricultural

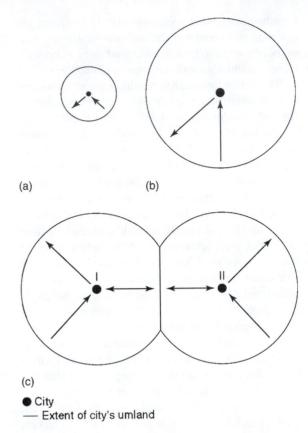

● City
— Extent of city's umland

Figure 3.6 (a), (b), and (c) The economic and population growth of a hypothetical city and its trade area.

trade center. Its umland is small. Its spatial interaction is limited to a small radius. The small center serves a restricted agricultural area for retail goods and services. Surplus agricultural products are moved to the center for sale. The village, along with its trade area, is basically self-sufficient. In Figure 3.6b, the center, now a town, has grown in population as a result of (1) improved transportation access and/or (2) the establishment of an industry. The outcome is an enlarged trade area. Finally, Figure 3.6c suggests that this expanding single center (I) and its larger trade area now encounter competition from another town (II) of approximately equal size. The circular trade areas in Figures 3.6a and 3.6b are modified through spatial competition to form a hypothetical straight line between the two centers.

Urbanization and Industrialization Among U.S. Urban Centers

As the Pred model suggests, U.S. urban settlements evolved from local market centers for retail and service activities to centers of manufacturing industries. In fact, the U.S. urban economy, until recent decades, has been driven almost entirely by the process of industrialization. The Pred model applies to this initial development of industries but it also applies to the period of rapid intensification of U.S. manufacturing, during which time innovations, inventions, and patents were essential to industrial success and urbanization. The most intense period of industrial-driven urbanization began after the Civil War (1861–1865) and lasted until approximately 1970.

Borchert's Transport Epochs and American Metropolitan Growth

We previously mentioned that improved modes of transportation were a driving force behind the growth of U.S. cities. To demonstrate this point, John Borchert (1967) identified four epochs in American urban history, each of which was characterized by fundamental changes in transport technology. Each epoch brought about changes in the spatial interactions among urban areas as well as changes in the internal arrangement of activities and functions of urban regions. Here we concentrate on the transformations that occurred among American cities and metropolitan areas, especially those metropolises near the top of the urban hierarchy. We term Borchert's four epochs (1) the "Horse and Wagon Epoch" (1790–1830), (2) the "Regional Railroad Network Epoch" (1830–1870), (3) the "National Railroad Network Epoch" (1870–1920), and (4) the "Automobile-Airplane Epoch" (1920–1960). (Chapter 5 treats the contemporary era based on information exchange).

Horse and Wagon Epoch, 1790–1830 During the first epoch, all sizable urban areas were located on the Atlantic coast, or on bays, estuaries, or navigable rivers (e.g., the Connecticut, Delaware, Hudson, and Savannah rivers). These cities served as Atlantic ports with geographically limited hinterlands and strong economic ties to Western Europe, forming the **Atlantic Alliance**. Also during this epoch cities began to grow in the eastern Midwest and along the Erie Canal (Syracuse, Albany), the lower Great Lakes (Buffalo, Cleveland, Detroit), and the Ohio River (Cincinnati, Louisville).

Regional Railroad, 1830–1870 Beginning in the 1830s, the development of the steam-driven railroad and its rapid expansion from the major population centers into surrounding regions bestowed an initial advantage on the largest urban centers of the horse and wagon epoch. Also during this period, the emergence of the steamboat greatly increased the tonnage of goods and commodities that were hauled on the Great Lakes and the Ohio-Mississippi-Missouri river systems. By 1870 water transportation had linked with the evolving regional railroad networks to create a proto-national transportation system, which sped urban development. Mississippi River centers prospered, notably New Orleans (the largest city in the South) and St. Louis, but also Omaha, Minneapolis-St. Paul, and Memphis. Kansas City dominated the Missouri River. Chicago, the quintessential railroad center, sprang out of the swamp left over from glacial Lake Chicago as it receded to today's Lake Michigan, providing a flat site at the lower end of the lake for the railroad. Some small inland urban centers evolved in the Midwest (Indianapolis, Columbus, and Lansing) and in the South (Atlanta), nodes on the railroad network.

National Railroad Network Epoch, 1870–1920 With the full integration of a standardized rail system after 1870, the contemporary distribution of major metropolitan areas was emerging and being set in place. The large industrial urban centers of the Northeast and Midwest continued to grow in importance, and largely maintained their position at the upper end of the urban hierarchy. The river cities of St. Louis, Louisville, and New Orleans declined within the urban hierarchy, as rail centers such as Chicago in the Midwest, Atlanta in the South, and

Dallas-Fort Worth in the mid-continent region of Texas gained ascendancy. Western urban centers, most notably San Francisco, but also Los Angeles, Seattle, and Denver also began to grow rapidly, though their greatest growth was yet to come. Pittsburgh achieved its most rapid growth during this period as the leading and relatively low-cost producer of iron and steel. The demand for steel for rails, locomotives, boxcars, skyscrapers, and later automobiles skyrocketed. The national rail system penetrated into the isolated areas of the South and West, as small centers such as Knoxville, Tennessee, Birmingham, Alabama, Lubbock, Texas and Phoenix, Arizona, began a growth spurt. Tiny Washington D.C. also began to increase in population through its role as the nation's political capital.

Automobile-Airplane Epoch, 1920–1960 The automobile-airplane epoch began with the decline of railroads, coal-based energy, and steam power and the rise of the internal gasoline and diesel engine (Figure 3.7). The result was an overall internal dispersal of urban areas into suburban and rural locations, and the regional and national diffusion of population down the metropolitan hierarchy. Not only did automotive technology tremendously

improve during this period, but spectacular highway construction also took place, reaching into small and isolated spaces never penetrated by the geographically limited and fixed rail lines. Satellite cities, previously a part of a large urban center's trade area, were incorporated into the growing and spreading metropolitan suburbs. Metropolitan areas in Florida, California, and the Southwest attracted massive migration flows. Small urban centers in the Midwest, the Great Plains, and the Piedmont South grew to metropolitan status by the end of the epoch.

Air passenger transportation also developed and thrived during this period, as the number of rail passengers declined. It was of course the largest metropolitan areas that acted as the principal air hubs, forming an early air-passenger hierarchy. This hierarchy was dominated in 1960 by New York, Chicago, and Los Angeles, the three largest metropolitan areas, followed by Boston, Detroit, Philadelphia, Pittsburgh, and San Francisco (Taaffe, 1962). Increased air transportation contributed to the growing affluence of the U.S. middle class after World War II (1941–1945) and especially to the expansion of the consumer service economy (e.g., fast-food restaurants, hotel services). Business travel became more important. Most businesses and

Figure 3.7 A view of O'Hare International Airport in Chicago (Chi-town). In 2006, the airport began undergoing the largest expansion in U.S. history, a 7-year, $15 billion project, attesting to the importance of passenger and freight movement to the economic viability of Chicago and metropolitan areas in general.

corporations were located in metropolitan areas, especially those at the upper end of the urban hierarchy. Borchert (1967, p. 307) concluded: "Hence in the auto-air age, even more than in the preceding epoch, growth breeds growth."

URBANIZATION PROCESSES

An understanding of the urban systems and the urban hierarchy forms a good foundation for a discussion of several **urbanization processes**, that is, the operation of urban growth and change over time. We wish to take up in turn (1) urbanization curves, (2) central place theory, (3) rank-size relationships among urban centers, and Kondratiev waves.

Urbanization Curves

Plotting changes in urbanization over time typically produces an S-shaped curve (Figure 3.8). At first an area begins to urbanize slowly. At some point in time, the urbanization process takes hold, and urban areas grow rapidly. This fast-growth phase is followed by a slowing down of urban growth as high levels of urbanization are achieved. The urbanization curve in Figure 3.8 shows a lag compared with world population growth, as human livelihood remained resource based for most of human history. Only recently—during the past 10,000–12,000 years—did humans begin to cluster in settlements in any considerable numbers.

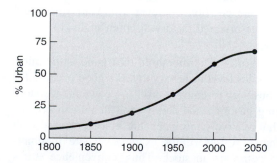

Figure 3.8 World urbanization trends, 1800–2050, follows the S-shaped curve.

Central Place Theory

Central place theory is concerned with the optimal or ideal spatial distribution of settlements over a landscape. The foundations for this theory were laid by Walter Christaller (1933, 1966) and August Lösch (1938, 1954), a German geographer and a German economist, respectively. Their initial purpose was to establish the optimal location of a single good (a loaf of bread, for example) for a dispersed population. They then considered the optimal locations for many goods and services. Christaller's theory emphasized the location of retail and services (tertiary) businesses, whereas Lösch's analysis also applied to secondary (manufacturing) industries. Many geographic studies of central places were conducted in the late 1950s and 1960s based on Christaller and Lösch's theories. Central place theory deals with the lower end of the urban hierarchy, small settlements such as hamlets, villages, towns, and cities. Despite the theory's simplification of reality, central place theory offers considerable conceptual insight into an important aspect of the urbanization process at the lower end of the urban hierarchy. Thus, central place theory helps us understand some of the forces shaping the urban hierarchy, though not all of the forces.

Central place theory seeks to explain the **size**, **spacing** and **functions** of relatively small urban settlements or central places (Figure 3.9). These three features are interrelated and interdependent. Five key principles guide these relationships:

- The larger the size of a central place, the greater the distance it will be located from another central place of the same or larger size.
- The larger the size of a central place, the greater the number of retail and service functions or activities found in that central place.
- The larger the size of a central place, the larger the trade area (umland) served by that central place.
- The larger the size of a central place, the higher the order of the functions served by that central place, with larger centers having **higher-order functions** and smaller centers having **lower-order functions**.
- The larger the size of a central place, the fewer such places, with smaller central places being larger in numbers.

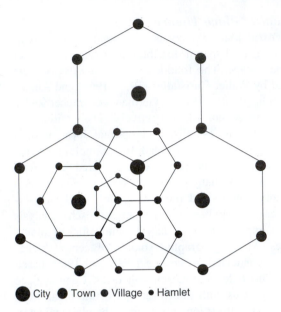

● City ● Town ● Village ● Hamlet

Figure 3.9 The optimal central place hierarchy showing the size and spacing of hamlets, villages, towns, and cities.

Figure 3.9 shows an optimal central place landscape, obeying the five principles highlighted above. The four largest centers (cities) are located an equal distance from one another. These four large centers are also located at the greatest distance from one another. These large centers have the largest trade areas (hexagonal in shape), and the smallest centers (hamlets) have the tiniest trade areas. Although it is not explicit in the figure, we know that the largest centers offer the widest range or highest order of goods and services, thus attracting consumers from the greatest distances and thereby creating the largest trade areas.

To more fully understand central place theory, we introduce four basic concepts: centrality, range of a good, threshold, and hexagonal trade areas. These concepts are based on two primary assumptions. The first is the **isotropic plain**, meaning that the central place landscape is *uniform* in climate, and landforms, that is, no natural physical or human-made features such as slopes, rivers or roads exist. Further, the population is equally distributed throughout the trade areas. The second assumption is that consumers of

retail and service functions will travel to the nearest central place that offers that particular good or service. Because the isotropic plain is uniform, the consumers will theoretically travel "as the crow flies," geodesically, directly to the closest center.

Centrality   The population size of a central place is directly related to its **centrality** or the degree to which the place is centrally located to serve a surrounding population. The chief characteristic of a town is to be the center of a region. The lower level of the urban hierarchy (villages, towns, cities) is based on the centrality of a place with respect to other places (Figure 3.9).

Range of a Good   The **range of a good** is the maximum distance a consumer is willing to travel to purchase a retail good or service. Thus, the range of a good defines the outer extent of a central place's trade area. Lower-order goods, such as a loaf of bread, a six-pack of beer, or a chocolate candy bar, have a small range. These goods are widely available in both small and large central places, and the consumer will make such purchases in small nearby places. The consumer, however, is willing to travel farther—and will have to travel farther—to purchase higher-order goods or services, such as computers, French restaurants, and tuxedo rentals. Clearly, smaller central places do not have a trade area large enough to support such high-order goods and services. In fact we see many enterprises go out of business because of an inadequate or too small a local market. Central place theory was developed before the creation of Super Wal-Mart stores and interstate-oriented factory discount malls.

Threshold   The **threshold of a good** is the minimum sales level necessary to sell a good in order for the business to enjoy a profit. A convenience store selling gasoline and handy food items can operate with a relatively low sales threshold compared with a Super Wal-Mart, for example, where innumerable items are in stock. Thus, convenience stores are common on the landscape within a metropolitan area or in small central places, whereas department

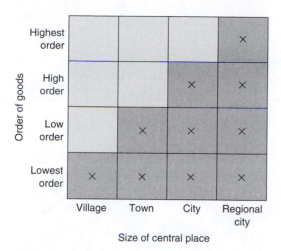

Figure 3.10 The relationship between the population size of a central place and the order of goods available in that place. The symbol *X* illustrates that large central places not only have higher-order goods but also have the full array of lower-order goods.

stores (Sears) are found widely separated in only the larger cities and urban areas. The threshold of a good or service is related to trade area size and the size of the central place.

Figure 3.10 illustrates the relationship between the population size of a central place and the order of goods available in that place. Lower-order goods with a low sales threshold and a small consumer range or travel time are found in both small and large central places. For example, barbecue shacks in the U.S. South, especially in the past, were widely scattered throughout rural landscape. Thus, lower-order goods may be said to be **ubiquitous**, meaning they are found in every center, or literally *found everywhere*. In contrast, a premier woman's shop with dresses created by world-famous designers will be able to operate at a profit only in the largest metropolitan centers.

Hexagonal Trade Areas   If a single central place existed in isolation, having no contact with other places, such a central place would theoretically have a perfectly circular trade area. However, since central places do not exist separately, they in fact compete with one another. As we saw in Figure 3.9 with competition over space or **spatial competition**, centers of equal size will equally divide their two trade areas. In a central place system, where a large central place will be surrounded by the trade areas of six other centers of equal or smaller size, the trade areas will take on an hexagonal or six-sided shape. The four cities in Figure 3.9 share the largest trade areas. In contrast, towns share intermediate-sized trade areas, and the villages have the smallest trade areas. (Trade areas for the hamlets are not shown.) At this point you might want to go back to the five "bullet" items on page 73 and apply them to Figure 3.9.

Rank-Size Rule
The **rank-size rule** demonstrates the relationships among a system of cities at the regional or national scale. Zipf (1949) is credited for bringing the rank-size concept to the attention of geographers and economists through his **principle of least effort**. This principle holds that humans, all other things being equal, will tend to behave in such a way as to minimize the energy they utilize to achieve a given task. For example, in central place theory, consumers will travel to the nearest place that offers a particular good or service. In migration, most residential moves involve short rather than long distances. Likewise, when traveling to work, most commuters prefer to travel short distances. This principle of least effort also translates to the human interactions that create a system of cities. The result, as we have just seen in central place theory, is that there will be a multitude of small centers and a decrease in the number of large centers as the size of the centers increases. This relationship between a city's population size and its regional or national rank gives rise to the rank-size rule.

Figure 3.11 shows the theoretical rank-size rule, where the rank of city size is plotted on the horizontal (x) axis and the population sizes of cities are shown on the vertical (y) axis. The main point is that both axes are plotted in logarithm form to form a negative linear relationship. Thus, the rank-size rule enables us to predict the population size of any

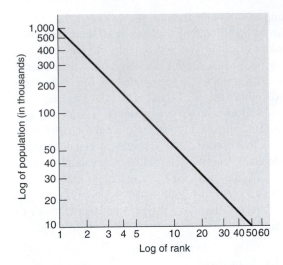

Figure 3.11 The plot of the log of population size for cities (vertical axis) versus the log of rank in population size (horizontal axis) produces a negative straight-line relationship according to the rank-size rule.

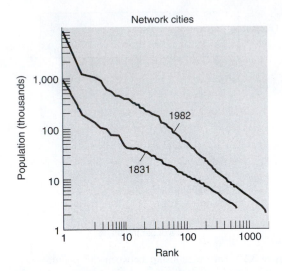

Figure 3.12 Rank-size distributions of French urban agglomerations, 1831 and 1982. Both years essentially follow the rank-size rule, with Paris at the top peaking somewhat higher than expected. (*Source:* Batten, 1995, p. 319).

given urban center by simply knowing that center's rank within the urban system and the populations size of the largest urban center:

$P_i = P_1 \cdot R_i^{-1}$ where P_i is the predicted population of the urban area to be calculated.

P_1 is the population of the largest urban area.

R_i is the rank of the urban area to be calculated.

If we wish to calculate the population of, say, the third largest city in a region or country where the population of the largest city is 1 million, we would proceed as follows:

$$P_i = 1,000,000 \cdot 3^{-1}$$

or

$$P_i = 1,000,000 \cdot 1/3$$

and

$$330,000 = 1,000,000 \cdot .33$$

If we calculated the predicted value of the top 50 cities using this rank-size procedure, we could plot the distribution on double-log paper (log of population on the vertical axis and log of rank on the horizontal axis), which would result in a negative

or inverse straight line (Figure 3.11). This would be the theoretical or predicted relationship, which then may be compared with the actual relationship for French cities (Figure 3.12), following Batten (1995). The degree of correspondence between the predicted and the actual lines determines the extent to which a particular region or country follows the rank-size rule. For example, China follows this rule, as does the United States and Russia, all large countries geographically.

Kondratiev Waves

The urban history of the United States largely follows a cycle of economic expansion and contraction, known as **Kondratiev waves**, named after the Russian economist Nikolai Kondratiev (1935). The long waves, or periods of economic dominance by one set of technologies, last approximately 50 to 60 years. These periods of urban market dominance (economic growth or long-wave peaks) are followed by downturns or retrenchments as the once-dominant technologies become obsolescent. These downturns or "valleys" in the urban economy are then followed by new, substitute technologies that stimulate a new wave of growth. In the United States and the United Kingdom these waves have coincided because of the close historic economic ties between the two countries. The advanced economies of Japan and European countries also closely follow these waves. In fact, as urbanization and urban systems become more mature and extend to more and more regions of the world, all urban areas are increasingly following these cycles of expansion and contraction.

There have been four complete Kontratiev waves, and we are now in the beginning of the fifth wave. These waves reflect changes in prices within the capitalist system. The 50- to 60-year waves are divided into two parts: (1) the expansion phase (25 to 35 years) and (2) the contraction phase (25 to 35 years). When did each of the four waves reach their peaks and how may we best characterize these waves?

- *The First Wave:* The Industrial Revolution (1770–1815)
- *The Second Wave:* The Steam Engine (1840–1865)
- *The Third Wave:* Fordism (1890–1920)
- *The Fourth Wave:* Consumer Goods (1945–1980)
- *The Fifth Wave:* Digital Telecommunications (2000–2035)

Berry (1991) offers the basic reason for the expansion phase of the long waves. It is the time required to develop the necessary infrastructure from a "take-off" to market saturation, that is, the planning, financing, the physical development of the network system. Infrastructure building, from start to the *long-wave turning point*, takes 50 to 60 years. Why then does the urban economic system retrench after the peak and reach a period of **stagflation**, defined as the condition of rising inflation and decline in business activities, including high unemployment? The main reason for the economic retrenchment is **market saturation** or exhaustion based on the older technological system. A crossover between the older technologies and the emerging new technological system takes place midway between the wave peaks, as we are experiencing today between the trough of the fourth wave and the rapid expansion of the fifth wave. The term **Fordism** is shorthand for the mass-production assembly-line manufacturing process, first achieved by Henry Ford.

URBAN GROWTH IN AMERICA

The growth and development of early cities in the United States and Canada may best be understood through the examination of two models of city creation and growth. These are (1) the Meyer-Wyckoff model of frontier cities and (2) the Vance mercantile cities model.

The Meyer-Wyckoff Frontier Cities Model

The **Meyer-Wyckoff model of frontier cities** (1980, 1988) explains how an urban place gradually becomes integrated into the national urban system. Wyckoff used the origin and development of Denver as an example of a frontier city. The model suggests that a frontier town evolves through three stages (Figure 3.13). The stages are based on the level of intensity of interregional linkages between the newly emerging frontier settlement and other urban centers.

In Stage I, the frontier town has strong ties with larger nearby urban centers that act as **gateway cities**. In the United States gateway cities are those which settlers pass on their way westward, such as St. Louis and Kansas city. Figure 3.13 shows the hypothetical frontier town G with strong linkages with gateway centers F and E. These linkages include the movement of people and commodities, with the predominant flow from the gateway centers to the frontier town. The ties with more distant national centers A and B are weak. Other small and distant centers (C and D) have essentially no linkages at all with the frontier town G. If G represents Denver in its early years (ca. 1859), then gateway centers F and E may identify Kansas City and St. Louis. National centers A and B may stand for New York and Philadelphia. Cities C and D may represent Birmingham and Detroit.

Stage II involves a considerable growth in the size and economic functions of all urban centers, G through A. The frontier center itself is able to provide more and more of the commodities formerly provided by centers E and F. In fact, linkages with E have declined. The major change in Stage II, however, is the strong links that have been

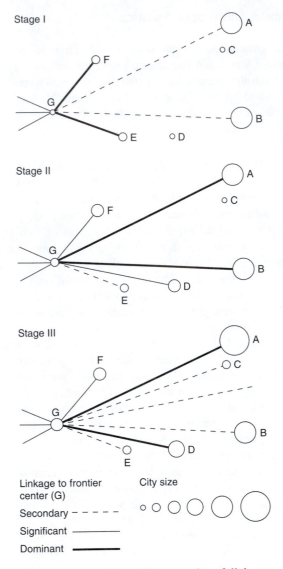

Figure 3.13 The dynamic geography of linkages between a frontier center and the national urban system. (*Source:* Wyckoff, 1988.)

established with the national centers *A* and *B*. Even an intermediate link is established with *D* (Detroit). These long-distance links rely on improved and less expensive modes of transportation, that is, the railroad in the 1860s and 1870s.

In Stage III of the Meyer-Wyckoff model, the differential growth and prosperity of regional and national centers and the considerable growth of *G*, the former frontier town, greatly modify the linkage pattern. A single dominant national center (New York) has now emerged with increased links with the frontier town, whereas the linkages with a former national center (Philadelphia) have weakened and a growing interaction has developed with the earlier small center *D* (Detroit). The entire urban system has matured and center *G* (Denver) itself is evolving into a major regional center that is increasingly tied to the national urban system.

The Vance Mercantile Cities Model

The dictionary defines "mercantile" as "characteristic of merchants or trade." **The Vance mercantile cities model** (1970) seeks to explain the development of the North American urban system based on (1) the role of merchants during five stages or eras and (2) the role of long-distance trade. The first era, *exploration*, is characterized by small North American settlements based on local markets and weak trade ties with Great Britain. The second, *harvesting of natural resources*, constitutes a period in which North American resources—for example, codfish, timber—are shipped to Great Britain. Small settlements become established at fishing ports and timber camps. The third era, the *emergence of farm-based staple production*, witnesses the development of central places in agricultural regions for the production of cotton, tobacco, and grains for export in return for manufactured goods from Great Britain. Atlantic ports such as New York, Baltimore, Boston, Charleston, and Savannah grow in importance to handle this two-way trade.

The fourth era is known as the *interior gateway cities*, which functions as collection centers for agricultural and natural resources. These gateway cities act as warehouses for commodities and typically were located along rail lines. This era also saw the development of local-market manufacturing in certain strategically located cities. Increased resource-based exports from North America were met with increased imports of manufactured goods from Great Britain and other European countries. The fifth and last era in the Vance model is *economic maturity and central place infilling*. At this point the North American market has grown to a sufficient size to accommodate both large-scale domestic manufacturing and the development of several large and growing urban areas. A system of central places emerges in formerly agricultural areas, and a national urban hierarchy develops that is based on widespread long-distance trade. Higher-order goods and services become available in both local and distant markets.

CONTEMPORARY URBAN-ECONOMIC RESTRUCTURING

From 1790, when the first U.S. Census of Population was taken, and for nearly the next 200 years, North American urban areas owed their population growth to manufacturing. Urban areas that occupied strategic locations on water or rail routes had significant cost advantages over inland centers. Manufacturing jobs attracted migrants from rural areas and immigrants from overseas, initially from Western Europe primarily but later from Southern and Eastern Europe. Virtually all of these immigrants settled in the largest urban areas where many manufacturing jobs were available. The multiplier effect also came into play to attract more workers. Urbanization and industrialization walked hand in hand for nearly 200 years.

It is no wonder that—starting quietly in the 1970s, gradually accelerating in the 1980s, exploding in the 1990s, and encompassing the early years of the twenty-first century—many scholars of the city were slow to recognize that by the late twentieth century manufacturing was no longer the backbone and primary instrument of metropolitan growth. Gradually, however, most scholars came to recognize that services had become the new engine running metropolitan economies. These were not the **consumer services**, such as basic retailing or fast-food restaurants, hotel maid and bellhop services, security guards, custodians, and auto parts workers. These consumer services pay relatively low wages, often starting at the minimum wage. In contrast, the metropolitan

economics were being driven by **advanced services**, also called **producer services**. These producer services are knowledge-based and include legal services, advanced financial services, marketing, advertising, engineering and architecture, accounting, investment banking, and telecommunications. They employ high-paid professional workers who usually possess advanced college and university degrees (law degrees, MBA degrees, or MAs in geography), and knowledge-based employment. Information technology has increasingly become tightly linked with the various producer service jobs. Importantly, these jobs are found almost exclusively in metropolitan areas, especially in the very largest metropolitan areas, including New York, Los Angeles, Chicago, and San Francisco-San Jose.

Empirical Examples

As we have noted, legal services are a key component of producer services. Warf and Wije (1991) studied the locations of the 500 largest U.S. law firms and found a high degree of concentration of these law firms, especially in New York and Washington D.C. (Table 3.4). The nine cities (not metropolitan areas) constitute nearly 60 percent of the total employment among the 500 largest law firms in the United States and over 50 percent of the 500 law firms themselves. This particular producer service—law firms—shows a high degree of agglomeration in the nation's

Table 3.4 Legal Employment in Major U.S. Cities

Cities	Total Legal Employment
New York	13,964
Washington, D.C.	7,571
Chicago	6,075
Los Angeles	5,258
Philadelphia	3,091
Boston	2,998
San Francisco	2,964
Dallas	2,383
Atlanta	1,620
Total	45,924

Source: Warf and Wije, 1991, p. 161.

BOX 3.2   BLACK, HISPANIC, WHITE, OLD, AND POOR IN METROPOLITAN AREAS

This chapter presents the concepts of urban hierarchies based on such attributes as population size, primary occupied office space, and air passenger flows. Urban hierarchies may also be based on race, ethnicity, age, and levels of poverty. An examination of these hierarchies or rankings reveals that black, Hispanic, white, elderly, and poor people are concentrated in certain metropolitan areas in particular parts of the United States.

Table B3.2 shows the top ten U.S. metropolitan areas ranked by the percentage of the population classified as black. Note that all of these metropolitan areas are located in the Census-defined South, including Baltimore and Washington, D.C. The

Table B3.2   Leading Metropolitan Areas in Percent Black,[a] 2004

Rank	Metropolitan Area	Percent
1.	Memphis, TN	45.1
2.	New Orleans, LA	38.2
3.	Baton Rouge, LA	34.8
4.	Columbia, SC	33.8
5.	Virginia Beach-Norfolk-Newport News, VA	32.2
6.	Richmond, VA	30.8
7.	Atlanta, GA	30.4
8.	Baltimore, MD	28.7
9.	Birmingham, AL	28.2
10.	Washington, D.C.	26.8

Source: County and City Extra, 2006.
[a]Not Hispanic or Latino.

Table B3.3   Leading Metropolitan Areas in Percent Hispanic or Latino, 2004

Rank	Metropolitan Area	Percent
1.	McAllen, TX	89.1
2.	El Paso, TX	80.7
3.	San Antonio, TX	52.1
4.	Fresco, CA	46.1
5.	Los Angeles, CA	43.2
6.	Albuquerque, NM	42.9
7.	Bakersfield, CA	42.5
8.	Riverside, CA	41.7
9.	Miami, FL	37.0
10.	Oxnard-Thousand Oaks-Ventura, CA	35.5

Source: County and City Extra, 2006.

percent black is even higher in the politically defined or inner cities of these metropolitan areas.

The ten leading metropolitan areas in percent Hispanic or Latino are all located in the Sunbelt South, particularly in California and Texas (Table B3.3). Of course, Miami, located near the island of Cuba, ranks seventh in Hispanic population. Mexican immigrants have settled widely across the United States, many in small towns and cities.

While there are vast white-only areas across the rural Midwest, Great Plains, and interior West, the leading metropolitan areas in the percentage of Caucasian or white population are found in the Northeast and Midwest (Table B3.4). The Pittsburgh

largest cities. Washington, D.C., is something of an exception, in that the population size of the city is the smallest of those included in Table 3.4, but it is of course the city's government function that explains its important legal role.

An indirect general measure of producer services among metropolitan areas can be derived by analyzing the concentrations of occupied office space.

An extremely high degree of concentration exists among the largest U.S. metropolitan areas. In fact the 43 metropolitan areas with populations exceeding 1 million account for 70 percent of the total occupied office space in the United States. New York alone has 12 percent of all occupied office space. New York clearly dominates, followed by Los Angeles and Chicago, the second- and

Table B3.4 Leading Metropolitan Areas in Percent White,[a] 2004

Rank	Metropolitan Area	Percent
1.	Pittsburgh, PA	89.6
2.	Albany, NY	87.6
3/4.	Akron, OH	85.7
3/4.	Worcester, MA	85.7
5.	Allentown, PA	85.6
6.	Cincinnati, OH	85.1
7.	Providence, RI	84.6
8.	Minneapolis, MN	84.2
9.	Omaha, NE	83.4
10.	Louisville, KY	83.1

Source: County and City Extra, 2006.
[a]Not Hispanic or Latino.

Table B3.5 Leading Metropolitan Areas with Population below the Poverty Level, 1999

Rank	Metropolitan Area	Percent
1.	McAllen, TX	35.9
2.	El Paso, TX	23.8
3.	Fresno, CA	22.9
4.	Bakersfield, CA	20.8
5.	New Orleans, LA	18.3
6.	Baton Rouge, LA	17.1
7.	Los Angeles, CA	16.2
8.	Memphis, TN	15.6
9.	San Antonio, TX	15.1
10.	Riverside, CA	15.0

Source: County and City Extra, 2006.

Table B3.6 Leading Metropolitan Areas in Percent of Population over Age 65, 2004

Rank	Metropolitan Area	Percent
1.	Tampa, FL	17.6
2.	Pittsburgh, PA	17.3
3.	Miami, FL	15.6
4.	Buffalo, NY	15.5
5.	Allentown, PA	14.9
6.	Cleveland, OH	14.3
7.	Tucson, AZ	14.2
8/9.	New Haven, CT	13.9
8/9.	Honolulu, HI	13.9
10.	Dayton, OH	13.8

Source: County and City Extra, 2006.

metropolitan area leads with virtually 90 percent white population. Several of the areas in the top ten are old industrial cities.

The poorest metropolitan areas typically have a high percentage of their population in minority categories (black as with Memphis and New Orleans, and Hispanic as in the case of McAllen, El Paso, Fresno, Bakersfield, and Los Angeles (Table B3.5).

Metropolitan areas with a high percent of their population 65 and older include several centers in the U.S. Northeast (New Haven, Buffalo, Allentown, and Albany) (Table B3.6). Also included are the Florida metropolitan areas of Tampa and Miami. Finally come the old industrial cities whose manufacturing jobs have suffered heavy loses: Pittsburgh, Buffalo, Allentown, and Cleveland.

third-largest metropolitan areas. Other large metropolitan areas of note include San Francisco, Boston, Philadelphia, Washington, D.C., Dallas and Detroit. (Box 3.2 presents different measures of the urban hierarchy).

Manufacturing has undergone a decades-long decline in the United States, both in relative and absolute importance. Producer services, in contrast, have been growing as the metropolitan economics have switched from a manufacturing base to a service-information base. It is in the high-pay producer services that new jobs are being created, and it is these jobs—not manufacturing jobs—that are driving metropolitan economies and generating population growth. This shift from goods production to advanced services results in an overall

BOX 3.3   Technology and Urban Geography

Changing Population Density Among the Ten Largest U.S. Metropolitan Areas, 1970–2000

What recent changes have occurred in the American urban system beyond the rapid growth in population numbers since 1970? A fundamental change has been in the density of the population *within* metropolitan areas, both large and small. Jason Hackworth 2005 has provided some interesting answers to the question of the internal population shifts. He used correlation-regression analysis to measure the decline of population density away from a centroid in the CBD.

Correlation-regression analysis is one of the most common statistical techniques used in the social sciences and elsewhere. Here we focus on bivariate (two-variable) analysis. Hackworth identified population density (the number of people divided by the area in which they reside) as the dependent variable—the variable to be explained or the issue of interest. He wanted to know how this density declined with distance from the center of the city into the suburban, peripheral parts of the metropolitan area. Distance was then the second—the independent—variable, used to explain changes in density. Thus, a negative relationship was expected between density and distance. Hackworth used the

exponential form of the correlation-regression model in which the data or observations of density and distance were transformed by taking their exponents.

Output from the model results in a correlation coefficient, R, that indicates the degree to which the two variables are related (correlated):

$$R = \text{density} - \text{distance}$$

If R equals zero, then there is no statistical association between the two variables, and if R equals ± 1.0 then there is a perfect association. A negative correlation, as Hackworth expected between the two variables, would result when one variable had large values and the other low values and vice versus. Thus, Hackworth expected that population densities would be high in the inner city—where distant values from the center were low—and densities would be low in suburban areas where distance from the center had high values (Figure B3.1).

In order to determine the amount of variation in density that is "explained" or associated with distance, the value of R is squared, R^2. Hackworth presented the R^2 values for 1970 and 2000 for the ten largest U.S. metropolitan areas in 2000 (Table B3.7).

It is apparent that for all ten metropolitan areas the role of distance in explaining population density has considerably lessened from 1970 to 2000.

change in the geographic arrangement of economic growth, stagnation, and decline within metropolitan areas, especially the contrast between inner cities and suburbs. Telecommunications technologies now form the base for producer services and are bringing about the fracturing of the geography within cities and among the system of cities (Wheeler, Aoyoma, and Warf, 2000) (Box 3.3).

Amenities

Recent population growth has been fastest in high-amenity locations. Therefore, we conclude our

discussion of the evolution of the American urban system by focusing on amenities. We recognize, of course, that the kind of amenities that are attractive for one person may differ from the amenities that another person values. Nevertheless, features such as temperate climate, proximity to the ocean coast, live entertainment performance venues per capita, dry climate, and restaurants per capita have been identified as important examples of amenities and of fast population growth.

Table 3.5 shows the ten highest-ranked and lowest-ranked metropolitan areas in the United

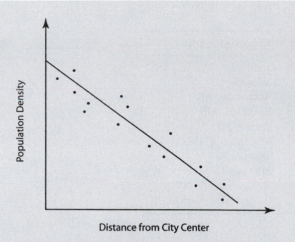

Figure B3.1 Bivariate scatterplot relating population density and distance from a centroid in the inner city. Dots represent observations or data points and the straight line shows the overall relationship between the two variables.

Table B3.7 R^2 Values for Population Density Gradients for the Ten Largest U.S. Metropolitan Areas, 1970–2000

Metropolitan Areas	R^2 Values[a] 1970	2000
Boston, MA	.42	.30
Chicago, IL	.60	.47
Dallas-Fort Worth, TX	.45	.31
Detroit, MI	.60	.39
Houston, TX	.46	.30
Los Angeles, CA	.42	.30
New York, NY	.53	.43
Philadelphia, PA	.44	.27
San Francisco, CA	.30	.13
Washington, D.C.	.61	.20

Source: Hackworth, 2005, p. 504.
[a]Exponential bivariate correlation-regression.

What this change means is that the largest U.S. metropolitan areas have been transformed over these three decades from a largely monocentric form to an increasingly polycentric structure. In 1970, "older," well-established manufacturing centers such as Chicago and Detroit displayed especially monocentric features, as shown by their large R^2 values. Likewise, New York, centered on lower Manhattan Island, and Washington, with its District of Columbia, also had a monocentric forms in 1970, while in 2000, New York ranks second to Chicago as the most monocentric major center.

More remarkable, however, is the metamorphosis to a polycentric urban order by 2000. Washington showed the most dramatic drop in R^2 value, and San Francisco manifests the most polycentric population density configuration of the ten metropolitan areas studied. The classic 1970 (and earlier) commute to the central city has long since been replaced by the reverse commute (central city to suburbs) and especially the suburb-to-suburb commute.

States based on amenity estimates by Glaeser, Kolko, and Saiz (2001, p. 37). All of the highest amenity urban areas are located in California, except for Honolulu, Hawaii, which ranks first (Figure 3.14). California meets the criteria noted above: ocean coast, dry temperate climate, and entertainment centers. This is especially true of Los Angeles, the second largest U.S. metropolitan area. In fact, Los Angeles—and to a lesser extent San Francisco and San Diego—has become a major center "of image-producing industries such as film, music recording...fashion clothing," and these "image-producing industries...[display] a strong proclivity to geographic agglomeration" (Scott, 2001, p. 11).

It is somewhat ironic that Honolulu holds first rank in amenities, given the "brain drain" from the state of Hawaii. According to the U.S. Bureau of the Census, approximately 17,000 more people left Hawaii for the mainland than moved from the mainland to Hawaii between 1997 and 1998. Significantly, many of those who move to the mainland are young and well educated, the best and the brightest. Honolulu has high housing prices and relatively

Table 3.5 Ranking of Top and Bottom U.S. Metropolitan Areas According to Estimated Amenity Value

Highest Rank	Metropolitan Area	Lowest Rank	Metropolitan Area
1.	Honolulu, HI	1.	Samford, CT
2.	Santa Cruz, CA	2.	Norwalk, CT
3.	Santa Barbara, CA	3.	Anchorage, AK
4.	Salinas-Seaside-Monterey, CA	4.	Rochester, MN
5.	Los Angeles-Long Beach, CA	5.	Detroit, MI
6.	San Francisco, CA	6.	Midland, TX
7.	San Jose, CA	7.	Trenton, NJ
8.	Santa Rosa, CA	8.	Minneapolis-St. Paul, MN
9.	Oxnard-Ventura, CA	9.	Nassau-Suffolk, NY
10.	San Diego, CA	10.	Bloomington-Normal, IL

Source: Glaeser, Kolko, and Saiz, 2001.

limited job opportunities in the producer services. Despite high foreign immigration and a relatively high birth rate, Hawaii has the third-lowest population growth rate in the United States. Honolulu citizens show a gradual rise in average age, as the migrating young, many from the University of

Figure 3.14 A view of a beach scene, Honolulu, Hawaii, a high-amenity location.

Hawaii, disproportionately leave for the U.S. mainland.

Attracting Young Educated People

Whereas manufacturing acted throughout American history—until recently—as the principal catalyst for urban population growth, today human resources are at the forefront of metropolitan viability. Specifically, **baby boomers** (born from 1944 to 1964) are retiring, and the next generation of college-educated (25- to 34-year-old) people are being attracted to selected urban areas. This "young and the restless" generation, their numbers actually declining, constitute a desired urban "creative class." They are mobile and are attracted to urban areas that already have a share of other young, educated, culturally sophisticated people. Metropolitan areas with such concentrations are assured of strong economies for the next generation. During the 1990s San Francisco and Atlanta showed the most rapid percentage increase in college-educated 25- to 34-year-olds. Meanwhile, for example, the New York metropolitan area lost more than 9,400 people in this age and educated cohort. While places such as Chicago, Los Angeles, Miami, and Philadelphia lost people in this desired group, other places—in addition to San Francisco and Atlanta—that had notable gains, especially from 1995 to 2000, include Las Vegas, Charlotte, Austin, and Portland, Oregon (see Derwan, 2006) (Box 3.4).

BOX 3.4   RELIGIOUS DIVERSITY WITHIN THE NORTH AMERICAN URBAN SYSTEM

Warf (2006, p. 552) remarked that "The U.S. is arguably the most religiously diverse society in the world," following Eck 2001. In contrast, European countries are relatively more secular, with Canada more moderate in religiosity. Whereas both Canada and the United States have ethnically diverse societies, religious pluralism is rooted in U.S. colonial history: Great waves of Roman Catholics came to the United States from Ireland, Italy, and Poland to diversify the Protestant country, followed more recently by Hispanics, as well as adherents to Islam, Buddhism, and Hinduism. Warf (2006, p. 552) stated that "About 40 percent of the U.S. population claims no explicit religious identification...including 7 percent who self-identify as atheist or agnostic."

To measure religious diversity, Warf used the Shannon index (H), derived from entropy theory:

$$H = -\sum pi \cdot \ln Pi$$

Where p is the proportion of a metropolitan area's adherents in religion i. The larger the value of H, the higher is the level of diversity.

Religious diversity is generally greater in the United States than in Canada, though Toronto is an exception (Table B3.8). Largely Catholic New England and upstate New York renders this area one of the least diverse in the U.S. Moreover, the Upper Midwest, dominated by Lutherans, and Utah, with its concentration of Mormons, are also lacking in diversity. Religious diversity tends to increase with city size—contrast New York with Baptist Bainbridge, Georgia, located near where Georgia, Alabama, and Florida meet.

Table B3.8   Index Of Religious Diversity By Selected U.S. And Canadian Metropolitan Areas

Metropolitan Areas	Shannon Index[a]
United States	
Boston, MA	1.48
Chicago, IL	1.80
Cleveland, OH	1.98
Dallas, TX	2.16
Detroit, MI	1.97
Houston, TX	1.80
Los Angeles, CA	1.92
Miami, FL	1.83
New York, NY	1.96
Philadelphia, PA	2.19
Phoenix, AZ	1.86
San Diego, CA	1.86
Canada	
Toronto	1.91
Montreal	1.08
Vancouver	1.74

Source: Warf, 2006, p. 561.
[a]Larger values indicate greater diversity.

Houston is the most Protestant of all major U.S. metropolitan areas. New York is highly religiously diverse, with more than 13 percent of its population Jewish. Montreal is two-thirds Catholic. The majority of people in Miami, Phoenix, San Diego, and Vancouver have no religious affiliation. For both the U.S and Canada, religious diversity is highest in the east and declines gradually as one moves westward in the North American urban system.

Recent Metropolitan Population Shifts

Approximately 31 percent, or 111 of the 361 U.S. census-defined metropolitan areas, lost White population between 2000 and 2004. One reason for this decline in the White population is the influx of Hispanics into metropolitan areas in the Sunbelt and Western states. A second reason is the accelerating rate of "return migrants," that is, blacks moving from the old industrial urban areas in the North to metropolitan areas in the South, especially in the states of Georgia, Texas, North Carolina, and Florida. Third, Asian immigrants have been increasing rapidly in such urban centers as Las Vegas, Atlanta, Phoenix, Dallas-Fort Worth, and Orlando. What is driving these population shifts among these minorities? It is the fast-growing job markets in these Sunbelt and Western metropolitan areas? The success of a metropolitan area during the 2000–2004 period in attracting minorities into the workforce directly translates into the economic viability of that metropolitan area. At the same time, White retirees from large metropolitan areas in the Northeast and Midwest are moving to small communities in the South.

WRAPPING UP

In this chapter we traced the development and early evolution of the American urban hierarchy, from approximately 1630 through the present. We studied the dominance of growing metropolitan areas and their changing economic viability by examining Pred's model and Borchert's four transport eras, which tied evolving transport technology to American metropolitan growth. This chapter presented four urbanization processes. Urbanization curves displayed the S-shaped growth of the urban population over time. Classic central place theory explained the regularity of small urban settlements on the landscape, especially in rural areas. The rank-size rule focused on another urban regularity, the interdependent growth of a system of cities. Kondratiev waves shed light on the rise and fall of particular technologies over 50 to 60-year cycles, as we find ourselves at the start of the twenty-first century entering the digital telecommunications age. Early urban growth in America was explained by the Meyer-Wyckoff model of frontier settlement and the Vance mercantile model. Bringing our discussion of metropolitan America up to date, we commented on contemporary urban-economic restructuring and the role of amenities and young educated people in recent urban growth.

READINGS

Batten, D. F. 1995. "Network Cities: Creative Urban Agglomerations for the 21st Century," *Urban Studies,* Vol. 32, pp. 313–327.

Berry, B. J. L. 1991. *Long-Wave Rhythms in Economic Development and Political Behavior*. Baltimore, MD: Johns Hopkins University Press.

Berry, B. J. L., E. J. Conkling, and D. M. Ray. 1997. *The Global Economy in Transition*. 2nd ed. Upper Saddle River, N.J.: Prentice Hall.

Borchert, J. R. 1967. "American Metropolitan Evolution," *Geographical Review,* Vol. 57, pp. 301–332.

Brunn, S. D., and J. F. Williams. 1993. *Cities of the World: World Regional Urban Development*. 2nd ed. New York: Harper Collins College Publisher.

Christaller, W. 1933. *Central Places in Southern Germany*. Translated in 1966 by W. C. Baskin. Englewood Cliffs, NJ: Prentice-Hall.

Derwan, Sheila. 2006. "Cities Compete in Hipness Battle to Attract Youth," *The New York Times,* November 25, pp. A1, A10.

Eck, D. 2001. *A New Religious America: The World's Most Religiously Diverse Nation*. San Francisco, CA: HarperCollins.

El Nasser, H. 2006. "Sun Belt Suburbs Get More Diverse," *USA Today,* March 7, p. A1.

Glaeser, E. L., J. Kolko, and A. Saiz. 2001. "Consumer City," *Journal of Economic Geography,* Vol. 1, pp. 27–56.

Gottmann, J. 1961. *Megalopolis*. New York: Twentieth Century Fund.

Hackworth, J. 2005. "Emergent Urban Forms, or Emergent Post-Modernisms? A Comparison of Large U.S. Metropolitan Areas," *Urban Geography,* Vol. 26, pp. 484–519.

Henrie, C. J. and D. A. Plane. 2006. "Decentralization of the Nation's Main Street: New Coastal-Proximity-Based Portrayals of Population in the United States," 1950–2000, *The Professional Geographer,* Vol. 58, pp. 448–459.

Kondratiev, N. 1935. "The Long Waves in Economic Life," *Review of Economic Statistics,* Vol. 17, translated by W. P. Stolper.

Lösch, A. 1938. *The Economics of Location*. Translated in 1954 by W. H. Woglom. New Haven, CT: Yale University Press.

Meyer, D. R. 1980. "A Dynamic Model of the Integration of Frontier Urban Places into the United States System of Cities," *Economic Geography,* Vol. 56, pp. 120–140.

Morrill, R. L. 2006. "Classic Map Revisited: The Growth of Megalopolis," *The Professional Geographer,* Vol. 58, pp. 155–160.

Pred, A. R. 1966. *The Spatial Dynamics of U.S. Urban Industrial Growth, 1800–1914: Interpretive and Theoretical Essays*. Cambridge, MA: MIT Press.

Scott, A. J. 2001. "Capitalism, Cities, and the Production of Symbolic Forms," *Transactions, Institute of British Geographers,* Vol. 26, pp. 11–23.

Taaffe, E. J. 1962. "The Urban Hierarchy: An Air Passenger Definition," *Economic Geography,* Vol. 38, pp. 1–14.

Vance, J. E. 1970. *The Merchant's World: A Geography of Wholesaling*. Englewood Cliffs, NJ: Prentice Hall.

Warf, B. 2001. "Global Dimensions of U.S. Legal Services," *The Professional Geographer,* Vol. 53, pp. 398–406.

Warf, B. 2006. "Religious Diversity across the North American Urban System," *Urban Geography,* Vol. 27, pp. 549–566.

Warf, B. and C. Wije 1991. "The Spatial Structure of Large U.S. Law Firms," *Growth and Change,* Vol. 22, pp. 157–174.

Wheeler, J. O., Aoyama, Y., and Warf, B. 2000. *Cities in the Telecommunications Age: The Fracturing of Geography*. New York and London: Routledge.

Wyckoff, W. 1988. "Revising the Meyer Model: Denver and the National Urban System, 1859–1879," *Urban Geography,* Vol. 9, pp. 1–18.

Zipf, G. K. 1949. *Human Behavior and the Principle of Least Effort*. Cambridge, MA: Addison-Wesley.

CHAPTER 4

GLOBALIZATION AND THE URBAN SYSTEM

The world is my idea.

—SCHOPENHAUER

The purpose of this chapter is to introduce the concept of "World Cities," sometimes referred to as global cities, and the process of globalization. In this chapter we focus on (1) how and why the world urban economy has become so incredibly interlinked and (2) what roles the world or global cities play in the process. The role of multinational corporations and world financial centers is also reviewed.

Globalization processes are tied to selected world cities, not necessarily the largest cities in population, but rather to cities whose engines drive the world economy and whose telecommunications links are the information base allowing these cities to function as if they were all located next to one another. These cities are headquarters to giant corporations that act globally and manage control of the world economy. In the next chapter we will see how telecommunications leads to the fracturing of traditional geographic concepts such as distance and accessibility.

Let us begin by asking, what is globalization? Globalization refers to the movement of capital, information, goods and services among huge multinational corporations, largely ignoring the traditional role of national boundaries. **Globalization** reflects (1) the geographic reorganization of industrial production and service provision, especially capital availability and financial services; (2) the interpenetration of corporations across national boundaries (countries producing and distributing goods and services in many countries); (3) the worldwide diffusion and deliberate creation of

markets being offered identical or nearly identical consumer goods; (4) the internal movement of populations within developing countries to large cities, and the immigration of people from developing economies to the United States, Canada, and Western Europe; and perhaps (6) the emerging worldwide preference for democracy.

Globalization has taken place, at first gradually and now at a quickened pace, only within the last 30 years or so of human history. Humans evolved in highly localized settings, tribes, and communities. Even when human settlements became large enough to be termed cities or urban areas, their focus was local. As capitalism grew and as countries or nation-states were established, these sovereign or independent political units engaged in economic relations with one another. These were international relationships, such as international trade, international diplomacy, and world wars. With the growth of large multinational corporations, the term "globalization" has come to replace "internationalization" as a feature of today's economic, cultural, and political environment. National boundaries have become less significant in many parts of the world. Multinational corporations are the movers and shakers of the modern global economy. Money surges from country to country as if national boundaries do not exist. We will see in Chapter 5 how telecommunications can act to funnel information to all parts of the globe. Even small companies can access the World Wide Web to reach global markets.

WORLD CITIES

Multinational corporations have thus freed themselves from operations in a single country and have established a global network of industrial production, service provision, and distribution. These multinational corporations are headquartered in **world cities**, which act as places where these corporations locate their management headquarters. From these headquarters in world cities, these giant corporations exercise the command and control of their global operations (Figure 4.1). Through the concentrated telecommunications infrastructure in these select world cities, the multinationals coordinate their far-flung enterprises. They draw upon a wide network of financial services and other producer services, such as advertising, marketing, legal assistance, and cyberspace maintenance and aid. A small number of world cities are the functional and operational nodes of the contemporary global economy. Whereas many areas in Africa, Asia, and Latin America are not much more global than they were 100 years ago and largely lack true or mature world cities, the multinational corporations have nevertheless reached out to these areas for low-cost labor for the production of many inexpensive items enjoyed and purchased by consumers in the developed world.

The World City Hierarchy

Where are these world cities located? According to Saskia Sassen (2006) New York, London, and Tokyo are the three world or global cities at the top of the hierarchy. Beyond these, various interpretations prevail. One interpretation, proposed by John Friedmann (1986) is the **world city hypothesis**: The world city hypothesis is about the spatial organization of the new international division of labor (p. 69). By the **international division of labor**, Friedmann meant the separation of management, financial, and production (labor) functions, that is, the division of the capitalist world economy into specialized roles occurring in different locations. These locations are cities at the international, national, regional, and local scales.

Included in Friedmann's hypothesis is the **world city hierarchy**, a ranking of major cities that function as world cities (Table 4.1). Friedmann divided world cities into (1) cities in the capitalist world's core or heartland (developed economies, such as the United States, Canada, Western Europe, Japan, Australia and New Zealand) and (2) those in the semiperiphery, that is, developing economies such as Mexico and Brazil. He further divided these two categories into primary and secondary world cities. Friedmann identified nine world cities in the

Figure 4.1 Chicago Transit Authority. The "El" Station, located on the "Brown" and "Purple" lines, looking southwest toward the downtown, the "Loop," so named because of the circular pattern of the transit route encircling Chicago's central business district. The station is directly above the north-south running Franklin Avenue, at east-west Chicago Avenue. Formerly mostly warehouses, and more recently an artists' loft district, this area is experiencing a condo-style redevelopment. The station is located on the northwest edge of the Loop, where many multinational corporations are headquartered.

Table 4.1 Friedmann's World City Hierarchy, 1986[a]

Core Countries		Semiperipheral Countries	
Primary	*Secondary*	*Primary*	*Secondary*
Chicago	Brussels	São Paulo	Bangkok
Frankfurt	Houston	Singapore	Buenos Aires
London	Madrid		Caracas
Los Angeles	Miami		Hong Kong
New York	San Francisco		Johannesburg
Paris	Sydney		Manila
Rotterdam	Toronto		Mexico City
Tokyo	Vienna		Rio de Janeiro
Zurich			Seoul
			Taipei

Source: Friedmann, 1986, p. 72.
[a]Cities are listed alphabetically.

primary core: three U.S. cities (New York, Los Angeles, and Chicago), five Western European cities (London, Paris, Frankfurt, Rotterdam, and Zurich), and Tokyo, Japan. He also listed nine secondary core world cities, three in the United States (San Francisco, Miami, and Houston), four in Western Europe, one each in Australia (Sydney) and Canada (Toronto). Of the semiperipheral world cities, only São Paulo and Singapore were included in the primary designation. The secondary semiperipheral

world cities consisted of five Asian centers, three Latin American cities, and one African city (Johannesburg, South Africa).

Friedmann's 1986 map of the world city hierarchy, reproduced as Figure 4.2, does not exactly correspond to his listing in Table 4.1, but it is instructive in that it reflects a more detailed breakdown of the hierarchy and shows linkages among selected world cities. Figure 4.2 depicts, from west to east (left to right), Tokyo, Los Angeles, Chicago, New York,

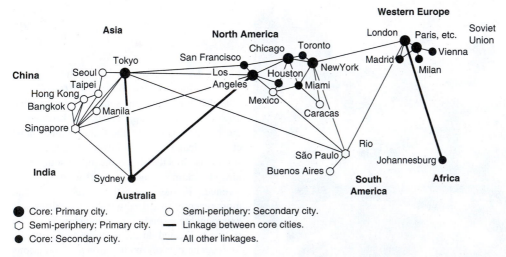

Figure 4.2 The hierarchy of world cities, 1986. (*Source:* Friedmann, 1986).

London, and Paris as the six world cities at the top of the hierarchy. At the next level of the hierarchy, again glancing at Figure 4.2 from left to right, are Sydney, San Francisco, Houston, Miami, Toronto, Madrid, Milan, Vienna, and Johannesburg as core secondary world cities. The figure also shows two other hierarchy levels: (1) primary semiperipheral cities and (2) secondary semiperipheral cities. Linkages among core world cities are shown in the thick lines.

It is interesting to compare Friedmann's world city hierarchy with the more contemporary hierarchy listed in Table 4.2. Several East Asian and certain Latin American cities have increased in rank since the 1980s, as have some European centers. Of special interest are the enhanced positions of the Chinese cities of Beijing, Shanghai, and Guanzhou, as well as the Japanese city of Osaka. Also notable is the rise in rank of Hong Kong, Singapore, Mexico City, Seoul, São Paulo, Osaka, and Beijing, as well as Istanbul, Shanghai, Bogotá, Jakarta, Berlin, Dallas, Melbourne, Santiago, Dublin, Lisbon, Guangzhou, Athens, and Rome.

Figure 4.3 shows the world city hierarchy among the top 50 cities based on the number of corporate headquarters and first-level subsidiaries of

Table 4.2 The 50 Top-Ranked World Cities by Headquarters and First-Level Subsidiary Locations Among the World's 100 Largest Corporations

Rank	World City	Number of Headquarters and First-Level Subsidiaries	Rank	World City	Number of Headquarters and First-Level Subsidiaries
1	New York, USA	69	24	Caracas, Venezuela	18
2	Tokyo, Japan	66	24	Istanbul, Turkey	18
3	London, UK	50	24	Toronto, Canada	18
4	Hong Kong, China	40	28	Dusseldorf, Germany	17
5	Singapore	35	29	Shanghai, China	17
6	Milan, Italy	30	30	Vienna, Austria	16
7	Paris, France	29	31	Bogotá, Colombia	15
8	Mexico City, Mexico	28	31	Jakarta, Indonesia	15
8	Madrid, Spain	28	31	Manila, Philippines	15
10	Seoul, Korea	26	34	Berlin, Germany	14
11	São Paulo, Brazil	25	34	Houston, USA	14
11	Zurich, Switzerland	25	34	Melbourne, Australia	14
13	Osaka, Japan	24	38	Panama City, Panama	13
14	Beijing, China	23	38	Santiago, Chile	13
15	Bangkok, Thailand	22	40	Dublin, Ireland	12
15	Brussels, Belgium	22	42	Athens, Greece	11
15	Chicago, USA	22	42	Dallas, USA	11
15	Frankfurt, Germany	22	42	Rome, Italy	11
15	Sydney, Australia	22	45	Barcelona, Spain	10
20	San Francisco, USA	21	45	Budapest, Hungary	10
21	Los Angeles, USA	20	45	Guangzhou, China	10
21	Taipei, Taiwan	20	45	Hamburg, Germany	10
23	Buenos Aires, Argentina	19	45	Kuala Lumpur, Malaysia	10
24	Amsterdam, Netherlands	18	45	Rio de Janeiro, Brazil	10

Source: Godfrey and Zhou, 1999, p. 276.

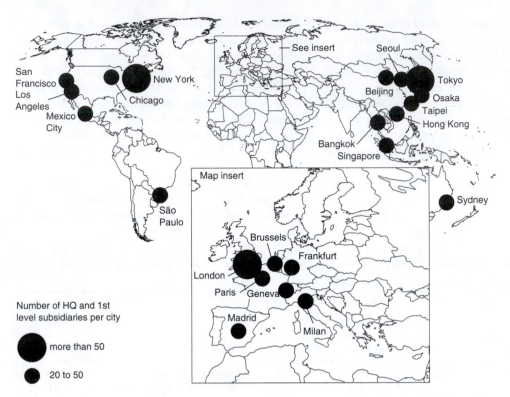

Figure 4.3 World cities with 20 or more corporate headquarters and first-level subsidiaries of the 100 largest multinational firms. (*Source:* Godfrey and Zhou, 1999).

the 100 largest multinational firms (Godfrey and Zhou, 1999). With more than 50 headquarters and first-order subsidiaries, New York, Tokyo, and London stand out as the top three world cities. Second-ranked world cities are found in Europe (19), East and Southeast Asia (13), Latin America (8), the U.S. and Canada (7), and Australia (2) (Table 4.2). Thus, since the 1980s second-ranked world cities have developed an important presence in Europe, the United States and Canada, as well as in a growing number of countries in East and Southeast Asia. Africa has no world city, not even Johannesburg, as defined based on headquarters and first-level subsidiaries locations.

Changing Functions of World Cities

Since the 1970s, world cities have changed some of their important economic functions. Then, and now,

however, world cities have continued to perform the following multiple roles:

- Centers of national and international tourism, commodity trade, and foreign investment
- Centers of commercial banking, investment banking, insurance, and other financial services
- Centers of political power at the national and international levels and the locations of many nonprofit institutions, associations, and organizations related to government
- Centers of consumption of specialized luxury goods by the wealthy elite and of mass-produced goods consumption by the middle and lower class
- Centers of advanced professional services in such areas as medicine, law, higher education, and the application of scientific knowledge and technology
- Centers of high-order information production and export (diffusion) of this knowledge (often proprietary information, data, and reports) to individuals as well as to

selected institutions, governments, and major corporations

- Centers of a concentration of large corporations and associated advanced producer and business services, agglomerating in these centers for mutual benefits
- Centers of culture, arts, entertainment, and clothing and other designs

These above activities, then, characterized world cities of the 1970s as well as today, representing a kind of **historical inertia**. Historical inertia suggests simply that most of the important economic functions of world cities have not changed too much. Having gotten a head start on other cities, these world cities have been able to maintain their primary activities at a high level of competition over other cities.

One dominant function of world cities today, however, has been added. At the same time, one paramount activity of world cities of the 1970s has been largely lost. The added new function and the lost activity are related. As noted in Chapter 3 at the national level, we see the same change as at the global level: (1) the rise in the **informationalization** of the world economy, especially in advanced services, as articulated through the world city network and hierarchy and (2) the decline in manufacturing jobs in the leading world cities. Informationalization involves telecommunications that are concentrated in relatively few places around the globe, particularly in locations in world cities. Because world cities manage the capitalist world economy, they require the rapid, high-volume, and secure transfer of information and data. The growth in international investment of the multinational corporations and the need to finance and service these titanic firms have also led to increased demand for informationalization. Fiber-optic cables laid beneath the Atlantic and Pacific oceans greatly facilitate this high-speed, high-volume transfer.

At the same time that world cities took on the added function of information production and dissemination, however, they became less important in the production of manufactured goods. The United States and Canada, as well as the industrialized world of Western Europe, Japan, and Australia and New Zealand, have massively lost jobs in manufacturing since the 1970s. This process, known as **deindustrialization**, results in large employment losses in local manufacturing in world cities. Deindustrialization in the developed countries occurs when lower-cost locations in the developing regions become more competitive, usually because of substantially lower wage rates and land costs. In addition, markets for manufacturing goods may become saturated; for example, how many dishwashers does a typical household need?

The result is that the industrial-based world cities have eroded at the same time that their high-order information-rich economic functions have grown enormously. The relatively modest-paying industrial jobs have been replaced by much higher-paying informationalization-based employment. These specialized cyberspace-related jobs require much higher levels of education and expertise, thus attracting to these world cities smart and talented people from surrounding regions but also people from all around the world, most of whom receive their higher education in colleges in world cities and/or in universities in the United States, Canada, and the United Kingdom. More routine information-based tasks may take place via telecommunications in developing economies such as India. As industrial jobs are lost, the low-skilled workers may be forced into the lowest paid jobs in consumer services and retailing.

CAPITALISM, POWER, AND WORLD CITIES

The engine that drives economic globalization is capitalism, especially as articulated throughout the network and hierarchy of world cities. **Capitalism** is a distinct economic and social organization in which labor (the factory or industrial worker) is *separated* from ownership of the means of production and the manufactured product itself, as physical work is transformed into a product that the owner sells in a market, while the worker is paid a wage. Capitalism has existed in the West since the sixteenth century, when firms located in different nation-states engaged in trade. Often the basis for international trade was the extraction of raw materials (minerals and agricultural produce) from developing countries and their importation to the more economically advanced countries or nation-states. The advanced economies, the principal producers of manufactured goods, would then export these industrial goods to countries in the less developed world.

Only since the late twentieth century has the world economy become global. With the new information economy operating in the age of telecommunications, the planetary urban system has been operating as a **single economic unit**. This concept of the world as a single economic unit provides the core definition and understanding of the process of globalization (Figure 4.4).

In the geographic context of the emergence of world cities, we have seen the *transformations* of the relatively autonomous cities of the nineteenth

Figure 4.4 Headquarters of a major multinational corporation.

and early twentieth centuries serving primarily local, regional, and, in cases such as New York, London, and Paris, national markets, to a larger number of mature world cities functioning as a hierarchial network to form a single world economic unit. The huge capitalist multinational corporations are the glue holding globalization together. Also in this geographic context is the *division* of the global economy (and therefore world cities) into **core**, **semiperiphery**, and **periphery** relationships. As we have already alluded to earlier in this chapter, the core world cities act as the dominant producers of high-order information for export and serve as the command and control (management) points of the power-based capitalist global economy. Semiperiphery cities are moving toward world city status as their economies continue to mature and prosper. The peripheral cities are the "controlled" or managed cities and operate ecomically on the margins or periphery (edge) of the global economy. Examples of core cities are, of course, New York, Tokyo, and London. Semiperiphery cities include Hong Kong, São Paulo, Seoul, and Singapore. Peripheral cities include Auckland, New Zealand; Lagos, Nigeria; Lima, Peru; Liverpool, United Kingdom; Madras, India; Novosibirsk, Russia; and St. Louis, United States.

John Short (2004) described **black holes** and **loose connections** in the global urban network. He defines black holes as cities with a population of more than three million that are *not* classified as world cities. The concept of loose connections refers to cities whose connectivity is less than expected by their population size (Tables 4.3 and 4.4). The nonworld city status of black holes reflects high levels of poverty, an indication of a limited market and an insufficient number of affluent consumers to support advanced producer services. Not only are these black-hole cities themselves poor, but also the countries in which they are located are among the poorest countries in the world. Moreover, Khartoum and Kinshasa have experienced recent social unrest and anarchy. In addition, national ideologies have not encouraged advanced capitalist economies in the case of Tehran, Iran, and Pyongyang, North Korea.

Table 4.3   Black Holes

City	Country	Population (in millions)
Tehran	Iran	10.7
Dhaka	Bangladesh	9.9
Khartoum	Sudan	7.3
Kinshasa	Congo	6.5
Lahore	Pakistan	6.5
Baghdad	Iraq	4.9
Rangoon	Myanmar	4.7
Algiers	Algeria	3.9
Abidjan	Ivory Coast	3.8
Pyongyang	North Korea	3.6
Chittagong	Bangladesh	3.1

Source: Short, 2004, p. 297.

The ten cities listed in Table 4.4 have the lowest degree of connectivity with the global urban network of all large cities in the world, compared to their populations. The least connected cities are Calcutta, Lagos, and Karachi, extremely large cities in extremely poor countries. The Ukraine economy has recently collapsed and Pittsburgh, perhaps a surprise inclusion, has experienced severe deindustrialization.

Examples of World City Globalization

Looking at particular examples of world city globalization is helpful in illustrating general characteristics of world city features. We begin with a

Table 4.4   Loose Connections

Rank	City	Country
1	Calcutta	India
2	Lagos	Nigeria
3	Karachi	Pakistan
4	Chennai	India
5	Guangzhou	China
6	Kiev	Ukraine
7	Rio de Janeiro	Brazil
8	Pittsburgh	USA
9	Casablanca	Morocco
10	Lima	Peru

Source: Short, 2004, p. 300.

look at the overall relationship between world cities their economic power and wealth. We then focus on the location of U.S. law firms in world cities.

Powerful World Cities

One way to view the hierarchy of world cities is through the degree of power they exhibit. A significant degree of this power is based on the level of connectivity of a given center to the entire network of major world cities. Power is expressed both as internal characteristic of cities as well as the city's position or rank on the world urban interlocking network. Taylor et al. (2001) has provided four different measures of power among the leading world cities: highly connected cities, dominant centers, command centers, and gateway centers (Table 4.5).

Ten cities are classified as highly connected. In addition to the top three world cities of New York, London, and Tokyo (Sassen, 2006) are the North American urban areas of Chicago, Los Angeles, and Toronto (Box 4.1). European centers include Milan and Paris. Asian cities that are highly connected with the world city network are Hong Kong and Singapore. Only seven cities are considered dominant centers, all also highly connected centers, with the addition of Frankfurt, Germany.

Command centers number eleven. These are cities that have world or regional headquarters of major transnational corporations, especially the 100 largest global service firms. Regional office headquarters now play an increasingly important role in critical decision making, as their knowledge of local and regional conditions are more extensive than the more remote and often "less informed" world headquarters.

Finally, highly connected gateway cities typically are not dominant centers or command cities. These cities serve important national economies, as for example São Paulo, Brazil; Mexico City, Mexico; and Melbourne and Sydney, Australia.

World Cities and Wealth

Since world cities are magnets for the wealthy (billionaires) and their business and financial activities, one wonders, at the same time, if world cities tend to somehow polarize

BOX 4.1   NEW YORK CITY'S POPULATION CHANGES

In the year 2000, the City of New York—consisting of the five boroughs of The Bronx, Brooklyn, Manhattan, Queens, and Staten Island (Figure B4.1)—had approximately 60 percent of its households with annual incomes of less than $50,000 (*New York Times,* 2006, February 19, p. 26). It is not easy to live in New York, especially on high-cost Manhattan Island, with such a marginal income. Do these figures suggest that the City of New York is about to lose population?

Nay, according to a recent study by Regina Armstrong, of Urbanomics, quoted in *The New York Times,* who projects an increase of the City's population of 1.2 million from today's 8.2 million (7.8 million in 2000) to 9.4 million by 2025, a 20 percent jump with Queens and Staten Island growing by 25 and 33 percent, respectively (Table B4.1). Whereas the City lost people from 1970 to 1980, since 1980 the population has steadily increased, particularly after 1990. This growth has been driven largely by immigration, which is forecast to continue apace over the next two decades. Asian immigrants will expand rapidly by some 1.3 million people between 2000 and 2025, as will Hispanics by some 575 thousands, both through immigration and natural increase. Whites will decline by more than 880 thousands by 2025, whereas the number of African Americans will remain largely unchanged.

Table B4.1   Projected Population Change in the Five Boroughs of New York City, 2000–2005 (in millions)

Boroughs	2000	2005	Percent Change
The Bronx	1.3	1.5	16
Brooklyn	2.4	2.8	12
Manhattan	1.5	1.7	10
Queens	2.2	2.8	25
Staten Island	.4	.6	33
Total	7.8	9.4	20

Source: Regina Armstrong, Urbanomics, quoted in *The New York Times,* 2006, February 19, p. 26.

What will drive the growth in jobs in New York City will of course be the advanced service economy, which geared up notably since the early 1980s. The projected change in household income of $100,000 and more (in 1999 dollars) for the five boroughs suggests a boost from 14 percent in 2000 to 36 percent by 2025. This percentage gain will mean a decrease in households with incomes of less than $100,000 from 86 percent in 2000 to 74 percent in 2025. Still the excessively poor will remain.

employment opportunities such that world cities have a disproportionate concentration of the very poor, the unemployed, and the homeless. What exactly is the connection, if any, between a city's position in the world city hierarchy and the social well-being of its inhabitants?

One widely held argument is that at the same time world cities have attracted high-paying professional and advanced service occupations, they have also experienced an increase in low-paying jobs, unemployment, and homelessness. Thus the

rich and the poor coexist in world cities. The same city in which corporate executives are chauffeured in limousines containing all sorts of sophisticated telecommunication devices to offices in modern buildings will also be home to homeless people sleeping in makeshift cardboard boxes on the sidewalk or low-income employees walking to work in the inner city. The haves and the have-nots are both packed in the same city space, but they exist in slightly different locations and in very different social, economic, and political conditions.

Figure B4.1 The five boroughs of New York City: The Bronx, Brooklyn, Manhattan, Queens, and Staten Island.

What would cause such economic polarization? One explanation is the **new international division of labor**. This concept divides work into low-pay production or manufacturing jobs in large cities in poor developing countries, such as Mexico or the Philippines, and the high-paying employment associated with the administrative and management functions of gargantuan multinational corporations, which are concentrated in developed countries. The *new* division of employment types has meant massive declines in manufacturing jobs in world cities (New York and Chicago are prime examples) and associated reductions in jobs supplying materials to the manufacturers. How many cases have we heard in the United States of, say, an automobile worker losing a job that paid $22 or $27 per hour and having to take a virtually minimum-pay job (Figure 4.5)?

This bifurcated or polarized employment picture, then, results from the changed economic functions

Table 4.5   Measures of Powerful World Cities

Cities	Highly Connected	Dominant Centers	Command Centers	Gateway Centers
Amsterdam			X	
Brussels			X	
Boston			X	
Buenos Aires				X
Chicago	X	X	X	
Frankfurt		X	X	
Hong Kong	X	X		X
Jakarta				X
Kuala Lumpur				X
London	X	X	X	
Los Angeles	X			
Madrid				X
Melbourne				X
Mexico City				X
Miami				X
Milan	X			X
Mumbai				X
New York	X	X	X	
Paris	X	X	X	
São Paulo				X
Singapore	X		X	X
Sydney				X
Taipei				X
Tokyo	X	X	X	
Washington D.C.	X			X
Zurich			X	

Source: Taylor, Walker, Catalano, and Hoyler, 2001.

Figure 4.5 Hope, a temporarily homeless lady is interviewed by a college professor as they sit on a bench in the median of Broadway in New York City. She sleeps in nearby Riverside Park, facing the Hudson River. In good weather, she picks flowers in Riverside Park, makes bouquets, and sells them on the corner of Broadway and 110th Street. She has been homeless a short time after losing her job, then her car, and then her apartment. She continues to seek work. She does not use alcohol or drugs. Estimates are that approximately one-third of homeless people are alcohol and/or drug dependent, one-third have mental conditions, another one-third are simply individuals who, like Hope, are temporarily facing unexpectedly tough times.

of world cities and emerging world cities and the different locations of production-oriented employment centers compared to high-level telecommunications and management centers (Box 4.1). While the underemployed and unemployed grow and accumulate in numbers in world cities, so too do the highly educated and technically skilled workers. Many of these skilled workers are attracted from afar, often from all around the world. The source regions for these knowledgeable workers experience a brain drain, a loss of what would otherwise have been local talent. The world cities gain the fruits of highly educated, technologically advanced workers drawing lofty incomes. As Saskia Sassen (2006) has noted, global cities attract a disproportionate number of highly educated workers in the producer services. In addition, there appears to be a worldwide preference among producer service workers for locations in cities with a democratic form of government. The developing areas lose their "best and their brightest." Polarization reigns (Box 4.3).

U.S. Law Firms in World Cities

The United States has become known as a litigious society, which the dictionary defines as quarrelsome individuals or groups given to carrying out lawsuits. The media are full of examples of outrageous lawsuits over trivial matters. It is no wonder that the United States has more lawyers by far than any other country. In addition, many U.S. law firms are huge and several operate globally, providing services to multinational corporations. For example, the world's largest law firm—Baker and McKenzie, headquartered in Chicago—bills themselves as "The Global Law Firm." Similarly, White and Chase, originating in New York, publicly declare themselves a "Global Law Firm."

U.S. law firms concentrate their offices outside the United States in eight principal world cities (Table 4.6). We should not be surprised to see that Hong Kong ranks second in number of foreign offices of U.S. law firms, outranking even Tokyo. All the Asian world cities are primary financial

Table 4.6 Non–U.S. World Cities with Offices of U.S.-Headquartered Law Firms

World City	Number of U.S. Law Firms Represented
London	63
Hong Kong	36
Paris	28
Tokyo	24
Brussels	22
Moscow	17
Singapore	14
Frankfurt	12

Source: Beaverstock et al., 2000, p. 131.

centers, requiring high-level legal services. Hong Kong is easily accessible to U.S. legal services, in contrast to the much more restricted and closed Japanese legal system. Four of the world cities with offices of U.S.-based law firms are located in Western Europe. The demise of the Soviet Union has resulted in U.S. law firms concentrating in Moscow during the lengthy and fitful transition to a market economy. The eight world cities shown in Table 4.4 represent the locations of more than one-half of the foreign offices of U.S.-headquartered law firms. This is indeed a highly bunched pattern. Moreover, these firms consist of exceptionally talented attorneys who deal with extremely complicated issues involving the multinational legal system.

Where are the U.S. headquarters of these global law firms? As Figure 4.6 shows, they are concentrated in the largest three metropolitan areas, plus Washington, D.C. The inclusion of the national capital is not surprising, given its fundamental political role. New York is the clear leader with 33 law firms with foreign offices, far ahead of second-ranked Washington, DC (11) and third-ranked Chicago (10). Significantly, Los Angeles, the second-largest U.S. metropolitan area, has only seven firms with foreign offices, fewer than Chicago. This reflects the fact that Chicago has occupied a high rank within the U.S. urban hierarchy for a much longer period of time than Los Angeles has.

BOX 4.2 Skilled Labor Migration Among World Cities

We typically think of a **brain drain** in terms of migration from countries with developing economies to the developed countries. Sometimes these migrants move to developed countries to obtain an education. Because developed countries offer much greater financial opportunities and other amenities, these now-educated people often remain in the same country in which they obtained their education. They typically become a part of the corporate and academic communities. The result is a brain drain in which the most educated workers are drawn away from the source region to attractive metropolitan areas in developed economies. Increasingly, these magnet cities are world cities and emerging world cities.

What is far less known, however, is another kind of international migration of skilled workers *from* world cities to other world cities and other dominant urban centers (Figure B4.2). Here we take the example of London's foreign banking. Globalization of skilled worker migration follows the path of the globalization of financial capital.

Major London-based banks that lend money in foreign locations must have personnel highly knowledgeable in sound investment practices. A London investment bank may rather *trust* an officer from its London headquarters to operate in Sydney or Hong Kong, for example, than a local banker. Many London bankers are eager to spend a year or two in an overseas world city out of interest in diversity and for extra financial gain.

Take another look at Figure B4.2. Taking only one example of London's many banks doing business overseas, NipponBank sends its bankers from its London headquarters to world cities and emerging world cities to perform highly skilled financial investment tasks for a one- or two-year assignment. In this particular example, Paris is the leading destination for the bankers, followed in order by New York, Tokyo and Milan. The London-based BritBank is more oriented to Asia and North America, and sends bankers to Hong Kong, Singapore, Toronto, and Washinton, D.C.

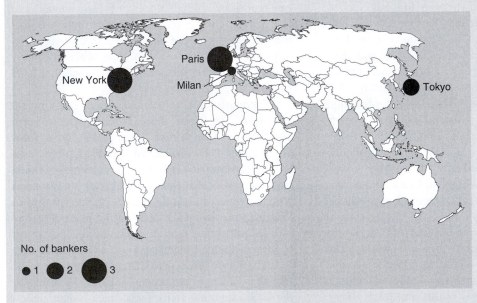

Figure B4.2 NipponBank's London headquarters to world cities and emerging world cities. (*Source:* After Beaverstock and Smith, 1996.)

BOX 4.3   U.S. TREASURY SECURITIES

The global economy may be viewed from many dimensions. One, though little considered by most observers, is through the ownership of U.S. Treasury securities. Americans currently own less than half of the U.S. Treasuries, and quite a variety of other countries count in the top ten in ownership (Table B4.2). Foreign ownership of these securities may be regarded in fact as international loans to the United States, rendering the U.S. a debtor to these nations.

Whereas some countries with the greatest ownership of U.S. Treasury securities are among the expected lenders because of their international financial status (e. g., Japan, the United Kingdom, and Germany), others may astonish casual observers with their importance as U.S. financial linkages. Perhaps the most astoundingly is Mexico, ranked tenth in lending to the United States. Whereas Mexican immigration to the U.S. has been widely discussed and debated, at the same time a financial ownership flow to the U.S. has been quietly occurring, a reverse flow to immigration. Also a perhaps unexpected country on the top ten list is Brazil, with

Table B4.2   Top Ten Foreign Countries Holding U.S. Treasury Securities

Rank	Countries	Holdings (in $ billions)
1	Japan	644
2	People's Republic of China	339
3	United Kingdom	201
4	South Korea	67
5	Taiwan	66
6	Germany	51
7	Hong Kong	50
8	Canada	47
9	Brazil	43
10	Mexico	42

Sources: Norris, 2006, and U.S. Treasury and Federal Reserve.

its size and rapidly advancing economy. China and its quickly emerging market economy ranks second only to the mature Japanese economy. It is less astonishing that the Asian tigers (South Korea, Taiwan, and Hong Kong) are in the leading ten in holding U.S. Treasury securities. (Based on Norris, 2006).

INTERCONNECTIONS AMONG WORLD CITIES

Although we know that the world cities are defined by the many kinds of interconnections among them, obtaining flow data to study these interrelationships is difficult. Much of the data are proprietary, highly specialized, and idiosyncratic for individual corporate enterprises. Only in the aggregate can we obtain a complete picture of the true interconnections among world cities.

One study used data from FedEx letters, packages, and boxes shipped from the United States to overseas destinations (Figure 4.7). FedEx is, of course, only one company providing service to foreign locations, and does not serve all parts of the world equally. Hence, Brussels, for example, shows up as more important than London, the country of

Puerto Rico as more significant than Mexico City. Nevertheless, Figure 4.7 provides a crude indication of linkages among world centers. In terms of shipments of information from the United States as international exports, New York alone accounts for 35 percent of the total. The four regional centers of Atlanta, Chicago, Dallas-Fort Worth, and Los Angeles send 40 percent, and all other urban areas ship the remaining 25 percent.

Interaction Among World Cities

One indirect measure that has been used to determine the interconnections among world cities is air passenger flows. Among which world cities are people most likely to travel by airplane? Table 4.7 shows the ranking of the top ten world cities based on air passenger travel and a second ten emerging

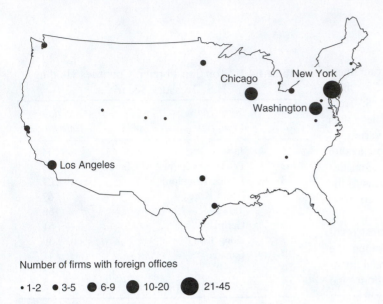

Number of firms with foreign offices

• 1-2   ● 3-5   ● 6-9   ⬤ 10-20   ⬤ 21-45

Figure 4.6 The number of U.S. law firms with foreign offices. (*Source:* Beaverstock, 2000).

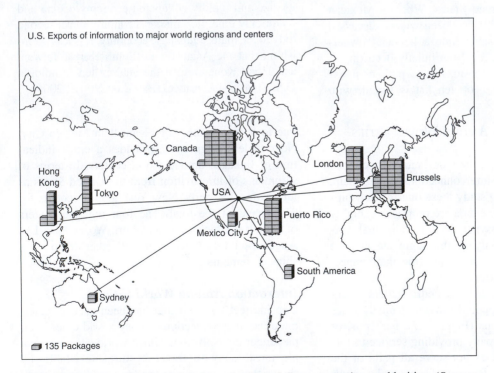

Figure 4.7 Exports of information from the United States to major world cities. (*Source:* Mitchelson and Wheeler, 1994).

Table 4.7 A Ranking of World Cities and Emerging World Cities Based on Air Passenger Travel

Rank	World Cities	Emerging World Cities
1	London	
2	Paris	
3	New York	
4	Tokyo	
5	Hong Kong	
6	Amsterdam	
7	Singapore	
8	Frankfurt	
9	Los Angeles	
10	Chicago	
11		Mexico City
12		Zurich
13		Milano
14		Madrid
15		Miami
16		San Francisco
17		Seoul
18		Houston
19		Boston
20		Montreal

Source: Smith and Timberlake (2001).

world cities. These rankings emphasize the role of more "central" cities within the travel network, such as London, Paris, Amsterdam, and Frankfurt in Western Europe. These more centralized cities have much heavier passenger flows to more world cities than do the more peripheral cities such as Mexico City, Miami, Seoul, and Montreal.

Corporations that operate globally have to decide in which cities to locate their foreign offices. Measuring the global office location strategies of advanced producer-service firms provides another way to study interconnections among world cities. One recent study found that the three dominant world cities of New York, London, and Tokyo have nearly identical links among the leading five world cities based on intrafirm global linkages (Table 4.8). Clearly, these cities are at the apex of the global network and may be said to act as command and control centers.

If we shift our attention specifically to the United States, we find that New York is by far the most connected of all U.S. urban areas in terms of its linkage with the largest number of other U.S. urban areas. Let us again use FedEx shipments as a measure of interconnections among urban areas. As Figure 4.8 indicates, FedEx materials flow from New York to cities throughout the country. Distance is obviously no obstacle to New York's reach. For example, New York, the East Coast global city, is most strongly tied to Los Angeles, the West Coast global city, as the major destination.

Not only does New York dominate the top of the urban hierarchy over Los Angeles and Chicago, but New York also rules over the smallest urban areas in the country. For example, Athens, Georgia, with an estimated 2006 population of only approximately 180,000 (including some 33,000 students at the University of Georgia) is clearly a small metropolitan area. Yet if we ask with which U.S. metropolitan areas Athens has its strongest ties, the answer is first with nearby Atlanta and second with New York. All the FedEx letters, packages, and boxes that are shipped out of Athens over, say, a month have New York as the second-leading destination. In addition, the leading sender of packages to Athens is New York. New York will rank first or second for virtually all metropolitan areas in the United States, from Los Angeles to Cheyenne, Wyoming.

The Tourist World City

Tourism involves not only the mass movement of people but also the consumption of tangible goods such as food and drinks, hotel accommodations, airline fares, rental cars, cruise ships, and souvenirs. Tourism has become a major entertainment industry as more and more people are experiencing more and more leisure time and as more and more people, including retirees, have the financial resources to travel. Even business travelers, in their times of leisure, may become temporary tourists. Advertising, television, and the Internet have touted various tourist locations—the selling of cities.

Major cities and world cities in particular are the strategic sites for the global entertainment industry.

Table 4.8 Interoffice Links Among New York-, London-, and Tokyo-Based
Advanced Producer-Service Firms Among World Cities

New York		London		Tokyo	
Rank	Cities	Rank	Cities	Rank	Cities
1	London	1	New York	1	New York
2	Hong Kong	2	Hong Kong	2	London
3	Tokyo	3	Tokyo	3	Hong Kong
4	Singapore	4	Singapore	4	Singapore
5	Paris	5	Paris	5	Paris
6	Frankfurt	6	Los Angeles	6	Frankfurt
7	Los Angeles	7	Milan	7	Los Angeles
8	Milan	8	Frankfurt	8	Milan
9	Chicago	9	Chicago	9	Chicago

Source: Beaverstock, Smith, and Taylor, 2000.

This industry requires the infrastructure provided by world cities in order to coordinate its diverse activities. New York and Los Angeles dominate the global entertainment industry. Only in these two world cities can we find a sufficient number of adequately creative professionals such as actors, television personalities, writers, and directors to maintain the kind of quality entertainment that can be exported worldwide. Only in these places can the entertainment industry find both the high-level

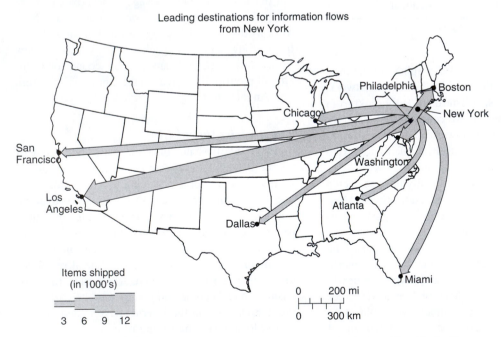

Leading destinations for information flows
from New York

Items shipped
(in 1000's)

3   6   9   12

0   200 mi

0   300 km

Figure 4.8 Leading destination for Federal Express information flows from New York. (*Source:* Mitchelson and Wheeler, 1994, p. 96).

technology and the experts capable of operating it to allow the global export of a high-caliber entertainment product, a product that is good enough to export to eager worldwide consumers.

Two factors have played a vital role in the growth of the international media markets: (1) technological innovations and (2) government deregulation. The globalization of the entertainment industry has been accelerated by mergers in which giant enterprises are buying smaller but still large media firms. We now have a relatively small number of major media conglomerates dominating the industry. Niche markets are filled by many small, specialized companies. The giant conglomerates are able to sell a standardized product to an enlarged international market.

Not only are world cities sites of tourist and other entertainment products, but these world cities have also become major consumers of the industry. Theme parks encourage customer loyalty, an area in which the Walt Disney Company has had a long tradition. Theme parks have vast shopping malls offering, for example, Disney products of all sorts. The Disney Store has long been a part of the traditional suburban shopping mall. The reach of the tourist and entertainment industries is extensive. For example, the recent redevelopment of Times Square, the entertainment core of Broadway in Manhattan, was heavily financed by the Walt Disney Company. Similarly, the Summer Olympics hosted by Atlanta in 1996 gave increasing testimony to Atlanta's role as a world city.

New York and Los Angeles as Tourist Cities

New York and Los Angeles, America's two leading global cities, rely heavily on tourism as a key component of their economies. In Los Angeles, tourism ranks third among all industries in employment. Although tourism is a more important part of the Los Angeles economy, New York—because of its size—attracts more total tourists. Travelers are drawn to these two centers for a variety of reasons. For example, New York, the national and global financial and corporate center, attracts a large number of international business travelers, as well

as those interested in the arts and entertainment. *The New York Times* daily publishes a "The Arts" section. Los Angeles also attracts many international business travelers, especially from Asia, as well as a substantial number of conventioneers. In fact, business travelers and conventioneers constitute 33 percent of New York's tourists and 25 percent of all tourists in Los Angeles.

Although New York and Los Angeles share many tourist features, the geography of tourism between these two centers is distinctive. In New York, as with global cities in general, tourism tends to be highly concentrated in the central area. Within the New York metropolitan area New York City accounts for about 80 percent of the tourism market, and Manhattan Island for nearly 80 percent of the New York City market. Manhattan contains 93 percent of the hotels in New York City and 80 percent of the jobs in the amusement and recreation service industries. Most of the tourism market is located between 96th Street and lower Manhattan.

In contrast, the tourist geography of Los Angeles is widely dispersed. For example, only 5 percent of overnight visitors to the metropolitan area stay in downtown Los Angeles. In fact, the ten most popular tourist submarkets combined account for only 55 percent of the total overnight visitors. Not surprisingly, Hollywood is the most popular tourist spot in the Los Angeles metropolitan area, accounting for 25 percent of all overnight visits. The last time this author stayed in Los Angeles, he was part of that small 5 percent of downtown sleepers, and he could look out his 21st-floor window and see the famous Hollywood sign on the hill staring back at him. Beverly Hills is the second most visited area, accounting for just over 15 percent of all overnight tourist visits.

The Impact of 9/11

The September 11, 2001, terrorist attacks in New York on the twin 110-story World Trade Center towers and on the Pentagon in Washington, D.C., had devastating impacts on America and Americans. In addition to all the emotional, psychological, and social consequences, these terrorist attacks had real economic impacts on the

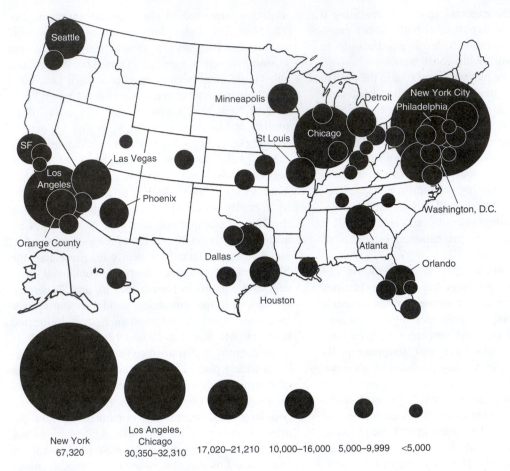

Figure 4.9 The 50 U.S. metropolitan areas most affected by the September 11th terrorist attacks: job losses in 2002 in the most impacted industries (aerospace, airlines, defense, entertainment, finance, tourism, and travel). (*Source:* Johnson, 2003).

U.S. economy. The repercussions hit hardest in the three U.S. global cities of New York, Los Angeles, and Chicago (Figure 4.9). Although the effect was immediately felt in tourism and related industries, the fallout rebounded everywhere and was felt throughout the U.S. economy. Tourism, the airlines, entertainment, and travel in general experienced the greatest job losses, but the financial services and even retailing sectors also suffered significant job losses. Many small companies and major corporations alike were hurting and were forced to lay off workers. The entire economy suffered a massive jolt.

Naturally, the greatest absolute job losses were in New York, numbering 70,000 in the most impacted industries. It is estimated that more than 15 percent of all jobs were lost in tourism, airlines and other travel, and entertainment, as well as in finance and retail combined. Los Angeles and Chicago were also seriously hurt, as each city lost approximately 30,000 jobs. Las Vegas and Orlando took hard hits of 20,000 people being thrown out of work—tourist and entertainment capitals outside the global city system.

As Figure 4.9 demonstrates, however, the flattening of the economy was a nationwide phenomenon.

For example, Washington D.C. lost some 20,000 jobs. The economic damage was also felt in the regional capitals of the United States: San Francisco, Seattle, Atlanta, Dallas-Fort Worth, Houston, St. Louis, Minneapolis, Detroit, Boston, and Philadelphia. The injury to the economy was felt in smaller metropolitan areas, such as Salt Lake City, Nashville, Louisville, and Charlotte. No place escaped the economic crippling. Nevertheless, the three U.S. global centers took the hardest hits. Why? Because these three cities, especially New York and Los Angeles, are the primary places where the tourist, entertainment, and airline industries are concentrated.

MULTINATIONAL CORPORATIONS

As we have seen throughout this chapter, multinational corporations realize that to remain competitive in today's market they must operate on a global level. Giant corporations cannot afford to limit their market to a particular country, not even a large and affluent market such as the United States. U.S. firms reach overseas and include Canada in their market strategy. European companies cannot ignore the plump U.S. market. And the rapidly expanding Asian market is an attraction to all. Japan of course, is especially attractive, as is South Korea. The People's Republic of China, which provides a vast array of manufactured products that are consumed in America and Europe, is itself a huge market that is still in the early stages of evolution and investment from multinational corporations. To multinational firms headquartered outside the United States, becoming global means penetrating the U.S. market.

How many Americans filling their vehicle tanks at the green BP station realize that BP stands for British Petroleum, which is headquartered in the United Kingdom? How many Americans chomping a Whopper at Burger King are aware that their mouthful is being provided by a company headquartered in the United Kingdom? How many Americans sleeping at a Holiday Inn, which was founded by a man from Memphis, are aware that Holiday Inn is now

British-owned? Brooks Brothers, providing the latest in styles, is Italian-owned. This writer's 1998 red Toyota Camry, manufactured by Toyota Motors of Japan, was actually assembled in California with parts both from Japan and the United Sates. So, am I driving a Japanese or an American automobile? And so on.

U.S. Multinational Corporations

Table 4.9 lists the leading U.S. multinational corporations. This group is clearly dominated by petroleum and automobile firms. In fact, Wal-Mart is the only retail firm among the top 20 U.S. multinationals, though Wal-Mart derives some 83 percent of its revenue domestically. Wal-Mart, however, owned more than 700 stores in Mexico in 2006, 290 stores in Britain, 260 in Canada, and 66 in China (Hugill, 2006). Wal-Mart operates the second largest computer network in the world, following only the Pentagon, and has the largest motor truck fleet in the world. The petroleum companies derive the majority of their revenue from foreign operations. For example, Texaco derives 72 percent of its total revenue from foreign activities, Exxon Mobil 69 percent, and Chevron 45 percent. Other major multinationals that are heavily dependent on foreign sources of revenue are the technology firms of IBM (58 percent foreign revenue) and Hewlett-Packard (56 percent).

Where are the U.S. headquarters of these multinational corporations? Of the top ten multinationals, four are located in the greater New York region (Table 4.9). Two are in the San Francisco metropolitan area, two (Ford and General Motors) are in Detroit, and one is in Dallas (Exxon Mobil). And then there are Wal-Mart Stores, headquartered in Bentonville, Arkansas. This tiny town of only some 26,000 people is tucked into the extreme northwestern corner of the state, only 5 miles south of Missouri and only 25 miles east of Oklahoma. However, Wal-Mart is a special case, as we will see shortly.

In 2005, Exxon Mobil replaced Wal-Mart as the leading U.S. corporation in revenue or sales, a position Wal-Mart had held since 2001. Home Depot,

Table 4.9 The Twenty-Five Largest U.S. Corporations in Total Revenue, 2005 and in Percent Change, 2004–2005

Rank	Corporations	Headquarters	Total Revenue (in $ millions)	Percent Change in Revenue, 2004–2005
1	Exxon Mobil	Irving, TX	339.9	25.5
2	Wal-Mart Stores	Bentonville, AK	315.6	9.6
3	General Motors	Detroit, MI	192.6	−0.5
4	Chevron	San Ramon, CA	189.4	28.1
5	Ford Motor	Dearborn, MI	177.2	2.9
6	Conocophilips	Houston, TX	166.7	37.0
7	General Electric	Fairfield, CT	157.2	2.8
8	Citigroup	New York, NY	131.0	21.0
9	American International Group	New York, NY	108.9	11.1
10	IBM	Amonk, NY	91.1	−5.4
11	Hewlett Packard	Palo Alto, CA	86.7	8.5
12	Bank of America	Charlotte, NC	83.9	32.6
13	Berkshire Hathaway	Omaha, NE	81.7	9.8
14	Home Depot	Atlanta, GA	81.5	11.5
15	Valero Energy	San Antonio, TX	81.4	50.9
16	McKesson	San Francisco, CA	80.5	15.8
17	J. P. Morgan Chase & Co.	New York, NY	79.9	40.3
18	Verizon Communications	New York, NY	75.1	5.0
19	Cardinal Health	Dublin, OH	74.9	15.0
20	Altria Group	New York, NY	69.1	7.3
21	Kroger	Cincinnati, OH	60.5	7.3
22	State Farm Ins. Co.	Bloomington, IL	59.2	0.7
23	Marathon Oil	Houston, TX	58.9	29.7
24	Procter & Gamble	Cincinnati, OH	56.7	10.4
25	Dell	Round Rock, TX	55.9	13.6

Source: Fortune, April 17, 2006, p. F-1.

headquartered in Atlanta, is the only other retail firm in the top 15 in revenue. General Motors, long the top corporation in the world, ranked third in 2005 in revenue. Newcomers since 2001 to the top 10 U.S. corporations in 2005 are merged Conocophilips and American International Group. Also included in the leading 10 U.S. corporations in 2005 revenue are Chevron (petroleum), Ford Motors (automotive), General Electric (diversified), Citigroup (financial), and IBM "blue supercomputers."

In terms of number of employees, Wal-Mart holds a huge lead over second-ranked McDonalds (Table 4.10). Five of the top six U.S. corporations that are **worker-dependent** are retailers; Kroger and Albertson's (groceries) are in the leading 15. General Motors and Ford Motors laid off massive numbers of workers in the mid-2000s.

The five fastest growing sectors of the U.S. economy during 2005 were pipelines, Internet services and retailing, securities, petroleum refining, and mining and crude oil refining (Table 4.11). Internet companies showed profits, but not a return to the dot-com bubble of the late 1990s. And of course petroleum-based corporations reflected an extremely strong growth in revenue and profits, following hurricane Katrina and its extended aftermath.

Table 4.10   The Fifteen Largest U.S. Corporations in Employees, 2005

Rank	Corporations	Headquarters	Number of Employees (in thousands)
1	Wal-Mart Stores	Bentonville, AR	1,800
2	McDonalds	Oak Brook, IL	447
3	United Parcel Post	Atlanta, GA	407
4	Sears	Hoffman Est., IL	355
5	Home Depot	Atlanta, GA	345
6	Target	Minneapolis, MN	337
7	Intl. Business Machines	Amock, NY	329
8	General Motors	Detroit, MI	327
9	General Electric	Fairfield, CT	316
10	Citigroup	New York, NY	303
11	Ford Motors	Dearborn, MI	300
12	Kroger	Cincinnati, OH	289
13	Albertson's	Boise, ID	240
14	United Technologies	Hartford, CT	222
15	Verizon Communications	New York, NY	217

Source: Fortune, April, 17, 2006, p. F-31.

Fordism, known as assembly-line mass production, today has largely given way to **flexible production**, whereby computer-assisted manufacturing processes can produce X numbers of product A for a specific customer and Y numbers of product B for another. Whereas setting up a new assembly line in the past was a time-consuming and expensive process, flexible production can result in change with the press of a button. Thus, whereas manufacturers under Fordism simply provided a standardized product for retailers and mass consumers, flexible production *responds* to retailers' demands for a specific product with particular desired characteristics. It is now the retailer—read "Wal-Mart"—that is telling manufacturers what to make, how it should look, how it should be packaged, and what it should cost. That is how Wal-Mart climbed up the U.S. corporate mountain. Wal-Mart, and its cousin Sam's Club, purchase goods in gargantuan quantities at very low unit costs, and pass these low costs on to consumers who can do one-stop shopping in the Super Wal-Mart or high-quantity buying at Sam's warehouse-like stores.

The Wal-Mart Example   Sam Walton was born in Kingfisher, Oklahoma, in 1918. After operating different discount stores that were barely profitable, located in small towns in northwest Arkansas, he opened the first Wal-Mart on July 2, 1962, in the tiny town of Springdale, Arkansas. Sam Walton was now a middle-aged 46-year-old, only a marginally profitable but determined retailer. One observer who was at the Wal-Mart opening made the following observation:

It was the worst retail store I had ever seen. Sam had brought a couple of trucks of watermelons in and stacked them on the sidewalk. He had a donkey ride out in the parking lot. It was 115 degrees, and the watermelons began to pop, and the donkey began to do what donkeys do, and it all mixed together and ran all over the parking lot. And when you went inside the store the mess just continued, having been tracked all over the floor. Sam Walton was a nice fellow, but I wrote him off.

Writing Sam Walton off, however, was a major mistake. In fact, Wal-Mart became so successful

Table 4.11 The Fifteen Fastest Growing U.S. Industrial Sectors in Revenue, 2005

Rank	Industry	Percent Growth in Revenues in 2005
1	Pipelines	46.0
2	Internet Services & Retailing	39.2
3	Securities	37.2
4	Petroleum Refining	35.7
5	Mining, Crude-Oil Refining	34.3
6	Homebuilders	29.4
7	Engineering, Construction	23.2
8	Oil & Gas Equipment, Services	22.0
9	Commercial Banks	20.7
10	Wholesalers: Diversified	19.0
11	Energy	16.8
12	Wholesalers: Health Care	15.0
13	Industrial & Farm Equipment	14.5
14	Hotels, Casinos, Resorts	14.4
15	Network, Communications Equipment	14.0

Source: Fortune, April, 2006, p. F-25.

that in 1985 *Forbes* magazine declared Sam Walton the "richest man in America." Now Sam Walton was 67. When asked why he drove a pickup truck, Sam replied, "What am I supposed to haul my bird dogs around in, a Rolls-Royce?" The richest man in America today is Bill Gates, head of Seattle-based Microsoft, which ranks only 48th among Fortune 500 companies. Microsoft had revenues of a mere $40 billion in 2005, compared to Wal-Mart's $315 billion.

Graves (2006) outlined how Wal-Mart was able to attract Northern capital financing from New York, California, Massachusetts, Illinois, and Pennsylvania, as well as from Germany and France (the global economic core) to "what was once the least developed portion of the American economic periphery" (rural, northwestern Arkansas) (p. 52). In fact, Sam Walton "brought more capital to the South than Coca-Cola and Bank of America combined" (Graves, 2006, p. 52).

Let's recount now how Wal-Mart grew over its 45 years of success. After the initial store opening in 1962, Sam Walton opened 17 more Wal-Marts in the 1960s: 10 in Arkansas, five in Missouri, and two in Oklahoma (Figure 4.10a). These stores were intentionally located in small towns not otherwise served by discount stores and poorly served by retail stores in general. Formerly the residents of these towns had to travel a sometimes considerable distance to a large town or city where they had to make multiple store stops. After a Wal-Mart opened close to them, however, they could do local discount one-stop shopping. While schools of business all across America taught MBA students that retail firms should locate in large cities and metropolitan areas to achieve market access, Sam Walton, who held only a BA degree in business from the University of Missouri (1940), had a different geographic or locational plan: locate in small, underserved and noncompetitive markets.

The Wal-Mart plot and strategy—some call it "**plotegy**"—was to expand its stores slowly, gradually, and primarily in small towns (Figure 4.10b). The geographic pattern of new Wal-Mart store openings was centered around the original Wal-Mart in northwest Arkansas. As late as 1979, Wal-Mart stores were found only in Arkansas, Missouri, Oklahoma, Texas, Mississippi, Louisiana, Tennessee, Iowa, Kentucky, and Alabama. In contrast, during the period 1980–1984 Wal-Mart stores opened as far west as New Mexico, as far north as Iowa and Nebraska, as far east as South Carolina, and as far south as Florida. Still most states were not served (Figure 4.10c).

The spatial spread of Wal-Mart continued rapidly in the late 1980s, with the pattern thickening. During this period, Wal-Mart decided to move into small and large metropolitan areas (Figure 4.10d). The new locational plotegy targeted particular large metropolitan areas, including Dallas-Fort Worth, Houston, Atlanta, St. Louis, Indianapolis, Memphis, as well as metropolitan areas of eastern and western coastal Florida. Despite the new metropolitan plotegy, many new Wal-Marts continued to locate in rural areas in such states as Kansas, Nebraska, Colorado, New

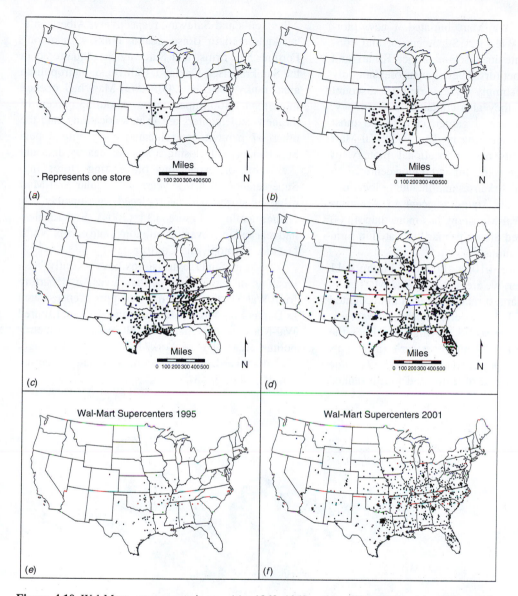

Figure 4.10 Wal-Mart store openings: (a) 1962–1969; (b) 1975–1979; (c) 1980–1984; (d) 1985–1989: (*Source:* Graff and Ashton, 1994). Wal-Mart Supercenters: (e) 1995; (f) 2001. (*Source:* Graff, 2002, 2004).

Mexico, and Arizona. As the result of this expansion, the unbelievable occurred: Wal-Mart, in less than 30 years, surpassed Sears, the grandfather and icon of American retail sales to become the largest retailer in the United States. Meanwhile, Sears restructured and closed many of its retail outlets. Wal-Mart pursued a *stand-alone* store location policy, whereas Sears had located most of its stores in shopping malls.

In the 1990s, Wal-Mart initiated a new plot-egy by opening Wal-Mart Supercenters, and continued to dominate its discount Super Kmart and SuperTarget competitors. These megastores not only offered an astonishingly wide variety of discount merchandise, but they also contained a pharmacy, an automotive center, a garden center, and most notably, a full-service grocery. By 1995, Wal-Mart had reverted to its earlier locational plotegy of opening Supercenters in a limited region centered on its headquarters in Arkansas and including locations primarily in the six states adjacent to Arkansas (Figure 4.10e). Wal-Mart now has more than 4,000 stores in the United States, primarily located in rural and suburban locations.

Compare Figure 4.10f (2001) and Figure 4.11 (2004). Remember, we are watching Wal-Mart grow into the world's largest retailer. Wal-Mart accounted for 20 percent of U.S. groceries sales, is the largest grocery chain in the world, having four times the sales of its nearest competitor, Kroger's (headquartered in Cincinnati, Ohio, and ranked 21st by *Fortune* in 2005) and far ahead of third- and fourth-ranked Albertson's and Safeway, respectively. Albertson's, headquartered in Boise, Idaho, ranks 47th among Fortune 500 firms, and Safeway, headquartered in the San Francisco-Oakland, California, metropolitan area, ranks 50th. By 2005, Wal-Mart had opened more than 1,400 Supercenters. About 33 percent of the new Supercenters are in new locations, and the other 67 percent are relocations (opening a new Supercenter and closing a smaller nearby discount Wal-Mart) or expansions of existing stores into Supercenters. In a few years, all regular Wal-Mart discount stores will be replaced by Supercenters. Glance again at Figure 4.11 (2004). Supercenters had reached into every contiguous state except North Dakota, Vermont, and California.

Wal-Mart Supercenter stores have recently been locating in large metropolitan areas, a departure from Wal-Mart's early small-town preferences, such as Dallas-Fort Worth, Houston, and Atlanta. Limited Wal-Mart presence has been felt in the large metropolitan areas of New York, Los Angeles, Chicago, Philadelphia, Detroit, Boston, and San Francisco (Graff, 2006, p. 58).

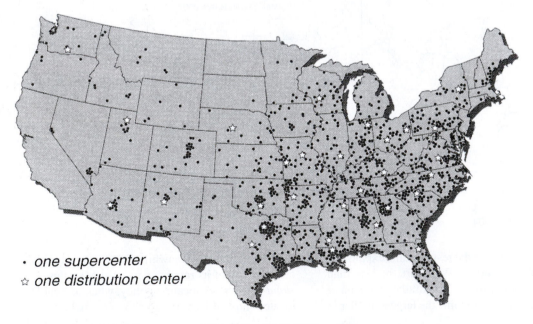

· one supercenter
☆ one distribution center

Figure 4.11 Wal-Mart Supercenters, 2004 (After Graff, 2006, p. 60).

Wal-Mart was criticized early on by many local merchants in the small towns, where the firm initially located, for putting Mom and Pop stores out of business, such as lawn and garden stores, camera and film stores, and even supermarkets. More recently, Wal-Mart has had a hand in forcing Kmart, directly competing with Wal-Mart for the low-price market, into bankruptcy. SuperTarget, on the other hand, largely avoids direct competition with Wal-Mart by offering somewhat more upscale merchandise at a slightly higher price, thus defining a different niche market from Wal-Mart. Nevertheless, Wal-Mart executives correctly argue that they employ many workers (100,000 added between 2003 and 2004) and offer consumers quality products at considerable savings.

Graff (2006, p. 63) succinctly summarized the current state of issues facing Wal-Mart:

> A new array of nonretailing challenges has emerged to confront Wal-Mart. As the largest retailer in the world, Wal-Mart is the subject of much public interest and scrutiny. Its pricing policies, personnel practices, employment compensation, antiunion activities, supplier relations, [and] impacts on communities...have become the subject of much critical public inquiry ... The Wal-Mart corporate executives who have succeeded Sam Walton have lacked the public relations acumen and folksy charisma of the firm's founder. In short, the public has begun to evaluate Wal-Mart Stores Inc. on far more than low prices and huge sales volumes.

From Bentonville to Beijing The People's Republic of China offers Wal-Mart a pivotal opportunity to tap this huge foreign market with its growing middle class, establishing itself as one of the few non-Chinese-owned retail chains in the country. China's retail market has been expanding at a rate of 15 percent per year over the past few years. Wal-Mart is buying Taiwanese-owned Trust-Mark for $1 billion to become China's largest retailer, where it joins Mexico and Canada as those countries' largest retail firms. In contrast, Wal-Mart

has not been successful in certain other countries, departing out of Germany and South Korea, for example (see Barboza and Barbaro, pp. A1 and C9).

Micro-Multinationals

In the last few years, driven by telecommunications, a new form of transnational enterprise has emerged, the **micro-multinationals**. These small-to-tiny firms are global in their organization, using advanced technologies and employing only a handful of employees up to, say, 25, high-paid workers. These are high-tech companies, not firms that normally outsource routine work to overseas electronic sweatshops. Moreover, the company CEO knows the language, culture, and customs of employees in the different world locations. Micro-multinationals today constitute more than 60,000 firms worldwide (Box 4.4).

Sundia is an example of a micro-multinational, a watermelon juice and fruit company headquartered in the CEO's San Francisco home. The firm employs workers across the United States, as well as the Philippines, Great Britain, Singapore, and India. The company is involved in manufacturing and distribution. Growers ship watermelons from Mexico and California to Washington State, where they are processed into concentrate and shipped to bottlers in California. A customer in, say, Philadelphia orders the juice by calling a number in San Francisco. An automatic phone system forwards the call to customer service in the Philippines, whereupon the order is sent to the nearest warehouse—Wisconsin in this example. The warehouse electronically notifies the accounting office in India and ships the product to the consumer. The Indian office sends an invoice to the San Francisco home headquarters, which thereupon bills the customer. In this example, Sundia mixes high-skilled and low-wage workers in a micro-multinational enterprise that is entirely Web-based. Without Sundia's global reach, the company would be forced, it argues, to provide U.S. workers with health insurance, worker's compensation, and perhaps unionization. So this micro-multinational simply moves watermelons around the world (based on Copeland, 2006, pp. 106–114).

BOX 4.4 Technology and Urban Geography

The Gravity Model in Local and Regional and Global Context

The classic **gravity model** has long been a workhorse of urban-economic and transportation geography. It is a model that compares volume of flows or levels of spatial interaction between or among two or more places based on mass (population) and distance between the places (Figure B4.3a). It looks like this:

$$I_{ij} = k \frac{(P_i P_j)}{D_{ij}^b}$$

where I_{ij} is the level of interaction or flow volume between origin i and destination j, b is an empirically determined exponent of distance, k is a constant, P_i is the population size of origin i, and P_j is the population of destination j, and D_{ij} is the distance between i and j.

This form of the gravity model has proven flexible, as other measures of mass than population may be used (such as retail sales or employment totals) just as distance may be calibrated as travel time or dollar cost. Operationally, the gravity model typically takes the following form of the well-known regression equation:

$$\text{Log } I_{ij} = \log k \,(\log P_i \times P_j - D_{ij})$$

where the terms are as before.

The gravity model has proven effective in explaining commuting flows, the journey to shop, social trips, commodity freight exchange, as well as migration patterns. The model thus has widespread

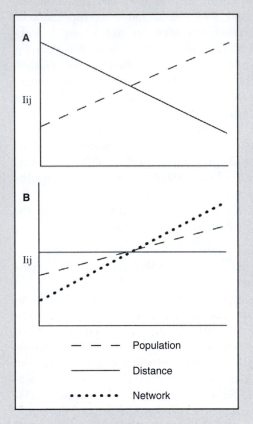

Figure B4.3 (a) Components (population and distance) of the local and regional gravity model. (b) Components (population, distance, and network connectivity) of the national and international telecommunications gravity model.

Wrapping Up

Globalization, as mediated through selected cities, has replaced international relations among countries only since the 1970s. Whereas international trade, for example, refers to commodity movement among countries, globalization refers to the movement of capital, information, goods, and services among huge multinational corporations, largely ignoring the traditional role of national boundaries. Multinational corporations are heavily concentrated in a relatively small number of world cities. The application and is here referenced as the **local and regional gravity model** (Figure B4.3a).

When measuring spatial interaction at the global scale, however, the classic gravity model falls short. A modified or **global gravity model** is called for (Figure B4.3b). Here, in addition to population and distance, a new component must be introduced: **network connectivity**. The degree to which world cities are connected, especially through telecommunications, is a more important factor than population size or distance. As we saw earlier in this chapter, several large cities (Tehran, Dhaka, Khartoum, Baghdad, and Lahore, for example) were referred to as black holes or loose connections (Calcutta, Logos, Karachi). Although their populations are large, they do not function as world cities. Thus, the role of population is greatly weakened.

Likewise, distance plays essentially no role in the spatial interaction of global cities, hence the horizontal line in Figure B4.3b. New York, London, and Tokyo are spaced far apart.

The essential and overarching feature of world cities is their close corporate and capitalist ties. The hallmark of the global gravity model is network connectivity:

$$I_{ij} = \log k \, (\log P_i \times P_j \times \log N_i \times N_j - \log D_{ij}$$

where all terms in the equation are as identified before, except that the N_i and N_j represent the network origin and network destination, respectively.

Derudder, Witlox, and Taylor (2007, p. 84) used airline data to measure the global network effect. Specifically, they utilized enplaned passengers to measure the global connectivity (network connectivity) of U.S. cities (Table B4.3). Although they did not employ the gravity model, their findings showed New York, Los Angeles, Chicago, and San Francisco to be the four U.S. cities with the strongest global airline connections, with New York, London, Los Angeles, and Tokyo as the major world tourist attractions. The business and corporate connections round out the top 20 U.S. cities with global linkages.

Table B4.3 Global Connectivities of U.S. Cities Based on Airline Data

Rank	Cities	Number of Connections (in millions)
1	New York, NY	10.6
2	Los Angeles, CA	8.3
3	Chicago, IL	5.2
4	San Francisco, CA	5.2
5	Atlanta, GA	3.8
6	Miami, FL	3.7
7	Washington, D.C.	3.7
8	Dallas, TX	3.7
9	Boston, MA	3.6
10	Houston, TX	2.9
11	Denver, CO	2.5
12	Seattle, WA	2.4
13	Minneapolis, MN	2.3
14	Detroit, MI	2.2
15	Philadelphia, PA	1.8
16	San Diego, CA	1.7
17	St. Louis, MO	1.6
18	Portland, OR	1.4
19	Kansas City, KS	1.3
20	Cleveland, OH	1.1

Source: Derudder et al., 2007, p. 84.

hierarchy of world cities has shifted over time with the economic growth of East and Southeast Asian cities, European cities, and cities in developing regions of Latin America. U.S. multinational firms dominate the global economy, especially petroleum, and Japanese companies are among the leading automotive corporations. People in developed parts of the world who are less than 30 years old have only experienced living in a global economy, which increasingly reaches to people in developing cities of the world. Only older people have experienced and remember the local, regional, and nation-based world and its sudden transformation by the information age into a multinational-based globalized unit.

READINGS

Barboza, D. and M. Barbaro. 2006. "Wal-Mart Acquiring a Chain in China." *New York Times,* October 17, pp. A1 and C9.

Beaverstock, J. V. and J. Smith. 1996. "Lending Jobs to Global Cities: Skilled International Labour Migrations, Investment Banking and the City of London." *Urban Studies,* Vol. 33, pp. 1377–1394.

Beaverstock, J. V., R. G. Smith, and P. J. Taylor. 2000. "World City Network: A New Metageography?" *Annals of the Association of American Geographers,* Vol. 90, pp. 123–134.

Bergdahl, M. 2006. *The Ten Rules of Sam Walton*. New York: John Wiley & Sons, Inc.

Brunn, S. D., ed. 2006. *Wal-Mart World: The World's Biggest Corporation in the Global Economy*. New York: Routledge.

Copeland, M. V. "The Mighty Micro-Multinational," *Business 2.0,* Vol. 7, pp. 107–114.

Corey, K. E. and M. Wilson. 2006. *Urban and Regional Technological Planning: Planning Practice in the Global Economy*. New York: Routledge.

Derudder, B., F. Witlox, and P. J. Taylor. 2007. "U.S. Cities in the World City Network: Comparing Their Positions Using Global Origins and Destinations of Airline Passengers," *Urban Geography,* Vol. 28, pp. 74–91.

Elliott, James R. 1999. "Putting 'Global Cities' in Their Place: Urban Hierarchy and Low-Income Employment During the Post-War Era," *Urban Geography,* Vol. 20, pp. 95–115.

Friedmann, John. 1986. "The World City Hypothesis," *Development and Change,* Vol. 17, pp. 69–84.

Godfrey, B. J. and Y. Zhou. 1999. "Ranking World Cities: Multinational Corporations and the Global Urban Hierarchy," *Urban Geography,* Vol. 20, pp. 268–281.

Graff, T. O. 2001. "Very Unequal Competition among Chains of Supercenters: Kmart, Target, and Wal-Mart." paper presented in New York, meeting of the Association of American Geographers.

Graff, T. O. 2006. "Unequal Competition among Chains of Supermarkets: Kmart, Target, and Wal-Mart," *The Professional Geographer,* Vol. 58, pp. 54–64.

Graff, T. O. and D. Ashton. 1994. "Spatial Diffusion of Wal-Mart: Contagious and Reverse Hierarchical Elements," *The Professional Geographer,* Vol. 46, pp. 19–29.

Graves, W. 2006. "Discounting Northern Capital: Financing the World's Largest Retailer from the Periphery." In Stanley D. Brunn, editor, *Wal-Mart World: The World's Biggest Corporation in the Global Economy*. New York: Routledge.

Hugill, P. L. 2006. "The Geostrategy of Global Business: Wal-Mart and Its Historical Forbearers." In Stanley D. Brunn, editor, *Wal-Mart World: The World's Biggest Corporation in the Global Economy*. New York: Routledge.

Johnson, J. H. Jr. 2001. "Immigration Reform, Homeland Defense, and Metropolitan Economics in the Post 9-11 Environment," *Urban Geography,* Vol. 23, pp. 201–212.

Mitchelson, R. L. and J. O. Wheeler. 1994. "The Flow of Information in a Global Economy: The Role of the American Urban System," *Annals of the Association of American Geographers,* Vol. 84, pp. 87–107.

Norris, Floyd. 2006. "Accessory for a U.S. Border Fence: A Welcome Mat for Foreign Loans." *New York Times,* November 4, p. B.3.

Sassen, Saskia. 2002. *Global Networks, Linked Cities*. New York: Routledge.

Sassen, Saskia. 2006. *Cities in a World Economy*, 3rd ed. London: Pine Forest Press.

Short, John. 2004. "Black Holes and Loose Connections in a Global Urban Network" *The Professional Geographer,* Vol. 56, pp. 295–302.

Smith, D. A. and M. F. Timberlake. 2001. "World City Networks and Hierarchies, 1977–1997," *American Behavioral Scientist,* Vol. 44, pp. 1656–1678.

Taylor, P. J., D. R. F. Walker, G. Catalano, and M. Haylor. 2001. "Diversity and Power in the World City Network." http://www.lboro.ac.uk/garge/rb/rb56.html.

Walton, Sam. 1992. *Made in America: My Story*. New York: Doubleday.

CHAPTER 5

TELECOMMUNICATIONS AND THE CITY

Our historic time is defined fundamentally by the transformation of our geographic space.

—MANUEL CASTELLS, 2000

The purpose of this chapter is to examine how modern technology is impacting contemporary urban geography. The specific focus is on telecommunications. The chapter begins with a brief history of computing and the Internet. It asks whether telecommunications has led to a dispersal or concentration of economic and social activities. The chapter then discusses the immensely important role of fiber-optic cables at both the national and global scales, offers a comparison between satellite and fiber-optic carriers, and discusses the "digital divide" among different groups of personal computer users. It also shows that telecommunications is of great significance to urban society and to the urban economy. Finally, the chapter concludes by examining the ways in which telecommunications has created a new urban geography that is fractured in certain unexpected ways.

Recall that the automobile fundamentally transformed life starting in the early part of the twentieth century, much as the railroad did the century before. At first the automobile was not very reliable because of frequent engine breakdowns and even more frequent flat tires. In addition, the early road and highway infrastructure was primitive. Gradually, however, automobiles improved in quality, and limited-access multiple-lane interstate highways allowed high volumes of traffic to flow. The automobile caused fundamental mutations in society, culture, and the economy. As a result, people could

travel greater distances and conveniently go from door to door, door to store, and door to work using a single mode of transportation. Remote areas became less isolated, local market monopolies faced nonlocal (now global) competition, and concentrated work places (the central business district) attracted an even greater concentrations of jobs. An entire way of life was metamorphosed.

Today, telecommunications is similarly transforming the economy, society, and culture, not only within metropolitan areas but also nationally and globally. We are still in the early stage of the information age. The **World Wide Web (WWW)**, an interactive medium and a system of documents that can be accessed and viewed from anywhere in the world if one is connected online to the Internet, was developed only in 1993. As of 2006, more than 75 percent of Americans were online at home or at work, and this number was up considerably from three years before. Thus, the Internet has drastically changed how we spend our work time, our money, and our leisure, with many more changes to come. For example, children increasingly have computers in their bedrooms, where they can communicate with their friends and with chatting strangers. Sitting alone, they in effect bring strangers (not all welcome) and friends into their home. They do homework on the computer, and they can examine all manner of mainstream and exotic information on the Web. A recent survey indicated that, as of late 2005, 50 percent of young people ages 13 to 16 have cell phones. If all teens were included, the number would likely be 70 percent. A stroll across most college and university campuses would no doubt indicate an even higher percentage of users.

Cell phones have become as common as watches. Parents may read newspapers on the computer, order all kinds of products via e-commerce, and in some instances even work at home (telecommute to work) (Box 5.1). More than 70 percent of Americans who

BOX 5.1   TELECOMMUTING

Although **telecommuting**, defined as working at home on a computer, has often been hailed by the popular media as a way to transcend "the tyranny of distance" in getting to work, scholarly studies have largely debunked the myth that telecommuting will significantly relieve morning and evening traffic congestion by allowing masses of people to work at home. Technologically deterministic futurists have created three myths:

- The unnecessary workplace;
- The unnecessary city; and
- The unnecessary need to travel.

Gillespie and Richardson (2000, p. 228) argued, on the contrary, that workplaces in cities "are highly functional and efficient forms of human organizations, and as a result are likely to prove considerably persistent more and resilient than the technologically futurists would have us believe."

The two kinds of work that may be most suitable for working at home (telecommuting) are (1) low level repetitive tasks such as data entry or filling out insurance or other types of forms, where the need for face-to-face contact is minimal, and (2) professionals engaging in occasional "quiet time" thinking and creativity. Even so, most workers prefer the social aspects of work and shared workplace experience. In addition, managers have difficulty in monitoring workers in remote locations, although the technology now exists to permit supervisors to "peer" onto telecommuters' home computer screens to see what tasks are being carried out. Empirical studies have shown that only an extremely small percentage of the workforce is involved in telecommuting on a regular basis.

Nonetheless, let us consider an imaginary worker: Mr. Andy Garcia, who lives in Santa Ana, California. His wife, Rita, commutes 26 miles each way daily, bumper to bumper, to downtown Los Angeles on the Santa Ana Freeway (I-5). As the automatic garage door closes and Rita pulls out of the driveway on her way to her job as a loan officer for Bank of America, Andy enters his office-study and boots up his computer. He makes a note that his eight-hour workday is starting at 7:17 a.m. Andy is in his mid-fifties. His coffee is perking on the table behind his computer desk. He will spend the next several hours—with breaks—filling out auto insurance claims that clients have sent him by e-mail and routing these claims to different company headquarters located in Akron, Ohio; Nashville, Tennessee; and Oshkosh, Wisconsin, making sure his work schedule is at least eight hours.

By 5:11 p.m. his workday is done, and he places a casserole in the microwave and turns on the L.A. murder report on the 27-inch television. At this time, Rita is walking through the Bank of America parking deck ready for her 26-mile bumper-to-bumper trip home. Whereas Rita has had her fill of people, phone, and "boss" stimulation at her job, Andy now decides that he needs to visit a neighbor over coffee just to have someone to talk with. After all, he has spoken to no one for several hours, and he is under some vague stress knowing that *his* boss may have tuned on his computer screen off and on all day, checking on his work habits. Will telecommunicating ever become common for most Americans?

use the Internet now consider online technology to be their most important source of information, ranking it higher than all other media, including television and newspapers.

Cyberspace has become cyberculture, cybereconomics, cyberpolitics, and—most of all—cyberhumans. Lévy (2001, p. ix) attributes "the growth of cyberspace [to] an international movement of young people eager to experiment collectively with forms of communication other than those provided by traditional media." Now traditional media—television, music, video, movies, news, advertising, and more—have been amalgamated into cyberspace.

A History of Computing and the Development of the Internet

The **Internet**, a complex network of networks linking tens of millions of computers worldwide, is a recent development, only an eyeblink in the history of *homo sapiens*. Conceived only in 1989 by researchers in Geneva, Switzerland, as a way of accessing documents stored in many different computers, the WWW did not begin until 1993, when it was principally used by a small number of academics. By 1995, more than 20,000 host computers had registered domain names as part of this document exchange system. **Domain names** represent locations on the Web.

In the early years (1960–1970) of computer development, the cost of the machine itself, including the hard drive, monitor, and printer, was relatively high—from 60 to 80 percent of the total operating cost, which also included software and other ancillaries. Over time, the cost of the computer and its auxiliary equipment has been reduced through improved manufacturing technology, while the relative cost of ever-more sophisticated software has risen from approximately 20 percent in 1960 to 40 percent in 1970 to just over 80 percent since 1985. Since 1985 the ratio of hardware-to-software cost has changed little.

The Internet was originally a product of the U.S. military during the Cold War that followed World War II. The Internet "was not originally to be a medium for interpersonal communications; it was intended to allow scientists to overcome the difficulties of running programs on remote computers" (Abbate, 1999, p. 2). The initial attempt to link computers with computers in a network of networks ended up connecting people with people through electronic mail, or e-mail. Originally conceived as a computing system by linking supercomputers together for analysis of massive data sets, the resulting Internet turned out to be a communications system that now connects hundreds of millions of people worldwide. E-mail had many advantages over the telephone and postal mail, as the electrons carrying digital information coded as words (principally in English) moved at the speed of light. E-mail on the Internet drastically changed the way corporations communicated within the firm and with others around the world. Paper memos and lengthy paper reports were no longer placed in workers' mailboxes or sent via the postal mail. Rather, they were sent as e-mails and e-mail attachments, although recipients could choose whether or not to print out the messages and reports on their own printers.

Transformed from a data manipulating, small research network, the Internet became a popular communications medium during the 1990s. This open communications system allowed individuals to expand the network and develop innovative applications, the World Wide Web being the most common example. The Internet originated in the United States, but other countries—Australia, Canada, Germany, Japan, Norway, Sweden, and New Zealand—also developed their internal data networks, which eventually became linked to the Internet (Carpenter et al., 1987). The Internet links with the United States occurred only after the Internet became privatized. The use of English as the "native language" of the Internet has raised some controversy, as in France, for example, with Chinese as the fastest growing language on the Internet.

The extraordinary growth of computer use and the Internet led to dramatic changes in the types of jobs held by U.S. workers. Figure 5.1 traces employment patterns in the United States during the period 1800–2005. Economists traditionally have identified three sectors of the economy: (1) the

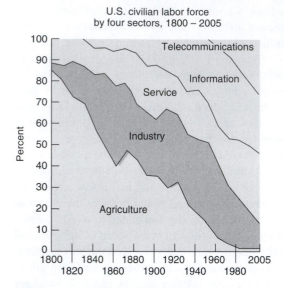

U.S. civilian labor force
by four sectors, 1800 – 2005

Figure 5.1 The U.S. civilian labor force by five sectors, 1800–2005. The telecommunications sector has been the fastest growing sector since 1970. (Updated from Lemon, 1996.)

primary sector, comprising agriculture and mining; (2) the secondary sector, including manufacturing and construction; and (3) the tertiary sector, consisting of retailing and consumer services. As Figure 5.1 illustrates, during the period 1800 to 2005 employment shifted from the primary sector to the secondary and tertiary sectors. Given more recent developments in medicine, law, higher education, and scientific research, a fourth sector has been recognized, termed the quaternary sector, or advanced services. In 1800, 86 percent of the workforce was involved in agricultural activities. Another 12 percent provided consumer services, and a mere 2 percent held what could be classified as industrial or manufacturing jobs. Industrial jobs, however, grew rapidly during the nineteenth century, while service jobs expanded somewhat. Meanwhile, jobs in agriculture declined rapidly. Although some information-based jobs were found in all three basic sectors of the economy, since approximately 1980, employment in the quaternary sector (information-based jobs) has grown most rapidly.

Moreover, beginning very slowly in the 1950s and rapidly accelerating especially after 1985 (when personal computers became more widely available), telecommunications employment in particular has risen most rapidly.

In summary, the original meaning of the word "computer" referred to a *person* whose job it was to solve mathematical equations. Thus, the original electronic digital computer was invented to solve equations much faster and more accurately than a person could. Although computers still perform this task for many scientists, engineers, and accountants, most of us today think of computers as communication devices. After World War II, the term "computers" came to refer to *machines*. In our contemporary **Information Age**, computers "store and retrieve data, manage networks of communications, process text, generate and manipulate images and sounds, fly air and space craft, and so on" (Ceruzzi, 2000, p. 1).

Mainframe Computers

The mainframe computer became standard in the 1960s, and research universities, governments, and other large data-processing institutions vied for ever-larger, faster, and more expensive machines. A mainframe computer was a physically massive, single computer occupying one site and serving many users who would provide hand-carried software and data on punch cards or magnetic tape to those who operated the machines. Competition among universities for bigger and faster mainframe computers—made by IBM or Control Data Corporation—led to "bragging rights," whether or not scientists and other university researchers actually needed or used these mainframes for analyzing large quantities of data. The data and software programs or algorithms were encoded on 90-column cards (3.25 × 7.375 inches), called *punch cards*. Keypunch machines punched rectangular holes in the cards, with each hole representing a number or letter of the alphabet.

Minicomputers to Personal Computers

Scientific research into solid-state physics, electronics, and internal computer instruction operations or codes led to the development of **microcomputers**. At first, the minicomputer was not a competitor to the large mainframes, but it opened new kinds of applications to a growing number of people as a personal interactive computer. The minicomputers evolved into the **personal computer** (PC). During the 1980s, growing numbers of people purchased PCs and PC software for *personal* use. By the mid-1980s, IBM had sold millions of PCs for homes and offices. **Moore's Law** states that chip density doubles every 18 months. In fact, memory chip density has been basically doubling every 18 months since 1970, leading to faster and faster and faster PCs.

TELECOMMUNICATIONS: DISPERSAL OR CONCENTRATION?

A general impression among the lay public, derived from many articles and stories in newspapers and popular magazines, is that the advent of the Internet and access to the World Wide Web has meant the "death of geography." In other words, where one is physically located, whether on Wall Street or in an obscure rural village in Thailand, makes no difference in accessing the Internet. Thus, information-based activities are increasingly being dispersed throughout the globe. Does this "distance doesn't matter" concept hold true? The answer seems to be that it is true for some smaller-scale functions but not for global corporate capitalism. In the following section we will discuss certain activities that have become decentralized as a result of telecommunications. We will then focus on many functions and occupations that have become more concentrated.

Telecommunications and Geographic Dispersal

As previously stated, telecommunications has allowed certain activities to be performed from decentralized locations. For example, a reporter in the field can transmit a story to the editorial office of a newspaper located in a distant city. Another example of dispersal involved **back-office activities**, which are defined as office functions consisting of routine data and paper processing that follow standardized procedures (Figure 5.2). In these typically repetitive, even monotonous, office operations, employees work for low pay in an environment that somewhat resembles a factory assembly line. Back-office functions can be carried out via telecommunications almost regardless of where the office is located. Back offices can be found in small towns and rural areas, on back streets, in small shopping centers, and even on the second floor of some convenience stores. The essential

Figure 5.2 An example of a back-office building is a low-rise suburban location.

Figure 5.3 Wall Street in Athens, Georgia, is a dead-end street, whose cul-de-sac houses the headquarters of Golden Pantry, a regional convenience store. A worker from El Salvador plants pansies.

locational requirement of back offices is low rents or inexpensive land (Figure 5.3). Omaha, Nebraska, because of its location with respect to the Eastern Time Zone and the Pacific Time Zone, is an advantageous location for telemarketing. Places that are too small, however, may not be able to supply an adequate work force for even low-paid workers.

One of the more interesting examples of back-office operations is a major financial service company headquartered in the Midwest. This company moved 85 percent of its telephone customer service calls to Bangalore, India. Thus, today a client calling from St. Louis to ask about a dividend check or a portfolio change will speak to a highly educated woman in Bangalore who has gone to school to learn to speak perfect American-accented English. The client assumes he or she is talking with someone at the financial company's headquarters in Toledo, Ohio. If the specifics of the call are not routine and are too demanding and precise and therefore

beyond the capabilities of the woman in Bangalore, she says, "Just a minute, please," and pushes a button on the phone, and the customer is now speaking with someone in Toledo. The relatively low-paid but highly educated Indian female not only allows the American firm to take advantage of a considerable wage differential but also to alleviate the problem of high turnover rates among U.S. workers, as it is often difficult to get Americans to do such repetitive and relatively boring jobs for low pay, even at U.S. pay scales.

Telecommunications and Geographic Concentration

In contrast to the dispersed activities, many other occupations and functions have become more concentrated as a result of telecommunications. In the following section we discuss geographic concentration in three areas: (1) front-office activities, (2) universities and (3) Web sites.

Front Office Activities Whereas back-office operations are repetitive and low paying, **front-office** occupations are highly skilled and specialized and attract well-educated, highly paid professionals. Examples of front-office occupations are legal and financial services, marketing, sales, advertising, engineering and architectural activities, and management and public relations. Because front-office activities involve face-to-face discussions and high-level decision making, major corporations tend to select grandiose and spacious office buildings that can accommodate large numbers of employees. These front offices often bring together people with specialized and technical knowledge to manage data and information collected from diverse locations that is processed by a team of corporate decision makers. They are concentrated in the largest metropolitan areas atop the urban hierarchy. Within these metropolitan areas they tend to locate in high-rise buildings in downtown locations and in newer suburban business concentrations, sometimes known as edge cities. International air connections are vital to bring together people from many global locations for the face-to-face communications that are a part of high-level decision making within multinational corporations.

In contrast to back-office operations, which locate in low-rent areas, front-office activities seek out conspicuous, prestigious, and prominent locations, and firms occupying these offices are willing to pay high rents or land cost. Thus, a front-office firm might select a Broadway, Fifth Avenue, or Wall Street address in Manhattan, a Peachtree address in Atlanta, a North Michigan Avenue address (and eastward toward Lake Michigan) in Chicago, or a Market Street address in San Francisco. The prestigious location is a part of the cost of advertising (Figure 5.4).

Universities Intellectual talent is greatly sought after among the leading research universities, just as it is in the private sector among major corporations. But like the front-office requirement of knowledge-based firms, intellectual talent relies powerfully on telecommunications. A person can

Figure 5.4 Wall Street in Manhattan, the financial capital of the world.

log onto an e-mail server from anywhere in the world to find a message or to send one. I did not need to be physically in my office this morning to receive the message sent eight hours ago to me by Steven Graham from Newcastle, England, five time zones away. The message was patiently awaiting me as I slept and then had breakfast at the Waffle House. Just as large volumes of electronic data and information require major corporations to make decisions in face-to-face conferences, leading them to concentrate in the largest metropolitan areas, so too do world-class universities seek to bring together on their campuses the most brilliant and productive faculty members.

William Mitchell (2001, p. 145), a professor of Architecture and Planning at MIT, explains:

> My occupation is knowledge work. I create value . . . out of "thin air." I rarely need direct access to raw materials or to production facilities; I mostly require quick and reliable access to knowledge, which increasingly appears as a torrent of Internet-delivered bits. This might suggest that I could locate myself anywhere—perhaps [on a] famous isolated mountaintop. But that

turns out to be far from the case. The density of daily intellectual contacts, the urbanity that derives from a highly educated and culturally sophisticated population, the frequency of useful chance encounters, and the knowledge spillover effects provided by Cambridge, Massachusetts—with its two world-class universities [MIT and Harvard University] and its information and biotech industries—give Cambridge a unique and powerful locational advantage for many knowledge workers . . . Places with stimulating and attractive local communities, good electronic connections, and well-served airports turn out to be locations of choice in the globalized world. These will be the home bases of the knowledge-worker elite and the hubs of the global workflows.

On the "death of distance" debate or the question of whether Internet communications lead to dispersal or concentration of economic activities, Saskia Sassen (2004, p. 196) writes:

> While the new telecommunications technologies do indeed facilitate geographic dispersal of economic activities without losing system integration, they have also had the effect of strengthening the importance of central coordination and control functions for firms and, even, markets. . . . For firms in any sector, operating a widely dispersed network of branches and affiliates and operating in many markets has made central functions far more complicated. . . . Major centers have massive concentrations of state-of-the-art resources that allow them to maximize the benefits of telecommunications and to govern new conditions for operating globally.

Web Sites Another source of evidence relating to the concentration of the Internet is its usage of Web sites. A person new to the World Wide Web may contentedly browse from one hyperlink to another in a kind of leisurely and eclectic fascination. There is so much to see; "a kid in a candy store" mentality prevails. Studies have shown, however, that after a certain period of time the Web surfer tends to focus on a small number of Web sites that are habitually consulted. It is like shopping at a familiar grocery store where you know the location of the items you typically buy. More specifically, a majority of Internet users regularly consult only about a half-dozen sites for such items as news stories, sport scores, weather forecasts, stock listings, travel information, and the like.

NATIONAL AND GLOBAL FIBER-OPTIC NETWORKS

It seems clear, then, that the advancements in telecommunications technology and usage have concentrated knowledge-rich information in relatively few places around the world. Likewise, in the United States it is the largest metropolitan areas—with certain exceptions—that generate and receive the greatest volumes of proprietary, valuable, and technically advanced information. New York, London, and Tokyo, the three leading world cities, are therefore intensely linked in telecommunications by fiber optics and satellites, especially for their financial firms, stock markets, and largest and most spatially complex corporations. "The growth of international investment and trade and the need to finance and service such activities have fed the growth of these functions in major cities" (Sassen, 2006, p. 32). In addition, international loci, such as the United Nations building in New York, is connected with every major city and nation in the world, as well as regional centers (Figure 5.5).

Massive concentrations of giant corporations and their close ties with needed producer services in the largest cities in the world, as well as in North America, are linked by shared fiber-optic networks. Concentrating huge capitalist firms in cities allows them to share costly fiber-optic cables, as well as facilitating face-to-face communications. The extremely expensive infrastructure investments needed to create and maintain a major telecommunications center means that only a limited number of cities in North America or worldwide will be able to fulfill these communications functions. For example, the

Figure 5.5 A view of the United Nations building, the tall shiny structure in the center of the photograph, as seen from the East River in New York City. This building is connected by telecommunications with every major city and country in the world, as well as many regional centers.

centralization of corporations in Manhattan allows them to access precise global information while retaining local ties to ancillary producer service firms.

Fiber-Optic Cables

Facsimile technology, more commonly known as FAX machines, were not widely used until the late 1980s. FedEx began delivery of overnight mail, packages, and boxes in 1974, but it was only in the 1990s that overnight delivery became a standard operating requirement for many companies, institutions, and even the general public. The Internet was conceived only in 1989, although the U.S. Department of Defense developed a progeny of the Internet much earlier during the Cold War to prevent a nuclear bomb from disabling all military computers. The linking of computers allowed for "backup" computers to continue to function and to store and access data. The early Internet operated over copper lines. Starting in 1998, fiber-optic cables began replacing copper telephone lines, thus allowing much more rapid telecommunications and at an amazingly greater volume. Prior to 1992, voice paths across the Atlantic Ocean were dominated by satellites. Whereas the total number of voice paths via satellite has continued to grow, the growth has been slow. Since 1992 Atlantic voice paths have been overwhelmed by the fantastic explosion of fiber-optic cable connections.

Fiber optics entails using glass fiber, as thin as a human hair, to transmit messages. A number of fibers may be packaged within a single cable. Digital laser light pulses (zeros and ones) are pumped through each fiber to constitute a message. The lasers split light into colors, permitting, for example, 2.5 million simultaneous voice messages to be transmitted through a single cable beneath the Atlantic Ocean between North America and Europe. Currently more than 600,000 miles of fiber-optic cable connects some 175 countries. A link with the People's Republic of China handles more than 4 million messages at one time.

Despite the globally interconnected, high-capacity broadband fiber-optic networks, many major metropolitan areas continue to be challenged by the **last mile**. Here is the expensive and messy local-link problem of "threading fiber optics under congested roads and pavements of the urban fabric to the smart buildings, dealer floors, headquarters, media complexes and stock exchanges that are the most lucrative target users" (Graham, 2004, p. 139).

Which world cities are the most connected via Internet backbone capacity? Figure 5.6 displays the ten most connected cities in the world. London ranks number one in total backbone connections followed by Amsterdam. New York and Paris are in a virtual tie for third and fourth rank. Three other West European cities, Frankfurt, Brussels, and Geneva,

The most connected cities

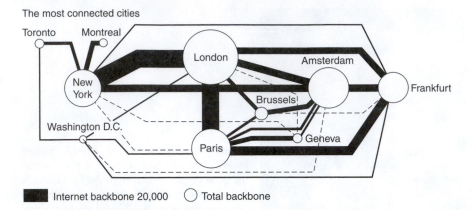

Internet backbone 20,000   ◯ Total backbone

International internet carriers

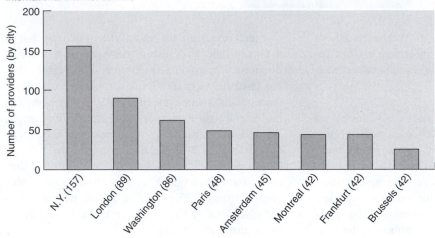

Figure 5.6 The ten most connected cities in the world via the Internet.

are ranked in the top ten. Two Canadian cities, Toronto and Montreal, are also included in the top ten list. Besides New York, the only U.S. city among the top ten is Washington D.C. The largest Internet backbone capacity exists between New York and London and between London and Paris. Of the ten major cities, Washington D.C. has the weakest Internet capacities within the world city system. Another way to measure global Internet dominance is to count the number of international Internet Service Providers (ISPs). Using this measure, we see a different ordering of the top ten world cities (Table 5.1). Here, New York is the dominant world city, followed by London and Washington D.C. Despite the differences in rank between Internet

backbone capacity (Figure 5.6) and the number of Internet carriers by city (Table 5.1), the same ten world cities appear on both lists. Significantly, despite Tokyo's world city status in banking and finance and other global measures, the city does not appear on either list.

U.S. Internet Urban Linkages
Not only are fiber optics preeminent in global communications, but they have also come into ascendancy within the United States in connecting the major metropolitan areas. Figure 5.7 shows the number of direct fiber-optic links between Atlanta and other major U.S. metropolitan areas. Washington D.C. has the greatest number of connections

Table 5.1   International Internet Carriers by Top Ten Cities

City	The Number of International Internet Service Providers
New York	157
London	89
Washington, D.C.	66
Paris	48
Amsterdam	45
Montreal	42
Frankfurt	42
Brussels	22
Toronto	16
Geneva	15

Source: 2001 TeleGeography, Inc.

with Atlanta. Almost all of the other direct fiber-connections are with metropolitan areas in the South, including Dallas-Fort Worth and Miami. Other major centers linked with Atlanta via fiber optics include Charlotte, Orlando, Houston, Nashville, Tampa, Richmond, Birmingham, and Jacksonville. Atlanta also has direct fiber-optic ties with the national centers of New York, Chicago, San Francisco, as well as many more indirect fiber connections. Once again we see that it is the largest metropolitan areas that dominate the Internet via intermetropolitan links. Thus, we are again reminded that the Internet has brought about a concentration of telecommunications, not a universal dispersal of activities.

Table 5.2 provides a different perspective regarding the metropolitan dominance of fiber-optic telecommunications by comparing Internet accessibility

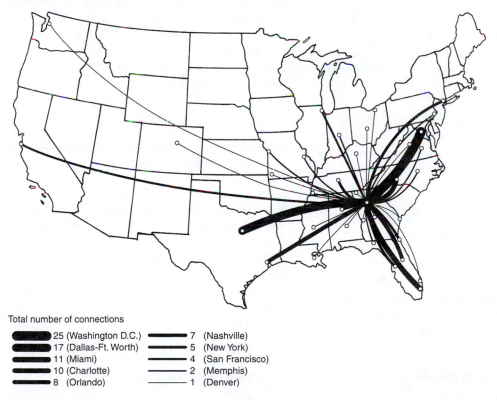

Total number of connections

- ▬▬ 25 (Washington D.C.)
- ▬▬ 17 (Dallas-Ft. Worth)
- ▬▬ 11 (Miami)
- ▬▬ 10 (Charlotte)
- ▬▬ 8 (Orlando)
- ▬▬ 7 (Nashville)
- ▬▬ 5 (New York)
- ▬▬ 4 (San Francisco)
- ▬▬ 2 (Memphis)
- ▬▬ 1 (Denver)

Figure 5.7 The number of direct fiber-optic links between Atlanta and other major metropolitan areas in the United States. (*Source*: Walcott and Wheeler, 2001.)

Table 5.2   Comparison of Internet Accessibility Among U.S. Metropolitan Areas

Rank	Metropolitan Area	Number of Hubs
1	Chicago	38
2	Washington, D.C.	36
3/4	Dallas	35
3/4	New York	35
5	Los Angeles	34
6	Atlanta	32
7	San Francisco	29
8	Seattle	28
9/10	Denver	24
9/10	Houston	24
11	San Jose	22
12/13	Boston	20
12/13	Miami	20
14	Philadelphia	19
15	Kansas City	17
16/17	Cleveland	16
16/17	Phoenix	16
18/19	Detroit	15
18/19	Orlando	15
20	San Diego	14

Source: Walcott and Wheeler, 2001.

among U.S. metropolitan areas. In 2002, the 41 major Internet Service Providers (ISPs) made available networks extending from major **backbone**, or extremely high-capacity service-hub centers. Of these 41 ISPs, 38 have hubs in Chicago, 36 have hubs in Washington D.C., whereas only 14 have hubs in San Diego. Thus, the ISPs constitute an urban hierarchy—although one that does not exactly correspond with the population hierarchy. For example, Atlanta ranks sixth in terms of hub dominance although it ranks only 11th in population. Conversely, the nation's fourth largest city, Philadelphia, ranks 14th in Internet hub activities. What other discrepancies can you find between population totals and numbers of ISPs?

Competition Between Fiber-Optics and Satellites

As Warf (2006, p. 1) pointed out, "International telecommunications traffic relies entirely on two modes of transmission, satellites and fiber optics" to link the transatlantic and transpacific economies. Global corporations, with their diverse, complex, and specialized activities, are crucially reliant upon sophisticated communications systems. The couple of dozen satellite companies overwhelmingly dominate mass media communications. Television has traditionally used satellite services, but has also begun to rely on fiber optics with cable television. Major companies, especially financial institutions, prefer to use the 1,000 or so fiber-optic firms because of their greater security and capacity to transmit large volumes of data quickly. Many enterprises and institutions use both satellites and fiber optics.

Geographically, satellites are better suited to serve remote and rural areas, as satellite transmission costs are unrelated to distance, whereas fiber-optic costs depend on the length of the fiber. Fiber-optic firms, in contrast, are well suited to large metropolitan areas where multiple clients are concentrated to realize scale economies or savings. New York and London, with their clustering of large corporations, including financial institutions, constitute the densest set of fiber-optic links in the world.

Fiber-optic carriers have significantly increased at the expense of satellite transmissions over the past several years, both for the transatlantic and transpacific markets. Over 96 percent of all voice paths, for example, across the Atlantic and Pacific oceans are now by fiber optics, compared to only 16 percent in 1988. Overall, 94 percent of international communications goes via cable. The concentration of high-volume users in the largest world cities has fundamentally shifted the balance of competition to fiber optics. The growth in the global fiber-optic network across the Atlantic and Pacific Oceans in recent years has been to serve giant world city clients (Warf, 2006).

OVERNIGHT INFORMATION FLOWS

Long before the Internet and its electron speed-of-light communications around the globe, there was overnight package and letter delivery. Whereas it remains difficult to map the ebb and flows of Internet messages from place to place, great insight into Internet flows may be achieved indirectly through the study and analysis of overnight package and letter flows. Although it is true that overnight packages and boxes may contain computer or automobile parts, for example, the overwhelming number of overnight movements are documents and letters that follow the same general pattern of flows as do Internet messages. In both Internet and overnight delivery, speed of communication is paramount and vital.

Just as an Internet electronic communication may be sent anywhere in the United States or the world without concern for the distance between the origin and destination of the message, overnight package and letter communications are also largely independent of the distance between where the overnight message originates and where it is delivered. Distance does not really matter—it is the necessity or convenience of speed that is essential. The information content may be said to be **perishable**.

If distance is not an especially important factor in Internet and overnight information flows, then what determines the locations from which the information is sent and where it is received? Studies of FedEx information flows among major metropolitan areas in the United States show that the population size of the urban area is the best indicator of the pattern of overnight information flows, and hence by extension to Internet e-mail communications. Information flows in general follow the metropolitan hierarchy.

Figure 5.8 shows FedEx overnight letters, packages, and boxes shipped from 48 major U.S. metropolitan areas. Because these shipments are generally related to the metropolitan hierarchy, we are not surprised to find that New York is the largest source of overnight information, followed by Los Angeles, and Chicago, the second- and third-ranked urban areas in population size.

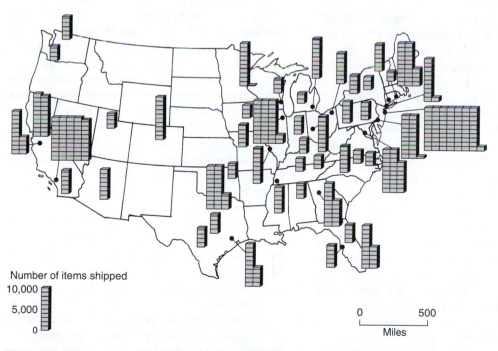

Number of items shipped

10,000

5,000

0

0   500

Miles

Figure 5.8 The number of FedEx overnight letters, packages, and boxes shipped by major metropolitan areas in the United States. (*Source*: Wheeler and Mitchelson, 1989.)

Table 5.3   The Top 15 U.S. Metropolitan Areas in Generating Overnight Information Via FedEx

Rank	Metropolitan Area
1	New York
2	Los Angeles
3	Chicago
4	Washington, D.C.
5	Boston
6	Dallas-Fort Worth
7	Philadelphia
8	San Francisco
9	Atlanta
10	Miami
11	Houston
12	San Jose
13	Denver
14	Minneapolis
15	Detroit

Source: Mitchelson and Wheeler, 1994.

A closer examination of Figure 5.8 and a look at Table 5.3 show that there are several exceptions to the rule that the largest metropolitan areas generate the most information. For example, the fourth- and fifth-ranked metropolitan areas are not Philadelphia and Detroit, as we might conclude based on population size, but rather Washington D.C. and Boston. Philadelphia actually ranked seventh and Detroit 15th in information origins. In fact, the old industrial cities ("Rust Belt" cities of the 1980s) of the Midwest and Northeast do not dominate the centers of information generation. Rather, it is the service-based metropolitan economies of the U.S. West and South that stand out. Of the leading 15 senders of overnight information via FedEx, nine (including Washington D.C.) are located in the West and South. San Jose, a modest-sized urban area compared with the other metropolitan areas in Table 5.3, ranks 12th nationally, ahead of larger centers such as San Diego, Pittsburgh, Phoenix, and St. Louis. Not coincidentally, San Jose is the major city and heartbeat of the Silicon Valley.

Because FedEx flies its letters, packages, and boxes from city to city, sorting them in its main facility in Memphis as well as in Newark, Indianapolis, and San Jose, the company relies on airports to collect the packages at day's end. FedEx likewise relies on airports to deliver the packages the next morning, after which they are delivered door to door by truck. Where are the most-frequently used airports for FedEx pick up and delivery located? The answer is in five major metropolitan areas: New York (LaGuardia, JFK, and Newark), Los Angeles (LAX), Chicago (O'Hare), Atlanta (Hartsfield-Jackson International Airport) and Dallas-Fort Worth. Each of these airports serves a number of smaller subregional urban centers. Atlanta serves and dominates many urban centers in the Southeast, that is, Atlanta sends many more FedEx messages to these centers than these centers send to Atlanta. For example, Atlanta dominates Tampa and Orlando in Florida; Charlotte, Greenboro, and Raleigh-Durham in North Carolina; Memphis, Nashville, and Knoxville in Tennessee; Louisville, Kentucky; and Birmingham, Alabama, as well as numerous smaller centers in the Southeast.

Despite the exploding growth of electronic mail, the rapidly expanding use of fax, the decreasing and low cost of long-distance telephone calls, the utilization of overnight delivery by FedEx and other overnight carriers continues to increase. It is not really true that the world is becoming smaller, as is often said or written. Rather, we can simply reach greater and greater distances on the globe ever more cheaply from a single place, whether it be a giant world city such as New York, London, or Tokyo or a small metropolitan centers such as Macon or Rome, both located in Georgia.

Table 5.4 shows the cumulative FedEx information flows from both Macon or Rome to the ten leading U.S. metropolitan destinations. Macon is located in the center of the state, and Rome northwest of Atlanta. In both instances the nearby center of Atlanta is by far the major destination for overnight flows. It might surprise you to find that New York is ranked second. As we continue down the list, we see that Macon and Rome are linked principally with the large U.S. metropolitan areas including Los Angeles, Chicago, and Dallas-Fort Worth. Based on Table 5.4, we can generalize that small metropolitan

Table 5.4 Leading Cumulative Overnight Flows to Major U.S. Metropolitan Areas Via FedEx From Macon and Rome, Georgia

Rank	From Macon	Cumulative Percentage	Rank	From Rome	Cumulative Percentage
1	Atlanta	24.5	1	Atlanta	23.0
2	New York	34.1	2	New York	31.3
3	Dallas-Fort Worth	38.3	3	Chicago	36.3
4	Los Angeles	41.9	4	Dallas-Fort Worth	40.3
5	Philadelphia	45.6	5	Los Angeles	43.9
6	Boston	48.9	6	Miami	47.5
7	Chicago	52.1	7	Boston	50.4
8	Washington D.C.	55.0	8	Orlando	53.1
9	Jacksonville	57.9	9	Houston	55.6
10	Sacramento	60.7	10	Washington D.C.	58.1

Source: Wheeler, 1999.

areas and even nonmetropolitan areas are strongly tied to the upper end of the metropolitan hierarchy, as well as to nearby regional centers. The information flows with Atlanta represent the city as both a national and regional center. The data in Table 5.4 show that the U.S. metropolitan system is very strongly interlinked, even with small centers. We conclude that the U.S. metropolitan as well as the nonmetropolitan economy has achieved a high level of maturity, or integration initially assisted by the telephone, later by overnight information flows, and now by electronic mail, fax, and cheap long-distance telephone usage. In recent years, of course, the Internet has led the way (Box 5.2).

TELECOMMUNICATIONS AND URBAN SOCIETY

The largest urban areas in the United States and around the world, far from creating an equitable, democratic, and open society, have increasingly utilized modern infrastructure technologies to separate the wealthy and powerful elite from the marginalized and poor people. *Forbes* magazine reports that the world's 450 wealthiest billionaires (mainly Americans) possess a wealth that is greater than the yearly income of the world's poorest 3 billion people, who constitute nearly one-half of the over

6.6 billion people on the earth. It is estimated that 1.3 billion people—or 20 percent of the world's population—live on less than one American dollar per day. Although these massive discrepancies in wealth have long existed, there is growing evidence that they are being enlarged by the rise of new electronic technologies. Telecommunications networks have advanced the power of the small privileged class at the same time that they have reduced the power of the poor and politically weak members of society.

Even when the rich and poor coexist in the same areas within the metropolis, their social and economic networks are almost totally separated. The gap in the use of the Internet between the rich and the poor has been termed the **digital divide** (Box 5.3). Electronic technology encourages the rich to live and interact with other rich people, and the poor to live with and interact with other poor people. The rich may gentrify previously poor neighborhoods, "islands of affluence within a sea of poverty," as Brian Berry phrased it. The rich may also live in high-rise condominiums, sometimes literally in the clouds above the street people, forcing them to call the lobby to find out if it is raining down there.

The well-to-do work in segregated places, office buildings in the downtown or in suburban office parks known as edge cities. They shop in upscale

BOX 5.2   TECHNOLOGY AND URBAN GEOGRAPHY

INTERNATIONAL INTERNET CAPACITY AND VOLUME OF INTERNATIONAL TELEPHONE CALLS

The most fundamental understanding of the geographic functioning of the global economy may be achieved by viewing world Internet capacity (Figure B5.1). These links among the world's leading countries and cities clearly show the much greater power of the transatlantic ties than the transpacific links. The United States has its strongest Internet links with the most developed European countries (United Kingdom, France, Germany, and Italy) and their principal cities. Canada, despite its relatively small population size, is the single leading North American country in Internet links with the United States (compare with Mexico). The transpacific ties are primarily with Japan, but also with Korea, China, and Taiwan. The developing economies of Latin America have only weak links with the United States, principally Brazil, and those links with Africa are so few that they are not included on Figure B5.1.

Interestingly, international telephone calls reveal similar patterns to those of Internet transmissions capacity (Figure B5.2). Again, the volume of telephone calls is greatest with the major urban centers in the most economically developed countries of Europe and Canada. The width of the telephone flow lines is proportional to the volume of calls in annual millions of minutes for 2003. The telephone linkages between the United States and India are stronger than they are with China because

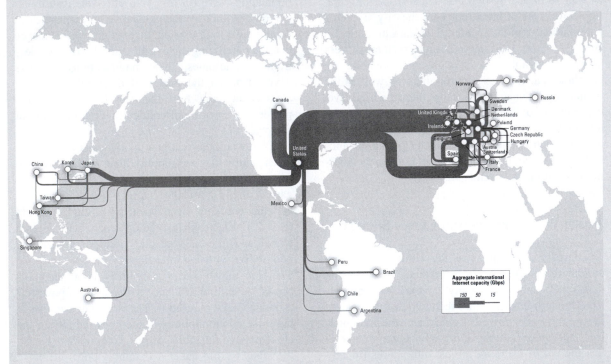

Figure B5.1 Global Internet map, showing Internet capacity (Gbps) among major cities and countries. Reproduced with permission of TeleGeography, Inc., 2003.

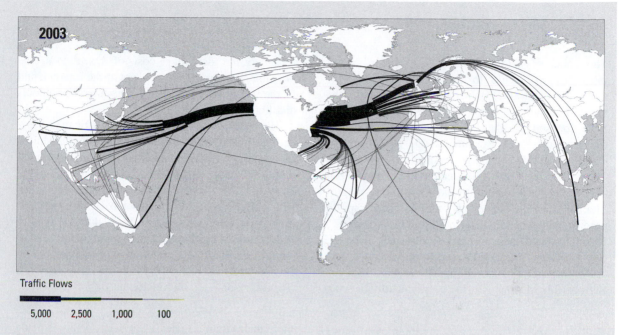

Traffic Flows

5,000   2,500   1,000   100

Figure B5.2 Global communications cable map, showing international outbound telephone calls. Reproduced with permission of TeleGeography, Inc., 2003.

of corporate telephone services provided primarily by English-trained, young females. The Indian ties are even slightly greater than those of Japan. Singapore stands out in the number of telephone ties with the United States, as does the United Kingdom, Germany, France, and Italy. In Australasia, strong links exist between China and Hong Kong (now a part of China), Australia and New Zealand (not shown on Figure B5.1). Japan's telephone ties are greatest with China, the Philippines, and Korea—in that order.

The European Internet backbone capacity among major urban centers clearly demonstrates the role of London as a world city, as well as that of Paris and Frankfurt (Table B5.1). The rank order of European cities in total Internet capacity connected to other cities is (1) London, (2) Paris, (3) Frankfurt, and (4) Amsterdam. Hamburg, Stockholm, and Copenhagen are in a virtual tie for fifth,

Table B5.1   The European Urban Internet Backbone Capacity, 2006

Rank of Route Capacity	Linked Cities
1	New York and London
2	London and Amsterdam
3	London and Paris
4	Paris and Frankfurt
5	London and Frankfurt
6	Washington D.C. and London
7	Paris and Madrid
8	London and Washington D.C.
9	Frankfurt and Amsterdam
10	New York and Paris

Source: TeleGeography, 2006.

sixth, and seventh rank. Madrid (ninth) and Brussels (tenth) round out the 10 leading centers in Internet capacity.

BOX 5.3   THE DIGITAL DIVIDE

The concept of the digital divide relates to the inequality in access to the Internet or to personal computer (PC) ownership among racial, ethnic, class, and income groups. Most such studies have focused on the United States. Recent data (Charkraborty and Bosman, 2005, p. 395) have shown that "while income inequalities among PC owners (households) have decreased between 1994 and 2001 in all regions and states, the magnitude of this inequality has declined more rapidly among whites compared to African Americans." Income-related inequalities are greatest in the U.S. South (having a higher percentage of African Americans) and smallest in the Pacific mountain regions. Part of this closing gap in the digital divide may

relate to the declining cost of home PCs, the growing numbers of young users of the Internet, and to the greater availability of computers in schools and libraries.

Hispanics now have exceeded African Americans as the largest minority population in the United States, bringing a new perspective on the digital divide. In 1998, among people over age 18 in the United States, 42 percent of whites used the Internet, whereas only 23 percent of African Americans did. Forty percent of English-speaking Hispanics had access to the Internet. By 2006, 75 percent of white adults used the Internet, and 80 percent of English-speaking Hispanics did so, compared with 54 percent of African Americans.

malls and use highways and automobiles to move about the metropolis to their favored places. They may live in gated or "fortressed" communities with entrance guards. They disproportionately utilize air transport and have customized security devices in their homes and offices. They disproportionately use the urban intrastructure of energy, sewers, water, and even downtown skywalks to navigate among buildings in too-cold or too-hot weather, eschewing the common and perhaps dangerously perceived streets below. However, nowhere is the disparity between the affluent and the less well off greater than in the realm of electronic communications. The social and economic landscape of the city has been increasingly transformed by the presence of sophisticated telecommunications technologies amid communities lacking telephones, automobiles, and most notably online computer connections.

The different geographic patterns of residential location of urban affluent and poor means that Internet users and nonusers are found in different parts of U.S. metropolitan areas. Prominent Internet users include those of higher socioeconomic status, more whites than minorities, more young than elderly, and

more males than females. American society is made up of computer haves and have-nots. Inner-city African Americans and Hispanics have notably less computer access than young, white, and suburban Americans. These differences are, however, converging, although slowly.

Telecommunications and the Transformation of Urban Space

Not only is telecommunications influencing where people live, work, socialize and shop, but it is also altering the kinds of activities that take place within the family home, the office and other workplaces, the classroom, financial institutions, and even within the automobile. The Internet is a hub for social relationships, contacts between grandparents and grandchildren, leisure-time activities, news reporting, shopping, dating services, and even organized crime to list a few.

Manuel Castells (2004, p. 83), a leading theorist on the Informational City, views the

> process of urbanization [as] concentrated disproportionally in metropolitan areas of a new kind: urban constellations scattered throughout huge territorial expanses, functionally integrated

and socially differentiated around a multicentered structure. I call these new spatial forms metropolitan regions.... Advanced telecommunications, Internet, and fast, computerized transportation systems allow for simultaneous spatial concentration and decentralization, ushering in a new geography of networks and urban modes throughout the world, throughout countries, between and within metropolitan areas.

Greater efficiency and increased productivity are achieved in the workplace, as e-mail often makes more inconvenient telephone conversation unnecessary. The e-mail message will be patiently awaiting the receiver's e-mail check in. Fewer U.S. mail ("snail-mail") letters need be sent. Activities that are highly time-dependent can proceed rapidly. An editor checking with an author on missing page numbers in a bibliographic citation, for example, can clear up such issues in a hurry. Reports and manuscripts can be quickly forwarded as e-mail attachments. Information on reprogramming a manufacturing machine to produce an additional 500,000 blue widgets instead of white ones can be instantly communicated to the appropriate engineer from a headquarters anywhere in the world. And so on and on.

Although some scholars have predicted the "death of cities" as a result of information being equally abundant everywhere in the country or world, as we have seen telecommunications can both centralize and decentralize urban activities. Past urban planning and policy approaches saw the city as made up of distinct and discrete zones of residential, commercial, and industrial land use maintained by zoning ordinances. This industrial-era perspective has become obsolete in the telecommunications age. The contemporary large city, far from being bypassed by spaceless communications and the death of distance, has become a concentrated constellation of computers principally linked with other major cities, themselves the control points of national and global economics and the ensuing social and cultural consequences. As Michael Batty (1997) aptly expressed it:

Computers which were once thought of as solely being instruments for a better understanding for science are rapidly becoming part of the infrastructure [along with highways, airports, shopping malls, theme parks, and energy and water services], and thus affecting space and location. In one view, the line between computers being used to aid our understanding of cities and their being used to operate and control cities has not only become blurred but has virtually dissolved. In another sense, computers are becoming increasingly important elsewhere and the asymmetry posed by their exclusive use for analysis and design in the past and their all-pervasive influence in the city is now dispersing. In both cases, the implication is that computers will have to be used to understand cities, which are built of computers.

Telecommunications has allowed physical distance to be relatively meaningless—"the death of distance"—but not the death of cities. Rather, telecommunications has resulted in the "dominance of cities," especially the largest ones.

As a result of the Internet, individuals who share particular hobbies, beliefs, and experiences can establish social communication networks. These individuals may be located in many different cities and locations. At the same time local communities can share neighborhood information, to oppose the development of a halfway house in the community, or to lobby for road repair or the addition of speed bumps. The Internet, then, can bring local communities closer together and can create strong links among individuals who live far apart.

The Internet accommodates the global flows of information, people, money, commodities, entertainment, and cultural symbols. This near-instantaneous telecommunications has overpowered many times over the historic and geographic spread of the telegraph, telephone, radio, newspaper, and even television (although it is also a part of telecommunications). Telecommunications has clearly enhanced the cultural and symbolic content and images of cities around the world and it has advanced the tourist industries. These sectors of the economy are almost exclusively located in large cities, for example New York, Los Angeles, Chicago, Boston, and Atlanta, in the United States. Image-producing industries, such as television news centers (Atlanta, New York, and Washington D.C.), film production and music recording (Los Angeles), and women's fashion clothing (New York, Paris, and Los Angeles) have found satellite and fiber-optic telecommunications increasingly essential to maintaining a creative global cultural economy.

TELECOMMUNICATIONS AND FINANCIAL MARKETS

At the core of modern capitalism is the need to overcome space and time. In the past the transcending of space and time was achieved by use of better transport technology, that is, faster and larger jet airplanes, improved automobile performance, larger trucks, and wider and upgraded interstates and other highways. Today telecommunications is essential for the geographical and economic functioning of contemporary global capitalism. Mobility and near-instantaneous telecommunications form the basis of corporate power and control, scientific and engineering discourse, and governmental legitimation of the capitalist economy. The ideal of global capitalism is to create a "spaceless world," to bring all cities functionally into one location. To put it another way, national and global transurban relations have surpassed the local, city-hinterland relations for the world's giant megacities. These dominant intercity linkages are perhaps best expressed through the flow of capital among financial markets.

The three world cities of New York, London, and Tokyo dominate the global financial markets. New York is the primary recipient of capital, London is the leading processor of international capital, and Tokyo is the main exporter of capital. These three cities form the core of the 24-hour global financial marketplaces. These financial transactions among these centers as well as among stock markets in many other cities

around the world—from Chicago, Hong Kong, and Singapore to Bangkok, Manila, and Istanbul—are carried out by advanced systems of telecommunications. These network links depend upon satellites and increasingly upon fiber-optic cables.

Telecommunications networks allow worldwide financial investors to take advantage of minor but significant fluctuations in stock values and exchange rates. Digital trading systems allow nearly instant communications with clients. Investors of funds search the globe for the highest rates of return and suffer no delays in financial trading. In financial transactions, widely separated cities maintain closer ties with one another than they do with their local and regional hinterland economies.

Most financial institutions and other data-intensive corporations, governments, and institutions maintain backup systems in several locations across the United States in the event of a natural disaster or a human terrorist attack, as occurred on September 11, 2001, with the destruction of the twin towers World Trade Center and damage at the Pentagon. For example, the Teachers Insurance and Annuity Association–College Retirement Equities Fund (TIAA-CREF), headquartered at 730 Third Avenue in New York, and not physically harmed by the horrifying tragedy of 9/11, has backup service and data centers in Denver and Charlotte. Social Security and military data are likewise protected by multiple backup locations. Interestingly, the Internet was little affected by the 9/11 attacks because of its inherent multiple access from computers around the world.

TELECOMMUNICATIONS AND OFFICE ECONOMIES

As noted earlier in this chapter, service activities may be classified into front-office and back-office functions. The former activities are associated with advanced services or producer services, such as engineering and architectural services and legal and financial services. These high-order services typically require face-to-face communications as well as advanced telecommunications and therefore tend to concentrate in the largest metropolitan areas. In contrast, back-office functions involve routine activities that pay relatively low wages and are performed at low-cost locations.

Intrametropolitan Locations of Professional and Business Services

Office locations for producer services in metropolitan areas are typically concentrated in the traditional CBD or in edge cities found at major interstate highway exchanges. The decentralization of certain producer services (back office) began in the 1970s and accelerated in the 1980s. At the same time, the CBD in most U.S. urban areas has experienced a renewal in producer services. Whether in the CBD or suburban edge cities, producer services have tended to **agglomerate**, that is, they characteristically locate near one another.

Table 5.5 shows the location of selected office activities in the Atlanta metropolitan area. It provides two examples of front-office activities, and two instances of back-office functions. Note that the front-office activities, as one would expect, are more centrally located than the back-office functions. The most centrally located of these front-office activities are accounting, auditing, and bookkeeping. Twenty-four percent of these firms are located in the CBD and another 48 percent are located within five miles of the CBD. This is a prime example of a concentrated front-office activity. At first glance, the second front-office activity, advertising firms, would seem to be less concentrated, as fewer than 2 percent are located within the CBD. However, a closer

look reveals that 75 percent are found within five miles of the CBD, and only 10 percent are located beyond ten miles of the Atlanta CBD.

In contrast, back-office firms, represented in Table 5.5 by credit reporting and collection agencies and by research and testing facilities, are more widely dispersed. Neither type of operation has a notable presence in the CBD. Moreover, nearly 25 percent of credit reporting and collection firms and almost 30 percent of research and testing facilities are found beyond ten miles from the CBD. Both types of firms seek out low-cost locations, may rely on a female labor force, and pay relatively low wages. Some research and testing firms, in contrast, may employ PhDs and scientists at high pay, and the more suburban orientation of these firms may reflect the preference of these professional workers to live in suburban locations and close to their place of work.

Ó hUallacháin and Leslie (2007) examined the spatial distribution of producer services in Phoenix, Arizona, a fast-growth metropolitan area. Densities of establishments and employment of these producer services showed an overall concentration of activities in the city core as a result of accessibility and productivity advantages (Table 5.6). Density is calculated simply as

$$D = \frac{N}{A}$$

Where D is density, N is the number of establishments or employees, and A is the study area. Legal establishments were especially clustered in

Table 5.5 The Percentage of Intrametropolitan Locations of Selected Business Services in the Atlanta Metroplitan Area, 1997

Economic Sectors	CBD	0–5 miles	6–10 miles	11–20 miles	Rest of MSA	Total[a]
Front-Office Activities						
Accounting, Auditing, Bookkeeping	24.3	48.1	13.3	11.2	2.8	100.0
Advertising	1.3	74.7	14.0	8.7	1.3	100.0
Back-Office Activities						
Credit Reporting and Collection	1.8	56.2	8.2	19.8	4.0	100.0
Research and Testing	0.9	32.2	37.1	26.9	2.9	100.0

Source: Gong and Wheeler, 2002.
[a]Does not always equal 100% because of rounding errors.

Table 5.6   Establishment and Employment
Density of Producer Service Firms
in Phoenix, Arizona

Geographic Sectors	Establishment Density	Employment Density
0–3 Mile Ring	18.1	487.6
3–6 Mile Ring	8.1	180.5
6–15 Mile Ring	2.6	46.2

Source: Ó hUalracháin and Leslie, 2007, p. 1594.

the CBD, as well as accounting and computer services. Based on the three concentric zones identified in Table 5.6, it is evident that producer services in Phoenix are highly concentrated in the inner zone (0–3 miles from the CBD) and decline notably with distance to the suburban periphery.

Intrametropolitan Fiber-Optic Loops

As we discussed earlier, during the past few years Internet Service Providers (ISP) have been busily laying fiber-optic cable within major metropolitan areas. The cheapest way to route fiber cables is to string them along existing electric power lines. Such cables are easily subject to interruption when, for example, vehicles strike the electric poles or ice storms and snow may pull lines down. The cost of burying an underground cable varies from more than $100,000 per mile in a congested downtown location to $25,000 per mile in a suburban area. Underground cables are of course much less vulnerable to natural or human-created disruption and therefore more secure.

Fiber-optic cables are typically built in loops in and around metropolitan downtown and in suburban locations. To save costs, fiber-optic lines are often laid out along existing rail, electric and natural gas rights of way. Fiber-optic loops are built for two basic reasons. One is to extend Internet service to large, established corporations and institutions, usually located in downtown areas (Coca-Cola in Atlanta, Wachovia Bank in Charlotte, or Citibank in New York). Here the Internet comes to them.

The second reason for building fiber optics in metropolitan areas—and this construction is usually found in suburban areas—is to provide fiber-optic service to attract new or relocating firms to these suburban sites. In these cases information-hungry firms are being lured to locations where fiber-optic services are available. Despite the high cost of making fiber optics available, knowledge-based companies and institutions find these services essential to their business operations.

A telecommunications advantage for many downtown locations is the ample supply of aging buildings that are increasingly unsuitable for their original purpose but are uniquely suited for Internet rewiring due to their spaciousness, proximity to rail lines for fiber-optic rights-of-way, and high-floor-load carrying capacity. These buildings are located near the downtown fiber-optic loops; they can thus provide corporations and institutions with a broadband **superhighway** ("fat pipe" in business jargon) that can handle multiples messages simultaneously, ensuring thereby speedy, high-volume data transmissions. Some experts have likened the Internet to a hierarchy of roads, with the superhighway able to move many vehicles (messages) rapidly side by side. In contrast, copper telephone lines on backroads may become congested even with limited traffic volume. Downtowns thus serve as a prime location for large telecommunications-intensive corporations because of building infrastructure, nearness to the downtown fiber-optic loops, and the availability of railroad, electric, telephone, and natural gas rights-of-way in which fiber-optic cable can be buried. The Atlanta metropolitan area, with its 28 counties as of the 2000 U.S. Census, has more than 400,000 miles of fiber-optic cable, a huge asset in attracting business and jobs within the region (Walcott and Wheeler, 2001).

Figure 5.9 illustrates this locational pattern by showing the concentrations of five important Internet clusters within the Atlanta metropolitan area. All of these clusters except for the CBD-Midtown cluster (southeast Cobb at the intersection of I-20 and I-75) are located in high-income suburbs in north Atlanta. The Cumberland-Galleria cluster (southeast

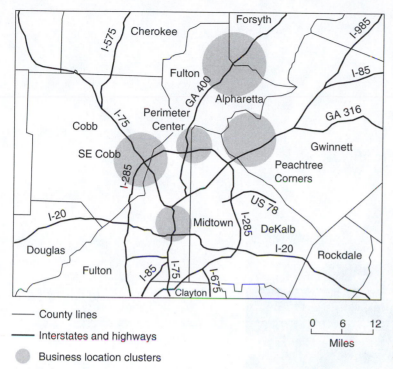

Figure 5.9 Location clusters (shaded) of high-bandwidth-demand businesses in the Atlanta metropolitan area. Shading shows the extent of business locations. (*Source: Customer and Business Services Locations*, Georgia Power, Inc., 1999, and Walcott and Wheeler, 2001.)

—— County lines

━━ Interstates and highways

⬤ Business location clusters

Cobb at the intersection of I-285 and I-75) and Perimeter Center (at the intersection of I-285 and Georgia 400) are at major highway interchange points. The Alpharetta and Peachtree clusters are associated with multilane Georgia 400 and 316 respectively. All four suburban centers are also sites of large shopping malls, which formed the original nucleus of these centers.

WIRELESS TELECOMMUNICATIONS

In addition to fiber optics, another key component of the telecommunications revolution has been the phenomenal growth in the use of cellular telephones, commonly called cell phones (Figure 5.10). This increase has been particularly dramatic in recent years as costs have gone down and competition among carriers has increased. Not surprisingly, the ten largest wireless phone markets in the United States are found in the nation's largest metropolitan regions (Table 5.7). Cell towers are being built all across America, many visible along interstate highways, and others blending in with the built landscape on top of urban buildings and other features. The construction of these towers follows heavily traveled vehicle routes and population clusters in cities and suburbs, especially suburban areas with affluent residents. Many people consider cell towers to be eyesores and oppose building them in their neighborhoods. Nonetheless, these same residents expect to have cell phone service wherever they travel. Many cell towers are hidden atop tall buildings or otherwise camouflaged from view.

Globally, there are more than 3.0 billion cell phone users active, up from only 600 million in 2000. Surprisingly, nearly 60 percent of cell usage is in developing, not developed, economies. Nearly one-half of the world's 6.6 billion people have access to cell phones. Africa is now the fastest growing world region in cell phone usage, as few conventional land phone lines exist. Africa had 152 million subscribers as of 2006, up from only 12 million in 2000. The Congo has 3.5 million

Figure 5.10 A tall cell tower located at a relatively high elevation. Cell towers are being built in both urban and nonurban locations, especially along interstate highways, sometimes hidden on tops of buildings and sometimes exposed in the open.

cell phone customers, with over 8,000 customers being added each day. More than 700 cell towers have been built across Congo, giving coverage to 70 percent of Congo's 60 million people (Sullivan, 2006). Thus, developing countries such as Congo are "jumping" the land phone stage of development.

The Automobile as Wireless Internet

We conclude this chapter by considering the telecommunications function of the automobile. Many homeless people, if they have a car—even if it does not run—may use it as shelter and a place to sleep. For those at the other end of the socioeconomic spectrum, the automobile is a kind of mobile office that can be in constant connection with remote places. A driver arriving in Indianapolis on I-65

Table 5.7 The Ten Largest Wireless Phone Markets in the United States

Rank	Metropolitan Region	Estimated Number of Wireless Users (in millions)
1	Los Angeles	3.2
2	New York	2.2
3	Chicago	2.1
4	Washington/Baltimore	1.6
5	Miami/West Palm Beach	1.5
6	San Francisco/San Jose	1.4
7	Detroit	1.2
8	Atlanta	1.2
9	Philadelphia	1.1
10	Boston	1.1

Source: Atlanta Journal Constitution, January 10, 1999, E-1.

North wants directions to Market Square, where the Indiana Pacers will play the Boston Celtics in three hours. She thus activates General Motors's OnStar service, headquartered in Troy, Michigan. Thanks to the car's Global Positioning System receiver and wireless connection, the OnStar advisor can find the car's exact location. He then guides the driver to the proper off-ramp and then to the Market Square parking lot. Another driver in Denver contacts Ford/Qualcomm's Wingcast center, headquartered in San Diego, California, and inquires as to the location of the nearest Italian restaurant. Again, detailed information is provided to the hungry driver.

WRAPPING UP

We are in the initial stage of the telecommunications age and its impacts on cities. Nonetheless, we are already seeing the fracturing of geography, as world cities and other megacities have become the principal nodes in the newly emerging economic and social order. These large, interlinked urban centers form the skeleton of globalization, connecting the world capitalist system via huge multinational corporations. This skeleton is physically held together by hair-thin glass fibers, some lying in cables on the ocean floor, some buried in the soil, and some strung on telephone poles. This chapter has demonstrated how telecommunications, particularly the Internet, is remaking urban areas and the relationships among national and world cities through front-office and back-office activities.

READINGS

Abbate, J. 1999. *Inventing the Internet*. Cambridge, MA: MIT Press.

Albrechts, L. and S. Mandelbaum, eds. 2006. *The Network Society*. New York: Routledge.

Batten, D. F. 1995. "Network Cities: Creative Urban Agglomerations for the 21st Century," *Urban Studies*, Vol. 32, pp. 313–327.

Batty, M. 1997. "The Computable City," *Online Planning 2*. http://www.casa.ucl.uk/planning/articles2/city.htm.

Carpenter, B. E. F., J. M., Fluckiger, J.M. Gerard, D. Lord, B. Segal. 1987. "Two Years of Real Progress in European HEP Networking: A CERN Perspective," *Computer Physics Communication*, Vol. 45, pp. 83–92.

Castells, M. 2004. "Space of Flows, Space of Places: Materials for a Theory of Urbanism in the Information Age." In Stephen Graham, ed., *The Cybercity Reader*. London and New York: Routledge, pp. 82–93.

Ceruzzi, P. E. 2000. *A History of Modern Computing*. Cambridge, MA: MIT Press.

Chakraborty, J. and M. M. Bosman. 2005. "Measuring the Digital Divide in the United States: Race, Income, and Personal Computer Ownership." *The Professional Geographer*, Vol. 57, pp. 395–410.

Corey, K. E. and M. I. Wilson 2006. *Urban and Regional Technology Planning: Planning Practice in the Global Economy*. New York: Routledge.

Gillespie, A., and R. Richardson. 2000. "Teleworking and the City: Myths of Workplace Transcendence and Travel Reduction." in James O. Wheeler, Yuko Aoyama, and Barney Warf, eds., *Cities in the Telecommunications Age*. New York: Routledge, pp. 228–245.

Gong, H., and J. O. Wheeler. 2002. "The Location and Suburbanization of Business and Professional Services in the Atlanta Metropolitan Area," *Growth and Change*, Vol. 33, pp. 341–369.

Graham, S. 2004. "Excavating the Material Geographies of Cybercities." in Stephen Graham, ed., *The Cybercity Reader*. London and New York: Routledge, pp. 138–142.

Hanley, R. E. 2006. *Moving People, Goods, and Information in the 21st Century*. New York: Routledge.

Lemon, J. 1996. "Liberal Dreams and Nature's Limits: Great Cities of North America since 1600," *Annals of the Association of American Geographers*, Vol. 86, pp. 745–766.

Lévy, P. 2001. *Cyberculture*. Translated by Robert Bononno. Minneapolis: University of Minnesota Press.

Mitchell, W. 2001. "Where I'm @," *Journal of the American Planning Association*, Vol. 67, pp. 144–145.

Mitchelson, R. L., and J. O. Wheeler. 1994. "The Flow of Information in a Global Economy: The Role of the American Urban System in 1990," *Annals of the Association of American* Vol. 84, pp. 87–107.

Ó hUallacháin, B., and T. F. Leslie. 2007. "Producer Services in the Urban Core and Suburbs of Phoenix, Arizona," *Urban Studies*, Vol. 44, pp. 1581–1601.

Sassen, S. 2004. "Agglomeration in the Digital Era?" in Stephen Graham, ed., *The Cybercities Reader*. London and New York: Routledge, pp. 195–198.

Sassen, S. 2006. *Cities in a World Economy*. 3rd edition London and Thousand Oaks, CA: Pine Forge Press.

Segaller, S. 1998. *Nerds 2.0.1: A Brief History of the Internet*. New York: TV Books, L.L.C.

Sullivan, K. 2006. "Bridging the Digital Divide," *Washington Post Weekly*, July 17–23, Vol. 23, No. 39, pp. 10–11.

Walcott, S. M. and J. O. Wheeler. 2001. "Atlanta in the Telecommunications Age: The Fiber-Optic Information Network," *Urban Geography*, Vol. 22, pp. 16–39.

Warf, B. 2006. "International Competition between Satellite and Fiber Optic Carriers: A Geographic Perspective," *The Professional Geographer*, Vol. 58, pp. 1–11.

Wheeler, J. O. 1999. "Local Information Links to the National Metropolitan Hierarchy: The Southeastern United States," *Environment and Planning A*, Vol. 31, pp. 841–854.

CHAPTER 6

URBAN LAND USE: THE CBD AND THE GROWTH OF THE SUBURBS

The crystallization of mass about a nucleus is part of the elementary order of things.

—WALTER CHRISTALLER, 1933

The purpose of this chapter is to survey urban land uses and land-use changes, with specific focus on **central business districts (CBDs)** and on **suburbanization**. The primary interest is with U.S. cities, as cities in other parts of the world are treated in Chapters 14, 15, and 16. We begin by detailing central-city decline as a backdrop to examining the traditional CBD. We then discuss the development of the traditional CBD. Following this discussion we analyze how the CBD has changed in its spatial structure, activities, and functions in contemporary America. The second major part of this chapter focuses on the suburbs and how they have changed over the past decades. We use the Erickson and the Hartshorn and Muller models to describe these basic changes. We conclude the chapter with a brief look at suburban sprawl.

CENTRAL-CITY DECLINE

Many **central cities** (political cities or incorporated municipalities) in the United States are in various stages of decline, and have been since 1970 and in some cases even since the 1960s. During this period population numbers in many central cities have remained stagnant or even declined. This is true not only of small metropolitan areas, but also of some of the country's largest metropolitan areas. The initial stimulus to population decline was the closing of manufacturing plants located near the CBD, also referred to as the downtown. Some older plants closed because their facilities and equipment became obsolete, because they needed to expand, or because of traffic congestion it became extremely difficult for trucks to bring in materials and move final products to markets. These plants, which had relied on rail transportation, found their locations ill-suited to modern truck transportation, including the recently instituted **just-in-time delivery**. Instead of depending on large stockpiles of parts stored in huge nearby warehouses, just-in-time delivery means that parts and materials are hauled in by truck at precise hours immediately prior to assembly, thereby eliminating the costs of warehousing and maintaining inventory. Why pay to store all kind of items in warehouses when they can be guaranteed to be delivered just as they are needed? For all these reasons, old plants and their outmoded assembly lines closed down. Many relocated into the low-cost suburbs, where physical space was abundant and modern computer-assisted manufacturing equipment could be wired into the building, thus allowing production to thrive (Figure 6.1).

Next to leave the central city was retailing. With the decline in population and therefore purchasing

Figure 6.1 A deteriorating CBD area with vacant and rundown stores.

power, retail shops abandoned the central city for locations in suburban strips and later in suburban malls. The first suburban shopping centers were tiny by today's standards, but they were a welcome and accessible convenience compared to the long traffic-congested shopping trip to downtown stores. Department stores often tried to remain in their loyal downtown locations until it became absolutely clear that they could not compete with the larger, more modern suburban department stores, and they were forced to close. Many consumer and business services and professional workers (e.g., doctors, dentists, and lawyers) remained downtown, but they soon found their markets were mainly in the suburbs and therefore relocated.

The consequences for central cities have been catastrophic. Their tax base has dropped sharply as people, industrial plants, and commercial activities have all moved away. Left behind in the central cities are a disproportionate share of the poor, who live in aging residential areas. The infrastructure of old buildings, many vacant and in disrepair, narrow and poorly maintained streets, ancient and often leaking sewage and water pipes, and lack of "green" space gives many central cities and CBDs a desolate look. The shrinking tax base prevents the local government from taking actions that a more affluent municipality would normally take to maintain and improve the infrastructure.

CBD CENTRALITY

Central business districts were established at places having accessible linkages to other places and to the surrounding population, a concept known as **centrality**. Cities initially grew up at focal points to serve a local, surrounding population. Some of this adjacent population resided within the settlement (or city) itself, while other people resided in agrarian locations outside the central city. The essential function of the CBD was to perform services not only for the surrounding city, but also for the adjacent agricultural region.

The Development of Central Business Districts

Central business districts initially sprang up in four general kinds of locations. The first were port locations, or **break-of-bulk points**. At break-of-bulk points freight and commodities were transferred from one mode of transportation onto another, such as unloading from an ocean-going vessel and reloading to a rail car (Figure 6.2a). It was therefore common to undertake manufacturing operations at a port break-of-bulk location so as to avoid an additional loading and unloading at some interior location. Because port break-of-bulk locations required stewards or longshoremen, as well as industrial workers, it was natural that commercial activities such as retailing would also develop at these central locations. The need for workers led to migration to the break-of-bulk employment magnets. Because transportation in the pre-automobile era was slow and costly, these workers settled close to the emerging CBD, as did the commercial activities that served them. Thus, the CBDs of developing port cities became centers of longshoremen functions as well as manufacturing, wholesaling, warehousing, retail, consumer services, banks, and government activities. These activities occupied central locations for their own, their workers', and their customers' benefits.

The second type of location in which the CBD developed was also associated with transportation, especially the railroad. Figure 6.2b illustrates the linear arrangement of transport cities in which small

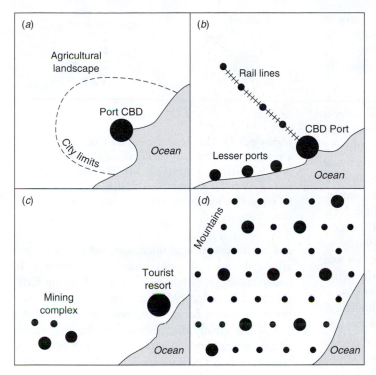

Figure 6.2 (a) CBD development at a port break-of-bulk site, where freight is unloaded from an ocean-going ship onto freight rail cars. The CBD also serves a surrounding local and agricultural population. (b) CBDs developing along rail lines and coastal ports in linear patterns. (c) The emergence of special-function CBDs in association with mining sites and tourist resorts. (d) The development of CBDs in market centers or central places that provide retail and service functions to both local and surrounding agricultural populations.

centers perform break-of-bulk activities principally between regional railroads and local distribution by wagons and later by motor trucks. It also provides an example of a major ocean port (e.g., Baltimore) and the linear arrangement of lesser ports, such as Charleston, Savannah, and Jacksonville. The CBD served as the anchor for these centers on the rail line and for the smaller string of ports.

A third location for CBDs was special-function cities. Examples of special-function cities shown in Figure 6.2c are mining cities and tourist resorts. Within these cities CBDs performed the same functions as import and railway cities and perhaps such additional functions as ore smelting, tourist-oriented retail shops, or varied restaurants and nightspots. Examples of mining cities include coal-mining centers in West Virginia and Eastern Kentucky and petroleum centers in Texas and Oklahoma. Famous tourist centers include Las Vegas and Orlando.

A fourth kind of location leading to a CBD cluster was at market sites. These towns and cities, referred to as **central places**, served the local and surrounding population principally as retail and consumer service sites. Figure 6.2d illustrates how these central places were fairly evenly spaced from one another in the pre-automobile era and continued to be so spaced even in the first few decades of the early automobile era, although their patterned location was modified by the growth of manufacturing. These early central places had well-developed CBDs featuring retail and service activities, including grocery stores, drug stores, shoe and shoe repair stores, and dry cleaners, as well as doctor and lawyer offices, banks, and sometimes a small hospital or clinic. They were generally arranged in a hierarchy at the lowest level of the urban hierarchy, with CBDs in larger central places serving a wider area and having a greater variety of retail and service activities.

Later some of these central places, especially the larger ones, attracted manufacturing industries, which located in or near the CBD. As manufacturing plants moved into these cities, warehouses and wholesale companies also relocated nearby. These central places would also act as collection points (hence warehousing) for the produce of farmers in surrounding areas (wheat, corn, lumber, cotton) and as distribution centers for certain foodstuffs, cloth, furniture, soft drinks, and other items not generally produced locally.

Although we have differentiated four types of locations, in reality, a number of CBDs were a composite of these four kinds of locations. That is, some were ports or other transport break-of-bulk points but also served as central places to provide retailing and services to the population. Likewise, some ports were resort or tourist centers. Examples of early composite centers were Philadelphia, New Orleans, Boston, New York, Baltimore, and Toronto.

In all cases, centrality—that is, accessibility to consumers and workers as well as businesses and service providers—was paramount. All of the activities present in the CBD were dependent on central access. Radial streetcar routes and later highways focused on the CBD and railroads passed through or near the CBDs of a great many small towns and cities. Because the CBDs were so accessible, they became the centers of all types of urban activities. In addition to business and financial institutions, local government offices, courthouses, police departments, and jails were located in the CBDs. So, a **monocentric city** was created, a city with a single center, the CBD. The people resided in areas around this vibrant central point.

When centrality was in the ascendancy, the CBD functioned as:

- A *collection and distribution node* for agricultural produce and industrial products to be shipped to markets elsewhere, initially by rail and then by truck—a *transshipment point*;
- A *workplace* for merchants, retail clerks, manufacturing, warehousing, and wholesale workers, as well as professional employees (doctors, lawyers);
- A *shopping node* for the city and nearby rural population;
- A *cultural, social, and entertainment center*—churches, taverns and bars, movie and other theaters;
- An *administrative center* for government offices (courthouses, mayor's office, jails).

Sometime in the early 1960s, the forces of centrality, in decline following World War II in 1945,

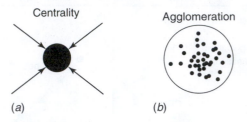

Figure 6.3 (a) The importance of the CBD as a point of urban centrality, a dominant feature of U.S. CBDs until the 1960s. (b) The dominance of post-1960 function of U.S. CBDs as centers of agglomeration or urbanization economies.

and the forces of agglomeration, notably activated after 1945, were of approximately equal intensity in understanding the dynamics of the changing CBD (Figure 6.3). After 1960, the role of centrality as a principal reason for the continued functions of the U.S. CBD greatly diminished, and the importance of agglomeration as an explanation for the existence and expanding functions of the CBD rose mightily.

The Decline of CBD Centrality and the Rise of Agglomeration Economies

We can define centrality simply as the most accessible location (the CBD) with respect to a surrounding population. **Agglomeration**, on the other hand, is the clustering of similar as well as dissimilar economic, social, cultural, and governmental activities in a given location, such as the early CBD and later suburban business location clusters or centers (Figure 6.4).

The concept of agglomeration is normally broken down into two types: **localization economies** and **urbanization economies**. The term "economies" refers to time and money savings that are generated by the clustering of economic and other activities. These savings apply to retailers, consumers, service providers, corporations, and business services, as well as customers and clients. Localization economies result when like or similar activities locate near one another. An example of localization economies is a health care center in which several medical doctors occupy offices in the same or nearby office buildings, which are often located

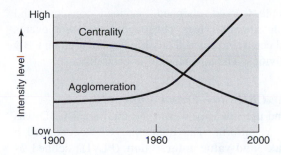

Figure 6.4 The decline of centrality and the rise of agglomeration in CBD functions in the U.S. during the 20th century.

close to a hospital. Other examples of localization economies are multiple shoe stores in the same large regional shopping mall and the fast-food strips that are so common along heavily traveled highways and at interstate interchanges. In contrast urbanization economies refer to clusters of unlike activities. Examples of urbanization economies are shopping malls and clusters of varied merchandise within a single store such as a Wal-Mart Supercenter and other discount retailers such as Kmart, and Target.

CBD Agglomeration Linkages Four kinds of agglomeration linkages are important in understanding the workings of localization and urbanization economies in the CBD, especially after 1960. These are **ancillary linkages**, **competitive linkages**, **companion linkages**, and **complementary linkages**.

1. *Ancillary linkages* represent one type of urbanization economy, specifically, clustering of *unlike* activities to serve a mutual market, client, or corporation. Figure 6.5a shows an example of an ancillary linkage, in this case a major corporation headquartered in the CBD and doing business with a legal services firm, an advertising firm, and an accounting firm. Another example is a large office complex in which workers make purchases at lunchtime and before and after work at restaurants and cafes, and specialty shops. Again, these are unrelated activities serving customers who work in a downtown office complex.

2. *Companion linkages* are a second type of urbanization economy; they refer to savings derived when several *different and unlike establishments* depend upon a common supplier or service (Figure 6.5b). Our example is taken from Atlanta: Coca-Cola (the soft drink company), Bank of America (a financial institution), and

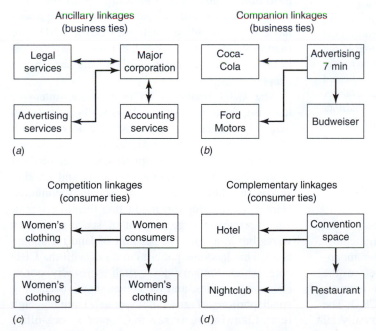

Figure 6.5 (a) Examples of ancillary linkages. (b) Companion linkages. (c) Competitive linkages. (d) Complementary linkages.

CNN (cable television), all using the same large advertising agency. These are unlike enterprises, but they are companions-in-advertising when they are all the clients of a large advertising agency headquartered in New York.

3. *Competitive linkages* are extremely common and, although once confined almost exclusively to the CBD, they now explain the competitive clustering of retail and service establishments in shopping malls. Competitive linkages facilitate comparison shopping, as, for example, when several women's clothing stores are located within a regional shopping mall. Competitive linkages refer to consumer ties, whereas ancillary and companion linkages are related to business or corporate links. Whereas ancillary and companion linkages are examples of urbanization economies (clustering of unlike activities), competitive linkages may represent both urbanization and localization economies. In Figure 6.5c, the example of women's clothing stores clearly demonstrates clustering of *like or similar* retail establishments, a reflection of localization savings. If, however, we view the entire CBD or the regional mall as agglomerations of unlike establishments, then these *concentrations* are examples of competition among primarily unlike establishments, or urbanization economies.

4. *Complementary linkages* occur when a clustering of *related functions* serve the same market. As with competitive linkages, these complementary linkages are consumer-based ties. One example is a professional convention, for example, the annual meeting of the Association of American Geographers in Chicago in 2006 (Figure 6.5d). The related consumer-oriented establishments serving this convention include a cluster of hotels such as the Hyatt Regency and the Marriott, a number of good- to high-quality restaurants, and a few strategically located nightclubs.

TRADITIONAL CBD CHARACTERISTICS

Before we explore the primary functions of the contemporary CBD, it is instructive to remember what the traditional CBD was like in the monocentric city, or single-centered city, before the suburbs, multicentered **polycentric developments**, known as the city, overwhelmed the old CBD. The monocentric city was *the* place where virtually all

people worked, shopped, obtained consumer and professional services, and sought out cultural events and entertainment. All city life was focused on CBD activities. The advantage was centrality.

The CBD Core-Frame Concept

Land-use intensity within the traditional CBD was never uniform. The traditional CBD contained a **peak land-value intersection** (PLVI), defined as the cross-street intersection having the highest land values. The PLVI was where the competition for land was greatest and therefore, where the highest price or rent could be charged for this most centrally located and most prized land. Commonly, the PLVI had the greatest volume of pedestrian traffic and some of the tallest buildings within the CBD.

Spreading away from the PLVI is the **CBD Core**, the part of the CBD that has the tallest buildings, high land costs, and most intensely utilized space (Figure 6.6). The core has heavy horizontal pedestrian traffic on sidewalks and skywalks, but it also has considerable vertical pedestrian traffic on elevators and escalators in the high-rise structures. Banks and other financial institutions, company head offices, government buildings, posh entertainment spots, and professional offices were representative of the traditional activities of the CBD core in monocentric cities. We will consider the activities in the core for the modern CBD a little later in this chapter.

The **CBD frame** is an area of less-intensive land use, fewer pedestrians, low-rise buildings, and generally different land-use types compared with the CBD core (Figure 6.6). In the frame, manufacturing, warehouses, hospitals and other medical services, and transportation terminals and parking spaces (machine spaces) were especially common. Here, for example, you might find furniture stores, which require a large amount of space to display wares but at a low cost per unit of land (or square foot). This land-use pattern contrasts with the CBD core, which contains stores such as jewelry stores, chocolate cookies, and ice cream shops, occupying small portions of ground floors at extremely high rents. Likewise, as we saw in Chapter 5, back-office

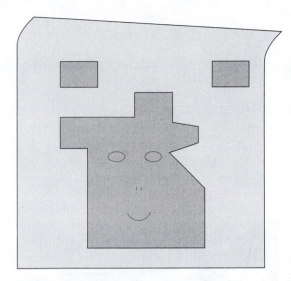

Figure 6.6 The CBD core-frame concept, with the core in dark shading and the frame in light shading.

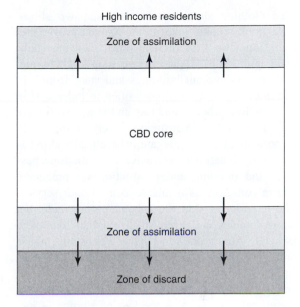

Figure 6.7 The zone of assimilation and the zone of discard.

activities, such as collection agencies or standardized billing services, which involve routine paper handling, may locate in the lower-cost land of the CBD frame. In contrast front-office activities which handle high-order, individualistic, and face-to-face information services, need to locate in CBD cores in spite of high rents.

Zones of CBD Assimilation and Discard

Not only is the use of the CBD, especially in large metropolitan areas, undergoing constant land-use change, but the CBD core itself may be expanding in certain directions and retracting in others. In the core, obsolescent buildings that are considered too costly to refurbish are imploded in a matter of seconds with precisely placed explosives to create a giant, but carefully confined, rubble and dust heap. After the building rubble is hauled away, giant construction cranes appear, indicating that a modern high-rise building is springing up that will modify the city skyline.

If we examine CBD land-use change over a period of time, we can find an underlining order or pattern to this change. CBD growth and expansion typically takes place in a **zone of assimilation** (Figure 6.7). This zone of assimilation is usually

found in one of two locations. First, CBD expansion often occurs in the direction that is closest to higher income residential areas. These residential areas "draw" investments in CBD activities because they are home to the more highly skilled and educated workers who may be attracted to the jobs that are relocating to the zone of assimilation.

Second, the zone of assimilation commonly expands into a former zone of discard. The **zone of discard** represents an older and rapidly decaying edge of a formerly vibrant part of the CBD that has been left behind. Land values in the zone have declined. Whereas at first, no real investment is made in this zone of discard because of the area's generally undesirable appearance, the proximity of the area to the dynamically functioning part of the CBD may bring about revitalizations—often large-scale redevelopment—that may be either entirely privately supported or partially financed by the government. It should also be noted that CBD functions may expand and contract within existing buildings. The zone of discard thus becomes the zone of assimilation.

The zone of discard is characterized by marginal retail outlets and entertainment venues, such as used clothing stores, tattoo parlors, pawn shops, bars, honky-tonks, juke joints, X-rated movie theaters, adult book stores and other adult entertainment, gun shops, liquor stores, soup kitchens and shelters, and vacant buildings and store fronts. In addition, the zone of discord often includes a **skid row** section, where homeless and others who have "dropped out" of mainstream society—temporarily or permanently—congregate, where panhandling is common, sometimes aggressive and sometimes passive, and pimping and prostitution are practiced, and in some places available as a 24-hour service. The majority of skid row inhabitants are male, but many females and even small children live there as well. About one-third have a substance-abuse problem (alcohol and/or drugs), another one-third suffer from mental and emotional difficulties, and another one-third have recently suffered an economic calamity such as the loss of a home, a job, or a car—or all these—or an abusive wife, husband, or other sexual partner.

Daytime-Nighttime CBD Populations

Especially evident in the traditional monocentric CBD, but also characteristic of the modern polycentric metropolitan area, are the marked changes in CBD population densities during 24-hour weekday periods (Figure 6.8). In 1950, very few people actually lived in the CBD core. Only a slightly greater number lived in the CBD frame, in boarding houses, converted hotels, and the occasional apartment building or converted large home. The nightlife population was sparse in the CBD, but it increased fairly rapidly as one moved away from the CBD. Here were small houses typically occupied by families with several children. The nighttime population density would commonly peak between one and three miles from the CBD and then decline in a fairly regular manner to the edge of the city. Because relatively little suburban sprawl existed in 1950, as compared with later decades, the limits or edges of the city were rather distinct from the surrounding noncity landscape.

Despite some increase in the number of CBD and near-CBD residents in high-rise condominiums

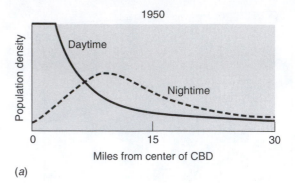

(a)

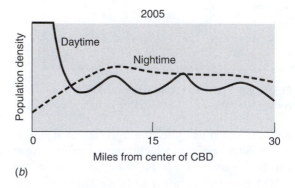

(b)

Figure 6.8 (a) The daytime-nighttime population density of the 1950 monocentric city. (b) The daytime-nighttime population density of the contemporary metropolitan area.

and luxury apartments, the heart of the CBD core in many of the largest American urban areas is taken over at night by people who contrast greatly with the daytime men and women workers in their well-tailored business suits. These nighttime people are the vendors and buyers of the bundle of illicit activities of the illegal and underground economy. Here are the street hustlers, gamblers, protection gangs, drug users, and the anonymous audiences and clients of strip joints, adult movie theaters, and gaming houses.

The daytime or working population densities have also changed remarkably since 1950. As we have seen in the monocentric city, almost all jobs were located within the CBD. Thus, the daytime densities dropped off precipitously away from this central location and were at extremely low levels in the newly emerging suburbs. In contrast, by the mid-2000s, many job concentrations had sprung up in both the inner suburbs (5 to 15 miles from the CBD, depending on the size of the metropolitan area) and the newer outer suburbs that had sprawled far into the once-rural regions. The relative importance of the CBD as an employment center had waned. Although traffic congestion to CBD workplaces has continued unabated into the present, traffic congestion is typically even worse near suburban workplaces on interstate highways, particularly perimeter highways. Most of us have experienced waiting motionless on a freeway while a traffic accident, sometimes several miles ahead, is cleared. The polycentric city has clearly spread clustered workplaces outward and has extended the vehicular traffic problem to nearly all parts of the metropolitan area.

The ebb and flow of people into and out of the CBDs of large American metropolitan areas may be compared to a sponge. This CBD **sponge model** soaks up water (people, whose bodies are mainly water anyway) starting from approximately 6:30 to 9:30 a.m. and stays saturated until late in the afternoon and early in the evening. Then, from as early as 3:30 p.m. until 6:00 or 6:30 p.m., the water (people) is rapidly squeezed and evaporated until the sponge is almost dry. Stand on a downtown street corner in, say, Pittsburgh from 5:00 to 7:00 p.m. First you will see the great rush of people, primarily middle- and upper-class CBD workers, heading for parking decks or parking lots, taxis, or buses.

By 6:00 p.m. this throng of scurrying bodies is almost gone. Some scampering people glance nervously over their shoulders. A few enter a McDonalds to grab a take-out burger, knowing that the fast-food eatery closes at 7:00 p.m. The whole CBD is shutting down. By 8:00 p.m. you may see a man or a woman sorting through the public wastebasket outside the McDonalds for a half-eaten sandwich, some thrown-away fries, or a half-consumed Coca-Cola. Later, there might be some hiccups of illicit activity around certain adult entertainment spots, but by 3:00 a.m. the CBD is largely deserted.

CONTEMPORARY CBD RETAILING

The decades are long past when the heart of retail activities was centralized in the CBD. The shopping malls in the early developing suburbs initiated the demise of the downtown as the retail kingdom, and they constituted the first serious assault on the CBD core of the monocentric city. The loss of inner-city manufacturing jobs, many in the CBD frame, had previously foretold the future fading of CBD efficacy. The phenomenal growth of ever-larger suburban shopping malls with more and more diversified selections and endlessly varied, upscale, and niche-targeted merchandise has curtailed and severely diminished CBD retailing. Today, except in such subway-oriented rapid transit centers such as New York (Manhattan) and Toronto, CBD retailing has become essentially restricted to three basic types: (1) mass-appeal consumer goods, (2) specialty goods and services, and (3) convenience goods. Department stores have largely disappeared from the CBD.

Mass-appeal consumer goods serve a *captive market* made up primarily of nearby inner-city residents, some of whom are welfare-dependent. Merchants cater to these residents who typically have moderate to low incomes. These inner-city residents often do not own automobiles and have at best only limited transportation to the suburban shopping malls (most bus and transit systems are focused on getting to the CBD and the inner city and not the suburbs.) These confined shoppers are basically dependent on the nearby stores for modestly priced clothing, including used clothing. The merchandise is designed to appeal to the widest possible shoppers because relatively little variety or selection is available. These mass-appeal stores emphasize haberdasheries, women's cosmetics, women's clothing fashions, wig shops, barbershops, and household goods as well as higher-priced package stores. CBD retailers typically provide a specialized array of mass-appeal goods to particular racial or ethnic groups, such as African Americans, Hispanics, and others, who may reside in the inner city. Especially in large, older, East Coast and Midwestern industrial cities and cities in the South, African Americans often comprise a significant proportion of inner-city residents.

Other CBD retailers offer **specialty goods and services**. These retailers seek to appeal to people who work in the CBD and to tourists, convention-eers, and those people who are engaged in transitory downtown business activities. These are the tempo-rary daytime CBD "prisoners," also part of the cap-tive market. Specialty goods and services include nice restaurants and cafes, quick in-and-out cafes, fast-food joints, flower shops, bead and bauble and knick-knack stores, tourist-oriented gift shops, travel agencies, night clubs, cocktail lounges, beer and wine package and liquor stores, and discreet adult amuse-ment spots. They also include the nightlife activi-ties that appeal to many conventioneers, especially in such places as Atlanta, Las Vegas, and New Orleans.

Convenience stores constitute a third type of CBD retail type. Convenience stores, many of which are open 24/7, are not confined to the CBD frame or to inner-city locations. Rather, they are ubiqui-tous throughout metropolitan areas and at strategic highway sites and interstate interchanges, as well as in small towns and other rural locations. The typi-cal patron is in and out of the convenience store in less than three minutes. He or she simply wants to pick up a newspaper, chewing gum, or cigarettes, a root beer, tampons, candy, beer or wine, or pay for gasoline. Significantly, he or she is willing to pay higher prices (except for gasoline) for the con-venience of saving time. Here the patron is not a prisoner trapped by the circumstance of inner-city residence, nor is he or she a hostage to the deliber-ate choice of working, visiting, or doing business downtown. Rather, the convenience store patrons voluntarily become part of the CBD captive market.

CBD REDEVELOPMENT AND REVITALIZATION

Beginning in the 1950s, however, downtowns began to deteriorate as manufacturing jobs declined in the CBD frame and in nearby inner-city loca-tions. Many retail shops went out of business or relocated to suburban malls or other suburban loca-tions. Likewise, middle- and upper-income people left for the safer, newer, more spacious homes and green yards of suburbia, taking their buy-ing power with them. By the 1960s, CBDs had declined precipitously as the areas became associ-ated with high crime rates, vacant stores, homeless people, marginal business, downscale merchandise, and low-quality consumer services. CBDs in the 2000s typically account for less than 3 percent of a metropolitan area's total retail sales.

Beginning in the mid- to late-1960s, downtown businesspeople, stunned by the rapid decline of their sales and the general degeneration of the CBD, embarked on a number of revitalization schemes. Local governments have joined CBD mer-chants, bankers, financiers, real estate developers, planners, and even labor unions to bring about downtown revitalizations. Such coalitions of inter-est groups became known as **growth machines**. Federal agencies also became part of the growth machines. Their goal was to return prosperity to the once-mighty CBD.

Packaging the Entrepreneurial CBD

The results of these growth machine efforts across America are mixed and idiosyncratic. Downtown after downtown has attempted to "sell" an image of itself, often based on real or fictional themes from its past. For example, Detroit's Renaissance Center is a megastructure—a city within a city—surrounded by block after block of urban decay. This one fortress of luxury has not attracted investment into adja-cent areas, and has brought about little positive spillover or neighborhood effects. Despite its name, the Renaissance Center has not brought about a downtown renaissance. In contrast, Baltimore's Har-bor Place has been much more successful, building on the theme of Baltimore's port functions. But even here the decay and social deprivation in nearby com-munities has changed only modestly.

Nearly all large cities today have developed and packaged unique complexes to attract tourist as well as to coax suburbanites downtown, if only for a con-cert, an art exhibit, or an ethnic festival, or for upscale shopping and fine dinning. Some downtowns have developed enclosed shopping malls, such as the Eaton Centre in Toronto, the Horton Plaza in San Diego, and the Gallery in Philadelphia. Philadelphia also developed Penn Central, a corporate center in Center City. Penn Center experienced a tall-building spurt in the 1980s when the law changed to allow skyscrapers to be built taller than the hat on the William Penn statue atop City Hall.

Many different strategies have been employed by large metropolises and small towns alike to make downtown areas more attractive and more economically and socially viable. The downtown growth machines have gradually recognized that the modern CBD cannot compete one-on-one with the affluent suburbs, with their huge upscale shopping malls, their spacious industrial and technology parks, and their rapidly growing clusters of regional and national corporate offices and headquarters. Consequently, the growth machines have spawned a variety of strategies to rekindle downtown prosperity. Here are a few of the most common downtown development strategies:

• Historic preservation and architectural integrity
• Downtown housing
• Convention center
• Improved parking facilities (machine space)
• Transit improvements
• Waterfront development
• Nightlife and entertainment
• Cultural attractions
• Tourism
• New office construction and old building refurbishment and cyberspace wiring
• Sport stadiums and arena
• Pedestrian spaces
• Police protection and presence

Naturally the success of these strategies has varied greatly from downtown to downtown.

CONTEMPORARY CBD ACTIVITIES

With the demise of manufacturing and warehousing in the CBD of the monocentric city, new land-use activities have come to dominate the contemporary downtown business district. Significantly, many of these modern CBD activities are also found in suburban areas. Most CBD employment today consists of office jobs. For example, corporate headquarters may remain concentrated in downtown areas, but also in suburban locations. Banks and other financial institutions remain especially loyal to high-rise CBD headquarter locations. Government office buildings also continue to be located in the CBD. Expensive hotels and convention facilities are concentrated in central parts of the CBD core, with less-expensive hotels scattered within the CBD frame. In addition to banks and other financial institutions, corporate headquarters, hotels and convention complexes, and government buildings, office employment in the contemporary CBD is also prominently associated with advanced producers services, such as accounting, advertising, auditing, bookkeeping, computer and data processing services, consulting services, marketing and sales, and public relations.

Business and Professional Services in Atlanta

Atlanta provides an excellent case study of the location of different kinds of business and professional services. Examine Table 6.1 closely and note the varied percentages of jobs in nine different business and professional service sectors among the four locational categories: (1) the CBD; (2) the rest of the city of Atlanta (which contains only approximately 6 percent of the 5.2 million inhabitants of the 28-county metropolitan area); (3) the inner suburbs (extending some 10 miles away from the CBD); and (4) the outer suburbs (extending more than 45 miles from the CBD to the edge of the U.S. Census-defined metropolitan area). Overall, only 5 percent of Atlanta's employment in these services is within the CBD and only about 23 percent in the city of Atlanta, leaving over 77 percent of these business and service jobs in the Atlanta suburbs.

When we look at the nine individual service sectors, we can identify five rather distinct groupings (Table 6.2). First are *low-order, proximity-dependent activities*, best exemplified by mail, copying, fax,

Table 6.1 The Percentage of Employment in Business and Professional Services in the Atlanta Metropolitan Area

Service Sectors	CBD	Rest of City	Inner Suburbs	Outer Suburbs	TOTAL
Mailing and Copying	26.8	19.8	42.2	11.2	100%
Accounting and Auditing	24.6	17.7	43.7	14.0	100%
Management and Public Relations	7.6	21.5	54.3	16.6	100%
Engineering	5.3	18.7	58.8	17.2	100%
Computer and Data Processing	4.7	12.7	65.5	17.1	100%
Personnel Supply	1.9	14.9	60.7	22.5	100%
Credit Reporting and Collection	1.8	6.8	67.6	23.8	100%
Advertising	1.3	39.1	49.6	10.0	100%
Research and Testing	0.9	7.8	61.5	29.8	100%
TOTAL	5.0	17.8	58.7	18.5	100%

Source: Calculated by Gong and Wheeler (2002) from U.S. Bureau of Census, 1997.

and e-mail services. Nearly 27 percent of these jobs are located in the CBD. These are routine, low-cost services, but they must locate near their clients. Mailing and copying services in particular have been slow to leave the CBD. In contrast are the *low-order, back-office services* such as credit reporting and collection agencies that locate in the suburbs (especially the inner suburbs) to avoid the high rents of the CBD and the city of Atlanta. As Table 6.1 indicates, less than 2 percent of jobs in credit and

collection agencies are located in the CBD, and less than 9 percent are found within the city of Atlanta. Personnel supply firms have suburbanized at a more moderate rate. In summary, then, although these two sectors both provide low-order services, they prefer different locations for different reasons.

Three groups of business and professional services represent high-order activities. *High-order, face-to-face-dependent activities*, which are best represented by accounting and auditing firms, are

Table 6.2 Locational Characteristics of Business and Professional Service Jobs in Atlanta

Service Sector Groups	Locational Preference	Rates of Suburbanization
Low-Order Proximity Dependent-Activities:		
Mailing and Copying	CBD	Slow
Low-Order Back Offices:		
Credit Reporting and Collection	Inner Suburbs	Fast
Personnel Supply	Inner Suburbs	Medium
High-Order Near-CBD Activities:		
Advertising	City of Atlanta	Medium
Management and Public Relations	Inner Suburbs	Slow
High-Order Footloose, Amenity-Seeking Activities:		
Research and Testing	Inner Suburbs	Medium
Computers and Data Processing	Inner Suburbs	Medium
Engineering	Inner Suburbs	Medium
High-Order Face-to-Face Dependent Activities:		
Accounting and Auditing	CBD	Slow

Source: Derived from Gong and Wheeler (2002).

heavily concentrated in the CBD. Such firms have been relatively slow to suburbanize. These services require considerable face-to-face interaction with other businesses and corporations, not all of which are located in the CBD. As businesses have developed in the suburbs, accounting and auditing firms have also followed. Today, 58 percent of accounting and auditing jobs are located in suburban Atlanta, in contrast to only 25 percent in the CBD. A second service-sector group is the *high-order, near-CBD activities*, consisting of advertising agencies and management and public relations firms. These two kinds of activities, and especially advertising agencies are particularly attracted to locations in the city of Atlanta outside the CBD. In fact, less than 2 percent of advertising jobs are found within the CBD. Again, however, the majority of the jobs in both advertising and public relation firms are found in the suburbs. The movement to the suburbs, however, has been slow to moderate.

A third group of high-order business and professional services are *high-order, footloose, amenity-seeking activities*. These activities include research and testing laboratories, computer and data processing services, and engineering companies. They are predominately suburban, with the suburbs having over 90 percent of the research and testing jobs, 82 percent of the computer and data processing jobs, and 76 percent of engineering jobs. These firms are classified as footloose because they can locate nearly anywhere. They employ people with high levels of expertise who prefer to work near their private suburban homes.

Location of Accounting Services Although suburbanization of producer or advanced services has undergone recent expansion, they remain largely concentrated in the CBD, the central city, and the inner suburbs. Gong and Wheeler (2002) found only 14 percent of accounting and auditing firms located in the outer suburbs in Atlanta. A more recent study (Nelson, 2006) of public accounting firms in the Chicago and Minneapolis metropolitan areas shows that central cities are favored over suburbs. Moreover, central city firms offer a more

complex array of services, are larger and pay more per employee than suburban firms. The considerable importance of face-to-face interaction, however, was found to be significant both in central city and suburban locations.

AMERICA'S NEW DOWNTOWNS

Larry Ford's *America's New Downtowns* (2003) offers considerable insight into the revitalization and reinvention of downtowns in U.S. cities. He points out that "Downtowns are no longer simply central business districts" (p. 198). Downtown activities have now expanded well beyond the traditional compact (core and frame) CBD into more space-extensive land uses. Ford identified four major features of new downtown expansion and change in large American cities. The first he characterizes in shorthand as "fun zones," **major attractions**. These are entertainment and cultural attractions, including sports venues, museums, cultural centers, theater and performing arts facilities, and "a few miscellaneous semidowntown activities such as zoos and harbor excursions" (p. 199). These so-called fun zones cater primarily to suburbanites, rather than to inner-city dwellers, as well as to tourists.

Second, Ford points to **historic districts** as gaining momentum in American downtowns. The historic preservation movement, in part a reaction to massive urban renewal, highway construction, and "glass box" office towers, made headway in the 1970s. "Instead of a sea of decay, civic leaders saw precious remnants" (pp. 223–224). Preserved areas and buildings were promoted as tourist attractions and new business sites. Again, these historic initiatives have done little economically to positively impact inner-city residents.

Ford identified a third recent change as downtown and near-downtown **residential neighborhoods**. Whereas the traditional CBD was almost entirely devoid of residential land uses, the past 25 years have seen an increasing "back-to-the-city" or "back downtown" movement. This movement involves suburbanites, individuals and couples without children who work downtown and enjoy the downtown social life, as well as new migrants to the city. Despite this recent downtown residential trend, the total number of people living downtown in American cities is still extremely low compared with the vast suburban population.

Downtown residential neighborhoods consist of three features: (1) gentrification, (2) conversion of old industrial and warehousing areas into "lofts," and (3) construction of new condominium and apartment complexes. Gentrification involves the transformation of older, once gracious, and often architecturally unique houses, now occupied by low-income households, into modernized and elegant structures. When entire neighborhoods follow this path, the neighborhood is said to be gentrified or revitalized. The higher-income new occupants are quite different from the previous residents, who become displaced. Only interesting historic neighborhoods are likely to undergo gentrification and thus not all American downtowns have experienced this process.

The conversion of old, abandoned industrial areas into residences began primarily during the 1980s. These areas are not found in the traditional CBD but rather in fringe areas. Loft living often provides ample and relatively inexpensive space compared with comparable suburban housing.

New housing in the CBD core consists of highrise condominiums. Lower-rise apartment and townhouse complexes are most likely found in the downtown fringe. Some of the high-rise buildings are "mixed use," including retail, office, and hotel activities, in addition to residential functions.

A final feature of downtown change is **transportation innovations**. These include light rail, new subways, freeways, and bus corridors. The automobile has transformed downtowns into large parking lots and decks, as well as underground parking. Freeways have been constructed around and through the downtown, one-way streets established, and mass transit provided. Most downtown rail yards have been removed. Mass transit, highly touted by some, is often an expensive, revenue-losing

enterprise, as Americans, unless they cannot afford it, continue to prefer the automobile and are willing to live with congestion and pollution and high gasoline prices.

MODELS OF SUBURBAN EVOLUTION IN NORTH AMERICAN METROPOLISES

Several quantitative models of urban land uses were developed in the 1960s that explained what kinds of activities would be found in which urban areas. These models, however, applied basically to the monocentric city, which was already giving way to a polycentric structure. In the following section we will review a model of the location of various land uses in an idealized urban area before we examine the evolution of the suburbs.

Location Rent and Urban Land Use
One prominent model of urban land use focuses on **location rent**, defined as profit per unit of land. According to the location rent concept, different land uses compete with one another. Some land uses, such as banks, corporate headquarters, insurance companies, and law offices, are able to compete for the more expensive and intensively used land in the CBD. In contrast, land uses at the fringe of the urban area typically are less intensively utilized, less desired, and therefore less expensive. These peripheral areas, often quasi-agricultural land, are given over to scattered residential land use.

Figure 6.9 illustrates a simplified and hypothetical urban land-use pattern that results from competition for the most desired spaces. Land-use types that locate within the CBD require the most central location and are able and willing to pay the high land costs or location rents associated with these locations. For example, high-income people who desire a five-acre lot for their residents cannot compete with the intensely used CBD skyscrapers. Figure 6.9 also shows low-income people living close to the CBD. How is it possible that low-income people can compete for relatively accessible land? The answer is because of their high residential densities

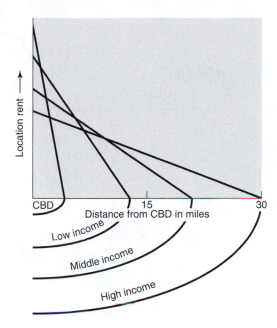

Figure 6.9 The concept of location rent and resulting residential land use.

in multistory apartments and public housing and extremely small lots. The poor live in high-density, accessible locations but each household consumes only a small portion of the area. The net effect is a high location rent yield per unit of land. The wealthy, on the other hand, consume large quantities of less accessible land with lower unit costs. The poor are not only attracted to cheaper inner-city housing in the monocentric city, but they also can save on transport costs to nearby CBD workplaces. The rich, however, can afford not only expensive housing but also the higher transport cost of traveling to work.

Location rent may be understood by a simple formula that demonstrates how residential land use is parceled out in a hypothetical urban area:

$$LR = H(P - C) - HTD$$

where:

LR = location rent (profit per unit of land per square mile)

H = number of households (dwellings) per unit of land (per square mile)

P = rent (dollars per month)

C = cost (dollars of upkeep per month)

T = transportation cost (dollars per mile per month)

D = distance from the center of the city

In the monocentric city, the variable D (distance) plays a crucial role in determining land-use types.

Land and Property Values If the location rent model is approximately accurate in the real world, then the generalized pattern of urban land and property values should decrease as we move away from the peak land-value intersection (PLVI) within the CBD and decline as we move toward the edge of the metropolitan area. Figure 6.10 shows the gradual decline in property values away from the highest values in the twin cities of Minneapolis and St. Paul. Other studies have measured the decline in land values in Chicago with distance away from Lake Michigan. The Chicago Loop (CBD) lies adjacent to Lake Michigan, as does high-value residential land use, especially to the north of the Loop. Some recent studies suggest that the old pattern of a steady decrease in land values away from the CBD has now been modified by the increase in land values related to the growth of business clusters and the associated high-value residential areas in the suburbs.

Erickson's Model of the Evolution of the Suburban Space Economy

Rodney Erickson (1983) developed a general spatial model of the process of suburbanization of North American metropolitan areas. His was a broad conceptualization, covering some 80 years of the evolution of the suburban space economy. The **Erickson model** emphasized the location and development of employment centers from approximately 1920 (just after World War I) to 1980. It is a hypothetical model put forth to illustrate the overall characteristics of the suburbanization process in North American cities. Its intent is to apply generally to all large cities as they evolved into full-fledged metropolitan areas.

The Erickson model divides the evolution of modern suburbs into three time periods or phases,

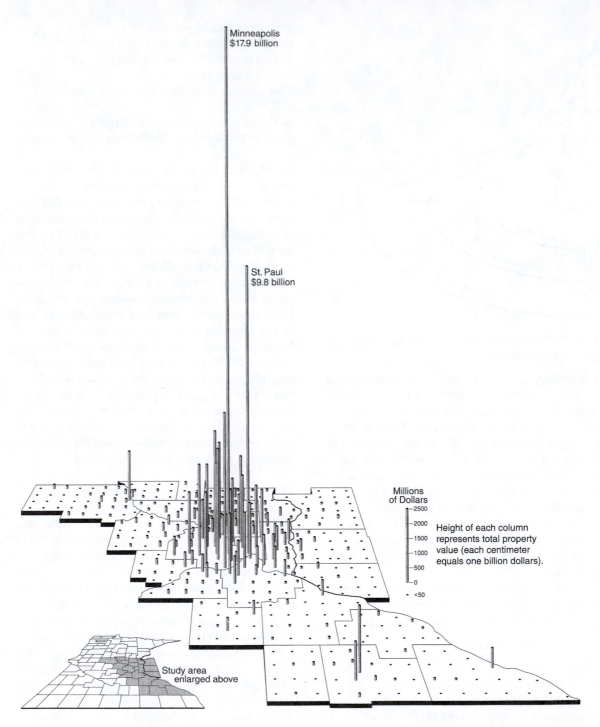

Figure 6.10 The gradual decline in property values away from the PLVI for Minneapolis and St. Paul.

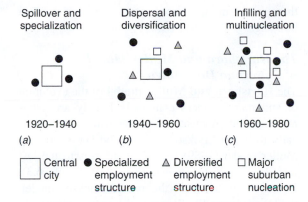

Spillover and specialization	Dispersal and diversification	Infilling and multinucleation
1920–1940	1940–1960	1960–1980
(a)	(b)	(c)

☐ Central city   ● Specialized employment structure   △ Diversified employment structure   ☐ Major suburban nucleation

Figure 6.11 Erickson's Model of the spatial and structural evolution of the suburban space economy. (a) The pattern of spillover and specialization. (b) Dispersal and diversification. (c) Infilling and multinucleation.

each of which encompasses 20 years. The three phases are: (1) spillover and specialization, (2) dispersal and diversification, and (3) infilling and multinucleation (Figure 6.11).

Spillover and Specialization The **spillover and specialization** phase occurred between 1920 and 1940, which roughly corresponds to the period between the end of World War I and the start of World War II (Figure 6.11a). In a sense, this period was one of *proto-suburbs*. My dictionary defines "proto" as primitive or first in time. Before 1920, cities were confined to their municipal or city limits. Rural and urban areas were distinct from each other. The jobs were nearly all in the city, almost all of them in the CBD. All of the people lived and shopped and socialized within the politically defined city limits.

During the inter-war period, manufacturing employment "spilled out" of the city proper into adjacent suburban land. Nevertheless, manufacturing jobs still needed to be near workers' residences. Therefore, the manufacturing enterprises typically located along inter-city rail lines and sometimes along waterways. The rail lines provided links to freight terminals and access to regional and national markets. Although some commercial development spilled over during this first phase, most of the spillover involved industrial jobs. Selected suburban

areas specialized as either industrial districts, commercial districts, or purely residential communities. Still, the preponderance of manufacturing, shopping, and socializing continued to take place within the traditional CBD.

Dispersal and Diversification The second phase, **dispersal and diversification**, extended from approximately 1940 to 1960. With improvements in transportation, the range of locational choices greatly expanded (Figure 6.11b). Private automobile ownership greatly expanded, the quality and reliability of automotive transportation was notably improved, and the interstate highway and intracity roadway system was significantly enlarged. All of these elements combined to favor the suburbs. Not only did high-income white people flock to the suburbs, but working-class suburbs also emerged, located near industrial districts in the suburbs. Substantial *dispersal* of people and economic activities occurred. Motor freight, of growing importance, favored the more accessible suburban locations over the congested CBD. Large-tract land development encouraged low-density residential land use. This dispersal of a combination of people and jobs, of retail, industrial, and service activities led inevitably to a suburban landscape of *diversification*.

Infilling and Multinucleation In the third phase, **infilling and multinucleation** (1960–1980), the large amount of developable land left over from the previous dispersal and diversification phase was gradually filled in. In one sense, this infilling of "jumped over" spaces was a continuation of dispersal. Districts where industrial and commercial activities had settled prior to 1960 now attracted nearby residential development. Conversely, residential areas that had developed in the suburbs prior to 1960 subsequently invited commercial opportunities to locate during infilling. Again, the role of transportation access, especially freeway proximity, was vital to the infilling process.

Multinucleation in the suburbs also became fully evident during this period. It was no longer efficient to serve a dispersed population from the monocentric city or the single core. Therefore, multiple cores sprang up, first in the inner suburbs (those closest to the political city) and later the outer suburbs. Agglomeration economies led to an increasing concentration of employment in a relatively few selected suburban nucleations. Many of these nucleations prospered around large regional shopping malls. Furthermore, as we have seen, as customers increasingly focused their retail shopping on these malls, service providers such as branch banks, restaurants, and doctors began to relocate there as well. The multipurpose shopping trips expanded into favorable access to many goods and services.

At the same time, many office activities were attracted to these emerging retail and service concentrations. Here was open land, relatively inexpensive, noncongested, with ample parking. Moreover, it was near workers' residences. Regional, and even national headquarters of corporations settled into these suburban nucleations, often in high-rise office buildings.

The Hartshorn and Muller Model of Suburban Downtowns

The **Hartshorn and Muller model** of the evolution of suburban business centers is largely an elaboration of multinucleation. As such, it follows logically from the Erickson model. The Hartshorn and Muller model (1989) roughly conforms to the last five decades of the twentieth century (Table 6.3). In contrast to the more theoretical Erickson model, the Hartshorn and Muller model is more empirically based, or more grounded in specific events.

Sprawl The first stage of the model is referred to as **sprawl**, or undifferentiated and "unexplained" suburban development. This sprawl was characterized by dispersal and residential expansion during the

Table 6.3 The Hartshorn and Muller Model of the Evolution of Suburban Business Centers

Periods	*Major Characteristics*
1. Sprawl—1950s:	a. Bedroom Communities b. Convenience Retailing c. Arterial Highway Radial Access d. Air Conditioning
2. Independence—1960s:	a. Freeways b. Regional Shopping Malls c. Office and Industrial Parks d. Residential Diversification
3. Magnet—1970s:	a. Mid-Rise Office Buildings b. Hotels/Conventions c. Corporate Headquarters d. High-Income Residential Areas e. Circumferential Freeways f. Support Services (Restaurants)
4. High—Rise/High-Tech—1980s:	a. High-Rise Offices and Hotels b. Low-Rise, High-Tech Buildings c. Increased Residential Densities
5. Mature Town Center—1990s to Present	a. Cultural, Social, Recreational Activity b. Maturing Government Functions c. Community Mismatch d. Infastructure and Planning Problems

1950s, creating *bedroom communities*. The operative concept here is that these sprawled residential areas served merely as places for workers to sleep, as their daytime activities were still focused on the political city and the CBD. The only type of shopping available in these rambling and spotty enclaves was *convenience retailing*. Any serious shopping venture entailed a trip to the still-dominant CBD. Finally, these spread-out areas were dependent on the private automobile and the *arterial highway layout,* like an artery pulsating with machines instead of blood. The highway arteries were arranged in a radial pattern, like spokes on a wheel converging on the yet-mighty CBD. Whereas *air conditioning* today is a taken-for-granted and a ubiquitous fact of life, it was of course not always so. Except for department stores, theaters, and the like, few homes had air conditioning prior to World War II. Wealthy southerners disliked air conditioning, preferring their high ceilings or summer homes in the Appalachians to stay cool. In any case, beginning in the 1950s and accelerating into the 1960s, air conditioning accompanied sprawl to the suburbs. Especially in the hot summer Sunbelt cities, air conditioning rapidly caught on. Automobile air conditioning only took hold in the 1960s after the too-heavy air compressors could be reduced in weight to accommodate their installation in vehicles.

Independence   During the 1960s a fundamentally different suburban landscape emerged. The suburbs became an entity in themselves. They declared their independence from the central city and the CBD. This autonomy was made possible by *freeway construction* during the decade, which facilitated movement through and around the urban area. This freeway pattern diverged significantly from the arterial highways, which were organized around the downtown. During the 1960s *regional shopping malls* sprang up in the suburbs at important freeway interchanges, making the suburbs increasingly self-sufficient. It was no longer necessary to shop in the CBD. Why not shop in the new, nearby and less-congested suburban mall with its ample

parking, where it never rains inside, and where you can enjoy considerable comparative shopping?

New *office and industrial parks* were attracted to these mall locations. Companies found locations near the malls ideal for their office operations. Industries, featuring quiet, "light," and automated (high-tech) manufacturing, located relatively close to the growing and emerging suburban business centers. *Residential diversification* occurred during the 1960s, as infilling took place on prime locations near these suburban business centers. New "downtowns" were being formed in the suburbs of large metropolitan areas of North America.

Magnets   The Hartshorn and Muller model described the 1970s as a **magnet** period. If the suburbs became independent of the city during the 1960s, then they became magnets to entice growth and investment during the 1970s. The short office buildings of the previous decade gave way to *mid-rise office buildings* of five to 12 stories. *Hotels and convention facilities* once confined to CBD locations thrived in the suburban business centers. Likewise, *corporate headquarters*, regional or national in scope, flourished in these locations, forsaking their traditional CBD locations. *Circumferential freeways* (beltways) facilitated automobile and motor truck traffic around the metropolitan area, providing superior access to these suburban business centers. Many *support services*, such as restaurants, night spots, and medical centers settled in *high-income residential areas* often hidden behind "gated" communities, where the entrance to the subdivision is guarded to exclude nonresidential traffic, and what some might consider riffraff, and other disreputable kinds of humanity! These high-income areas, only a few of which were gated, were located within commuting proximity to these suburban business centers.

High Rise/High Tech   In the 1980s, **high-rise/high-tech** became the order of the day. Office buildings became taller to accommodate more firms and more workers. Multiple-story hotels crowded into the business centers. Many low-rise (often only one floor), high-tech companies providing computer-related services settled at the periphery of these centers. Not only did the employment densities in these centers greatly increase during the 1980s, but the residential areas surrounding these centers swelled with the spread of apartments and condominiums.

Mature Town Center By the 1990s the suburban business centers had developed into **mature town centers**. Now we see the true polycentric city. These mature town centers are fully stand-alone centers that function not only as business concentrations but also as clusters of *cultural, social, and recreational activities*. Furthermore, these centers are increasingly taking on *maturing government functions*. These mature town centers offer everything that the surrounding residents need. Only rarely do suburban residents need to travel to the CBD or to the inner city. Some metropolitan areas continue to have major sports events near the downtown (Atlanta's Turner Field), but others (Detroit) have suburban locations.

However, although the evolution of suburbs into mature centers provided many benefits and conveniences, it also created several difficulties. These centers sprang up rapidly at locations where freeways formed interchanges. The result has been a series of *infrastructure and planning problems*. One consequence is that these centers often lie astride more than one local political boundary. Whereas many residential suburbs and satellite towns have names such as Santa Ana, Long Beach, Pasadena, and Burbank—all located in California—these suburban centers often have no official name or even a single postal address or ZIP code.

Another problem is the *commuting mismatch* between where people work and live. In general, there is no mismatch for the higher-income workers in these centers. These workers typically choose to live either in relatively expensive single-family detached homes or in luxury condominiums, both of which are located close to the business centers.

For the less-skilled clerical or blue-collar workers, however, the mismatch may be a serious problem. They cannot afford to live in the expensive neighborhoods that are located close to business centers. Therefore, they live far away and are commonly forced to commute long distances. These less-skilled workers either (1) live in the inner city and may have to reverse commute by bus or (2) live in the rural fringe and must travel by car because no public transportation is available.

Beyond the Hartshorn and Muller Model: Twenty-First Century Big City Suburbs

The initial decade of the Twenty-First century is seeing the proliferation of high-rise condos in the inner suburbs near interstate locations and major employment concentrations, such as office parks and shopping malls. These condos, from 12 to 30 stories tall, cater to higher-income households. Thus, the population of the suburbs is gaining density, in contrast to the earlier view of the suburbs as scattered single-family residences. Most large American metropolitan areas are experiencing these **big city suburbs**, which are simply residential extensions of the Hartshorn and Muller suburban downtowns (theirs based largely on commercial activities). When the cost of land rises, real estate developers prefer to build upward. Thus, *suburban vertical living* leads to mixed-use activities, including quality restaurants, specialty shops and niche services. Local governments often favor the development of such big city suburbs because of the greater tax base they provide.

SUBURBAN SPRAWL

Suburban sprawl is typically viewed by the media and the general public as a negative feature of metropolitan development (Box 6.1). Although the issue of sprawl has generated many pro-and-con arguments, sprawl has been, in fact, a normal and natural result of suburban growth and expansion (Box 6.2). Based on a study by Zeng, Sui, and Li (2005), we identify

BOX 6.1 CASH CROPS IN THE SUBURBS

A basic feature of the 1996 farm law, the Freedom to Farm Act, includes a provision to allow homeowners as well as tenant farmers to receive an annual cash subsidy from the U.S. Department of Agriculture (USDA), even if they raised no crops (see Morgan, Gaul, and Cohen, 2006). The purpose of the Act was to phase out government subsidies. Since 2000, the USDA has made payments of $1.3 billion to people who do not farm.

Suburban developments on land that once grew a subsidized crop such as rice, wheat, corn, or cotton are eligible for these annual payments, even though housing may have sprung up on these former agricultural fields. For example, a landowner of, say, 20 acres of a former field may build a house on one acre, leaving the other 19 acres undeveloped and thereby eligible for a "farm" payment. Real estate agents southwest of Houston, for instance, have bought up tracts of former rice land, divided it, and resold it for housing. Nonfarmer suburbanites have purchased these peripherally located lots and built housing, leaving the majority of the land "underdeveloped," though the back yard may support a family horse. One suburban owner of former rice land some miles from Houston, for example, has received more than $5,000 since 2002 on his nine acres of "agricultural land."

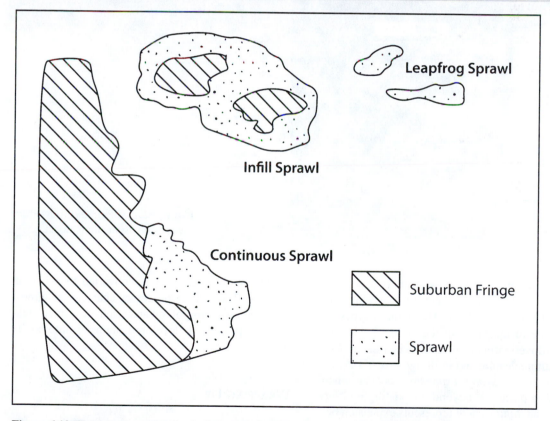

Figure 6.12 Three basic types of suburban sprawl: continuous, infill, and leapfrog development. (*Source:* After Zeng et al., 2005, p. 417.)

BOX 6.2 TECHNOLOGY AND URBAN GEOGRAPHY

USING GIS TO SIMULATE SUBURBAN SPRAWL

Suburban sprawl has been simulated using a computer model and applied to the urbanized area

surrounding the lower Lake Michigan region, including the states of Illinois, Indiana, Michigan, and Wisconsin (Torrens, 2006). The model incorporates exogenous (external) growth, as with migrants from

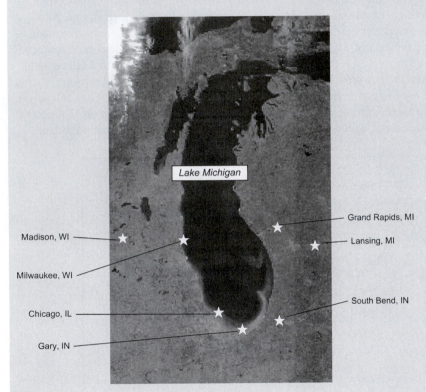

Figure B6.1 Sites in the Midwestern Megalopolis simulation model.

three types of naturally occurring suburban sprawl: continuous, infill, and leapfrog development (Figure 6.12, on page 163). These three types of sprawl relate to the three stages of the Erickson's model: spillover/specialization, dispersal/diversification, multinucleation and infilling/(Box 6.3).

Continuous suburban expansion occurs when growth takes place just beyond an existing built-up suburban area. *Infill growth* represents expansion beyond a previously leapfrog cluster. *Leapfrog sprawl* refers to the process whereby underdeveloped land

beyond the built-up area is converted to suburban land use. These three processes characterize almost all American metropolitan areas and are intrinsic features of peripheral development in an automobile society.

WRAPPING UP

The monocentric city, focused on the CBD, proudly served as the standard for North America for nearly outside the city system, and endogenous (internal) population growth or decline. Sprawl is a newer form of the traditional urbanization process that occurs on the low-density periphery of urban areas, a rather homogeneous group of single-family homes and ribbon commercial stores reflecting a piecemeal and fragmented pattern of loosely planned development that is almost entirely automobile oriented.

Torrens's simulation model of suburban sprawl was applied to the lower Lake Michigan area, the Midwestern Metropolis (Figure B6.1). The model is designed to show how sprawl develops under conditions of population diffusion from a specific land unit to compact neighborhood areas at a given radius. The Torrens sprawl model incorporates the notions of irregular growth, leapfrogging, and developments along roadways. "The simulated city-system began developing as a loose constellation of urban clusters in the immediate vicinity of [certain specified cities]. The relative dominance of Chicago and urbanized lower Wisconsin is evident" (p. 264) (Figure B6.2).

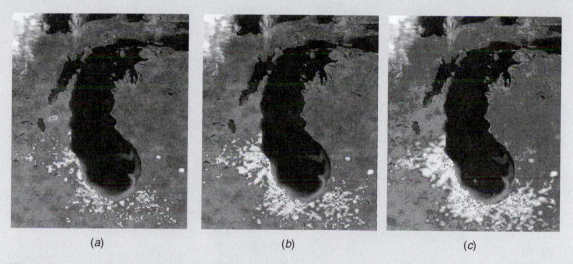

(a) (b) (c)

Figure B6.2 Simulated Midwestern sprawl over three stages: a, b, and c.

two centuries. In the latter part of the twentieth century, however, the suburbs broke away and overwhelmed the inner city in population and in economic, social, cultural, and political vigor. The CBD remains a major employment center, although agglomeration advantages have eclipsed former centralization functions. The metropolitan economy consists both of the central city with its CBD and the suburban business centers in a competitive but also symbiotic, that is, mutually beneficial relationship. Each subeconomy interacts with the others to provide a variety of services, goods, and especially information. New downtown activities are transforming the area in a variety of ways.

The new service economy is both centralized and decentralized within metropolitan areas. This economy is hungry for well-educated and technically trained workers, most of whom prefer suburban residences and who may commute to the CBD or nearby suburban business centers, the now mature town centers or edge cities. Although suburban areas may be characterized by sprawl, such

BOX 6.3 OUTSOURCING FAST-FOOD DRIVE-THROUGH ORDERS

Outsourcing occurs when a parent firm utilizes production processes or services of another firm or entity to provide cost-efficient assistance in the overall operations of the parent enterprise. The term **outsourcing** is often used to refer to an American company relying on a foreign source to provide a good or service (offshoring), as for instance Indian telephone operators fielding helpline calls from Americans.

In the example here, fast-food restaurants outsource drive-though orders. The way it works, a customer drives up to a Wendy's order window in

Columbia, South Carolina. The order is received by an attendant at a call center in Wilmington, Delaware, who flashes it, via Internet phone lines, to the cook in Columbia. When the driver reaches the pickup window, the order is ready. The purpose of the telecommunications outsourcing of drive-through orders: (1) faster service and (2) eliminating confusion in the no longer needed order booth, where several orders would otherwise be jumbled. It is retail outsourcing, where one call center with a dozen agents can handle the orders of a dozen restaurants at peak hours.

development is a natural expansion process. While the new telecommunications-based suburbanization has grown apace and has challenged the central city economy and the CBD, the continued, although weak, symbiotic links between city and suburbs provides opportunities for progress and positive change for the future.

READINGS

Erickson, Rodney A. 1983. "The Evolution of the Suburban Space Economy," *Urban Geography*, Vol. 4, pp. 95–121.

Ford, Larry R. 2003. *America's New Downtowns: Revitalization or Reinvention* (Baltimore, MD: Johns Hopkins University Press).

Gong, Hongmian, and James O. Wheeler 2002. "The Location and Suburbanization of Business and Professional Services in the Atlanta Metropolitan Area," *Growth and Change*, Vol. 33, pp. 341–369.

Hartshorn, Truman A., and Peter O. Muller 1989. "Suburban Downtowns and the Transformation of Metropolitan Atlanta's Business Landscape," *Urban Geography*, Vol. 10, pp. 375–395.

Morgan, D., G. M. Gaul, and S. Cohen, 2006. "Subsidized Suburbia," *Washington Post National Weekly*, July 10–16, pp. 6–8.

Nelson, Marla K. 2006. "Interseating Producer Services: The Public Accounting Industry in Chicago and Minneapolis-St. Paul," *Urban Geography*, Vol. 27, pp. 45–71.

Torrens, Paul M. 2006. "Simulating Sprawl," *Annals of the Association of American Geographers*, Vol. 96, pp. 248–275.

Zeng, H., D. Z. Sui, and S. Li, 2005. "Linking Urban Field Theory with GIS and Remote Sensing to Detect Signatures of Rapid Urbanization on the Landscape: Toward a New Approach for Characterizing Urban Sprawl," *Urban Geography*, Vol. 26, pp. 410–434.

CHAPTER 7

LANDSCAPES OF PRODUCTION

We will now discuss in a little more detail the struggle for existence.

—CHARLES DARWIN *The Origin of Species,* 1859

Industrialization—manufacturing—has been the principal engine that has driven city-building since the start of the Industrial Revolution in Britain just before the turn of the nineteenth century. The Industrial Revolution spread from Britain to the United States and Canada, to Western Europe, to Japan and Australia, and to other developed or industrial countries. Today, it has come to flourish in the People's Republic of China, Korea, Taiwan, and Singapore. In the United States, manufacturing cities, first located along the East Coast and later throughout the Midwest, grew to dominate the urban landscape, only much later spreading to Los Angeles and other selected urban centers in the West and South. The past 50 years or so, however, have seen a fundamental change in U.S. manufacturing jobs as the advanced service economy has surged in importance. Not only has this transformation from manufacturing to services impacted different urban centers and different regions of the United States and Canada in particular ways, but it has also affected the location of the industrial landscapes within American metropolitan areas.

The purpose of this chapter is to lay out certain theoretical and conceptual notions involving industrial location and locational change. We also focus on specific empirical evidence of manufacturing change, both at the interurban (between cities) and intrametropolitan (within cities) levels. We begin by considering basic and nonbasic economic activities that relate to urban population growth. Next we provide a generalized historical overview of urban industrial change, focusing on the traditional industrial city, the twentieth-century industrial metropolis, and the postindustrial (advanced capitalist) metropolitan area. After reviewing certain conceptual frameworks for understanding the location of manufacturing at both the interurban and intraurban levels, we provide empirical information on recent changes in the urban industrial landscape. We end the chapter by examining political economy approaches. The basic themes of this chapter relate to (1) the decline in manufacturing employment in the developed countries and the rise of the new advanced service economy and (2) the different locational requirements of the industrial and service economy within metropolitan areas and within different regions of the United States.

UNDERSTANDING THE ECONOMIES OF CITIES

We want to start by making a basic point. People living in cities must have some way to make a living. The most basic division of labor is between those economic activities that directly produce the means of survival (e.g., food), and those that do not. For cities, economic activity has an inescapable impact on the spatial form of the city: cities must accommodate economic activities. As the nature of economies change over time, the nature of urban economic landscapes also necessarily changes. We begin this chapter by exploring some fundamental aspects of urban economic activity. Our intent here is not to present a course in economics, but rather to provide a grounding for our later discussion of the impact of economic activity on urban landscapes.

Basic and Nonbasic Economic Activities

Every city must generate income as a result of its economic activities. At the most fundamental level, we can divide economic activities into two groups—basic and nonbasic. This dichotomy allows us to start to understand something about urban economies.

Basic vs. Nonbasic Activites **Basic** economic activities *generate* income for the residents of the city. These activities export goods and services produced within the city and sell them outside of the city—the engine for economic growth. Up until the last several decades, basic activities were typically associated with manufacturing—the making of things through a system of divided labor. Today, advanced services are also an important part of basic urban activities.

In contrast, **nonbasic** economic activities *circulate* income within the city—rather than bringing in income from the outside. Nonbasic activities were traditionally associated with retailing and other consumer services, although we will soon see that this view has changed to include advanced services. Figure 7.1 illustrates the differences between basic and nonbasic activities.

All economic activity is classified as either basic or nonbasic, as the following equation shows:

$$TA = BA + NBA$$

In this equation, TA stands for total economic activity, BA stands for basic economic activity, and NBA represents nonbasic economic activity.

Multipliers One of the reasons that we make the distinction between basic and nonbasic economic activities is that basic activity is the engine for economic growth for the city. Without basic activity,

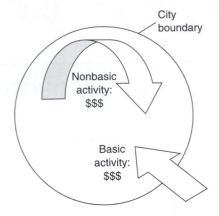

Figure 7.1 Conceptual diagram of the difference between basic and nonbasic economic activities.

no income will be brought to the city. In a very real sense, every resident of the city depends on the income brought into the city by the people working in the basic sector. Consider the hair stylist. His or her income is based on people coming into the shop and paying for the service. Without someone bringing in the income, the hair stylist cannot make a living. If the shop patron lives within the urban area, say, next door to the hair stylist shop, the transaction would be considered a nonbasic activity, because money is simply being circulated within the city. If, however, the client lives outside the urban area—perhaps a business person traveling from another city—the financial exchange is classified as basic, because money is being brought into the city.

One of the ways that basic activity supports other city residents is through primary and secondary multipliers. Together these multipliers are the impact of basic activity on the total employment of the city. Typically we think in terms of adding one additional job in the basic sector to the city. For example, a manufacturing company located in the city that is doing well might hire an additional worker to increase production to meet rising demand. The multiplier can be shown using the terms in the first equation:

$$TA = m \times BA$$

In this equation, *m* is the multiplier—it tells how much of an overall impact this one extra job will have on the urban economy. For example, if there is no multiplier effect, adding 10 jobs to the local urban economy will net only 10 jobs. In that case, *m* = 1. In reality, however, multipliers are always greater than 1. That means that some nonbasic activity will be supported based on the income brought into the city by the workers in the basic sector. The new workers will, for example, acquire housing (either renting or buying), they will have to eat (buy groceries), they will need transportation to work (either using public transportation or buying a car). All of these activities require spending some of the income earned, but *within* the local area. These nonbasic activities circulate the income, and generate extra jobs in the local economy. If the factory hires 100 new workers, perhaps the grocery store will need to expand to keep up, and perhaps a new gas station will open up. So the total impact of one additional job in the basic sector is greater than that one job.

Circular and Cumulative Causation

One of the reasons that we need to know something about multipliers is that they play an important role in an important theory called **circular** and **cumulative causation**. In this theory, **primary multipliers** describe the **direct economic linkages** between a basic activity and other local businesses with which it might do business. **Backward linkages** are those between a company and other companies that provide it with materials or services that it uses in its own production process (e.g., raw materials or equipment repair). **Forward linkages** are those in which a company sells its goods or services to other local businesses. Here, primary multipliers increase employment in the city due to direct connections between a company and other companies in the same city.

Secondary multipliers are more like our previous example—the money spent by workers employed in the basic sector circulates within the local urban economy, several times and for multiple ends, and supports the employment of nonbasic workers. For example, a basic worker who spends, say, $100 on groceries within the local metropolitan economy will contribute a portion of the $100 to help pay the wages of the produce manager, who in turn spends a part of his or her wages on a fast-food item, which contributes to the salary of an Elise Watts, who works at Burger King. And so on. Eventually, if enough basic sector workers (and nonbasic sector workers supported by them) are able to live in the city, new kinds of goods and services will be offered or produced. Think, for example, about car dealerships. Many small cities in the United States have Ford or Chevrolet dealerships—these companies sell standard U.S.-made automobiles at relatively low costs. Not every city has a Lexus or an Audi dealership, however. For these cars—more features, higher prices—a larger population is needed. A similar example may be medical services—all cities will have doctors, but only larger cities will have neurosurgeons. This relationship between the population of an area and the type of goods and services found there is called **threshold**. There needs to be a threshold of population with enough spending power to support certain kinds of higher-level economic activities.

When we put together primary and secondary multipliers, we have the basic insight of circular and cumulative causation—economic activities that bring income and jobs into a local urban economy feed growth, which then feeds more growth, and so on. The process of economic growth is circular and cumulative—it keeps going, feeding off of itself. Now, of course, you are thinking that this picture may be a bit too optimistic. You are correct. Smaller places, in particular, are economically vulnerable—if a local factory closes or has to cut production because their product is not doing well, the process will work in reverse. The grocer may have to lay off workers, a gas station may have to close, and eventually people may have to leave. It was once thought that when cities grew to a sufficiently large size—say 250,000 people—they were largely immune to the process working in reverse, at least with regard to population. With large enough populations, local urban economies are going to be robust and be able to withstand downturns. However, large cities can and have experienced population loss, especially those in the old manufacturing areas of the Midwest, such as Buffalo, Chicago, Cleveland, Detroit, and many more.

Putting these pieces together, we see that production, at a fundamental level, must be defined as basic economic activity—activity that generates income for the local community by exporting a product or service. As industrial capitalism grew and developed, manufacturing was considered to be a basic activity. Factories brought in new basic sector workers, who then supported local consumer-oriented service sector workers. Services were always thought to be local and nonbasic.

As we discussed in Chapters 3 and 5, however, the economy has changed radically since the 1970s. Although manufacturing still generates most of the nation's aggregate income, it employs a much smaller segment of the overall workforce. By replacing people with machines in the process of producing things, manufacturing employs many fewer workers than it used to. In one sense, this process represents increased productivity, that is, producing more things with fewer people. In another sense, however, these economic changes present us with a difficulty: if manufacturing no longer provides the jobs that support the entire local urban economy, then what does?

One answer is services—but not the way we have been talking about services so far. Here we refer to **advanced services**. For example, the grocery store is not a basic economic activity because it does not bring income into the city from outside (unless it is particularly large or offers specialty goods that people from surrounding communities will travel for). Rather it primarily circulates income already present within the local urban economy. Indeed, as we have seen, the global economy increasingly relies on these high-end services to coordinate its far-flung activities. So, instead of the factory worker being the basic sector worker who supports the local economy, lawyers and accountants and investors now play that role by attracting customers from outside the city. In some ways the multipliers associated with high-end service workers are greater than the multipliers associated with

industrial workers because service workers make, and thus spend locally, more money. Thus, the shift from a manufacturing-based metropolitan area to an advanced service-based center results in greater multiplier effects. Cleveland, Ohio, for example, which suffered massive economic shocks as manufacturing jobs were lost, has now regained economic strength as the new advanced service sector has gradually achieved significance. Secondary multiplier effects are now bringing prosperity to many, though not all.

Agglomeration

The concept of **agglomeration economies** holds a classic place in urban and economic geography. This classic concept formed a part of Alfred Weber's (1909) theory of the location of industries. The advantages of agglomerative locations have been applied both to interurban and intraurban location of manufacturing, as well as more recently to services.

Agglomeration refers to clustering, or a locational concentration of activities. Economies is a synonym for savings. In other words agglomeration economies reflect savings that can be achieved through a concentration of economic activities—manufacturing in our example. The result may be industrial districts or industrial parks.

Two types of agglomeration economies have been identified, **localization economies** and **urbanization economies**. In the former, savings occur when there is a concentration of *similar* kinds of manufacturing. Classic examples include steelmaking in Pittsburgh, automobile manufacture in Detroit, and cattle slaughtering (meat packing) in Chicago.

Urbanization economies are savings that accrue when there is a clustering of *unlike* activities, as occurs in urban areas. Here the benefits are the result of sharing the urban infrastructure, such as highways, water and sewage systems, and a skilled workforce. Urbanization economies are extremely important in understanding why industry concentrates in metropolitan areas and helps explain the concept of industrialization in the evolution of American cities.

Thus, agglomeration economies reflects the reduction in average cost of a unit of production. In the case of urbanization economies, the cost reductions result from the shared urban infrastructure; should the same firm locate in a remote rural area, the firm would have to provide itself with the infrastructure components on its own—at a considerably higher cost. Before the massive transformation to the advanced service economy, it follows that the major manufacturing centers of the early and middle twentieth century were the largest cities: New York, Chicago, Detroit, Cleveland, Pittsburgh, Buffalo, Milwaukee.

INTERURBAN INDUSTRIAL PRODUCTION AND LOCATION

In this section we briefly survey two conceptual models of industrial production and locations as they relate to urban areas and city growth: the growth pole model and the Stanback model. Here our interest is on manufacturing location and change among a system or group of urban centers.

The Growth Pole Model

The **growth pole model** is a way of showing changes in the location of manufacturing over time among a group of urban areas. The model may apply on a national scale as with the United States or Canada, or a regional scale as with the U.S. West, or at a state level as with Alabama or Michigan. An essential component of the growth pole model is that the location and productivity of manufacturing activity is inherently uneven geographically. There will be one **key center** and many smaller ones. The key center will be the growth pole. It will have a disproportionate level of industrial productivity and will experience the most rapid population growth. Examples are Los Angeles in the U.S. West, Vancouver in the Canadian Pacific Southwest, Detroit in Michigan, and Birmingham in Alabama. The rest of the area outside the key urban growth center is the **periphery**, a slow-growth set of urban areas as well as nonmetropolitan rural regions. New and expanded industrial enterprises will be attracted to the key or growth urban center, leading to futher population growth and economic prosperity.

At the same time, manufacturing establishments in the periphery may be linked to firms in the growth center through purchases of goods and services as centers for the sale of goods produced in the key urban area. These kinds of links between the growth center or core of the region and the periphery are known as **trickle-down processes**. These are positive elements in regional urban industrial growth.

Negative elements are known as **polarization processes**, or the harmful effects of uneven geographical growth. Small manufacturing establishments in the periphery are often unable to compete with rival industries in the urban growth center. Typically, the manufacturing firms in the largest urban center will be most efficient, have lower costs, and be more high-tech oriented. In addition, outmigration of workers from the periphery to the key urban growth center will drain the lagging region of its most highly skilled workers, who will be attracted to the high wage rate of the growth center. Capital investment is much more likely to be made in the large, more profitable urban center, siphoning off funds from the small peripheral urban centers and further retarding their growth. Thus, polarization implies a wide and often long-lasting gap between the key urban centers and the peripheral centers, often more powerful than the trickle-down effect.

The Stanback Model

Whereas the growth pole model is a conceptual or theoretical model, the Stanback Model is largely based on empirical observation and data. Thomas Stanback has written several books in which he examines the transformation of the American metropolitan economies from production based to service based. The **Stanback model** is characterized by the radical decline in manufacturing, especially the loss of jobs over the last quarter of a century, and the corresponding explosion of jobs in business and professional services and in the nonprofit sector (Figure 7.2). There are two basic tenets of the Stanback model. First, metropolitan areas

Figure 7.2 A once-productive factory, Barrow Manufacturing Co. in Statham, Georgia, now shut down and abandoned.

that were highly specialized in industrial production experienced a slower and more difficult adjustment to the new service economy. The massive employment losses in manufacturing made it more difficult for metropolitan areas such as Buffalo and Cleveland to develop flourishing service-based economies. In contrast, metropolitan area such as Atlanta and Phoenix, which never were major manufacturing centers, quickly became leaders in the new urban service economy and experienced major population growth.

A second tenet of the Stanback model is that major corporations require many kinds of *advanced* or *producer services*, including financial and legal services, advertising, accounting, auditing, marketing, and insurance activities as well as central administrative services (headquarters). A metropolitan area having a concentration of corporate headquarters thereby creates the need for these services both from within the metropolitan area as well as from other large metropolitan areas around the United States.

The changes Stanback wrote about are referred to as **structural changes**, meaning changes that are permanent, not fleeting or temporary. (Take a sheet of paper and fold it crisply down the middle. The crease cannot be removed no matter how hard you try to smooth it. You have created a structural change.) These structural changes of the past 25 to 30 years will not be reversed and, in fact, are

being accelerated by the new information age. In summarizing Stanback's model, we may paraphrase and update a statement issued by the U.S. National Research Council:

> Powerful and deeply rooted structural changes in the national and international economy over the past quarter of a century have transformed urban areas and the economic functions they perform. A new metropolitan system has emerged, with a growing polarization between urban places where corporate headquarters and producer services are concentrated and those urban centers that have been more specialized in manufacturing activities.

The massive decline in the goods-producing sectors as providers of jobs in the U.S. metropolitan economies has had major consequences for metropolitan areas in general. Stanback (2002) has offered five key observations in this regard:

1. The increasing importance of services as a source of job creation;
2. The dominant role of metropolitan, in contrast with nonmetropolitan, economies;
3. The economic specialization of metropolitan areas such as in manufacturing, finance, health services, and resort amenities as broken down by population size;
4. The wide-ranging differences in patterns of growth in employment, earnings, and income among metropolitan areas;
5. The increased importance of nonearned income as a source of aggregate demand within metropolitan areas.

In addition to the dominant growth of service jobs in large metropolitan areas, and the decline in manufacturing jobs, metropolitan areas are overrepresented in employment totals compared with nonmetropolitan areas. For example, the 170 largest metropolitan areas (those with a population of more than 250,000), which make up 50 percent of all metropolitan economies, account for 90 percent of all metropolitan employment. Moreover, the 21 largest metropolitan areas (2 million or more in population), which constitute only 12 percent of the 170 largest metropolitan areas, account for 40 percent of all metropolitan jobs. Metropolitan areas with important resort and retirement components are among the fastest-growing centers, whereas metropolitan areas that emphasize manufacturing are the slowest-growing centers. Consider fast-growth Charlotte, North Carolina, in contrast with slow-growth Youngstown, Ohio. Youngstown, in the core of the manufacturing belt, has lost manufacturing jobs and has not been successful in attracting investment in the advanced service sector. In contrast, Charlotte, ranking only behind New York among the top banking centers in the United States, has the charisma to entice a variety of jobs in the advanced services. Because manufacturing in general is no longer a job creator, other sectors, including the nonearned income sector, contribute to aggregate demand. Nonearned income, including dividends, interest, rent payments, and transfer payments (Social Security, Medicare, Medicaid, and welfare), indirectly creates the demand for labor and thus new jobs.

Table 7.1 illustrates the percentage change in U.S. employment among industrial categories between 1960 and 1997. Not surprisingly, the greatest decrease is in manufacturing, a drop from 31 percent of the U.S. workforce in 1960 to 15 percent in 1997. The largest increase is in services, up from just over 13 percent in 1960 to nearly 30 percent in 1997. Other notable changes include the decrease in employment percentage in the federal government and the increase in local government jobs. Retail jobs have also shown growth over this time period.

Manufacturing versus Service Cities One example highlights the differences among large U.S. metropolitan areas, following the Stanback model. Corporate headquarters were classified into seven economic sectors for the 30 largest U.S. metropolitan areas. The percentage of headquarters in each of the seven sectors was calculated and the 30 metropolitan areas were grouped into two essential types: manufacturing centers and service centers. Table 7.2 shows the percentage distribution in these seven categories between Cleveland (a manufacturing center) and Phoenix (a service-based center). The basic differences between these two metropolitan areas are (1) the high percentage of jobs in the manufacturing sector for Cleveland (49 percent) compared with Phoenix (18 percent) and (2) the high percentage of jobs in services in Phoenix (30 percent) in contrast with Cleveland (17 percent). Other differences between the two cities may be noted for construction, wholesaling, and finance,

Table 7.1 Percentage Change in U.S. Employment among Industrial Sectors, 1960 and 1997

Industrial Sectors	1960	1997
Mining	1.31	0.48
Construction	5.32	4.63
Manufacturing	30.97	15.21
TCU[a]	7.38	5.21
Wholesale Trade	5.54	5.42
Retail	15.46	17.94
FIRE[b]	4.92	5.78
Services	13.69	29.37
Government		
Federal	4.19	2.20
Local	11.21	13.75
Total	100.00	100.00

Source: U.S. Bureau of Labor Statistics.
[a]Transportation, Communications, Utilities.
[b]Finance, Insurance, and Real Estate.

Table 7.2 Percentage Corporate Headquarters in Cleveland and Phoenix by Economic Sectors

Economic Sectors	Cleveland	Phoenix
Manufacturing	49.4	17.8
Services	17.1	29.7
FIRE[a]	5.7	12.6
Construction	4.5	10.2
Wholesale Trade	11.4	17.8
TCM[b]	3.3	3.4
Retail	8.6	8.5
Total	100.0	100.0

Source: Compiled by author.
[a]Finance, Insurance, and Real Estate.
[b]Transportation, Communications, Utilities.

insurance, and real estate (FIRE). The significance of the contrasting percentage between Cleveland and Phoenix is that Phoenix, the service-based center, made a smooth transition to the new advanced service economy and enjoyed rapid population growth. In contrast, Cleveland, the manufacturing-based center, has lost many industrial jobs since 1970, had a difficult transition to the new advanced service economy, and the metropolitan area faced slow population growth, with the city of Cleveland actually losing population since 1970.

Figure 7.3 shows the regional distribution of manufacturing-based and service-based U.S. metropolitan areas. All of the metropolitan areas in the Midwest emphasize manufacturing, except for the state capitals of Columbus, Ohio, and Indianapolis, Indiana. Likewise, the East Coast cities are manufacturing-based, except for Washington and Boston.

In California, only San Diego has a service emphasis. All of the midcontinent centers in Texas (Dallas-Fort Worth, Houston, San Antonio) are classified as manufacturing centers. In contrast, within the Sunbelt, only Tampa is classified as a manufacturing center.

Recent U.S. Manufacturing Changes The United States has been losing manufacturing jobs for decades, though the media in general highlights industrial job loss as something contemporary. "A manufacturing plant in Oshkosh, Wisconsin, has closed and 120 people are out of work!" And so on.

Between 1994 and 2002, for example, the United States lost more than 3.7 million jobs in manufacturing, from 18.1 million jobs in 1994 to 14.4 million in 2002—a decline of more than 20 percent. During the same time period, the share of manufacturing

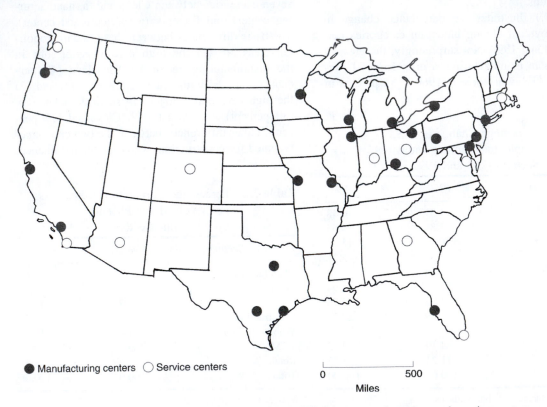

● Manufacturing centers   ○ Service centers

0   500
Miles

Figure 7.3 The largest 30 U.S. metropolitan areas classified into manufacturing and service centers. (*Source:* Wheeler, 1986.)

jobs to all U.S. jobs dropped by approximately 6 percent from 18.7 percent in 1994 to 12.8 percent in 2002. The states with the highest levels of job losses from 1994 to 2002 are the Southern states of Alabama, Mississippi, North Carolina, and South Carolina—along with Michigan (the automobile industry), Delaware, and Rhode Island (Bowen, 2006).

Job losses in manufacturing in the United States varies by industrial sector and by region. For example, job losses in the iron and steel industry and in automobile manufacturing greatly impacted the Midwest, and other particular cities. In the South the hardest hit industries were textiles and apparel. The automobile industry—thanks in large part to foreign manufacturers—has seen employment growth in the South, somewhat offsetting other job losses.

What is nearly always forgotten, however, especially by the media, is the fact that U.S. manufacturing productivity is increasing. Based on manufacturing output per labor hour, the period 1994 to 2002 shows an increase in productivity of 42 percent, compared with only a 23 percent increase in productivity for all U.S. nonfarm businesses. Likewise, exports of U.S. manufactured goods rose by 38 percent, reaching $555 million in 2002. U.S. imports of manufactured goods, in contrast, jumped by 75 percent between 1994 and 2002, totaling more than 925 million dollars, leaving a negative trade balance of some $420 million in 2002.

Manufacturing job losses have not been uniform across the United States. Bowen (2006) studied manufacturing job loss using data on trade-induced job loss. He finds that the primary pattern of losses due to trade is correlated with U.S. areas of low income and low educational attainment. Moreover, these poor areas that are most negatively impacted by the North America Free Trade Association (NAFTA) are also the areas which are least competitive in attracting alternate industry. The states most negatively impacted by NAFTA are the Southern states of Alabama, Mississippi, North Carolina, and Tennessee. In the Pacific Northwest, Oregon and Washington have suffered from trade-induced job loss, as well as Maine in the Northeast.

Despite serious problems in the U.S. manufacturing sector, certain recent developments have led to high-technology change, flexible production (Box 7.1) and just-in-time delivery (Box 7.2).

The 1980s Rust Belt According to Stanback, metropolitan areas with a high concentration of employment in manufacturing had a more difficult time in adjusting to the new service economy than centers that already had a strong service component. Thus, Cleveland, Buffalo, Chicago, and Detroit, for example, were slow to make the transition to the new service economy. When manufacturing jobs were lost, the workforce was generally ill prepared to shift to services, especially advanced or producer services (Figure 7.3).

Figure 7.4 shows the manufacturing employment change from 1980 to 1987 in one part of the so-called **Rust Belt**: Indiana, Ohio, and the lower peninsula of Michigan. The term Rust Belt implies an area of aging factories, decreasing production of such products as steel and automobiles, and diminishing populations. Figure 7.4 shows the 40,000 job loss in Cleveland and the 30,000 job loss in Gary, Indiana, the steelmaking center at the southern tip of Lake Michigan. Notable losses also occurred in Cincinnati, Indianapolis, and Detroit. Job loss in manufacturing characterized all metropolitan areas in the region, except for South Bend in Indiana, Columbus and Dayton in Ohio, and Grand Rapids in Michigan (Box 7.3).

In contrast to the job losses in manufacturing during the 1980s, service employment increased in all metropolitan areas in this region (Figure 7.5). The largest gains were in Detroit. Cleveland, which suffered the greatest job loss in manufacturing, was able to gain some 50,000 service jobs between 1980 and 1987.

Comparison of Figures 7.4 and 7.5 shows the changes in the metropolitan economies in a part of the Midwest during the 1980s. Fortunately, the steady growth in service employment in subsequent decades has more than offset the decreases in manufacturing jobs. Consequently, the term Rust Belt is now of only historic significance.

BOX 7.1 FLEXIBLE PRODUCTION

Henry Ford was the first to develop efficient mass manufacturing production with the Model A and Model T Ford. This system of mass production of identical automobiles allowed for economies of scale or savings per unit of production. This system came to be known as **Fordism** and was the dominant technological system for three or four generations. Fordism gradually spread from the United States to Canada, Western Europe, and Japan. Fordism relied upon mass markets to consume the growing output of large, highly efficient manufacturing plants. At some point after approximately 1980, consumption of mass-produced goods lagged behind global production capacity of these goods, leading to new technologies and a post-Fordism system of production.

This new system is known as **flexible production**, which relies upon advanced computer software development and high-quality telecommunications. Large, centrally controlled corporate and labor relations became transformed away from mass production to a flexible system whereby programmable tools and robots replicate a series of actions to produce many somewhat different products on the same "assembly" line. Whereas in Fordism, manufacturers made products that the wholesaler or retailer is/was more or less forced to buy, flexible production now allows the retailer—especially large retailers such as Wal-Mart—to order the kind and number of products it wants from the manufacturer. For example, the Kroger grocery corporations, headquartered out of Cincinnati, can now tell Breyers ice cream how many half-pound orders of Breyers French Vanilla, Cherry Vanilla, and Chocolate it wants, as well as how many half-gallons of Kroger Chocolate Chip, Strawberry, and Natural Vanilla it wishes to order. The flexible production system

at Breyers processes and produces the Kroger order.

In addition to the flexible manufacturing system that relies on an integrated system of design, manufacturer, and distribution, a flexible employment system has come into place, in part supplanting unionized labor. This system entails increased reliance upon part-time and temporary workers and on subcontracting. Moreover, production lines are fed continuous information about external market demand directly from large retailers to speed distribution of desired products straight to them. For example, a carpet sales office may communicate directly with a carpet mill as to how many square feet of beige carpet it wants delivered in two days and how many square feet of light blue. The operator at the carpet mill, where there are very few workers but highly flexible (programmable) carpet machines, pushes a button and now the machine will produce the requested X number of square feet of beige carpet, rolled up for easy transport by the 18-wheeler waiting for loading behind the carpet mill. Both large and small companies are involved in flexible production, giving consumers ever-wider choices.

As Scott (1988, p. 182) has noted, "modern capitalist production systems have evidently been evolving over the last couple of decades away from relatively rigid Fordist industrial structures towards more flexible forms of production organizations." The result has been a "pronounced displacement of the locational foundations of modern capitalism." Modern flexible production systems avoid older inner-city locations and seek out areas in the suburban periphery. At the regional level the Sunbelt metropolitan areas, which have had little direct contact with "big industry" and labor unions, have become favored locations for flexible production.

BOX 7.2   TECHNOLOGY AND URBAN GEOGRAPHY

JUST-IN-TIME DELIVERY

Somewhat related operationally to flexible production is the practice of **just-in-time** (JIT) delivery. JIT is an inventory strategy that eliminates inventory and warehousing. Instead of storing the many parts that go into a finished product in a nearby warehouse to avoid running short of parts and thus having to shut down the assembly line, parts are delivered just in time to be used on the assembly line. Huge warehousing inventory costs are eliminated. JIT depends on an efficient transportation system, whereby the same part, for example, may be delivered several times in one day. The entire process is driven by a series of signals, or *kanbans*, that inform the production process when the next part is needed. Thus, new stock is ordered when the stock drops to the re-order level. JIT has proven to be extremely cost effective.

Traditionally, manufacturers simply created products that were then made available to retailers, the manufacturers pushing the retailers (Figure B7.1). Led by retailing giant Wal-Mart, retailers are now pushing manufacturers to create exactly and specifically what the retailer wants and when and where it must be delivered, just in time.

Henry Ford in 1922 recognized the benefits of a small but adequate inventory, but the transportation system at the time (still rail-dependent) did not permit JIT delivery: "We have found in buying materials that it is not worthwhile to buy for other than immediate needs. With bad transportation one has to carry larger stocks."

JIT practices are common in the automobile industry in the United States. In Japan, and now the United States, Toyota Motor Corporation is well-known for early JIT operations, as Japanese land was in short supply. Since it is extremely costly to shut down an assembly line, Toyota usually uses two suppliers of parts and forms long-term relationships with suppliers rather than short-term, price-based competitive ties. The goal is to maintain high-quality relations with Toyota's entire supplier network.

Increasingly, manufacturers are moving to made-to-order products, instead of carrying large stocks of finished goods, another example of the retail push. Made-to-order manufacturing is greatly facilitated by the JIT system. *Kanban*!

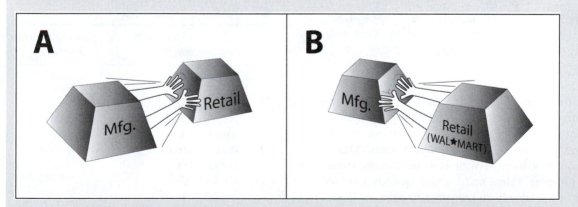

Figure B7.1 In the traditional industrial system, manufacturers created products that were then made available to retailers (a). However, led by such retail giants as Wal-Mart, increasingly retailers are telling manufacturers what they want, how many, in what color, in what shape, and where and when delivery should be made (b).

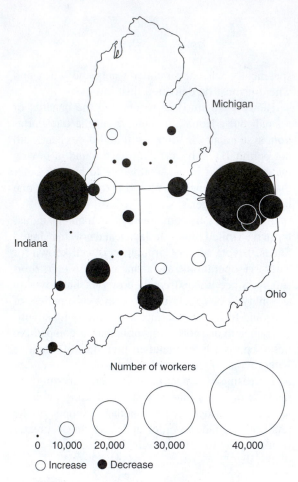

Number of workers

0   10,000   20,000   30,000   40,000

○ Increase   ● Decrease

Figure 7.4 Change in manufacturing employment, 1980–1987, by metropolitan area in Indiana, Ohio, and the lower peninsula of Michigan.

Human Talent and the Location of High-Technology Industry The urban geography of human resources or talent is highly concentrated in only a few major U.S. metropolitan areas. "Talent is strongly associated with high-technology industrial location. Talent and high-technology industry work independently and together to generate higher regional incomes" (Florida, 2002, p. 174). Certain metropolitan areas attract talented people, especially highly educated people (human capital) who are mobile in their choice of location. There is a strong

relationship between amenities or quality of life in selected metropolitan areas and their ability to attract talented workers, as well as the attraction of higher wages. Both market (economic) and non-market (quality of life) forces operate in these cities. Florida (2005, p. 54) provides an especially insightful measure of talented people with his index of the number of software workers per million population by metropolitan area (Table 7.3). It is the same familiar list of centers that are the leaders in the advanced service economy, with San Jose (Silicon Valley) and Washington, D.C., leading the parade.

Figure 7.6 shows the number of professional and technical workers per thousand population in 50 U.S. metropolitan areas. Eight metropolitan areas stand out: Atlanta, Austin, Denver, Minneapolis-St. Paul, Richmond, San Francisco, and Washington. Mighty Los Angeles, the nation's second largest metropolitan area, ranks fiftieth in per capita professional and technical workers, due largely to a lesser-skilled Latino population. The most educated metropolitan area in the United States is Washington, D.C., with approximately 42 percent of the population holding a bachelor's degree or above in 1990. Five other metropolitan areas had more than 30 percent of their population with bachelor's degrees or above: Atlanta, Austin, Boston, San Francisco, and Seattle. Las Vegas, ranked

Table 7.3 Software Workers per Million by Metropolitan Areas

Rank	Metropolitan Areas	Software Workers per Million
1	San Jose, CA	24,348
2	Washington, D.C.	22,562
3	San Francisco, CA	17,633
4	Boston, MA	16,871
5	Atlanta, GA	11,633
6	Dallas-Fort Worth, TX	11,345
7	Denver, CO	11,258
8	Oakland, CA	9,700
9	Minneapolis, MN	9,408
10	Raleigh-Durham, NC	9,309
11	Austin, TX	9,157
12	Seattle, WA	8,366

Source: Florida, 2005, p. 54.

BOX 7.3   RESTRUCTURING AMERICA'S RUST BELT CITIES

Wilson and Wouters (2003) have focused on two themes in explaining how former Midwestern manufacturing rust belt cities became economically transformed during the mid-1980s and 1990s. Their two themes were (1) the accelerated competition among Midwestern cities in the new global era and (2) the role of entrepreneurial leadership and growth coalitions within those cities. These two forces gradually brought about the restructuring of the rust belt centers and the growth of service-sector jobs. The shrinking, closing, and relocating of manufacturing jobs had massive impacts on city populations and municipal revenues.

Table B7.1 shows the decline in population and in manufacturing employment for the cities of Cleveland and St. Louis between 1970 and 1990. The city population in both Cleveland and St. Louis dropped by over 30 percent. The number of manufacturing jobs in the two cities combined dropped by more than 120,000, a 52 percent decline. Significant in this decline were the closure or relocation of major manufacturing plants, such as U.S. Steel in Cleveland and Chrysler Plant No. 1 in St. Louis.

Rust belt cities began seriously competing for new jobs and investments as manufacturing employment dramatically declined. The Midwestern cities had to compete on a global scale, recognizing that investment decisions made in New York, London, and Tokyo, as well as a host of regional centers, impacted their economic recovery in the rapidly evolving new service economy. These cities had to discover and highlight their strengths and comparative advantages, the Mississippi River in St. Louis and

Lake Erie in Cleveland, for example. The city image was important in global competition. Jobs were being created in advanced services, such as financial and legal firms and in high-technology enterprises. White-collar markets grew all across America, raising demand for quality housing, entertainment, and restaurants, for example.

Entrepreneurial leadership became manifest through growth coalitions made up of builders, realtors, developers, the media, government actors such as mayors, and dominant corporations. For example, in St. Louis Anheuser-Busch, Monsanto, and Ralston Purina played prominent roles. The leadership involved cooperation between public and private interests. The results were efforts at downtown revitalization; inner-city gentrification; the transformation of the CBD to advanced service employment; entertainment, museums, and cultural venues; the construction of sports stadiums and the sport complexes; and often waterfront development. The purpose was to market a nourishing physical, business, and social environment that would attract investment and create jobs.

The result of (1) accelerated competition among Midwestern rust belt cities in the new global economy and (2) innovative entrepreneurial leadership within public-private growth coalitions has been that the former rust belt cities have established a much stronger economic base and have gradually restructured themselves into the contemporary service sector.[1]

[1] This textbox is based on Wilson and Wouters, 2003.

Table B7.1   Population and Manufacturing Employment Change

	Cleveland		St. Louis	
	1970	1990	1970	1990
Population	751,046	505,616	662,236	396,685
Manufacturing Employees	131,000	59,400	97,600	48,700

Source: Wilson and Wouters, 2003.

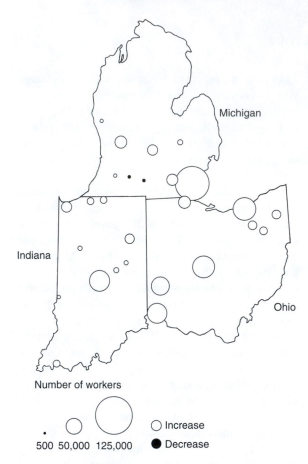

Number of workers

500 50,000 125,000

○ Increase
● Decrease

Figure 7.5 Change in service employment, 1980–1987, by metropolitan area in Indiana, Ohio, and the lower peninsula of Michigan.

fiftieth, had just 14 percent of its population holding bachelor's degrees or above. Not only is talent strongly associated with the location of high-technology industry, but high-technology industry generates regional population growth and high metropolitan and regional incomes.

Another feature of human talent is reflected in patent activity. While the traditional sources of patents has been in metropolitan areas in the U.S. Northeast and Midwest, Johnson and Brown (2004) find that there has been a regional "inversion" in patents granted over the past 25 years. It is now the Pacific Northwest and Southwest that are the hotbeds of these innovative inventions.

They explain this change principally as a result of industrial shifts and changing demographics away from the relatively stagnating Northeast and Midwest metropolises to the more vibrant centers of the U.S. West. The location of patent activity has paralleled areas of economic growth over the past 25 years, as related to population growth, economic endowments, and technological infrastructure.

INTRAURBAN INDUSTRIAL PRODUCTION AND LOCATION

In this section, we introduce two conceptual ways of understanding changes that have been occurring in the location and production of manufacturing within cities and metropolitan areas: The Wheeler-Park model and the product cycle model. Whereas these are general models identifying major structural forces relating to the locational change of manufacturing within metropolitan areas, Walker and Lewis (2005) focus on three key functional processes that account for the spread of industry from central city to suburban locations. First is urban geographical industrialization, that is, urban expansion has its base in industrial growth and capital accumulation. That creates new places attracting a labor force and new technologies, resulting in industrial districts in suburban locations. A second factor is the investment in real estate, where profits are made on the suburban fringe that lead to industrial concentrations, as well as to residential development and highway improvement. Third is the role of political processes, guided by business and government leaders. Thus, Walker and Lewis shed light on the processes that underpin the general Wheeler-Park and the product cycle models.

The Wheeler-Park Model
The **Wheeler-Park model** captures the basic changes in manufacturing location within metropolitan areas since approximately 1850. It focuses in particular on differences and similarities between central cities and suburbs (Figure 7.7). The Wheeler-Park model involves five phrases. Note that the curved lines on

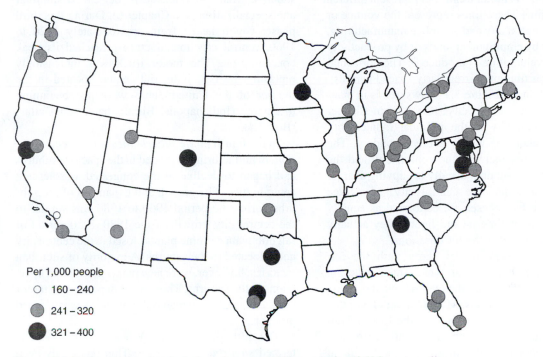

Figure 7.6 Professional and technical workers per 1,000 people for 50 U.S. metropolitan areas.

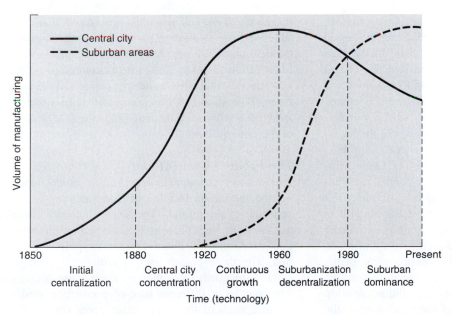

Figure 7.7 The five-phase Wheeler-Park model of idealized metropolitan manufacturing locational change. (*Source:* Wheeler and Park, 1981.)

Figure 7.7 follow similar trends but represent different periods of time. These lines represent the volume or intensity of central city and suburban manufacturing, as measured by employment totals or by productivity (number or value of units produced). The horizontal axis measures time over irregularly spaced periods.

The solid line in Figure 7.7 shows trends in manufacturing in the central city. Recall from Chapter 1 that a central city is the political municipality or the area enclosed within a city boundary. The metropolitan area includes the central city and the suburbs, with the suburbs usually occupying a larger geographic area than the central city. Also, note that while the five phases are calibrated as equally spaced periods of time on the figure, they actually represent periods of different durations.

The Wheeler-Park model starts with the *initial centralization phase* in which manufacturing first comes to locate in the central business district (CBD) or its environs. Manufacturers favor this downtown location because it was the focus of rail lines and commercial activity. It was also accessible to the city labor market. The time frame for initial centralizations is approximately 1850 to 1880. Many cities during this period were oriented more toward commercial than to industrial activities.

The second phase, *central city concentration*, represents the heyday of the railroad and the period (1880–1920) when certain large cities of the East Coast and the Midwest developed into preeminent manufacturing centers. Large East Coast cities had Atlantic port advantages (New York, Philadelphia, Baltimore, and Boston), and most Midwest industrial centers had port accessibility via the Great Lakes (Chicago, Detroit, and Cleveland) or the Mississippi and the Ohio River systems (St. Louis, Minneapolis, and Cincinnati). Industry concentrated not only in the environs of the CBD but also along rail lines emanating outward from the CBD but still in the central city, long before the suburbs appeared.

The third phase is labeled *continuous growth*. In one sense, this third phase is a continuation of the second phase, but in another sense it is not (see Figure 7.7). Significantly, this phase did not develop from the initial emergence of manufacturing in the

suburbs, what the Erickson model called spillover and specialization (see Chapter 6). During this third phase, which lasted from approximately 1920 to 1960, central city manufacturing reached its peak concentration. The motor truck was increasingly replacing the rail. Industrial centers located in the interior of the United States were just beginning to emerge (Indianapolis, Birmingham, and Dallas) (Box 7.4).

In the fourth phase *suburbanization-decentralization*, manufacturing exploded in the spacious suburbs and began to decline in the congested, obsolescent central cities. The growth and expansion of the suburbs during the period 1960 to 1980 was similar to the central city growth of the 1880–1920 period of rail dominance. Some plants closed in the central city and relocated to the suburbs. A majority of suburban factories, however, were new plants that started operations in the suburbs. These firms depended on motor trucks to supply raw materials and take away finished products.

The fifth phase of the Wheeler-Park model is termed *suburban dominance*. This phase has been characterized by further rapid decline in central city manufacturing and the ascendancy of the suburbs. High-tech manufacturing principles have become the norm. A skilled suburban workforce is accessible, leaving central city residents isolated from the new suburban jobs. The suburbs encompass vast tracts of low-cost land, often many counties, in contrast to the typically more circumscribed central cities. This suburban dominance, in place since at least 1980, continues unabated into the first decade of the new millennium.

The Product Cycle Model

The second conceptual approach to understanding the intraurban location of manufacturing is the **product cycle model**. The cycle involves three phases, with each phase associated with a different kind of intrametropolitan or nonmetropolitan location. The three phases are (1) *initial*, (2) *growth*, and (3) *standardized or mature*. Each phase is characterized by a different mix of production costs. In turn, each of the three mixes gives rise to the

BOX 7.4   REVITALIZING CITIES THROUGH SPORTS VENUES

Almost all large cities turned to the development of sports facilities to revitalize downtown development. As Austrian and Rosentraub (2002, p. 550) have noted, "Baltimore, Buffalo, Cleveland, Dallas, Dayton, Detroit, Los Angeles, [and] Oklahoma City . . . used sports as an anchor for [downtown] redevelopment." This construction boom that began in the late 1980s accelerated in the 1990s and continues apace today. This expansion "can be attributed to league expansion, franchise relocation, and the real or perceived need for new facilities for existing franchises" (Newsome and Comer, 2000, p. 105). Thus, "instead of competing for auto plants, cities competed for sports teams" (Turner and Rosentraub, 2002, p. 489). Further, "corporations found they could hitch a ride on the enthusiasm for downtown sports facilities by purchasing naming rights to stadiums and ballparks" (Turner and Rosentraub, 2002, p. 489). Coors Field in Denver is one example. Table B7.2 shows the intraurban locations of stadiums, coliseums, and hockey rinks as of 1997. Overall, the downtown locations account for more than 50 percent of the combined venues for the National Football League (NFL), Major League Baseball (MLB), the National Basketball Association (NBA), and the National Hockey League (NHL).

Table B7.2   Intraurban Locations by Sports, 1997

Location	NFL	MLB	NBA	NHL	Total	Percent of Total
Downtown	14	9	18	17	58	51.3
Central City	4	12	6	4	26	23.0
Suburbs	12	7	5	5	29	25.7
Total	30	28	29	26	113	100.0

Source: Newsome and Comer, 2000, p. 113.

different location preferences of the manufacturing firms (Figure 7.8).

In the initial phase of the model, a new product is being developed and improved upon. This initial phase is also the risk phase, as many new products are not successful in sustaining profits. The most important costs during this phase comprise (1) *research and engineering* in the creation, development, and upgrading of the product and (2) *urbanization economies*. Urbanization economies represent cost savings that result from an urban location in which the urban area provides many infrastructural advantages, including roads and highways, water and sewer services, access to a workforce, the provision of necessary consumer retail and other services, and access to business services. Relatively little capital is required during this phase,

only routine management functions are needed, and unskilled labor is not in demand. The firm in this initial risk phase relies on this urban infrastructure as a basic necessity and as a way to minimize cost. Not surprisingly, firms in this initial phase favor an urban location. In the past, they favored a central city location, but today they prefer a location in or near a suburban business center.

The second phase is the growth segment of the product cycle. Assuming profits and success during the initial phase, the manufacturing firm now finds demand for the product to be high in the growth phase. The firm is highly profitable. In some instances, the innovations achieved in phase one generates super profits in the growth phase. Some firms may find themselves as part of an **oligoloply** with respect to their product. An oligopoly exists

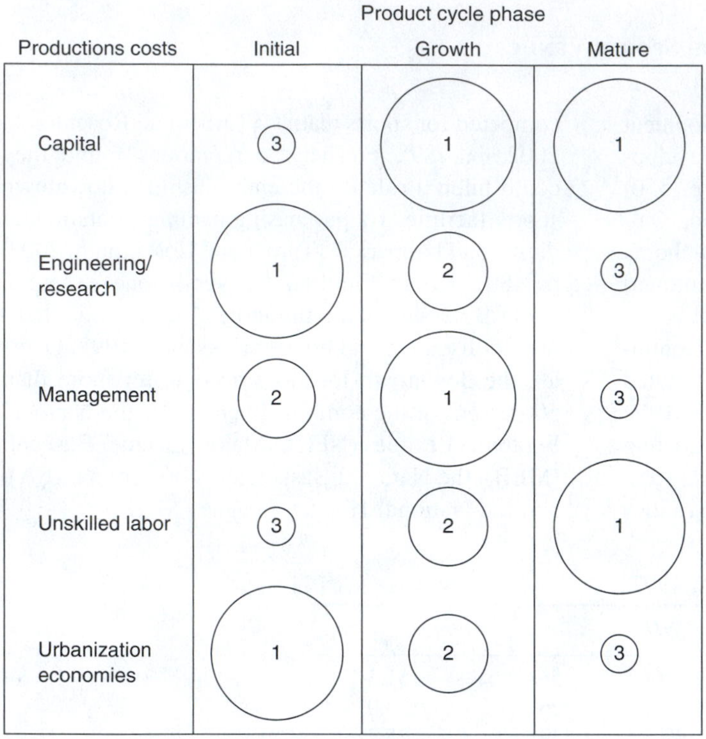

Product cycle phase

Productions costs	Initial	Growth	Mature
Capital	3	1	1
Engineering/research	1	2	3
Management	2	1	3
Unskilled labor	3	2	1
Urbanization economies	1	2	3

Figure 7.8 The relative importance of production costs in each of the three phases of the product cycle model.

when only a handful of firms provide the product because of severely restricted competition. These firms have simply jumped ahead of the would-be competition.

In this growth phase, urbanization economies become much less important, as the firm may seek out a production location on inexpensive suburban land. A new and enlarged production facility is needed. Likewise, little additional research or engineering work is required. But what now becomes of great importance is the management of this rapid growth. Management costs suddenly rise, as more levels of management and sales become essential to continued success. In addition, greatly enhanced capital sources are needed to produce high volumes of the product. Other necessities include plant enlargement, added space, and material and product transportation. A location at the edge of the metropolitan area is typically sought out, not a location in or near a suburban business center.

In the third phase of the product cycle, the firm may be said to become mature. The product has become standardized, with little innovative research and development improvement. Competition has increased as other firms are producing essentially the same product. Instead of amassing super profits as during the growth phase, the firm now achieves normal profits in a kind of market equilibrium. In this mature phase, production costs shift once again. Capital is still required to maintain the day-to-day operations. However, unskilled, low-paid workers are now essential to the success in this third phase. Because the product is standardized, unskilled workers can carry out the production process. Management functions shrink in relative importance during the routine operations of the third phase. The need for an urban location disappears. As a result of the shifts in the relative role of production costs, the firm might relocate to either a nonmetropolitan or an out-of-country location. For many decades rural areas in the U.S. South supported manufacturing firms in the mature phase through a branch plant economy in which the branch plant headquarters were located in New York, Chicago, or Atlanta, for example. More recently, production facilities in Mexico and overseas offer labor at a fraction of the cost of using the U.S. workforce, creating a significant negative impact for many workers (Figure 7.9). Remember that these overseas operations work best for firms and products in the mature phase of the cycle, e.g., textiles and apparel.

POLITICAL ECONOMY APPROACHES

Most of our effort so far in this chapter has been to focus on traditional ways of understanding the organization of urban economic and industrial landscapes. However, as cities have changed tremendously in the last two and three decades, so have the methods and research approaches in the social sciences. In this section of the chapter we review some alternative notions about urban landscapes of economic production. In particular, most of the ideas we have discussed already in this chapter begin (either explicitly or implicitly) with the assumption that groups and individuals make economic decisions in a rational manner. In contrast, the approaches we discuss in this section of the chapter do not rest on this assumption. One approach in particular that rests on different assumptions can be called **political economy**. This perspective, which was first developed in the 1970s, attempts to understand the deeper structural relations that create the observable economic landscape, though the foundations for this viewpoint go back many decades. Although neoclassical economics identifies economically rational decision making as the primary force, political economy perspectives do not agree, as is evident in the summary of the following basic concepts.

Basic Concepts

There are several basic notions common to political economy approaches to urban geography. First, cities are embedded within a larger structure, specifically, the structure of production that defines the role and character of cities. North American cities are embedded within a system of capitalist economic production. Over the last several centuries, capitalism has taken on a series of different configurations—called **modes of production**. The mode of production includes basic economic relations like methods of combining materials with labor to produce products. The mode of production

Figure 7.9 This forlorn-looking gentlemen has just given over his automobile title for some quick cash. He has been unemployed since July, 1999.

also includes the broader social relations that make production possible. The primary social relations concern the ownership and control of the means of production, that is, the factories, machines, and companies. There is an inherent conflict within capitalism between those who own (or control) the means of production and the laborers. Most often this conflict is referred to as **class conflict**. Importantly, this inevitable class conflict from time to time manifests itself as **crisis** in the system, that can sometimes have large impacts on the mode of production. In other words, changes in the broader structures of capitalist production are brought about by the expression of crises that emerge from the very structure of capitalism.

Crises emerge from class conflict, but they take different forms. One of the key themes of political economy theories is that capitalists are motivated by a need for **capitalist accumulation**, which is a basic motive of human economic behavior. Capitalist accumulation depends on the ability of capitalists to extract surplus value from laborers. In other words, the economic value of products produced by laborers must exceed the economic cost of paying wages to laborers. Herein lies the conflict. On the one hand, if laborers are paid a wage that reflects the value of the products they produce, then capitalists reap less profit. On the other hand, if labor is not paid enough to buy the products they produce, then the demand for these products will be inadequate, and capitalists will lose profit. Capitalists face competitive pressure to keep wages low, but if low wages become pervasive enough, the system experiences a crisis of **underconsumption**. Other crises also plague capitalist production, including fiscal crises that emerge from the need for governments to take an increasingly active role in managing economic affairs.

Circuits of Capital

David Harvey is one of the primary proponents of political economy approaches to urban geography. He argues in particular that the political economy approach is relevant to understanding the urban space economy (Harvey 1989). He recognizes that

some of the basic categories are more complicated than previously discussed. For example, not all capitalists are the same. Some make money from participating in manufacturing, whereas others make money by participating in the global financial market. These groups differ in their behavior, their needs, and their mark on the city. Similarly, not all workers are the same. Line workers in a heavy manufacturing plant differ from computer engineers who design high-tech machinery. They have different needs and resources, and they impact the city in different ways. Even so, the most important force affecting urban geography is still the class conflict engendered by capitalism itself.

Harvey also detailed the impact of the capitalist economic system on urban space by advancing a theory of **circuits of capital**. Circuits of capital are the most common ways that investment takes place. Harvey describes three circuits. The **primary circuit of capital** reflects the basic economics of making profit from industrial production. Industrialists must invest capital in the raw materials, labor, and means of production (machines and tools) in order to make commodities that can be sold. If the exchange value (value of the commodities that can be realized in a market) of the commodities produced is greater than the exchange value of the raw materials, labor, and means of production, then the industrialist realizes excess value, or profit. When industrialists invest excess value in producing more things, this constitutes the primary circuit of capital. Of course, the actual processes are more complex than we have described here; Figure 7.10 illustrates some of the complexities involved. There are important distinctions between the interests of individual capitalists and the interests of capitalists as a group. Individual capitalists tend to overinvest in the primary circuit, resulting in overaccumulation and excess capacity.

The **secondary circuit of capital** includes investments that are necessary for, but not directly related to production. This is where the theory explains the urban space economy. Harvey identifies these investments as providing aids, rather than direct inputs, to production and consumption. **Fixed capital assets** (outside of the immediate production

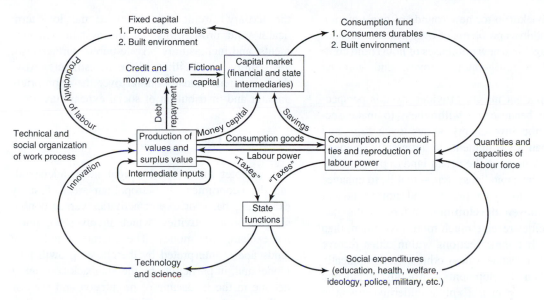

Figure 7.10 David Harvey's diagram of circuit of capital.

process, that is, not factories or machines) form the physical framework for production or the **built environment for production**. In a parallel fashion, **consumption fund assets** form the **built environment for consumption**. Examples of fixed capital in the built environment include power-generating facilities and transportation infrastructure. Examples of consumption fund investments include housing, schools, and sidewalks. Some features of the urban built environment function as both fixed capital and consumption fund assets; for example, roads and highways are used both by workers to travel back and forth to work, play, and shop, and by producers to transport raw materials and finished commodities.

Although secondary circuit investment is necessary to the capitalist system, it presents problems. First, the built environment tends to require large capital investments that make it difficult for individual capitalists to invest directly. Complex financial markets that provide credit and governments that regulate financial markets and levy taxes are important institutions that facilitate these investments. Second, the built environment is geographically fixed and long-lived; thus investments in the secondary circuit of capital tend to be for long

periods of time. Although initially facilitating production and consumption, the built environment can outlive its usefulness and ultimately prove to be a hindrance. Unlike other forms of capital, like labor and machines, the built environment cannot be moved without destroying it.

In times of economic crisis or restructuring when the built environment is no longer useful to production and/or consumption, substantial segments of the urban built environment may be abandoned or rebuilt. At other times, new rounds of investment in the secondary circuit of capital results in new built environments of cities. For example, suburbanization (addressed in greater detail in several chapters including Chapters 6 and 9) has been explained by political economists as a way to avoid the extreme costs of rebuilding older portions of cities. New investments in consumption fund assets (houses, parks, and sidewalks) and fixed capital assets (highways) are cheaper and easier on the undeveloped fringe of cities. These investments were made necessary in part because of overproduction in the primary circuit and by the aging of the built environment. Older transportation systems can inhibit new production systems. Building new housing provides an important backdrop for new rounds of consumption needed to address problems of overproduction. With new housing come new purchases of household commodities like refrigerators, stoves, and washing machines.

One important insight provided by this perspective is that because the willingness to make secondary sector investments varies over time and space, urban development is inherently uneven. Major investments in the urban landscape are made to promote the capitalist system—that is, to enhance the potential to make profit—and not to benefit workers. **Uneven development** refers to the fact that some cities receive much more investment than others and that some sections within cities receive much more investment than others. Geographically uneven urban development is not just accidental to capitalism, however. Explicit underinvestment in some places provides the necessary preconditions for future rounds of capitalist development. Some people have argued, for example, that central cities were underdeveloped in the last two or three decades of the twentieth century in part to provide a outlet for later development pressures when the suburbs stagnate. Some arguments about gentrification (the upgrading of old residential neighborhoods) (discussed in Chapter 9) reflect this perspective.

Harvey also identifies a **tertiary circuit of capital**. This circuit also involves investments that are useful to the long-term health of the capitalist system but are further removed from the direct production of commodities. On one hand, there are investments in scientific and technological capacity that are needed to increase productivity and to design new commodities. On the other hand, there are social expenditures that increase the quality of labor, often in the form of education and government-funded benefits. Sometimes these social expenditures can be in the form of a safety net provided to catch individuals and families that fall through the cracks of the system. For both research and development and social expenditures, there is a problem with the individual motivations of capitalists to overinvest in the primary circuit, and underinvest in the tertiary circuit, even though

the tertiary circuit contributes to the long-term health (and profitability) of the system. Governments, and increasingly private-public partnerships, are required to facilitate these investments. Also, there is often intense conflict over the appropriate amount and distribution of social expenditure.

WRAPPING UP

This chapter has offered insight into understanding the economics of metropolitan areas, first by examining basic or export activities versus nonbasic economic activities, which involves the internal exchange of money. The interurban industrial landscape is interpreted by the classic growth pole model and, in particular, by the Stanback concept of decline in the landscape of production and the rise of the new service metropolitan economy. The intraurban location of manufacturing is illustrated by the Wheeler-Park model and, especially by the product cycle model. The chapter ends with an analysis of political economy approaches, which provides a useful lead-in to the next chapter on social landscapes of cities and models of social geography.

READINGS

Austrian, Ziona and Mark S. Rosentraub. 2002. "Cities, Sports, and Economic Change: A Retrospective Assessment," *Journal of Urban Affairs,* Vol. 24, pp. 549–563.

Bowen, John T. Jr. 2006. "The Geography of Certified Trace-Induced Manufacturing Job Loss in New England," *The Professional Geographer,* Vol. 58, pp. 249–265.

Florida, Richard. 2002. "The Economic Geography of Talent," *Annals of the Association of American Geographers,* Vol. 92, pp. 743–755.

Florida, Richard. 2005. *Cities and the Creative Class.* New York: Routledge.

Harvey, David, 1989. *The Urban Experience.* Baltimore and London: The Johns Hopkins University Press.

Johnson, Daniel K. N. and Amy Brown. 2004. "How the West Has Won: Regional and Industrial Immersion in U.S. Patent Activity," *Economic Geography,* Vol. 80, pp. 241–160.

Newsome, Tracey H. and Jonathan C. Comer. 2002. "Changing Intra-Urban Location Patterns of Major League Sports Facilities," *Professional Geographer,* Vol. 51, pp. 105–120.

Scott, Allan J. 1988. "Flexible Production Systems: The Rise of New Industrial Spaces in North America and Western Europe," *International Journal of Urban and Regional Research,* Vol. 12, pp. 171–185.

Stanback, Thomas M. Jr. 2002. *The Transforming Metropolitan Economy*. New Brunswick, NJ: Center for Urban Policy Research, Rutgers University.

Turner, Robyne S. and Mark S. Rosentraub. 2002. "Tourism, Sports and the Centrality of Cities," *Journal of Urban Affairs,* Vol. 24, pp. 487–492.

Walker, Richard and Robert D. Lewis. 2005. "Beyond the Crabgrass Frontier: Industry and the Spread of North American Cities, 1850–1950." In Nicholas R. Fyfe and Judith T. Kenny, eds., *The Urban Geography Reader*. New York: Routledge, pp. 121–127.

Weber, Alfred. 1909. *Theory of the Location of Industries*. Trans. C. J. Friedrich 1929. Chicago: University of Chicago Press.

Wheeler, James O. 1986. "Similarities in Corporate Structure of American Cities," *Growth and Change,* Vol. 17, pp. 13–21.

Wheeler, James O. and Sam Ock Park. 1981. "Locational Dynamics of Manufacturing in the Atlanta Metropolitan Region, 1968–1976," *Southeastern Geographer,* Vol. 20, pp. 100–119.

Wilson, David and Jarad Wouters. 2003. "Spatiality and Growth Discourse: The Restructuring of America's Rust Belt Cities," *Journal of Urban Affairs,* Vol. 25, pp. 123–138.

CHAPTER 8

FOUNDATIONS OF URBAN SOCIAL LANDSCAPES

*The processes of segregation establish moral
distances which make the city a mosaic of little
worlds which touch but do not interpenetrate.*

—PARK, 1921, P. 313

In Chapters 6 and 7 we discussed how cities are orga-nized as economic landscapes; in this chapter we begin to discuss cities as **social landscapes.** We ask, "Is there a pattern to the way social groups are dis-tributed across urban space?" and "Do social groups occupy distinct parts of cities?" Most of us will rec-ognize that we carry around notions of a social land-scape. Think of a major city that you know well, perhaps the one you live in. Are there sections of town that you go to for ethnic foods, perhaps a "China-town"? Are there sections of town where you will find old large homes with meticulously maintained lawns? Are there sections of town where you might feel uncomfortable walking alone at night? Have you ever wondered why these sections of town are located where they are? Have you ever been amazed at how quickly you can move from one section of the city to another, perhaps just by walking across the street? All of these questions have motivated scholars to try to understand the spatial organization of urban society.

This chapter considers basic theories that have attempted to explain urban social structure. We start by looking at ideas that compare urban social land-scapes to ecological communities, followed by a series of simple attempts to represent cities diagram-matically. We then consider more realistic ideas that discuss various dimensions along which cities are organized, and we finish by looking at contemporary cities.

We focus in this chapter on the broad processes that differentiate residential areas in cities; we con-sider more specific topics in chapters that follow. Chapter 9 discusses housing markets and the cru-cial role they play in shaping the patterns of cities; Chapter 10 focuses on an issue of major policy concern—the concentration of the urban poor in spe-cific neighborhoods; Chapter 11 discusses the issues of residential segregation and immigration.

ECOLOGICAL APPROACH TO CITIES

The industrialization that started in England in the mid-eighteenth century and spread across continen-tal Europe over the following century led to rapid and dramatic urbanization (see Chapter 2). Indus-trialization radically changed European cities, and many observers were concerned about its negative effects on society. The general argument contrasted the nature of "traditional" society characteristic of villages and small towns with that being observed in cities. Many of these observers (for example Fer-dinand Tönnies [1855–1935] and Emile Durkheim [1858–1917]) thought in terms of "ideal types" that epitomize distinct kinds of places—typically the large industrial city as one ideal type and the small agrarian village as the other ideal type. It helps to think of these as end points on a continuum of place

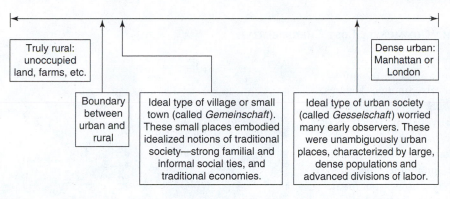

Figure 8.1 Ideal place types and the urban continuum. Although urban (for example, Manhattan) and rural places are easy to distinguish from one another, it is difficult to identify a firm dividing line between the two ends of the continuum.

types (Figure 8.1). Apparent differences in social behavior between urbanites and small town residents were of particular concern to these observers.

"Community Lost": European Perspectives on Cities

Community is a slippery concept that still motivates a lot of concern today. The European scholars that first began to think about cities typically contrasted them with ideals of **community** life experienced in a small village. In a village, the family or kin-group is the basic unit of society, and social relationships are characterized by depth, continuity, cohesion, and fulfillment—people are bound together in caring, familial ways. Social bonds are constructed on the basis of likeness, common beliefs, and common rituals and symbols. The population is socially homogenous, and people are united without having to think very much about how they relate to one another. Controls over individual behavior are exerted through the informal discipline of family and neighbors.

In contrast, European scholars described urban **society** as fundamentally distinct from traditional community. Social relationships rest on the rationality, efficiency, and contractual obligations made necessary by new patterns of economic organization. Most social interactions tend to be short-lived and superficial. People are bound together by formal ties to institutions and organizations. Controls over individual behavior are exerted through impersonal, institutionalized codes. Social order is based

on differences—it rests on complex divisions of labor, with people specializing in different occupations. Specialization requires mutual dependence. In general, urban societies provide greater opportunities for individual freedom and choice at the cost of a weakened social fabric.

Other European scholars (for example, Georg Simmel [1858–1918]) worried about the psychological impact of living in cities. They were concerned, in particular, that moving to a city would transform an individual from wholesome to corrupt and sinful. Simmel (1903) identified several adverse influences of the city. **Dynamic density** refers to the much higher population density in cities than in small towns. Because of the variety of people and ways of life found in cities, informal social controls on behavior are weaker in cities. More social interactions are with people you don't know personally and it is possible to "get away" with behaviors found unacceptable in the small town. **Rationality/impersonality** results from the increasing influence of economic relationships on social interactions: People had to interact on the basis of economic rationality as opposed to the deeper social basis of traditional society. **Overstimulation** reflects the stress created by the greater population diversity found in cities than in small towns or villages. People have difficulty dealing with the press of people and tend to withdraw socially to try to preserve a sense of privacy. Cities present people with too much stimulation and people shut down psychologically because of it.

BOX 8.1   REBUTTING THE "COMMUNITY LOST" PERSPECTIVE

Not all observers of urban life were as pessimistic as the early European observers Simmel, Tönnies, and Durkheim. We review here some of the major challenges to their "community lost" perspectives of urban social life. One of the problems that worried the early observers of modern large cities was the presence of strangers—the anonymity that stood in contrast to the "everybody knows your name" kind of small town community. Some observers, however, do not view interactions with strangers as negative; indeed, they view such interactions as vital to healthy cities. One of the chief concerns with cities is safety, especially personal safety on the streets. Jane Jacobs, writing in the late 1950s and early 1960s in opposition to the grand urban redevelopment schemes then popular and the ethos of modern city planning, argued that in order for sidewalks to be safe, they had to be constantly used and open (Figure B8.1). The tendency to retreat and create secluded pockets with limited access actually increases danger on the street.

Figure B8.1 Jane Jacobs celebrated the diversity of the street, especially as expressed on sidewalks, in her defense of traditional densely settled and heavily used urban spaces. This photograph of a Greenwich Village Street shows the kind of constant use essential to Jacobs' view of cities.

In settlements that are smaller and simpler than big cities, controls on acceptable public behavior, if not on crime, seem to operate with greater or lesser success through a web of reputation, gossip, approval, disapproval and sanctions, all of which are powerful if people know each other and word travels. But a city's streets, which must control not only the behavior of the people of the city but also of visitors from suburbs and towns who want to have a big time away from the gossip and sanctions at home, have to operate by more direct, straightforward methods. It is a wonder cities have solved such an inherently difficult problem at all. And yet in many streets they do it magnificently. (Jacobs 1961, p. 35)

William Whyte shared Jacobs's optimism about urban public space, and he conducted years of detailed research on how people used public spaces. He articulated a series of design features that facilitate constructive interaction. He also argued that public use of urban space is an essential element of safety because spaces unused by the public become useful for illicit purposes (Figure B8.2).

URBAN VILLAGES AND "COMMUNITY SAVED"

Reacting against the prevailing pessimism of existing urban theory, sociologist Herbert Gans (1962) studied the West End, a predominantly Italian inner-city neighborhood in Boston about which considerable irony existed. The urban planning establishment, enthralled with urban revitalization,

(a)

(b)

Figure B8.2 These photographs illustrate the importance of design for urban public space. (a) The first space in Washington Park, New York City is open and invitingly designed, and well used by the public. (b) The second space in downtown Baltimore, although accessible to the public, is sterile and sparsely used.

had targeted this neighborhood for redevelopment based on its density and low socioeconomic status, characteristics typically referred to in descriptions of "urban blight." At the same time, many of the professional planners busy plotting the destruction of the West End thoroughly enjoyed visiting the neighborhood. Gans's study articulated a perspective that "community" in the sociocultural sense is indeed possible within a densely settled urban environment; indeed, these pockets of urban community shared much in common with the traditional rural villages that served as contrast to cities in earlier theories.

"COMMUNITY TRANSFORMED"

Herbert Gans (1967) was also a major voice in articulating another theoretical perspective that countered prevailing wisdom. This time, Gans studied the new large-scale, mass-produced housing subdivisions built by Abraham Levitt and others (discussed in more detail in Chapter 9). The prevailing wisdom was that these new suburban residential environments, although in many ways the epitome of the post-World War II American Dream, lacked soul and were bereft of community. Based on ethnographic research (he bought a house in Levittown and lived there!), Gans argued that community existed in Levittown, just in a different form. Specifically, community was based initially upon pioneer eagerness (the willingness of newcomers to form new bonds because all residents are new) and later on bonds of common interests, including undergoing common life-cycle stages, raising children, and protecting and enhancing property values.

Two other phenomena that European scholars, in particular Durkheim, associated with urban life are anomie and deviant behavior. **Anomie** refers to both the social isolation that stems from the weakening of traditional informal social bonds and the resultant moral confusion and/or normlessness that urban people experience. **Deviant behavior** can be the result of anomie, which renders people less capable of avoiding the ever-present temptations found in the city.

The "community lost" perspective advanced by the early European scholars was pessimistic about cities and continues to hold strong influence today. Opinions about cities are fundamentally mixed in the United States. Many of the fears expressed by European scholars more than 100 years ago are still evident (and indeed have been since the beginning of the country; Thomas Jefferson was committed to an agrarian future in part because of his distrust of cities). Not all scholars, however, have agreed with this perspective. Herbert Gans (1962), William Whyte (1988), and Jane Jacobs (1961) each made spirited defenses of cities, presenting a "community saved" perspective (Box 8.1). In fact, even Durkheim, who was generally suspicious of cities, ultimately argued that cities offered enough social opportunity to outweigh the risks.

The Chicago School of Sociology

Soon after starting the nation's first academic department of sociology in 1892, the University of Chicago hired a group of scholars, including Robert Park in 1914 and Ernest Burgess in 1919, who had trained in Europe and were heavily influenced by the perspectives we have just discussed (Burgess, 1925; Park, 1925). These scholars and the students they trained developed what is now known as the **Chicago school of sociology,** which has had a major impact on North American social science. They developed an "objective" and empirically oriented research approach that has marked urban studies and urban geography ever since. They emphasized the need to directly observe social groups in urban contexts. Park had been exposed to Simmel in Europe and shared some of the Europeans' misgivings about

the detrimental impact of cities on community and mental health. Still, the Chicago school was very concerned with having a positive social impact, and they shared the Progressive movement's qualified optimism and commitment to reform. Much of the Chicago research focused on "deviant" behavior, a practice many scholars now feel uncomfortable with. More important, however, was their conceptual understanding of how urban society is organized spatially, the perspective we now call **spatial or urban ecology**.

Written in a period ranging from the mid-1910s through the early 1930s, the work defining the ecological approach was affected by a diverse array of historical factors and reflects the spatial structure of cities at that time. Cities were much smaller in population and spatial extent and were denser than they are today. They had a single dominant business district and factories were typically housed in multistory buildings close to the downtown area. Cities were just beginning to feel the impact of technologic innovations in transportation. Public transportation encouraged the spatial spread of cities, first with horse-drawn vehicles carrying small numbers of professional and middle-class residents, and later with larger and cheaper electrically powered vehicles running on tracks built into roads. These transportation routes also began to change the shape of cities: Cities spread unevenly, with housing and retail being constructed along the transportation routes in a pattern that resembled the arms of a starfish.

Urban populations grew very rapidly during this period as advanced industrial capitalism increasingly fueled the national economy, especially in the manufacturing cities of the Northeast and the upper Midwest. With the exception of the World War I years, and ending with passage of legislation restricting immigration in the 1920s, manufacturing cities had been destinations for millions of immigrants coming to North America to take advantage of the economic opportunities (see Chapter 11). Many manufacturing cities had more people born in Europe than in the United States.

Several other factors affected the nature of the ecological approach. First, this approach argued for the use of scientific methodologies to study human society (i.e., the social *sciences*) as opposed to the more philosophically oriented social reflections that characterized European scholarship. Second, biological sciences were also developing rapidly, changing in response to and incorporating evolutionary thinking. Especially prominent was the field of community ecology, whose practitioners attempted to understand how the numbers and types of plant and animal species in a particular place, or ecological niche, change over time in a rational and predictable manner.

The Chicago sociologists described cities as being like ecological communities. Basically they felt that there was a rational and predictable pattern in cities that emerged from the competition among social groups over resources, in much the same way that plant species compete for access to sunlight and soil moisture. Central to this approach is the notion of **social distance,** which argues that social groups want to have as little contact with other groups as possible. Moreover, groups realize their dislike for other groups by living as far away from them as possible. In other words, they enforce or protect social distance by creating **spatial distance.** The natural result is an urban social landscape marked by a variety of groups living in distinct neighborhoods that are often identified with the group that lives there.

The ecological approach maintained that occupants of neighborhoods change over time in a predictable process called **invasion and succession.**

If we observe an abandoned agricultural field, we will note that the plant and animal species that occupy that field change over time in a predictable manner. For example, grasses and small woody shrubs may be replaced by short-lived fast-growing trees, which may be replaced (eventually) by a relatively stable assemblage of trees similar to the forest that was cut down to create the field in the first place. Applied to urban neighborhoods, invasion and succession views the group occupants of neighborhoods as changing over time. Given the historical context of Chicago (and northern industrial cities more generally), groups were often defined on the basis of their national origin, with members of one immigrant group replacing members of another immigrant group within a neighborhood. From the perspective of a neighborhood, the Chicago scholars viewed the invasion and succession process as ongoing: any given neighborhood will be occupied by a series of immigrant groups over time.

Looking at the city as a whole, the arrival of immigrants often functioned like tossing a pebble into the middle of a pond: the impact radiates outward in concentric circles. If we consider one immigrant group and its occupation of a particular neighborhood, Figure 8.2 shows how the process might work. As a new immigrant group begins to arrive in a city, they will find housing in neighborhoods close to the jobs they get (most cannot afford any form of transportation other than walking), which at the beginning of the twentieth century

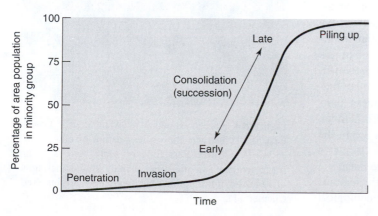

Figure 8.2 S-shaped curve showing the typical stages of neighborhood invasion and succession, based on the percentage of the area's population who are of the "invading" group. (*Source:* From R. J. Johnston, *Urban Residential Patterns*. London: Bell, 1971, Figure 6.3, p. 253.)

were located close to the core of cities. As more and more immigrants from the same country arrive they tend to find jobs in the same factories and live in the same neighborhoods as the "pioneer" immigrants that preceded them. Eventually, enough immigrants from the same origin country live in a neighborhood to make their presence visible, and a rapid transition ensues. The former residents begin to leave, often because of the discomfort of living close to a "foreign" group, and the new group increases rapidly. The old residents of the neighborhood may begin a new round of invasion and succession in another neighborhood.

An important related idea that we will take up in more detail later in this chapter comes from the Chicago sociologists' use of biological metaphors: Cities are viewed as being comprised of **natural areas.** The processes that distribute groups across urban space are natural and stem from the competition among groups for control over space. Thus, the fact that different groups occupy different parts of the city is not viewed as fundamentally problematic. The attempts to work toward reform were conducted within the distinct parts of the city.

Even though the writings of the Chicago sociologists are almost a century old, we still observe processes that resemble those that they described. Consider, for example, the traditional Chinatown in Manhattan in New York City. As its population has been increased by renewed immigration from mainland China and Taiwan (not to mention other East Asian countries) over the last several decades, Chinatown has been expanding into surrounding areas. Chief among them is Little Italy, an adjacent area that still carries its association with the Italian immigrants who shaped it in the early decades of the twentieth century. As Chinatown expands, however, you can now see blocks with the traditional Italian restaurants and grocers next to Chinese markets (Figure 8.3). On the other side of Chinatown, Korean and other East Asian immigrants are in the early stages of occupying neighborhoods formerly in various stages of abandonment (Figure 8.4).

Even though we still observe many of the features of urban society seen and described by the ecological

Figure 8.3 Chinese signage in Little Italy, Manhattan, illustrates the changing ethnic nature of immigrant neighborhoods. Little Italy, the traditional Italian neighborhood, is undergoing an uneven transition.

approach, there are important problems with this approach that other perspectives have attempted to deal with. First, social groups are defined superficially based solely on country of origin for immigrants. In fact, many other factors shape and influence social identity in today's complex metropolitan areas,

Figure 8.4 Korean signage in Manhattan's Lower East Side illustrates the restless nature of ethnic districts. The Lower East Side of Manhattan, a traditional tenement district, increasingly shows the signs of renewed immigration, but from new origins (see Chapter 11).

including race, gender, sexuality, age, and lifestyle. Second, the ways in which groups interact are treated too superficially. For example, the assertion that every group "naturally" wants to avoid other groups and live among its own is only partially true, and it ignores many other factors that influence the residential landscape. Third, the foundational attitudes about the negative influence of cities and the focus on groups perceived as "deviant" doesn't match current sentiments. Fourth, human societies cannot be treated as if they are simple biologic elements in a large urban ecosystem. To do so ignores the complex array of social, economic and political forces that shape human behavior and the social landscapes of cities. Even with these problems, however, the ecological approach is still very important and motivates (sometimes only implicitly) much contemporary work on cities. Empirical urban research (including increasingly popular ethnographic work) almost always bears some connection methodologically with precedent set by the Chicago scholars. The notion that intergroup relations are related to revealed spatial patterns and dynamics also remains important.

TRADITIONAL MODELS OF URBAN SPATIAL STRUCTURE

Our concern so far has been with the basics of how the Chicago school approached the study of cities. The interplay of social and spatial processes is central to their approach. We shift in the following section to explicitly consider the typical spatial form of the city, starting with the one derived from the Chicago school writings and finishing with two other major models.

Burgess Concentric Zone Model

The spatial pattern of cities produced by processes of invasion of succession was described in visual form by Burgess (1925) in his **concentric zone model** (Figure 8.5). This model captures significant elements of the social ordering of industrial cities in the early twentieth century. It is not the most important contribution of the Chicago School,

but it is often the most widely remembered. Note that the industrial sector is located just outside the downtown business district (the Loop) and is spreading outward into the oldest residential districts (the Zone in transition). The mixed residential/industrial zone is the area into which most European immigrants first settled, setting off the successive rounds of invasion and succession described above.

Recalling our discussion of location rent in Chapter 6, note that both this theory, often called bid-rent theory, and the concentric zone theory propose a concentric zone structuring of cities. There are similarities and differences between the theories that deserve mention. Both theories are based in some way on notions of competition—economic competition between land users in bid-rent theory and social competition between social groups in the ecological approach. The object and form of the competition, however, are quite different. In bid-rent theory, the objects of competition are the spatial attributes of urban land that contribute to profit or utility. This competition occurs between individuals in "free" land markets that operate according to principles of neoclassical economics. In ecological theory, the competition revolves around the control of urban spaces needed to maintain social distance between groups. The competition is social, not economic. Both theories rest on rather simplistic notions of human behavior that do not recognize politics, power, and other forces that shape society. Both theories fail to account, either by omission or intent, for the growing impact of intra-urban transportation, and both fail to account for fundamental changes in the economic logic of cities. Still, the social spatial pattern predicted by the two theories is very similar, and it is useful to think of these in relation to each other, even though they were articulated almost 50 years apart by academics with few intellectual connections with one another.

Hoyt Sector Model

Homer Hoyt (1936-1937, 1939), an economist employed by the Federal Housing Administration during the 1930s, also worked for insurance and lending institutions. He conducted a variety of empirical

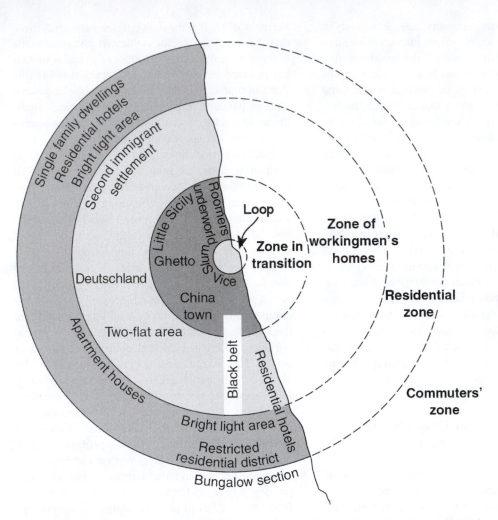

Figure 8.5 Burgess's concentric zone model of urban spatial structure, based on empirical research conducted by the Chicago school of urban ecology. (*Source:* Modified from Ernest W. Burgess, 1967/1925.)

studies of urban land markets, and he proposed a theory known as the **Hoyt sector model** that also resulted in an alternative visual model of urban spatial structure (Figure 8.6).

The basic notion Hoyt described was based on his observations of how cities grew. Very often, as cities grew the highest income groups moved into new homes in new neighborhoods. These neighborhoods were often located along transportation routes on the periphery of the city. In other cases these neighborhoods offered aesthetic views, such as prominent landscape features like river bluffs and hilltops, or proximity to other important landmarks like parks or universities. As high-income groups moved into new houses, their old houses became available for other households to occupy. Hoyt described an often top-down process in which families with lower class standing subsequently occupied the housing left behind by the outwardly mobile upper classes.

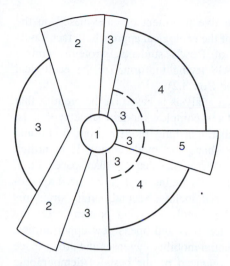

1. Central business district
2. Wholesaling and light manufacturing
3. Lower-class residential
4. Middle-class residential
5. Upper-class residential

Figure 8.6 Hoyt's sector model of urban spatial structure based on empirical observations of housing market dynamics in the 1920s and 1930s. (*Source:* Modified from C. D. Harris and E. L. Ullman, 1945.)

Hoyt recognized that people search for new housing in areas close to where they currently live, often following major transportation routes. This leads to radial rather than zonal expansion and results in a sectoral rather than a concentric pattern. Note that some of the social dynamics central to the ecological approach are obliquely incorporated in Hoyt's model. For example, high-income sectors tend to be insulated from low-income sectors by middle-income sectors in both models. Also, Hoyt's sector model does not specifically address racial and ethnic clusters. Note also that Hoyt's model was also based on a city with a single major commercial core.

Harris and Ullman Multiple Nuclei Model

Chauncy Harris and Edward Ullman (1945) wrote a short article immediately following World War II that has had a surprisingly enduring impact on urban

geography. They recognized in relatively early form many of the trends that came to characterize cities during the last decades of the twentieth century well before most observers. Rather than the concept of a single central business district that was common to the concentric zone and sector models, Harris and Ullman recognized that cities were developing multiple centers, or "nodes," that shaped land values and surrounding land uses (Figure 8.7). Thus, Harris and Ullman's model became known as the **multiple nuclei model.** In this model the nodes did not all have the same function; some were business parks, others were significant institutions like hospitals or

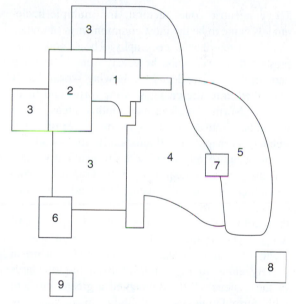

1. Central business district
2. Wholesale light manufacturing
3. Low-class residential
4. Medium-class residential
5. High-class residential
6. Heavy manufacturing
7. Outlying business district
8. Residential suburb
9. Industrial suburb

Figure 8.7 Harris and Ullman's multiple nuclei model of urban spatial structure. Rather than a single dominant urban core, Harris and Ullman identified several "nodes" around which urban land use clustered. (*Source:* Modified from C. D. Harris and E. L. Ullman, 1945.)

universities. Even so, the multiple nodes all had significant effects on their surroundings, and together they fundamentally altered the spatial structure of cities. Although many urban places prior to 1950 resembled the zonal and sectoral models in that they had a single dominant center, cities increasingly grew spatially complex through the later half of the twentieth century. Thus, Harris and Ullman's observations ultimately proved to be much more accurate descriptions of what cities would look like in the late twentieth and early twenty-first centuries.

MORE COMPLEX MODELS

The concentric zone, sectoral, and multiple nuclei models came to be the most common ways of understanding urban social geography. These models, as presented in textbooks, however, were descriptive and simplistic. The decades following World War II witnessed dramatic changes in the forms and functions of North American metropolitan areas. There were also dramatic changes in the nature of social science. Perhaps most dramatically, the social sciences began to rely ever more on quantitative data and the new analytical techniques designed to take advantage of the new data. The study of cities during this period was still heavily influenced by the ecological tradition, especially the portion of that perspective that emphasized the careful assemblage of empirical data. As the study of urban society came to be evaluated from the standards of the "sciences," there emerged a greater concern with formulating and evaluating "hypotheses." In this section we consider a series of more complex models of urban structure that reflect the growing reliance on scientific methodology and quantitative analysis.

Social Area Analysis and Factorial Ecology
Eshref Shevky and Wendell Bell (1955) formulated an approach called **social area analysis** that explicitly built on the earlier writings of Park and his students, but in a more deductive formal way. (Significantly, this was not the first attempt to develop

a more deductive treatment of cities based on the empiricism of the ecological approach. In fact, Louis Wirth, one of Park's students, wrote a seminal article in 1938 trying to formalize the ecological approach; see Box 8.2)

Social area analysis is based on the premise that the city reflects complex modern society; that is, the forces distinguishing modern from traditional society also shape the modern city. It identified three primary forces that shaped urban spaces. First, advanced job skills are increasingly required for success in industrial society. Second, family structures change as the rapidly evolving postwar economy makes new demands and opens new opportunities. Third, residential mobility increases and urban space becomes reorganized on the basis of demographic categories such as race and ethnic identity.

Social area analysis further hypothesized that each of these three forces would have a different spatial expression that could be mapped empirically. To begin with, **socioeconomic status** differentials reflect the increased range of economic activities in the post-World War II industrial economy. Well-educated, high-income households tended to live in sectors similar to those identified by Hoyt.

Family status differentials (also referred to as **urbanization** differentials) reflect the increasing importance of family and household demographic structure in determining housing needs and preferences. The post-World War II decades witnessed a dramatic increase in childbearing, often called the "baby boom," that became associated spatially with the rapidly expanding suburbs on the fringes of cities. Singles, young childless couples, and older households tended to live towards the center of the city in older, smaller housing stock. Finally, **ethnic status** differentials reflect the growing importance of racial and ethnic identity stemming from the increased mobility of modern urban society as immigrants and migrants from the rural South poured into cities.

An important aspect of social area analysis was the use of large data sets about urban neighborhoods created by the U.S. Census Bureau. Shevky and Bell adopted specific variables from the census

BOX 8.2 WIRTH'S "URBANISM AS A WAY OF LIFE"

A seminal article was published in 1938 by sociologist Louis Wirth, who had trained at the University of Chicago under Park and Burgess and also with Simmel in Europe. Wirth reacted against the empiricism of Chicago school of ecological research, arguing that it was too inductive (an approach to science that starts with detailed observations and draws generalizations from those observations). He offered a much more deductive (moving from abstract thought to specific expectations) discussion of cities and social life. He differentiated between *urbanization* as a related set of economic and demographic trends producing rapid and dramatic changes in cities and *urbanism* as an interrelated set of social and psychological responses to these trends. Wirth identified three main attributes of urbanization:

- *Population size.* Increasing numbers of people bring about greater cultural and occupational diversity. Large populations, especially when driven by migration and immigration, increase the potential for different groups to come into close contact. Greater diversity brings about greater need for formal control systems, such as legal systems. Large differentiated populations lead to highly divided and specialized occupational structures. In sum, social interactions are increasingly depersonalized, based more on functional and formal roles than on personal relationships. Ultimately, there is a real risk of social disorganization and disintegration.
- *Physical density.* The crowding of ever-larger populations into inadequate amounts of urban space intensifies the effects of increased population size, producing spatial

fragmentation and segregation. The social-psychological effects of crowding and diversity include geographic stereotyping and the attempts to maintain social distance as antidotes to the press of people of different backgrounds. On a more positive note, crowding and diversity may lead to a greater toleration of differences.
- *Heterogeneity.* As we have already mentioned in passing, increasing social heterogeneity is a basic attribute of urbanization. In particular, we observe heightened social mobility across caste and class lines, weakened family ties, and an increase in the valuation of personal achievement. Social mobility is also connected to spatial mobility which then feeds back to weakened ties to community. Heterogeneity also increases the commercialization and rationalization that lead to the erosion of personal relations.

Wirth also identified three consequences of urbanization, which he defined as urbanism:

- *Adaptive individual behavior* appears in response to the changing urban context. People behave in more aloof and impersonal ways and do not restrain their behavior because of the liberties provided by the urban environment.
- *Neurotic individual behavior*, mental illness, alcoholism, and other "deviant" behaviors increase because of the lack of effective social controls. There is a greater reliance on institutionally enforced forms of social control.
- *Social fragmentation* becomes mapped into spatial segregation of groups, and social activities become much more compartmentalized.

data to represent each of their hypothesized forces, or, as they called them, "factors." Using these variables, they identified "social areas" specifically related to the natural areas previously described by Park:

> The social area generally contains persons having the same level of living, the same way of life, and the same ethnic background; and we hypothesize that persons living in a particular type

of social area would systematically differ with respect to characteristic attitudes and behaviors from persons living in another type of social area (Shevky and Bell 1955, p. 20).

Social area analysis compellingly demonstrated how quantitative data analysis could be combined with deductively derived hypotheses about the social patterning of cities. During the 1960s and 1970s much more data became available at the same time that rapid progress was made in computer technology. Many of the social sciences, including geography, embraced the application of ever-more complex ways of doing quantitative analysis of larger and larger data sets. The use of a set of quantitative techniques loosely known as "factor analysis" and now known as **factorial ecology,** became popular as a way to examine the ideas suggested by Shevky and Bell. Basically, the forces creating the spatial patterning of the city will be evident in empirically defined "factors" discovered inductively through analysis of large data sets. The quantitative empirical analysis is conducted first, and the factors are identified afterwards. Despite apparent methodological differences between social area analysis and factorial ecology, the two empirical approaches generally found evidence in support of three main factors responsible for organizing urban form: (1) socioeconomic status, (2) family status, and (3) ethnic and racial segregation.

The Urban Mosaic

An enduring difficulty with the social science study of urban spatial structure during the 1960s and 1970s was the apparent discrepancies among the spatial structures suggested by Burgess's concentric zone model, the Hoyt sector model, and the Harris and Ullman multiple nuclei model. Many studies were conducted to see which of the three visual models most closely reflected the reality of urban spatial structure. Ultimately, these studies found only weak support for any of the three. The emerging results of factorial ecologies, of which many were conducted during this period, provided a possible way to reconcile the three visual models.

Robert Murdie (1969) most clearly articulated this approach by describing the existence of an **urban mosaic** that resulted from the intersection of the three primary forces repeatedly identified by social area analysis and factorial ecology. Murdie suggested that the socioeconomic status factor most often exhibited a sectoral pattern similar to that described by Hoyt, with higher-income families

typically located in a specific sector of the city. Family status most often exhibited the concentric zone model described by Burgess, with young singles and the elderly living in the apartments and smaller houses located towards the center of the city and families raising children located on the periphery of the city. Ethnic and racial concentrations typically reflect historic concentrations and cut across the other factors. This can be argued to resemble, if only loosely, the Harris and Ullman notion of multiple nodes. When these three spatial patterns are overlain, the result is the urban mosaic (Figure 8.8).

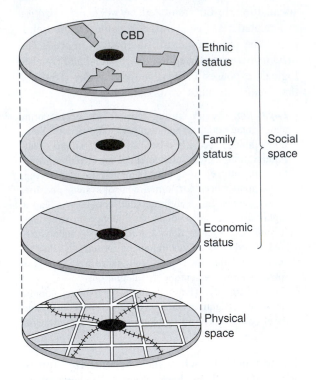

Figure 8.8 Murdie's idealized model of urban residential structure, based on studies of factorial ecology, helped to resolve the apparent disagreements among the zonal, sectoral, and multiple nuclei models of urban spatial structure by suggesting that different groups of neighborhood characteristics were distributed across urban space by different processes and thus took on different spatial patterns. (*Source:* Modified from R. A. Murdie, 1969.)

CONTEMPORARY URBAN SOCIAL SPACE: GLOBALIZATION, POSTMODERNISM, AND CITIES OF DIFFERENCE

Most of our effort so far in this chapter has been to present traditional ways of understanding the organization of urban social space, ways that enjoyed their greatest acceptance in the 1970s. However, cities and the social sciences have changed tremendously in the last three decades. Some of these changes we have already discussed in earlier chapters. In this section we review some more recent notions about contemporary social landscapes of cities. Some of these ideas reflect changes in cities themselves, while others reflect changes in the ways we think about cities. In particular, most of the ideas we have discussed already in this chapter begin (either explicitly or implicitly) with the assumption that groups and individuals choose where they live in a fairly rational manner. Although these choices may reflect a desire to maintain social distance (as in the ecological approach) or economic utility (as in neoclassical economics), the ability to choose remains an important aspect of these approaches. This assumption that social landscapes reflect the accumulated choices of individuals is challenged by the perspectives discussed in the last section of this chapter.

We discussed the political economy perspective in Chapter 7, where we focused on landscapes of industrial production. Here we want to discuss briefly how this perspective helps us understand the social landscapes of cities. The important insight from political economy is that the social landscapes of the city do not occur naturally as the result of individual decisions. They are part of a larger economic system from which they draw their meaning, and to which they contribute. In particular, social groups come to inhabit different and distinct parts of cities, not so much because they want to but rather because broader forces place them there. **Power,** thus, is a crucial concern of these approaches. Who has power? Who does not have power? And how is power created and used? Power derived from political structure or conflict and power derived from

economic structure are the primary foci of much of this research.

One of the central defining features of capitalism is class conflict between those that own (or control) the means of production and laborers. The division of urban space along social lines, known as **residential differentiation,** serves an important function in maintaining and reproducing this system. Recall from Chapter 7 that investment in the secondary circuit of capital results in the creation of the built environment for consumption (also known as the consumption fund) consisting of housing, parks, and roads among other features. On the one hand, these features are necessary to stimulate new rounds of consumption of industrial commodities, which is necessary to avert crises of overproduction. On the other hand, however, residential differentiation is recognized as being essential to the process of **social reproduction.** In order for the capitalist system to keep going, the basic classes must be reproduced. This requires socialization into group norms: value systems, ideologies, expectations, attitudes, and behaviors. Socialization often takes places in neighborhoods—in schools and parks and playgrounds. Socially homogenous neighborhoods facilitate this process. Children of working-class parents are socialized to become members of the working class in part because they grow up in working-class neighborhoods; children of the affluent are socialized to become members of the bourgeoisie in part because they grow up in elite neighborhoods.

Political economy perspectives also help us understand the sometimes startling polarities embedded within the urban social landscape. Capital investment and development is inherently uneven. This in part explains why cities contain places of extravagant wealth as well as places of despairing poverty. The dynamics and geographic logic of investment, disinvestment and reinvestment are discussed later in this chapter, and in Chapters 9 and 10.

The remainder of this chapter focuses on three major themes: **globalization, postmodernism,** and **cities of difference.** In particular, we ask what impact these trends have had on the social patterning of urban space. Our purpose here is both to discuss the forces that are changing urban social landscapes (whether or not they are "new") and to identify and describe some of the types of areas seen today that you probably would not have seen in decades past. Globalization, in particular, rests on the insights of the political economy approach, whereas postmodernism and notions of cities of difference, according to some theorists, rest on very different propositions that we will discuss briefly below.

Globalization: General Trends

Globalization represents interrelated economic transformations that include the shift from manufacturing to advanced services, the increasing speed and global scale of economic (especially financial) interactions, and the increasing mobility (some would say hyper mobility) of goods and people on a global scale. The impacts of these economic transformations upon the social landscapes of cities is our concern in this section.

To focus our discussion, we ask two questions. First, which general aspects of globalization have the potential to remake urban social geography? The profound economic changes that characterize globalization have deepened economic and **social polarization,** such that today the numbers of both rich and poor are increasing while the high-income working class and the middle class are shrinking. This process has the potential to affect cities because the increasing numbers of the wealthy and the increasing numbers of the poor both place new demands on cities for housing and residentially based services and amenities. International migration flows, especially from less-developed regions of the world into the largest global cities, are creating new opportunities for social groups to interact socially and economically. New opportunities for discrimination and conflict also arise.

Second, what are the geographic correlates of these trends within cities? The literature suggests that we should see several spatial trends along with globalization. Most generally, we should see increased spatial concentration and separation of social groups—a **spatial polarization** to accompany

social polarization. Although some degree of social separation has always marked cities, globalization is argued to have accentuated the extent and intensity of separation. New, and newly configured, enclaves of a variety of types mark the globalizing city.

Increased concentration and separation are also marked by the increased fortification of urban space, often with use of barriers such as walls and gates between sections of the city and heightened surveillance. The wealthy, and increasingly the professional classes, seem to want to "wall out" unwanted groups due to fear of increased social disorder and crime. Although defensive and exclusive "fortresses" always have marked some parts of the city, their use has widely expanded. On the other side of the polarized social spectrum, the poor are increasingly walled into abandoned and unwanted areas of cities.

The intensified tendencies toward concentration and separation are marked by internal self-sufficiency—referred to as *totalization* by some observers. Here we note the increasing tendency of the spatially separated parts of the city to provide a more comprehensive range of employment, service, retail, and entertainment opportunities *within the separated part of the city*. As a result, the historic role of cities as the loci of public interactions between disparate groups may be diminishing as social groups increasingly need not leave their part of the city for any purpose. This trend can be observed in suburban areas as professional office buildings and large complex retail centers have been constructed in outlying areas. Similarly, downtown residential areas are now providing a wider array of retail and entertainment opportunities. Note, for example, the increased presence of national and international retail chain stores, typically found in suburban malls, in urban areas such as New York's Times Square.

Elements of the Global City

Having identified some of the trends affecting globalizing cities, we now ask, what do these cities look like? What is the emerging urban social landscape? Based on the examples of the most important cities in the global economy, New York, London, and Tokyo, Saskia Sassen (1991) and other early observers (e.g., Mollenkopf and Castells, 1991) described a **dual city,** sometimes referred to more generally as a **divided city.** In the dual city, the most important forces are economic polarization and the functional and spatial links between the polarized segments of society. The increase in the number of lower-income workers at the bottom is linked to changing lifestyles at the top: higher-level workers increasingly meet basic functions of life by hiring someone else to perform them. For example, professional families often eat out more frequently and hire people to clean their homes, wash their cars, and watch their children. This pattern highlights renewed flows of immigrants into global cities, as immigrants, rather than existing minorities, often perform these low-level, low-income service tasks.

Spatially, the dual city hypothesis predicts that the social landscape of cities will be marked increasingly by intense spatial divisions reflecting the deepened social polarization generated by economic globalization. It frequently identifies two types of neighborhood transformations: upgrading and downgrading. On one hand, there is an *upgrading* of neighborhoods to accommodate the new affluence of the professional class. Older neighborhoods that had deteriorated during the middle decades of the twentieth century, yet contained interesting architecture, experienced what can be called **gentrification.** Here, "pioneers" willing to take considerable financial risks move into poor neighborhoods and renovate their houses. As more and more houses are renovated, the neighborhood undergoes a more widespread transformation and can eventually become a place with high-priced housing that only a few are able to afford. The in-town location of these neighborhoods, with convenient access to employment and to urban entertainment, makes them attractive to the new professional classes, often called "yuppies" (young urban professionals). Exclusive and private new in-town neighborhoods for the truly wealthy also have come to symbolize the new affluence of the global economy.

On the other hand there is an expansion of poor neighborhoods, often called *downgrading* or

filtering, with associated social problems. As the number of poor residents increases (from both economic dislocation and immigration), the spatial extent of the city devoted to housing the poor also grows. The poor are now more likely to live in poor neighborhoods, and the places where poor people live are now more likely to be populated by other poor people. This growing spatial concentration of poverty is tied to a series of social problems.

The metaphor of the dual city, marked by the increasing polarization of the contemporary global city into poor and rich that is driven by economic globalization, captures only a small part of contemporary trends. Peter Marcuse, in a series of publications (1996, 1997), identifies a number of other components of the globalizing city. Summarizing and rephrasing his work somewhat, there are three fundamental elements that constitute the globalizing city: the citadel, the enclave, and the ghetto, sometimes with important subelements, such as a distinction between the traditional ghetto and a new "outcaste ghetto." In between these basic elements lay urban landscapes of gentrification, working-class housing, and increasingly totalized suburbanization.

The Citadel "Citadels are enclosed, protected, insulated areas of upper-income residence, often, particularly if located downtown, combined with office and commercial uses" (Marcuse and van Kempen 2000, p. 13). **Citadel** residents tend to be at the highest levels of income and power, whereas residents of gentrified neighborhoods (see below) tend to be managers and professionals associated with the expanding sectors of the new information economy. The wealth necessary to live in these areas may be inherited or generated by the opportunities of the postindustrial global economy. Often, citadel residents desire proximity to downtown but fear the dangers that contemporary cities represent. For this reason, newly constructed developments often are surrounded by high protective walls and guarded by armed "rent-a-cops." Such citadels reflect both the increase of wealth and the increased desire of the wealthy for social isolation (Figure 8.9).

Figure 8.9 Battery Park City in New York demonstrates that citadels have become a prominent feature of many urban landscapes. They are often located close to downtown cores, offering proximity to urban amenities, and are often heavily fortified for protection.

The Enclave The enclave represents spaces of social concentration where the forces creating the spaces are more *voluntary* than imposed. Marcuse distinguishes three types of enclave: cultural, immigrant, and exclusionary. The **cultural enclave** is an area where residents participate in and share common cultural interests. For example, areas with cheap rents and studio space attract artists and musicians. The **immigrant enclave,** as its name implies, houses a population that consists of a particular immigrant group. Here, the distinction between contemporary concentrations of immigrants and the traditional immigrant ghetto of the industrial city needs to be articulated. Although some immigrants with fewer economic resources still congregate in the classic immigrant ghettos of a hundred years ago (e.g., Manhattan's Chinatown), a new form of immigrant enclave is emerging—the **ethnoburb.** Possessing both economic resources, and, increasingly, political influence, immigrants (and second-generation households) are voluntarily clustering in suburban locales, transforming both our impression of what suburbs are and our notions of immigrant communities.

Perhaps the most troubling type of enclave is the **exclusionary enclave,** populated by upper-middle-class households seeking to reside in areas where they are not exposed to ethnic and/or racial diversity or especially to poverty and crime. The point of the exclusionary enclave is to keep others out—to reproduce residential homogeneity. These enclaves are often associated with high-income suburban jurisdictions that enforce homogeneity through the imposition of exclusionary zoning, restrictive building codes, and other local regulations. Increasingly, however, exclusive enclaves are also being created in other parts of the city, including some gentrified and redeveloped inner-city neighborhoods.

The Ghetto Ghettos represent spaces of congregation created and maintained by forces external to the choices and desires of their residents. Historically, ghettos have had an ethnic component to them; for example, Jewish Quarters in the cities of Medieval Europe (Chapter 2). In the United States, ghettos were given a racialized meaning during the decades of the Great Migration of southern blacks to northern industrial cities when residential segregation reached unprecedented levels (Chapter 10). Recent trends have created ghettos that also have substantial implications in terms of poverty. Marcuse thus recognizes two kinds of ghettos. The **traditional ghetto** is based on ethnic and/or racialized identity, and residents typically serve an economic function (e.g., as the source of low-cost labor) for the broader society. The **excluded ghetto,** (sometimes refered to as the outcaste ghetto) in contrast, houses groups of the population for whom there is no economic role. This representation of the ghetto is often based on the work of sociologist William J. Wilson, who wrote about the development of an isolated and structurally impoverished underclass living in abandoned central-city neighborhoods. The lack of current economic usefulness for the residents of the excluded ghetto differentiates it from the historically antecedent traditional ghetto and other working-class and poor areas.

"In Between" Neighborhoods in the Global City

If citadels, enclaves, and ghettos constitute the major "ideal types" of the spatial elements of contemporary cities, other types of areas exist in between. These areas are often transitional, both in the sense that they exist spatially in between citadels and ghettos, for example, and in the sense that they can be neighborhoods temporally in the midst of transitioning from one type to another. Regardless of the temporal longevity of these forms, they are important components of the contemporary social landscape.

The Gentrified City Gentrification represents the movement of upper- and middle-income, predominantly white residents into older neighborhoods that typically contain architecturally valuable housing stock. These neighborhoods often are in close proximity to downtown business and entertainment districts, though they can also be located in older suburbs. The process of gentrification is closely related to housing value cycles in urban housing markets: it typically begins when a few so-called "urban pioneers," often gays or artists, purchase devalued older housing stock and renovate and upgrade the properties with "**sweat equity.**" Housing values often begin a rapid increase. An often-observed demographic sequence can ensue where pioneers are followed by "yuppies" and childless couples. For a time, gentrifying neighborhoods often are quite diverse in terms of social identity and economic resources. Very often, however, rents and home prices escalate to the point where former residents can no longer afford to live in the neighborhood and are displaced. Eventually, given a complete transition, the residents of gentrified neighborhood may be quite like those of wealthier suburban enclaves—predominantly white and upper income (Figure 8.10).

The Suburban City Suburbs are not new to global cities. Indeed, as we discuss more fully in other chapters, the general process of decentralization, and specific locations called suburbs, have been associated with urbanization for several centuries. Automobile-oriented residential suburbanization was one of the dominant forces affecting urban areas in the post–World War II decades. In many

Figure 8.10 The Alamo Square Victorians shown in this photograph of San Francisco demonstrate the increasing prevalence of gentrified neighborhoods in inner-city areas of many North American cities. Older neighborhoods with interesting architectural features have become popular with affluent urbanites willing and able to renovate the properties. Critics point out that gentrification displaces the poor who formerly lived in these neighborhoods and reduces the supply of affordable housing throughout the city.

ways the mythology of the homogenous, mostly white, middle-class, conventional family-oriented suburb is an enduring force, affecting not only the reality of the social geography of the city but also how we view the contemporary city. Several recent trends have tremendously impacted suburbs, however, perhaps fundamentally changing the very nature of the territories on the outer edges of metropolitan areas.

First, **edge cities** (also called stealth cities, suburban downtown and totalizing suburbs, which are discussed in greater detail in Chapter 6) have formed. Journalist Joel Garreau popularized the term in his 1991 book of that name (Figure 8.11). The trend is for high-rise office buildings, comprehensive retail centers, and entertainment opportunities to anchor what were formerly only residential communities. Increasingly, suburban locations contain the majority of a metropolitan area's jobs and retail businesses, in addition to the majority of housing. Thus, suburban residents do not need to leave the suburban environment for any of their needs.

Figure 8.11 Tysons Corner, Virginia, demonstrates the increasing importance of edge cities in many metropolitan areas since the 1980s. Formerly nonurban spaces were made accessible by interstate freeways, especially where radial freeways intersected with circumferential or beltway freeways. Edge cities are remarkable for their concentration of higher order service functions, among them corporate command and control functions.

Second, suburban environments are increasingly marked by defensive design. Comprehensive walled developments spring up next to older developments that add walls, gates, and guards in a defensive attempt to shield out the dangers of the city. Both edge cities and defensive designs can be seen as part of the polarization that results from the economic changes brought by globalization, in that they are attempts to maintain spatial distance and isolation against the spreading troubles of the inner city.

The Working-Class City

Cities long functioned as the residential location of the laboring classes that undergirded industrial capitalism. Especially in cities that matured during the last half of the nineteenth and first half of the twentieth centuries, the neighborhoods occupied by the working classes have experienced a variety of fates. In many U.S. cities, working-class neighborhoods built in the two decades following World War II are undergoing substantial downgrading. Many (though certainly not all) of these inner-ring working-class suburbs will be ghettos in just a few years. In Los Angeles, for example, many of these areas already have poverty rates and associated rates of crime similar to those

in the ghettos of northeastern cities. Other working-class areas face extreme upward pressure as households search for ways to deal with rising housing costs. Some properties are purchased simply for their location so that the house can be torn down and replaced with a new and typically larger house.

Overall, the globalization thesis describes many trends that we observe in contemporary cities. Indeed, many of these trends occur in cities of all sizes, not just the largest cities described as global cities. In addition, we also observe trends and patterns in the largest cities that are not consistent with the trends described. For example, contemporary cities remain deeply divided by race (Chapter 10), a pattern that predates globalization and seems resistant to recent changes.

Postmodern Urbanism

Many scholars identify a major historical shift in the fundamental nature of society dating to the late 1960s and early 1970s. As the economy in developed nations shifted from industry to advanced services and simultaneously became more globalized and more fragmented, culture also changed. Observers understand these changes as part of an epochal shift from a long period of modernism to an emergent period of postmodernism. The advent of postmodernism in architecture and other design fields resulted in the incorporation of various past (sometimes pre- or early-modern) elements into new designs. The sometimes glaring juxtaposition of elements from different traditions is thought to provide opportunities for constructing new meaning and can be seen across a wide variety of building types, ranging from residences to commercial establishments to high-rise office buildings. Postmodernism is also thought to have dramatic yet shifting impacts on urban form. Paul Knox (1993) describes the constantly changing postmodern metropolis as a "restless urban landscape." The basic elements of postmodern design are contrasted with modern design elements in Table 8.1.

One example of postmodern urban design that we talk about more in Chapter 13 is the increasing tendency to adopt multiple land uses in close

Table 8.1   Differences between Modern and Postmodern Architecture

Modern	Postmodern
"Less is more" (Mies van der Rohe)	"Less is a bore" (Robert Venturi)
International style, or "no style"	Double-coding of style
Utopian and idealist	Real-world and populist
Abstract form	Responsive and recognizable form
Deterministic form ("form follows function")	Semiotic form ("form follows fiction")
Functional separation	Functional mixing
Simplicity	Complexity and decoration
Purist	Eclectic
Protechnology	Disguised technology
No historical or vernacular references	Mixed historical and vernacular palette
Innovation	Recycling
No ornamentation	"Meaningful" ornamentation
Context ignored	Contextual cues
"Dumb box"	Scenographic

Source: Table 6.1 from Knox, 1994, p. 166 (his sources: After C. Jencks, *The Language of Post-Modern Architecture*, New York: Rizzoli, 1977; and J. Punter, "Post-Modernism: A Definition," *Planning Practice and Research* 4 (1988): 22.)

proximity, sometimes on the same parcel or even in the same structure. In particular, **New Urbanism** (also called neo-traditional town planning) is a movement to retrieve urban and architectural design from a past era (typically thought of as the central portions of late-nineteenth and early-twentieth century towns and small cities and the streetcar suburbs of larger urban regions). Often presented as an antidote to automobile-dependent, environmentally destructive suburban sprawl, **New Urbanism** also more generally celebrates design diversity and the absence of highly segmented urban landscapes. In many New Urbanist developments, housing combines contemporary amenity and space sensibilities with nostalgic designs, such as large front porches, no visible automobile garages, narrow lots or connected housing, and sidewalks. Moreover, residential land use is located close to, or interspersed with, commercial and industrial land uses, and has easy access to public transportation facilities.

A stronger discussion of "postmodern urbanism" emerged from scholars working in and focusing on Los Angeles. Los Angeles developed without the strong center epitomized by Manhattan or downtown Chicago and is characterized by a highly decentralized and fragmented social landscape. The so-called "LA school" scholars have since the early 1980s seized upon Los Angeles' distinctiveness and argued that rather than being unique, it is the model of postmodern urbanization. Drawing on earlier discussions of economic restructuring and globalization, Dear and Flusty's (1998) iconic presentation accentuates cultural interpretations of urban form. For example, they identify the increasingly isolated neighborhoods for the wealthy and the professional classes (citadels and some gentrified neighborhoods discussed earlier) as **dreamscapes**—places increasingly disconnected from broader realities and thus given over to artificial and contrived meanings. They refer to the powerful controllers of the global economy as the **cybergeoisie,** ever more interested in consuming urban dreamscapes, and the increasingly disenfranchised and exploited masses as the **protosurp,** relegated to marginalized urban spaces. They argue that the depth of spatial fragmentation based on deepening social polarization in Los Angeles foreshadows the future of urbanization in other metropolitan regions.

As an alternative to the concentric-ring theory and its sectoral and multinucleated variations that we have already discussed, Dear and Flusty offer a game-board model of city space (Figure 8.12).

> It is evident that the traditional, center-driven agglomeration economies that have guided urban development in the past not longer apply. Conventional city form, Chicago-style, is sacrificed in favor of a noncontiguous collage of parcelized, consumption-oriented landscapes devoid of conventional centers yet wired into electronic propinquity and nominally unified by the mythologies of the disinformation highway. Los Angeles may be a mature form of this postmodern metropolis; Las Vegas comes to mind as a youthful example. The consequent urban aggregate is characterized by acute fragmentation and specialization—a partitioned gaming board subject to perverse laws and peculiarly discrete, disjointed urban outcomes. (Dear and Flusty, 1998, p. 66)

While Dear and Flusty's model is perhaps the most exaggerated and extreme of attempts to theorize the postmodern metropolis, it illustrates important themes present in much of the literature: (1) individual parcels of urban land have direct connections with globalized capitalism (i.e., individual uses of land owe more to their utility in the global economy than to local rationales); (2) there is little apparent connection between parcels in use; and (3) the uses of land can be shuffled—mixed and redistributed.

Cities of Difference

An important perspective on the social geography of cities shares with postmodernism respect for the importance of culture, especially as related to the major axes of social differentiation (race, gender, sexuality, etc.). While the material we address in this section is not dominated by a single research tradition or theory, much of it (especially in recent years) prioritizes questions of social **identity** and builds, in some fashion, on notions of a **socio-spatial dialectic.** This is a way of thinking about the back-and-forth and simultaneous relationships between the configuration of space and social identity. For example, we might say that

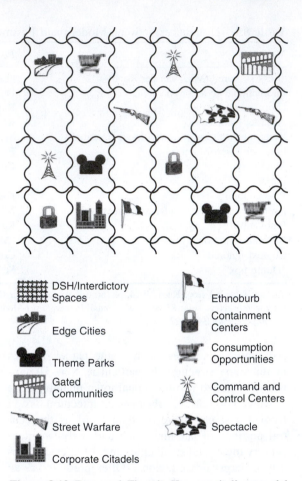

DSH/Interdictory Spaces

Edge Cities

Theme Parks

Gated Communities

Street Warfare

Corporate Citadels

Ethnoburb

Containment Centers

Consumption Opportunities

Command and Control Centers

Spectacle

Figure 8.12 Dear and Flusty's Keno capitalism model of urban (non)structure, based on applying a postmodern perspective. (*Source:* Modified from M. Dear and S. Flusty, 1998.)

the development of gender identity *reflects* the spatial structure of the city, while at the same time gender identity *affects* the spatial structure of the city. Because many scholars in recent years are increasingly uncomfortable with the idea that identity (whether gender, race, or sexuality, among other dimensions) can be permanent or stable, some have argued that we should focus instead on the processes that generate social **difference.** From this perspective, we recognize that differences are socially constructed (as opposed to biologically determined), mutable, and multiple (e.g., the experience of a lesbian black women looking for a neighborhood to live in will be shaped by her racialized difference *and* by her gendered difference *and* by her sexualized difference). This last point is sometimes referred to as the **intersectionality** of the multiple dimensions along which social difference is produced and experienced. We review in this section two of the dimensions along which social difference is produced and interacts with urban spatial configurations: feminist theories of urban space and theories that deal with sexuality in urban space. We will address issues of racialized difference more fully in Chapter 10.

Women and the City   Women have been scarcely mentioned in this chapter. This largely reflects the fact that the traditional models of urban social space do not consider the relationship between urban social space and womens' identities and experiences in and of the city. Historically, the feature of urban social space that held perhaps the greatest importance is the separation of work from home, which began during the period of preindustrial modernism and intensified as part of the industrialization of capitalist production. Reflecting patriarchal social relations, space came to be understood culturally in gendered terms. Public space was the realm of work and commerce and the domain of men working outside of the home in a wage economy. Private space was the home and the domain of women whose domestic labor was not wage compensated. This overly simplistic dichotomy has been mapped onto geographic space at several scales (Box 8.3). Domosh and Seager (2001), for example, note that in Renaissance Europe, cities were seen as masculine and the countryside as feminine. Industrialization deepened and rearranged this mapping by requiring large new urban districts devoted to production (including factories, warehouses and transportation facilities): these spaces became part of the masculine public realm. Housing (for the nonlaboring classes) became increasingly separated from the spaces of production and commerce in new suburban districts. Accordingly, private feminine space became associated with suburban areas within cities, while public masculine space identities adhered to cities' downtowns and sites of capitalist production. This simplistic dualism of public masculine city versus private feminine suburb still has cultural power today, reflected in the opinions and politics of urban space.

This simplistic dualism, of course, does not adequately reflect the complexities of the lives that women lead in cities. Domosh and Seager (2001), for example, draw attention to the many contradictions presented by shopping. As industrialization progressed during the nineteenth century, mass production made available to the expanding middle class an ever-widening range of consumer products at more affordable prices. As the gendered household division of labor deepened, women were expected to take the primary role in running the household, which increasingly required that women take responsibility for managing the household budget and purchasing household items. Department stores and other retail spaces required for the circulation of mass-produced goods were located downtown, which required that women travel from the private feminine realm of suburban home to the public masculine realm of downtown. These daily mobilities produced social anxieties, and much effort was expended on regulating how and when women could "appropriately" move through urban space.

Over the last five or six decades, women have greatly expanded their presence in the workforce. Even so, the patriarchal division of labor in the household continues to require that women hold the vast majority of domestic responsibilities for the household, even while working. These dual responsibilities interact with urban space in several important ways. The **spatial entrapment** thesis contends that women must make career sacrifices in order to accommodate their dual responsibilities. The job must be located close to home, and often have flexible or part-time hours, to facilitate domestic responsibilities. Many women end up working in jobs stereotypically known as "women's work" (e.g., nursing, teaching, clerical work) for relatively lower salaries and fewer advancement opportunities. An important associated trend is for large corporations

BOX 8.3   TECHNOLOGY AND URBAN GEOGRAPHY

WOMEN AND GIS?

We are portraying throughout this text examples of GIS applied to urban issues. The profound theoretical changes that have deeply affected urban social geography over the last several years, including feminist theories in particular, have called into question the appropriateness of using GIS research methods. Mei-Po Kwan, a leading GIS scholar, has engaged this idea by arguing that GIS and

feminist research are indeed compatible. The feminist critique argues that in terms of both practice (what people using GIS techniques *do*) and theory, GIS is gendered male. In particular, GIS relies on approaches that overly emphasize (if not exclusively validate) the analyst's view from above, as if flying over a landscape. This perspective troubles feminist scholars who value a way of understanding that centers on the subject's view. Kwan has developed several innovative ways of collecting,

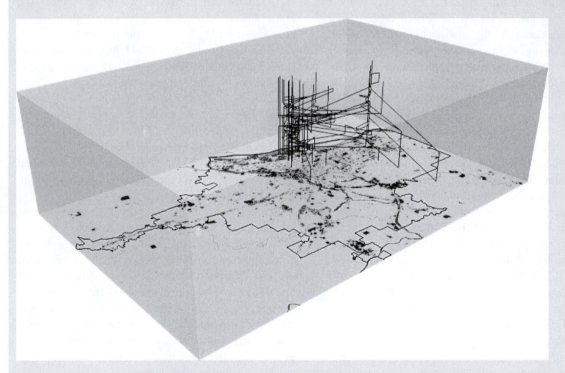

Figure B8.3 The space-time paths of a sample of African-American women in Portland, Oregon. (*Source:* Kwan, Mei-Po, 2002, Fig 1.)

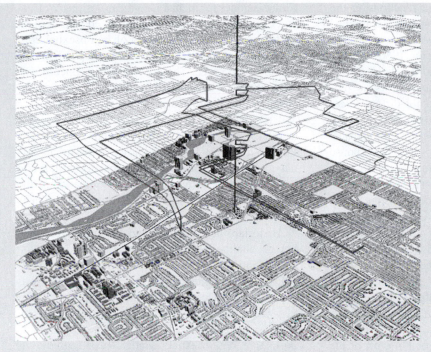

Figure B8.4 A space-time path, as a continuous trajectory in three-dimensional space, is a useful means for visualizing a person's daily movement in space and time. In this figure, the vertical axis represents the temporal progression of such movement, while the horizontal plane represents the geographical extent of a person's activity space. This path shows a woman's feeling (color coded in the original figure) about the urban environment while traveling outside her home in Columbus, Ohio. (*Source:* http://geog-www.sbs.ohio-state.edu/faculty/mkwan/Gallery/STPaths.htm)

analyzing and visually representing information that she argues addresses this critique. For example, Kwan (2002) uses very detailed travel diaries for a sample of people living in Portland, Oregon, and incorporated the space-time information into a three-dimensional GIS (Figure B8.3), which she used to argue that African-American women in Portland have much more constrained activity spaces than other gender/ethnic groups in the sample. Figure B8.4 shows a close-up of a single woman's space-time path through urban space (Coumbus, OH) where Kwan color-coded (in the original figures) the path according to the woman's feelings about the urban space she was traveling through. Addressing the philosophic critiques, Kwan argues that

The geometry of women's life-paths and the processes of identity formation and women's experience of places are mutually constitutive. The movement of women's bodies in space-time is also an active element in the production of gendered spaces. Through this reimagining, the lines representing women's life paths in space-time are no longer abstract lines in the Cartesian space of GIS. Instead, they are the material expressions of women's corporeality and embodied subjectivities—a mapping of their bodies onto space-time that emanates from their prediscursive practices of everyday life. In this light, I argue that feminist geographers can *appropriate* GIS methods for illuminating women's spatiality, while recognizing the apparent privilege given to the physicality of the body by GIS methods. (Kwan 2002, 653) to locate clerical and back-office functions in the suburbs to take advantage of the spatially entrapped labor pool of educated suburban women seeking proximate and flexible jobs (Nelson, 1986).

Hanson and Pratt (1995) and England (1993) argued that the spatial entrapment thesis as presented here is too simplistic, but for different reasons. Hanson and Pratt emphasize the multiple ways that geographies of work vary across urban space. In particular, women offer their labor in response to very localized norms and values (i.e., the local context matters), and employers are very sensitive to these contextual variations. Class also matters, as working-class women seem to experience greater spatial entrapment than middle- and upper-class women who are able to use paid labor to attend to domestic responsibilities. England (1993) accentuates the diversity of motivations and strategies that characterize women working outside of the home, and argues that spatial entrapment is not ubiquitously applicable.

Dolores Hayden (1981), also building off of the distinctions between public masculine versus private feminine space, critiques the highly privatized design of urban space, focused on single-family ("dream") homes, as being dysfunctional for working women with dual responsibilities. Tellingly, the emphasis on privacy in the single-family home superficially seems to accentuate the private realm of domestic femininity, yet burdens women with unnecessary domestic work stemming from the isolation of the household from the community resources, including the option of housing shared between multiple families, that would make domestic labor much more feasible. Hayden, a noted Yale architect, goes beyond critique to propose several alternative models of house design and urban design that foundationally build on the needs of working women, especially those in nontraditional households (i.e., single women, single mothers, widows, etc.).

Sexuality and the City

Is there an urban geography of sexuality? Mort (2000) identifies the mid-1950s maps of prostitution and male homosexuality produced by London's Metropolitan Police Commissioner for inclusion in the notorious Wolfendon Commission Report (which proved instrumental in decriminalizing some forms of homosexual conduct in Britain) as perhaps the first maps of homosexual urban space. The government's concern was to locate the spaces of sexual impropriety as a precursor to eliminating them through the monitoring and regulation of those spaces (much as a public health campaign might begin with maps of disease). Prior to this, very little was known about urban sexual geographies. Mapping gay space continues to be an attractive activity: note the popularity of the Urban Institute's *The Gay and Lesbian Atlas* (Gates and Ost, 2004).

Historians and other scholars disagree over when homosexuality became socially recognized as a distinct identity in opposition to normative heterosexuality: some contend that sex between men was a public and accepted part of life in many cities of antiquity. Others argue that a distinct homosexual social identity, understood in opposition to normative heterosexual identity, was forged during the industrialism of the mid-nineteenth century as capitalism fixed the nuclear family as the site of social reproduction. Most scholars agree that a public social identity began to take spatial form in the cities of the early twentieth century. As a starting point, cities were attractive as locations for homosexual activities because of their size, diversity and anonymity relative to rural or small town contexts. Within cities, gay men increasingly utilized public and semi-public spaces to meet and pursue sexual encounters. Parks, bathhouses and public restrooms became known as spaces for gay cruising—though it was necessary to always be watchful for police and/or unwanted public observation. Given that homosexual activity was still illegal in most Western societies until the 1960s or later, more permanent spaces were created in bars and social clubs, which were often located in city districts that were already known for sexual tolerance.

Spaces for gay males shifted dramatically in the 1960s, in part due to increasing social tolerance for homosexuality and the emergence of an active gay rights movement after the 1969 Stonewall riots in Greenwich Village. One result has been a shift from the ephemeral and covert spaces of public restrooms and secret bars to a pronounced residential clustering in many large U.S. cities: Levine (1979) popularized the term "gay ghetto." As mentioned earlier in this chapter, gay males are often popularly associated with gentrification. Simplistic but only partially accurate arguments contended that because gay males did not carry the financial burden of rearing children, they enjoyed greater disposable income, even if their jobs did not pay any more than heterosexual men. Seeking the relative permissiveness and anonymity of the cities, they were well-positioned to be pioneers in inner-city neighborhoods that had suffered from decades of deterioration and neglect yet were located in close proximity to the lifestyle amenities and job opportunities of the city. They were able to leverage their lifestyle and financial resources by investing in real estate in marginal neighborhoods, and through renovation and sweat-equity begin the process of gentrification. While not all gentrification has been associated with concentration of male gays, some of the first and most visible examples clearly were (e.g., San Francisco's Castro district, New York's Greenwich Village, New Orleans' Marigny neighborhood).

Lawrence Knopp has written extensively on the development of homosexual urban spaces. One of his more influential arguments (Lauria and Knopp, 1985) is that gay men, in particular, congregate in specific urban neighborhoods as a strategy of creating gay territories that serve to establish and defend gay social identity. Moreover, these gay neighborhoods also provide a territorial basis for developing economic and political power (Knopp 1990, 1998), though the specific goals and methods varied considerably among cities.

Benjamin Forest (1995) took this line of research to a broader scale in his analysis of the successful effort to incorporate the city of West Hollywood. The area had long been known as a gay part of the greater Los Angeles area, but with the strong support of the local gay community, as reflected in several gay newspapers, it became perhaps the first predominantly gay city. Forest focused on the symbolic features of gay social identity that were attributed to West Hollywood's place identity in the effort to win the incorporation vote, and which in turn solidified a narrative of what it meant to be gay. He identified seven elements of this gay social/place identity: "creativity, aesthetic sensibility, an orientation toward entertainment or consumption, progressiveness, responsibility, maturity, and centrality" (Forest 1995, p. 133).

Most of the published research on urban space and sexuality has focused on gay males rather than lesbians. Some (e.g., Castells 1983) have argued that lesbians are less likely to congregate in visibly "lesbian neighborhoods," attributing this, in part, to an innate male desire to dominate territory. This is an overly simplistic view that perpetrates gendered stereotypes. Note that while there is ongoing interest in mapping gay spaces (Box 8.4), recent research criticizes these approaches on several grounds. First, there are real problems in the data that used to create maps; while census data capture households with same-sex partners, gays and lesbians live in a wide variety of household types. Moreover, many gay men and lesbians deliberately conceal ("closet") their sexual identities. Second, even when gay spaces are mapped, most often there are many non-gays living in these neighborhoods at the same time that many gays and lesbians live (and work and play) in other spaces of the city. Third, the focus on gay spaces glosses over the more basic fact that all spaces in the city have sexual identity.

WRAPPING UP

Our focus in this chapter has been on the social landscape of the city—in particular upon traditional and contemporary ways of understanding how distinct social groups come to inhabit separate parts of the city. Many of the models presented in the first part of the chapter came under severe criticism over the last three decades. Part of this criticism reflected changing tastes for theoretical frameworks. Part of the criticism, however, reflected the fact that the

BOX 8.4 MAPPING GAY AND LESBIAN SPACES

Gary Gates of the Urban Institute has extensively explored the potential of U.S. Census data to count and map gay men and lesbians—work that is attractively portrayed in *The Gay and Lesbian Atlas*. While their images cannot be reproduced in color here, Michael Brown and Larry Knopp (2006) have rendered several of their maps in gray scale: these image portray the neighborhood distribution of female (Figure B8.5a) and male (Figure B8.5b) same-sex households in Seattle, based on Census

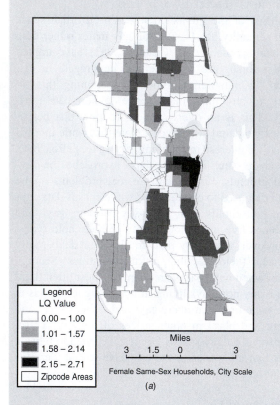

Legend
LQ Value
- 0.00 – 1.00
- 1.01 – 1.57
- 1.58 – 2.14
- 2.15 – 2.71
- Zipcode Areas

Miles
3   1.5   0   3

Female Same-Sex Households, City Scale
(a)

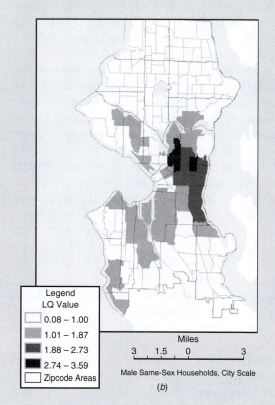

Legend
LQ Value
- 0.08 – 1.00
- 1.01 – 1.87
- 1.88 – 2.73
- 2.74 – 3.59
- Zipcode Areas

Miles
3   1.5   0   3

Male Same-Sex Households, City Scale
(b)

Figure B8.5 Maps of gay and lesbian urban spaces in Seattle. (*Source:* Adapted from Brown, M. and Knopp, L., Figure 2, Figure 3, and Figure 4, 2006.)

traditional models based on rings and sectors simply no longer described what most people (not to mention scholars) observed in cities. For example, most people living in cities are acutely aware of the rapidly changing nature of suburbs with their increasing presence of jobs and entertainment, and the expansion of gentrified neighborhoods at the center.

Much of the last half of this chapter thus is devoted to understanding the contemporary social landscape of the city from newer theoretical perspectives. We end our discussion by asking a simple question: Are cities really all that different than they were in the past? Or are we simply seeing the end result of processes already in place a century ago? It is interesting

2000 data. While there are substantial methodological problems with their approach, Brown and Knopp confirmed that the maps roughly correspond with urban spaces locally known as being "gay" or "lesbian." Even so, they also note that a slightly different way of treating the data produces a very different looking map (Figure B8.5c shows the redrawn

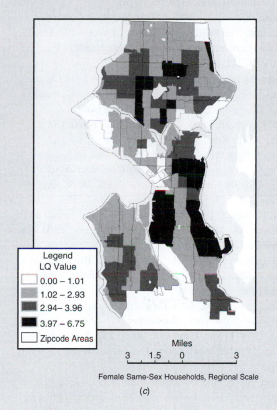

Legend
LQ Value

☐ 0.00 – 1.01
▨ 1.02 – 2.93
▩ 2.94– 3.96
■ 3.97 – 6.75
☐ Zipcode Areas

Miles

3   1.5   0   3

Female Same-Sex Households, Regional Scale

(c)

Figure B8.5 (*Continued*)

map of female same-sex households) that doesa better job of illuminating some neighborhoods that are known to be home to substantial numbers of lesbians. Brown and Knopp provide a much more extensive engagement with Gates' mapping project than we can explore here. Gates' work with census data shows up in a very different context. Richard Florida has received tremendous attention in recent years for his "Creative Class" arguments (2002, 2005), where he claims that cities with a diverse, tolerant and vibrant bohemian cultural life win economically by attracting the kinds of innovative and creative labor that start companies like Google and eBay. Florida collaborated with Gary Gates to create a "Gay Index" as a way of identifying culturally diverse and tolerant cities that the new "creative class" prefers to live in.

to consider some of the authors that we presented earlier in this chapter. Take Peter Marcuse, for example, who presented strongly worded arguments in articles and chapters throughout the 1990s about how significantly cities are changing in the era of economic globalization. In a more recent book, published in 2000, Marcuse backs away from these arguments.

Instead of a "new spatial order" evident in globalizing cities, Marcuse concludes that although the forces affecting change in the globalizing city are real and have real effects, there are also significant continuities with past processes and past spatial patterns.

A similar reaction can be seen with regard to arguments about an emergent postmodern city. If stripped of the new phraseology, arguments about postmodern urbanism (and Los Angeles's archetypal status) sounds surprisingly similar to arguments made a century ago when the Chicago school was coming to prominence. This is not to suggest that we do not see substantial changes in the social landscapes of contemporary cities—we do. We simply suggest that these changes are the result of long-standing processes as well as new processes deriving from macro-changes in the nature of economic activity. A popular and nonacademic presentation of the changing structure of cities is evident in the rapidly growing area of geodemographics. This field takes advantage of the social patterning of cities that we have been talking about in this chapter for business use. Businesses target residential "clumps" for special marketing and to help determine potentially profitable locations for their establishments. Most major data vendors (companies that package and process data from a variety of sources in formats useful to businesses) have some sort of neighborhood classification scheme. In subsequent chapters we examine specific aspects of the social landscape of cities in greater detail: housing (Chapter 9), poverty (Chapter 10), and immigration (Chapter 11).

READINGS

Berry, Brian J. L., and John D. Kasarda. 1977. *Contemporary Urban Ecology*. New York: Macmillan Publishing Co., Inc.

Brown, Michael, and Larry Knopp. 2006. "Places or Polygons? Governmentality, Scale, and the Census in *The Gay and Lesbian Atlas*," *Population, Space and Place*, Vol. 12, pp. 223–242.

Burgess, Ernest W. 1925/1967. "The Growth of the City: An Introduction to a Research Project." In R. Park, E. Burgess, and R. McKenzie, *The City*. Chicago: University of Chicago Press.

Castells, Manuel. 1977. *The Urban Question: A Marxist Approach*. Cambridge, MA: MIT Press.

Castells, Manuel. 1983. *The City and the Grassroots*. Berkeley: University of California Press.

Dear, Michael, and Steven Flusty. 1998. "Postmodern Urbanism," *Annals of the Association of American Geographers*, Vol. 88, pp. 50–72. See also the 1999 special issue of *Urban Geography* (Vol. 20) evaluating Dear and Flusty's paper.

Domosh, Mona, and Joni Seager. 2001. *Putting Women in Place: Feminist Geographers Make Sense of the World*. New York: Guilford Press.

Durkheim, Emile. 1893/1964. "Mechanical Solidarity through Likeness;" and "Organic Solidarity Due to the Division of Labor" In *The Division of Labor in Society*. New York: The Free Press.

England, Kim V. L. 1993. "Suburban Pink Collar Ghettos: The Spatial Entrapment of Women?" *Annals of the Association of American Geographers*, Vol. 83, pp. 225–242.

Florida, Richard. 2002. *The Rise of the Creative Class . . . And How It's Transforming Work, Leisure, Community and Everyday Life*. New York: Basic Books.

Florida, Richard. 2005. *Cities and the Creative Class*. New York: Routledge.

Forest, Benjamin. 1995. "West Hollywood as Symbol: The Significance of Place in the Construction of a Gay Identity," *Environment and Place, D: Society and Space*, Vol. 13, pp. 133–157.

Gans, Herbert J. 1962. *The Urban Villagers: Group and Class in the Life of Italian-Americans*. New York: The Free Press of Glencoe.

Gans, Herbert J. 1967. *The Levittowners: Ways of Life and Politics in a New Suburban Community*. New York: Pantheon Books.

Garreau, Joel. 1991. *Edge City: Life on the New Frontier*. New York: Doubleday.

Gates, Gary J., and Jason Ost. 2004. *The Gay and Lesbian Atlas,* Washington, D.C.: The Urban Institute Press.

Hanson, Susan, and Geraldine Pratt. 1995. *Gender, Work, and Space*. London and New York: Routledge.

Harris, Chauncy, and Edward L. Ullman. 1945. "The Nature of Cities," *Annals of the American Academy of Political and Social Sciences*, Vol. 242, pp. 7–17. See also the 1997 special issue of *Urban Geography* (Vol. 18) commemorating the 50th anniversary of the publishing of "The Nature of Cities."

Hayden, Dolores. 1981. "What Would a Non-Sexist City Be Like? Speculations on Housing, Urban Design, and Human Work." In C. R. Stimpson, E. Dixler, M. J. Nelson, and K. Yatrakis, eds., *Women and the American City*. Chicago: University of Chicago Press.

Hoyt, Homer. 1936–1937. "City Growth and Mortgage Risk." In Homer Hoyt, ed., *According to Hoyt; Fifty Years of Homer Hoyt. Articles on Law, Real Estate Cycle, Economic Base, Sector Theory, Shopping Centers, Urban Growth, 1916–1966*. Washington, D.C.: Homer Hoyt.

Hoyt, Homer. 1939. *The Structure and Growth of Residential Neighborhoods in American Cities*. Washington, D.C.: Federal Housing Administration.

Jacobs, Jane. 1961. *The Death and Life of Great American Cities*. New York: Vintage Books.

Knopp, Lawrence. 1990. "Exploiting the Rent-Gap: The Theoretical Significance of Using Illegal Appraisal Schemes to Encourage Gentrification in New Orleans," *Urban Geography*, Vol. 11, pp. 48–64.

Knopp, Lawrence. 1998. "Sexuality and Urban Space: Gay Male Identity Politics in the United States, the United Kingdom, and Australia." In Ruth Fincher and Jane M. Jacobs, eds., *Cities of Difference*. New York and London: Guilford Press.

Knox, Paul L., ed. 1993. *The Restless Urban Landscape*. Englewood Cliffs, NJ: Prentice-Hall.

Kwan, Mei-Po. 2002. "Feminist Visualization: Re-envisioning GIS as a Method in Feminist Geographic Research," *Annals of the Association of American Geographers*, Vol. 92, pp. 645–661.

Lauria, Mickey, and Lawrence Knopp. 1985. "Toward and Analysis of the Role of Gay Communities in the Urban Renaissance," *Urban Geography*, Vol. 6, pp. 152–169.

Levine, Martin. 1979. "Gay Ghetto," *Journal of Homosexuality*, Vol. 4, pp. 363–377.

Marcuse, Peter. 1996. "Space and Race in the Post-Fordist City: The Outcast Ghetto and Advanced Homelessness in the United States Today." In Mingione, Enzo, ed., *Urban Poverty and the Underclass: A Reader,* Cambridge, MA: Blackwell.

Marcuse, Peter. 1997. "The Enclave, the Citadel, and the Ghetto: What has Changed in the Post-Fordist U.S. City?" *Urban Affairs Review*, Vol. 33, pp. 228–264.

Marcuse, Peter, and Ronald van Kempen. 2000. *Globalizing Cities: A New Spatial Order?* Oxford; Malden, MA: Blackwell.

Mollenkopf, John H. and Manuel Castells, eds. 1991. *Dual City: Restructuring New York*. New York: Russell Sage Foundation.

Mort, Frank. 2000. "The Sexual Geography of the City." In Gary Bridge and Sophi Watson, eds., *A Companion to the City*. Oxford: Blackwell.

Murdie, R. A. 1969. *Factorial Ecology of Metropolitan Toronto, 1951–1961*, Research Paper no. 116, Department of Geography, University of Chicago.

Nelson, Kristin. 1986. "Labor Demand, Labor Supply, and the Suburbanization of Low-Wage Office Work." In A. J. Scott and M. Storper, eds., *Production, Work, Territory: The Geographical Anatomy of Industrial Capitalism*. Boston: Allen and Unwin.

Park, Robert E. 1915. "The City: Suggestions for the Investigation of Human Behavior in the Urban Environment," *American Journal of Sociology*, Vol. 20, pp. 577–612.

Park, Robert E. 1925/1967. "The City: Suggestions for the Investigation of Human Behavior in the Urban Environment." In R. Park, E. Burgess, and R. McKenzie, *The City*. Chicago: University of Chicago Press.

Sassen, Saskia. 1991. *The Global City: New York, London, Tokyo*. Princeton, NJ: Princeton University Press.

Shevsky, Eshref and Wendell Bell. 1955. *Social Area Analysis: Theory, Illustrative Application and Computational Procedures*. Stanford, CA: Stanford University Press.

Simmel, Georg. 1903/1971. "The Metropolis and Mental Life." In *Individuality and Social Forms*. Chicago: University of Chicago Press.

Tönnies, Ferdinand. 1887/1955. *Community and Association (Gemeinschaft and Gesellschaft)*. London: Routledge and Kegan Paul.

Whyte, William H. 1988. *City: Rediscovering the Center*. New York: Doubleday.

Wilson, William J. 1987. *The Truly Disadvantaged: The Inner City, the Underclass, and Public Policy*. Chicago: University of Chicago Press.

Wirth, Louis. 1938. "Urbanism as a Way of Life," *The American Journal of Sociology*, Vol. 44, pp. 1–24.

CHAPTER 9

URBAN HOUSING MARKETS: SPRAWL, BLIGHT, AND REGENERATION

The everyday American landscape is a vast, confusing, and dangerous terra incognita, braved in recent years by a hardy band of enthusiasts in America's fastest-growing outdoor adventure hobby. These are the intrepid, if sometimes carsick, *navigators of uncharted highway interchanges, the daring runners of overflowing arterials that, in full spate, become Class V rapids choked with Detroit and Yokohama iron.*

—CARBONELL, 2004, P. 5

In Chapter 8 we discussed general spatial arrangements of social groups in cities, that is, the social structure of cities. Although we did not draw explicit attention to the fact, housing comprises a very important feature of urban social landscapes. As you continue to think about the various parts of cities you have been in, consider how important housing is to your perceptions. Some neighborhoods consist of brand new, large suburban houses located along curving streets ending in cul-de-sacs. Other neighborhoods consist of attached row houses on narrow streets close to downtown. Still other neighborhoods consist of large apartment complexes. Much of what we call to mind when we think of the city's social landscape is symbolized by housing! In this chapter we address some of the major forces that have shaped, and continue to shape, housing in North American cities. Specifically, we look at notions of blight, sprawl, and various forms of neighborhood regeneration. We begin, however, by looking at some of the basic features of housing and housing markets.

BASICS OF HOUSING AND HOUSING MARKETS

What is housing? On a very fundamental level, housing is a basic need of human existence: shelter, protection from the elements, a place to sleep and eat and recreate. Housing, however, has a much broader meaning in North American society. Housing represents most households' largest single expenditure as well as significant investment potential. Most of us choose housing that works for us in a functional sense, but many of us also attempt to find housing that expresses some aspect of our personality or that reflects something of our values. Housing affects us in a variety of ways: it can serve as a canvas to express our personality and values, but it can also make us sick if lead paint peels or if radon floats into our air. Housing separates our private lives from our public lives, but public issues sometimes intrude into our homes. So, what are the basic processes that shape how people select housing? How is housing provided? How have cities changed over time in terms of housing?

Sectors of Housing Tenure

What kinds of housing exist in North American cities? What kinds of arrangements govern the way that households occupy housing? A common way of differentiating housing is based on the notion of **tenure** (based on the Latin *tenere*, "to hold"), which refers to the various ways in which residential units are secured and occupied. Most simply, analysts distinguish rental from owner-occupied housing. *The Encyclopedia of Housing* points out that the renter/owner distinction is secondary to more basic factors that divide housing into sectors. Table 9.1 shows four possible sectors based on private versus public ownership and market versus nonmarket conveyance.

The ownership distinction is rather self-explanatory: Does a public entity or branch of government hold the title to the property, or is the property privately owned? **Conveyance** describes the pricing mechanism: Do markets set the prices and terms of occupancy, or are they established outside of markets? Of these four possibilities, publicly owned housing conveyed by markets is quite rare. Private market housing (comprised of renter-occupied and owner-occupied housing) and public nonmarket housing are the most common. In the United States, more than 90 percent of housing units are conveyed via private markets. Public nonmarket housing, although important for many reasons discussed below, constitutes a small share of total units.

Table 9.1 Housing Market Sectors Based on Ownership and Conveyance

		CONVEYANCE	
		Market	*Nonmarket*
OWNERSHIP	*Private*	Private Market Housing	Private Nonmarket Housing
	Public	Public Market Housing	Public Nonmarket Housing

This sector constitutes a greater share in Canada and many other industrialized nations. The third type of housing evident in industrialized nations, called by some **third-sector housing,** or social or nonprofit housing, contains units that are privately owned but are not conveyed by traditional markets. Many community activists favor this kind of housing as a possible solution to critically low supplies of affordable housing.

Housing as a Commodity

Most housing in North America is privately owned and conveyed through private markets. Thus, whether occupied by a renter or by the owner, housing is in a very basic sense a commodity—a thing that is bought, sold, and rented. What does that mean? First, like all things bought and sold, housing can be analyzed in terms of **markets,** using ideas and concepts from economics. Second, housing is unlike many other commodities in that it is not moveable (usually); it is expensive, durable, and subject to strong neighborhood effects; and it simultaneously possesses strong use value (the often intangible benefits we derive from housing) and exchange value (the economic value of housing that is realized when sold). These features, especially geographical immobility, introduce many complexities into our ability to understand housing.

We want to understand the forces that determine how much housing is produced (built or renovated), where that housing is produced, and who purchases that housing. Let's start by applying the conceptual tools of neoclassical economics: We need to understand forces shaping the *supply* of housing, the forces shaping the *demand* for housing, and the impact of the interaction of supply and demand forces.

Housing Demand People everywhere and throughout time have always needed shelter, thus creating a demand for housing. Understanding demand, however, requires more than counting the number of households and the number of housing units. Demand also involves housing **amenities,**

a dwelling's features that determine its economic value. Think about the last time you (or a friend or family member) looked for a place to live. You probably faced a trade-off between how much you could afford to pay (whether in monthly rent or a mortgage payment) and the amenities of the housing unit.

As you examined potential dwellings you probably asked some basic questions about each one: How many bedrooms are there? How many bathrooms are there? How big is the kitchen? Is there off-street parking? Is there a pool in the apartment complex or in the neighborhood? Is there central air-conditioning? Each of these amenities carries a use value (utility) and an exchange value.

When people purchase rather than rent housing, they pay even more attention to the amenities of the house or condominium. The trade-off is how much we can afford to pay—our budget. Even when we do not sit down and write out an explicit monthly budget, most of us still make economic choices with a sense of how much we can afford. Significantly, each housing amenity has individual value. Indeed, one approach to housing research attempts to quantify the value of each of these attributes, an approach called hedonic price modeling (Box 9.1). In most cases, however, amenities are evaluated collectively. In other words, we evaluate *amenity bundles*.

A second attribute of housing as a commodity that deserves our attention is explicitly geographic. The value of housing depends not only on the amenities of individual housing units but also on the **geographic location** of the housing unit. When you look for housing, you are not just trading off the cost of housing with your budget, you are also making an explicitly spatial decision—you are choosing a location in which to live.

Location matters at several geographic scales. First, at a relatively detailed scale, site characteristics affect housing value. Is the site shaded? Is there a stream or a swamp on the property? Is the soil rocky or sandy? Second, the location of the property relative to immediately proximate properties matters (Box 9.2). Is the house or apartment on a busy street or next to a railroad track? Are the neighboring houses larger, nicer, and in better shape than the one you are considering?

BOX 9.1 HEDONIC HOUSE PRICE MODELS

Economists have developed a way of thinking about, and studying, house prices. They put together large databases on a large number of houses in a city. For each house, the database contains the sale price and detailed information about the house: the number of bedrooms, the number of bathrooms, square footage, finished basements, and so forth. With this information, they can detect the impact of each characteristic on the overall sale price. This approach is based on multivariate regression modeling, a statistical technique that allows us to determine the *net* contribution of each characteristic on the price. For example, what happens to the price of a house if the owners add an extra bathroom, keeping everything else in the house the same? The regression model presented below captures, over the set of houses in the database, the typical relationship:

$$\hat{\$} = 125,000 + 1,750 \times BATH + 3,250 \times$$
$$BEDROOM + 5,050 \times FINISHED\ BASEMENT$$

In this example, that extra bathroom adds, on average, an extra \$1,750 to the sales price of a house that doesn't change in any other way. This is not to say that any particular homeowner will get exactly \$1,750 more in sales price. In reality, some will get more, and some less. Rather, this formula just captures the general relationship. This approach is called **hedonic price modeling** and has been used extensively to understand the forces that shape house prices.

BOX 9.2   NIMBY, LULUS, AND BANANA: HOW HOMEOWNERS REACT TO ADJACENT LAND USES

One of the intriguing aspects of understanding home prices in a society where we treat houses as commodities is the impact of *local context*. Real estate agents tell us that the three most important attributes of a property are location, location, and location. In practical terms this means that the characteristics of the area surrounding a house are important, in addition to the attributes of the house itself. Imagine a four-bedroom suburban house with two-car garage, and all the typical amenities. Now imagine that house located across the street from an automobile parts recycling facility (i.e., auto junkyard). That house will sell for less money than if it were located on a leafy cul-de-sac, miles away from the nearest nuisance.

The problem with local context is that communities change over time. A house when built may be miles away from anything. Over time, however, the surrounding parcels of land are often developed, or redeveloped. If the new land uses are perceived to have a detrimental impact on the value of the property, the homeowner may wish to resist or protest that land use. Sometimes homeowners in an area join together to resist a planned development in defense of their property values. Sometimes this resistance extends to an entire suburban jurisdiction. This kind of political power in suburban areas has been noted as a potent force shaping how cities grow. Some critics have suggested that suburbanites can take on an attitude that rejects any land use other than more suburban housing, preferably priced at least as high as their own housing. Thus, suburbanites have resisted such things as apartment buildings (especially if they are publicly financed or subsidized), group homes, low-income housing, and nonresidential land uses. This is especially true if these land uses have any

negative **externalitites**, that is, spillover effects in terms of noise, odor, aesthetics, and so forth. This resistance at times has been fierce, earning it the nickname NIMBY (Not In My Back Yard).

Variations on that theme have been referred to as LULUs (Locally Unwanted Land Uses) and in its extreme form as BANANA (Build Absolutely Nothing Anywhere Near Anything). All of these terms reflect the attitude, often problematic, that stems from treating housing as a commodity. Given that we invest wealth in our houses, houses are more than the places where we live. Another way to say the same thing is that in a capitalistic economy, our houses have **exchange value**, that is, the fact that housing is a form of investment from which most homeowners profit, in addition to **use value**, that is, the enjoyment and utility that homeowners derive from their housing. We defend the exchange value in our houses, even though that defense can end up detrimental to the community at large. For example, everyone in a metropolitan area can agree that effective sewage treatment is necessary for all, just don't build the treatment facility upwind from my neighborhood. The problem is that there are essential and socially important land uses that no community wants within their boundaries.

As previously mentioned, controversies regarding land use often center on facilities with obvious negative externalities, such as a sewage treatment facility or a plant to generate electricity from burning trash. Very often, given the highly fragmented state of affairs in metropolitan areas, these land uses end up being located in parts of town that are not efficient or, worse, in parts of town where the poor and minorities live, who do not have the same political power to resist them.

A third consideration—the location of housing—always positions you within the spatial configuration of your daily activities. You need to travel from home to school or work. You need to purchase food.

You want to recreate and relax, perhaps by taking a run in a park. This leads to several questions: How close is your housing to work or school? Would you be required to drive or could you take public transportation or even walk? How complicated will it be for you to go to the grocery store or to the video store? How accessible is this housing unit to the airport?

All of these considerations affect the market value of the housing unit and how much you are willing to pay for it. Keeping in mind the trade-offs that we have talked about, some of you probably chose housing with an attractive amenity bundle but had to accept a less-favorable location to keep the costs down. Or perhaps you valued a location close to work or school and chose to sacrifice some of your desired amenities to make sure you were in a good location.

Housing Supply Housing supply is a complicated subject with many facets. First, housing typically is produced on site in the very place where it will be used. This affects production methods—housing typically is not assembled in a factory and then transported to the place where it is consumed. Rather, laborers gather materials on site to construct the housing. Economic cost savings that mass production and assembly line production techniques provided for mobile commodities have been more elusive in housing. Attempts by builders to realize some of the economic benefits of mass production and assembly-line production procedures, especially after World War II, led to dramatic impacts on the nature of the housing (i.e., the tendency towards larger subdivisions, standardized housing floor plans, and extensive site preparations, including bulldozing away topographic irregularities and cutting down trees).

A politically charged issue related to the supply of housing revolves around the adequacy of affordable housing units. In particular, can households with low incomes or members with disabilities find adequate shelter at a price that they can afford? An old rule of thumb suggests that most households will spend approximately one-third of their income on housing. Low-income households typically pay a much greater proportion of their income for housing. Activists and some scholars claim that

the markets fail to provide an adequate supply of housing. Low-income households are thus forced to make very difficult decisions—either they have to devote such a high proportion of income to housing that they risk financial instability, or they must accept housing conditions that most North Americans find unacceptable, for example, several families sharing a one-room apartment. Moreover, the trend during the last several decades has been towards a shrinking supply of affordable housing. Conventional economic theories of housing markets suggest that markets do supply enough housing for low-income households through processes that we will discuss below—filtering and vacancy chains. We turn next to traditional theories about how housing markets function.

Housing Market Geographies
Our discussion so far has mostly focused on how housing markets work in the abstract. Housing markets have very explicit geographies, however. In the next section, we discuss various ways of understanding spatial aspects of urban housing markets.

Urban Ecology and Housing Markets: Invasion and Succession We introduced the Chicago school of sociology's perspective on urban spatial structure in the last chapter (i.e., concentric zones defined by social status and degree of social assimilation surrounding a central business district and industrial zone). The ecological approach also provided an important understanding of how housing markets work spatially. According to ecological theory, cities' housing stocks grow from the inside out. Recall from Chapter 8 our discussion of neighborhood invasion and succession caused by the most recent arrival of immigrants from foreign countries. We noted that the impacts of immigration ripple outward, as previous residents of neighborhoods close to the factories that provided immigrants' jobs leave and seek housing in neighborhoods farther out (Figure 9.1). The spatial mobility into the next zone outward is propelled by the desire for social distance from the most recent arrivals, but it is made

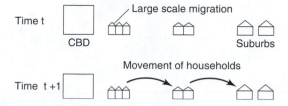

Figure 9.1 Housing market impacts of invasion and succession. (*Source:* From Short, John R. 1984. *An Introduction to Urban Geography*. London and Boston: Routledge and Kegan Paul, Fig. 7b.)

possible by upward socioeconomic mobility and cultural assimilation into a nonethnic mainstream.

Filtering and Vacancy Chains

Homer Hoyt (1939), the housing economist that developed the sectoral model of urban structure introduced in Chapter 8, explicitly considered the spatial implications of housing market characteristics. Based on U.S. house price data collected and mapped in the 1930s, he identified several patterns that he considered inherent to the spatial functioning of urban housing markets. In contrast to the notions derived from ecological theory, Hoyt felt that cities grew from the outside in.

Hoyt felt that the highest-income households propelled urban growth on the edges of cities (Figure 9.2). As their incomes rose, homeowners desired larger houses with more amenities, and had them built on the edge of the existing city, typically close to existing lines of transportation. When the homeowner moved into their new home, their old home became vacant and available for occupation by a new household—typically one who was younger and possessed fewer financial resources. Importantly, the new occupant of the housing unit vacated by the upper-income family had also moved up and out of a neighborhood closer to the central city, thus creating a new vacancy. Hoyt called this process of successive vacancies, each one in a progressively smaller and older housing unit closer in to the core of the city, **vacancy chains.** From this perspective, housing units in the core neighborhoods of cities became available to new arrivals

(i.e., immigrants and domestic migrants) through this process of vacancy chains. New units are added at the edge of the city for the highest-income groups, and the rest of the housing stock sequentially and progressively becomes available for lower-income groups.

Filtering is an important associated concept. There are several ways to understand filtering. First, from the perspective of the whole city, the impact of constructing one additional housing unit on the edge of the city for an upper-income family filters its way through vacancy chains to result in a vacant housing unit close to the core of the city, available to newly arriving low-income households. Second, individual households filter upward through the housing market, successively occupying larger, more expensive housing. Imagine, for example, a young couple initially renting a small apartment close to the core of the city. As their financial resources increase through occupational advancement, the couple is able to move into a larger, newer apartment farther out. This couple can now afford the longer commute and can maybe even buy a car (recall that Hoyt wrote in the 1930s). After several years, the couple decides to start a family and moves into a small starter house even farther out from the core of the city. As their children grow, they desire a larger house (maybe with a second bathroom) and become more concerned with issues of school quality and neighborhood social stability. Consequently, they move still farther out into a larger house. When the children are in high school (before the financial shock of college!), the family buys a newly built dream home on the edge of the city.

A third, and perhaps the most common, interpretation of filtering applies to the fate of housing units and neighborhoods. Hoyt observed during the 1930s that lower-income families, immigrants, and racial minorities increasingly were occupying once-fashionable neighborhoods with large houses. Some of these neighborhoods even became "slums" (a notion we will address later in the chapter). Hoyt explained that filtering applied to neighborhoods in the sense that each new occupant of a housing unit was often of lower income and social standing than

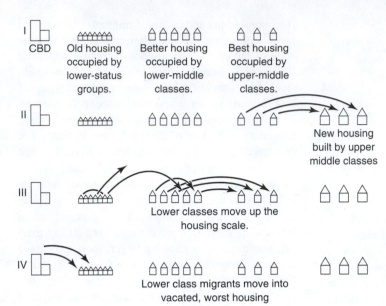

Figure 9.2 Hoyt's process of filtering in urban housing markets. (*Source:* From Johnston, R. J. *Urban Residential Patterns: An Introductory Review*, London: G. Bell (1971), Fig. 3.8, p. 98.)

the departing household. Thus, over time, the once fashionable in-town neighborhood built and initially occupied by a high-income urban gentry became outdated in terms of the modern conveniences it offered. The bedrooms now felt too small, there was too little closet space, it was difficult to find a place to park the new car on the street, and the kitchen lacked the latest technologically advanced conveniences. When the upper-income family built a new home, they sold their old home to a family with fewer means, probably with a lower income than they had when they built the house originally. When the middle-income family moved out several years later, they sold to a lower-middle-class family, which then sold some years later to a lower-income family or landlord.

Large single-family homes were at some point subdivided into multiple apartments. The neighborhood thus filtered downward in terms of the income and class levels of the households who resided there. Hoyt saw downward neighborhood filtering as a natural feature of a healthy urban housing market because it reflected the growth of housing stock and made housing units available to expanding numbers of low-income households in the very locations that were attractive for their easy

access to the still-centralized industrial employment. Downward filtering of the housing stock in some cases eliminated housing from the available stock if its physical condition deteriorated beyond the willingness of property owners to invest in repairs.

Some observers and policy makers argue that inefficient filtering and premature demolition are the main explanations for inadequate supplies of affordable housing. When construction of new housing for higher-income households was stymied during the Depression, vacancy chains were broken, filtering stopped functioning, and overcrowding of housing ensued. As we will see below, Hoyt's ideas about the natural and proper functioning of urban housing markets had a strong impact on federal housing policy and subsequently on the radical post–World War II restructuring of the North American metropolis. Basically, housing policies reflected Hoyt's argument that the proper role of governmental involvement in housing markets (if needed) should be to stimulate the construction of new housing for higher-income households. Housing for lower-income households would be provided in due course by the natural processes of filtering and vacancy chains.

Life-Cycle Notions of Neighborhood Change

Other urban theorists have developed several similar life-cycle or stage models of neighborhood change. Each agreed with Hoyt's basic notion that as the housing stock in neighborhoods ages and becomes more out of date with contemporary tastes, the neighborhood inevitably decays, both physically and socially. This process was held to be inevitable because it was a natural byproduct of properly functioning economic markets for housing.

Edgar M. Hoover and Raymond Vernon (1962) developed a stage model of neighborhood evolution based on their observations of the New York metropolitan area in the 1950s. The housing market processes they describe are similar to filtering as described by Hoyt, and the evolution of neighborhoods resembles the predictions drawn from the Chicago school's discussion of invasion and succession. Hoover and Vernon identified five stages in their attempt to understand how neighborhoods' housing stocks changed along with their demographic characteristics:

- *Stage 1:* Initial Urbanization—typically occurs on the fringe of the city.
- *Stage 2:* Transition—population growth continues, density increases, and multifamily housing begins to be built.
- *Stage 3:* Downgrading—older housing stock is converted to multifamily use, densities continue to increase, and the housing stock physically deteriorates.
- *Stage 4:* Thinning—population declines, household size shrinks, housing units become vacant and are abandoned.
- *Stage 5:* Renewal—obsolete housing is replaced with multifamily buildings, and the intensity and efficiency of land use increase. Renewal was thought to often require public sector involvement.

Other scholars have modified the Hoover and Vernon stage model. Anthony Downs (1981), for example, conceived of neighborhoods in stages along a continuum between health and viability. His five stages are: (1) healthy and viable, (2) incipient decline, (3) clearly declining, (4) accelerating decline with heavy deterioration, and (5) abandoned and nonviable. Significant changes in the social composition of the neighborhood occur in stages 3 and 4, as renters replace owners, the poor replace the working class, and the fate of the neighborhood is deeply questioned. Unlike Hoover and Vernon, Downs recognized that neighborhoods can move in both directions along the continuum; they can be revitalized through changes in the housing market and/or through public interventions.

MARKET REALITIES: ONGOING DEBATES OVER EQUAL ACCESS TO HOUSING

We have treated housing so far in a somewhat idealistic way, as if conventional understandings of markets apply to housing. In this section and the next we discuss two ways in which housing market realities differ from the abstract theories. We first consider the failure of housing and finance markets to provide equal access for all groups in U.S. society. Then we discuss the dependency of U.S. housing markets on government involvement. We describe the implementation of the federal government's loan guarantee programs during the Depression, followed by a discussion of recent federal policy transformations that impact contemporary housing markets. In both sections, we reveal how institutions and governments wield consider power over the functioning of housing markets.

Unequal access has characterized urban housing markets for many decades. As we will discuss in Chapter 11, immigrants flooding into industrial cities in the late nineteenth and early twentieth centuries often lived in very poor housing conditions—overcrowded tenements and physically deteriorated housing stock. Inadequate and overcrowded housing conditions also plagued later immigrants—African Americans migrating from the rural South. Although low income undoubtedly explains part of the problem, housing markets did not function the same for immigrants or blacks as they did for whites. Participants at the time clearly recognized this fact, intentionally creating a dual housing market, one for whites and the other for blacks. We discuss in Chapter 10 some of the tactics used to create and enforce racial segregation. Here we examine how these tactics affected the functioning of housing markets.

Real Estate Agents and Differentiated Access

Several forms of discrimination are experienced in housing market transactions. Both renters and homeowners experience discrimination throughout the process of acquiring housing. A useful framework for thinking about discrimination as part of the housing market transaction is provided by John Yinger (1995) in Figure 9.3.

Housing discrimination was routine and overt in the early twentieth century. Some landlords simply refused to rent to minorities. Some white real estate agents did not conduct business with blacks. Some black real estate agents also contributed to the creation and maintenance of segregated neighborhoods by showing blacks properties only in black areas, or, in times of housing shortages, in neighborhoods adjacent to black areas. Black real estate agents have been accused of spurring racial transition by practicing block-busting techniques (discussed more fully in Chapter 10).

Laws to ban explicit discrimination on the basis of race were passed in the 1960s and 1970s as the civil rights movement gained success. Nevertheless, claims of racial discrimination in housing markets continued. We have seen a reduction over time in the amount of explicit discrimination by housing market gatekeepers and an increase in more subtle forms of discrimination. Research conducted in the 1970s and 1980s confirmed that landlords, property managers, and real estate agents practiced a variety of discriminatory techniques.

Margery Austin Turner and Stephen Ross coordinated the most recent national examination of racial discrimination in housing market transactions, called the Housing Discrimination Study (HDS2000) using a methodology referred to as **fair housing matched pairs auditing.** Previous national studies were conducted in 1977 (the Housing Market Practices Study, or HMPS) and in 1989 (HDS). Carefully trained pairs of applicants (called testers or auditors), matched on all employment and financial characteristics, were sent to inquire after publicly advertised available housing units. The only difference between pairs was race—some were black, some white, and some Hispanic or Asian. Detailed notes were kept by testers

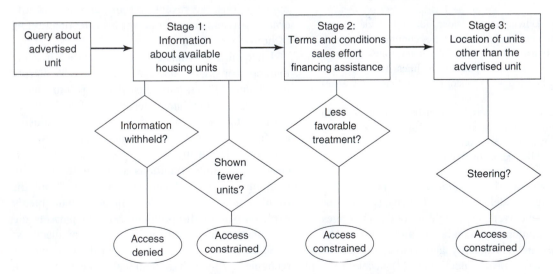

Figure 9.3 Potential discrimination in the stages of a housing market transaction. (*Source:* Adapted from J. Yinger, 1995, Fig 3.1.)

of the transaction, including the actions of real estate and rental agents. The information was analyzed in order to evaluate how often the pairs received differential treatment. The studies interpret differential treatment as indicative of systemic racial discrimination when white auditors consistently received preferential treatment over the minority auditors.

HDS2000 results (Turner et al. 2002, Turner and Ross 2005) clearly show that nonwhites still experience considerable discrimination in housing market transactions. Direct and blatantly racist forms of discrimination (e.g., refusing to talk with blacks or other minorities, slamming doors, and so forth) are less common today than in earlier decades. Indirect forms of discrimination, often carried out with a smile and a handshake, are now more common. Table 9.2 lists the multiple parts of any rental or sales housing search where preferential treatment can happen. Table 9.3 shows the areas where racially differentiated treatment is significant—the numbers in the "gross upper bound" column indicate

the percentage of time the white testers received more favorable treatment than the minority testers. Given that some differences in treatment are not related to race (e.g., the advertised unit might have been rented in between the two visits), the study also presents a very conservative minimum "net lower bound" estimate of the number of times white testers are treated preferentially over minority testers. Figure 9.4 shows a summary measure of preferential treatment across the individual parts of the rental and sales housing transactions. Two points are clear: (1) discrimination in housing transactions remains significant for blacks and Hispanics, even though (2) discrimination has declined since 1989.

The simple incidence of racially differentiated treatment by real estate agents does not tell the whole story. Most people looking for housing look at multiple properties, often talking to several potential agents. John Yinger (1995) calculated, using the conservative "net lower bound" measure and the 1989 HDS study data, that blacks experienced being

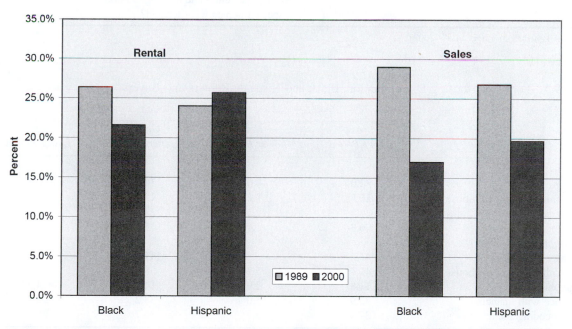

Figure 9.4 Discrimination in housing markets by blacks and Hispanics. The height of the bars indicates the percentage of times that an auditor received consistent adverse treatment relative to a white auditor. (*Source:* Adapted from Exhibit ES-1, p. iii, Turner, M. A., S. L. Ross, G. C. Galster, and J. Yinger, 2002.)

Table 9.2 Indicators of Adverse Treatment in Rental and Sales Housing Transactions

Rental Housing Transactions	Housing Sales Transactions
1. *Comparable Information?* • Was the advertised housing unit available? • Were similar units available? • How many available units were recommended? 2. *Ability to Inspect Units?* • Was the advertised unit inspected (if available)? • Were similar units inspected (if available)? • How many units were inspected? 3. *Housing Unit Costs* • Was an application fee required? • Were rental incentives offered? • What security deposit was required? • How much was the rent for the advertised unit (if available)? 4. *Agent Helpfulness* • Did the agent make follow-up contact? • Was tester told s/he was qualified to rent? • Were arrangements made for future contact? • Was the tester asked to complete an application?	1. *Comparable Information?* • Was the advertised housing unit available? • Were similar units available? • How many available units were recommended? 2. *Ability to Inspect Units?* • Was the advertised unit inspected (if available)? • Were similar units inspected (if available)? • How many units were inspected? 3. *Mortgage Finance Options* • Was help with financing offered? • Were specific lenders recommended? • Were down payment requirements discussed? 4. *Agent Helpfulness* • Did the agent make follow-up contact? • Was tester told s/he was qualified to buy? • Were arrangements made for future contact? 5. *Neighborhood Difference* • Average percent white for neighborhoods where recommended homes were located? • Average percent white for neighborhoods where inspected homes were located?

Source: Adapted from Turner et al. (2002).

Table 9.3 Forms of Housing Discrimination, Black and Hispanic Renters and Buyers

	Black		Hispanic	
Form of Discrimination	Gross Upper Bound	Net Lower Bound	Gross Upper Bound	Net Lower Bound
Rental treatment				
Housing availability	32.0	4.6	34.4	12.4
Opportunities to inspect housing	26.5	7.2	25.8	8.0
Housing costs	21.5	...	23.0	4.4
Agent encouragement	36.3	...	35.9	...
Sales treatment				
Housing availability	46.2	...	47.2	...
Opportunities to inspect housing	41.7	5.7	38.5	...
Geographic steering	11.8	3.9	14.8	4.3
Assistance with financing	33.9	5.0	38.2	13.4
Agent encouragement	37.5	5.9	34.7	...

Source: Turner and Ross, 2005, Table 4-1, p. 88.
Note: All reported measures are statistically significant at the 90 percent confidence level or higher.

excluded from a rental housing unit, one of the most extreme forms of discrimination, 10.7 percent of the time they visit a single real estate agent. The chances of encountering this form of discrimination at some point in the housing search process increase dramatically with the number of visits—estimated to be 20.2 percent with two visits and a dramatic 49.2 percent with six visits!

Steering is an inherently geographic form of discrimination, defined as "behavior that directs a customer toward neighborhoods in which people of his or her racial or ethnic group are concentrated" (Yinger 1995, 51–52). The HDS2000 study shows that the incidence of steering *increased* between 1989 and 2000, even though other measures of systemic discrimination showed decline. The HDS2000 study conducted a more detailed examination of steering. The study identified three *techniques* that agents use to steer: racially differentiated neighborhood recommendations, racially differentiated inspections of housing units, and racially differentiated commentary or editorializing about neighborhoods. They also identify three *forms* of steering, each of which uses the three techniques

of steering. *Information steering* means that whites are given information about a wider variety of neighborhoods than minorities. *Segregation steering* means that whites are encouraged to take housing in more predominantly white neighborhoods than minorities (or its converse, minority households are steered to racially diverse or predominantly minority neighborhoods). *Class steering* occurs when whites are directed towards more affluent neighborhoods than similar minority households, who, in turn, are directed towards mixed- or lower-income neighborhoods. Table 9.4 reports the incidence of these forms of steering for blacks and Hispanics. One paradox is that U.S. metropolitan areas have generally become more racially diverse over the last several decades, which should have increased the chances for both white and minority households to find attractive housing in diverse neighborhoods. The worsening of steering by real estate agents seems to work in the opposite direction by pushing white households towards more affluent and less diverse neighborhoods, while effectively restricting the choices of minority home seekers to minority and less-affluent neighborhoods.

Table 9.4   Housing Discrimination through Geographic Steering Black and Hispanic Homeseekers

	Black		Hispanic	
	Gross	Net	Gross	Net
Form of Geographic Steering	Upper Bound	Lower Bound	Upper Bound	Lower Bound
Information steering				
Homes recommended	14.1	. . .	15.4	. . .
Homes inspected	10.0	. . .	9.9	. . .
Commenraty	38.5	15.0	35.0	. . .
Segregation steering				
Homes recommended	16.5	3.8	17.1	. . .
Humes inspected	12.1	3.8	15.0	5.0
Commentary	37.1	13.7	35.1	6.2
Class steering				
Homes recommended	6.9	. . .	7.0	. . .
Homes inspected	5.2	. . .	5.1	. . .
Commentary	34.9	11.5	30.7	. . .

Source: Turner and Ross, 2005, Table 4-3, p. 95.
Note: All reported resources are statistically significant at the 90 percent confidence level or higher.

Discrimination in Lending

Race has long played an important role in housing finance markets. Private market lenders discriminated against minorities in several ways well before the Depression. First, they often practiced blatant discrimination; that is, they refused service to minority customers. Even if black customers had sufficient income and wealth for a down payment, many banks simply refused to lend them the money necessary to purchase housing.

Second, lenders devised a way of evaluating risk that denied capital to black and minority areas of the city based on the premise that the presence of blacks, Jews, and other ethnic minorities in a neighborhood would be detrimental to the long-term value of properties within those neighborhoods. This practice came to be know as **redlining** because neighborhoods deemed unacceptably risky due to racial and ethnic composition were often bounded in red on the maps used in the loan approval and appraisal processes (see Figure 10.4).

Redlining was adopted by the federal government in home finance programs established during the Depression. Under the auspices of the Federal Housing Authority (FHA) loan guarantee program, redlining had devastating consequences that we discuss in more detail in Chapter 10. Here it is sufficient to note that federally supported redlining had the dual impacts of denying much-needed capital to minority and central city areas *and* excluding blacks and other minorities from the rapid suburbanization of the post–World War II decades.

The federal government eventually prohibited redlining in its own programs and passed laws banning discrimination by private lenders. The 1975 Home Mortgage Disclosure Act (HMDA) required that lenders report the amounts and locations of the loans they make. The 1977 Community Reinvestment Act (CRA) required lenders to make loans in the areas from which they drew deposits, including central city and minority neighborhoods. Claims of lending discrimination persist despite the federal government's policy changes: community activists used HMDA data to show that lenders kept making the majority and highest dollar value of their mortgage loans to predominantly white and suburban areas throughout the 1980s.

The discrimination debate shifted in the 1990s from redlining, a primarily geographic notion, to applicant-level discrimination. Research generally supports claims that black and minority applicants are more likely to have their applications denied, even when controlling for borrower characteristics that banks use to evaluate risk. A major study by the Boston Federal Reserve Bank, which had access to much more information than do typical studies, found substantial racial differences in rates of loan denial after controlling for employment history, current debt, and the applicants' history in dealing with credit and paying bills.

The debate over lending discrimination shifted again in the late 1990s and early 2000s to issues of **predatory lending.** Because of major changes in the housing finance markets in the late 1990s, lenders are now much more willing to lend to applicants who would have been considered unacceptably risky two or three decades ago. In fact a whole industry segment called **subprime lending** has developed to handle many of these loans. To compensate for the higher risks, subprime lenders are allowed to charge higher fees and higher interest rates. Certainly, not all companies making subprime loans are guilty of predatory lending practices; they provide a much needed services to customers who need credit but have flaws in their credit history. Claims of predatory lending emerge when lenders unethically steer applicants into the subprime market even when they otherwise would qualify for a conventional loan (Table 9.5). Predatory lenders are also accused of using unscrupulous marketing tactics to generate business from unsophisticated homeowners, often the elderly. More specifically, they are accused of making home improvement and refinancing loans that strip the existing equity out of properties and can, in the worst cases, force current homeowners into foreclosure (Box 9.3). Central to the concerns of analysts and community activists is that fact that subprime and predatory lending are unduly concentrated in minority and low-income neighborhoods. A widespread crisis emerged in 2006 and 2007

Table 9.5 Typology of Predatory Lending Practices and Loan Terms

Type of Predatory Behavior	Examples
Sales and marketing	• high pressure, door-to-door sales • targeting vulnerable populations (e.g., those with health debts, elderly, less educated) • steering to higher-cost loans despite borrower qualifying for lower-cost credit • flipping—excessive refinancing • home improvement scams, in which contractors act as loan brokers
Excessive fees	• "packing" loans with unnecessary fees, including credit life insurance, which are often financed in the loan • padded closing costs or third party fees • excessively high points or origination fees • high broker fees, including yield spread premiums
Terms that trap borrowers into unaffordable financing	• balloon payments, which conceal the true cost of financing and may force repeated refinancing or foreclosure • negative amortization, in which payments are less than interest, resulting in an increasing principal balance and decreasing owner equity • prepayment penalties • "asset-based" lending, ignoring repayment ability
Other fraudulent or deceptive practices	• reporting inflated income figures • forgeries • insufficient or improperly timed disclosure • inflated appraisals, in part to enable secondary market sale

Source: Immergluck, Dan and Marti Wiles, 1999, Table 1, p. 8.

because of excessive subprime lending to financially risky homebuyers. The impact of the crisis has been felt globally because of the extensive reach of the secondary mortgage market (see discussion later in this chapter, pages 237–238). The impact was also detrimental locally because of a sharp increase in foreclosures, which deflate the value of surrounding homes and make lenders less willing to extend credit.

Accumulated Impacts of Housing Market Discrimination

Having shown that housing and lending markets are discriminatory, we now ask: what are the impacts of this discrimination? Many of the consequences of discrimination are indirect, creating and reinforcing residential segregation, as we discuss in greater detail in the following chapter. To conclude our discussion here, though, we present some more of the work by John Yinger (1995). Yinger estimated the direct financial costs of the various forms of housing market discrimination. To summarize his findings, discrimination (1) restricts minority households' access to housing by reducing the number of units they see, (2) makes the search process more unpleasant for minority households, increasing the effort (time and money) required of them, (3) increases the difficulty in finding appropriate

BOX 9.3   Sub-Prime Mortgage Lending and the Racial Geography of Foreclosure

Much of the policy and public concern about predatory lending has been the sometimes substantial personal financial loss suffered by its victims. One of the extreme consequences can be the loss of property due to foreclosure. Unfortunately, foreclosure is a broader problem that has substantial impacts on the residential geography of cities. Critics claim that the suite of policies that enabled the extension of low-cost credit to financially risky homebuyers during the 1990s, especially that credit made available through the subprime market, is now imperiling many minority and low-income neighborhoods. First, note that foreclosures have skyrocketed over the last several decades (Figure B9.1). Second, foreclosure rates are much higher among subprime loans.

While on face value this is not too surprising, given that subprime borrowers are generally more financially risky, critics point out that subprime lending is heavily concentrated in minority and low-income neighborhoods and that many low-risk borrowers are steered into subprime loans. Third, there is a strong association between the geographic location of foreclosures and the geographic concentration of minority and low-income populations.

Dan Immergluck and Geoff Smith (2004, 2005) studied the distribution of foreclosures relative to underlying racial patterns, and document the clear concentration of the growing number of foreclosures in Chicago's minority neighborhoods (Figure B9.2). Their statistical analysis shows a strong relationship

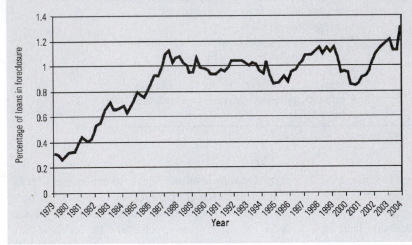

Figure B9.1 Percentage of outstanding mortgages in foreclosure. (*Source:* Immergluck and Smith 2006a, Figure 1 [*Original Source:* National Association of Realtors, Research Division 2004.])

financing (minorities are given less assistance in locating lenders and in making sure their applications meet minimum requirements), (4) increases the chances that mortgage loan applications will be denied, and (5) increases the actual costs of moving.

A black household seeking to move will pay between $3,000 and $4,200 (1990 dollars) more for housing, depending on the assumptions one makes,

and a Hispanic household will pay between $3,300 and $4,400 more for housing. Yinger defines as a **discrimination tax** the extra housing costs created by discrimination against nonwhites. When we add up the number of black and Hispanic households who move over a three-year period, the total costs of discrimination to black households range from $7 billion to $10 billion, and the costs to Hispanic between the concentration of subprime lending in minority and low-income neighborhoods, and the subsequent concentration of foreclosures. In more recent work, Immergluck (2006a, 2006b) shows that the increased number of foreclosures in minority and low-income neighborhoods is exacerbating

neighborhood crime rates and deflating the property values of surrounding residential properties. Thus, dysfunctions in housing finance markets are having negative impacts that extend well beyond the individuals that often serve as our image of the victims of predatory lending.

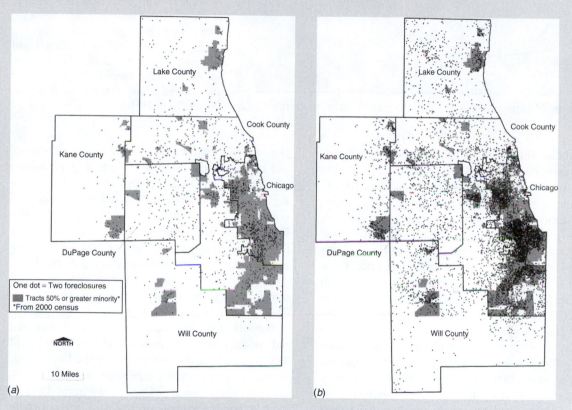

Figure B9.2 Foreclosures in Chicago, relative to minority neighborhoods, (a) 1995 and (b) 2002. (*Source:* Figure 4 and Figure 5, Immergluck, Dan and Geoff Smith 2004.)

households range from $4 billion to just under $6 billion. As these estimates suggest, housing market failings are not trivial. Rather, they impose considerable direct financial costs upon minority households. Moreover, these estimates do not include any of the indirect costs associated more generally with residential segregation!

HOUSING MARKET REALITIES: GOVERNMENT INVOLVEMENT

Prior to the Great Depression, the purchase of housing was limited to those with considerable means. Historical data show that a far smaller portion of the population owned their own house during this period

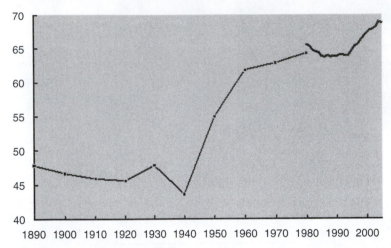

Figure 9.5 Home ownership over time in the twentieth century. (*Source:* Drafted by authors with data from U.S. Bureau of the Census, Department of Commerce [http://www.census.gov/hhes/www/hvs.html], and as reported in Exhibits 1 and 2, p. 44, in Eggers, 2001. The data are annual estimates from 1980 to 2005 and are derived from the decennial census from 1890 to 1980.)

than today (Figure 9.5). One of the reasons that home ownership was less prevalent was because the economy generated less wealth. Yet a more important reason was the nature of housing finance.

Historically, as today, purchasing a house requires more money than most households have within easy access. Most people buying houses must borrow at least a portion of the purchase price. Prior to the Depression, lending institutions were much more restrictive in the way they lent money to buy houses. First, borrowers had to have a large portion of the total purchase price in cash—upwards of 30 percent to 50 percent. Second, lending institutions were willing to lend money only for short periods, often no more than six to seven years. Borrowers had to be able to afford a larger monthly payment. Finally, lending institutions shouldered their own risk: They charged high interest rates on home purchase loans. From a supply perspective, most housing was not built speculatively. Rather, it was constructed only when a household was financially able to enter into a contract with a builder.

Securing Home Ownership through Loan Guarantees

The Great Depression greatly affected the nature of home ownership. Its economic dislocations reduced the income even of upper-income households.

Demand for new owner-occupied housing dried up, and the economic troubles experienced by households with existing loans further imperiled the banking industry. The construction industry stalled significantly. The federal government under President Franklin Roosevelt recognized the importance of the housing and housing finance industries to the nation's economic prospects. Housing demand was considered too sensitive to economic cycles and too narrowly restricted to upper-income households. The federal response was to focus on the financing of housing. Although many of the changes instituted did not have their maximum effect until after World War II, the foundations were laid in the Depression.

President Roosevelt established the Home Owners Loan Corporation (HOLC) early in the Depression to provide immediate relief to home-owning households. Loans were provided directly to homeowners who had already been, or were about to be, foreclosed upon. As with many of the New Deal programs, the HOLC represented the involvement of the federal government in economic markets in new and unprecedented ways, this time in housing markets. The scope of the HOLC's impact was necessarily limited by the fact that the federal government had to provide the capital loaned to homeowners and the fact that the beneficiaries of the program already owned homes.

Later, in order to reduce the financial burden on the federal government while at the same time broadening the impact of its policy, Roosevelt began a new finance program under the auspices of a new agency, the Federal Housing Authority (FHA). Initial FHA programs operated differently than the HOLC, ultimately having a much more dramatic impact on housing markets. Rather than directly providing loans, the FHA provided *incentives* for private market lenders to increase lending for home ownership by providing a guarantee to the lender on behalf of the homeowner. More specifically, the federal government promised to pay lenders if borrowers were not able to maintain payments on the loan.

Federal loan guarantees had several important features. First, lending institutions were required to fully amortize the loans over a longer payback period. At first this period was 20 years. It was later extended to 25 and then again to 30 years. Monthly loan payments thus would be considerably reduced. Second, smaller down payments were required—20 percent versus the 30 to 50 percent previously required. Borrowers thus needed less cash to buy a house. Third, interest rates dropped dramatically because the federal government ultimately bore the financial risk. Together, the new programs significantly reduced the total and monthly costs of buying houses.

Another major aspect of federal housing policy put into place during this period, though not formally part of the FHA program, is the mortgage interest income tax deduction. Homeowners can deduct the amount they pay on mortgage interest from their income when computing federal taxes. Significantly, in the early years of a long-term fixed mortgage, most of the monthly payments go to paying interest. Therefore, being able to deduct these payments is a substantial financial benefit, and it provides households with an extra incentive to purchase houses. As we discuss below, suburban areas enjoyed the greatest benefit from federal programs in general and from the tax policies in particular.

The impacts of the FHA program were just beginning to be felt when World War II erupted and halted housing construction, providing an alternatively stimulus for the economy. The program remained in effect, however, and was expanded after the war, dramatically contributing to decentralization and sprawl, issues that we turn to later in the chapter. In terms of the basic issue of stabilizing and even expanding the demand for housing and thus stabilizing the construction and banking industries, the new federally supported housing finance system was a success.

A New System of Housing Finance: The Secondary Mortgage Market

The Depression-era system of housing finance had its greatest impact in the economic boom years of the post–World War II decades, when the FHA and the similar Veterans Administration (VA) loan guarantee programs enabled millions of households to purchase housing at reasonable costs. Homeownership rates increased dramatically (note the steep increase between 1940 and 1960 in Figure 9.5). In addition, as we will discuss later in this chapter, the spatial form of cities changed dramatically because built-in biases of the system favored newly built housing in suburban areas.

The postwar system of housing finance has undergone significant change in recent decades. The system initially depended on commercial depository banks and smaller savings and loan (S&L) institutions (also called thrifts) to provide the majority of housing capital. A significant portion of housing finance capital was guaranteed through the FHA and VA programs. Nevertheless, a shortage of finance capital increasingly plagued the market, a trend exacerbated by the failure of many S&Ls during the 1980s. As federal regulators and politicians struggled to craft a politically feasible solution to the S&L failures, they created a new system that would change the nature of housing finance during the 1990s and first decade of the twenty-first century.

The federal government sought to allow financial institutions to offer investment securities backed by housing mortgages in order to increase the availability of housing finance capital. Federal laws prohibiting these kinds of transactions had to be changed, and the federal government had to foster institutions that could facilitate these new financial arrangements. Two privately held corporations had been chartered during the 1930s to facilitate the sale of mortgages backed by the FHA and VA. The Federal National Mortgage Association (Fannie Mae) and Federal Home Loan Mortgage Corporation (Freddie Mac) were authorized to purchase government-secured mortgages from the institutions that originally made the loans. These corporations played an important role in keeping mortgage capital flowing. As part of the S&L bailout, Fannie Mae and Freddie Mac's charters were expanded, allowing them to purchase (and to help third parties to purchase) conventional loans (i.e., loans not guaranteed by the government through the FHA or VA programs). They could then package mortgages together and sell them again on a new **secondary mortgage market** to investors seeking a return on their investments. Given their important role in facilitating the circulation of capital through housing markets, we now refer to Fannie Mae and Freddie Mac as *government-sponsored enterprises* (GSEs).

The secondary mortgage market has a significant impact on urban housing markets by making additional capital available to homebuyers over the last two decades. It is easier to get a mortgage loan today, and the costs of borrowing are generally lower. By selling loans into the secondary market, lending institutions now have the ability to pass on the financial risk inherent in making long-term loans. Individual investors are protected from risk by buying bundled securities that are not immediately threatened by the failure of individual loans. The GSEs minimize their risk by issuing guidelines for loans that they are willing to acquire and package for resale on the secondary market. If lending institutions comply with these guidelines, they are guaranteed the ability to sell the loans.

The GSEs have also relaxed many of the requirements traditionally considered necessary to qualify for loans, in part because the risks of loan failure are spread through bundled securities, and in part to comply with regulations issued by the Department of Housing and Urban Development (HUD, the federal agency responsible for overseeing the GSEs). Under President Clinton during the 1990s, HUD required that the GSEs increase lending to traditionally underserved markets—low- and moderate-income families and minorities—in order to increase homeownership rates. Down payment requirements were relaxed so that a borrower could qualify for loans with as little as a 3 percent down payment. New GSE guidelines also allowed higher debt levels for home buyers and became more flexible on requirements regarding employment and credit histories.

The goal of many of these policies has been to expand homeownership to populations who formerly could not afford it. Although the policy goals are similar to those of the FHA program, the means are very different. Current policies rely on public-private partnerships to stimulate the desired results. Although a complete assessment of these policies cannot yet be conducted, empirical evidence suggests that lending has increased to low- and moderate-income households, especially in low- and moderate-income and minority neighborhoods. It is difficult, however, to tell whether these increases could have been achieved without the new standards or whether they resulted primarily from the economic growth of the 1990s.

SPRAWL AND THE SUBURBANIZATION OF HOUSING

In the last half of this chapter we explore several aspects of urban housing markets in light of our discussions so far. More specifically, we discuss housing in the context of suburban sprawl, and we consider the fate of older inner-city neighborhoods through decades of blight, redevelopment, and regeneration.

Perhaps the dominant geographic trend to characterize housing in North American cities in recent history has been the rapid and extensive spreading out of cities—suburbanization and urban sprawl.

As Box 9.4 shows, sprawl can be defined in several ways. When and how did this happen? We have discussed various aspects of suburbanization in previous chapters; our concern here is the housing that gets built on the edges of cities. Although many experts correctly identify the decades following World War II as a key period of suburbanization, we start further back in history—because the tendency to build new housing on the edges of cities is not a new phenomenon.

Antecedents and Preconditions of Post–World War II Suburban Sprawl

As we begin our discussion of suburbanization, we need to recall a fundamental shift in the geography of housing that took place several centuries ago during the Industrial Revolution. Through most of urban history, people lived close to where they worked: cobblers lived in the apartments above their ground-floor shop; tanners lived adjacent to their shops and the stables. With industrialization, however, urban dwellers increasingly lived in areas distant from their shops. This work/home separation was an essential precursor to suburbanization.

An early notable example of suburbanization is eighteenth-century London. Newly wealthy industrialists and merchants wanted nice housing within the city yet far from the dirt and congestion of the factories. Thus, they built large houses in suburban estates—tracts of land adjacent to the existing city. Townhouses were also constructed for wealthy aristocrats who needed to attend to financial or business matters in the city or simply wanted to maintain social connections. The first suburbs were quite exclusive and limited to the wealthy; they did not resemble most post–World War II suburbs. Yet their precedent remains important.

The trend towards suburban housing development did not generally characterize North American cities in the early years. Indeed, many North American cities were quite small and compact during the Colonial period. They have been described as **walking cities** because they lacked alternative forms of transportation (Figure 9.6). Functional segmentation of these urban places was much more limited than we see today. For example, housing for all classes was interspersed between commercial land uses, warehousing districts, and the docks. In addition, social segmentation was much less than we observe today, as individuals of all economic classes and social positions lived relatively close together.

North American cities expanded unevenly as they grew. They expanded outward along transportation routes that were being put into place in many cities. We mention at several points in this chapter the relationship between urban spatial form and the predominant mode of transportation. Figure 9.7 illustrates this relationship in a very generalized way. As cities grew, they spread outward along transportation routes. When transportation routes were fixed as they were during the nineteenth and early twentieth centuries (railroads, streetcars, and so forth), the developed portions of cities followed these routes, creating a starfish shape. As the car was adopted later in the twentieth century, the spaces in between the arm of the starfish were filled in with new development. Late twentieth-century freeways spurred new rounds of development that followed the transportation routes farther out.

As new forms of urban public transportation were introduced in the late nineteenth and early twentieth centuries, new housing was built alongside public transportation routes. This housing very often was restricted to the professional and upper-middle classes. Public transportation was affordable only to households with means. The form often taken by this new housing was the **streetcar suburb** (Figure 9.8). Streetcar suburbs provided quick accessibility to the public transportation routes: Residents working downtown could walk out of their house and down the street (note the extensive use of sidewalks) and catch the streetcar along the main artery. Other features include relatively narrow lots to maximize the number of households with convenient access to public transportation, houses placed close to the front of the lot with a broad porch on the front face of the house, and the absence of an attached garage.

BOX 9.4   Technology and Urban Geography

Wrestling with Sprawl: Using GIS to Measure Urban Form

Ask people what they do not like about suburbia, and you are likely to get a response involving the term "sprawl." In fact, suburban sprawl has become a shorthand for so much that is bad about new commercial and residential developments and why they are often resisted. In the words of Duany, Plater-Zyberk, and Speck (2000):

'cookie-cutter houses, wide, treeless, sidewalk-free roadways, mindlessly curving cul-de-sacs, a streetscape of garage doors . . . Or, worse yet, a pretentious slew of McMansions, complete with the obligatory gate house. You will not be welcome there, not that you would ever have any reason to visit its monotonous moonscape.'

In addition to housing sprawl, critics decry modern retail development, with big box stores swimming in a sea of parking—sometimes called retail sprawl.

Such descriptions have come to embody our perceptions of sprawl, but they have not really helped to define or measure it. There has been considerable recent activity devoted to developing new ways to understand and measure sprawl, using the sophisticated tools offered by GIS. Unfortunately, there isn't uniform agreement on how best to measure sprawl. We present two different approaches here.

First, one team of scholars, including George Galster, Hal Wolman and Jackie Cutsinger, has focused on using available data to create *multiple* measures of sprawl for entire metropolitan areas. The team conceptually identified seven dis-

tinct dimensions along which metropolitan land use varies: density, continuity (Figure B9.3), concentration, centrality, proximity, nuclearity, and mixed use. Sprawl is conceptualized as extremes on each of these dimensions.

To measure these seven dimensions, the team used a variety of GIS techniques. (1) They used satellite imagery from United States Geological Survey's National Land Cover Data Base (NLCDB) to identify land that has been or can be developed. By excluding land that cannot be developed and focusing on what they call the Extended Urbanized Area (EUA), their measures are much more accurate and allow them to capture urban growth on the fringe of metropolitan areas. (2) They used Census information on housing and jobs at the small spatial unit possible, and (3) They used GIS to overlay all the data, using for most measures a grid with one square mile cells. They computed 14 measures of the seven dimensions for 50 large metropolitan areas, which they subsequently used in a variety of analyses.

In one analysis (Cutsinger and Galster 2006), they identified four "types" of metropolitan sprawl based on their data—dense but deconcentrated, leapfrog, compact and core-dominant, and dispersed. Some of the results from this analysis confirm common conceptions; for example, Atlanta is highly sprawled in a configuration that they term "leapfrog," which is marked by high job concentration, but low housing and job density, low continuity, low housing centrality, and low mixed land use. Figure B9.4 illustrates several of these characteristics for the distributions of housing and jobs. Other results are more surprising; Los Angeles, for example, is characterized by high density of jobs and housing, high continuity, but low job proximity

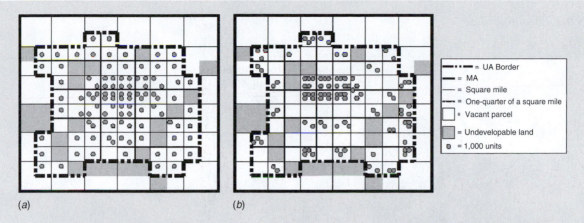

Figure B9.3 Aspects of discontinuity. (a) High continuity suggests that land has been developed in a relatively unbroken fashion. (b) Low continuity results from "leapfrog" development. *(Source:* Galster et al. 2001, Fig. 2.)

and low job concentration. One of their consistent points is that sprawl is too eclectic of a concept to rely on a single measure—their analyses illustrate the necessity of GIS techniques to address a complex measurement problem *and* that sprawl is a multifaceted problem.

Song and Knapp (Song 2005, Song and Knapp 2004) rely on a different approach that also uses GIS to measure sprawl, but ends up with neighborhood-specific measures rather than measures that describe entire metropolitan areas. Like the Galster, Wolman, and Cutsinger team, they also conceive of sprawl as a multifaceted problem that requires multiple empirical measures. Rather than focusing on the spatial patterning of jobs and housing, however, they focus instead on characteristics of the built environment. They use a GIS based on detailed parcel and road network layers. Their measures are organized into five themes; *street design and circulation systems* (street connectivity within neighborhood, median block perimeter, number of blocks per housing unit, median length of cul-de-sacs, street connectivity exterior to the neighborhood),

density (median lot size of single-family development, single-family residential density, median floor space of single-family units), *land use mix* (acres of commercial, industrial and public land uses per number of housing units), *accessibility* (median distance to the nearest commercial land use, median distance to the nearest bus stop, and median distance to the nearest park), and *pedestrian access* (percent of single-family dwelling units within a quarter-mile of existing commercial uses and percent of single-family dwelling units within a quarter-mile of all existing bus stops). In their empirical examples, they demonstrate that New Urbanist and Smart Growth policies in Portland, OR have had an effect on neighborhood design since the early 1990s by increasing single-family dwelling density, internal connectivity (i.e., less use of cul-de-sacs), and pedestrian access to commercial land use and bus stops. Even so, external connectivity has decreased, land use mixing remains limited, and house sizes continue to increase.

(continued)

BOX 9.4   (*Continued*)

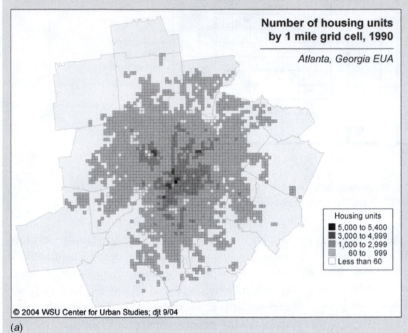

**Number of housing units
by 1 mile grid cell, 1990**

Atlanta, Georgia EUA

Housing units
■ 5,000 to 5,400
■ 3,000 to 4,999
■ 1,000 to 2,999
□ 60 to 999
□ Less than 60

© 2004 WSU Center for Urban Studies; djt 9/04

(*a*)

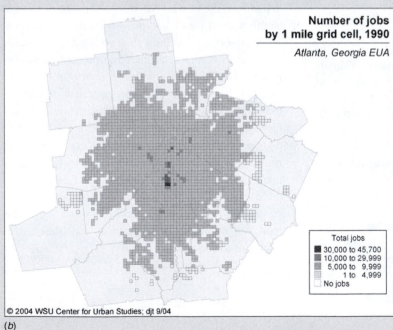

**Number of jobs
by 1 mile grid cell, 1990**

Atlanta, Georgia EUA

Total jobs
■ 30,000 to 45,700
■ 10,000 to 29,999
■ 5,000 to 9,999
□ 1 to 4,999
□ No jobs

© 2004 WSU Center for Urban Studies; djt 9/04

(*b*)

Figure B9.4 Using GIS to study urban sprawl, these maps demonstrate the leapfrog nature of Atlanta's urban sprawl. (a) Shows a dispersed low density distribution of housing, with a fragmented edge, while (b) shows jobs to be concentrated in the central business district and numerous peripheral subcenters. (*Source:* Figure 1 and Figure 2, Cutsinger, Jackie and George Galster 2006.)

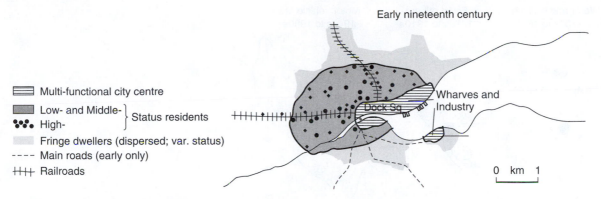

Figure 9.6 Diagram of a walking city. Cities in early North America were compact spatially and incorporated a mixture of land uses.

Streetcar suburbs formed the empirical backdrop for Hoyt's notions of filtering, vacancy chains, and neighborhood life cycles. In other words, they demonstrated downward neighborhood transition as middle-class households moved beyond them to the next ring of housing. Even so, these neighborhoods are today very attractive again. Some never deteriorated, and many others are experiencing various forms of renewal and renovation, contrary to the expectations of traditional theories. In addition, as we saw in Chapter 8, New Urbanism touts the sidewalk-oriented design and narrow lots of streetcar suburbs.

Automobiles, introduced in the first decade of the twentieth century, ultimately have had a tremendous impact on the North American metropolitan areas. As automobiles usage increased, local governments were forced to make critical decisions about physical infrastructure. Cars and all other independently powered vehicles (e.g., trucks and buses) needed paved roads, traffic control, and parking. Cities could continue to invest limited fiscal resources in expanding public transportation, or they could divert these resources to the physical infrastructure needed by the automobile. Most North American cities fatefully chose the automobile over expanding (or even continuing) fixed-route public transportation systems. Some observers suggest that heavy political pressures were brought to bear on these decisions in many cities, with oil companies and automobile manufacturers joining forces to pressure local decision makers to abandon public transportation in favor of road building.

Urban form changed as automobile usage increased and local governments invested resources into developing auto-related infrastructure. Even before the Depression and World War II, roads were paved and extended, and housing was built in areas where it was previously infeasible because of inaccessibility to public transportation routes. The spaces in between the fixed routes of existing public transportation systems began to fill in, and some greenfield (previously undeveloped, often agricultural) sites were developed.

Automobiles also began to impact housing design in the prewar years. Existing neighborhoods had to be retrofitted to accommodate cars. Households either converted existing outbuildings into garages, built garages and carports, or found parking on streets that increasingly seemed crowded and narrow.

Postwar Sprawl

Part of the explanation for post–World War II suburban sprawl is economic. World War II ultimately proved to be a very effective economic stimulus. The United States found itself in a remarkable position after the war. Most economic competitors had been defeated in the conflict or had been so drained

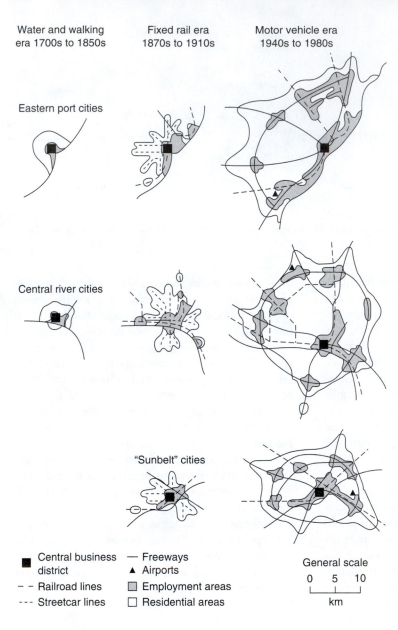

Water and walking
era 1700s to 1850s

Fixed rail era
1870s to 1910s

Motor vehicle era
1940s to 1980s

Eastern port cities

Central river cities

"Sunbelt" cities

■ Central business — Freeways
district   ▲ Airports
- - Railroad lines □ Employment areas
--- Streetcar lines □ Residential areas

General scale

0   5   10
|____|____|
km

Figure 9.7 Relationship between transportation infrastructure and urban spatial form. Note the influence of the automobile in particular. (*Source:* Fig. 5.4 in Knox, 1994, *Urbanization*, New York: Prentice Hall [original in T. Baerwald, 1984, "The Geographic Structure of North American Metropolises," paper presented to the 25th International Geographical Congress, Paris.])

by the war effort as to offer little real competition. The United States was the world's unchallenged economic leader, and it experienced robust domestic economic expansion for several decades.

Supply and Demand Factors The nature of housing demand partially explains the suburban

focus of postwar growth. Postwar economic prosperity unleashed several decades of pent-up housing demand that had characterized the Depression and war years. Cities grew rapidly after World War II as thousands of workers found relatively high-paying jobs in the factories that propelled the postwar economy. Most residents could find work, and wages

(a)

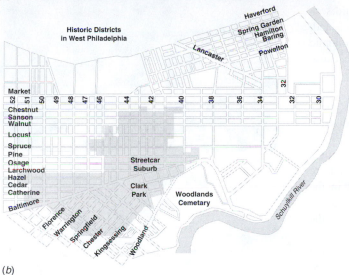

(b)

Figure 9.8 (a) Aerial view of Scranton, PA, showing typical form of streetcar suburbs with narrow lots, sidewalks, and houses close to the street. (b) Map of Philadelphia shows a streetcar suburb designated as a Historic District. (*Source:* Adapted from http://www.uchs.net/Historic Districts/HistDistmap.html.)

were rising. Economic prosperity meant that households had extra economic resources that could be used to purchase housing. It was easier for households with higher incomes to save money for a down payment and to afford the monthly mortgage payments. Households that previously had to make do with crowded and cramped rental housing now were now able to move up and out.

Demographic trends also dramatically affected the demand for housing. Millions of military service personnel returned to civilian life after the war. Many married, began or restarted careers, and started families, creating the baby boom. The result was a sudden increase in the number of households with young children. Many of these households sought housing with amenity bundles considered conducive to raising children, and many wanted to buy their own houses. The powerful social ideal of the American Dream—owning your own home (with a white picket fence, a dog, 2.4 children, a two-car garage and a station wagon [later a minivan and more recently a SUV] in the driveway)—became entrenched in the American psyche during these decades.

The intense postwar demand for housing was at first only inadequately met, as home construction had been limited for more than a decade. Providing new housing units quickly became one of the problems facing the housing industry. The industry also wanted to keep costs low enough so that new households could afford the newly built housing. Several dramatic trends occurred during the postwar decades in the arena of housing supply.

Several innovations in the production process, pioneered by developer William Levitt, made the construction of housing less expensive. In the Northeast, some of the economic principles of mass production based on a division of labor were applied to housing construction. The key was to build several houses simultaneously on a large tract of land. Large-scale developers realized several economic advantages. First, supplies were cheaper because suppliers typically charge less per item on large orders. Second, improved production times were derived from using standardized building plans and dividing the building process into discrete units.

Rather than having a single work crew building a house from the ground up, task-specific crews were organized that moved from site to site within the development. For example, framers would enter a site after foundations had been laid and build the frame for a house. They would proceed to the next site and frame that house while electricians and plumbers worked on the first house. Each crew, by specializing on a limited set of tasks, could speed up the process, especially as the building plans were standardized. Crews knew in advance exactly what would be required to complete their tasks.

The trend towards speculative housing development in large subdivisions had several impacts on the nature of housing. First, the new ways of building housing met the goal of making housing affordable to the rapidly growing segments of the market: young families with moderate incomes. Combined with the FHA and VA loan guarantee programs, mass-production construction techniques enabled many households to buy houses for the first time. Second, these processes created a new kind of community—a large number of very similar, relatively small houses occupying relatively small lots. The houses and streets were much more uniform (Figure 9.9). Not all postwar suburban housing was constructed on the same scale as the Levittowns, but many of the building and design innovations were subsequently adopted.

(a)

(b)

Figure 9.9 (a) Aerial photo of Levittown, developed on former potato fields in 1947. (b) Close-up of street in Levittown.

Sprawl and the Federal Government: Housing Finance Rapid development of suburban housing did not result simply from increased housing demand interacting with new ways of increasing housing supply. The new housing finance system put into place during the Depression years had a major impact on the degree and nature of suburbanization. As we discussed above, this system helped many households to purchase housing for the first time. The question of *where* the new housing would be constructed had not yet been answered, however.

First, recall that one of the goals of the FHA and VA loan guarantee programs was to expand homeownership. By increasing homeownership, these programs intensified the demand for new housing, most of which was being built in new suburbs. In addition, these programs had a marked geographic bias, directing most benefits to newly constructed housing located on the suburban fringe. FHA and VA lending guidelines specified that houses had to meet minimum physical standards as a safeguard against substandard housing (owners are more likely to default when the structure is in disrepair or would require infusions of cash to fix it up). These standards were relatively stringent and ended up disqualifying much older housing stock. Builders of new housing typically built to FHA standards in order to qualify for the program.

The discriminatory appraisal standards (redlining) used by the FHA and VA programs until the late 1960s also had a spatial bias. Racial and ethnic heterogeneity characterized inner-city neighborhoods, and redlining prevented homebuyers using the FHA and VA programs from considering houses in many inner-city areas. Ultimately, the vast majority of the millions of dollars in FHA-guaranteed mortgage loan capital was excluded from inner-city neighborhoods, instead financing suburban sprawl.

Sprawl and the Federal Government: Automobiles and Interstate Freeways The federal government played another critical role in spurring suburban development when it authorized and financed the national interstate freeway system. The plan gained approval during President Eisenhower's administration with the passage of the Federal-Aid Highway Act of 1956 (commonly known as the Interstate Highway Act) and called for a national network of limited-access highways to be built connecting all major urban areas.

The impact of the interstate freeways on suburbanization was enormous. The network (Figure 9.10) at first connected just the major urban areas, providing for easier, quicker, and cheaper long-distance travel. Importantly, the new interstate freeways were sited through the core of most major urban areas, providing new pathways from the core into the hinterland, and between the core and fringe areas of cities. Economically, the interstate system provided a boon to the trucking industry and led to a gradual decline in long-distance rail as a means of transportation.

The impacts that concern us here, though, are those on the cities themselves. The interstate freeways opened up many areas farther and farther from existing urban cores to new residential development. Residents could commute farther distances in about the same amount of time, thus allowing households to live farther away from existing employment centers. Many of the processes we have already discussed regarding the changing nature of housing in postwar cities were amplified by the interstate system. It became easier to speculatively develop large greenfield tracts of land into residential subdivisions given the improved access provided by the interstates.

Cities expanded in the late 1950s and 1960s along the new interstate arteries. Several features mark this expansion. For one thing, it was based on the premise of automobile-based commuting rather than public transportation—a notion that we call **automobility.** Residential development based on public transportation is by nature denser, because residents must be able to get from home to the public transportation stop. In contrast, interstate-stimulated, automobile-based residential development has tended to be much more dispersed and lower in density. Thus, compared to the compact streetcar suburb, the automobile-dependent suburb consumed much more land, often at a rapid pace. Moreover, as we discussed

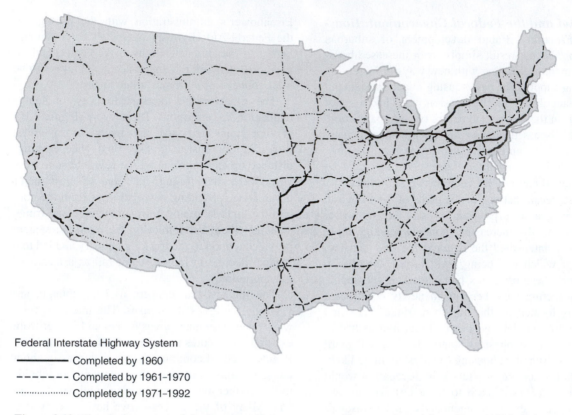

Federal Interstate Highway System
——————— Completed by 1960
- - - - - - Completed by 1961–1970
················ Completed by 1971–1992

Figure 9.10 Historical progress of the interstate highway system. (*Source:* adapted from Knox, 1994, *Urbanization*, New York: Prentice Hall, Fig. 3.1.)

in Chapter 6, given the distances that increasingly characterized cities in the postwar decades, shopping centers, business parks, and a variety of other economic functions also decentralized out of urban cores along with the residential areas.

Circumferential links were constructed between the radial spokes of the interstate system beginning in the 1960s. Most urban areas eventually had complete beltways or loops at some distance from the core. The intersections between the radial and circumferential portions of the interstate system have many economic advantages and have become major nodes of economic activity. Think of a city where you live or have visited. You probably can identify a large cluster of shopping malls, business parks and office buildings, and apartments surrounding one of these intersections. We discuss many

of these features of the economic landscapes of cities—sometimes called edge cities—in Chapters 6 and 8. In terms of housing, the continued expansion of the interstate system had two major impacts. One, it provided economic rationale for a greater diversity of housing types farther from the core. Two, it provided a greater diversity of employment opportunities farther from the core, allowing residents to live yet farther from the core of cities.

"BLIGHT" AND THE FATE OF INNER-CITY HOUSING

We next turn to the fate of inner-city housing in the decades following World War II. Recall that housing construction lagged during the Depression and stalled during the war. The federal loan guarantee programs were in place and reached their full impact during the postwar years as housing construction boomed. At the same time, inner-city neighborhoods were undergoing a different kind of transformation, often involving a bulldozer. What happened to these areas dramatically changed the function and structure of many cities during the postwar decades.

Blight and Growing Redevelopment Pressures

Much of the nation's urban housing stock in the first half of the twentieth century consisted of overcrowded and physically deteriorating neighborhoods in close proximity to the downtown retail core of many cities. This geographic arrangement had been functional for generations of immigrants and in-migrants moving to cities looking for work because these areas were close to the industrial areas of cities and the jobs they provided. These areas grew even more crowded and conditions worsened during World War II because of the general stagnation in the housing market. Of particular concern were the aging and structurally unsound tenements. Community activists pressed for public action to improve conditions. The housing stock in some areas was truly dangerous and could not be readily repaired. Thus, demolition appeared to be the only antidote. (Recall Hoover and Vernon's last stage of neighborhood evolution.)

The problems of an aging housing stock increasingly considered unsuitable were compounded by postwar suburbanization. Recall that suburbanization predated World War II and was already accompanied, though only to a minor extent, by retail decentralization: early suburban shopping centers were constructed well before the war started.

This presented a problem for the large downtown retailers like Macy's and Gimbels. They foresaw that suburbanization was going to continue and that their preferred clientele would increasingly live in the newly developing suburban areas. As new shopping centers were being built to service the decentralizing population, suburban residents began to feel that traveling into the core for shopping was more and more of a hassle. Retailers saw the blighted neighborhoods close to the retail districts as a problem: they feared that suburban residents would become less willing to travel through these blighted areas to shop downtown.

Local political leaders, in concert with local economic leaders—sometimes referred to as local growth machines—pushed hard in many areas for federal aid to resolve the blight problem. Beginning with the Housing Act of 1949, the solution increasingly took the form of bulldozers followed by bricks and mortar—in other words, demolish older neighborhoods and replace them with new development. These efforts would involve complex public-private partnerships in which governments spent money acquiring and clearing blighted properties before making the land available to private developers.

Through the 1950s and 1960s and into the 1970s, billions of dollars were spent on massive urban redevelopment schemes in the downtown areas of cities across the country. Many of these areas had been residential. In most cases, they were labeled as blighted, torn down, and often replaced with large-scale projects (although some areas razed by bulldozers were never redeveloped and remain barren today). Think of a downtown are that you are familiar with. There probably is a civic center or a university or hospital campus that was constructed or expanded significantly during this period (Figure 9.11).

The Housing Dynamics of Redevelopment

Several problems confronted urban redevelopment efforts. Where were the displaced residents going to live? This problem was intensely compounded in many cities by the fact that many of the residents of the worst neighborhoods were racial minorities who faced limited housing choices because of discrimination. What kind of development was to replace the old overcrowded neighborhoods? Would housing be provided, or would the newly cleared land be used for some other function? How would financing and responsibility be allocated?

The solution was a complex program of initiatives authorized in large part by federal legislation, for example, the Housing Act of 1949.

Figure 9.11 The University of Illinois opened its Chicago Circle campus (later renamed the University of Illinois at Chicago) in 1965 after immigrant and minority neighborhoods were cleared as part of Chicago's urban renewal efforts.

The government condemned older neighborhoods designated as blighted by local officials and obtained property ownership through **eminent domain,** which empowers the government to obtain ownership of land if it is in the overriding public interest, as long as the government pays fair market value. Once properties were obtained in this manner, they were cleared of existing structures and made available to private developers for new construction.

The blight designation became highly problematic. Instead of describing the worst housing that probably could not be renovated, blight became a self-fulfilling prophecy in many areas. Many neighborhoods destroyed during this period were poor yet economically and socially viable, having served for decades as gateways for new immigrants and rural-to-urban migrants. Once designated

as "blighted," however, these viable neighborhoods inevitably deteriorated very rapidly.

Physical decay proceeded very quickly after a blight designation, in part because of housing market dynamics. Property owners had no financial incentive to maintain properties following a blight designation because ownership was certain to be obtained by the city at some point. The problem was that exerting the power of eminent domain could get bogged down in legal proceedings, and the acquisition of *all* properties in an area (necessary before construction could start) could be significantly delayed. Property owners wanted to maintain an income flow in the mean time and therefore continued to rent out properties but withheld maintenance. The result was severely substandard housing for the very portions of the population least able to move to other neighborhoods.

Decisions about what to build in replacement for the blighted neighborhoods were also heavily shaped by the local growth machines. Seeking to retain the attractiveness of downtown areas for suburban consumers, most cities pursued development that would not be occupied by the poor. Downtown hospitals and universities sought land to expand. City governments built downtown convention centers and sports facilities. Freeway engineers sought the least expensive land possible to build the new interstate system. Private developers sought to build mixed-use, often high-rise, structures that would provide an income stream. These new structures often combined office and retail space with higher-income residential units. Community groups protesting downtown redevelopment claimed that the purpose of the redevelopment essentially was to depopulate the inner city of the poor, especially poor racial minorities.

Displacement and Public Housing The problem of providing housing for the residents displaced by downtown redevelopment was serious. Political leaders who wanted to pursue redevelopment schemes often encountered serious opposition from community residents. Many cities turned to public housing as a partial solution and in the process co-opted what at the time were only nascent efforts to provide publicly financed housing.

Many European industrial nations turned to publicly owned housing in response to the suffering of the Depression. The United States resisted the notion of public housing, favoring instead the series of financial incentives discussed earlier to increase homeownership. The theory behind much of this policy orientation rested on Hoyt's ideas about vacancy chains and filtering: If enough housing was provided for the upwardly mobile on the fringe of the city, natural housing market processes would make ample housing available to the poor.

Even so, beginning in 1935 the federal government funded the construction of a limited number of public housing units in cities around the country through the auspices of local housing authorities. The initial intent of this housing was very different than what you might think today. Local housing authorities applied stringent selection criteria and envisioned the housing as temporary shelter for intact nuclear families with good prospects of subsequently finding employment. Public housing was envisioned as transitional housing for the deserving poor disadvantaged by the unfortunate economic circumstances surrounding the Depression (Figure 9.12). Most often, this early public housing was reserved for white families only.

As World War II drew to a close, local housing authorities were very aware of the potential problems created by the return of millions of service personnel into overcrowded housing markets with few vacancies. Federal policies encouraged homeownership and stimulated new house construction—long-term strategies dependent on efficient filtering. Local housing authorities worried that the filtering process would not operate quickly enough to address the housing needs of returning veterans. They therefore sought to construct new public housing for returning veterans. This housing was not stigmatized in the way that it is today; rather, most people thought of it as a well-deserved benefit for veterans.

Public housing, despite noble initial goals, was eventually co-opted by downtown redevelopment initiatives to provide a political solution to the prob-

Figure 9.12 This public housing project built in 1937 was typical of early public housing. Buildings were generally small, and tenants were typically white and working poor.

lem of displacement. Under pressure from local growth machines (and some community organizers), many local housing authorities began to reconceive public housing. No longer was public housing to be a temporary and transitional form of housing. Rather, it was to become a place to house the most disadvantaged residents displaced by urban renewal programs. The very laws that authorized many of the redevelopment schemes (e.g., the Housing Act of 1949) also provided federal funding to local housing authorities to greatly expand the supply of public housing with the intent that it be filled with displaced residents. The social composition of public housing very quickly changed from intact families and returning veterans to the long-term poor, often the residents of demolished neighborhoods who were least able to find their own alternative housing.

Not surprisingly, decisions concerning the locations of the newly configured public housing projects generated intense political controversies. On the one hand, providing public housing for residents displaced from blighted neighborhoods became an essential part of the political selling of downtown redevelopment projects. (Note, however, that the number of units destroyed by redevelopment projects far exceeded the number of units built via public housing. Indeed, the number of units destroyed exceeded the total number of housing units ever constructed in those areas, counting even high-income units.) On the other hand, as it became clear that public housing was going to house the truly poor and racial minorities, communities increasingly resisted siting of projects. Indeed some of the worst urban violence in post–World War II decades centered around the siting of public housing and the racial composition of its residents. White communities frequently gathered to violently resist occupation by black residents, even black military personnel with intact nuclear families and good jobs (see Figure 10.6).

Eventually, many of the largest and most densely occupied public housing projects came to be located in marginal areas with little perceived economic value—in or adjacent to old abandoned industrial areas or in areas cut off by railroad lines or the newly built interstate system. In some cities, public housing built during this era came to occupy very large tracts of land and became a very visible symbol of poverty. A major example of this process was the Pruitt Igoe housing development, built in St. Louis in the mid-1950s (Figure 9.13), and heralded upon its completion as a triumph of modern city planning and social engineering.

Figure 9.13 Aerial view of Pruitt Igoe Homes, completed in 1955. Architect for the project, Minoru Yamasaki, won an award from the American Institute of Architects. The project represents the commitment to modernist design and massive scale.

High-density, high-rise projects were sold to the public not as the warehouses of the destitute that they became, but as a way to improve the lot of the unfortunate people who formerly lived in dirty, crowded, blighted neighborhoods. Unfortunately, the presumed triumph of modern architecture over the social ills of industrial capitalism ultimately failed. Very quickly after construction, many of these high rise projects became plagued by high crime rates. For example, a short two decades after their initial construction, the massive Pruitt Igoe homes of St. Louis were demolished in 1972 (Figure 9.14). The American Institute of Architects had recognized the architect, Minoru Yamasaki, for the design of the project. Even so, the modernist design of the projects made it difficult for housing authorities, police officers and residents to supervise activities in the buildings. As a result, crime rates were unacceptably high and social life was difficult to sustain. The residents actually lobbied to have the projects destroyed. Rather than serving as a testament to the power of modernist design, public housing came to represent its failure. Today the federal government is spending billions of dollars to tear down and reconstruct public housing.

NEIGHBORHOOD REVITALIZATION: GENTRIFICATION

Despite their apparent blight, many inner-city neighborhoods have enjoyed a remarkable turnaround in recent years. This trend is not unique to last few decades. For example, Brian Berry (1985) described "islands of renewal in a sea of decay" in the mid-1970s. In fact, selective renewal in older run-down neighborhoods was occurring during the 1960s in some North American cities. Gentrification describes the trend in some neighborhoods for predominantly white, middle-class residents to purchase and restore or revitalize houses in poor minority neighborhoods.

Revitalizing housing entails ripping out subdivided rental units and restoring the structure to

(a)

(b)

Figure 9.14 Demolition of the Pruitt Igoe Homes in St. Louis. (a) The degree of violence and abandonment in 1969, that led to (b) the demolition of the projects in 1972.

a single-family residence. Owner-occupiers invest significant sweat equity into the property, doing much of the renovation work themselves. Many gentrifying pioneers initially had difficulty in securing financing. Once the neighborhood had accumulated enough renovated properties, however, it would undergo a rapid transition from poor minority renters to white, middle-class owner-occupiers. Housing values would skyrocket, reflecting the considerable amenities that in-town neighborhoods provide to certain segments of the population.

David Ley (1996) and others favored explanations for gentrification that focus on the diversification of housing demand, especially the emergence of a new consumer-oriented, affluent middle and professional class. Homebuyers are now more socially diverse than in the immediate post–World War II decades. There are many more childless households, as young people choose to not have or at least to postpone childbearing. Also, many more singles are maintaining independent households, as are many more gays and lesbians. These are the populations that tend to pioneer gentrification. They are attracted to neighborhoods with older houses possessing interesting architecture and convenient access to urban amenities.

Alternative explanations for gentrification focus on the geographic nature of land values in urban neighborhoods, arguing that decades of disinvestment in the inner neighborhoods of cities creates new opportunities for speculative investment. According to Neil Smith (1996), urban land occupied by the poor is undervalued by land markets, creating a **rent gap** between the current value of the land and the higher potential value of the land under a new or different (gentrified) use. The rent gap represents profit potential that can be exploited via gentrification for investors willing to risk their capital, especially in periods when real estate investment more generally makes economic sense. Smith concluded that the economic motivations were more important in explaining gentrification than cultural or demand-centered explanations.

Gentrification stimulates very contrary responses. Its supporters applaud the return of middle-income (white) populations to the central city after decades of suburbanization. City governments argue that tax rolls increase, and demands on costly city services decrease, as higher-income households choose to live in the city. Problems associated with concentrated urban poverty (see Chapter 10 for a more detailed discussion of urban poverty) are eliminated, or at least moved elsewhere. Also, gentrification is often accompanied by the return of some of the retail businesses lost to the suburbs in previous decades.

Critics, however, contend that gentrification is another example of the exploitation of the poor. Federal housing policy and discriminatory housing institutions forced the poor to occupy inner city neighborhoods with old and deteriorating housing stock at a time when economic activity was rapidly decentralizing. At least the old neighborhoods were accessible to public transportation and proximate to what remained of inner-city employment opportunities. Now, when the attractions of in-town living are re-emerging, the poor are again being displaced from their neighborhoods. This time, they are being displaced into housing stock that really possesses little advantage—the small postwar suburban housing inaccessible to public transportation and distant from most urban services and employment opportunities. These criticisms thus focus on the power relations that lead to the appropriation of neighborhoods from the disadvantaged residents.

WRAPPING UP

In 1999 Robert Fishman (2000) surveyed a group of urban professionals who were members of the Society for American City and Regional Planning History, an interdisciplinary professional organization composed of urban historians, social scientists, planning faculty, and working planners and architects. He asked them to rank the 10 most important influences shaping the past 50 years, and the future, of the American metropolis. The results are as follows:

1. The 1956 Interstate Highway Act and the dominance of the automobile,

2. Federal Housing Administration mortgage financing and subdivision regulation,
3. Deindustrialization of central cities,
4. Urban renewal: downtown redevelopment and public housing projects (1949 Housing Act),
5. Levittown (the mass-produced suburban tract house),
6. Racial segregation and job discrimination in cities and suburbs,
7. Enclosed shopping malls,
8. Sunbelt-style sprawl,
9. Air conditioning, and
10. Urban riots of the 1960s.

Note that four out of the top 10 influences relate to housing and are discussed in this chapter. As Fishman notes, many of these influences reflect the direct and indirect, intended and unintended consequences of government involvement, in particular the 1956 Highway Act, FHA loan guarantee programs, and the 1949 Housing Act. The urban geography of housing is a fundamental feature of modern metropolitan areas.

READINGS

Berry, Brian J. L. 1985. "Islands of Renewal in Seas of Decay." In Paul Peterson, ed., *The New Urban Reality*. Washington, D.C.: Brookings Institution.

Carbonell, Armando. 2004. "Forward." In Dolores Hayden, *A Field Guide to Sprawl*. New York and London: W. W. Norton & Company, pp. 5–6.

Cutsinger, Jackie and George Galster. 2006. "There is No Sprawl Syndrome: A New Typology of Metropolitan Land Use Patterns," *Urban Geography,* Vol. 27, pp. 228–252.

Cutsinger, Jackie, George Galster, Harold Wolman, Royce Hanson, and Douglas Towns. 2005. "Verifying the Multi-Dimensional Nature of Metropolitan Land Use: Advancing the Understanding and Measurement of Sprawl," *Journal of Urban Affairs,* Vol. 27, pp. 235–259.

Downs, Anthony. 1981. *Neighborhoods and Urban Development*. Washington, D.C.: Brookings Institution.

Duany, A., E. Plater-Zyberk, et al. 2000. *Suburban Nation: The Rise of Sprawl and the Decline of the American Dream*. New York: North Point Press.

Eggers, Frederick J. 2001. "Homeownership: A Housing Success Story," *Cityscape: A Journal of Policy Development and Research,* Vol. 5, pp. 43–56.

Fishman, R. 2000. "The American Metropolis at Century's End: Past and Future Influences," *Housing Policy Debate,* Vol. 11, pp. 199–213.

Galster, George, Royce Hanson, Michael Ratcliffe, Harold Wolman, Stephen Coleman, and Jason Freihage. 2001. "Wrestling Sprawl to the Ground: Defining and Measuring an Elusive Concept," *Housing Policy Debate,* Vol. 12, pp. 681–717.

Hoover, Edgar M. and Raymond Vernon. 1962. *Anatomy of a Metropolis.* New York: Doubleday-Anchor.

Hoyt, Homer. 1939. *The Structure and Growth of Residential Neighborhoods in American Cities.* Washington, D.C.: Federal Housing Administration.

Immergluck, Dan and Geoff Smith. 2004. *Risky Business: An Econometric Analysis of the Relationship Between Subprime Lending and Neighborhood Foreclosures.* Chicago: Woodstock Institute.

Immergluck, Dan and Geoff Smith. 2005. "Measuring the Effect of Subprime Lending on Neighborhood Foreclosures," *Urban Affairs Review,* Vol. 40, pp. 362–389.

Immergluck, Dan and Geoff Smith. 2006a. "The External Costs of Foreclosure: The Impacts of Single-Family Mortgage Foreclosures on Property Values," *Housing Policy Debate,* Vol. 17, pp. 57–79.

Immergluck, Dan and Geoff Smith. 2006b. "The Impact of Single-Family Mortgage Foreclosures on Neighborhood Crime," *Housing Studies,* Vol. 21, pp. 851–866.

Immergluck, Dan and Marti Wiles. 1999. *Two Steps Back: The Dual Mortgage Market, Predatory Lending, and the Undoing of Community Development.* Chicago: Woodstock Institute.

Jackson, K. T. 1985. *Crabgrass Frontier: The Suburbanization of the United States.* New York and Oxford: Oxford University Press.

Ley, D. 1996. *The New Middle Class and the Remaking of the Central City.* Oxford and New York: Oxford University Press.

Smith, N. 1996. *The New Urban Frontier: Gentrification and the Revanchist City.* London and New York: Routledge.

Song, Yan. 2005. "Smart Growth and Urban Development Pattern: A Comparative Study," *International Regional Science Review,* Vol. 28, pp. 239–265.

Song, Yan and Gerrit-Jan Knaap. 2004. "Measuring Urban Form: Is Portland Winning the War on Sprawl?" *Journal of the American Planning Association,* Vol. 70, pp. 210–225.

Turner, M. A., S. L. Ross, G. C. Galster, and J. Yinger. 2002. *Discrimination in Metropolitan Housing Markets: National Results from Phase I HDS2000.* Washington, D.C.: U.S. Department of Housing and Urban Development.

Turner, M. A. and S. L. Ross. 2005. "How Racial Discrimination Affects the Search for Housing." In X. d. S. Briggs, ed., *The Geography of Opportunity: Race and Housing Choice in Metropolitan America.* Washington, D.C.: Brookings Institution Press.

White, M. J. 1987. *American Neighborhoods and Residential Differentiation.* New York: Russell Sage Foundation.

Yinger, John. 1995. *Closed Doors, Opportunities Lost: The Continuing Costs of Housing Discrimination.* New York: Russell Sage Foundation.

CHAPTER 10

SEGREGATION, RACE, AND URBAN POVERTY

Every large city in the United States, whether economically vibrant or withering, has areas of extreme poverty, physical decay, and increasing abandonment. Most city residents will go to great lengths to avoid living, working, or even driving through these areas. Usually, these neighborhoods are seen only on nightly news broadcasts after a gang-related shooting or drug raid, or they are depicted on television shows populated with every stereotype. But millions of Americans cannot keep a safe distance from them because they live in one.

—JARGOWSKY, 1997, P. 1

While the 1990s brought a landmark reversal of decades of increasingly concentrated poverty, the recent economic downturn and the weakening state of many older suburbs underscore that the trend may reverse once again without continued efforts to promote economic and residential opportunity for low-income families.

—JARGOWSKY, 2003, P. 1

This chapter addresses urban poverty and the people who experience it. Urban poverty remains an enduring problem, even after the robust economic growth of the 1990s. It has real and intense effects on the lives of the people that experience it. Moreover, poverty has become part of the way we imagine the city. Ask people what comes to mind when they think of the city, and they undoubtedly will mention "ghettos," "barrios," "slums," or other manifestations of poverty as part of the urban landscape.

Even worse, popular images of the urban poor too often carry a nonwhite face. If you live in a city or receive television broadcasts from a large city, recall the nature of stories about the urban poor. Very often, stories are about people in dire straits—crime victims, abandoned children, and so forth. Very often the people depicted are ethnic and racial minorities. Many aspects of these depictions greatly concern us. To begin with, most of the poor living in U.S. cities are, in fact, white. The problem goes deeper than this, however. As anyone, including the authors of

this textbook, the instructors of the classes you take, and you, talk about ethnic and/or racial identity in association with economic disadvantage, there is the potential to offend, or even to stigmatize, groups of people, even when we are trying not to.

A large measure of this problem centers on the complex nature of identity. The terms *ethnicity* and *race* are fluid and imprecise concepts that take on fixed meanings in part because governments and institutions use categories that only imperfectly reflect the complex realities in which people live. The text box in Chapter 11 discusses the notion of ethnicity; we discuss the concept of race in this chapter. To highlight the problematic nature of these notions, many authors have as a matter of course started enclosing the words in quotation marks. We do not follow this practice, though we do agree that the concepts are highly problematic in ways that we discuss. We stress in this chapter that talking about segregation and poverty using these vague and imprecise categories of identity is loaded with moral weight, especially regarding minority groups that ended up living in North America against their choice.

We start here with the tricky and problematic categories of race. This concept emerged centuries ago as European nations encountered diverse human populations during periods of exploration, nation-building, and colonial exploitation. Three human races were identified—Caucasians, Mongoloid, and Negroid—based on the global geography of where populations were "discovered" and the physical characteristics of the populations who lived there. Mongoloid and Negroid groups were considered by Europeans to be inferior, a belief used to justify colonial control over their homelands.

Genetic research refutes any meaningful biological basis to human races, yet the idea persists. Many people still talk as if race identifies inherent characteristics that explain behavior—and economic disadvantage. We, the authors, reject such notions. When we talk about race, we recognize that all differences between groups are created by society in specific historical and geographical contexts. Still, to understand the social landscapes of cities, we are forced to confront forms of oppression based on wrong-headed notions of racial and ethnic identity. Cities are the way we observe them today because people, institutions, markets, and governments acted (and still act) on the basis of racial ideas. These ideas are wrong, but they have had, and continue to have, a very important impact on the nature of cities that any student of cities needs to understand.

When we refer to race in the context of North American cities, we refer to populations at least partially descended from Africans involuntarily brought to North America on slave ships. Consider the variety of names that have been used to refer to this group: Colored, Negro, black, Afro-American, African American. There is today no universally accepted term that we can use. We generally use *black* and *African American* interchangeably, although without implying any biological basis to the differences that we describe. A better way to think about the complex issues of race and disadvantage in urban areas is conveyed by the concept of **racialization,** which describes the process whereby the

majority in society systematically imposes a racial identity upon a minority group with less social, economic, and political power.

CURRENT PATTERNS OF RACIAL RESIDENTIAL SEGREGATION

Most African Americans still lived in the rural South at the conclusion of the Civil War when U.S. slavery was finally abolished. This pattern changed dramatically in the twentieth century when rural blacks migrated to northern cities in large numbers. In the process of this major demographic shift from the rural South to the urban North, African Americans ended up in urban spaces unlike those experienced by any other group. We begin this section by exploring the degree of segregation that currently marks U.S. cities, including intense and multifaceted forms of residential segregation that concern many observers. We then provide a brief historical narrative of how African Americans came to live in these circumstances, and we consider how these conditions may be related to poverty.

Census 2000 Figures
In Chapter 11 we discuss the role of immigration in shaping the social landscapes of U.S. cities, with a particular focus on the residential segregation of immigrant groups in particular neighborhoods. This segregation has taken multiple forms in different cities and historical eras. Although people have worried over the years that immigrant segregation may hamper social and cultural assimilation, many people find ethnic neighborhoods enjoyable places to visit and recognize that they provide many economic, social, and cultural benefits to immigrants. This chapter discusses racial forms of residential segregation that have had much more adverse impacts on urban life.

Black/White Patterns U.S. Census data collected in April 2000 reveal some remarkable things about segregation by race. These data show that African Americans experience very high levels of

BOX 10.1   Types and Measures of Segregation

To think effectively about the issues that concern us in this chapter, we need to understand some basic ideas about residential segregation. Segregation is a fundamental concern of urban geographers, and we touch on this issue in all of the chapters in this section. Here, we want to focus particularly on the very long-standing and large academic interest in the segregation of African Americans. To do this, we need to discuss some of the ways that scholars have measured residential segregation. At one level it is easy to identify segregated neighborhoods. Recall a city that you live in or have visited. Most large cities have areas that commonly are identified with African Americans, often called *ghettos* (though recall from Chapter 2 that the term *ghetto* originally described areas of Medieval European cities into which Jews were segregated). As scholars and policy makers have struggled with issues of poverty and race, however, they have pondered questions such as this one: *how* segregated is this city, relative to the past and to other cities? Many ways of measuring segregation have been developed to address these questions. Today, our discussions of segregation are very much influenced by the most common quantitative measures of segregation. We discuss the two most common measures: index of dissimilarity and indices of exposure and isolation.

EVENNESS AND THE BASIC DISTRIBUTION OF GROUPS

By far the most common way of thinking about segregation is tied to the most common way of measuring segregation. The basic notion is to compare the distribution of a group or groups across neighborhoods within a city to some ideal, and then to measure quantitatively how different the actual distribution is from the ideal. The benchmark distribution against which segregation is most often measured is **evenness**. Imagine, for example, that a

group constitutes 10 percent of a city's population. An "even" distribution of that group across neighborhoods would result in that group's constituting 10 percent of each *neighborhood's* population. The degree to which that group's distribution differs, on average, from that ideal constitutes one way of measuring segregation in that context. Put another way, given the current distribution of a group across neighborhoods, what would be required to eliminate segregation (resulting in an "even" distribution of that group across neighborhoods)? The most common measure of the evenness interpretation of segregation is often called the **index of dissimilarity** (D), and it is computed easily from standard Census data. The formula is:

$$D = \frac{1}{2} \times \sum_{j=1}^{J} \left| \frac{x_j}{X} - \frac{y_j}{Y} \right|$$

The subscript j in the formula refers to the neighborhoods—in most cases census tracts or block groups, although sometimes other types of areas are used (e.g., voting districts, or wards, are often used when studying cities historically before census tracts were created). The vertical bars indicate that the absolute value of the difference is to be taken, the Greek character sigma (Σ) tells us to add up everything that follows. The symbols x_j and y_j refer to the numbers of people in group X and group Y, respectively, that live in census tract j. The symbols X and Y refer to the total numbers of people in group X and group Y, respectively, that live in the city as a whole.

For each group and each census tract, we divide the number living in the tract by the total living in the city. When we do this division for each census tract, we have the **proportional distribution** of that group across census tracts. We then add up the absolute value of the difference between the two proportional distributions, and divide by two. Look at Table B10.1 for an easily worked example. The index for the city is one-half of the

Table B10.1   Calculation of the Index of Dissimilarity *(D)* for a Hypothetical City

Subarea	Subarea Population		Proportional Distribution		Absolute Difference
	x_j	y_j	$\frac{x_j}{X}$	$\frac{y_j}{Y}$	$\left\| \frac{x_j}{X} - \frac{y_j}{Y} \right\|$
Part A					
1	110	10	0.44	0.02	0.42
2	100	40	0.40	0.08	0.32
3	15	140	0.06	0.28	0.22
4	25	150	0.10	0.30	0.20
5	0	160	0.00	0.32	0.32
Sum	250	500	1.00	1.00	1.48
Part B					
1	5	10	0.02	0.02	0.00
2	20	40	0.08	0.08	0.00
3	70	140	0.28	0.28	0.00
4	75	150	0.30	0.30	0.00
5	80	160	0.32	0.32	0.00
Sum	250	500	1.00	1.00	0.00

sum of the absolute differences: 1.48/2 = .74, or as often presented, multiplied by 100 to get 74. The value is also interpreted as the percentage of the minority group that would have to relocate to different neighborhoods in order to achieve an even distribution. In this example 74 percent of black residents would have to move in order to achieve an even distribution. Part B of Table B10.1 shows one possible pattern when members of group X relocate to subareas where they were formerly underrepresented. Note that in Part B group X now constitutes one-third of each subarea's population, as it does in the city as a whole.

The index of dissimilarity ranges from a minimum value of 0, representing perfect evenness, to 100, representing absolute separation of the groups. Traditionally, values between 0 and 30 are thought of as low, values between 30 and 70 are thought of as moderate, and values over 70 are thought of as high. Note, however, that the size and shape of geographic subareas affect the values of this index. Smaller areas, for example (relevant, perhaps, when we use block groups instead of census tracts) will generate higher values of the index even if the underlying residential distribution is identical.

EXPOSURE AND ISOLATION

The index of dissimilarity has been a very useful and durable measure of segregation. Even so, there are problems with the measure. Our ability to use it to compare places over time or across space is hampered by its sensitivity to the spatial characteristics of subareas and their location relative to one another. Even more troubling is the conceptual interpretation of the index—as a measure of evenness, the index compares actual proportional distribution against the ideal of an "even" distribution. Socially, however, we are often more concerned with what neighborhood residents might experience within their neighborhoods. The second most common segregation measure captures (though imperfectly) notions of **isolation** and **exposure**. This *P**, or *P*-star, index popularized by Stanley Lieberson (1981) is actually a related family of indices that take the form:

$$ _xP_y^* = \sum_{j=1}^{j} \left(\frac{X_j}{X} \right) \times \left(\frac{Y_j}{T} \right) $$

(continued)

BOX 10.1   *(Continued)*

The symbols are the same as in the formula for the index of dissimilarity (T = the total population of each tract). The exposure index attempts to measure the chance of encountering a person of another group within one's neighborhood rather than measuring the "average" difference between the distributions of two groups across neighborhoods. There will be a very low probability that group X individuals will encounter a group Y member in their neighborhood if most live in areas where few group Y members live. Another way to think about it is in terms of the average group composition of the neighborhood of a member of group X, on average. Specifically for the formula depicted here, what is the proportion of group Y members living in the neighborhood of the average member of group X? If neighborhoods where group X members disproportionately live are characterized by large proportions of group Y members, the index will have a

large value. Conversely, if they are characterized by large proportions of their own group, the index will have a small value. The index ranges from 0 to 1 (commonly multiplied by 100), with large values representing greater "residential exposure" of group X to group Y. A closely related and more commonly used variant of this index is the isolation index:

$$_xP^*_x = \sum_{j=1}^{J} \left(\frac{x_j}{X}\right) \times \left(\frac{x_j}{T}\right)$$

The difference is that the isolation index measures the average neighborhood proportion of group X members for other members of group X. In other words, what is the typical neighborhood percentage black for black residents of a city? Large values indicate that group X members live in neighborhoods, on average, dominated by their own group; that is, they are residentially isolated from other groups.

segregation—higher than any immigrant group in any U.S. city at any point in history. Before we can understand this, however, we need to understand something about the way we measure levels of segregation—a topic that we address in Box 10.1. Both the index of dissimilarity and the isolation index, our most commonly used indices, are quantitative measures of segregation that characterize the level of segregation across an entire metropolitan area. Values range from 0 to 100, with 100 indicating the maximum possible level of segregation.

Table 10.1 shows that African Americans remain extremely segregated several decades after the civil rights movement. We interpret the index of dissimilarity as the percent of the minority population that would have to exchange residences with members of the majority in order to achieve an even distribution between the two groups. In nine out of 10 of the Metropolitan Statistical Areas (MSAs) with the largest black population, more than two-thirds of blacks would have to move to eliminate segregation. The isolation index tells us, on average, the percent

of your own group living in your neighborhood. In seven out of the 10 MSAs listed in Table 10.1, blacks, on average, live in neighborhoods that are well over 50 percent black, demonstrating a high level of racial segregation. These numbers become even more dramatic when we compare them with the percent black in each MSA as a whole. For example, the average percent black in Chicago neighborhoods with black residents (73) is almost four times the percent black for the MSA as a whole (19). Even Los Angeles, with an isolation index of only 34, the average percent black of neighborhoods with black residents is more than three times the percent black for the MSA as a whole.

Hispanics and Asians   The categories *Hispanic* and *Asian* are not terribly meaningful. Hispanics come from a wide range of countries, and because the race and ethnicity questions on census forms are asked separately, Hispanics can be any race. Asians come from an even wider range of countries, and the category includes very different populations, from

Table 10.1 Residential Segregation in Metropolitan Areas with Largest Black Population

	2000				1990	
	Black Population	% of Total	Black-White Dissimilarity	Black Isolation	Black-White Dissimilarity	Black Isolation
New York, NY	2,217,680	23.8	81.8	60.4	82.3	62.7
Chicago, IL	1,575,173	19.0	80.9	72.9	84.5	77.9
Washington, D.C.	1,312,419	26.7	63.1	58.8	65.7	62.0
Atlanta, GA	1,202,260	29.2	65.6	62.6	68.7	65.3
Philadelphia, PA-NJ	1,040,144	20.4	72.3	62.3	77.2	67.7
Detroit, MI	1,037,674	23.4	84.7	79.0	87.7	81.2
Los Angeles-Long Beach, CA	950,765	10.0	67.6	34.4	73.6	42.8
Houston, TX	734,732	17.6	67.5	47.3	67.6	54.4
Baltimore, MD	712,002	27.9	67.9	66.1	71.9	70.0
Dallas, TX	537,789	15.3	59.4	42.0	63.6	50.7
Average			71.1	58.6	74.3	63.5
Average, large MSAs (Population > 1 Million)			62.2	41.6	66.9	46.9
Average, All MSAs			51.4	27.7	55.6	27.5

Source: Segregation indices calculated by the Mumford Center from U.S. Census data, 1990 and 2000 [http://mumford1.dyndns.org/cen2000/WholePop/WPdownload.html]. Copyright © 2002 by Lewis Mumford Center for Comparative Urban and Regional Research, The University at Albany.

descendants of Chinese immigrants who arrived in the late nineteenth century to Laotian immigrants who have lived in the United States for only a few years. Still, these categories are frequently used, and they are the best ones available at this time.

Tables 10.2 and 10.3 show segregation index values computed for Hispanics and Asians, respectively. Overall, Hispanics are more segregated than Asians, although neither group is as severely segregated as blacks. This is true for both the particular metropolitan areas in which each group is most frequent and for all metropolitan areas. Los Angeles, New York, and Chicago provide an interesting point of comparison because they appear on each group's top 10 list. New York and Chicago follow the general trend, with segregation highest for African Americans followed by Hispanics and Asians. Los Angeles deviates from the pattern. According to the index of dissimilarity, Hispanic segregation is on par with African American segregation. And, according to the isolation index, Hispanics are *more* segregated

than African Americans—a result that stems in large part from the fact that Hispanics now constitute 44 percent of the city's population.

Recent Change

Although the indices tell us that African Americans are highly segregated in U.S. metropolitan areas, especially in those areas where they live in the greatest numbers, they also indicate some improvement in this area. During the 1990s, segregation decreased for each of the MSAs depicted in Table 10.1 (by an average of 3 points based on dissimilarity and 5 points based on isolation). Segregation decreased in all regions of the country and in cities of all sizes: on average, segregation dropped by 4 to 5 points. A few cities saw increases in segregation, but the size of the black population in these cities is generally small. Viewed over the course of the twentieth century (Figure 10.1), we see that African American segregation rose through

Table 10.2 Residential Segregation in Metropolitan Areas with Largest Hispanic Population

	2000				1990	
	Hispanic Population	*% of MSA*	*Hispanic-White Dissimilarity*	*Hispanic Isolation*	*Hispanic-White Dissimilarity*	*Hispanic Isolation*
Los Angeles-Long Beach, CA	4,242,213	44.6	63.2	63.3	61.3	57.7
New York, NY	2,339,836	25.1	66.7	46.3	66.0	43.8
Chicago, IL	1,416,584	17.1	62.1	48.0	63.4	42.7
Miami, FL	1,291,737	57.3	44.4	71.3	51.1	67.9
Houston, TX	1,248,586	29.9	55.7	49.2	50.1	40.5
Riverside-San Bernardino, CA	1,228,962	37.8	43.0	49.8	36.9	38.1
Orange County, CA	875,579	30.8	56.0	53.7	50.8	45.4
Phoenix-Mesa, AZ	817,012	25.1	52.5	45.8	49.3	36.0
San Antonio, TX	816,037	51.3	51.0	65.8	53.7	65.1
Dallas, TX	810,499	23.0	54.1	44.8	50.6	32.2
Average			54.9	53.8	53.3	46.9
Average, large MSAs (population > 1 Million)			47.5	25.5	45.8	19.3
Average, All MSAs			38.6	16.7	39.8	10.1

Source: Segregation indices calculated by the Mumford Center from U.S. Census data, 1990 and 2000 [http://mumford1.dyndns.org/cen2000/WholePop/WPdownload.html]. Copyright © 2002 by Lewis Mumford Center for Comparative Urban and Regional Research, The University at Albany.

Table 10.3 Residential Segregation in Metropolitan Areas with Largest Asian Population

	2000				1990	
	Asian Population	*% of MSA*	*Asian-White Dissimilarity*	*Asian Isolation*	*Asian-White Dissimilarity*	*Asian Isolation*
Los Angeles-Long Beach, CA	1,232,085	12.9	48.3	28.7	46.6	22.7
New York, NY	913,199	9.8	50.5	26.5	49.3	20.7
San Jose, CA	459,401	27.3	41.7	37.9	39.1	25.6
Oakland, CA	449,146	18.8	41.5	29.4	39.8	21.4
San Francisco, CA	430,146	24.9	48.7	39.6	50.2	36.0
Orange County, CA	424,828	14.9	40.3	25.7	34.2	16.7
Chicago, IL	415,244	5.0	44.4	14.8	47.1	11.9
Washington, D.C.	366,991	7.5	39.0	13.8	37.4	9.4
San Diego, CA	294,966	10.5	47.0	21.7	48.4	18.1
Seattle, WA	270,728	11.2	35.1	18.6	37.7	15.5
Average			43.6	25.7	43.0	19.8
Average, large MSAs (population > 1 Million)			39.9	10.2	43.9	7.6
Average, All MSAs			35.5	5.6	44.0	1.9

Source: Segregation indices calculated by the Mumford Center from U.S. Census data, 1990 and 2000 [http://mumford1.dyndns.org/cen2000/WholePop/WPdownload.html]. Copyright © 2002 by Lewis Mumford Center for Comparative Urban and Regional Research, The University at Albany.

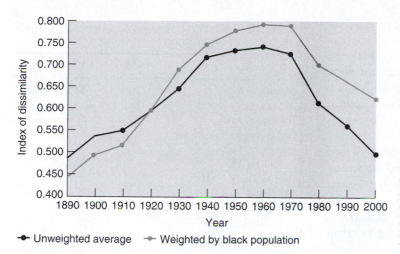

- **Unweighted average** - **Weighted by black population**

Figure 10.1 Trend in residential segregation as measured by the index of dissimilarity, 1890–2000. (*Source:* Modified from Glaeser and Vigdor, 2001, "Racial Segregation in the 2000 Census: Promising News," Center on Urban and Metropolitan Policy Survey Series, The Brookings Institution, Washington, D.C.)

the first two-thirds of the century to reach its highest levels in the 1960s. Following the passage of landmark antidiscrimination laws in the 1960s and early 1970s (see Chapter 9), accompanied later by the economic boom of the 1990s, segregation levels declined.

In contrast to the downward trend in African American segregation over the last several decades, segregation for Hispanics increased notably during the 1990s. Although indices of Hispanic segregation are not as high as those for African Americans, these increases are nonetheless very troubling. The increase in the isolation index values for Hispanics stems in part from their rapid increase in numbers due to recent immigration. (Note that there are more Hispanics in the top 10 Hispanic MSAs than there are African Americans in the top 10 African American MSAs.) Census Bureau data confirms that Hispanics are now more numerous than African Americans, making Hispanics the largest minority group.

Hypersegregation

Our discussion so far has explored two ways of thinking about and measuring segregation, reflected in the index of dissimilarity and the isolation index. Douglas Massey and Nancy Denton (1988) proposed a more sophisticated model that delineates five ways of thinking about segregation:

1. **Evenness** describes the similarity in the distribution of groups across neighborhoods (measured by the index of dissimilarity).
2. **Exposure/isolation** captures the typical composition of neighborhoods where group members live (measured by the isolation index).
3. **Centralization** describes the degree to which group members live close to the center of the city, relative to other groups.
4. **Clustering** is the degree to which group members live in neighborhoods that are close together within the city. (Note that the other measures do not distinguish between segregated neighborhoods located next to each other and segregated neighborhoods that are located on opposite sides of the city.)
5. **Concentration** describes the extent to which a group lives in a restricted amount of urban space; that is, the extent to which the group lives in high-density settings.

These forms of segregation are somewhat similar yet are also distinct. Massey and Denton argue that a group experiences **hypersegregation** when it faces multiple forms of segregation simultaneously. In other words, a group is hypersegregated when it is spatially uneven, isolated, concentrated, clustered, and centralized at the same time. Hypersegregation appears to compound the negative impacts of segregation.

Massey and Denton (1989, 1993) found in an empirical examination of 1980 U.S. Census data that only African Americans were highly segregated on multiple dimensions. They defined a group as hypersegregated when it had high segregation on at least four out of five indices. African Americans were hypersegregated in 16 metropolitan areas: Atlanta, Baltimore, Buffalo, Chicago, Cleveland, Dallas, Detroit, Gary, Indianapolis, Kansas City, Los Angeles, Milwaukee, New York, Newark, Philadelphia, and St. Louis. They point out that "these sixteen metropolitan areas are among the most important in the country, containing six of the ten largest metropolitan areas in the United States. Together they house 35 percent of the nation's black population, and 41 percent of all blacks living in urban areas" (Massey and Denton 1993, p. 77).

An updated analysis using 1990 Census data (Table 10.4) found that 14 out of the 16 areas hypersegregated in 1980 remained so in 1990 (Denton, 1994). Only Dallas and Atlanta dropped from the list, experiencing significant declines in evenness and concentration. Several additional metropolitan areas had become hypersegregated by 1990. Though many of these were smaller, several large metropolitan areas were added to list, including Birmingham, Cincinnati, Miami, New Orleans, and Washington, D.C. By 2000, black-white segregation had declined in many metropolitan areas, and the number of hypersegregated areas also declined (Table 10.4). Notably, however, all of the metropolitan areas that dropped from the list still had very high levels of racial segregation and several areas joined or rejoined the list, including Atlanta (Wilkes and Iceland, 2004). Also, Wilkes and Iceland report that Hispanics were hypersegregated in Los Angeles and New York in 2000—the first time that any group other than blacks have been found to be extremely and extensively segregated from whites.

We will look at Massey and Denton's claim that segregation has negative consequences for African Americans later in the chapter, where we talk about the intersection of racial segregation with high levels of poverty concentration. First, however, we explore some of the factors that account for the residential segregation that we have just observed. We first

Table 10.4 Hypersegregated Metropolitan Areas, 1980–2000

Metropolitan Area	1980	1990	2000
Albany, GA		X	X
Atlanta, GA	X		X
Baltimore, MD	X	X	X
Baton Rouge, LA		X	X
Beaumont-Port Arthur, TX		X	X
Benton Harbor, MI		X	
Birmingham, AL		X	X
Buffalo-Niagra Falls, NY	X	X	X
Chicago, IL	X	X	X
Cincinnati, OH		X	
Cleveland, OH	X	X	X
Dayton-Springfield, OH			X
Dallas-Fort Worth, TX	X		
Detroit, MI	X	X	X
Flint, MI		X	X
Gary, IN	X	X	X
Indianapolis, IN	X	X	
Kansas City, KS	X	X	
Los Angeles-Long Beach, CA	X	X	X
Miami, FL		X	
Milwaukee, WI	X	X	X
Mobile, AL			X
Monroe, LA		X	X
New Orleans, LA		X	
New York, NY	X	X	X
Newark, NJ	X	X	X
Oakland, CA		X	
Philadelphia, PA	X	X	X
Saginaw-Bay City, MI		X	X
Savannah, GA		X	
St. Louis, MO	X	X	X
Trenton, NJ		X	
Washington, D.C.		X	X

Source: Massey and Denton (1989, 1993), Denton (1994), Wilkes and Iceland (2004).

Note: There are some differences in methodology and sample of candidate metropolitan areas between the studies that examine hypersegregation. We used the most conservative and consistent numbers that we could obtain in order to create this table.

consider the debate over the causes of segregation, and we then consider in greater historic detail the evolution of racialized ghettos.

What Causes Segregation?

Social scientists often specify three forces or factors that cause residential segregation: economics, discrimination, and preferences. The first of these forces suggests that what appears to be racial segregation simply results from the fact that most minorities earn lower incomes and possess less wealth than whites. In other words, they simply can't afford to live in the same neighborhoods, and higher-income neighborhoods thus end up predominantly white as a natural and unproblematic outcome of the ways that housing markets work. Empirical research does not support this suggestion. In fact, it suggests just the opposite; that racial segregation occurs at all income and wealth levels.

The second force points to institutionalized discrimination on the part of real estate agents, lenders, appraisers, and so forth (see Chapter 9 for a detailed discussion of discrimination). According to this perspective, discrimination remains integral to the maintenance of segregation. Critics of this theory point to the successes of the civil rights movement and the empirical decreases in segregation levels indicated by the decennial censuses. As documented in Chapter 9, however, discrimination in the housing market has not ended.

The third force—preferences—has received the most recent attention. There are two versions of this argument, which have very different implications. Proponents of the first version maintain that segregation results from voluntary self-separation practiced by minorities. Looking at immigrant neighborhoods (today and in the past), these observers note that segregation provides benefits—cultural reinforcement, job contacts, and so forth. They conclude that minorities are segregated because they want to live close to other members of their group.

Although there is some support for the notion that immigrant groups at least partially choose to live in immigrant neighborhoods, there are some important distinctions between immigrant groups and African Americans. Immigrant neighborhoods are not now, and never have been, as segregated as African American neighborhoods have been through most of the twentieth century and remain today. Immigrants of a single group almost never constitute the vast majority of a single neighborhood. They may constitute the majority of a neighborhood, yet undoubtedly there will be members of other groups also living in those neighborhoods.

More importantly, when we look at the best available evidence on the residential preferences of African Americans, we see little evidence to support the argument that blacks want to live in segregated neighborhoods. The Multi-City Study of Urban Inequality (MCSUI), funded by the Ford Foundation and the Russell Sage Foundation, used an innovative methodology to investigate the issue. They interviewed thousands of people in Los Angeles, Boston, Detroit, and Atlanta, asking questions about what these people wanted in terms of the racial composition of their neighborhoods. Residents were asked to rank in order of preference a series of "show cards" that depicted various combinations of racial composition. This research shows very clearly that blacks "prefer" neighborhoods that are around 50 percent white and 50 percent black. Completely segregated neighborhoods clearly are not the ideal.

The MCSUI research provides strong support for a second way of viewing the issue of preferences, namely, that the preferences of whites matter more than the preferences of blacks. Whereas black respondents indicated that integrated neighborhoods were most desirable, white respondents indicated that anything more than a minimal minority presence was problematic. White respondents thus are more likely to move out of neighborhoods that undergo integration and to avoid moving into neighborhoods where minorities constitute a noticeable presence. These findings are consistent with other research from the 1970s (Schelling 1971) that suggested that white residents react to a **tipping point**: When racial composition goes beyond a certain threshold (and there is some evidence that the threshold has moved slightly higher over the last three decades), the neighborhood will inevitably "tip." That is, the neighborhood will turn completely over from white to black as whites leave the neighborhood very quickly in a process known as **white flight.** Viewed from this perspective, preferences are not such a benign force.

Although the debate over the causes of segregation has been intense, it still leaves too much unanswered. The level of African American segregation remains amazingly high and had reached extreme levels by the 1960s and 1970s. How did we get there? Are the forces that created the ghettos still in force? Or are other factors at play today, maintaining levels of segregation that were created in earlier decades by different forces? The next section lays out the complex history of segregation in the United States, an account of which is necessary to make sense of the contemporary patterns.

RACE AND THE NORTH AMERICAN GHETTO

Only small numbers of African Americans lived in cities during the late nineteenth century. Levels of segregation were not remarkable. Urban African American communities in many ways were not that different from communities of European immigrants

arriving in large numbers at the same time. Indeed, the few African Americans who were able to achieve some degree of middle-class standing often lived in predominantly white neighborhoods.

The "First" North American Ghetto

The first major migration stream of African Americans to northern cities, called the "Great Migration," occurred during and just after World War I between 1915 and 1920. It was fueled by the devastation of southern agriculture at the hands of the boll weevil and by severe wartime industrial labor shortages in northern cities. Northern industrial capitalists had previously used southern black labor in small numbers to break the strikes of the increasingly influential labor movement during the years prior to the outbreak of World War I. They turned again to southern black labor when faced with the need to increase war production at the same time that European immigration was suddenly curtailed by the conflict (see Chapter 11).

As a result of the Great Migration, the number and percentage of blacks in many northern cities increased dramatically. For example, the black population of Chicago grew from about 14,000 in 1890 to more than 100,000 in 1920 (Table 10.5). The sudden increase in the number of blacks in northern cities squeezed an already limited housing market. Very few new units were made available during the

Table 10.5 Growth of Chicago's Black Population, 1850–1930

Year	Total Population	Black Population	% Black	% Increase Total	Black
1850	29,963	323	1.1		
1860	109,260	955	0.9	265	196
1870	298,977	3,691	1.2	174	286
1880	503,185	6,480	1.1	68	75
1890	1,099,850	14,271	1.3	119	120
1900	1,698,575	30,150	1.9	54	111
1910	2,185,283	44,103	2.0	29	46
1920	2,701,705	109,458	4.1	24	148
1930	3,376,438	233,903	6.9	25	114

Source: Philpott (1991), Table 5.1.

war years. These pressures on local housing markets created wartime crises in many cities. The response of cities to the suddenly larger African American populations *after* World War I, however, resulted in the first African American ghettos.

Dual Housing Markets, the "Color Line," and Ghettos

Ghettos are not "natural" outcomes of acceptable social and economic processes. Rather, *people*—individuals, institutions, and governments—create and maintain ghettos. This becomes clear when we examine the emergence of the first racial ghettos. Fear and racism increasingly characterized northern whites' response to industrialization and large-scale labor migrations (including the Great Migration). There were pronounced increases in sentiments and expressions of white racism against blacks, Jews, and other minority groups during the early decades of the twentieth century. African American migrants to northern cities, though better educated and more skilled than nonmigrants in the South (and many blacks already in the North), were perceived to be culturally backwards, ignorant, and dangerous, both by white society and by the established black elite.

Whites in northern cities acted out their fears and hostilities by spatially isolating blacks into distinct ghettos. (African Americans also ended up residentially segregated in southern cities, though to a lesser extent.) To understand the creation of the early twentieth-century racial ghetto, we need to understand the tools that whites used to inscribe the color line on the residential landscape of the city.

Whites' response to the Great Migration can best be described as a combination of informal and institutional efforts intended to minimize social and economic contact with African Americans. Through these efforts, whites succeeded in limiting blacks' housing choices to predominantly black neighborhoods. Blacks living in predominantly white neighborhoods prior to the war were sometimes driven out, and the numerous in-migrants from the South were forced to settle in the consolidating ghettos. Areas of town known before World War I as "black," but which in fact were only about 25 to 30

percent black, became much more exclusively black after the war.

African Americans increasingly faced personal violence and hostility. When a black family lived or moved into an area that white residents wished to make or keep all white, angry crowds of whites would gather to throw stones, start fires, and even fire-bomb black residences in the middle of the night (Philpott 1991; Spear 1967). Racial violence was not limited to northern cities, but it became increasingly common in these cities as contact between the races increased. The brunt of this racial violence was directed against black communities that grew most rapidly. The areas most prone to violence were adjacent to, and in the growth path of, the consolidating black ghettos. During the worst episodes of white-on-black violence, gangs of white youths would pull blacks off of public transportation lines to beat them (Philpott 1991; Spear 1967). During the 1919 Chicago race riot, white gangs even went through black neighborhoods searching for black victims. Although housing issues did not always spark the worst examples of racially motivated violence, the goal of the violence was always to enforce social separation of the races. Figure 10.2 illustrates the impact of racial violence on blacks.

Figure 10.2 The 1919 race riot in Chicago forced many blacks to leave their homes, increasing residential segregation and leading to a racially segmented housing market.

White residents also tried to exclude blacks from their neighborhoods through more subtle means. Faced with blacks' desperate need for housing and their inevitable "incursion" into white neighborhoods, white homeowners and neighborhood leaders often organized **neighborhood improvement associations** to do whatever they could to exclude blacks. These associations attempted to convince white owners and landlords not to sell or rent to blacks. They collected money and attempted to buy outright properties that were "threatened" with racial transition. They encouraged banks to not lend money to blacks and pressured real estate agents to treat as unethical the showing of properties in white neighborhoods to blacks. Perhaps most important, they devised and instituted the **restrictive covenant,** which made it illegal for white owners to sell property to blacks if a majority of the neighborhood residents opposed such a transaction.

More formal mechanisms of concentrating blacks in racially defined ghettos emerged during this period, although they became much more prevalent in the post–World War II period. For example, there were brief attempts at direct legal segregation (i.e., prescribing by law where blacks could and could not live) between 1910 and 1917, mostly in southern and border states, which were struck down by the Supreme Court as unconstitutional (Rice 1968). The most influential role of law during this period was to support the legality of restrictive covenants until 1948, when they were ruled unenforceable.

Institutional practices played an important role in creating a **dual housing market,** with very different rules for whites and blacks, during this period. Some real estate agents practiced racial steering: blacks (even those who could obviously afford it) were not shown property in white neighborhoods, and whites were not shown property in mixed or transitional neighborhoods. Other real estate agents (black and white) profited from block-busting, in which they would generate racial fear by bringing a black family into a white neighborhood and then playing up the situation to white neighbors in hopes that the neighbors would sell cheaply. Real estate agents often would buy property themselves and either resell or rent it to blacks. Subdividing apartments into small kitchenettes and charging exorbitant rents were also common practices. Lending institutions and insurance agencies contributed to the problem by redlining black neighborhoods and denying mortgages to blacks.

Postwar Institutionalized Ghettos

The patterns of racial segregation established in the early decades of the twentieth century largely remained in place until after World War II. After the war, much could have changed, but did not. In Chapter 9 we discussed many of the changes sweeping across North American cities during the postwar years: unprecedented economic growth, massive increases in housing stock (in the form of suburban development), rapid increases in home ownership fueled by revolutionary changes in the housing finance system, and notable successes by the civil rights movement. These forces easily could have ended the racial ghetto. Instead, divides between the racial ghetto and the rest of urban society were deepened and strengthened.

Urban historian Arnold Hirsch (1983) argues that during this period a "second" racial ghetto was created, continuing yet distinct from the first. These newly created ghettos occupied a larger area, housed a much larger population, and imposed increasing levels of social and spatial isolation on their residents. Chicago is illustrative: in 1920, although the outlines of the first ghetto had been drawn, no blacks lived in a census tract that was more than 90 percent black. By 1960, however, more than 50 percent of Chicago blacks lived in almost exclusively black tracts (Figure 10.3). Understanding the second ghetto is crucial to our understanding of contemporary issues of race, segregation, and poverty.

The dual housing market inscribed into cities during the 1920s prevailed for several decades. Conditions in the post–World War II decades quickly deteriorated, however. Significantly, the migration of southern rural blacks into the industrial cities of the North, Midwest, and West resumed during the war and continued through the 1950s and 1960s, fueled by increased demand for industrial

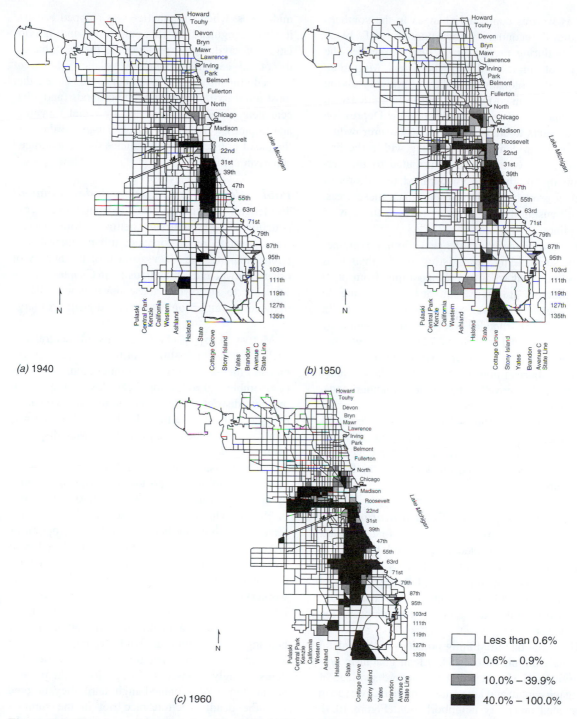

(a) 1940

(b) 1950

(c) 1960

Less than 0.6%

0.6% – 0.9%

10.0% – 39.9%

40.0% – 100.0%

Figure 10.3 Changing racial geography of post–World War II Chicago. (*Source:* From Hirsch, 1983, Maps 1–3.)

labor as well as continued changes in the southern agricultural economy. The numbers of black migrants during these years actually exceeded the number of migrants during the Great Migration. Even so, the color line inscribed on the city during the 1920s remained in place, and it combined with the stagnant housing market through the Depression and war years to create extraordinary overcrowding and bottled-up demand for housing within the first ghetto. This overcrowding contributed to the perception of "blight" and encouraged the efforts of the local growth machines to eliminate these areas. Public housing did not provide much in the way of real relief.

Pressure increased on the neighborhoods immediately surrounding the existing black ghettos as blacks, many of whom were benefiting from postwar economic prosperity, sought better housing. In the immediate postwar years, white residents in adjacent neighborhoods fiercely resisted attempts by blacks to cross old color lines. The pressure was too great in most areas, however. So, when newly constructed suburban housing became available, many whites rapidly moved out of older neighborhoods, surrendering them to black households in a process described as **white flight.** Note that these types of racial transitions took place relatively quickly and that they could have occurred only when new housing was being constructed for whites on the fringes of the cities.

Government-Supported Discrimination   The
second ghetto is distinct from the first, in part, because of the expanded role played by government regulation. Many of the changes in the housing finance system implemented during the Great Depression (described in Chapter 9) played a significant role in deepening racial segregation during the postwar years.

The adoption of redlining practices in the Federal Housing Administration (FHA) loan guarantee program, in particular, resulted in a severe shortage of mortgage capital and adequate insurance coverage in segregated inner-city neighborhoods (Figure 10.4). From the beginning of the FHA program through the

mid-1960s, when the practice was stopped because it was recognized as discriminatory and in violation of civil rights protections, the vast majority of all capital guaranteed by the FHA went to predominantly white neighborhoods. Given that most minority-dominated neighborhoods (and adjacent neighborhoods threatened by racial transition and tipping) were located in older parts of the city, the racial politics of FHA policies only encouraged suburban sprawl.

Public Housing and Urban Redevelopment
The federal government also contributed to the construction of the great urban ghettos in more concrete ways, through redevelopment, urban renewal, and public housing. We discuss much of the history of urban renewal and public housing in Chapter 9. Here we want to stress that these developments had a tremendous impact on the racialized ghettos of large cities.

Motivated by general patterns of central-city decline, powerful coalitions of business and governmental officials leveraged enormous sums of money to assemble and redevelop areas close to the central business districts of many cities. Racial segregation resulted both because the role of public housing was transformed and because poor blacks were displaced from these areas.

Public housing contributed to the creation of the second ghetto in the post–World War II decades by spatially concentrating and anchoring the poor in ghettos. This occurred for at least three reasons. First, public housing became the housing option of last resort for the poorest of the poor displaced from areas undergoing redevelopment (rather than temporary housing for upwardly mobile low-income workers). Second, most public housing was (and is) extremely segregated by race. Figure 10.5 illustrates the racial antagonism surrounding public housing. The Sojourner Truth Homes opened in 1942 to provide housing for veterans. White residents strongly opposed the integration of the project. Racial tensions remained high until they erupted into the deadly Detroit race riot in the summer of 1943. Note that violent resistance to the

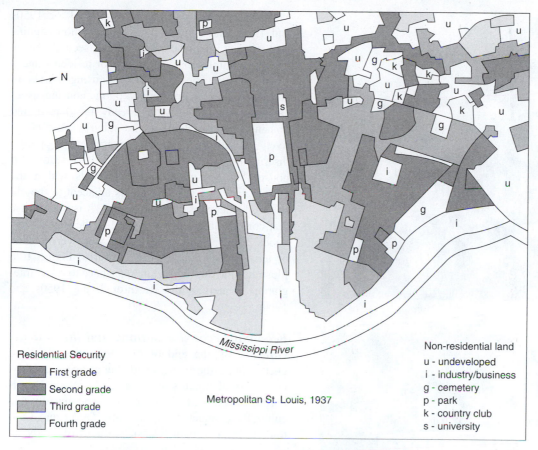

Residential Security

First grade
Second grade
Third grade
Fourth grade

Non-residential land

u - undeveloped
i - industry/business
g - cemetery
p - park
k - country club
s - university

Metropolitan St. Louis, 1937

N

Mississippi River

Figure 10.4 Redlining neighborhood risk in St. Louis. (*Source:* From Jackson, 1985, *Crabgrass Frontier: The Suburbanization of the United States*, New York and Oxford: Oxford University Press, Figure 11.1 as modified in Kaplan and Holloway, 1998.)

integration of public housing continued through the 1950s when as part of redevelopment schemes, local housing authorities placed poor displaced blacks into both existing and newly built public housing. Third, almost all public housing occupied by African Americans was sited in neighborhoods that were already (or soon to become) poor and minority-dominated. For example, in Chicago, 33 public housing projects were built between 1950 and the mid-1960s. All but one of these projects were built in areas at least 84 percent black (at the time of project completion). Overall, 98 percent of the 21,000 apartment units built during this period

were located in all-black census tracts (Hirsch 1983, 243).

Displacement occurred when bulldozers tore down "blighted" units that had provided affordable housing primarily to poor blacks and minorities. The displaced poor, especially the poorest of the poor who had the greatest difficulties finding housing in the private market, ended up in many existing and new public housing units. The pressure placed on public housing to provide housing for people displaced by redevelopment also reinforced the racist siting decisions being made by local political powers and housing authorities.

(a)

(b)

Figure 10.5 Public housing, originally designed for white working poor, was integrated beginning in the 1940s. Here, Detroit's Sojourner Truth Homes became the site of white hostility when black veterans attempted to move in. (a) shows the organized resistance of whites, (b) communicates the clear desire of whites for segregation.

The urban redevelopment projects of the 1950s and 1960s had another, and perhaps more significant, impact on the creation of the second ghetto. The large number of displaced poor residents intensified pressures on the private housing market in addition to placing pressure on public housing, especially for minorities who already faced restricted housing choices. Because the suburbs were effectively closed to them by government supported discrimination, blacks were forced to search for housing in non-ghetto neighborhoods within the city, typically in neighborhoods adjacent to the old ghetto. Under these circumstances, it is no surprise that considerable tension existed in these neighborhoods, especially among whites who were unable or unwilling to move to the suburbs. Figure 10.6 illustrates the ongoing white resistance to racial integration of neighborhoods through the 1950s and 1960s.

Economic Transformations and the Outcast Ghetto By the end of the 1960s the racialized ghettos of northern cities had changed considerably. Observers of ghettos at the close of World War II portrayed a racially isolated, but economically and culturally connected, community. Drake and Cayton (1945), in their classic exhaustive study of

Figure 10.6 White resistance to residential integration, sometimes violent, marked the 1950s and 1960s. This photo was taken in a Chicago suburb during the 1960s.

Chicago's "Bronzeville" in the late 1940s, depicted a thriving community. Robert Weaver noted in 1948 that

> The Negro [sic] ghetto of today is made up of people who are American to the core, who are part of the national culture and who share a common language with the majority of Americans ... Its inhabitants are better prepared and more anxious than ever before to enter the main stream of American life. Residential segregation, more than any other single institution, is an impediment to their realizations of this American Dream. (Weaver 1948, 7, quoted in Marcuse 1996, 180)

By the close of the 1960s, however, conditions had changed considerably. As a result of the institutionalization of the racialized ghetto, described in the previous section, the ghetto had become a less hopeful place. Kenneth Clark's problematic description still provides a useful summary:

> The dark ghetto's invisible walls have been erected by the white society, by those who have power, both to confine those who have no power and to perpetuate their powerlessness. The dark ghettos are social, political, educational, and—above all—economic colonies. Their inhabitants are subject peoples, victims of the greed, cruelty, insensitivitiy, guilt, and fear of their masters. (Clark 1965, 11, quoted in Marcuse 1996, 180)

Marcuse correctly notes that Clark's description still links the ghetto to the dominant society in that it provides an economic benefit to the dominant society. Nevertheless, Marcuse (1996) argues that ghettos of today are different in ways that he links to economic changes.

> Those in today's black ghettos are not productive for their masters; their masters get little benefit from their existence. As far as the dominant society is concerned, most residents of the new ghetto are only a drain on public and private resources, a threat to social peace, fulfilling no useful social role. They are outcasts; hence an outcast ghetto "defines, isolates, and contains" its victims. (Marcuse 1996, 181)

On top of these changes, volatile conditions in the racialized ghettos erupted into blatant violence in the summers of 1965 through 1968 (Box 10.2).

In the following section we discuss several major trends that have shaped the evolution of ghettos through the concluding decades of the twentieth century: civil rights advances, deindustrialization, and globalization. We conclude by addressing ways that scholars and policy makers have attempted to understand the new ghetto.

Civil Rights   One of the major features of the last decades of the twentieth century relevant to racial segregation is the implementation of—and subsequent retrenchment from—civil rights. Grass roots efforts to end legally recognized segregation (not just residentially, but in terms of equal access to all "public" facilities like transportation and bathrooms) swelled in the late 1950s, continuing through most of the 1960s. One target of these efforts was discrimination in housing markets (see the discussion in Chapter 9). The federal underpinning for redlining was struck down, and laws codified the federal government's opposition to racial discrimination throughout housing markets.

Several trends follow these civil rights successes. First, some African Americans were able to take advantage of freer access to education and reduced hiring discrimination to advance economically. Whereas the black middle class previously was limited to community-based entrepreneurial opportunities (i.e., businesses and services catered to a segregated black population), a much larger and more diverse black middle class began to emerge in the last two decades of the century. Although substantial wealth disparities remain between black and white middle-class families of similar income, there has been a limited convergence of income.

Second, the reduction of racial barriers experienced in the housing market allowed an increased number of black families, especially those with middle-class incomes, to move out of the traditional

BOX 10.2   Urban Riots of the 1960s

Between 1965 and 1968, some 83 U.S. cities experienced race riots. In the first nine months of 1967 alone, eight major events and 33 additional serious events occurred, including large-scale riots in Detroit and Newark. The report of the National Advisory Commission on Civil Disorders (commonly known as the Kerner Commission) appointed by President Johnson to study the events drew strong conclusions about the causes of the events. The commission rejected simplistic explanations that blamed the violence on rowdy youths or conspiracies or outsiders stirring up trouble. They pointed instead to structural racism reflected in deepening racial segregation combined with economic disadvantage experienced by urban minorities—the very themes that concern us in this chapter. They state: "This is our conclusion: our nation is moving toward two societies, one black, one white—separate and unequal" (U.S. Advisory Commission on Civil Disorders 1968, 1). "What white Americans have never fully understood—but what the Negro can never forget—is that white society is deeply implicated in the ghetto. White institutions created it, white institutions maintain it, and white society condones it" (U.S. Advisory Commission on Civil Disorders 1968, 2).

Although the commission was critical in its reflections on the causes of the urban unrest, they were cautiously optimistic in their proposals. They felt that the prosperity of the U.S. economy, if effectively motivated with new will and vision,

could make real changes. Unfortunately, the specific recommendations of the commission were largely ignored, and the trends towards racial separation that they predicted have in many ways come true. Although the Kerner commission urged that the unrest of the 1960s be used as a stimulus for concerted action to eradicate racism, the unrest actually intensified urban problems. Inner-city areas were increasingly seen as places of danger and unrest, which intensified white flight and economic decentralization, further deepening the racial geographic separations that we have discussed. In addition, some of the areas damaged in the 1960s conflicts have yet to be restored.

Significantly, urban unrest has not disappeared. In 1992, for example, Los Angeles erupted into conflict in response to the acquittal of the four police officers who had been videotaped beating black motorist Rodney King. Although many explanations for that conflict have been proposed, it is significant that many of the characteristics documented in the Kerner report also marked Los Angeles 25 years later. Johnson and Oliver (1996) further argue that recent immigration trends exacerbated the long-standing patterns of racism. Hispanics were replacing blacks in many Los Angeles neighborhoods, and Korean immigrant merchants had taken over many of the local retail facilities. New forms of interethnic conflict thus mark the Los Angeles conflicts, illustrating the ever-more complicated urban world of racialized identity and poverty.

black ghetto into suburban housing. Although many serious issues remain, including the resegregation of suburban areas and ongoing white flight once black families move in, there are substantially fewer neighborhoods that are completely devoid of black residents.

Deindustrialization and Globalization   The 1970s and 1980s witnessed a major deterioration

of economic and social conditions in the racialized neighborhoods of many major cities. Industrialized economies underwent dramatic changes during this period, in particular the loss of manufacturing jobs and the rise of globalization and advanced services as the economic base of cities. These changes were especially problematic because inner-city segregated neighborhoods (immigrant and African American) historically were located close to the factories that provided relatively stable and high-wage employment. During the 1950s and 1960s, even as blacks were migrating to cities to find employment, industrial activities began to move away from their historic inner-city locations, at first to suburban and nonmetropolitan locations, and later to sites in other countries. Their motivation was partially to lower labor costs and partially to disempower organized labor. At the same time that industrial production underwent radical locational changes, it also underwent other dramatic changes that compounded the adverse impacts on cities. Perhaps most significantly, computer and numerical technologies increasingly replaced human labor.

In combination, the relocation of industry away from urban core areas and the restructuring of industrial production away from labor intensive process were so dramatic that we refer to the result as **deindustrialization.** The pronounced impacts of deindustrialization were amplified because of all the other jobs in local areas that depend on manufacturing. The multiplier effects that we describe in Chapter 7 apply here, only in reverse. If one manufacturing job supports several nonmanufacturing jobs through local spending, the loss of that manufacturing job threatens all of those other jobs. Overall, these transitions removed thousands of job possibilities that had historically provided upward economic mobility for generations of immigrants and migrants.

The impacts on racialized ghettos were severe. Rates of joblessness and poverty skyrocketed during these decades. Thousands of people grew so discouraged with the lack of employment opportunities that they no longer tried to find jobs. Wilson (1987) documents that among 25- to 34-year-old nonwhite males, the share who held jobs declined from almost 88 percent in 1955 to just more than 76 percent in 1984. The decline in employment among teenage and young adult males was even more dramatic: more than 20 percentage points for 20- to 24-year-olds, 30 percentage points for 18- to 19-year-olds and 25 percentage points for 16- to 17-year-olds.

Job opportunities did not completely disappear from the inner city, however. In fact, as manufacturing jobs decreased, services, especially high-order services, expanded. Economic growth occurred in sectors tied to the increasingly global economy. Multinational transnational corporations grew, based in part on their multilocational production strategies. With basic product fabrication and assembly relocated to the developing world, many of these corporations were able to expand considerably during the decades. Many U.S. cities, especially the largest cities, grew increasingly important as locations where the globalizing economy was controlled and managed.

Thus, many of the same cities that suffered devastating manufacturing job losses due to deindustrialization also experienced growth fueled by globalization. In these cities, striking paradoxes increasingly emerged. The new, service-oriented economy required a labor force that was highly educated, professional, and upwardly mobile. Thus, employment opportunities began to increase for wealthier, better-educated people just as they were declining for lower-income blacks. As a result, devastating poverty increasingly coincided with excessive wealth. Many geographers refer to these contrasts as **social polarization**—the increasing gulf between the rich and poor. Racialized ghettos became increasingly isolated from the mainstream economy as deindustrialization devastated local economies.

Social/Spatial Isolation and the "Underclass" Question   Some observers link the two trends that we just discussed: deindustrialization and civil rights progress. Most prominent among them is sociologist William Julius Wilson (1987), who argues that the convergence of these trends pushed many black communities into crisis. Economic transformations made it impossible for an increasing share of inner-city blacks to hold stable jobs at the same time that upwardly mobile blacks were increasingly able to leave the traditional ghetto.

The result, according to Wilson, was the creation of an **urban underclass** of people effectively outside mainstream society. The concept of an underclass has become too controversial to have much current utility (some used it to blame the poor for their poverty by focusing on "underclass behaviors"), but Wilson effectively highlighted the severe problems faced by the residents of racialized ghettos. One of the more important aspects of his work was his focus on the linkage between **social isolation** and **spatial isolation.** The result of historical patterns of segregation overlain with economic distress was to create a community that had very few effective ties with mainstream society. Thus, we return to Peter Marcuse's view of the ghetto as an economically isolated place—an **outcast ghetto**—where socially unwanted groups are collected and stored as far away as possible from the core of mainstream society. Jargowsky and Yang (2006) analyzed 2000 Census data and found a dramatic reduction in neighborhoods that can be labeled "underclass," in large part because of reductions in the spatial concentration of poverty—a topic that we address in the next section.

POVERTY AND THE CITY

So far in this chapter, we have dealt mostly with racial segregation. As you can see, it is very difficult to talk about racial segregation and segregated places without also talking about poverty. But to end there would leave you with the incorrect perception that poverty is uniquely a black or minority problem. This is not true, so we want to discuss poverty more directly and more generally than we have so far.

We begin this section with some basic observations about poverty in cities. One of the most profound changes in the broad patterns of poverty in the United States over the last half-century is its persistent urbanization. At the end of World War II, cities (in this case we are talking about cities, not their suburban regions) housed less than one-third of the poor in the United States. By the end of the century, cities claimed almost half of the poor. When we broaden our view to include cities and their suburbs, Census 2000 reported that 78 percent of the U.S. poor lived in metropolitan areas. This shift in the location of the poor towards urban and metropolitan areas reflects broader patterns of the

urbanization of the general population discussed in earlier chapters. Yet this shift has been manifest in new ways within cities, as we now discuss.

Spatial Concentration of Urban Poverty

Once we start looking at the distribution of the urban poor across neighborhoods within cities, we note several disturbing trends. First, the **spatial concentration** of poverty within a set of extremely poor neighborhoods increased markedly from the 1960s through the 1980s. Paul Jargowsky (1997), in a study of all urban neighborhoods in the United States, reports that the number of high-poverty neighborhoods (defined as census tracts where more than 40 percent of the population is poor) more than doubled between 1970 and 1990. The number of people living in these areas increased from 4.1 million (3.0 percent of total) to almost 8.0 million (4.5 percent of total), and the number of poor people living in these neighborhoods increased from 1.9 million (12.4 percent of total) to 3.7 million (17.9 percent of total).

Returning to a theme introduced earlier in this chapter, there has been an ongoing debate over what really caused the increased spatial concentration of poverty in cities. Wilson (1987) argued that for blacks it was the combination of the black middle class increasingly taking advantage of opportunities to move out of the ghetto and increased joblessness due to deindustrialization. While Massey and Denton (1993) agreed with much of what Wilson described, they denied that improved housing opportunities for blacks were to blame. Just the opposite, they argued that ongoing racial segregation and racial discrimination in housing markets were to blame. The economic dislocations produced by deindustrialization were concentrated by racial segregation. Jargowsky (1997) takes a somewhat broader view, arguing that the multi-stranded economic restructuring of the 1980s and 1990s generally led to increased economic segregation, and specifically increased spatial concentration of the poor. He noted that different economic changes were responsible for this process in different areas; for example, deindustrialization was the chief factor in northeastern cities but not in Sunbelt cities. Common to all areas, however, is increased economic polarization and the inability of low-level service jobs to sustain populations above the poverty level.

The increased spatial concentration of poverty in urban neighborhoods did not affect all groups equally. Certainly, much of our discussion in this chapter (and almost all of the policy debate) has been about ghettos—areas simultaneously racially stigmatized and marked by poverty. And almost all research confirms that urban blacks have been disproportionately affected by the spatial concentration of poverty. For example, Jargowsky's (1997) analysis of 1990 Census data shows that while the black share of the total U.S. poor was 26.6 percent, the black share of poor persons living in extremely poor neighborhoods was 65.0 percent. At the same time, however, blacks are not the only group to experience concentrated poverty. Of the poor people living in extremely poor neighborhoods in 1990, almost 17 percent were white and almost 27 percent were Hispanic. Mulherin (2000) studied the concentration of white poverty and found that cities marked by concentrated white poverty (Figure 10.7) are not the same as the cities where blacks and Hispanics live in concentrated poverty. This pattern owes more to the regionally localized patterns of cyclical migration from the Appalachian Mountain region, which historically has been marked by pockets of concentrated rural poverty. In many of the cities where white poverty is most concentrated, it is recent in-migrants from Appalachian areas that constitute the residents.

Analysis of Census 2000 data (Jargowsky, 2003) shows hopeful signs (Figure 10.8). The number of high-poverty neighborhoods declined dramatically during the 1990s, from 3,417 in 1990 to 2,510 in 2000. The total number of residents in high-poverty areas declined by 24 percent, from 10.4 million in 1990 to 7.9 million in 2000. The number of poor residents similarly declined, from 4.8 million in 1990 to 3.5 million in 2000, even though the total number of poor people increased nationally, from just fewer than 32 million to just fewer than 34 million. Overall, the share of the poor that live in extremely

poor neighborhoods dropped from 15.1 percent to 10.3 percent. Reductions in the concentration of poverty were experienced by all racial groups, but most strongly by African Americans (30.4 percent to 18.6 percent) and American Indians (30.6 percent to 19.5 percent). The decline was regionally most prominent in the South and Midwest regions, but spread across the majority of metropolitan regions.

All was not good news, however. Several prominent metropolitan regions experienced increases in the concentration of poverty during the 1990s. In Los Angeles, for example, the share of the poor living in extremely poor neighborhoods increased from 17.3 to 21.3 percent for African Americans and from 9.1 to 16.9 percent for Hispanics. The concentration of poverty in extremely poor neighborhoods among Hispanics increased in several metropolitan areas in the West, particularly in California's Central Valley.

Also, across the nation, suburban areas did not share in the decline in the number of high-poverty neighborhoods or in the number of residents of such neighborhoods. Census 2000 reported that 42 percent of the U.S. poor lived in central cities and 36 percent in suburbs. Of the metropolitan poor, almost one-half (46 percent) lived in suburbs. Summarizing the largest U.S. metropolitan areas, Berube and Frey (2002, 7) report that:

> Cities and suburbs differed markedly in their overall population growth in the 1990s. Total population in the suburbs of the 102 largest metropolitan areas grew by 17 percent, compared to only 9 percent in the central cities. The city-suburb growth gap widened, moreover, when it came to poor populations. While the absolute number of people living below the poverty line increased by 8 percent in cities, the number of poor in suburbs grew by nearly 21 percent. As a result, over the decade, the share of all poor individuals in large metropolitan areas that lived in the suburbs rose from 46 percent in 1990 to almost half (49 percent) in 2000.

Cooke and Marchant (2006) provide a very important distinction between early post–World War II suburban areas and more recent sprawling

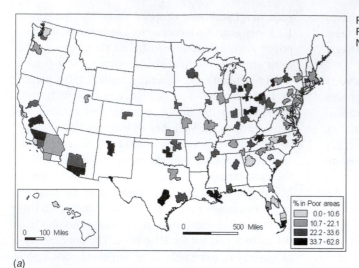

Poor non-Hispanic White
Population in 20% Poverty
Neighborhoods 1990

% in Poor areas
0.0 - 10.6
10.7 - 22.1
22.2 - 33.6
33.7 - 62.8

(a)

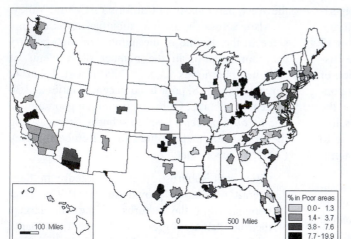

Poor non-Hispanic White
Population in 40% Poverty
Neighborhoods 1990

% in Poor areas
0.0 - 1.3
1.4 - 3.7
3.8 - 7.6
7.7 - 19.9

(b)

Figure 10.7 Whites living in concentrated urban poverty. (Adapted from Mulherin, 2000, Fig. 2 and Fig. 4.)

suburban areas. While their analysis generally supports Jargowsky's (2003) optimistic analysis, they report that the number of poverty neighborhoods increased in the urban-core areas of Northeastern metropolitan areas, in suburban areas of Los Angeles and Las Vegas, and in California's Central Valley metropolitan areas. If the spatial concentration of urban poverty is shifting away from core urban areas towards older first-ring suburbs, there may be significant consequences for jurisdictions that are less able to deal with the attendant problems.

Consequences of Concentrated Poverty: The Neighborhood Effects Debate
Scholars and policy makers disagree on how optimistically to assess current trends regarding the

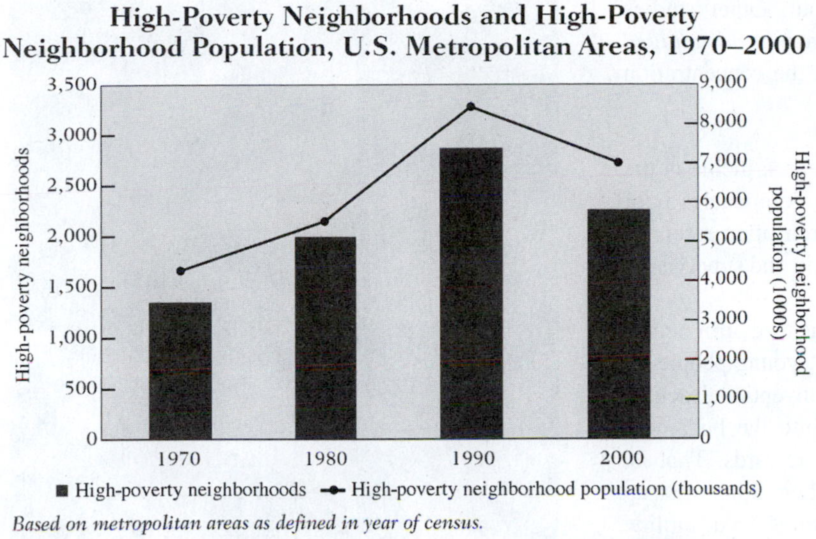
High-Poverty Neighborhoods and High-Poverty Neighborhood Population, U.S. Metropolitan Areas, 1970–2000
High-poverty neighborhoods
High-poverty neighborhood population (100s)
3,500
3,000
2,500
2,000
1,500
1,000
500
0
9,000
8,000
7,000
6,000
5,000
4,000
3,000
2,000
1,000
0
1970
1980
1990
2000
High-poverty neighborhoods
High-poverty neighborhood population (thousands)
Based on metropolitan areas as defined in year of census.

Figure 10.8 Changes in the Concentration of Poverty, 1970–2000. (Adapted from Jargowsky, 2003, Fig. 1.)

concentration of urban poverty. Some (for example, Jargowsky, 2003) point to the success of poverty dispersal policies that include the demolition of project-based public housing and the major change in welfare policy implemented in 1996. Others (for example, Goetz, 2002) argue that these policies are part of a broader neoliberal restructuring of urban governance that favors the advantaged (in terms of making inner-city neighborhoods available for gentrification and redevelopment) at the expense of poor families (in terms of reducing the overall availability of affordable housing). Even optimistic observers note that Census 2000 was conducted at the height of a significant economic expansion, and that conditions may be deteriorating in the leaner economic conditions of the current decade.

Even when scholars and policy makers disagree on the causes of concentrated urban poverty or its current trends, they share a concern with its consequences. We address here this important area of research and public policy innovation. The basic argument is that living or growing up in poor neighborhoods has negative consequences. Residents do worse in school, have greater problems finding stable work, and are more likely to engage in criminal activity. Much of the work in this field was stimulated by Wilson's 1987 book *The Truly Disadvantaged*, in which he argued that concentrated urban poverty has lingering effects. He called these effects *concentration effects*, but today most scholars refer to them as **neighborhood effects,** a term that suggests that neighborhoods matter in their own right. Before we evaluate these issues more thoroughly, we discuss some of the basic premises of neighborhood effects theory (see Brooks-Gunn, Duncan, and Aber, 1997, for detailed discussion).

Peer Effects The primary premise of neighborhood effects theory is that neighborhoods exert peer effects, especially upon young people. The neighborhood effects argument suggests that growing up in a neighborhood where more peers engage in problematic behavior will increase a young person's chances of also engaging in those behaviors.

This is a "common sense" way of evaluating neighborhoods: if I attempt to raise my children in a "bad" neighborhood, they may be corrupted by the bad behavior of their peers. Of course this is a highly problematic way of viewing the power of place, but it is one that characterizes a lot of policy making and academic research. Some empirical research supports this notion, but typically not as strongly as you might expect. Some studies suggest that only in the most heavily impacted neighborhoods does this effect seem to play out. Other studies suggest that the presence or absence of *advantaged* neighbors is more important than the concentration of *disadvantaged* neighbors.

Social Control   A broader research theme is the nature of social relationships that dominate in poor urban neighborhoods. This research often refers to two key mechanisms: role modeling and supervising public behaviors.

The **role model** argument suggests that in neighborhoods of concentrated poverty, young people do not see grown-ups engaged in conventional activities that help to socialize them into the behaviors and values that the labor market rewards. That is, growing up in an environment where adults get up and go to work each day demonstrates the discipline needed to succeed in getting a job. When there are no adults going to work, youths are deprived of positive role models and thus are never exposed to the small yet important behaviors and values necessary to find and keep jobs.

A variant of this argument focuses less on the psychology of role modeling and more on the ability of the community within the neighborhood to directly supervise and monitor activity in the neighborhood. Poor neighborhoods historically had a mixture of residents, some poor and some not. There was often considerable street-level activity, with people shopping and cars filling the streets. There were many "eyes on the street" in these contexts, monitoring behavior. Young people were known in the neighborhood, and if they got into trouble shop owners or neighbors would tell the parents. Young people knew that they would face the consequences of their behavior when they got home.

As poverty became more concentrated, however, especially in the areas that were redeveloped into superblock public housing projects, it became more difficult to monitor behavior informally. Sometimes this problem was related to the physical design of the neighborhood. Superblock public housing, built according to modernist architectural design principles, consisted of large, high-rise buildings interspersed with large open spaces (Figure 10.9).

Figure 10.9 Harlem's James Weldon Johnson Housing Project illustrates the superblock design (large high-rise buildings interspersed between open spaces) common of many public housing projects built during the 1950s and 1960s.

Instead of providing everyone access to the open space, however, this design made it very difficult to know neighbors and to informally supervise the activities of neighborhood residents (see the discussion and photographs of Pruitt Igoe in Chapter 9).

Another reason that behavior is more difficult to supervise in contemporary neighborhoods with concentrated poverty is that poor residents are very mobile—they move around a lot. Given the increasing crisis of affordable housing in most cities, adequate housing for the poor is a dominant problem. Poor residents often must move several times, even in a single year. With the increased rates of residential instability, informal social ties become more difficult to build and sustain, making it more difficult to informally monitor and discourage behavior that has negative effects on neighborhoods.

Opportunities and Resources Another variant of the neighborhood effects approach focuses more on neighborhoods' economic opportunities than on their social relationships. This approach ties in with the economic restructuring and deindustrialization arguments that we discussed earlier. One of the greatest ironies of late-twentieth century urbanization was the *spatial* disjuncture between where poor people live and where job opportunities are located.

The basic argument is fairly simple (in fact it was first powerfully made in a 1968 article written by economist John Kain). Jobs are being lost in the central city due to deindustrialization at the same that time that new jobs are being relocated to, or created in, the suburbs. The problem and irony is that the populations most in need of employment are increasingly distant from the opportunities they want. Thus, in the late 1980s and early 1990s, many central city neighborhoods experienced record high unemployment and joblessness at the same time that suburban employers faced a critical labor shortage.

This argument that central city residents are not able to take advantage of suburban job opportunities because of increasing geographic separation is often called the **spatial mismatch hypothesis.** It has received a tremendous amount of attention, both in public policy circles and in research (see Preston and McLafferty 1999 and Bauder 2000 for reviews). The research results are mixed. Some research supports the basic notion that there is increasing spatial separation between where the poor live and where they work, if they work. Other research goes further by demonstrating that spatial separation makes it more difficult for poor central-city residents to locate jobs that pay enough to compensate for the long and often expensive commutes. At the same time, housing market research clearly demonstrates that poor minorities continue to face daunting challenges in securing any housing, much less housing close enough to job locations to make a difference.

Empirical results also demonstrate, however, that the degree of spatial separation between the residences of the poor and job locations varies considerably in intensity across metropolitan areas. Moreover, the impact of spatial mismatch on employment and other labor market outcomes is inconsistent, and never seems to be the most important factor.

Institutions, Schools, and Businesses Another argument revolves around the differences in the ways that government institutions react to and service poverty neighborhoods. Police and other emergency service agencies are less responsive to calls from poor neighborhoods. Sanitation services do not keep these neighborhoods as clean as wealthier neighborhoods. Recreation departments do not provide the same services that they do in richer neighborhoods.

Perhaps the most damning criticism revolves around schools. Central city school districts are severely underfunded relative to their suburban neighbors, in large part because of the way the nation funds schools based on local property taxes. Even within school districts, poor and minority neighborhoods end up with the oldest buildings in the worst repair, and often times with teachers who are the least prepared and the least supported by the administration.

Poor inner-city neighborhoods also lack access to reasonable retail opportunities. Think about where in your city the cheapest clothing and school supplies can be found—most likely in a Wal-Mart, Target, or similar big-box retail outlet. Where are these stores located? In most cases, they are found in large complexes located in the suburbs. Even though central city neighborhoods provide a large consumer base interested in low-cost products, value-oriented retailers often do not locate there. Some central city neighborhoods don't even have a grocery store. As a result, residents are forced to undertake long commutes just to buy food at reasonable costs. The retailers that are located in central city neighborhoods are accused of gouging desperate residents with exorbitantly high prices and offering inferior products.

Stigma and Spatial Discrimination One last argument that we want to consider integrates neighborhoods with the broader society. Emerging from several strands, this theory maintains that most people carry with them perceptions and stereotypes about neighborhoods *and the people that live in them*. Regarding poor urban neighborhoods, research shows that employers have very particular impressions about the characteristics of people that live there. In particular, if a job applicant indicates an address in certain stereotyped neighborhoods, employers assume that the applicant has poor work habits, inferior schooling, and bad attitudes. Thus even if the applicant has none of these characteristics, she or he will have greater difficulty finding work, simply because of the reputation or stereotype associated with the place where she or he lives.

Evidence and Debates

In recent years a great deal of research has focused on the impact of living and/or growing up in poor neighborhoods. Yet much of this research is not conclusive. The most compelling research stems from an accidental natural experiment created by a U.S. Supreme Court decision.

The issue at the heart of the case was the location of public housing in Chicago. As we have discussed previously, public housing was most often sited in poor and minority communities—increasingly so as public housing was co-opted by redevelopment interests to warehouse the poorest of the poor, who were being displaced by redevelopment projects. A suit was filed for public housing residents against the Department of Housing and Urban Development (HUD), claiming discriminatory siting procedures.

After several court cases over several years, the Supreme Court ultimately agreed with the plaintiffs (Hills v. Gautreaux, 425 U.S., 1976). The Court issued a consent decree that required corrective action on the part of public housing agencies. The Gautreaux program was created as part of the implementation of this decree. The program subsidizes private apartments, either in the central city or in the (mostly white) suburbs, for public housing residents. What makes this a good test of the effects of residential location is that assignment to private apartments is made quasi-randomly with regard to central-city versus suburban location; that is, residents have little choice about their eventual location. In addition, the neighborhood environments that most of the public housing residents leave behind are almost uniformly bad.

Research has evaluated the results of relocating families out of extreme concentrations of urban poverty into other types of neighborhoods. For example, Rosenbaum (1995) reported that after low-income black students experienced some initial difficulties in adapting to white suburban schools, they performed far better after several years than did Gautreaux children living in city apartments. Moving to the suburbs also had similar benefits in the labor market, as shown in Table 10.6. Employment was uniformly higher among residents relocated to suburban apartments, even among those *not* employed prior to their move.

Table 10.6 Effect of Suburban Move on the Employment of Public Housing Residents in Chicago

	% Residents Employed	
	Participants Moving to Suburban Apartments	Participants Moving to Central-City Apartments
Before Move	64.3	60.2
After Move	63.8	50.9
After Move, of Those Employed Before Move	73.6	64.6
After Move, of Those Not Employed Before Move	46.2	30.2

Source: Rosenbaum and Popkin 1991, Table 1; Rosenbaum 1995, Table 3.

Poverty, especially urban poverty concentrated in particular neighborhoods, has always been a lightning rod of public debate. These debates over the sources and expressions of poverty are in many ways central to the way we define ourselves as a society. We do not have space to fully discuss these debates, but in the following sections we present something of the flavor of these debates. In the concluding section we discuss some of the major policy efforts to address these issues. George Galster (1996) describes a deep ambivalence in America towards poverty—one that results in sometimes dramatic pendulum swings in public opinion and policy initiatives:

> Rather, the center of gravity on the poverty issue seems to be defined by the deeply seated American ambivalence towards the poor. Are the poor somehow fundamentally different from the mainstream and undeserving of public support, or not? Are the observed behaviors of the poor indicators of their personal shortcomings or adaptations to the structural barriers that society has erected? Thus, although demographic and economic trends and new policy research can swing the pendulum in one direction or another, such changes will be often counteracted by this underlying ambivalence toward the poor.

Morality and Responsibility   One of the most enduring controversies surrounding poverty revolves around the issue of individual responsibility. Powerful political platforms have rested on opposing perspectives. Some platforms are centered on the assumption that individuals are responsible for their own behavior, and thus for their own poverty. Other platforms are centered on the assumption that individuals are not responsible for their own poverty, or at least not fully responsible. This fundamental split shapes all discussions of poverty.

We, the authors, take the view that all individuals are responsible for the choices they make. Even so, not all individuals have the same choices—and that the differences in choices that people face are related to structures of society and the economy. At one level, there is much merit to the observation that

market economies in a capitalist economy require some degree of poverty—the system will not continue to function if there is not a group of poor people that are useful to discipline the working class. The question then becomes, who are the poor, and when and where will their poverty be imposed? Within this framework, people still have choices, and they bear some moral responsibility for those choices. The choices, however, may not include leaving poverty. There is ample empirical evidence that adhering to the American Dream, (i.e., working hard, playing by the rules, and so forth) does *not* always result in a happy middle-class life.

Culture and Poverty versus Culture of Poverty   One of the flash points in the debates over urban poverty consistently has been culture. A commonsense argument is only one step removed from directly blaming individuals for their own poverty: whole cultures (or, perhaps more commonly, subcultures) are blamed for unequal distributions of poverty. If minorities living in central-city neighborhoods (or whites living in a rural Appalachian community, etc.) disproportionately experience poverty, then there is something wrong with "their culture." "They" don't teach the work ethic, or "they" have higher expectations than "they" ought to. These notions in their crudest forms signify cultural prejudice and are often reflected onto existing sociocultural divisions, including national origin (note the discussion in Chapter 11 of prejudice against immigrants, past and present), race, and geography.

Cultural arguments are not always so crude. One cultural argument that has inspired passionate debate emerged in the 1960s when anthropologist Oscar Lewis argued that the lack of economic opportunity creates ongoing structural disadvantages that lead to changes in the community's culture. These cultural responses (i.e., values and behaviors) are adaptive to the structural setting that defined the community's context, but they are not helpful for individuals who want to succeed in a market economy. Cultural adaptation may help the community deal with their poverty but simultaneously inhibit the community's ability to advance economically. Lewis's argument was distinctive in his suggestion that cultural adaptations can become permanently rooted in the culture. In other words, adaptive cultural responses are internalized and passed on intergenerationally.

Lewis's (1966, 1968) theory, which became known as the **culture of poverty** perspective, has come under intense criticism. Critics contend that Lewis's explanation put too much focus on the culture(s) of the poor. Whereas Lewis felt that adaptations made in response to sustained disadvantage can become a permanent characteristic of the culture, critics maintained that attention should be on the forces that create poverty and not on the cultural responses to poverty. They argued that the culture of poverty argument resulted in blaming the victims for their own poverty. They also argued that white, middle-class norms and values are too often imposed on minority families and communities.

William Julius Wilson's arguments (1987, 1996), which we have discussed in several parts of this chapter, attempted to revitalize and recast discussion of culture in the context of urban poverty. Wilson criticized Lewis for viewing cultural adaptation as a permanent cultural adjustment—he clearly rejected the culture of poverty argument. Instead, he argued that structural disadvantage stemming from economic restructuring created an environment in which counterproductive adaptive responses emerged. *But*, these responses were contingent on the ongoing presence of the structural disadvantages! In contrast to Lewis, Wilson held that if individuals, families, and communities were relocated or otherwise relieved of their structural constraints, the adaptive cultural responses would adjust to the new setting. In other words the "problematic" cultural responses were situational and were not passed intergenerationally.

Wilson's views were consistent with the relocation remedy put into play in the Gatreaux experiment discussed earlier, in that both concluded that changing geographic context affects behaviors that were too rigidly assumed to be permanent. People are smarter than often assumed: they can and do adjust their behavior to fit with their current circumstances. Wilson's arguments are problematic in many ways, including his continuing use of presumptive white, middle-class norms as the standard against which culture is measured. Nonetheless, his arguments were highly misrepresented and for many urban geographers have come to represent (we feel unfairly) an inherently and unavoidably flawed way of viewing urban poverty.

Oppositional Culture/Culture of Segregation Other scholars have attempted to understand the role that culture plays in poor neighborhoods. For example, Massey and Denton, in their work on residential segregation titled *American Apartheid* (1993), argue that situational cultural values are developed in opposition to whatever values are imposed on them from the outside, especially in settings where dominant cultural values are associated with social economic and political power that is perceived to be oppressive. In these circumstances, **oppositional culture** is developed—behaviors and outlooks are valued because they reject the values of the dominant society.

Massey and Denton go further by arguing that seemingly permanent racial segregation overlain with economic deprivation creates the conditions in which an oppositional **culture of segregation** is developed. They note, for example, the development and continuance of linguistic differences (for example, the debate over so-called ebonics or "black English") that reject white middle-class norms of spoken and written English. They argue that although these linguistic patterns may be important markers of cultural difference, and thus, provide benefit to the community, they also serve to further isolate these communities. The antidote, they argue, is to end the structural conditions that foster these oppositional cultural adaptations; that is, to end segregation.

RESPONDING TO URBAN POVERTY

In this last section of the chapter we turn to policy. Given the highly controversial nature of the issues we discuss throughout the chapter, it is not surprising that government attempts to respond to poverty are also controversial and often divisive. Before you proceed to this account of antipoverty policies that affect cities, recall that for decades the government has attempted to do something about poverty. As far back as the 1930s, the federal government instituted wide-ranging programs to address crushing poverty in the wake of the Depression's economic catastrophe. Below, we discuss selected policy efforts directed, at least partially, at alleviating urban poverty. The major trend that we observe is towards reduced direct government responsibility for social problems and increased government financial investment directed towards benefiting business.

War on Poverty

In the midst of the unprecedented prosperity of the post–World War II decades, poverty did not generally enter into public awareness. Nevertheless, in the midst of this prosperity, however invisibly, poverty persisted in the United States. In 1962 Michael Harrington published *The Other America*, a highly influential exposé of poverty in the United States that drew public attention to—and raised moral outrage against—the continued existence of poverty among the elderly, small farmers, racial minorities (increasingly moving to the cities), and the rural poor in Appalachia. At the same time, social scientists were asserting growing confidence in their ability to understand and counteract complex social problems. One prestigious report claimed in 1962 that "the elimination of poverty is well within the means of the federal, state, and local governments" (cited in Galster 1996, 41). "This hubris of the feasible conjoined with the morality of the desirable: if we were capable of eliminating poverty, it was unconscionable not to do so" (Galster 1996, 41).

Confident in the potential of federal governmental action to correct the remaining deficiencies of the market economy, President Lyndon Johnson declared a **War on Poverty** in 1964 (although the beginnings of many of the specific programs can be traced to President John Kennedy's administration). The initial proposals were heady with optimism and wide in scope. They rested on three

principles intended to improve the ability of the poor to earn enough money in the labor market to alleviate their poverty: (1) stimulate macroeconomic growth (to improve demand for low-skilled labor—"a rising tide lifts all boats"), (2) improve individuals' work-related skills, and (3) counter discriminatory or unresponsive social institutions. Several well-known programs began or were expanded as part of this federally oriented effort to combat poverty: Head Start, Job Corps, Upward Bound, Food Stamps, and so forth. Note that most of these efforts were designed to address what were perceived to be root causes of poverty, including inadequate education and job skills.

Many of the efforts of the War on Poverty, though not initially as apparent to the public, involved direct transfers of federal monies to select groups. Federal government expenditure on so-called "transfer programs" in 1965 constituted 10.5 percent of gross national product and rose to 16 percent by 1974. The impacts of transfer program expenditures, in one simple way, are quite profound. In 1965, 33 percent of the pre-transfer poor were pulled above the poverty line by federal cash transfers alone. By 1974, 44 percent were pulled above the poverty line by federal cash transfers, and an additional 16 percent by in-kind transfers (noncash benefits like food stamps or subsidized medical care). Note, however, that most federal antipoverty spending was directed towards the elderly, especially through the Social Security and Medicare programs. Not surprisingly, the greatest reductions in poverty that we just mentioned were among the elderly.

Important components of the War on Poverty focused on cities and urban poverty. The **Community Action Program** attempted to organize poor residents of poor neighborhoods to lobby for and define the nature of the government services they desired. Later, there were attempts to bring together and focus the various and sometimes conflicted elements of the broader War on Poverty efforts on specific poor neighborhoods. This **Model Cities** program (created by the 1966 Demonstration Cities Act) argued that federal investment should focus on just a few neighborhoods with significant demonstration potential. By concentrating massive federal investment in just a few places, this program would demonstrate to the nation, and the world, how government efforts could truly remedy the problems related to urban poverty.

Unfortunately, the same political process that created the Model Cities program also dramatically modified the program so that it was never implemented in its intended form. In order to gain political support for the demonstration project, the total amount of money spent had to be scaled back and distributed more broadly (each city and each neighborhood wanted a piece of the government largesse). Elected representatives wanted to ensure that the benefits of this new federal social policy extended to cities in their jurisdictions. As a result, the massive concentration of federal expenditure called for by the program's architects never materialized. Instead, a bastardized and ultimately unsuccessful blend of underfunded programs was put into place.

Retrenchment

The 1970s turned out to be a period of partial retrenchment. President Richard Nixon adopted a political philosophy called the **new federalism** that attempted to scale back and redirect federal involvement in the affairs of the nation's cities. Some observers claimed that the War on Poverty had been successfully concluded (noting especially the dramatic reduction in poverty among the elderly), while others grew frustrated with the escalating costs of antipoverty programs. These groups argued that antipoverty spending should be scaled back, if not eliminated. Others objected to what was seen as federal interference with local problems. Nixon's solution was to reduce total spending levels, and to give local governments more control over how funds were spent. For example, Nixon replaced Model Cities efforts with the **Community Development Block Grant** (CDBG) program. Funding levels for these grants were set by a formula that included metropolitan status and population. The grants themselves were made in response to applications from local governments. The scope of CDBG

funded programs was broader than the federally funded social programs they replaced.

President Ronald Reagan's administration furthered the retrenchment from federally initiated urban policies directed at reducing or addressing poverty. Philosophically, Reagan favored market-based solutions over government-based efforts. Two strands of research supported this position. The first emphasized the traditional belief that individuals were personally responsible for lifting themselves out of poverty. During the 1980s, public opinion and some academic writing increasingly came to favor individualistic explanations for poverty, arguing that in light of what they considered to be excessive governmental generosity, those that remained poor were poor because they weren't trying hard enough or because there was something wrong with them. It was here that the phrase *underclass* discussed earlier became associated with conservative politics: the underclass were popularly defined as those individuals who did not participate in mainstream society in part because they engaged in problematic behavior (crime, out-of-wedlock childbearing, welfare dependency, and so forth).

The second strand of research actually reversed the logic of the War on Poverty. Instead of proposing that government programs have tremendous potential to redress the causes of poverty, new arguments arose that blamed the government programs themselves for poverty. Government generosity was thought to create dependency and discourage individual initiative. Aid to Families with Dependent Children (AFDC) and other "welfare" programs (what came to be the label for means-tested programs where low income was required for participation) encouraged people to behave in ways counterproductive to their rising out of poverty. Proponents of this research encouraged the government to focus on market-based mechanisms and to dismantle the "entitlements" that presumably were sapping the moral fiber of urban communities.

Reagan's philosophy stressed that the proper role of government was much more limited than was previously held. Indeed, government was viewed as the *problem* that needed to be addressed by reducing taxes and eliminating regulations and piecemeal incentives to development. Reagan and other conservatives believed that private commerce and open markets were the best remedies for poverty and other problems. Consequently, during the 1980s severe funding cuts were implemented for many of the remaining entitlements and incentive programs.

Welfare Reform Policy efforts in the 1990s, especially under President Bill Clinton, represented a public consensus concerning a restricted role of the federal government. In part reflecting the political success enjoyed by Reagan, Clinton put into place major changes in the way that welfare is distributed. Focusing primarily on AFDC and other means-tested entitlement programs, Clinton's reforms combined work-related requirements (all recipients have to receive work training and seek employment) with time limitations (recipients now have a maximum lifetime cap on how long they can receive benefits—5 years in the first round of legislation). The number of aid recipients drawing support from the states decreased dramatically, with many recipients moving off the welfare rolls and into jobs.

At first glance, then, welfare reform would seem to be a success. The reality, however, is more complex. Significantly, at the time these reforms were implemented, the nation was experiencing dramatic economic growth and extreme labor shortages. It is not too surprising, then, that the new requirements that forced recipients to find work were not too difficult to meet. Moreover, most of the jobs that recipients went into were low-skill, low-paying jobs with few benefits.

Enterprise Zones One theme that has characterized the debate over poverty from the beginning is the need for enhanced labor demand. Even the architects of the War on Poverty recognized that additional job training would have little benefit if there were no jobs for workers to move into. Interestingly, efforts have been made throughout the last 40 years to stimulate economic development, and thus increase demand for labor, within areas targeted

as needy, that is, poverty areas. These efforts began with the Economic Development Act of 1965 that created the Economic Development Administration (EDA). Investment capital was made available to businesses at attractive rates along with grants to improve infrastructure.

During the 1980s Reagan attempted to increase the demand for labor by reducing or eliminating what he considered to be obstructions to free market activity that the federal government had put into place. He called for the creation of **enterprise zones** where businesses could flourish. These zones would reduce or eliminate burdensome corporate taxes (especially capital gains taxes) and regulatory obstacles (including those that protected environmental quality and labor rights). Limited incentives in the form of tax credits would be provided for investment in plants and equipment. Although Reagan's efforts to institute enterprise zones at the federal level failed, several states created enterprise zones of their own. Empirical evidence concerning the success of these zones has been mixed.

Empowerment zones were instituted under Clinton in the early 1990s and are similar to Reagan's proposed zones, except that they stress wage incentives over capital investments and they are accompanied by stronger links to community organizations. In addition, the Clinton administration instituted **community development banks** to encourage private investment in inner-city areas. During the late 1990s and early 2000s, **public participation GIS (PPGIS)** became more popular as a strategy to empower local community groups (Box 10.3).

Moving to Opportunity/HOPE VI/Homeownership One last area of new liberalism that we want to discuss returns us to the links between public housing and concentrated poverty. Encouraged by the success of the Gatreaux experiment in Chicago, the federal **Moving to Opportunity** program represented an expansion of the effort to enable residents of public housing to relocate to better neighborhoods. This would be accomplished through subsidizing housing vouchers that

BOX 10.3   TECHNOLOGY AND URBAN GEOGRAPHY

PUBLIC PARTICIPATION GIS (PPGIS)

Seen optimistically, Public Participation GIS (PPGIS, or sometimes Participatory GIS, PGIS, or P-GIS) promises to empower disadvantaged groups by putting in their hands the ability to produce and deploy geographic knowledge(s) contained within and enabled by GIS. Communities can also actively participate in the formation of this knowledge and thus increase their influence in participatory governance. Some critics claim that GIS can disempower or marginalize disadvantaged groups because of high cost and complexity of the hardware and software required, and problems with gaining access to data. Sarah Elwood (2002, Elwood and Ghose 2001, Elwood and Leitner 2003) has studied the use of GIS by community groups, trying to understand the extent to which, and the conditions under which community groups are empowered by access to and use of GIS. She notes that empowerment can be conceptualized

in three ways: *distributive empowerment, procedural empowerment*, and *capacity building*.

One of Elwood's (2002) case study organizations is the Powderhorn Park Neighborhood Association (PPNA), located in a declining area of south central Minneapolis. PPNA has been working towards neighborhood revitalization since the 1970s. Beginning in the early 1990s, PPNA invested in the development and use of a neighborhood housing database—a GIS (Table B10.2). Their initial intention was for the GIS to be accessible by the public. Though the complexity of the system means that staff members with GIS training do most of the analysis and mapping, community residents specify and use the information produced. Elwood found that PPNA's use of GIS both empowers and disempowers social groups, though at different scales of interaction and for different groups. The PPNA was most positively empowered in its relationship with the local state.

residents would use (potentially) to find housing in any neighborhood they wanted. (Of course, the success of these efforts depended in part on the willingness of landlords to rent to residents with vouchers.)

The **HOPE VI** program recognized the ongoing problems with public housing, associated in part with design flaws and in part with the impact of public housing on concentrating poverty and increasing segregation. It provides federal dollars to

Table B10.2   Elements of a PPGIS Database Used by the Powderhorn Park Neighborhood
Association in Minneapolis, MN

Property	Involved Individuals	Activities/Problems
Lot size	*Owner/taxpayer*	Past problems
Zoning	*Name*	PPNA actions
Property ID number	*Address*	Staff/resident
Age of structure	*Telephone number*	observations
Condition code	PPNA involvement	
Legal description	Volunteer skills	
Tenure status	*Rental license holder*	
Tax delinquent status	*Name*	
Sales history	*Address*	
	Telephone number	
	PPNA involvement	
	Volunteer skills	
	Caretaker/manager	
	Name	
	Address	
	Telephone number	
	PPNA involvement	
	Volunteer skills	
	Block leader	
	Name	
	Address	
	Telephone number	
	PPNA involvement	
	Volunteer skills	
	Tenants	
	Name	
	Address	
	Telephone number	
	PPNA involvement	
	Volunteer skills	

Source: Elwood 2002, Table 1.
Note: Italicized text indicates attributes for which data are obtained from local government sources and are maintained
for all neighborhood properties. All other information is locally collected and is known for some, but not all, properties
in the neighborhood.

local public housing authorities to redevelop public housing. Many of the densest projects have been torn down and replaced with mixed-income housing or have undergone extensive upgrading (Figure 10.10). These efforts are designed to reduce the physical and social isolation that had attended conventional public housing in previous decades. Considerable controversy surrounds these efforts, however, because the total number of units made available to low-income residents is being reduced

(a)

(b)

Figure 10.10 HOPE VI Public Housing Redevelopment in Atlanta: (a) East Lake Meadows is torn down and replaced with mixed-income project, (b) The Villages at East Lake.

and because the redevelopment process itself causes considerable disruption during the period of redevelopment.

Most recently, the federal government is attempting to promote homeownership through the auspices of HUD's oversight of the government-sponsored enterprises (GSEs; see Chapter 9) Fannie Mae and Freddie Mac. By relaxing the income and debt requirements associated with long-term mortgage lending, homeownership is being made available to low- and moderate-income households that formerly could not afford to purchase housing. By increasing homeownership, the federal government hopes to attach more people to the wealth escalator of home value appreciation while reducing the demand on the rental stock and alleviating some of the problems of affordable housing. As we discuss in Chapter 9, however, there is increasing evidence that the lending market practices that were implemented to increase homeownership among low- and moderate-income households are now growing burdensome and leading many households into foreclosure and bankruptcy.

WRAPPING UP

This chapter has addressed two urban issues that typically stimulate considerable debate: race and poverty. These issues are too often addressed as if they are a single issue: race and poverty have been conjoined in popular discussion, research, and policy debate. In part our hope has been to disentangle these issues—to show that race and poverty are not the same thing. Not all blacks are poor, and not all of the poor are black. As we mention, most of the urban poor are, in fact, not black. Moreover, blacks living in cities are present in all strata of society. Issues of racial segregation go beyond issues of poverty—and issues of poverty go beyond issues of racial segregation.

Although there have been several efforts to address the confluence of these two issues (i.e., black urban poverty), the debates surrounding these issues are too limited, especially the debate over the presence and size of an urban underclass. Even if we put aside the highly problematic behavioral dimensions of efforts to define and count the underclass, the best empirical estimates suggest that the size of such a group is almost trivially small and experienced a significant reduction during the 1990s (Jargowsky and Yang 2006). In the coming years, it appears that issues of urban poverty will focus on (a) the concentration of poverty in the older inner-ring suburbs and (b) the increasing presence of foreign-born and non-white/nonblack minorities in areas of concentrated poverty.

As you think about cities and these two issues, recognize that the most productive approaches will treat them separately: the causes and outcomes of segregation are not the same as the causes and outcomes of concentrated urban poverty. They are not unrelated, but they are also not indelibly linked. Keep an open mind, and ask critical questions.

READINGS

Bauder, Harald. 2000. "Reflections on the Spatial Mismatch Debate," *Journal of Planning Education and Research,* Vol. 19, pp. 316–320.

Berube, A., and W. H. Frey. 2002. *A Decade of Mixed Blessings: Urban and Suburban Poverty in Census 2000.* Washington, D.C.: The Brookings Institution.

Brooks-Gunn, Jeanne, Greg J. Duncan, and J. Lawrence Aber. 1997. *Neighborhood Poverty: Volume I Context and Consequences for Children; and Neighborhood Poverty: Volume II Policy Implications in Studying Neighborhoods.* New York: Russell Sage Foundation.

Clark, K. B. 1965. *Dark Ghetto: Dilemmas of Social Power.* New York: Harper and Row.

Cooke, Thomas, and Sarah Marchant. 2006. "The Changing Intrametropolitan Location of High-Poverty Neighbourhoods in the U.S., 1990–2000," *Urban Studies,* Vol. 43, pp. 1971–1989.

Denton, N. A. 1994. "Are African-Americans Still Hypersegregated?" in R. D. Bullard, J. E. Grigsby, III, and C. Lee, eds., *Residential Apartheid: The American Legacy.* Los Angeles: CAAS Publications, Center for Afro-American Studies, University of California, Los Angeles.

Drake, St. Clair, and Horase R. Cayton. 1945. *Black Metropolis: A Study of Negro Life in a Northern City.* New York: Harcourt, Brace and Company.

Elwood, Sarah. 2002. "GIS Use in Community Planning: A Multidimensional Analysis of Empowerment," *Environment and Planning A,* Vol. 34, pp. 905–922.

Elwood, Sarah, and Rina Ghose. 2001. "PPGIS in Community Development Planning: Framing the Organizational Context," *Cartographica,* Vol. 38, pp. 19–33.

Elwood, Sara, and Helga Leitner. 2003. "GIS and Spatial Knowledge Production for Neighborhood Revitalization: Negotiating State Priorities and Neighborhood Visions," *Journal of Urban Affairs,* Vol. 25, pp. 139–157.

Fainstein, N. I. 1993. "Race, Class and Segregation: Discourses about African Americans," *International Journal of Urban and Regional Research,* Vol. 17, pp. 384–403.

Galster, G. 1996. "Poverty." In G. Galster, ed., *Reality and Research: Social Science and U.S. Urban Policy Since 1960.* Washington, D.C.: The Urban Institute Press.

Goering, John, Judith D. Reins, and Todd M. Richardson. 2002. "A Cross-Site Analysis of Initial Moving to Opportunity Demonstration Results," *Journal of Housing Research,* Vol. 13, pp. 1–30.

Goetz, E. G. 2002. "Forced Relocation vs. Voluntary Mobility: The Effects of Dispersal Programmes on Households," *Housing Studies,* Vol. 17, pp. 107–123.

Harrington, Michael. 1962. *The Other America: Poverty in the United States.* New York: Macmillan.

Hirsch, A. R. 1983. *Making the Second Ghetto: Race and Housing in Chicago, 1940–1960.* Cambridge, UK, and New York: Cambridge University Press.

Iceland, J., D. H. Weinberg, and E. Steinmetz. 2002. *Racial and Ethnic Residential Segregation in the United States: 1980–2000,* U.S. Census Bureau, Series CENSR-3. Washington, D.C.: U.S. Government Printing Office.

Jargowsky, P. A. 1994. "Ghetto Poverty among Blacks in the 1980s," *Journal of Policy Analysis and Management,* Vol. 13, pp. 288–310.

Jargowsky, P. A. 1997. *Poverty and Place: Ghettos, Barrios, and the American City.* New York: Russell Sage Foundation.

Jargowsky, P. A. 2003. "Stunning Progress, Hidden Problems: The Dramatic Decline of Concentrated Poverty in the 1990s." *The Living Census Series.* Washington, D.C.: The Brookings Institution.

Jargowsky, P. A., and M. J. Bane. 1991. "Ghetto Poverty in the United States, 1970–1980." In C. Jencks and P. E. Peterson, eds., *The Urban Underclass.* Washington, D.C.: The Brookings Institution, pp. 235–273.

Jargowsky, P. A., and R. Yang. 2006. "The 'Underclass' Revisited: A Social Problem in Decline," *Journal of Urban Affairs,* Vol. 28, pp. 55–70.

Johnson, J. H. J., and W. C. J. Farrrell. 1996. "The Fire This Time: The Genesis of the Los Angeles Rebellion of 1992." In J. C. Boger and J. W. Wegner, eds., *Race, Poverty, and American Cities.* Chapel Hill and London: The University of North Carolina Press, pp. 166–185.

Kain, J. F. 1968. "Housing Segregation, Negro Employment, and Metropolitan Decentralization," *Quarterly Journal of Economics,* Vol. 82, pp. 175–197.

Kaplan, D. H., and S. R. Holloway. 1998. *Segregation in Cities.* Washington, D.C.: Association of American Geographers.

Lewis, Oscar. 1966. *La Vida: A Puerto Rican Family in the Culture of Poverty in San Juan and New York.* New York: Random House.

Lewis, Oscar. 1968. "The Culture of Poverty." In Daniel Patrick Moynihan, ed., *On Understanding Poverty: Perspectives from the Social Sciences.* New York: Basic Books.

Lieberson, Stanley. 1981. "An Asymmetrical Approach to Segregation." In Ceri Peach, Vaughan Robinson, and Susan Smith, eds., *Ethnic Segregation in Cities.* London: Croom Helm.

Marcuse, P. 1996. "Space and Race in the Post-Fordist City: The Outcast Ghetto and Advanced Homelessness in the United States Today." In E. Mingione, ed., *Urban Poverty and the Underclass: A Reader.* Cambridge, MA: Blackwell Publishers Inc.

Massey, D. S., and N. A. Denton. 1988. "The Dimensions of Residential Segregation," *Social Forces,* Vol. 67, pp. 281–315.

Massey, D. S., and N. A. Denton. 1989. "Hypersegregation in U.S. Metropolitan Areas: Black and Hispanic Segregation along Five Dimensions," *Demography,* Vol. 26, pp. 373–391.

Massey, D. S., and N. A. Denton. 1993. *American Apartheid: Segregation and the Making of the Underclass.* Cambridge, MA: Harvard University Press.

Mulherin, Stephen. 2000. "Affordable Housing and White Poverty Concentration," *Journal of Urban Affairs,* Vol. 22, pp. 139–156.

Philpott, T. L. 1991. *The Slum and the Ghetto: Immigrants, Blacks, and Reformers in Chicago, 1880–1930.* Belmont, CA: Wadsworth Publishing Company.

Preston, Valerie, and Sara McLafferty. 1999. "Spatial Mismatch Research in the 1990s: Progress and Potential," *Papers in Regional Science,* Vol. 78, pp. 387–402.

Rice, R. L. 1968. "Residential Segregation by Law, 1910–1917," *Journal of Southern History,* Vol. 34, pp. 179–199.

Rosenbaum, J. E. 1995. "Changing the Geography of Opportunity by Expanding Residential Choice: Lessons from the Gatreaux Program," *Housing Policy Debate,* Vol. 6, pp. 231–269.

Rosenbaum, J. E., and S. J. Popkin. 1991. Employment and Earnings of Low-Income Blacks Who Move to Middle-Class Suburbs. In C. Jencks and P. E. Peterson, eds., *The Urban Underclass.* Washington, D.C.: The Brookings Institution.

Schelling, T. 1971. "Dynamic Models of Segregation," *Journal of Mathematical Sociology,* Vol. 1, pp. 143–186.

Spear, A. H. 1967. *Black Chicago: The Making of a Negro Ghetto 1890–1920.* Chicago: University of Chicago Press.

U.S. Advisory Commission on Civil Disorders. 1968. *The Kerner Report.* Washington, D.C.: U.S. Government Printing Office.

Wacquant, L. J. D. 1997. "Three Pernicious Premises in the Study of the American Ghetto," *International Journal of Urban and Regional Research,* Vol. 21, 341–353.

Wilkes, R., and J. Iceland. 2004. "Hypersegregation in the Twenty-First Century," *Demography,* Vol. 41, pp. 23–36.

Wilson, W. J. 1987. *The Truly Disadvantaged: The Inner City, the Underclass, and Public Policy.* Chicago: University of Chicago Press.

Wilson, W. J. 1996. *When Work Disappears: The World of the New Urban Poor.* New York: Alfred A. Knopf.

CHAPTER 11

IMMIGRATION, ETHNICITY, AND URBANISM

Have we not reason to believe that while popery is losing ground in Europe, this land presents to the Pope a fine field of operations and that he is now sending out his minions to accomplish his fiend-like purpose, to prepare the way before him that he may make a grand and triumphant entry into this country when he shall be hurled from his tyrannous & polluted throne in Europe.

—TYPICAL NEWSPAPER EDITORIAL FROM THE 1850s

From their earliest inception, cities have attracted people from the outside. They have been viewed as centers of opportunity, of freedom, of culture, of ambition. The growth of cities has been driven by people moving into the city, rather than through natural increase alone. Rural to urban migration caused nineteenth- and twentieth-century American cities to swell as discussed in Chapters 2, 3, and 10. But during this period the United States also grew, thanks to immigrants from around the world. Many of these folks eventually made their way into U.S. cities. Today, we see this as a blessing but, as the quote above shows, urban immigration was not always viewed this way.

Throughout the history of the United States, Americans have had to come to grips with ever more culturally distinct arrivals; many have anguished over the perceived threat of immigration to American culture and its impact on the livelihoods of those already here. When the United States was founded, it was composed principally of men and women descended from the peoples of northwestern Europe: England, Scotland, Protestant Northern Ireland, along with some from Germany (mainly Pennsylvania) and Holland (New York and New Jersey).

Bordering the new country—to the north in Quebec and along the Mississippi—was a substantial French contingent. Sprinkled along the Florida and Pacific coasts as well as within the southwestern regions were several Spanish missions and other outposts. American Indian tribal lands straddled the ever-expanding frontiers of white settlement. And, of course, there were the peoples brought to participate involuntarily in the new country. Africans—some free but most slaves—comprised nearly 20 percent of the early U.S. population. Most lived within the rural South.

With the exception of the African American and Native American populations, the United States during its first 50 years of existence was mainly a homogeneous, white, Anglo-Saxon, Protestant (WASP) society. The nation had been founded on the principle that there was to be no established church and that all men were endowed with certain rights (ignoring the female half of the population). At the same time, it would be fair to say that "America" considered itself to be a rural, Protestant nation. Ninety-five percent of Americans lived in villages and on farms. Someone looking for a Catholic or Eastern Orthodox church, a Jewish synagogue, or a Muslim mosque would have been sorely disappointed. Such institutions—when they existed at all—were found only in the largest cities. Although, to our modern eyes, even the cities would appear homogeneous, cities were looked on suspiciously because they threatened the established order. Although it had rebelled politically against its mother country, the United States was clearly and forcefully a cultural extension of Britain.

Around 1820, this population pattern began to change. Until the government passed laws severely restricting immigration in the 1920s, up to 45 million people would arrive in the country, from ever more distant lands. After a brief hiatus, mass immigration to the United States resumed in the 1960s and continues to this day. In 2005, the Office of Immigration Statistics (the agency responsible for tracking the volume of immigration) reported an annual influx of 1,122,373 legal **immigrants**, counterbalanced by about 311,000 **emigrants** (data from *Estimates, Fiscal Year 2000* from the 2000 Statistical Yearbook of the Immigration and Naturalization Service). Immigrants are individuals who are entitled to live and work permanently in the United States, and are distinguished from tourists, students, temporary workers, and business visitors. Emigrants are individuals who have been accepted to live and work in some other country, although they often retain American citizenship. In addition, data from the Pew Hispanic Center estimates that about 800,000 individuals enter and remain in the country illegally every year. So-called "illegal immigrants" are foreigners who have no visa and are therefore defined as **undocumented migrants**. These undocumented migrants add substantially to U.S. population growth and account for 1 in 30 Americans. The presence of illegal or undocumented aliens on American soil has spurred a number of competing proposals. Some have called greater restrictions and enforcment to curb the numbers of illegal immigrants, including the development of a fence across the U.S.-Mexican border. Others have called for some amnesty provisions to allow people who are now in the United States an opportunity to acquire legal residency.

Immigration is the most dramatic step in the various stages of mobility. Each year, one out of every seven Americans change residences. The action of moving within the same region is called **intraurban mobility**. People are also likely to move across larger distances: from one state to another or from one part of a state to another part of a state. This is called **internal migration**. Immigration and emigration, known collectively as **international migration**, result from a move across international borders and are relatively rare.

In the world about 175 million people, out of a total of 6.5 billion, live outside their country of origin. This is just a little over 2.5 percent. Immigration can be viewed as a product of both (1) **push forces**, that is, those factors that cause a person to want to leave his homeland, and (2) **pull forces**, those factors that entice a person to move to a particular place. Many international migrants move voluntarily. They make a calculation as to the benefits of making such a dramatic move and usually have a destination in mind. However, a large number of international migrants are **refugees** who leave a country because they would be killed or imprisoned if they did not. They are pushed out of their homelands and generally have little choice as to where they end up. Such migrants often languish in refugee camps for years at a time. Significantly, most international migration occurs within less developed regions, rather than from poor to rich countries.

This chapter presents an overview of immigration and its effect on cities. We begin by examining the great era of overseas European immigration, which lasted from the early nineteenth century until the early twentieth century. In sheer numbers, this had the largest impact on American society and was augmented by the increasing urbanization of American life. We then look at the newest wave of immigration, which has played such a large role in the reshaping of our modern cities. Finally, we examine America's new ethnic patterns in light of location. Ethnic groups in the contemporary United States come from all over the world. They confront new challenges, but many have also made the most of the opportunities found in American cities and suburbs.

THE ERA OF IMMIGRATION AND U.S. URBANIZATION

Between 1820 and 1925, at least 33 million people and perhaps as many as 45 million people entered the United States (Figure 11.1). The bulk of these immigrants came in the last 40 years of that period. More than 1 million individuals arrived in six of the first 14 years of the twentieth century; during the other eight years more than 800,000 arrived. All told, more than 13 million people arrived during this critical period. When considered as absolute numbers, these figures exceed the immigration we have today. More significantly, they occurred when the U.S. population was about one-third of today's: 76 million in 1900 and 92 million in 1910. The impact was such that the foreign-born population in 1910 accounted for about one out of seven Americans, one out of four working Americans, and one out of two Americans working in the key industries of steel, mining, and meatpacking. Many female immigrants worked in the garment and food

processing industries. The impact on cities was even more astounding; in some of the nation's largest cities—New York, Chicago, Detroit—immigrants comprised a majority of the labor force.

It is easier to think about immigration as occurring in waves. The immigration that took place before 1820, when no records were kept, continued the British cultural domination. Between 1825 and 1880, immigrants came from more diverse areas in Northern and Western Europe. Historians term this the **old wave** of immigrants. Between 1880 and 1925, immigrants increasingly came from other parts of Europe, as well as from French Canada, and even some from China and Japan (See Box 11.1). Historians term this the **new wave**. Each of these groups encountered different experiences and different receptions from the native-born population and tended to have different settlement histories. These differences persist today, in the ethnic complexion of separate parts of the United States and in the differences among urban, small town, and rural America.

The New Catholic Arrivals
During the period between 1820 and 1880, the British Isles continued to be the primary source of immigration, with Germany running a close second.

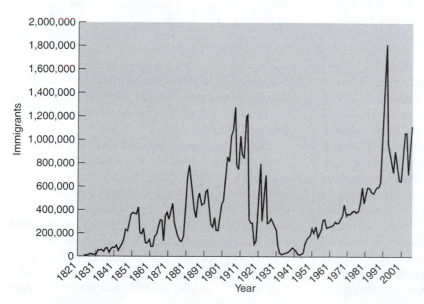

Figure 11.1 Number of immigrants to the United States by year, 1821–2005. Immigration has proceeded in a series of waves. Today, there are more immigrants than there have ever been.

BOX 11.1 STRANGERS FROM A DIFFERENT SHORE: CHINESE AND JAPANESE MIGRATION TO THE UNITED STATES

Although the majority of immigrants arrived in East Coast ports such as New York, Boston, and Philadelphia, San Francisco was also a significant port of entry. The last half of the nineteenth century witnessed migration from China and Japan. Beginning in 1850, Chinese migrants left a land of economic poverty and political chaos to try their luck in a land they called "Gum Shan" or "Mountain of Gold." They arrived on clipper ships—often debenturing themselves to pay the fare—and on arrival they took whatever low-level jobs were available to them: personal services such as doing laundry, cooking, and serving, railroad construction, mining, agricultural work, and some factory work. By 1890, there were about 110,000 Chinese in the United States, nearly all of them within the western states. That population was made up of men supporting families in China through remittances. Chinese laborers often treated their stay as a sojourn and had no plans to bring over their families. Many of the Chinese lived in small mining towns, laboring and performing services for the local population, but many also clustered in a few square blocks in distinct "Chinatowns" in San Francisco

(Figure B11.1), Los Angeles, Vancouver, and after a time in New York City. By the early twentieth century, the Chinese population remained concentrated in the West, but it was also found in other sections. It also became almost exclusively urban; the Chinese are now the most urbanized ethnic group in the United States.

The Chinese were probably treated worse than any other ethnic group, with the exception of African Americans and Native Indians. They were confronted with virulent racism that viewed them as depraved, disease-ridden, opium-addicted heathens. Because they were unwelcome, the Chinese were forced to stick together as a defense mechanism. As a result, they were accused of clannishness. These attitudes led to a series of immigration restrictions. Chinese women were excluded in 1875. Then in 1882, Congress passed a more general **Chinese Exclusion Act**, which restricted immigration to only a few males. Only in the 1940s was a more normal stream of Chinese immigration allowed.

Along with the Chinese, Japanese settlers began coming over to the United States in the late nineteenth century. Until the 1860s, the Japanese

Other areas, such as France, Scandinavia, and even Canada (some immigrants used Canada as a way station en route to the United States), each sent less than half a million people. Scandinavians, although they arrived mainly after 1880, are usually considered to be part of the old wave of immigration. In many respects, these arrivals helped to reinforce population patterns that already existed, adding to the considerable stock of English and Scots-Irish, while bolstering existing populations of Germans. Note, however, that the proportional volume of immigration during this period was larger than at any other time during U.S. history. In the peak decade of the 1850s, the number of immigrants

exceeded 12 percent of the existing American population. Even small changes in the composition of the population carried dramatic consequences for America's cities.

This immigration introduced several new elements. The large-scale German immigration brought people who spoke no English and who would often retain the native language. German continued to be used in Wisconsin parochial schools and parishes until World War I. The old wave of immigration also brought for the first time an enormous number of Catholics. The German immigrant population included many Catholic adherents. The Irish population, from the south this time, was overwhelmingly government maintained a closed door policy toward the outside world; only during the Meiji Restoration was Japan opened up and emigration allowed to proceed. Most immigration occurred from the 1890s up until the period before World War I. With the need for labor in the western United States, many large U.S. companies actively recruited Japanese laborers. Japanese immigrants also flocked to work on plantations in Hawaii, both before and after it became an American territory. In general, Japanese immigrants were far more agriculturally oriented than the Chinese. Many worked on farms and over time saved up enough money to buy their own land.

Attitudes toward the Japanese do not appear to have been as hostile as those toward the Chinese. After Chinese immigration was curbed in the 1880s, Japanese immigration made up some of the slack. But the Japanese were also discriminated against. Like the Chinese, they could not be naturalized as citizens. A **Gentlemen's Agreement** in 1907 curbed male labor migration, although it did allow for the families of immigrants to be brought over. Later, laws were passed in the 1920s that deprived Japanese immigrants of the right to own land, causing many to relocate in cities. And, the Japanese were singled out during World War II and forced into relocation centers or internment camps.

Figure B11.1 San Francisco Chinatown, 1952.

Catholic. As a result, Catholics went from less than 1 percent of the total U.S. population in 1790 to about 7.5 percent in 1850.

Geography of Immigration

A particular **geography of immigration** surfaced at this time because immigrants were likely to favor certain parts of the country over others. The large majority of immigrants disembarked in the port of New York. New Orleans, Boston, Baltimore, Philadelphia, and San Francisco were distant runners-up, although each "specialized" in a particular immigrant group. This had a clear effect on regional patterns of settlement, as did the perceived economic opportunities of different regions. With the exception of New Orleans, which attracted large numbers of Irish and Germans, immigrants generally avoided the South. The southern antebellum and postbellum plantation economy was unsuitable for new arrivals. The far West (especially California) increasingly attracted its share of immigrants, including a sizable number of Chinese and Japanese (Box 11.1). But it was in the northeast and Midwestern states that the foreign population predominated. By itself, New York State was home to one-quarter of the total foreign-born population in 1860.

Foreign arrivals of this period were more likely than native-born residents to settle in cities, and their urban orientation increased with time. Pre–Civil War immigrants encountered an agrarian society that was in the early stages of an industrial and urban revolution. The United States was still significantly behind Great Britain, which had reached a threshold of having half of its population located within cities. In 1860, only about 36 percent of all foreigners lived in the largest 43 U.S. cities, and half of these resided in the six major ports of entry.

There was a great deal of opportunity within the vast, untapped hinterlands. Prior to 1890, the frontiers of the United States continued to expand. Land was widely available for those who wished it, as long as they were willing to travel long distances. The Homestead Act made land available to those who agreed to settle and farm it. The railroad companies had an interest in selling vast swaths of land they had been granted by the federal government. Some Midwestern states even promoted themselves to prospective migrants, setting up recruitment offices and running advertisements overseas. They wished to grow, and immigration was an effective strategy for promoting growth. Many such states established a patchwork of intensely ethnic enclaves throughout the countryside: Swedes and Finns among Minnesota's Iron Range; German-dominated counties in southwestern Wisconsin and in northwestern Ohio, Norwegians in northeastern North Dakota.

Differences in Urban Orientation Urban orientation clearly varied among the major groups. Scandinavians were among the least likely to settle in cities, preferring the wide-open spaces of the upper Midwest and the upper Plains. By the late nineteenth century, only 28 percent of Scandinavians lived in cities with more than 25,000 people. The majority re-created the farms and villages of their homeland, residing in rural ethnic enclaves and showing little interest in interacting outside the group. Germans tended to divide evenly between farms and cities in the Middle Atlantic and Midwestern regions. Slightly less than half of all Germans lived in cities with more than 25,000 inhabitants. The Irish, on the other hand, were more likely to live in small, medium, and large cities, and were more likely to concentrate within the cities of the northeast, especially Boston.

A chart taken from geographer David Ward's *Cities and Immigrants* (1971) shows the variation in German and Irish urban settlement patterns (Figure 11.2). The chart places the 50 main American cities along a plot with the percentage of Irish increasing from left to right and the percentage of German increasing from bottom to top. Overall, the Irish made up a larger proportion of the total urban population (14.5 percent) than did the Germans (11.5 percent). But the regional differences are striking. Only New York City—the only city with 1 million people—had greater than average percentages of both groups. The other cities divided fairly evenly along ethnic lines. New England cities—and a few other northeastern cities—were clearly Irish oriented. Given Pennsylvania's original attraction to German settlers in the colonial era, it is also surprising to find that Philadelphia and Pittsburgh had higher proportions of Irish. Midwestern cities as well as Baltimore, Newark, and two upstate New York cities were clearly German. Cities in the South had smaller proportions of both populations.

Reception of Immigrants Another point of difference among the old immigrant groups came from the reactions they encountered among existing residents. Although individual experiences differed, the Scandinavians and Germans were largely welcomed at best, or at least tolerated. Scandinavians settled in remote areas and had often been targeted by recruiters. They did little to upset the status quo. Germans had an advantage of enjoying the sympathies of articulate spokesmen, and they were well represented among the skilled workers, specializing in a variety of handicrafts, brewing, and food processing. In addition, many came to the United States with some property.

Most animosity at the time was directed toward the Irish, for several reasons. The Irish were generally impoverished. Many emigrated as a response to a series of famines that swept the island. So most came with almost nothing in their pockets and no

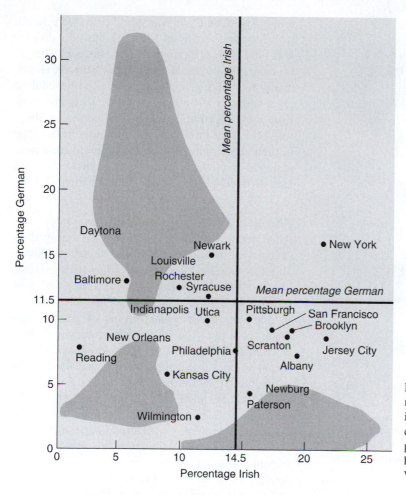

Figure 11.2 Irish- and German-born immigrant percentages of American cities in 1870. There was a strong regional distinction between cities with a high proportion of Irish and cities with a high German proportion. (*Source:* From Ward, 1971, p. 78.)

skilled trades to parlay into economic success. The bulk of Irish immigrants were employed in unskilled jobs and many were employed as domestic servants. As shown in Figure 11.2, the Irish tended to settle in older areas of the country, forcing them to adapt to existing social structures rather than be able to fully re-create their own societies. There was no opportunity for such immigrants to isolate themselves.

Finally, the Irish were Catholic. Unlike Germans who could be either Catholic or Protestant, Catholicism was clearly equated with Irish background. The Irish were also disparaged by the British upper class, whom the American upper class sought to emulate. The combination of these factors led to large-scale denigration, abuse, and exploitation of the Irish population. This culminated in the vicious editorials (such as the one at the beginning of the chapter), nasty cartoons that cast the Irish as subhuman (Figure 11.3), and discrimination. The addendum "Irish need not apply" or "None need apply but Americans" was a common part of want ads and job notices well into the twentieth century. Attempts by the Irish to improve their situation through organizing, political activity, and their ascendance in the Catholic Church hierarchy only infuriated "native" Americans.

Segregation Patterns   Despite the cultural difference of these European ethnic groups, there was little in the way of true **residential segregation** as we

Figure 11.3 Cartoon by Thomas Nast depicting both African Americans and Irish immigrants as subhuman. Unfortunately, such sentiments were typical in the late nineteenth century.

understand it today. In Latin, *segregation* means literally "to separate from the flock." In common usage, segregation refers to the geographical separation of people on the basis of ethnicity or race. Residential segregation in this case would entail the separation of people's residences. Other types of segregation can and do exist: segregation of businesses, segregation of schools, segregation by activity.

Within the countryside, segregation did occur as entire villages were populated by particular ethnic groups. But the city was something else entirely; here the Irish, German and other mid-nineteenth century immigrant groups were more residentially mixed. The absence of residential segregation was due largely to the nature of the urban form prior

to the American Civil War. Most cities were small, with little in the way of a central business district, with almost no separation of functions, and with little separation by social class. Cities were set up primarily for walking, and most people conducted their lives within a minimum of space. Rich and poor lived close together, sharing space across an alleyway often near their places of business. In this type of urban environment, even the despised Irish were scattered throughout the city, as evidenced by the map of Boston, circa 1850, shown in Figure 11.4.

The New European Immigration

After 1880, the nature of American immigration changed a great deal. For one thing, the overall totals increased dramatically. The steady stream of pre-1880 immigration became a flood of new arrivals as immigration doubled and then tripled. In addition, the national origins of most immigrants changed. The older immigrant populations of Germans, Irish, British, and Scandinavians continued to arrive. But they were joined by a series of peoples from southern and eastern Europe, the so-called "new immigrants." From 1880 until 1920, the main sources of immigration were from Italy, the Russian Empire, the Austro-Hungarian Empire, Greece, and Spain. Contained within some of these imperial jurisdictions was an array of ethnicities: Jewish, Ukrainian, Lithuanian, Polish, Hungarian, and Serbian, to name just a few. These groups were largely non-Protestant (divided among Catholics, Jews, and Eastern Orthodox), non-English speaking, and culturally distinct from the old immigration of the late eighteenth and early nineteenth centuries.

As was the case with the old immigration, the new immigrants were likely to favor particular areas of the country. If anything, the avoidance of the South was even more pronounced. With the exception of New Orleans, which attracted a fair number of Italian migrants, most newcomers came through New York and a few other eastern ports and either remained close by or traveled into the industrialized Midwest. In fact, it was the emerging industrial geography of the late nineteenth- and

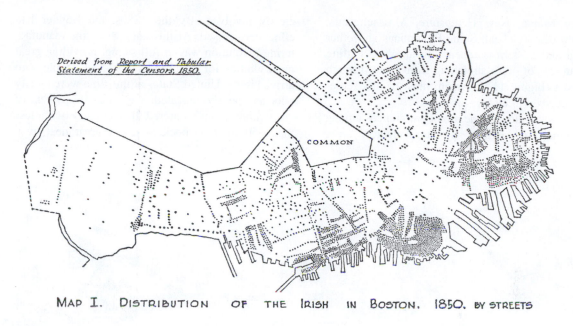

Derived from *Report and Tabular Statement of the Censors, 1850.*

COMMON

MAP I.   DISTRIBUTION   OF   THE   IRISH   IN   BOSTON,   1850, BY STREETS

Figure 11.4 Distribution of Irish in Boston, 1850. Although the Irish population avoided certain neighborhoods, they were generally dispersed throughout the city.

early twentieth-century America that most predicted where immigrants would locate.

Urban Orientation of New Immigrants   The new wave of immigrants differed in still another way from the older wave. Whereas the first wave of immigrants had been likely to move to both cities and rural areas, this second wave settled overwhelmingly in urban areas. Even though the United States as a whole was still predominantly rural, more than 90 percent of Jews, 85 percent of Italians, and 85 percent of Poles settled in cities. As was true of the old immigrants, the new immigrants exhibited a strong predilection to settle in particular cities.

In general, we can point to three types of urban settlements that attracted immigrants:

1. *Ports of entry* attracted immigrants without money to go any further and those who had found opportunity there. These were cities such as New York, Boston, New Orleans, Philadelphia, Baltimore, and San Francisco.

2. *Interior cities* served as major distribution and export centers, including Chicago, St. Louis, Cincinnati, Milwaukee, Cleveland, Detroit, and Akron.
3. *Small manufacturing towns* were located in New England and the Mid-Atlantic region, including Lowell, Fall River, Worcester, Scranton, and Toledo.

A result of all of this immigration and urbanization is that the foreign-born population of America's biggest cities soared. By the last quarter of the 19th century, immigrants and their children accounted for more than two-thirds of the urban population in the northeast and Midwest—the most populous and economically dynamic part of the country. Even as late as 1920, half of all the urban population in the country was of foreign birth or foreign parentage.

With regard to the different ethnic groups involved, certain patterns of settlement emerged. Jews settled primarily in Mid-Atlantic states, especially in New York. Italians were also found in Mid-Atlantic states, although many were also located in New England. Most French Canadians settled in New England, creating an extension from Quebec down through Maine, New Hampshire, Massachusetts, and into Rhode Island. Some Bohemians and other Central and Eastern Europeans went West, settling in a number of cities stretching from Ohio through Nebraska (Figure 11.5). Again, most of this settlement occurred in cities.

What accounted for the urban preferences among new immigrant settlers? Structural factors were clearly involved. By the 1880s, the frontier had effectively closed. At the same time, the manufacturing revolution was in full swing, providing great opportunities for unskilled labor. The people who arrived in the United States at this time were mostly poor and poorly educated. Well over 90 percent of "new immigrants" entered this country with less than $50 in their pocket—not a great deal even

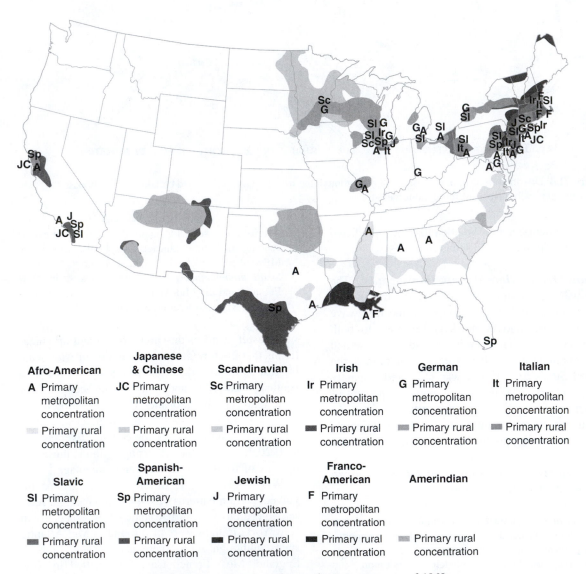

Afro-American	Japanese & Chinese	Scandinavian	Irish	German	Italian
A Primary metropolitan concentration	**JC** Primary metropolitan concentration	**Sc** Primary metropolitan concentration	**Ir** Primary metropolitan concentration	**G** Primary metropolitan concentration	**It** Primary metropolitan concentration
Primary rural concentration	Primary rural concentration	Primary rural concentration	Primary rural concentration	Primary rural concentration	Primary rural concentration

Slavic	Spanish-American	Jewish	Franco-American	Amerindian
Sl Primary metropolitan concentration	**Sp** Primary metropolitan concentration	**J** Primary metropolitan concentration	**F** Primary metropolitan concentration	Amerindian
Primary rural concentration	Primary rural concentration	Primary rural concentration	Primary rural concentration	Primary rural concentration

Figure 11.5 This map shows the primary location of several ethnic groups as of 1960.

in those days. Many new arrivals were illiterate, even in their own language. Among the arrivals, 50 percent of Lithuanians, 35 percent of Poles, 52 percent of southern Italians, and 38 percent of Russians could not read, and virtually none of the newcomers could read in English. This contrasts with the earlier wave of old immigrants, who tended to be literate and possessed some knowledge of English.

Occupationally, most of the new immigrant populations had few usable skills—more than 90 percent could be classified as laborers, peasants, and servants—reducing the prospects of securing well-paying jobs in the cities. But the prospect for some type of employment was usually good. In times of economic depression, when jobs were scarce, many of the new arrivals simply turned around and went back home. About one-fourth of immigrants returned to their homeland, although many of these were men who had always intended to remain in the United States for only a short time.

Neighborhood Locations   Given these circumstances, the bulk of new immigrants located where housing was available and where it was cheapest. Because the new immigrants were arriving at a time when cities were expanding and the middle class was moving into more spacious suburbs, a majority settled in inner-city neighborhoods that had been previously occupied by more established groups—an area termed the **zone of transition**.

The neighborhoods that the immigrants occupied were noted for their density and squalor. The demand for housing far exceeded the supply, meaning that families had to squeeze into ever smaller spaces. This did not necessarily mean that conditions were unhealthy—Russian Jews, for example, lived in extremely congested conditions but enjoyed fairly low mortality rates—but it highlighted the poverty of many arrivals. The conditions experienced by the turn-of-the-century immigrants horrified outside observers. Report after report testified to the substandard conditions experienced by the newest urban residents. Many commentators were indeed sympathetic to the plight of the people. Upton Sinclair's novel, *The Jungle,* exposed

the abuse of immigrant workers and families in Chicago. Others simply reported on the conditions they saw. One such reporter was Jacob Riis, a social reformer who fought to improve the conditions of many of New York's worst slums. His book, *How the Other Half Lives*, was published in 1890 and included text and redrawn photos chronicling the conditions of the time. Riis described cheap lodging houses, waifs, street Arabs, and tenements. A tenement of the time was described officially as a

> brick building from four to six stories high on the street . . . four families occupy each floor, and a set of rooms consists of one or two dark closets, used as bedrooms, with a living room twelve by ten. The staircase is too often a dark well in the center of the house, and no direct through ventilation is possible, each family being separated from the other by partitions. (p. 17)

Unofficially, tenements held significantly more people. As Riis exclaimed:

> It no longer excites even passing attention, when the sanitary police report counting 101 adults and 91 children in the Crosby Street house, one of twins, built together. The children in the other, if I am not mistaken, numbered 89, a total of 180 for two tenements! Or when a midnight inspection in Mulberry Street unearths a hundred and fifty "lodgers" sleeping on filthy floors in two buildings. (p. 17)

Conditions outside of New York were little better. One account of a Polish neighborhood in 1920 Chicago described it as 10 square blocks containing 14,000 people, making it three times more crowded than the most crowded portions of Calcutta, India. In this neighborhood, three-quarters of all apartments had less than 400 square feet of space, one-fifth of all people lived in basement apartments, and most of the residents had access only to outdoor plumbing. Such eyewitness accounts sparked reform legislation and gave rise to charitable institutions.

Segregation Patterns   As a rule, the new immigrant populations were far more concentrated than the older groups had been. These segregation patterns largely reflected changes in the shape of the American city. As the city expanded, functional separation was accentuated. Most cities developed a central business district (detailed in Chapter 6), a factory district, and residential districts divided on the basis of class. Because newcomers occupied the worst housing, they tended to be separated from native-born and even older immigrant groups. Distinct residential quarters characterized by a particular group emerged. Little Italy, "Jewtown," and other ethnically distinct neighborhoods became fixtures of some of the largest cities. Note, however, that few neighborhoods were occupied strictly by a single group, and so were not strictly consistent with the definition of a ghetto. To be sure, foreigners *were* segregated from the native born, but they were much less segregated from one another.

Table 11.1 illustrates the tendency of foreign populations to be segregated from the native population in 1910, 1920, 1930, and 1950. The table makes use of a segregation index or index of dissimilarity, as described in Chapter 10. The "new" groups, composed of Southern, Central, and Eastern Europeans are clearly more segregated than the "old" groups of Germans, Irish, and Scandinavians at each point in time.

Negative and Positive Impacts of Location

Whatever the facts of the situation, these urban ethnic neighborhoods combined in the American imagination. Many native-born Americans feared that immigrant groups, concentrated in cities, were undermining American culture. Many Americans

were wary of cities in the first place, but a city filled with foreigners was considered to be especially dangerous. The congested conditions of cities along with the high percentages of aliens appeared to many people to be a social tinderbox, waiting to ignite into riots and anarchy.

Nevertheless, these initial locations had a number of positive aspects. The first was one of *cultural expediency*. Immigrant ghettos were destinations that attracted family and friends from the old country. Neighborhoods furnished newcomers with a steppingstone into mainstream society. People were not forced to confront an unfamiliar and sometimes hostile environment. Many of the early immigrant neighborhoods were also fairly insular. The language of the streets was the immigrant language (in fact, in some parts it was virtually impossible to get around in English). Beyond this, a host of institutions developed to help the immigrants: churches and synagogues, welfare institutions, meeting houses, and businesses. All of these allowed for the creation of a "society within a society."

Economically, these immigrant neighborhoods were also *close to available employment*. Although the middle class had moved out, most of the major industries, warehouses, and services remained near the center of the city. Many immigrants were attracted to the availability of cheap housing located close by the manufacturing jobs. A central location also made it easier for unskilled laborers to find other jobs when they were laid off. Many such jobs required little in the way of skills and were distasteful to most native white Americans. Unemployment was therefore not nearly as large a problem as exploitation.

These particular advantages of cultural expediency and proximity to available employment eventually provided a springboard into mainstream society, propelling many immigrants upward and outward. By and large, immigrant communities were short-term phenomena that dissipated once large numbers of the ethnic groups—and especially the children of immigrants—made enough money to move into better housing further outside the city. After World War II, many of these neighborhoods began to

Table 11.1 Segregation Indices for Immigrants

		1910	1920	1930	1950
Boston	Old	20.6	23.2	26.2	25.4
	New	53.3	45.8	54.6	49.6
Chicago	Old	32.6	29.8	27.7	27.8
	New	52.6	41.1	47.1	41.4
Philadelphia	Old	21.6	21.1	29.3	28.4
	New	57.8	47.7	52.9	48.0

Source: Lieberson, 1963.

diminish. The inhabitants either died or became successful and left. Some ethnic neighborhoods survived into the 1940s and 1950s, becoming subjects of such studies as *Street Corner Society* and *The Urban Villagers*, but by the 1960s and 1970s, most had become relics. Newer populations had moved in or the neighborhoods were torn down in the name of urban renewal.

The loss of these distinct neighborhoods and the dispersal of second- and third-generation groups throughout the cities and metropolitan areas marked the long erosion of economic and social barriers between ethnics and native-born Anglo-Americans. This process is termed **assimilation**. Social scientists use the term to describe the process whereby an ethnic group becomes more similar (in culture, in employment, in attitudes) to the dominant group. Although cultural distinctiveness still remains, as manifested by religious devotion, political attitudes, and especially ethnic pride, over the course of the twentieth century, the massive European immigrant stock was incorporated into the American culture. Those who had once been reviled and scorned became a part of the establishment.

The Ethnic Kaleidoscope of Today

From World War I through the 1960s, immigration rates declined significantly. A great deal of this had to do with structural and external conditions. Two world wars, a global economic depression, and the desire of several oppressive governments after World War II to keep their subjects locked in reduced the number of potential migrants, although these forces did lead to several waves of refugees.

Immigration Legislation In addition to the causes listed above, the nation itself undertook several successful efforts to limit immigration through **immigration legislation**. By the 1920s, American attitudes toward immigration had become inconsistent. On the one hand, there was pride in American diversity. *Abie's Irish Rose*—a story about the marriage of a Jewish man and an Irish woman—ran for seven years on Broadway. Al Smith became the first Catholic to receive a major party nomination for president in 1928, although he lost the election decisively. On the other hand, more determined voices heeded the statements of President Calvin Coolidge that "biological laws tell us that certain divergent people will not mix or blend" (Barkan, 1996, p. 12) and that "America must be kept American" (Barkan, 1996, p. 2). Later on, President Herbert Hoover would complain to New York Congressman Fiorella LaGuardia that "Italians are predominantly our murderers and bootleggers...foreign spawn, who do not appreciate this country" (Martin, 2004 p. 76). In 1924, Congress passed restrictive legislation that used **national origin quotas** that effectively cut off most overseas immigration. This legislation imposed a ceiling of only 154,000 immigrants a year, almost three-quarters of which were designated for people from Great Britain, Germany, and Ireland. Earlier acts had eliminated Asian immigration, made it more difficult for certain people to obtain citizenship, and even stripped citizenship from some. The stringency of these restrictions became especially poignant as hundreds of thousands of refugees from Nazi Germany were denied entry to the United States, only to be returned to their doom.

These restrictions largely held until the 1960s. They led to a steady decline in the foreign-born population that would not be reversed until some 70 years later. They also left a substantial void in the mass migration to U.S. cities—filled in part by the migration of American blacks from the South.

In 1965, immigration laws changed dramatically. Congress passed a law abolishing the discriminatory national origin quotas of the 1924 act and replaced them with a series of preferences. Parents, spouses, and minor children of immigrants already in the country were exempted from the overall quota. By 1997, these groups comprised about 40 percent of the total legal immigration. This was followed by preferences for other family members, professionals, skilled workers, and refugees. Each country was expected to contribute no more than 20,000 immigrants a year (although initially inhabitants of the Americas were considered outside the quota; this was changed in 1976). Although the overall ceiling was not raised substantially at first, this law expanded both the numbers and the diversity of immigrants.

Immigrant Patterns The figures from the 1960s through 2005 show how the 1965 law and subsequent laws dramatically reshaped American immigration (Figure 11.6). To begin with, the overall volume of immigration has continued to increase. An average of 320,000 immigrants a year came to the United States in the 1960s; 430,000 in the 1970s; 630,000 in the 1980s; 978,000 in the 1990s, and 958,000 in the first years of the twenty-first century. In fact, by the first decade of the twenty-first century, immigration volumes finally attained the level of the first decade of the twentieth century, albeit within a much larger national population. In addition, the destinations favored by immigrants have changed a great deal. At the beginning of the twentieth century, New York City was the preferred destination, followed by several important cities in

the Northeast and Midwest: Chicago, Philadelphia, Boston, Cleveland, and Detroit. By the end of the century, New York continued to be the number one destination, but it was now followed closely by Los Angeles and a host of Sunbelt cities. In fact, nine of the 12 primary destinations between 1998 and 1999 were in southern or western cities (Figure 11.7).

Recent immigration data indicate that Miami is easily the top immigrant destination, in proportion to its population, with Fort Lauderdale also popular. They are followed by Jersey City, New York City, and Bergen County in northeastern New Jersey—all three within the New York greater metropolitan area. Several West Coast metropolitan areas—San Francisco, San Jose, Los Angeles, Oakland, Salinas, and Orange County—are highly popular as well. Other immigrant destinations are Seattle, Texas metropolitan areas like El Paso and Houston, and Boston.

Among the least popular destinations are cities in the Midwest, Mountain West, and South. Many of these cities are major magnets for domestic

	1820–1880	1881–1920	1921–1960	1961–2004
Germany	3,052,126	2,443,565	1,230,603	511,300
Ireland	2,829,206	1,529,144	290,358	138,872
UK	1,949,256	1,946,253	713,272	728,450
Italy	81,277	4,114,603	766,495	484,068
Austria-Hungary	80,769	3,988,034	207,044	104,015
Soviet Union	43,170	3,237,079	64,354	742,749
Other Europe	953,449	3,410,085	1,485,508	1,924,172
Canada	654,660	1,318,026	1,582,712	1,028,668
Mexico	25,119	271,530	842,006	5,710,305
Caribbean	63,490	293,080	263,217	3,402,928
Central America	1,220	26,304	88,046	1,484,290
South America	8,726	62,558	163,477	1,820,195
China	228,945	118,393	61,201	1,115,083
India	359	7,132	6,116	1,050,578
Philippines	–	–	24,526	1,703,506
Korea	–	–	6,338	871,741
Vietnam	–	–	335	862,494
Other Asia	1,385	590,058	220,415	3,161,212
Africa & Oceania	12,333	60,008	68,231	1,049,293

Europe	4,633,626
Canada	1,028,668
Latin America	12,417,718
Asia	8,764,614
Africa/Oceania	1,049,293

Figure 11.6 Changing composition of immigration, by nationality. Before 1880, most immigrants were from northern and western European countries. Between 1881 and 1920, most immigrants came from countries in southern and eastern Europe. Since 1960, Latin America and Asia have been the principal places of origin. (*Source:* Martin and Midgley, 1994, p. 25.)

Top immigrant destinations

● Immigrant destinations

☐ States

Figure 11.7 Top immigrant destinations, 1998–1999. Immigrants tend to be initially attracted to cities along the West Coast, Northeast corridor, and in Florida and Texas.

migration—Phoenix, Denver, Atlanta, Austin—but are less likely to experience immigration. The demographer William Frey (1998) has suggested that the immigration to a city may be inversely related to domestic migration, as natives seek to escape the diversity and move to more homogeneous metros. Recently, new patterns of immigration have seen an increase in Latinos and Asians in smaller cities, such as Raleigh-Durham, North Carolina, and Holyoke, Massachusetts.

Finally, the complexion of American immigration has changed. Before 1965, northwest Europeans were the dominant population, strongly favored by the preferential quotas. With the removal of these preferences, all types of nationalities were allowed to enter the United States. But rather than the southern and eastern Europeans, who had sparked the restrictions in the first place, well over 80 percent of immigrants came from Latin America and Asia.

Mexico alone accounts for more than 18 percent of the total. Five Asian countries—the Philippines, China, Korea, Vietnam, and India—account for another 23 percent of the legal total. When undocumented immigrants are added to the mix, the preponderance of Latin Americans and Asians is even more accentuated.

The country encountered by this newest wave of immigrants differs dramatically from the country entered by the major European immigrants of a century ago. Gone is the free and open land; gone also are the bustling, industrial cities. The America of today is far less rural, far less industrial, far more suburban, and far more oriented toward the West and the South. It is also a much more prosperous place, but one where education and skills are at a premium.

The newest immigration is composed of many different groups. Arrivals come from a wider variety

BOX 11.2   ETHNIC DIVERSITY WITHIN CANADIAN CITIES

Which city in North America can claim to be the continent's most diverse? People might consider New York or Los Angeles, but the honor most likely goes to Toronto. The largest city in Canada and the center of its economy, Toronto has emerged as a destination zone for millions of people from around the globe. According to the latest 2001 Canadian census, Toronto contained a higher proportion of immigrants (43.7 percent) than any metropolitan area in North America. In contrast, Miami and Los Angeles contained 38.6 and 30.5 percent "foreign-born" populations, respectively (a grouping that includes immigrants as well as some other legal and illegal visitors). Moreover, Toronto's makeup is far more diverse than that of Caribbean-dominated Miami or even Latino-dominated Los Angeles. Toronto has a substantial immigrant population from Europe, Asia, and Latin America. As a result, the city has

been transformed from a staid, somewhat stuffy, Anglophile city that shuts down promptly after dark and on Sundays to a cosmopolitan metropolis that hosts North America's largest Chinatown, Greektown, and Indian community, to mention just a few.

Toronto is the most visible exemplar of the astonishing speed by which immigration has affected Canada's cities (Figure B11.2). Vancouver, for example, is close behind Toronto in percentage of immigrants in the population. The consequences of this influx are that Canada's cities have been reshaped to an extent heretofore unseen. Canada's British and French heritage has given way to a **multiculturalism** borne of many different nationalities. The Canadian government policy has embraced multiculturalism, affording ethnic groups greater autonomy, linguistic privileges, and funding than is true of the United States. In addition, the

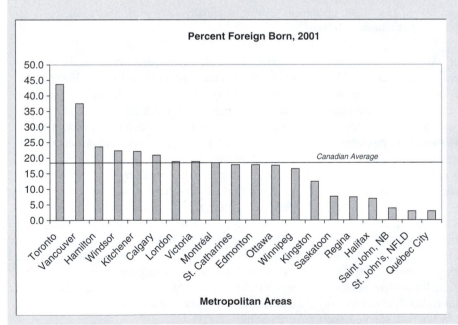

Figure B11.2 Percentage foreign born in Canadian metropolitan areas, 2001. Most immigrants arrive in Toronto, Vancouver, and Montreal, but some metropolitan areas in southern Ontario, Alberta, and British Columbia contain a high proportion of foreign born. (*Source:* From Statistics Canada.)

immigration of peoples from Asia, Latin America, the West Indies, and Africa has led to a rapid increase in what Canadians term **visible minorities**, or nonwhite ethnics. As is true in the United States, many nonwhite populations concentrate in the inner cities, forcing Canada to confront issues of race and urbanism. Other aspects of the influx of immigrants have to do with their growing presence across the urban landscape, found in markers like stores, schools, monuments, and signage (Figure B11.3).

Canadian immigration has occurred within a national and cultural context quite different from that of the United States. Canada has long styled itself a bilingual nation, split between English- and French-speaking peoples. All of the cities in Quebec contain a clear majority of French Canadians, while the cities in the rest of country began as overwhelmingly English. The capital city of Ottawa is a rare exception: It is truly bilingual in spirit as well as in letter.

French Canadians are suspicious of immigration for two reasons: first, because it might appear to challenge the French position as Canada's principle ethnic group and, second, because immigrants tend to acculturate into the English Canadian society, even those who arrive in Quebec. Recently, Quebec has taken steps to open itself further to immigration while ensuring that newcomers learn the language of the majority—French.

Figure B11.3 Chinese presence in Vancouver, British Columbia.

of places than before. They also bring tremendous differences in financial and human capital assets. For example, although immigrants are now less likely than native-born Americans to have finished high school, they are also more likely to have advanced degrees. Overarching all of this is the fact that the American economy exists more than ever within a globalized world, where labor, capital, and culture are far more integrated than ever before.

The diversity in immigration and its effects on U.S. cities defy easy categorization. Immigrant groups vary greatly from one another, and there are substantial differences within groups as well. Two main umbrella populations stand out in their contributions and in the way in which they are reshaping American cities: **Latinos**, arriving from the Caribbean, Central America, and South America, and new **Asian** immigrants. Together, these two broad

populations are expected to comprise one-third of the total U.S. population in 2050 (Figure 11.8). Non-Hispanic whites—themselves becoming a more diverse population with the incorporation of many immigrants from eastern Europe and the former Soviet Union—will at that time become a bare majority, as the United States completes its transformation into a **majority-minority** country. Box 11.2 discusses how cities in Canada are also heavily affected by immigration.

LATINO MIGRATION AND ITS IMPACT ON CITIES

In the last two decades of the twentieth century, nearly half of all immigration came from Latin America and the Caribbean. This was not a purely "Latino" migration—Afro-Caribbean groups such

Projected U.S. Racial and Ethnic Composition, 1999 to 2050

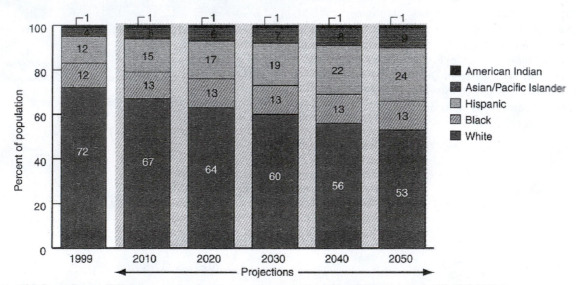

Source: U.S. Census Bureau. 1999 data accessed online at: www.census.gov/nation/e90s/e9999rmp.txt, on Jan.22, 1999; 2010 data accessed online at: www.census.gov/population/projections/nation/summary/np-t5-c.pdf, on Jan. 22, 2000; 2020 data accessed online at: www.census.gov/population/projections/nation/summary/np-t5-e.pdf, on March 14, 2000; 2030 and 2040 data accessed online at: www.census.gov/population/projections/nation/summary/np-t5-f.pdf, on March 14, 2000; and 2050 data accessed online at: www.census.gov/population/projections/nation/summary/np-t5-g.pdf, on March 14, 2000.

Figure 11.8 Projected racial and ethnic composition of the United States, 1999–2050. During the next several decades, the non-Hispanic white proportion will steadily decline, while the proportion of Asians and Hispanics will increase. (*Source:* Riche, 2000.)

as Haitians, Jamaicans, Guyanans, and Trinida-
dians contributed a significant proportion—but it
underscores the extent to which Spanish- and
Portuguese-speaking immigrants from the Western
Hemisphere continue to influence American society.
The result is that Latinos or Hispanics (both terms
are used) surpassed African Americans in the 2000
census as the country's largest ethnic group. Even
if no further immigration were to occur, the proportion of Latinos in the United States would continue
to expand, because fertility rates among Latinos are
the highest of all ethnic groups. But all signs point
toward continued high immigration and the likeli-
hood that Hispanics will comprise one-quarter of the
overall U.S. population in 2050.

The distribution of Latinos is geographically
uneven. Figure 11.9, taken from the 2000 census,
shows the proportion of Latinos by county. It gives
a good snapshot of where Latinos live today. There
are three distinct areas of concentration:

1. The largest and most visible by far, is a belt described
   by some as **Mex-America** that stretches from California's central valley and coast through the southwestern
   states of Arizona and New Mexico into Texas, especially along the Rio Grande. The vast majority of
   Hispanics within this region are of Mexican origin.
2. The second region is focused within southern Florida,
   with a clear focus on Miami. Miami is one of the
   growing number of American cities where Latinos
   constitute a clear plurality of the population. The leading Hispanic group in this region is Cuban, although
   diversity is growing within the Hispanic population,
   as Cubans are joined by a variety of nationalities from
   Central and South America.

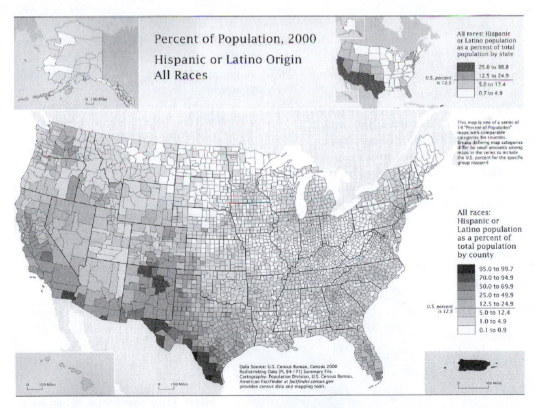

Figure 11.9 Percent of Latino origin population by county, 2000. Latinos are regionally concentrated in
the southwestern United States, California, and south Florida. (*Source:* Mapping Census, 2000.)

3. The third region stretches from New Jersey to New York City and into southern New England. Unlike the other two Hispanic belts, this area as a whole cannot be said to be dominated as much by the Latino population. Nevertheless, there are several strong concentrations within certain inner-city pockets, especially the Bronx. The leading Hispanic group in this region is Puerto Rican.

The three major Hispanic populations in the United States—Mexicans, Cubans, and Puerto Ricans—have quite distinct histories, vary in their socioeconomic status, and differ in their degree and conditions of urbanization. In general, Hispanics are very urban, with some 92 percent living in metropolitan areas as of 2000, compared with 78 percent of non-Hispanic whites. Six metropolitan areas—Los Angeles, New York, Miami, San Francisco, Chicago, and Houston—account for fully half of all U.S. Hispanics.

Mexicans

The largest group of Hispanics are Mexican American, making up some 58.5 percent of the total (Figure 11.10). The tradition of Mexican migration began mostly in the twentieth century, with many Mexicans moving to areas that had once been Mexico. The first surge of Mexican immigration took place during the 1920s, when Mexico emerged as a source of low-wage labor for farms. After World War II, the **Bracero program** renewed immigration activity. The Bracero program was an effort to bring in Mexican laborers to work on farms in the West, increasing the Hispanic presence in traditional states as well as in Idaho and Washington.

Although this program ended in 1964, Mexican immigration has continued at a steady pace. Mexico is what economists consider a middle-income country, and it is far wealthier than many other countries in Latin America. At the same time, the boundary between Mexico and the United States represents the most pronounced economic disparity among international border zones in the world. This creates an extraordinary series of push–pull forces that cause Mexico to be the greatest supplier of both legal and illegal immigration. The **North American Free Trade Agreement (NAFTA)** attempted to address these issues by creating a more rational economic framework that was supposed to decrease the amount of illegal entry. Thus far, there is little evidence that NAFTA has succeeded in this endeavor.

Urbanization Trends The initial Mexican settlement patterns were rural, largely because most Mexican immigrants were farm migrant workers. Over the course of the twentieth century, however, Mexican Americans became more urbanized. Los Angeles County, the largest urban county in the country, contains nearly 4 million Latinos, most of whom are Mexican. In fact, Los Angeles contains the largest Mexican population outside of Mexico City. Likewise, in San Antonio, Corpus Christi, El Paso, and Brownsville (all in Texas), a majority of the overall population is of Mexican origin. These

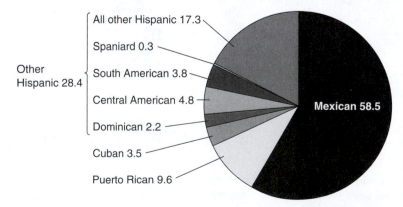

Figure 11.10 Distribution of the Latino population, by nationality, 2000. (*Source:* Census 2000 Brief.)

cities now contain extensive ethnic communities, with a host of institutions, businesses, and church and charitable networks. This layering of institutions that provide the needs of ethnic groups within a city has been defined as **institutional completeness**.

Los Angeles provides the clearest example. In 2000, the segregation index (or index of dissimilarity) for the Los Angeles metropolitan area stood at 63.1. The center of this city's Mexican community is Broadway Avenue, just east of Los Angeles's modern downtown. Broadway used to be the main street in Los Angeles for everyone; mass transit lines or "Red Cars" would bring in shoppers from far afield. Now Broadway is a Mexican shopping district (Figure 11.11). Hundreds of shops advertise in Spanish and cater to the needs of the population. Numerous bridal shops and stores selling dresses for the traditional Mexican 15th birthday celebration compete for attention with jewelry stores, electronics shops, and the Broadway Market, where all kinds of Mexican foodstuffs can be purchased.

Cubans

Cubans, another significant Latino group, are proportionally small in number, but heavily concentrated and politically and economically powerful. Unlike Mexican migration, which was driven largely by economic conditions, the migration of Cubans has a clear political genesis. When Fidel Castro took over the government, and Cuba became a Communist country, a number of people from the middle and upper classes were compelled to leave. Despite the existing immigration restrictions in the United States in the early 1960s, the Cubans were considered refugees from a Communist land and therefore were allowed free entry. Moreover, they have been treated better than any immigrant group in American history. Not only was legal entry quick and unquestioned, but about $400 million in financial assistance was offered, and a Cuban Refugee Emergency Center was established by the U.S. government.

Cuban immigration has continued in fits and starts since the early 1960s. Most of the Cubans who came over from 1960 through 1979 were fairly wealthy, highly educated, and mostly white. There

Figure 11.11 Broadway Avenue is just east of downtown Los Angeles. It is a major shopping street for Los Angeles's Latino population.

was a big spike in Cuban immigration in 1980, when Castro allowed 125,000 Cubans to leave from the Port of Mariel. Most **Marielitos** were less well educated and poorer than previous Cuban immigrants, and many were black or mulatto (mixed race). In addition, the presence of nonpolitical prisoners and mental hospital patients in this group prompted some concerns.

Florida Concentration Cubans are highly urbanized, with nearly all living in metropolitan areas. The metropolitan area of choice is Miami, with a much smaller number settled in New York. The relationship between Cubans and Miami began before Castro's takeover. After all, Cuba is only 90 miles away from southern Florida. It was during the early 1960s that the conduit between the two places deepened. Refugees from Communist Cuba desired to remain close to their homeland, and the growing Cuban community in Miami only strengthened that desire. The United States did attempt to resettle the Cuban population outside southern Florida, but with little success. As a result, the relationship between greater Miami and the Cuban ethnic population is unmatched anywhere else in the United States. More than half of all Cuban Americans live in Dade County (the county that includes Miami), and two-thirds live in Florida. This has enabled the Cuban population to parlay its relatively small population (just 4 percent of the Hispanic total) into enormous political and economic influence (Box 11.3). By and large, Cubans in Miami are prosperous (with the exception of some Marielitos), well organized (boasting an enormous array of economic, cultural, political, and social groups), and politically powerful. Today, most Cubans in the United States are citizens, and their influence is enough to support Cuban American local leaders and congresspeople, and to have an impact on U.S. presidential politics.

Although Cubans in Miami are fairly prosperous and can afford housing throughout the metropolitan area, they tend to be segregated from nearly every other group: Anglo (or non-Hispanic) whites, blacks, Asians, and even other Hispanic groups (Figure 11.12). The traditional center of the Cuban community is Little Havana, which at one time was a rundown area on the southwest side of Miami's central business district, but has now been rejuvenated with the concentration of Cuban residents and businesses (discussed later in the chapter). A newer, more prosperous core can be found in Hialeah, a suburb that is two-thirds Cuban. These neighborhoods and other adjoining areas are Cuban in every way: ethnicity, language, political organizations, stores, banks, and other businesses. In fact, the level of cohesion is so strong here that some have described the creation of a segregated **moral community**, one that includes a fierce anticommunism, the adoption of extremely conservative views,

and disapproval toward mavericks or non-Cubans in general.

Puerto Ricans

Puerto Ricans are the second largest Hispanic group, constituting about 10 percent of the total Hispanic population within the *mainland* United States. This distinction is important because, officially, the island of Puerto Rico is part of the United States (although it is not a state), and its residents enjoy U.S. citizenship. As a result, no immigration is necessary to go to the mainland, and there is substantial back-and-forth migration between the island and the mainland. This makes Puerto Ricans unique among Hispanic populations. Significantly, the population of Puerto Ricans living on the U.S. mainland—almost negligible before 1950—now almost equals the population of Puerto Rico itself. The conveyance of choice has been the airplane. By the 1950s, airlines were providing a one-way ticket for $35, with installment plans available for those who could not pay even that amount.

Spatial Patterns   Although the island of Puerto Rico contains a large rural population, Puerto Ricans in the mainland United States are almost exclusively urban. Historically, most Puerto Ricans have come to the New York metropolitan area. Higher populations are found in nearly every borough of New York City and in northeastern New Jersey. There is also a significant Puerto Rican concentration in southern New England and Pennsylvania. In cities like New Haven, Hartford, Springfield, Worcester, Boston, Philadelphia, and Allentown, Puerto Ricans are the predominant Hispanic group and are sometimes the largest nonwhite group (Figure 11.13).

By some measures, Puerto Ricans are the poorest major Hispanic group. A higher percentage of Puerto Ricans than Mexicans live in poverty and are on welfare, although Puerto Ricans have a slightly higher per capita income than Mexicans. In New York City, Puerto Rican neighborhoods like Spanish Harlem and the South Bronx are achingly poor, having greater problems of drug dependency, blight,

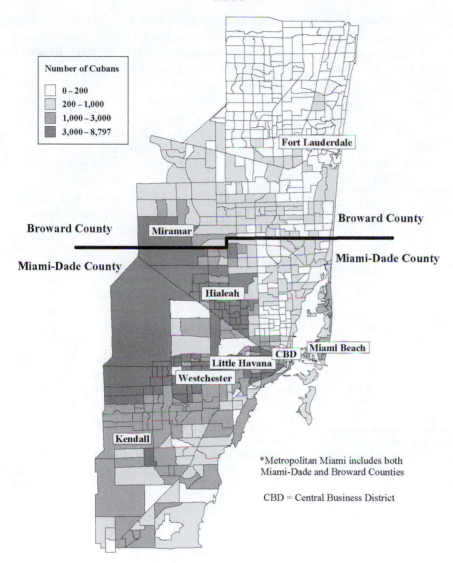

Cubans Living in Metropolitan Miami*
2000

Number of Cubans

- 0 – 200
- 200 – 1,000
- 1,000 – 3,000
- 3,000 – 8,797

Fort Lauderdale

Broward County

Broward County

Miramar

Miami-Dade County

Miami-Dade County

Hialeah

Miami Beach

CBD

Little Havana

Westchester

Kendall

*Metropolitan Miami includes both
Miami-Dade and Broward Counties

CBD = Central Business District

Figure 11.12 Cuban population in Miami, Dade County, Florida. Miami is the center of the Cuban community, most of whom have immigrated from Cuba since 1960. (*Source:* Courtesy of Tom Boswell, 2006.)

BOX 11.3   THE CREATION OF ETHNIC ECONOMIES

Several immigrant groups to the United States have chosen to open their own businesses—bypassing the mainstream economy (nonethnic economy) in favor of entrepreneurship (Table B11.1). The relative proportion of self-employment varies considerably by ethnic group and follows a long-standing process

Table B11.1   Business Ownership of Ethnoracial Minorities in the United States, 2000

All Industries	Self Employed
White	10.7%
Black	4.7%
Mainland Chinese	9.7%
Taiwanese	14.5%
Japanese	10.8%
Korean	21.3%
Asian Indian	9.8%
Pakistani	14.3%
Filipino	5.2%
Vietnamese	10.0%
Cuban	11.9%
Puerto Rican	4.6%
Mexican	9.8%
Entire Population	9.9%

Note: Earlier data suggests that Koreans, Indians, Japanese, Cubans, Chinese and Vietnamese ethnic groups are likely to employ co-ethnics. This often increases the ethnic presence of businesses by more than 150 percent.

pursued by immigrants from the nineteenth century onward. The reasons behind the decision to start one's own business are varied. For many individuals, self-employment is an opportunity to be one's own boss, a common factor among native U.S. residents as well. For immigrants, it may also be a way to avoid having to operate on the terms dictated by the majority. For still others, self-employment is a response to frustrated expectations, as people find that their education and skills are not appreciated in the American economy.

Ethnic business ownership depends on resources, and these certainly vary by group. The ability to open up a store or other business depends on access to four main types of resources: (1) financial capital, that is, gaining enough start-up money; (2) human capital, that is, previous experience and education; (3) social capital, defined as useful social networks, often based around one's membership in a particular class; and finally (4) ethnic capital, which refers to the resources of the particular ethnic group. Ethnic groups differ greatly in their access to the required resources. For example, the success of the Korean population can be attributed to a combination of these resources. Many Korean immigrants were highly educated and owned homes in Korea. Koreans also could take advantage of **pooled credit** among co-ethnics, as well as the loyalty of customers.

Figure B11.4 Chinese herbal shop in center of Asian immigration area in Los Angeles.

Cubans in Miami have also been able to parlay their human capital and ethnic capital advantages into initial predominance in some lucrative niches—apparel and construction—which then led to greater diversification.

The concept of an **ethnic economy** differs from simple ethnic business ownership. An ethnic economy consists of a group of businesses owned by members of a particular ethnic group that also employs members of that group (Figure B11.4). Ethnic economies differ tremendously in their scope. A series of stores and businesses run by an ethnic group certainly makes for an ethnic economy but it may not be. Some, but not all, ethnic economies are internally integrated. In other words, the businesses buy from one another and are otherwise linked. This integrated economy is sometimes described as an

enclave economy. A few groups have been successful at creating such enclave economies: California's Koreans in Los Angeles, Chinese in San Gabriel Valley, and Cubans in Miami. The Cuban enclave economy has developed a series of links among manufacturing, service, wholesale, and retail businesses. The result is an economy that is able to employ upward of 70 percent of all Cuban workers and that some argue is able to provide higher returns than the mainstream (nonethnic) economy.

Ethnic economies are often related to some form of **spatial clustering**. This need not be residential clustering. For example, Koreatown is a massive aggregate of Korean-owned businesses, but it is not where the Koreans live. Clustering or segregation may confer an additional spatial resource that allows ethnic businesses an opportunity to take advantage of a nearby customer base and labor supply. It may also foster links between businesses and can serve as a focus for a more broadly dispersed population.

The emergence of an Indochinese ethnic economy in St. Paul is best captured within the space of a few key blocks (Figure B11.5). This schematic transect of six blocks along University Avenue, a busy corridor about a kilometer from the downtown and extending west, shows activity at two different points in time. Asian-owned businesses have changed both in quantity and in diversity over the 13 years during the period that Southeast Asians have settled in St. Paul. As with many such ethnic economies, this business activity has grown out of residential clustering nearby.

BOX 11.3 *continued*

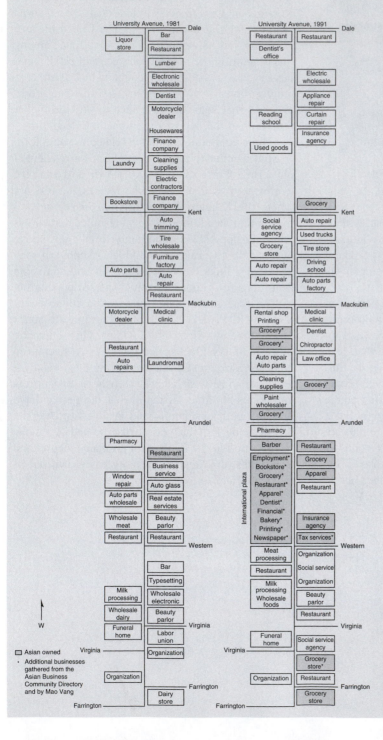

Figure B11.5 Changes in ethnic ownership on University Avenue, St. Paul, Minnesota. In the 10 years between 1981 and 1991, St. Paul's Southeast Asian population acquired many businesses along University Avenue, creating the rudiments of an ethnic economy. (*Source:* Kaplan, 1997.)

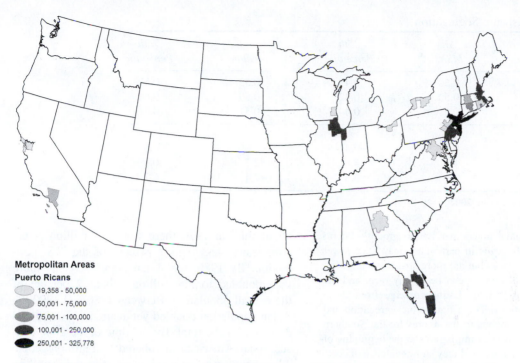

Figure 11.13 Puerto Rican population by metropolitan area, 2000 data. Most Puerto Ricans who live on the U.S. mainland are in New York, New Jersey, the southern New England states, and Florida. (*Source:* Map made by José R. Díaz-Garayúa.)

and social pathology than adjoining neighborhoods dominated by African Americans. This has become less common, however, as more Puerto Ricans have joined the middle class and moved to suburban neighborhoods. Puerto Ricans concentrate in particular neighborhoods, but they do not dominate to the extent that Mexicans and Cubans do in their respective enclaves.

Latino Influences

Latino migrations have profoundly altered the population composition of American cities. In addition to the three groups mentioned above, Hispanic groups such as Dominicans (from the Dominican Republic), Salvadorans, Colombians, and other nationalities are well represented among recent immigrants, although they have not had the same cultural or social impact on cities as the three groups mentioned above.

Significant Aspects   Several aspects of Latino immigration and ethnicity are significant:

1. First, Hispanic poverty is high and seems to be increasing slightly. Except for Native Americans, Latinos are the poorest ethnic group in the United States. However, this generalization masks some major differences among and within groups. Cubans, for example, are quite prosperous, with income levels that approach those of white non-Hispanics. Mexicans display a range of incomes but are primarily poor (especially when undocumented immigrants are included). Puerto Ricans are the worst off of the major groups and the most likely to be on welfare.

2. Segregation exists between Latinos and other groups, but it is not nearly as great as with blacks (Table 11.2). This is evidence that there is less discrimination toward Latinos than toward blacks and there is also less of a tendency for real estate professionals to "steer" prospective renters or buyers into exclusively Latino naeighborhoods. People studying segregation

Table 11.2 Hispanic Segregation

Dissimilarity Index	All MSAs	25th Percentile	Median	75th Percentile
1980	0.50	0.43	0.53	0.57
1990	0.50	0.42	0.50	0.61
2000	0.51	0.44	0.51	0.61
Percent Change				
1980–1990	−0.3	−0.4	−5.0	6.6
1990–2000	1.8	3.8	2.7	0.1
1980–2000	1.5	3.3	−2.4	6.7

Source: U.S. Census Bureau, 2002.

and income have noted that Latino groups—Puerto Ricans and Mexicans in particular—may have lower incomes than blacks but are more spatially integrated. Remember that Latinos can be of any race, and the experiences of "white" Latinos diverge from those of "black" Latinos. These figures on segregation and income are analogous to the figures for the Southern and Eastern European immigrants at the beginning of the twentieth century, and they show evidence of coming decline. What this means is that Hispanics now have an easier time escaping persistent ghettos.

3. The Hispanic influx into certain metropolitan areas has often increased **racial antagonism**. For instance, many Latinos have moved into neighborhoods formerly occupied by blacks (as in many of the neighborhoods affected by the Los Angeles riots of 1992). Latinos are also more likely to take low-wage jobs (owing to the undocumented status of several Latinos), and this creates friction with black workers who are competing for the same jobs.

NEW ASIAN IMMIGRATION

The Asian population of the United States has been increasing more rapidly than any other large group. Asian immigration began with the early introduction of Japanese and Chinese immigrants around the turn of the twentieth century (see Box 11.1), but then it was cut short by exclusionary legislation. The numbers of Asian Americans, which were small to begin with, increased very slowly and were not supplemented by new arrivals. The passage of immigration legislation in 1965 changed

all of this. In 1970 there were 1.4 million Asian Americans—less than 1 percent of the U.S. population. By 1980, the Asian population had more than doubled to 3.5 million—about 2 percent of the overall population. Between 1980 and 1990 the Asian population doubled yet again, and constituted 3 percent of the total. By the time of the 2000 census, Asian Americans numbered 10.2 million people when counted singly, and an additional 1.7 million when counted as part of a combination of races. Pacific Islanders, with whom Asians have sometimes been lumped for statistical purposes, numbered about 874,000. As a result, Asians now constitute 4 percent of the U.S. population today, and are projected to become about 9 percent of the population by 2050. No other group comes close to this rate of growth.

Variations in where Asians live has much to do with the favored destinations among Asian immigrants. By far the greatest concentration is within Hawaii, where about 42 percent of the population considers itself Asian, 9 percent are Pacific Islanders (including native Hawaiians), and 21 percent are mixed race that is mostly Asian.

There are also two regional concentrations of Asian residence outside of Hawaii (Figure 11.14). First is the West Coast, which contains about 40 percent of the total Asian population. In fact, about 36 percent of Asian Americans live in California alone. This reflects the historic tendency of Asians to immigrate across the Pacific Ocean and disembark in Los Angeles or San Francisco. Second, there

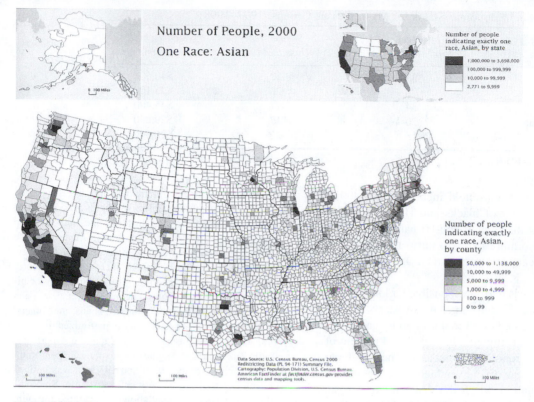

Number of People, 2000

One Race: Asian

Number of people indicating exactly one race, Asian, by state

- 1,000,000 to 3,698,000
- 100,000 to 999,999
- 10,000 to 99,999
- 2,771 to 9,999

Number of people indicating exactly one race, Asian, by county

- 50,000 to 1,138,000
- 10,000 to 49,999
- 5,000 to 9,999
- 1,000 to 4,999
- 100 to 999
- 0 to 99

Data Source: U.S. Census Bureau, Census 2000 Redistricting Data (PL 94-171) Summary File. Cartography: Population Division, U.S. Census Bureau. American FactFinder at factfinder.census.gov provides census data and mapping tools.

Figure 11.14 Percent of Asian population by county, 2000. Asians are regionally concentrated in the Northeast corridor, Hawaii, West Coast, Florida, Chicago and Detroit. (*Source:* Mapping Census, 2000.)

is the concentration of Asians along the Northeast megalopolis, centered in New York City but with sizable numbers at both ends: Boston and northern Virginia. These major cities, especially New York, continue to attract immigrants. Beyond these locations, Asians are found concentrated in a series of separated counties and cities: Chicago, Houston, St. Paul, Jacksonville, and many college towns. These concentrations stem from varied forces. College communities, like Ann Arbor, Michigan, host well-educated and sought-after Asian professionals who are involved in universities or related institutions and industries. The Asian population in St. Paul, by contrast, is the result of a refugee stream of poor Southeast Asians, especially the Hmong from Laos. Significantly, each census finds Asian Americans to be less concentrated in particular states and places.

Urban Orientation and Some Models of Asian Segregation

Asian Americans are highly urbanized—some 19 out of 20 live in cities—and are more likely to live in central or inner cities than are non-Hispanic whites. They enjoy a substantial presence in some cities, but they are a plurality in only one large city (Honolulu) and one smaller city (Daly City, just south of San Francisco). Otherwise, Asian Americans predominate in some smaller suburban towns such as Monterey Park, California, and especially in urban neighborhoods.

Asians as a whole enjoy socioeconomic advantages over other minority groups and white Anglos as well (Table 11.3). According to 1997 and 1998 data, nearly half of all Asians have a college degree, two-thirds are employed in a white-collar occupation (one-third as managers or professionals),

Table 11.3   Socioeconomic Status for Major Census Groups, 1997–1998

	Managerial Professional (%)	Semiskilled Unskilled (%)	Household Income
White	33	12	$40,600
African-American	20	20	$25,100
Asian	34	11	$45,400
American Indian	20	17	$29,200
Latino	15	22	$26,600

Source: Pollard and O'Hare, 1999, pp. 33, 36.

and their median household income of $45,400 is almost double that of blacks and Hispanics and is slightly higher than that of non-Hispanic whites. The Asians are also more likely to **naturalize**, that is to adopt American citizenship, than are other immigrant groups.

This success is partly responsible for lower levels of segregation. By and large, Asian Americans are the least segregated of all major minority groups. In 1990, Asians constituted a bit less than 4 percent of the overall metropolitan population. Their segregation index average of 39, weighted by the metropolitan area population, was lower than those of African Americans (64) and Hispanics (42). Other indices of segregation were likewise lower—much lower than for blacks and a bit lower than for Hispanics. Asian Americans are also more likely than any other major group to marry outside of the group—the practice known as *exogamy*. About 40 percent of all native-born Asian Americans marry outside of their ethnic group, although they may marry an Asian of another ethnicity. This practice clearly affects residential patterns because mixed-marriage partners and their children tend to locate in integrated neighborhoods. Substantial variations in Asian American residential patterns do occur, and we might usefully point to four types of Asian ethnic neighborhoods or enclaves (the names are from Chung, 1995, and Li, 1998):

1. *Traditional ethnic neighborhoods* These are the neighborhoods that have traditionally served as the first point of entry for Asian immigrants. For instance, big cities on the East and West Coasts have a well-recognized Chinatown that serves as an ethnic

crossing point for immigrants just entering the United States and for more established ethnics who still own businesses there, or who just use the area to shop and for social and other activities. In many of these cities, Chinatown has decreased its share of the overall Chinese population but has increased as a center for other Asian ethnic communities. Manhattan's Chinatown, for instance, now encompasses a pan-Asian population of Koreans, Southeast Asians, and others. Boston's Chinatown is likewise patronized by several Asian ethnic groups. Among Japanese Americans, Little Tokyo in Los Angeles serves the role of a traditional enclave. In the 1920s and 1930s, it was built as a center of business activity and social life. Since the 1960s, the Japanese population has scattered throughout the greater Los Angeles metropolitan area, but the neighborhood continues to hold special significance as a distinct ethnic place.

2. *One-step-up enclaves* These are neighborhoods within easy access to the traditional immigrant point of entry, usually the Chinatowns. Most of the residents of these neighborhoods are either in the middle class or close. The Asian population, while maintaining many ethnic ties, also interacts with the other groups present within the community. These communities are still recognizably urban, but they include people who plan to settle down, buy a house in the neighborhood, and send their children to the local schools.

3. *Ethnoburbs* The suburbanization of the American population has been joined by many Asian groups whose income and education make living in affluent suburbs far more feasible. This has given rise to a new type of ethnic settlement—what geographer Wei Li calls an **ethnoburb** but what might also be described as a suburban enclave, with features of both an ethnic neighborhood and a suburb. The populations residing within these neighborhoods tend to be affluent—belonging

to the upper-middle class—and are much more tied into regional and global economic flows. The San Gabriel Valley east of Los Angeles exemplifies this type of settlement. It includes high proportions of immigrants—from Taiwan, Hong Kong, China, and Indochina—and is characterized by substantial ethnic businesses, high educational status, white-collar occupations, and comfortable housing.

4. *New immigrant enclaves* These are enclaves located in poorer communities that include a large number of recently arrived immigrants. Many of the immigrants come from a more diverse set of countries (Vietnam, Laos, Cambodia, Korea, and South Asian countries) than was traditionally the case. They are also more likely to rent and to move out of these neighborhoods as they enjoy a bit of success. Although several such new enclaves are located close to the central business district, many are found further out, in outlying city neighborhoods and in inner suburbs.

Any discussion of Asian Americans as a whole masks some enormous distinctions among the experiences of different Asian groups. Although nearly all Asian Americans live in metropolitan areas, they differ in terms of urban location, levels of segregation, and socioeconomic status. This is true even in generally affluent neighborhoods like the ethnoburb, where the Indochinese and mainland Chinese populations fare much more poorly than do the immigrants from Taiwan and Hong Kong. Great differences also persist within groups as well. Some social scientists have described the status of Asians in terms of a **bipolar distribution**, meaning that Asians are overrepresented at both the bottom and the top of the socioeconomic scale. Table 11.4 shows how this relates to educational levels. It makes sense therefore to highlight some aspects of a few of these Asian populations.

Asian Indians

There is a saying that there is "no motel without a Patel" (Bhardwaj and Rao, 1990). By some estimates members of the Patel or Gujarati group—ethnic groups within India—own more than one-quarter of all motels in the United States. There is also a high concentration of South Asian physicians, engineers, professors, and other professionals in the United

Table 11.4 Asian Groups by Selected Educational Category, 2000

Group (single response)	No High School	College
Indian	13.3%	63.9%
Pakistani	18.0%	54.3%
Chinese	23.0%	48.1%
Korean	13.7%	43.8%
Filipino	12.7%	43.8%
Japanese	8.9%	41.9%
Thai	20.9%	38.6%
Vietnamese	38.1%	19.4%
Cambodian	53.3%	9.2%
Laotian	49.6%	7.7%
Hmong	59.6%	7.5%
All Asian	19.5%	44.2%
Total Population	19.6%	24.4%

Source: Census 2000 Summary File 4.

States. Overall, South Asians are a very successful immigrant/ethnic group that is in fact composed of many diverse groups. The South Asian population in the United States is still predominantly Asian Indian, which in itself includes about a dozen distinct ethnicities, but it also includes several groups with origins in Bangladesh, Pakistan, and Sri Lanka. Their influence on America's religious geography in particular has been profound. The introduction of Indians especially has created a significant Hindu community, whereas Pakistanis and Bengalis have augmented the Muslim population.

Between 1986 and 1998, Asian Indians accounted for about 12 percent of Asian immigration and about 4 percent of all immigration. Other South Asian groups together added an additional 2 percent of total immigration. As a rule, the Asian Indian immigrants and their descendants have done remarkably well. Nearly 60 percent have a college or graduate degree, and 44 percent are managers or professionals—higher than any single group. Their median incomes are likewise high.

This extraordinary level of economic success may help explain why few defined South Asian enclaves exist (but see Box 11.4). Large-scale regional concentrations do exist. Asian Indians are more likely to live in northeastern states, especially

BOX 11.4 TECHNOLOGY AND URBAN GEOGRAPHY

MAINTAINING SMALL ETHNIC COMMUNITIES VIA THE WORLD WIDE WEB

The traditional portrait of urban ethnic settlement involves colorful signs, banners and flags, festivals and parades, and a host of shops complete with exotic items exposed in the window. But the majority of ethnic communities do not enjoy the size thresholds needed to support these types of places. What is more, many ethnics move to the suburbs, where an automobile culture precludes much of the street life we associate with ethnic community. This dilutes the visibility of the ethnic group, and may also weaken the ties between members of the group, their homeland, and each other.

Computer technologies, in particular the World Wide Web, have emerged as a means by which ethnic communities can maintain their ties, even within the smallest community. There have always been ethnic media. Newspapers and radio served an important points of contact among ethnic groups. But the Internet offers something more. It provides a means of two-way communication that is instantly updateable, providing much of the bulwark for a virtual ethnic community.

This technology can be especially helpful for tiny communities. The number of Latvians in North American cities never exceeds more than about 7,500 (in Toronto) and 4,000 (in Chicago). For the most part, the community is externally invisible; most of the markers of ethnics are found within interior landscapes. It is through the Internet, however, that Latvian ethnics are able maintain their ties. One Latvian American woman points to the Internet as "a good way of meeting and staying in contact with Latvians all over the globe. From the Latvian camps she attended and those attended by her children, they have become acquainted with many other members. Her four children are always online with Latvians from North America and Europe, chatting away." (Woodhouse 2005, 170).

Larger communities also benefit from Internet communication. The Asian Indian ethnic group in the United States is the third largest of all Asian groups, and has been quite successful. But compared with many other American ethnicities, the Indian American community is not very visible. Much of this can be attributed to their geographic location in the suburbs. Without a set of concentrated settlement nodes, the Indians have come to exploit Internet technology as a means of cohesion. The Internet has allowed Asian Indians to create what Adams and Ghose describe as "bridgespaces" that allow them to communicate with each other and which also tie together the Indians in North America with the South Asian subcontinent.

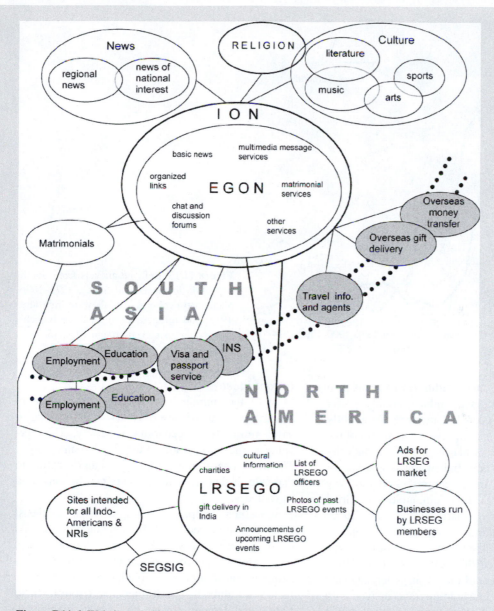

Figure B11.6 Websites used by nonresident Indians to maintain their diasporic identities: Indian Online Nodes (ION) are designed to help users navigate quickly to sites of interest to Indians in India and overseas; Ethnic Group Online Nodes (EGON) are multipurpose sites dedicated to a particular subethnic group; Local/Regional Sub-Ethnic Group Organizations (LRSEGO) are websites constructed by local or regional organizations in the USA (Adams and Ghose 2003).

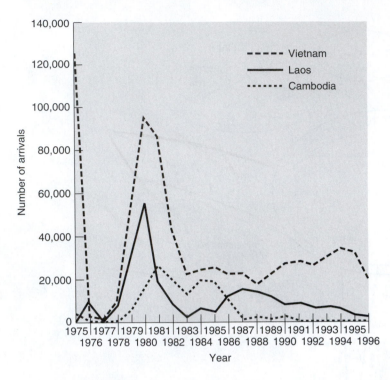

Figure 11.15 Refugee arrivals from Southeast Asia to the United States, 1975–1996. Vietnamese refuges arrivals were high after 1975, and refugees from all three Indochinese countries spiked around 1980. (*Source:* Airriess & Clawson, 2000.)

along the megalopolis, and in Illinois and Texas than in other states. And Asian Indians greatly prefer metropolitan areas. Asian Indians are only slightly more likely than whites to live in a metropolitan area's central city, for instance, and so the majority live in the suburbs. Few Indian towns are visible on the landscape (a major contrast with the very visible Indian and Pakistani communities in Great Britain). In one study, Bhardwaj and Rao (1990) indicated that Asian Indian segregation compared to whites was lower than that of any other Asian group. They attributed this pattern to (1) the high socioeconomic position of Indians in general, (2) the fact that many Asian Indian immigrants arrived with a firm knowledge of English, and (3) the fact that Hinduism as a religion may minimize segregation because its focus of religion is in the home rather than the temple. Within most metropolitan areas it is difficult to discern Asian Indian enclaves, although some defined residential and business enclaves can be found in neighborhoods of Chicago, Newark, Washington, D.C., and Cincinnati.

Indochinese

Most of the immigration that has taken place in recent years can be described as voluntary and/or based primarily on economic necessity. This certainly is true among most of the major Asian groups. The Indochinese immigration forms an exception to that rule in that most immigrants can be classified as refugees.

Indochina comprises that portion of southeast Asia once colonized by the French that now consists of the countries of Vietnam, Cambodia, and Laos. It includes at least five distinct ethnic groups: Vietnamese, Sino-Vietnamese (Chinese-ancestry Vietnamese), Cambodian or Khmer, Lao (from lowland Laos), and Hmong (from the Laotian highlands). These populations were all caught up in the Vietnam War. Between 1975 and 1996, about 1.1 million Indochinese refugees came to the United States (Figure 11.15). The Indochinese came in three distinct waves. The first wave involved well-connected individuals who fled as soon as the United States abandoned Saigon in 1975. The second wave took place between 1979 and 1982 and was composed of four main groups: (1) families of the initial refugees, (2) people who had ties with the United States and were thus in danger, (3) boat people from Vietnam, and (4) refugees from Laos and Cambodia who managed to escape across the border. The third wave has continued since the mid-1980s and includes people released from reeducation camps, Amerasian children (whose fathers were American servicemen), and some who had spent long years in United Nations refugee camps in Thailand.

The U.S. government initially hoped to disperse the flood of refugees from Southeast Asia. They enlisted the support of voluntary agencies, or **VOLAGS**, to act as sponsors for the immigrants. These VOLAGS were primarily church related—the United States Catholic Conference was the largest—and were scattered around the United States mainly in metropolitan areas. Over time, the immigrants, especially those in the second and third waves, began to reconcentrate in a few key places as they moved to where their compatriots and families lived. Yet the initial dispersion and use of VOLAGS did have some effect. Although California is the main settlement site, large concentrations of Southeast Asians are found in Texas, Virginia, and Louisiana (primarily Vietnamese), Minnesota and Wisconsin (Hmong and Lao), and Massachusetts and California's Central Valley (Cambodian). The Hmong are particularly interesting in that they have eschewed the usual immigrant hot-spots and are concentrated in cities like Fresno, California; St. Paul, Minnesota; and Eau Claire and La Crosse, Wisconsin.

By and large, the Indochinese are the poorest of Asian immigrants. The majority of adults came over with less than a ninth-grade education, and large numbers of Indochinese are still impoverished. In the short time they have been in the country, they have left a distinct imprint on many American cities. Studies of northern Virginia, Fresno, New Orleans, and St. Paul show the extent of "place-making" among various national groups. Although a significant number of Indochinese, especially Vietnamese, are fairly well off, large numbers of Southeast Asian American are quite poor. In St. Paul, Minnesota, for example, Southeast Asians occupy some 80 percent of the available public housing. In New Orleans, Vietnamese populate the public housing project known as Versailles. These are inner-city urban examples (akin to the new immigrant enclaves) and indicate a medium level of segregation, as new, poor immigrant populations live side by side. Looser suburban concentrations (akin to the ethnoburb and one-step-up examples given earlier) also have come into being. One notable district in Westminster, California, is called "Little Saigon" in recognition of the impact of Vietnamese merchants and residents across this suburban landscape. The Sino-Vietnamese appear to have been singularly successful in the establishment of businesses here. Another example is found in northern Virginia, where the Vietnamese have developed clusters of stores that replicate an urban market district in Vietnam (Figure 11.16).

Koreans

In Los Angeles, just to the west of the central business district, is an area of approximately one square mile known as Koreatown. In this district, strung along Wilshire Boulevard, one can see the makings of a vibrant Korean enclave. Signs in Hangul script (the Korean alphabet) predominate. Studios for Korean language television and radio locate off side streets (Figure 11.17). Hotels with names like the Hilton Koreana, banks, restaurants, travel agencies, and services make clear the ethnic identity of the neighborhood. Although Koreans have begun to have a profound effect in a number of American cities, Los Angeles clearly has a special significance for Korean life in the United States.

Korean immigration did not really begin until the 1970s. It was facilitated by easing restrictions on both the U.S. and South Korean ends (all immigrants are from South Korea; North Korea has remained completely closed off since the 1950s). There were about 350,000 Koreans in the United States in 1980; 800,000 in 1990; and about 1 million in 2000. Because they are recent arrivals in this country, most Korean Americans are foreign born, although

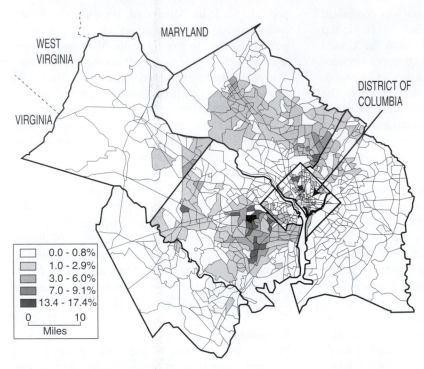

Figure 11.16 Southeast Asian population in Washington, D.C. 2000. Southeast Asian refugees, especially the Vietnamese, have a substantial presence within the Washington, DC metropolitan area, and in particular the suburbs of Northern Virginia. (*Source:* Courtesy of Chris Airriess.)

that percentage is declining. The volume of immigration is likewise declining somewhat, especially when compared to several of the other Asian groups. Today, the Koreans constitute about 10 percent of the Asian population. The regional distribution of Koreans indicates that they are concentrated on the West Coast (one-third of all Koreans live in California alone) though less so than other East and Southeast Asian groups. Significant concentrations also exist in the New York metropolitan area (especially in the borough of Queens), in Chicago, and in metropolitan Washington, D.C.

Like other Asian groups, Koreans are highly urbanized. In Los Angeles and in other cities, they are also highly entrepreneurial. The tall buildings and large firms of Koreatown in Los Angeles are one example of this. But a more frequent example is the small, Korean-owned mom-and-pop convenience/liquor store. In Los Angeles, such stores are frequent fixtures in poor African American and Latino neighborhoods. In the early 1990s, about 40 percent of all small grocery and convenience

stores were owned by Koreans. Within the inner city, where there continues to be a scarcity of supermarkets, 70 percent of stores are Korean-owned (Figure 11.18). This has sparked a great deal of resentment among residents of these communities, who complain that they are not treated fairly.

Significantly, Koreans do not live in these areas, nor even in the enclave of Koreatown, where the dominant residential population is Latino. In Los Angeles, most Koreans prefer to live in the San Fernando Valley or in Orange County, in fairly mixed neighborhoods. The tendency among Korean Americans is to scatter in suburbs. As a result, segregation indices among Koreans are low. Koreans have used business activity to create their own traditional enclaves in Koreatown and in scattered outposts of Korean ethnicity throughout the city of Los Angeles.

Asian Influences

The percentage of Asian Americans is still smaller than that of any other major immigrant group. At the same time, Asians are the fastest growing group

Figure 11.17 Koreatown is just to the west of downtown Los Angeles on Wilshire Boulevard. This is the main business center for the Korean community, although most Koreans live in other neighborhoods.

and one that has had great impact on particular cities and in particular niches. Several important Asian groups other than those we have just discussed have also made an imprint on U.S. society. Filipinos, for example, are second only to Chinese in their proportion of the Asian population. As a group, Filipinos are well represented in California cities and in greater Chicago. Certain middle-income neighborhoods host large populations of Filipinos. Daly City, just south of San Francisco, contains several such neighborhoods. Another group that is partly "Asian" in origin (though not usually considered as such) is the growing number of Arab Americans. They have a tremendous influence in cities like Detroit and

Toledo, Ohio. This is evidenced not only by population numbers, but by the presence of institutions, businesses, and political clout. Even more so than with Hispanics, it is difficult to try to accurately generalize across Asian groups and even within groups. However, a few key points can be made:

1. Asians are generally better off than other minority populations. Japanese and Asian Indians are among the wealthiest and best educated Americans—considerably exceeding the education and per capita income of the white population—and a large percentage of Chinese, Filipinos, and Koreans are also quite prosperous. Asian Americans tend to be overrepresented in many professions. They are also found in high numbers in elite colleges and universities.
2. High levels of exogamy characterize the Asian American population: More than any other group, they are likely to marry someone outside their ethnic group, often whites. This is a sign of assimilation, but it also threatens the maintenance of ethnic identity.
3. Asian Americans are found almost exclusively within metropolitan areas and other cities. However, they are more likely than other minority groups to live in suburban neighborhoods, and they exhibit the lowest levels of residential segregation. At the same time, Asian enclaves—Chinatowns and Koreatowns—are found within big cities, and these are growing in size. New suburban Chinatowns and other Asian enclaves are also found in the outer city.

WRAPPING UP

Any discussion of urban geography needs to contend with the issues of immigration and ethnicity. This chapter has focused on American cities, but immigration and ethnicity are issues of increasing relevance for cities around the world. Attitudes toward immigration, changing government policies, and changing source areas have had a profound influence on the evolving character of cities in North America. Although immigration is a continuous process, in this chapter, we have charted the separate "waves" of immigration that have characterized different periods in our history. In doing this, we have noted the different social and economic climates that

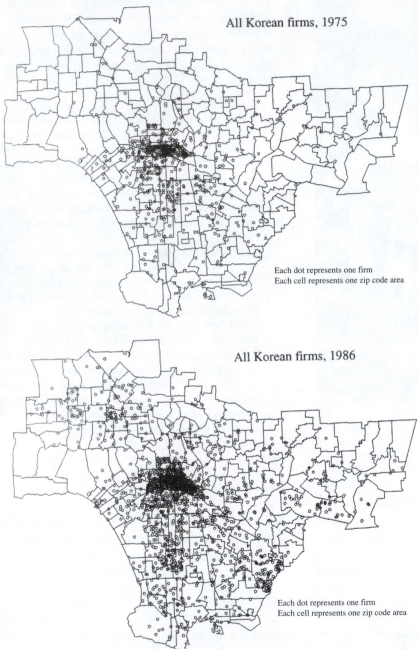

Figure 11.18 Korean businesses in Los Angeles, 1975 and 1986. (*Source:* Lee, 1995.)

have greeted the arrival of new Americans, how these climates affected their lives within American cities, and the nature of the cities themselves.

READINGS

Adams, Paul and Rina Ghose. 2003. "India.com: The Construction of a Space Between," *Progress in Human Geography,* Vol. 27, No. 4, pp. 414–437.

Airriess, Christopher, and David Clawson. 2000. "Mainland Southeast Asian Refugees." In J. McKee, ed., *Ethnicity in Contemporary America: A Geographical Appraisal.* Lanham, MD: Rowman and Littlefield.

Archdeacon, Thomas. 1983. *Becoming American: An Ethnic History.* New York: The Free Press.

Barkan, Elliott R. 1996. *And Still They Come: Immigrants and American Society 1920 to the 1990s.* Wheeling, IL: Harlan Davidson.

Bhardwaj, Surinder, and N. Madhusudana Rao. 1990. "Asian Indians in the United States: A Geographic Appraisal." In Colin Clarke, Ceri Peach, and Steven Vertovec, eds., *South Asians Overseas: Migration and Ethnicity.* Cambridge: Cambridge University Press, 197–217.

Boswell, Thomas. 1993. "Racial and Ethnic Segregation Patterns in Metropolitan Miami, Florida, 1980–1990," *Southeastern Geographer,* Vol. 33, pp. 82–109.

Boswell, Thomas, and Angel Cruz-Báez. 2000. Puerto Ricans Living in the United States. In J. McKee, ed., *Ethnicity in Contemporary America: A Geographical Appraisal.* Lanham, MD: Rowman and Littlefield.

Breton, Raymond. 1964. "Institutional Completeness of Ethnic Communities and the Personal Relations of Immigrants," *American Journal of Sociology,* Vol. 70, pp. 193–205.

Brown, Catherine, and Clifton Pannell. 2000. "The Chinese in America." In J. McKee, ed., *Ethnicity in Contemporary America: A Geographical Appraisal.* Lanham, MD: Rowman and Littlefield.

Chung, Tom. 1995. "Asian Americans in Enclaves— They Are Not One Community: New Models of Asian American Settlement," *Asian American Policy Review,* Vol. 5, pp. 78–94.

Espritu, Yen Le. 1992. *Asian American Panethnicity: Bridging Institutions and Identities.* Philadelphia: Temple University Press.

Frazier, John W. and Eugene L. Tettey-Fio. 2006. *Race, Ethnicity and Place in a Changing America.* Binghamton, NY: Global Academic Press.

Frey, William. 1998. "Immigration's Impact on America's Social Geography: Research and Policy Issues." presented at annual meeting of the Association of American Geographers, Boston, MA.

Handlin, Oscar. 1941/1976. *Boston's Immigrants.* New York: Atheneum.

Haverluk, Terence. 1997. "The Changing Geography of U.S. Hispanics, 1850–1990," *Journal of Geography,* May/June, pp. 134–145.

Herberg, Edward. 1989. *Ethnic Groups in Canada: Adaptations and Transitions.* Scarborough, Ontario: Nelson Canada.

Hing, Bill Ong. 1993. *Making and Remaking Asian America through Immigration Policy 1850–1990.* Stanford, CA: Stanford University Press.

Horowitz, Donald. 2000. *Ethnic Groups in Conflict.* Berkeley: University of California Press.

Isajiw, W. 1974. "Definitions of Ethnicity," *Ethnicity,* Vol. 1, pp. 111–124.

Kaplan, David H. 1997. "The Creation of an Ethnic Economy: Indochinese Business Expansion in St. Paul," *Economic Geography,* Vol. 73, pp. 214–233.

Kaplan, David H. 1998. "The Spatial Structure of Ethnic Economies," *Urban Geography,* Vol. 19, pp. 489–501.

Kaplan, David H., and Steven R. Holloway. 1998. *Segregation in Cities.* Washington, D.C.: Association of American Geographers.

Lee, Dong Ok. 1995. "Koreatown and Korean Small Firms in Los Angeles: Locating in the Ethnic Neighborhoods," *Professional Geographer,* Vol. 47, No. 2, pp. 184–195.

Lee, Sharon. 1998. "Asian Americans: Diverse and Growing," *Population Reference Bureau Population Bulletin,* Vol. 53, No. 2.

Li, Wei. 1998. "Los Angeles's Chinese Ethnoburb: From Ethnic Service Center to Global Economy Outpost," *Urban Geography,* Vol. 19, No. 6, pp. 502–517.

Lieberson, Stanley. 1963. *Ethnic Patterns in American Cities.* New York: The Free Press.

Lieberson, Stanley. 1980. *A Piece of the Pie: Blacks and White Immigrants since 1880.* Berkeley: University of California Press.

Light, Ivan, and Steven Gold. 2000. *Ethnic Economies.* San Diego: Academic Press.

Lin, Jan. 1998. *Reconstructing Chinatown: Ethnic Enclave, Global Change.* Minneapolis: University of Minnesota Press.

Martin, Philip. 2004. "The United States: The Continuing Immigration Debate." In Wayne Cornelius, ed.,

Controlling Immigration. Stanford, CA: Stanford University Press.

Martin, Philip and Midgley, Elizabeth, 1994. "Immigration to the United States: Journey to an Uncertain Destination," *Population Reference Bureau Population Bulletin,* Vol. 49, No. 2.

Martin, Philip, and Midgley, Elizabeth. 1999. "Immigration to the United States," *Population Reference Bureau Population Bulletin,* Vol. 54, No. 2.

Miyares, Ines, Jennifer Paine, and Midori Nishi. 2000. "The Japanese in America." In J. McKee, ed., *Ethnicity in Contemporary America: A Geographical Appraisal.* Lanham, MD: Rowman and Littlefield.

Pinal, Jorge, and Audrey Singer. 1997. "Generations of Diversity: Latinos in the United States," *Population Reference Bureau Population Bulletin,* Vol. 52, No. 2.

Pollard, Kelvin, and William P. O'Hare. 1999. "America's Racial and Ethnic Minorities," *Population Reference Bureau Population Bulletin,* Vol. 54, No. 3.

Portes, Alejandro, and Alexander Stepick. 1993. *City on the Edge: The Transformation of Miami.* Berkeley: University of California Press.

Riche, Martha F.. 2000. "America's Diversity and Growth: Signposts for the 21st Century," *Population Reference Bureau Population Bulletin,* Vol. 55, No. 2.

Riis, Jacob. 1890/1971. *How the Other Half Lives.* New York: Dover Publications.

Royce, Anya Peterson. 1982. *Ethnic Identity: Strategies of Diversity.* Bloomington: Indiana University Press.

Spain, Daphne. 1999. "America's Diversity: On the Edge of Two Centuries," *Population Reference Bureau Reports on America,* Vol. 1, No. 2.

Smith, James. 2006. "Little Tokyo: Historical and Contemporary Japanese American Identities." In Frazier and Tettey-Fio, eds., *Race, Ethnicity and Place in a Changing America.* Binghamton, NY: Global Academic Press.

Ungar, Sanford. 1995/1998. *Fresh Blood: The New American Immigrants.* Urbana: University of Illinois Press.

U.S. Census Bureau. 2002. *Census 2000 Special Reports: Racial and Ethnic Residential Segregation in the United States:1980–2000.* Washington, D.C.: U.S. Department of Commerce.

Ward, David. 1971. *Cities and Immigrants: A Geography of Change in Nineteenth Century America.* London: Oxford University Press.

Wood, Joseph. 1997. "Vietnamese American Place Making in Northern Virginia," *Geographical Review,* Vol. 87, No.1, pp. 58–72.

Woodhouse, Kathleeen. 2005. "Latvian Place Making In Three North American Cities." MA thesis, Kent State University.

Zhou, Min. 1992. *Chinatown: The Socioeconomic Potential of an Urban Enclave.* Philadelphia: Temple University Press.

CHAPTER 12

METROPOLITAN GOVERNANCE AND FRAGMENTATION

Once it is fully established, bureaucracy is among those social structures which are hardest to destroy. Bureaucracy is the means of carrying "community action" over into rationally ordered "societal action." Therefore, as an instrument for "societalizing" relations of power, bureaucracy has been and is a power instrument of the first order—for the one who controls the bureaucratic apparatus.

—MAX WEBER, IN GERTH AND MILLS (1958)

Most cities in the Western world and especially in the United States are paeans to private enterprise. The skyline of a city, composed of towering office buildings, hotels, banks, and apartment complexes, is constructed by private developers for the benefit of private interests. The hustle and bustle of a city comes from the movements of people shopping, working, and going to entertainment and from the myriad shops, restaurants, theaters, and other diversions meant to attract the money of all of those people. Indeed, the very distribution of people and functions in the city can be tied to differences in land rent, as discussed in Chapter 6, and the workings of the housing market, as discussed in Chapter 9.

The public aspect of such cities is less obvious, but it enables private enterprise to flourish. Over the decades, cities have grown to embrace many tasks and to accumulate a broad range of powers. Even in the most private, free-enterprise-oriented cities, public operations and regulations, controlled by municipal or metropolitan-area governments, play a major role in the city's shape and function. The expansion of such **collective consumption**—the consumption of goods and services by all or a portion of the urban citizenry—has led to a search for revenue: sales taxes, property taxes, personal and corporate income taxes, excise fees, user fees, and other sources. The provision of services, the regulation of activity, the imposition of taxes—these make the operation of the city, or what some refer to as the **local state**, important and immediate. Many people tune out when discussions of foreign aid or energy policy are debated at the federal level, but they pay attention when plans are proposed to put up a huge shopping center down the street or to increase property taxes. Everyone and every interest are affected by decisions made at the local level. Urban politics—who controls the levers of city government—is therefore of crucial importance.

This chapter focuses on the changing nature of urban governance and planning in cities. Such a topic is huge, both temporally and geographically. We focus mainly on cities in the United States, bearing in mind that such cities represent a particular bundle of powers and ideologies. Urban government within a socialist, politically centralized country such as China enjoys a far different mix of opportunities and constraints than does local government within the United States. We also discuss the geographical implications of governance, mentioning in passing some of the concepts, theories, and insights that have come from fields such as political science. It is for this reason that much of this chapter is devoted to metropolitan fragmentation, planning, and strategies of renewal.

URBAN GOVERNANCE AND THE GROWTH OF SERVICES

What is it that local governments do? An awful lot, it turns out. Much of a city's **infrastructure**—the streets, sidewalks, lighting, ports, airports, sewers, and water pipes that allow urban businesses and residents to thrive—are publicly owned. Some of the transportation itself, mass transit in particular, is under public control. Public safety is arranged through the city's operation of police departments, fire departments, and emergency squads. A city's public face also appears through the establishment and maintenance of parks—the green oases and emerald necklaces that characterize great cities—in recreational areas, and in monuments to great historical figures or to abstract ideals. The goal of universal education is manifest in the network of public schools, public universities, and free libraries. And the incomplete goal of universal housing and welfare is reflected in the varieties of public housing, free medical clinics, and income assistance programs.

An additional aspect of city and metropolitan governance has to do with its regulation of the conduct of private enterprise and of human activity. City operations are involved in zoning different land uses, requiring permits for almost any activity; regulating traffic, criminal, and potentially hazardous activity; inspecting facilities for health violations; levying taxes and user fees; and making the kinds of decisions that have repercussions throughout the city and its environs.

In the United States, local government preceded national government. Colonies were established along the eastern seaboard, and many towns and cities were settled and incorporated long before American independence. Cities established to the west—Cincinnati, Louisville, St. Louis—were established before their respective states of Ohio,

Kentucky and Missouri. Cities were instituted by **charter**, a document that recognized the legal basis of the city and that laid out its prerogatives. Cities varied in their levels of control. Some older cities like Boston had a broad range of powers that could not be usurped by the state. In contrast, many western cities were limited in what they could accomplish. For the most part, city charters established the city as a corporation; as such the city was **incorporated**. This designation ultimately gave the city the right to act as an "individual" with the power to raise capital by issuing bonds and borrowing money.

Expanding Urban Services

From the onset, American settlements differed from settlements in Europe. The physical differences were clear. American settlements rarely had walls or other man-made defenses. Land was also widely available, and new settlements were buffered by enormous tracts of unused (by Europeans) land. This allowed settlements to spread indefinitely, and it led to far less control over the emerging city shape than would have been necessary had there been a defined physical perimeter. Here, more than elsewhere, economic considerations—land value—determined what went where, often with the highest land value located at the city center (see Chapter 6). This spatial freedom—the ability for residents to pull up stakes and venture further out—marked and continues to mark American cities.

Urban government acquired more functions and responsibilities over time, especially as the population and complexity of settlements grew. In the early nineteenth century, governments exercised extensive control over a city's economic activities. Most cities owned at least one central marketplace, as well as dock and warehouse facilities. City authorities set standards of pricing and quality for the goods that came in from the countryside and were sold in the market. In 1819, for example, St. Louis enjoined butchers from selling "any blown stuffed unsound unwholesome tainted or putrid meat" (quoted in Wade, 1959, p. 81). Much of the early urban revenues came from the fees paid by stall owners and from the fines imposed on violators. Yet, the change toward a free-market system, where goods could be bought and sold in all locales and for all prices, spread throughout American cities shortly after independence. Government regulation of the economy declined, thereby eliminating one of the major functions of early urban governments. What replaced these functions was a movement toward a "service" city in which the government increasingly took charge of a wide variety of service functions—especially safety, education, and infrastructure—as well as the tax basis to pay for these functions.

Safety   The public safety functions of urban governments centered around firefighting and police services. In much of the nineteenth century, firefighting was done through voluntary organizations (in fact, the volunteer firefighter is still a staple of many small towns). At most, the city government might provide a station and a stipend for the fire chief. In return, urban residents received uneven service, including numerous strikes and brawls among rival fire companies.

Police services were likewise composed of volunteer brigades. Constables were paid mainly to serve the court, proffering summonses and the like. They also responded to citizen complaints and made money by arresting public nuisances. Volunteer night watchmen would patrol the streets after dark. By the last half of the nineteenth century, however, both police and fire protection had come under the authority of formal, uniformed organizations. Fire companies became hierarchical, professional, and technologically sophisticated. Police departments became proactive, seeking to prevent crime rather than simply to respond after a crime had been committed. Many duties of the new police forces, like animal control and health inspection, were later delegated to separate city institutions.

Education   Education is today the largest expense of local government, dwarfing the other functions of the city. Police and fire protection together cost less than one-fifth as much as elementary and secondary schools. Because education is so important, most cities and towns elect separate school boards. It is important to note that most of the operation

and financing of schools takes place through school jurisdictions that are independent of municipalities and sometimes cover a slightly different territory. Therefore, school expenditures are a smaller proportion of city and town budgets than of all local budgets.

Before the early nineteenth century, education was a private affair available to only the wealthy. Schools became public responsibilities only with the advent of compulsory and free education, and the burden fell on the shoulders of local government. Education was inaugurated at both state and municipal levels during the early nineteenth century. Individual cities made the decision to establish school systems before the states acted. Cincinnati, for instance, at first lobbied Ohio to institute a statewide system of education but ended up granting itself the authority in 1829. Such actions initiated the pattern of municipal, rather than state, control of primary and secondary schools. Eventually, state governments mandated that all students receive some education, although they left payment and administration largely up to the municipalities. In 1851, Massachusetts became the first state to require free and compulsory schooling. State governments also became largely responsible for public higher education, establishing land-grant universities and normal schools to educate the educators.

Infrastructure   As we have defined it before, *infrastructure* refers to the basic facilities, services, and installations needed for the functioning of a community, such as transportation, communications, water and sewer systems, and power plants. Each of these needs is most apparent at the local level, and demands for each became more pressing as villages became towns and towns became cities. For a small farming hamlet, a foot and bridle path may have sufficed for transportation, water and sewage needs could be accommodated by the nearby river, and communication was all face to face. But as communities grew and the technology became more essential and expensive, demand for infrastructure increased rapidly. We can see an example of this in recent history, as cellular telephones have necessitated the installation of cellular transmitters

BOX 12.1   STREET PLANS IN EARLY AMERICA

Until the mid-twentieth century, the grid was the dominant design for U.S. cities. In many respects it suited the American character. It was simple to demarcate, easy to visualize, and could be extended to the far horizon. The grid, as used by Americans, repudiated the closed cities of the Old World. Here the grid was employed as a way to stretch a city out into the horizon in endlessly repeating lines. Land was plotted without much regard to topography: The grid passed across rivers, over hills, on all kinds of land. From New York to Los Angeles, on flat land and hillocks, the grid began to characterize nineteenth-century urban expansion.

Several American cities did not begin with a grid, however. The earliest cities, like Boston and New Amsterdam (later New York), often developed

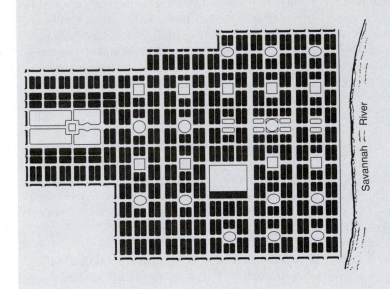

Figure B12.1 A view of colonial Savannah, Georgia.

and the expansion of area codes. During the nineteenth century, the most pressing needs were for paved streets and a means of getting water to the residents and taking sewage and other garbage out of the city. By the twentieth century, the needs had grown much more sophisticated and included electric power grids, telephone wires, asphalt-paved streets and fast highways, and other resources that urban residents now take for granted. Some of these needs were met privately or by publicly regulated but privately owned utilities; others became the province of city governments.

The provision of these services came fitfully and was often in reaction to intolerable situations. For example, early cities often set out "streets" that were public rights of way and that were not to be encroached upon. However, these were little more than paths, littered with animal carcasses, invaded by entrances to building cellars, dusty in dry weather and muddy in rain. Note, however, that except for the oldest cities, most American cities did develop a consistent street plan, usually a **grid plan**, that was an extension of the national survey of sections and quarter sections (Box 12.1). Maintenance was at first left organically, with no intentional design. In addition, several cities were designed in a more elaborate fashion. Philadelphia, Savannah, and New Haven were designed as a series of squares. These were meant to instill a sense of community.

Savannah, Georgia, was made up of large squares or *wards* (Figure B12.1). Each of the wards had a 2-acre open space surrounded by house lots. To encourage compactness, residents were granted a lot "in town," a 5-acre garden on the periphery, and a 45-acre farm lot clearly outside the city. However, they were expected to live around the central square of each ward. As the city grew, more wards were added, a process that continued until about 1850.

This helped to retain a centralized form to the whole. New Haven, Connecticut, was likewise established as a series of squares.

Philadelphia was set up on a larger scale, under the direction of William Penn. It was first divided into quadrants, and at the intersection of each quadrant was a large public square. The main street plan of the city incorporated a grid as well. But in this case the distances between the streets were established at an unwieldy 400 feet! These **superblocks** were soon carved up to allow for more development within the interior (Figure B12.2). In the process, much of the spaciousness of Penn's original plan was lost.

A City square
B Park

Figure B12.2 Plan of Philadelphia.

to private residents, but cities later began to pave their streets and to take responsibility for cleaning them, although they differed (and still do) on how to pay for these improvements. Some cities established special boards to regulate street development, extension, and maintenance; later the states intervened to coordinate the street patterns across neighboring municipalities. In the colonial period, Philadelphia appointed surveyors and regulators to lay out and maintain streets. By 1891, the Pennsylvania legislature had extended this practice to the entire state. In New York City, the Commissioners Plan of 1811 divided all of Manhattan

into 155 east–west streets and 12 north–south streets. This occurred at a time when 50,000 people were squeezed into the southernmost tip of the island. At times, state courts worked to circumvent a rational street-planning process by upholding private property rights and allowing people to build in the middle of prospective thoroughfares. Nevertheless, street planning persisted as a means of crudely designing the city and as an expression of municipal ambition.

Water and sewer systems likewise developed in response to growing needs. The use of on-site cesspools, perhaps adequate in a lightly populated landscape, imperiled growing cities. The wastes often contaminated the water supply, which came from nearby wells and streams. "Night soil" scavengers, who made a living from carting off human fertilizer to nearby farms, could not keep up with the growing populations. Garbage accumulated on the streets, mixing with mud and horse manure. By the mid-nineteenth century, cities began to plan elaborate sewer systems that would drain and divert rain water into "water carriage" sewer pipes—open-topped sewer pipes that could clean away water, animal carcasses, fecal matter, and other wastes—and then use gravity to direct the flow of wastewater out of the city.

Waterworks were established in some cities (originally in Philadelphia), but were inadequate to meet the cities' needs and were rarely truly sanitary. The need for clean water was brought home through the surveys done in London by John Snow that showed that cholera, one of the major scourges of nineteenth-century urban life, was a product of contaminated drinking water. The early twentieth century saw the introduction of modern filtration systems, the expansion of reservoirs, and the provision of water directly to the home. By the turn of the twentieth century, city dwellers in the United States were far ahead of urbanites in Europe in their access to clean water.

Over time, cities have been either persuaded or forced to add numerous new services to their existing load (Figure 12.1). Public health and public welfare, for instance, take a large slice of modern city budgets.

Cities help to subsidize local hospitals, cope with substance abuse, pay a proportion of welfare, engage in pollution control, and build and maintain some housing. Cities also work to promote their own growth through extensive redevelopment efforts. One of the most irritating trends, according to local officials, is the tendency of state legislatures, the federal government, and the courts to require that cities perform a function without giving them the money to pay for it. These are termed **unfunded mandates**. Examples are a requirement that shelters be provided for the homeless or a law that all public buildings be made accessible to people with disabilities. All of these regulations are well intentioned, but all are quite costly as well, with the costs normally passed on to the locality.

Financing the City

Each of the needs of collective consumption led to the expansion of civic responsibility. However, one of the paradoxes of municipal governance within the United States has been that the necessary financial resources and authority of cities has lagged behind the demands imposed on cities. The U.S. Constitution endowed states with a tremendous range of powers, but cities are considered simply "creatures of the states." They have historically been limited in their ability to raise **revenue**. State governments could and did intervene in urban affairs, amend city charters, establish other public bodies with local authority (such as school districts), and limit the amount of taxes a city could raise.

Local Government Expenditures 2002

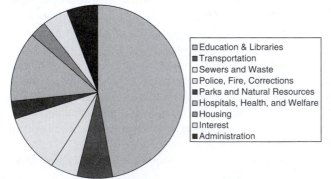

□ Education & Libraries
■ Transportation
□ Sewers and Waste
□ Police, Fire, Corrections
■ Parks and Natural Resources
■ Hospitals, Health, and Welfare
■ Housing
□ Interest
■ Administration

Figure 12.1 Local government expenditures, 2002. This pie chart shows how much counties, cities, towns, and other local governments spend on various services. Education accounts for a little over 40 percent of all direct expenditures. No other function accounts for more than 6 percent.

The main source of revenue for municipal services was and is **property taxes**, a tax based on the assessed value of one's property, sometimes referred to in terms of a **millage rate** or one-thousandth of the value. The advantage of this tax is that it is levied on very tangible wealth—real property—that could not be concealed and that has historically stood as an indicator of wealth. Today, property taxes constitute about three-fourths of all local revenue that is raised in the form of taxes, after intergovernmental revenue is accounted for (Figure 12.2). However, these property taxes have long gone to school districts that are often independent of the municipalities, as well as to counties. Property taxes constitute well over one-half of all revenue in cities and towns proper.

In growing cities, the value of existing property is rarely sufficient to keep pace with needs, and state legislatures, political uprisings, and economic considerations have often limited the millage rate. One of the most profound changes came in 1978, when California voters approved **Proposition 13**, which limited property taxes to 1975 levels and limited annual increases to only 2 percent. Massachusetts voters went even further by approving **Proposition $2\frac{1}{2}$**, which limited the property tax to $2\frac{1}{2}$ percent of the assessed rate.

The limitation of property taxes as a source of revenue has forced municipalities to find other sources of funding. One such source, **sales taxes**, has long been used to finance state governments. Local governments use these too, often piggybacking their levy onto the levy imposed by states. Sales taxes are **regressive** in that they impose a greater hardship on poor people than on the more affluent. Nevertheless, they are a fairly reliable source of income, they affect everybody who buys goods within the municipality, and they can be supplemented with special sales taxes on hotels, amusements, alcohol, and other items. **Hotel taxes**, for one, are popular because they affect outsiders and not voters.

City income taxes were rare before the 1940s but they have become quite a prominent source of funding in those cities that can assess them. Income taxes are often a flat percentage of one's income. In Ohio, for example, all incorporated municipalities assess some percentage of income, ranging from 1 percent to more than 2 percent of all income. These taxes are levied on city residents as well as on people who work in the city. Many states do not allow local income taxes, but these taxes have become a major source of financing for the 3,500 cities and towns where they are imposed. In such cities, local income taxes account for about half of all revenue.

Although taxes contribute to city revenues, they are not sufficient to finance city government and operations. Therefore the money has to be raised in a variety of other ways. Cities have long relied on grants from the federal and state governments

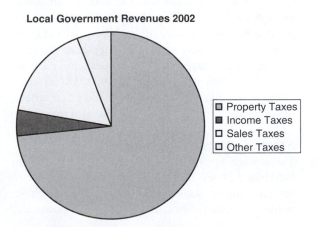

Local Government Revenues 2002

- ☐ Property Taxes
- ■ Income Taxes
- ☐ Sales Taxes
- ☐ Other Taxes

Figure 12.2 Slightly more than half of all local revenue comes from intergovernmental transfer. Of what is left, about three-quarters comes from property taxes. Sales taxes, income taxes, and assorted fees make up the remainder.

or on revenue sharing of taxes like the gas tax. These transfers go under the heading of **intergovernmental revenues**. In 2002, they accounted for forty percent of all local revenues. The problem is that this intergovernmental aid is always subject to cuts from state and federal government, either for fiscal reasons (they become too expensive) or for ideological reasons. For example, in the early 1980s the Reagan administration deeply cut federal aid to large northern cities, often by as much as two-thirds.

The other way for cities to raise revenue, especially for major development projects, is through the issuance of bonds marketed to investors. These **municipal bonds** were initiated in the nineteenth century as a way for growing municipalities to create the needed infrastructure for more and more residents, to help finance big projects, such as streetcar lines, port expansions, and integrated sewer lines, and to generally compete with all of the other cities and towns that struggled to be the biggest and the best. They continue to be a major source of urban funding. In 2002, for example, localities issued $197 billion in new long-term debt, with total long-term debt at nearly $1.1 trillion. These bonds pay for convention centers, sports facilities, museums, and often anything that the city estimates may be good for its long-run economic development. Investors are attracted to these municipal bonds because they are **tax exempt**, meaning that investors do not have to pay federal, state, or local taxes on the dividends. One danger associated with issuing bonds, for cities and investors alike, is that a city will default on its payments, although that has happened rarely.

Ideally, the revenues that local governments receive should be sufficient to pay for local expenses. In reality, many cities have run into financial difficulties. Local governments cannot operate a deficit the way the federal government can, and when they run out of money they are forced to cut services. Unfortunately, this happens most often in cities with the greatest need for services: cities with a large number of poor residents, with severe public health problems, and with an aging infrastructure. We discuss this predicament later in the chapter.

WHO GOVERNS THE CITY?

Urban governance in the colonial and early post-independence era was largely undemocratic, similar to the European model. There was no initial universal suffrage. Only **freemen**, a status that had to be purchased, were allowed a role in government. A ruling council of six or so members was often instituted, and both officials and voters had to own property. City government was dominated by the wealthiest of residents—merchants with a strong business orientation—and functioned somewhat like a chamber of commerce for mercantile interests. Juxtaposed against this was the beginnings of a strong American countercurrent of populism. In his book, on the New England town, Kenneth Lockridge (1970) describes how residents of Dedham, Massachusetts, began to circumvent the authority of the official selectmen by making more of their decisions in the town meeting, run by a moderator who was not necessarily a selectman himself. The push toward democracy in governance at all scales was singled out by de Tocqueville in his book, *Democracy in America*. This ideological thrust exerted a constant pressure on American cities.

Although wealth always conferred major advantages to urban politics, this overwhelming predominance would change over the course of the nineteenth and twentieth centuries as ethnic politics, interest group politics, and machine politics brought other perspectives to the table. In the early nineteenth century, suffrage was extended to all white men. After the Civil War, African Americans were granted the right to vote, although this was not truly in effect everywhere until a century later. Female suffrage was delayed even more, until the ratification of the 19th Amendment in 1920. Urban government was likewise opened up as old city charters were revised to reflect changing circumstances.

Stages in Urban Governance
There were several stages of urban governance in the United States. In the following section we focus on four major stages: elite dominance, machine politics, reform politics, and professional politics.

Elite Dominance In the first stage, cities were run by an elite—first patricians, by virtue of birth and breeding, but later simply those who achieved commercial success. This **elite dominance** lasted from the Colonial era into the mid-nineteenth century for most Northeastern and Midwestern cities and into the twentieth century within the urban South. The essential aspect of this type of governance is that government was run by the property-owning upper class, with little interest in accommodating the needs of poorer residents or immigrants, many of whom were not allowed to vote.

Machine Politics The mid-nineteenth century witnessed the growth of the political machine, especially in the Northeast and the Midwest. This second stage of urban governance—**machine politics**—consisted of a strong party organization that generated votes for favored candidates. The party would dole out favors—sometimes actual cash, sometimes patronage jobs, sometimes bail—in return for votes. Those people who did not vote correctly would be denied whatever the city might provide, especially services.

The machine had three especially important characteristics. First, the machine was **hierarchical**, with a clear leadership and organization. Each city had a strong party boss, a man who operated behind the scenes and often did not serve in a formal position. One such boss, William Marcy ("Boss") Tweed, the head of the Tammany Hall organization in New York City, was the favorite foil of cartoonists like Thomas Nast. But there were other bosses in cities throughout the industrial North. In recent years the first Mayor Richard Daley of Chicago acted much like a machine boss.

Second, the machine was **populist**, meaning that it appealed to the interests of the lower classes. Votes were votes, and it was easier to corral the votes of newly enfranchised ethnics and poorer residents than it was to gain support from the city elite. The machine delivered a slew of favors to the poorer residents in return for gratitude and votes. For example, at a time of widespread anti-Catholicism,

they provided money to the Catholic Church. Immigrants were especially grateful for help in finding jobs and housing and in becoming citizens. Of course, it helped that many of the machine's fiercest opponents were clearly **nativists** who felt the United States would be better off without new arrivals.

Finally, the machine was **territorial**. The city was divided into wards, precincts, and blocks, and the machine would place personnel at each level. These party workers, termed *block captains*, *precinct captains*, and *ward leaders*, would minister to the needs of the residents and on election day would make sure that everybody voted. Before the introduction of the Australian ballot—where votes could be cast in secret—party voting was easily identifiable.

The era of machine politics lasted for a long period of time. It was also clearly tied in with the introduction of ethnic politics in American cities, as immigrant groups matured and began to take the reins of power. The Irish, especially, but also the Italians, the Jews, and some Slavic groups ran the city for their own benefit.

Reform Politics. Even today some machines may be said to exist, albeit in a much weakened state. The reaction against machine politics, which tended to be secretive, undemocratic, and corrupt, led to the era of **reform politics**. The major tenet of the reform movement was that cities should be run by experienced administrators who applied scientific management techniques to serving the public interest. The kind of back-rubbing, log-rolling politics of the past was not good for the city as a whole and therefore needed to be swept away. A lot of different reforms were actually made in cities throughout the country. Among these were at-large elections, nonpartisan elections, and the council-manager form of government.

- *At-large elections.* Traditional machine politics had cities divided into wards, each of which elected a representative: councilors, aldermen, selectmen. In contrast, reformers felt that a city-wide election of every council member would better reflect the city's overall interest and would provide the city with the best representatives, regardless of where they lived. Today, most cities have at least some of their representatives elected at large. The problem is that such a system dilutes the influence of geographically concentrated groups. Minorities and the poor tend to inhabit certain parts of the city, and they have a great deal of difficulty electing people who represent them in an at-large system. Studies have shown that blacks, for instance, are far less likely to be elected under such a system.

- *Nonpartisan elections.* Although machines tended not to be ideological, they were based on a party, and voters were expected to vote for the party and not the man. To counter this practice, some reformers did away with partisan labels so that candidates would stand on issues alone and voters would form judgments based on the candidates' merits. Today, about three-fourths of urban elections are officially nonpartisan. One problem with nonpartisan elections is that they may actually lead to less emphasis on issues because candidates rely on saturation advertising and name recognition. Their stand on issues, for which a party label could provide some clues, may be unknown. Other factors, like the ethnicity of the candidate, may play a disproportionate role.

- *Council-manager form of government.* There are several forms of local government (Figure 12.3). Strong mayor systems place all control over city administration in the hands of the mayor. Weak mayor systems yield more control to the city council. Commissioner systems, which are often found in counties, establish separate administrative officers and place these under an elected commission. One form, the council-manager form of government, was instituted as a type of political reform. This system involved the introduction of a city manager, a professional appointed to head the city services and administer laws passed by an elected city council. A large number of cities moved to this form of government and still subscribe to it. The hope was that such an administrator would skirt ideology and favoritism. The disadvantage is that the city manager often becomes a very powerful figure in his or her own right, but is not directly accountable to the voters. It is difficult for city councilors, who often serve part time, to successfully oppose a persuasive manager.

One overall problem with these reforms is that they appeared to shift power away from the people and toward a meritocracy. In essence, they could be seen as a continuation of the style of governance that marked the era of elite dominance. Although machine politics was undoubtedly corrupt, it did distribute municipal resources to the poor. Neighborhood voting produced candidates who reflected the interests of neighborhood residents and often fought to keep these interests alive. Beneficiaries of at-large elections were those citizens powerful enough to equate their interests with the city's interest. Thus, professional administrators might think it expedient to tear down a neighborhood to make way for a new highway, something that was hard to accomplish when every neighborhood had a voice.

Professional Politics The modern era of urban politics corresponds with the rise of **professional politics**, at least in big cities. More and more, politics has moved from the "retail" style of knocking door-to-door (or getting people to knock door-to-door for you) to the "wholesale" style of advertising on broadcast media. Candidates must be telegenic, glib, and able to raise prodigious amounts of cash. Cities of the modern era have also been forced to deal with a large set of problems. The United States has become a suburban nation, and the big cities are just the central anchors in large metropolitan areas that exceed the city in area and population. The problems found in big cities may not be any bigger than problems of the past, but cities feel an obligation to deal with them lest they lose even more businesses and residents to the suburbs. Moreover, the cities are more connected to and dependent on political currents at the federal and state levels, and urban politicians must know how to get money from the federal government.

Power in the City
Students of urban politics have long debated the basis of urban power, especially in the modern city. Blatant manifestations of power, from business elites or political machines, have given way to a more subtle type of politics. But this does not mean that certain interests are not served. We can look at the urban order (to use geographer John Short's terminology) as composed of three sets of important players: households, businesses, and the local state. The **households** are the ultimate authorities

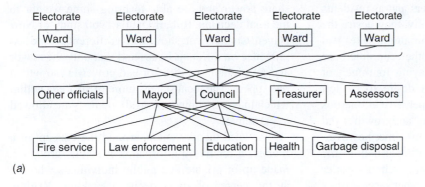

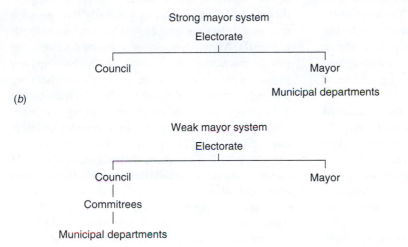

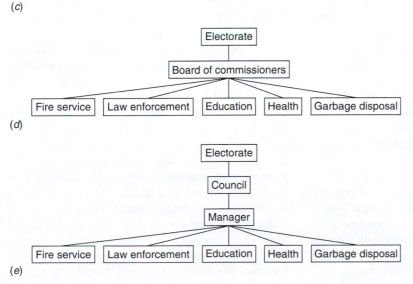

Figure 12.3 Types of local governments. The United States contains five basic local government types: (a) A mayor-council form, where top administrative officials are directly elected. (b) In a strong mayor system, the mayor appoints the heads of municipal departments. (c) In a weak mayor system, the council controls these departments. (d) A commission form, where an elected committee of upwards of three commissioners appoints the department heads. (e) The council-manager form entails the hiring of a city manager who reports to the council but ends up running the day-to-day business of the city. (*Source:* Short, 1996.)

as voters who elect the city leaders and as residents who use the city services. Basically, they desire the maximum of services for the minimum of taxes and fees. **Businesses** are essential to the economic base of a city, providing jobs and paying for much of the costs. They often profess a desire to be left alone, especially from what they perceive as onerous regulations and, sometimes, an "antigrowth" and "antibusiness" attitude. At the same time, however, business interests also seek government help in the forms of expanded roadways, quality schools, better fire and police protection, and the other services they see as beneficial to their operation. The **local state** plays a role as both a player in its own right, trying to serve the interests of the entire city, as a referee among competing interests in the city, and as one component of the overall machinery of government with very real limits to its authority.

Three basic theories concerning the sources of power in modern cities have been proposed: the elitist theory, the pluralist theory, and the regime theory. The **elitist theory** argues that urban political decisions are made by a relatively small number of select individuals. Power is concentrated among this group, who normally come from the business establishment, although other sectors (such as universities and big nonprofits) may also be represented. Although this elite may not be able to sway the voters, they can help frame what sorts of issues get discussed in the first place. They are also able to cut favorable deals with city officials. One well-known study of Atlanta, conducted in 1953 and 1980 by Floyd Hunter, showed that 40 individuals essentially controlled what transpired in the city. Many of these influential leaders were business owners, leading to a conclusion that the local state served as a handmaiden to powerful individuals and specific businesses.

The **pluralist theory** disputes this assertion of power concentration. Instead, it argues that power is distributed among several different groups. Business interests, of course, have great resources and influence, but they are often divided internally. Other interests—ethnic groups, labor unions, religious groups, neighborhood residents, special interests—

share power and are able to bring some weight to the final decision. Robert Dahl's 1960 study of New Haven, Connecticut, showed that different people had influence on different issues and that only the mayor and redevelopment director had power in more than one sphere. The local state is more of an arena within which interests compete, and all interests are allowed to participate.

The third theory centers around the concept of a *regime*, a relatively informal, but stable, grouping, made up of private and public individuals who are at the center of most decision making. **Regime theory** argues that each city generally has one such regime that has the capacity to act and accomplish key goals. Although business interests dominate the private fraction of the regime, public participation plays a role. This is not the kind of overwhelming power described by elitist theory for two reasons: (1) This group can rarely dictate everything that takes place and must operate within a broader political environment, and (2) depending on the city, regimes are composed of a more heterogeneous mix of interests including minorities, neighborhoods, and organized labor. Nevertheless, regime theory differs from pluralist theory, in which power is diffused. Although other actors can sometimes hold sway and participate in decisions, urban political power is clearly pooled in the dominant regime. However, the nature of the regime may vary, depending on what the chief objectives are.

Regimes act for specific purposes: maintaining the status quo, attracting more business and industry, creating a more equitable society. Political scientists Gerry Stoker and Karen Mossberger (1994) have identified an **organic regime** as one that seeks to keep things the way they are. This is mainly possible within more homogeneous, smaller communities that feel fairly satisfied with the status quo. An **instrumental regime** coalesces to accomplish a particularly big project or a string of projects. In the 1980s, for example, many big cities sought to redevelop their downtowns through constructing massive civic projects and attracting private capital. Instrumental regimes are made up of people who feel that this development will benefit themselves as well as people who see such development as promoting the general public interest. These regimes have also been termed **growth coalitions**. Some cities and towns have been guided by a **symbolic regime**, a coalition that looks to alter the city's image. Sometimes the alteration is toward more revitalization and more growth. In this respect, there is an attempt to create more of an urban "brand" that will succeed in better positioning the city among its competitors. Other times the goal is turning toward environmental, preservationist values. Such regimes have emerged in a number of towns and suburbs that seek to mitigate the effects of excessive growth. Over the long term, they are hampered by the opposition of many business interests and the realization that a perceived negative attitude toward growth may drive businesses and the tax base out to the suburbs. European cities are more likely to be dominated by a progressive symbolic regime.

CONTEMPORARY FRAGMENTATION IN THE METROPOLIS

Urban geographers are especially interested in issues of urban or metropolitan fragmentation. Complexity has grown as cities have grown, as urban regions have stretched far beyond municipal lines to include more and more rings of suburbs. Today the central cities and the suburbs that surround them are tied together loosely by the same history, a common economy, a metropolitan designation, and a perception of being part of the same urban region. Whereas people once hailed from the city of Chicago, they are now more likely to live in "Chicagoland," a vast complex of towns, small cities, counties, other urban districts—all anchored by the central city of Chicago. In the United States we term such regions *metropolitan areas*, and we draw lines to demarcate them. This general process of suburbanization, discussed earlier in Chapter 8, is common to most cities throughout the world, but it is more advanced within the United States than in any other country.

Cities are prone to some degree of fragmentation. Much of the material in this textbook is devoted to how cities are divided on the basis of economic functions, investments, housing quality, social groups, ethnicity, and the like. Suburbanization and the growth of complex metropolitan regions have overlaid a great deal of political fragmentation on top of this existing fragmentation. A metropolitan urban region may contain hundreds of different local governments that share certain interests but differ in other respects. The political separation is also fiscal, because each local government is required to provide services and is endowed with the capacity to generate revenue. The types of services required and the amount of revenue that can be generated differ widely.

Many of the best recent books dealing with metropolitan fragmentation have been written by urban politicians. One such individual, Myron Orfield, has represented a Minneapolis district in the Minnesota state legislature. In his book, *Metropolitics* (1997), he asserts that fragmented communities "concentrate the social and economic needs of the region on the weak resource base of the central cities and inner suburbs, those least able to resist" (p. 74). Another close observer of metropolitan fragmentation is David Rusk, former mayor of Albuquerque, New Mexico. In his book, *Cities without Suburbs* (1993), Rusk paints a picture of "inelastic" cities that are unable to expand and are hemmed in by competing suburbs. In this situation, the "very fragmentation of local government reinforces racial and economic segregation. Rivalry among jurisdictions often inhibits the whole area's ability to respond to economic challenge" (p. 47). For both of these politicians, the solution is the creation of a single, overarching local government. Orfield advocates a two-tiered regional metropolitan government, while Rusk promotes the value of *elasticity*—the ability of cities to annex surrounding land, thereby keeping suburbs within the city jurisdiction. We look more closely at these and other solutions later in this chapter.

Increasing Fragmentation

That there has been an increase in metropolitan fragmentation is largely indisputable. This process

Table 12.1 Types and Numbers of Governments in the United States

Type of Government	2002	1992	1982	1972	1962	1952
Total	87,900	86,743	81,831	78,269	91,236	116,805
Federal Government	1	1	1	1	1	1
State Governments	50	50	50	50	50	48
Local Governments	87,849	86,692	81,780	78,218	91,185	116,756
General Purpose:						
County	3,034	3,043	3,041	3,044	3,043	3,052
Subcounty	35,937	35,962	35,810	35,508	35,141	34,009
Municipal	19,431	19,296	19,076	18,517	17,997	16,807
Township	16,506	16,666	16,734	16,991	17,144	17,202
Special Purpose:						
School district	13,522	14,556	14,851	15,781	34,678	67,355
Special district	35,356	33,131	28,078	23,885	18,323	12,340

Source: http://www.census.gov/govs/www/cog2002.html

is not primarily the result of the shearing off of parts of existing cities. Rather, fragmentation can be traced to three main developments: (1) the physical expansion of metropolitan areas, (2) the increase in the number of incorporated suburban municipalities, and (3) the growth and variegation of service delivery areas. Taking a look at the United States as a whole, there were 87,900 governments as of 2002. Of these, 3,034 were counties (Table 12.1).

When we examine the process of political fragmentation more closely, a few trends become apparent. First, the number of school districts declined by almost 90 percent. The 1940s, 1950s, and 1960s witnessed the establishment of large regional school districts, often in rural and exurban areas. The idea was to increase economies of scale by allowing the creation of large new high schools and the primary schools to feed into them. In this sense, there was a tendency away from fragmentation and toward more consolidation. Second, the number of incorporated municipalities increased, largely at the expense of townships. Laws vary by state, but in most places it is impossible for a central city to annex an incorporated municipality without a mutual agreement. The proliferation of incorporated municipalities began in the late nineteenth century. Cook County, which includes Chicago, went from 55 incorporated municipalities in 1890 to 109 in

1920—and the trend proliferated. By 1930, all state legislatures "put the decision of whether suburbanites would or would not be annexed by the central city firmly into the hands of those who had already fled the city" (Judd and Swanstrom, 1994, p. 218). Conditions came to a point where some independent localities developed as tax havens. In Los Angeles County, for instance, the City of Industry was formed in the 1950s by a group of industrialists who wished to avoid paying for residential services.

By 1992, the average number of local governments per metropolitan area had risen to 90. This growth, although modest at the nationwide scale, was often quite dramatic and variable in particular metropolitan areas. By the 1980s, for example, the Chicago area included some 1,250 local governments. Data from the 1990 Census showed that metropolitan Detroit had 338 suburban governments; by the year 2000, the city government of Detroit proper governed about one-quarter of the entire metropolitan population.

Third, the largest increase came in the growth of special districts, which increased by four times over the period from 1942 until 2002. These include park districts, fire districts, housing districts, and sewerage water districts. The boundaries of these special districts do not need to coincide with municipal or township boundaries. For example, nearly half of Chicago's local governments are actually special districts, more than the number of townships, municipalities, or school districts.

But clearly the greatest contributor to metropolitan complexity lies in the expansion of metropolitan areas. The push to suburbanize has been intense. In the nineteenth century, as cities increased in population, residents moved further and further out. In addition, it often resulted in the extension of the physical boundaries of the big cities. Thus, Boston annexed Roxbury, Dorchester, and Brighton; New York annexed Brooklyn and Staten Island; and Cleveland annexed Ohio City, Glenville, East Cleveland, and West Cleveland. Although annexation continues in many cities, for many others metropolitan expansion has far outstripped central city governance. Beginning in the early twentieth century, each generation has constructed a ring of suburbs such that a modern metropolitan area resembles a pinwheel with the central city at the very center of a swirl of prewar, postwar, 1960s, 1970s, 1980s, and 1990s suburban municipalities.

Political fragmentation within the metropolis takes place under a fair degree of economic integration. Cities and suburbs exist within a single metropolitan economy. Generally speaking, their fates have been intertwined. As a recent book has argued, "there is an underlying local economic region of which the city and suburban governmental jurisdictions each comprise only parts" (Barnes and Ledebur, 1998, p. 40). Over time, however, the relationship between city and suburban income has changed dramatically. In 1960, cities were slightly wealthier as a group than the suburbs. By 1990, average city income was only 84 percent of suburban of suburban income (data from Barnes and Ledebur, 1998). Newer data suggests that by some income measures, the city-suburban income disparity has narrowed as cities enjoy better walkability, downtown attractions, and new condominium constructions. The relative rise in city incomes can be healthy for the entire metropolitan area. Data derived from the 2000 census suggests that metropolitan areas with smaller disparities

tend to enjoy more robust empoyment growth than metropolitan areas where suburbs are far wealthier than the metropolis as a whole (Figure 12.4).

A Positive View of Metropolitan Fragmentation

The two public officials quoted previously—Myron Orfield and David Rusk—help to make the case against excessive metropolitan fragmentation. Indeed such views have been most vocally expressed by concerned politicians as well as by academic social scientists. Because these experts have assembled a great deal of information, we will spend some time examining their case against excessive fragmentation. It would not be fair, however, to ignore those people who believe that metropolitan fragmentation, of the sort found primarily in the United States but also elsewhere, can have positive implications.

One approach that advocates fragmented government may be labeled **polycentrism**. Overarching this perspective is the belief that big metropolitan-scale governments can become remote and unresponsive to local interests. A citizen is likely to be more successful fighting city hall if the city is small. Moreover, anyone who has dealt with a vast urban bureaucracy knows that its size and complexity can be intimidating. Councilors may be responsible to tens of thousands of constituents, services are arrayed within hierarchical agencies, and citizens may have trouble just finding the right person to talk to in order to register a complaint.

A related point is that a greater number of suburban governments present people with greater options for where to live. The **Tiebout hypothesis**, named after economist Charles Tiebout, maintains that people seek a better fit between their tolerance for taxes and their demands for services. The choice of a community can be seen as a market decision. Some communities may offer more services, albeit at the cost of higher taxes, whereas other communities offer fewer services and lower taxes or perhaps some other trade-off, like the presence of a revenue-generating convention center or shopping mall. Young singles and the elderly may care little about the schools and choose not to live in

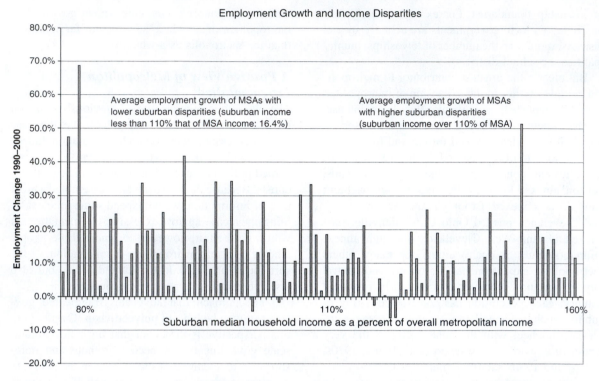

Figure 12.4 This graph examines the 99 largest MSAs in 2000 and ranges them from the metropolitan areas (on the left) where suburban income is less than metropolitan area income to those metropolitan areas (on the right) where suburban income is much greater than metropolitan income. Those metropolitan areas where suburban incomes are fairly close to metropolitan incomes (up to 110 percent of MSA incomes) enjoy more robust employment growth than metropolitan areas with much richer suburbs.

communities that offer and pay for quality public education.

Political or lifestyle arguments can be made for multiple municipal choices as well. For example, the incorporated city of West Hollywood, California, is dominated politically by gay men and lesbian women. As a result, gays and lesbians throughout the Los Angeles metro area can choose to live in a community whose laws, public officials, and services will be friendlier to their lifestyle (Figure 12.5). Other communities, like Monterey Park, cater to residents who are ethnically Chinese. The list goes on. Pick any large metropolitan area, and you will find clear variations in the character of the surrounding suburbs.

Even without this kind of variety, polycentrists argue that smaller communities provide a more personal touch. People have a greater voice in how government is run, and local government officials are more attuned to the needs of the people they serve. Some communities have gone so far as to establish a computer network linking all residents together (Box 12.2). Metropolitan fragmentation combines the interpersonal advantages of living in a small town with the benefits of residing within a big city. It is a win-win situation, according to the polycentrists, which is why people have consistently chosen this path through their residential choices, by voting against annexation, and through efforts to preserve local autonomy.

Figure 12.5 West Hollywood, California (in the Los Angeles basin) is one of the first cities run by an openly gay administration. Pride in this achievement is manifested by the pink triangles along Santa Monica Boulevard.

Finally, many observers of America's new municipal geography have noted the emergence of edge cities (discussed in Chapter 6). These new urban forms are often found outside the central-city boundaries, within incorporated suburbs or unincorporated county lands. The prosperity and capacity of edge cities have come to overshadow that of the traditional downtown. Proponents of edge city development, including those helping to build these complexes, feel that fragmented governments serve the logic of edge cities better than would a single consolidated government, which may be tempted to impose more rules and regulations.

Fiscal Disparities

Although metropolitan fragmentation has its proponents, it has also been decried for a number of reasons. These criticisms take many forms, but one factor that comes up repeatedly in various arguments is **fiscal equity**. As we discussed earlier, local governments are capable of assessing taxes. The problem is that they vary in their **tax base**, which refers to all of the taxable property within the local boundaries. It may also refer to sales receipts if the locality is given a share of sales tax revenues, or income if a local income tax is assessed. Other taxable items may be included as well. In most cases, however, property taxes are the dominant source, providing about three-quarters of local tax revenue. The tax base is important because it represents the "principal" or "wealth" from which revenue can be generated. To get the same amount of revenue from a small tax base as from a large tax base requires a higher **tax rate**, or the percentage of the base (be it property, income, sales, or whatever) that is assessed. Localities with large tax bases are able to offer their residents a lower tax rate. Conversely, localities with a lower tax base must assess a high tax rate in order to receive the same amount of revenue.

What accounts for differences in the tax base? In most places, the key factor is property values. Expensive housing generates much more revenue than moderately priced housing. A fully developed community enjoys higher property values than a community with a lot of undeveloped land. Localities also rely on taxes generated from commercial and industrial property. Factories, warehouses, stores, offices—all of these are subject to taxation. Clearly, more revenue will come out of places with a lot of nonresidential activity. Vacant storefronts, empty offices, and industrial "brownfields" (sites where factories were once located but that, because of cleanup problems, are difficult to reuse) procure no revenue (Figure 12.6). In some instances, commercial and industrial property is also taxed at a higher rate, which creates an even greater advantage to certain localities.

The differences in property values are one source of the fiscal inequities between central cities and surrounding suburban communities (Figure 12.7). The lower per capita property value can put central cities at a disadvantage. The simple dichotomy between poor central cities and rich suburbs masks a great deal of complexity. Remember, though, that historically central cities and their central business districts enjoyed high property values, mostly because they contained high-rise office buildings, luxury apartments, and the like. Several downtowns still enjoy this advantage: downtown revivals during the 1980s and 1990s led to a major enhancement in property values and helped to anchor city-wide fortunes. Myron Orfield (1997) has argued that the major

BOX 12.2   TECHNOLOGY AND URBAN GEOGRAPHY

NETWORKING COMMUNITY

Computer technology has been touted as a way to improve productivity, find quick answers to questions, and to engage with the wider world of information. But can computer technology help to enhance a sense of community? This issue has gained additional salience as observers have noted an increased isolation among families within modern cities and a decline of what we might consider "community." There were also some fears that computer technology, rather than aiding community, might in fact weaken it, summoning up visions of people isolated in their computer hutches and reluctant to engage people in the real world.

A number of communities are putting these notions to the test with the introduction of community networks, often placed within a subdivision, a set of buildings, or a small town. The value of these networks (often termed an intranet) is that it helps to link together all members of the community, providing a cyber-alternative to a physical community forum. It also becomes part of the promotional material of the community as well, promising a convenient source of information and input, all accessible via the family room.

Several studies have been conducted on the value of community intranets around the world. One study, written by Alladi Venkatesh and associates, examined a networked community in Orange County, California. This study showed that the community intranet served several roles. It was a central clearinghouse for announcements about community events, garage sales, and information from the local schools. It provided a meeting ground for people who might have shared interests, furthering different groups and social clubs. Finally, it provided a forum for community views and exchanges. Members could air their views about everything from "trash collection to more serious problems concerning traffic congestions to the planning of the next shopping mall" (Venkatesh et al., 2003). The use of this intranet varied, as might be expected, but it seemed especially useful for stay-at-home mothers and working women who were more likely to utilize the public forum aspects of the community intranet.

Probably the most comprehensive study has been conducted by urbanists Keith Hampton and Barry Wellman looking at the pseudonymously named "Netville," a suburb of Toronto (Figure B12.3). Survey research and participant observations indicated that the presence of a community intranet had a substantial effect on neighborhood interaction. Residents who used the intranet developed more ties with neighbors, people were more likely to sit on their front porches (despite most having spacious backyard patios) to watch the street, and neighbors often pursued topics first broached on the intranet. The intranet also became a forum for political action, reducing the barriers that busy suburbanites often experience. In sum, the use of community intranets help to enhance the sense of community.

Figure B12.3 Welcome to "The Smart Community."

Figure 12.6 Older industrial cities have been forced to contend with the decline in their industrial base and also the fact that factory land is often not safe for other uses. Brownfields—vacant lots where factories once operated—need to be cleaned and decontaminated before they can be used again.

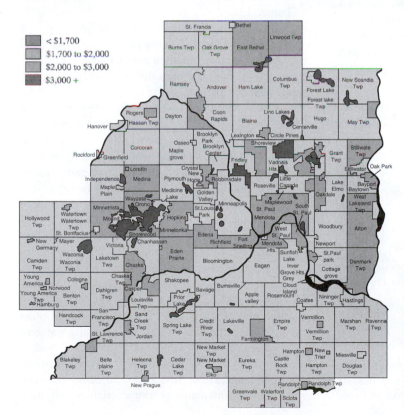

< $1,700
$1,700 to $2,000
$2,000 to $3,000
$3,000 +

Figure 12.7 This map shows fiscal inequities within the Minneapolis-St. Paul MSA. The effective net tax capacity is the potential tax revenue from a community's property tax base after any fiscal disparities or distribution are accounted for. In the southwest suburbs that Myron Orfield calls "the favored quarter," effective net tax capacity is high. In general, the tax capacity in the cities is lower. (*Source:* Orfield, 1997.)

discrepancies do not always exist between central cities and suburbs. Rather, the inner-ring suburbs, with declining tax bases and no large commercial centers, often get the worst of the deal. Often the worst-off areas are suburbs with a declining tax base and few assets. Camden, New Jersey; Chelsea, Massachusetts; and East Cleveland, Ohio, are among the fiscally worst-off places in the United States. Consider East St. Louis, Illinois (Figure 12.8):

> The city, which is 98 percent black, has no obstetric services, no regular trash collection, and few jobs.... Only three of the 13 buildings on Missouri Avenue, one of the city's main thoroughfares, are occupied.... Fiscal shortages have forced the layoff of 1,170 of the city's 1,400 employees in the past 12 years. The city, which is often unable to buy heating fuel or toilet paper for the city hall, recently announced that it might have to cashier all but 10 percent of the remaining work force of 230. In 1989, the mayor announced that he might need to sell the city hall and all six fire stations to raise needed cash.... East St. Louis is mortgaged into the next century but has the highest property-tax rate in the state. (Kozol, 1991, p. 8)

The list goes on: no garbage pick up, dysfunctional sewers, hemorrhaging budgets for police and fire

Figure 12.8 Some of the worst blight is found outside of major cities, in poor suburbs. This picture shows a scene from East St. Louis, Illinois, a suburb of St. Louis.

protection, and a city teetering on the edge of bankruptcy.

In Minneapolis-St. Paul, the affluent southern and western suburbs enjoy a tax base that is one-third greater per capita than those of the two central cities, the inner-ring suburbs and the working-class suburbs. The Twin Cities have worked to reduce such disparities.

Although they are worlds away from the distress of some inner-belt suburbs, the rapidly urbanizing places on the metropolitan fringe prompt some of the biggest demands for services, which can create fiscal problems of their own. New residents require new schools, new infrastructure, and greater protective services. People may be unwilling to pay for these services initially, but they do pay eventually. Studies that measure the revenue and costs associated with each type of development have shown, in fact, that the costs associated with new housing usually end up exceeding any revenue gain (see Chapter 13).

The other major aspect of fiscal inequity is a **differential need for services**. Central cities tend to include the metropolitan area's poorest residents, they tend to have the most difficulty with crime, and they also are likely to suffer an aging infrastructure. Moreover, central-city schools—a huge consumer of local monies—are burdened with these same problems of poverty, crime, and a substandard physical plant. Greater service needs, including welfare spending, police protection, street and sewer maintenance, and education, require more funding. It is often for these reasons that big central cities need more money relative to their population.

The combination of the differences in the tax base and the differential needs for services creates a situation of **metropolitan polarization** between resource-poor municipalities and resource-rich municipalities. Municipalities with a low tax base and a high need for social services must beg for more money from the state. They are generally unpleasant places to live because the strain on the budget makes it extremely difficult for them to provide the basic necessities, much less to afford luxuries like park maintenance or extracurricular activities.

Towns that enjoy a high tax base and a low need for social services can be good places to live, providing their residents with a lot of extras. These disparities lead to the flight of middle- and high-income residents—those with the ability to make housing choices—from resource-poor municipalities to resource-rich municipalities. Low-income residents, however, have no choice but to remain. Businesses also move and take with them their property tax dollars, which only serves to further increase polarization. Suburban communities may also use exclusionary zoning, discussed in Chapter 13, to keep out certain groups of people.

COUNTERING THE FRAGMENTED METROPOLIS

Several efforts have been made to reduce metropolitan fragmentation or to at least alleviate some of its worst effects. Here, disagreements often erupt because all types of coordination generally correspond with some loss in local control. Wealthy communities, for instance, may be less willing to cede autonomy to a large organization if it means that they lose some of their fiscal authority. Suburban communities often see the central city as a threat to their autonomy and may rightly believe that the big city will dominate any metropolitan organizations.

At the same time, all communities need to work together at some point in time for mutual benefit. Several projects that aid the economy and accessibility of all communities, such as airports, need to be handled at the metropolitan level. Likewise, the expansion of highways or other types of transit, such as commuter rail, need to be undertaken with the agreement of all affected communities or else the project will simply fail. Even if they are not politically united, metropolitan regions operate as a single economic entity and so need to coordinate policy to pursue particular goals. Likewise, metropolitan communities are also mutually affected by environmental decisions. Among these are the location of toxic dumps, watershed issues, and air pollution. So they need to coordinate on this basis as well.

Annexations

Several methods exist to counter metropolitan fragmentation, but the most simple is **annexation**. Annexation occurs when one municipality adds another incorporated municipality or unincorporated land to its territory. In the United States, cities long relied on annexation in order to ensure that their political reach extended as far out as their rapidly expanding population. A look at any state or metropolitan map confirms the legacy of past annexations: a region's major cities are generally much larger in area than the other towns and cities. They achieved this size through annexation.

There is a great deal of variation, however, among cities in terms of their areas. The most populous city, New York, grew rapidly in the nineteenth century and was able to annex significant territory, in effect combining the territory of five counties. Its area of 308 square miles is large, but it is smaller than the areas of Los Angeles, Houston, San Diego, Phoenix, San Antonio, Dallas, Indianapolis, Jacksonville, Nashville, Oklahoma City, Kansas City, Anchorage, Chesapeake, and Augusta. All of these are significantly smaller cities than New York, some only 1/40th the population size! You may also notice from the above list that, with the exception of Indianapolis, almost none of these territorially large cities are located in the Northeast or industrial Midwest. It is mostly the newer cities in the South and West that have successfully expanded through annexation. As a result, they have kept better pace with their expanding population. The older cities in the Northeast have not been able to expand, and, as a result, they capture a smaller percentage of suburban growth.

Elastic Cities
David Rusk (2003), the former mayor of Albuquerque, New Mexico, has hypothesized and provided evidence that "old cities are complacent—young cities are ambitious." He argues that annexation is the single best way for cities to remain fiscally healthy and economically prosperous. He contrasts elastic cities that can continue to annex with inelastic cities that can no longer annex and so are severely underbounded. By **elastic**

cities, he means cities that have expanded their city limits aggressively through either annexation (e.g., Houston, Columbus, and Raleigh) or consolidation (e.g., Indianapolis and Nashville) with their home counties. In contrast, **inelastic cities** (e.g., Detroit, Cleveland, and Milwaukee) "did not budge their city limits." Because elastic cities expand their city limits, they *capture* suburban growth. In contrast, inelastic cities *contribute* to suburban growth. Rusk further argues that all cities were elastic in their youth, but that several cities have lost the capacity to expand. Rusk designates a city by levels of elasticity: zero, low, medium, high, and hyperelasticity. Each level is a function of the degree to which a city's boundary expanded and the city's density levels. Table 12.2 shows some of the differences among these types of cities. Rusk further argues that higher levels of elasticity correspond with higher levels of job growth and a better bond rating, meaning better fiscal health. A city such as Tucson, Arizona, while hemmed in somewhat by federal and Native American lands, has plenty of room to expand its municipal boundaries and continues to map out new pathways of growth (Figure 12.9).

It is probably accurate to say that, given the choice, most cities would prefer to expand their territory. This would enable them to capture a more affluent tax base. What is stopping them are the desires of suburbs to maintain their autonomy and the policies of state governments, which have been notably stingy in allowing annexation to proceed. For example, most states mandate that the annexation of another incorporated area requires the consent of both jurisdictions, usually in the form of dual referenda. This requirement, combined with the ease by which suburbs can incorporate, means that cities can quickly be hemmed in by incorporated municipalities. For cities surrounded by unincorporated land, annexation is generally easier. Here again, state laws vary. In many states unincorporated lands can be annexed by the city without the approval of the residents of the territory to be annexed, provided there is some contiguity between the city and the other lands. Oklahoma, for instance, simply requires that a city surround an area on three sides. In other cases, resident approval is necessary, but there are enough incentives so that suburbanites accede to the request.

Even within the same state, cities can vary significantly in their ability to annex territory. Some cities have been able to pursue a more aggressive annexation policy. Several cities have been prescient in grabbing surrounding rural land before it gets too urbanized, offering the extension of city services to the new territory. For example, in the early part of the twentieth century, Los Angeles aggressively expanded by withholding water to recalcitrant suburbs. Before this time, San Francisco had more than three times the population of Los Angeles,

Table 12.2   How Annexation Strategy Affects the Characteristics of Cities

Type of Elasticty*	Metro Population within Central City %	City Density 1950	Change in Area %, 1950–2000	Average Size 2000 (mi. sq)	City-Suburban Income Ratio %	Manufacturing Job Growth % 1969–1999	Non-manufacturing Job Growth % 1969–1999
Zero Elasticity	25	12,720	1	58	68	−40	66
Low Elasticity	28	6,879	21	84	78	−23	92
Medium Elasticity	33	5,280	193	79	89	28	177
High Elasticity	36	4,822	342	146	97	18	168
Hyperelasticity	54	4,729	944	345	102	65	194

Source: Rusk, 2003.
*Examples: Zero Elasticity: New York, Chicago, Boston, San Francisco, Cleveland; Low Elasticity: New Orleans, Seattle, Atlanta, Los Angeles; Medium Elasticity: Denver, Charlotte, Madison, Portland (OR); High Elasticity: San Antonio, Phoenix, San Jose, Lincoln Hyperelasticity: Fort Worth, San Diego, Houston, Anchorage.

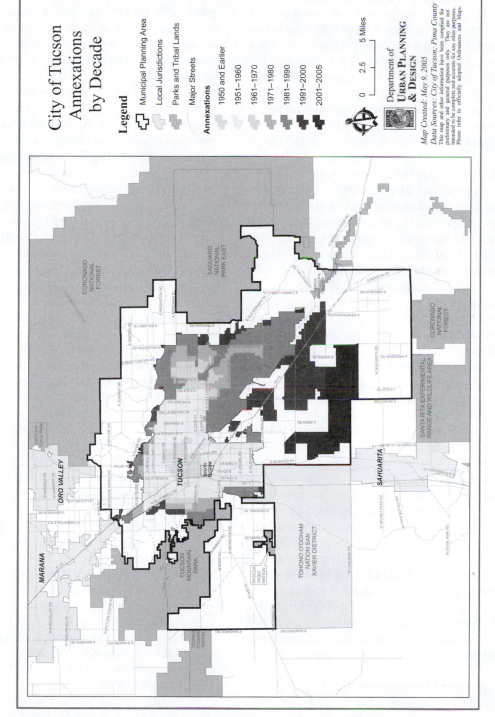

Figure 12.9 This map shows how Tuscon, Arizona, has continued to expand during the first decade of the 21st century.

but it now has only one-fifth its population and one-tenth its area. Similarly, in the latter part of the century, St. Louis and Kansas City have traded places; that is Kansas City has replaced St. Louis as Missouri's largest city. Whereas Kansas City has expanded to an area of 311 square miles, St. Louis is circumscribed at only 62 square miles. In these cases, Los Angeles and Kansas City took advantage of annexation opportunities and were able to avoid being hemmed in by incorporated municipalities.

City-County Consolidation   Another strategy that has been utilized by some cities has been the creation of large united governments, in essence effecting a mass expansion in one swift move. This is often accomplished through the consolidation of the central city with the surrounding county and is termed **city-county consolidation**. Indianapolis is one of the best examples of this strategy. In 1969, the state of Indiana merged the old city with Marion County, creating what was called "Unigov." The consolidation was not complete—several local governments and special districts were left intact, and the new city still was divided into 22 school districts—but the new city was able to capitalize on a much bigger tax base and enjoyed a major boost in population.

Another alternative to annexation is the creation of a **joint economic development district (JEDD)**. A JEDD may be defined as a joint contract for economic development between a city and an unincorporated township. The city provides specified services in exchange for some of the township's revenue. This approach has been used in Akron, Ohio, as a way of collecting some revenues from incorporated suburbs without a direct takeover. The advantage to the suburbs is that they are able to acquire city services while retaining their autonomy. The advantage to the city is that it is able to share in some of the new tax revenue that is created by the JEDD. Promoters of JEDD agreements argue that these agreements offer the benefits of annexation without the loss of local suburban control.

Metropolitan Government

Even within metropolitan areas in which annexation and consolidation are impossible, several levels of

coordination are seen among the various municipalities. To be effective, this coordination should be institutionalized in some way. Every metropolitan area contains metropolitan-wide organizations: transportation authorities, regional planning commissions, park boards, and so forth. In many cases the county government helps coordinate activities of its constituent cities and towns. True coordination, however, comes with the creation of a **metropolitan government** that enjoys a broad range of authorities superseding those of the municipalities, especially some form of fiscal authority. Some of the hallmarks of metropolitan government include direct election of a regional council, tax-raising authority (the ability to levy property taxes or sales taxes on metropolitan residents), tax base sharing (where wealthier municipalities within the metropolitan area subsidize poorer municipalities), and regional planning decisions (decisions on where future growth should be sited). Unlike consolidation, the local governments are left intact, but they cede many of their powers to the metropolitan scale of authority.

The creation of metropolitan governments has been complicated by the fact that suburban residents are often suspicious of what its impact will be on them and their autonomy. They want to avoid city taxes and city problems, and they wish to see themselves as still living in a small town, even if it happens to be right next to a big city! Urban residents may also be leery. This is often the case when urban minority groups have gained power within a city government and look on metropolitanization as a way of diluting their influence. Federal and state governments have gone back and forth in their policies, sometimes encouraging regional governments and other times promoting political decentralization. Certainly, the Canadian government promotes fiscal equalization among municipalities. Not surprisingly, metropolitan governments are found in all of Canada's largest cities, although with varying levels of efficacy. Toronto's metropolitan government has been notably successful, whereas Montreal's has been less so (Box 12.3).

Within the United States, true metropolitan governments are the exception rather than the rule.

BOX 12.3   METROPOLITANIZATION AND LANGUAGE IN MONTREAL

In the United States, metropolitan areas are marked by differences in race and class. In Montreal, there is also a linguistic aspect to these disparities. Once the largest city in Canada and still the major city in French-speaking Quebec, Montreal has long functioned as a bilingual city. English speakers, or Anglophones, continue to reside alongside French speakers, or Francophones. Immigrant groups that flock to Montreal are also part of this mix. Greater Montreal's linguistic geography has long complicated efforts to fashion a metropolitan solution to fragmentation. Despite a steady stream of outmigration among Anglophones—the English-speaking population declined by 13 percent between 1971 and 1991—this segregated pattern is still apparent (Figure B12.4).

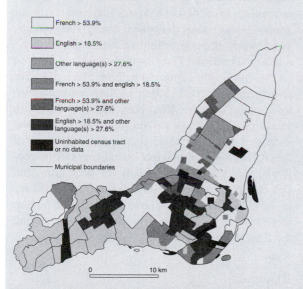

Figure B12.4 Linguistic distribution on Montreal Island in Quebec. This map shows the distribution of French, English, and other populations in relationship to their island-wide percentages. Clearly, the Anglophone population is concentrated on the western side of the island, whereas the Francophone population is found on the eastern side. Immigrant populations, who have other mother tongues, are more likely found in central Montreal itself. (*Source:* Germain and Rose, 2000.)

Embedded within the spatial segregation of the linguistic groups, there continues to be a pattern of institutional segregation. In 1978, a Quebec government commission declared that:

> Herein lies the explanation of this peculiar phenomenon of two communities living side by side without having to communicate with each other.... This double network of institutions and services...is seen at the legislative, judicial, educational and hospital levels; it is evident in the information media and entertainment fields; it applies in the area of culture and even at the...provincial administrative level. (Sancton, 1978, p. 69)

The twentieth-century history of annexation and municipal government in Montreal suggests that the city attempted to fashion metropolitan fragmentation in order to retain linguistic divisions. Once Montreal became a French-majority city, annexations clearly targeted French-majority territory. English-majority townships to the west were scrupulously avoided and to this day are home to solid Anglophone populations.

At well over half a million people, the English-speaking population in Montreal exceeds that of all but a few Canadian cities. It has the numerical substance to uphold key institutions. The spatial concentration of Anglophones in parts of Montreal city itself and in some suburban municipalities has enabled them to exercise a degree of political clout that would not have been possible had they been more evenly dispersed. It has also prevented many solidly English townships from being incorporated into the city of Montreal and risk losing their cultural autonomy. In fact, towns like Westmount and Mount Royal were so tenaciously independent that, as the city of Montreal expanded through annexation, they were virtually surrounded. Recent political acts, especially those related to the dominance of the French language, have undercut much of this political power, but it still exists and helps to shape Montreal's metropolitan configuration.

Reasons for this include the greater fiscal disparities between cities and suburbs, perceived differences in educational quality, the frequently significant differences in the racial and ethnic geography of cities and suburbs, and the fact that most metropolitan areas spill out beyond county lines. Despite these impediments, however, some metropolitan governments have emerged. For example, in 1957 Miami developed a strong metropolitan government with Dade County, but it has not been able to extend this into surrounding counties. Most urban geographers point to Portland, Oregon, and the metropolitan government of Minneapolis and St. Paul as the two most successful examples of multicounty metropolitan governments in the United States.

The Portland Metropolitan Services District was developed during the 1970s and has responsibility for regional planning, transportation policy, and environmental quality. Like Miami-Dade, Portland's metropolitan government is directly elected, giving it a legitimacy not often found elsewhere in the United States. It has been most noted for putting a relatively stringent land-use policy into effect, with a real growth boundary that concentrates development in certain areas. Portland's metro does not have a regional tax base sharing arrangement, however. Although the levels of fiscal disparities are lower in Portland than in most other metropolitan regions, pronounced differences still exist between wealthy suburbs with a high and growing tax base and poor suburbs with a lower and sometimes declining tax base.

The Twin Cities Metropolitan Council was created in 1967 and includes St. Paul, Minneapolis, seven counties, and dozens of suburban municipalities. The original charge was to develop long-range plans for the entire region by focusing growth in certain places. Over the years, the Metropolitan Council has also acquired jurisdiction over regional sewer, transit, and land-use planning. The council itself is not popularly elected, but appointed. However, the council has fiscal authority. It can raise its own revenues and issue bonds. One item that also aids in the metropolitan mission is the fact that the Twin Cities region has a partial tax base sharing program that allows each community to gain from development in the region by sharing the fiscal wealth, although strong disparities still remain. Compared to other metropolitan regions, the Twin Cities Metropolitan Council demonstrates remarkable success in promoting a true regionalist perspective. It has not altered the basic dynamics of fiscal disparities and metropolitan polarization, however, and it finds itself bypassed by the overall expansion of the metro area.

Wrapping Up

This chapter has shown how the economic and social development of the nineteenth and twentieth centuries helped spur the development of civic institutions. As cities became the places where most Americans lived and as the cities themselves became larger and more populous, urban government was compelled to expand. Services that we take for granted today, such as police, firefighters, streets, and sewers, became organized and supervised by urban governments. The increase of services required an expansion of revenue, something that cities have sometimes had trouble acquiring. Expansion has also led to more complex local governments, often with several power centers and shifting coalitions. In the latter part of the twentieth century, the expansion of the city beyond its municipal boundaries and the geographical disparities found between poor cities and rich suburbs have led to some acute fiscal problems in the old urban core and have encouraged efforts to solve what is at its heart a problem of trying to find the right political solution.

Readings

Barnes, William, and Larry Ledebur. 1998. *The New Regional Economies: The U.S. Common Market and the Global Economy*. Thousand Oaks, CA: Sage Publications.

Bender, Carrie. 2001. The Role of Community-Based Organizations and the Local Government in the Creation and Maintenance of Racially Integrated

Communities in the Cleveland Metropolitan Area. MA thesis, Kent State University, Kent, OH.

Brown, Richard. 1974. "The Emergence of Urban Society in Rural Massachusetts, 1760–1820," *Journal of American History*, Vol. 61, No. 1, pp. 29–51.

Dahl, Robert. 1961. *Who Governs? Democracy and Power in an American City*. New Haven: Yale University Press.

Germain, Annick, and Damaris Rose. 2000. *Montreal: The Quest for a Metropolis*. New York: Wiley.

Gerth, H. H., and C. Wright Mills. 1958. *From Max Weber: Essays in Sociology*. New York: Galaxy Books.

Gordon, Mary McDougall. 1978. "Patriots and Christians: A Reassessment of Nineteenth-Century School Reformers," *Journal of Social History*, Vol. 11 pp. 554–574.

Hamilton, David. 2000. "Organizing Government Structure and Governance Functions in Metropolitan Areas in Response to Growth and Change: A Critical Overview," *Journal of Urban Affairs*, Vol. 22, No. 1, pp. 65–84.

Hampton, Keith and Barry Wellman. 2003. "Neighboring in Netville: How the Internet Supports Community and Social Capital in a Wired Suburb," *City & Community*, Vol. 2, No. 4, pp. 277–311.

Harrigan, John. 1989. *Political Change in the Metropolis*. Glenview, IL: Scott, Foresman.

Hemmens, George, and Janet McBride. 1993. "Planning and Development Decision Making in the Chicago Region." In Donald Rothblatt and Andrew Sancton, eds., *Metropolitan Governance: American/Canadian Intergovernmental Perspectives*. Berkeley: Institute of Governmental Studies Press, University of California.

Hunter, Floyd, 1980. *Community Power Succession: Atlanta's Policy Makers Revisited*. Chapel Hill: University of North Carolina Press.

Johnston, R. J. 1982. *Geography and the State: An Essay in Political Geography*. New York: St. Martin's Press.

Judd, Dennis, and Todd Swanstrom. 1994. *City Politics: Private Power and Public Policy*. New York: HarperCollins.

Katz, Bruce and Robert Lang. 2003. *Redefining Urban and Suburban America: Evidence from Census 2000*. Washington, D.C.: Brookings Institution Press.

Kozol, Jonathan. 1991. *Savage Inequalities: Children in America's Schools*. New York: Crown Publishers.

Lockridge, Kenneth. 1970. *A New England Town: The First Hundred Years*. New York: W. W. Norton.

Lucy, William and David Phillips. 2006. "Cities' Performance Improves Since 2000 Census." http://www.virginia.edu/topnews/releases2006/20060410cities_study.html (accessed 5/15/2006).

Monkonnen, Eric. 1988. *America Becomes Urban: The Development of U.S. Cities and Towns 1780–1980*. Berkeley: University of California Press.

Orfield, Myron. 1997. *Metropolitics: A Regional Agenda for Community and Stability*. Washington, D.C.: Brookings Institution Press.

Ross, Bernard, and Myron Levine. 1996. *Urban Politics: Power in Metropolitan America*. Itasca, IL: F. E. Peacock Publishers.

Rothblatt, Donald, and Andrew Sancton, 1998. eds., *Metropolitan Governance Revisited: American/Canadian Intergovernmental Perspectives*. Berkeley: Institute of Governmental Studies Press.

Rusk, David. 2003. *Cities without Suburbs, Third Edition: A Census 2000 Update*. Washington, D.C.: Woodrow Wilson Press.

Sancton, Andrew. 1978. The Impact of French, English Differences on Government Policies. PhD Thesis, Univ. of Oxford.

Short, John. 1996. *The Urban Order*. Cambridge, MA: Blackwell Publishers.

Stoker, Gerry, and Karen Mossberger. 1994. "Urban Regime Theory in Comparative Perspective," *Environment and Planning C: Government and Policy*, Vol. 12, pp. 195–212.

Swanstrom, Todd. 2001. "What We Argue about When We Argue about Regionalism," *Journal of Urban Affairs*, Vol. 23, No. 5, pp. 479–496.

U.S. Census Bureau. 1999. *Statistical Abstract of the United States*.

Venkatesh, Alladi, Steven Chen, and Victor Gonzales. 2003. "A Study of a Southern California Wired Community: Where Technology Meets Social Utopianism." Paper presented at the Human–Computer 10th International Conference, Crete, Greece.

Wade, Richard C. 1959. *The Urban Frontier*. Chicago: University of Chicago Press.

CHAPTER 13

PLANNING THE BETTER CITY

Make no little plans. They have no magic to stir men's blood and probably themselves will not be realized. Make big plans; aim high in hope and work, remembering that a noble, logical diagram
once recorded will never die, but long after we are gone will be a living thing, asserting itself with ever-growing insistency.

—DANIEL BURNHAM, ADDRESS OF 1907,
FROM HALL, 1996, P. 174

Today, we may envision urban planning as something that occurs in a government office, undertaken by professional civil servants who work with elected politicians, community activists, and property developers. This is the image of urban planning as it evolved during the course of the twentieth century. Although accurate in part, this is an incomplete view. Planning is something that has been done from the very earliest human settlement, where villages were constructed according to constraints, customs, and, likely, the decisions of the society. Later, cities were clearly designed according to certain precepts.

Urban planning has a rich history, dating back to the ancient Greeks. It was Hippodamus who introduced the idea that settlements could be designed in a rational and orderly way. Of course, such sentiments did not always lead to ordered communities. Some communities were exceptionally well ordered, often along cosmological lines, with the city being set up as a microcosm of heaven on earth, and with particular attention paid to the orientation of the structures within the city and to the city itself. Many other communities, however, grew by accretion, as bits and pieces of the physical structure of the settlement—streets, houses, places of worship,

businesses, and industries—were added bit by bit. The resurgence of the capitalist city, discussed in Chapter 2, often included some planned elements: The wall, port facilities, canals, and marketplaces were maintained in the public interest. However, the sections of the city in which most people lived and worked were generally quite chaotic. Planning emerged as a means of instilling some order into the urban environment. Professional planning began to take form in the late nineteenth century, as urban areas grew larger and more complex. By the early twentieth century, planning moved away from the ideals of a few charismatic visionaries toward the practice of a cadre of dedicated and certified professionals.

Today, planning is carried out by many people who would not necessarily be considered professional planners. Planning takes place whether or not "planners" are involved. Professional planning has evolved as a means to add rational thought, methods, and experience to the process. Sometimes planners leave a bigger mess than they found, but often they perform an important function of minimizing costs and increasing benefits.

In this chapter we discuss the rationales, bases, and activities of modern urban planning. The tools of modern planning—the comprehensive plan, zoning, fiscal incentives, and others—developed throughout the course of the twentieth century. Today, some of these tools are under attack as helping to contribute to some of problems of modern urban society. At the same time, new planning solutions have been devised and are beginning to be implemented in various communities across the country.

MAKING THE CASE FOR PLANNING

Although they may differ over the extent and details of how cities should be guided, people of just about every political persuasion would agree that some form of urban planning is desirable. The alternative—a city based on the unfettered exercise of the free market—would just be too chaotic. For this reason, every city, town, and village in North America is planned to some degree. Likewise, planning has long been a key element of the development of cities. As we discussed in Chapter 12, demands for particular services—police, fire, education, water, streets—made it necessary to expand the power and authority of municipal governments. During the nineteenth century, the demand for these services grew along with the urban populations. Unprecedented rates of urban growth in North America and Europe, as a consequence of the Industrial Revolution, created an awareness of unprecedented problems and a desire to help alleviate some of these problems. With industrialization, cities expanded at a terrific pace, defying any attempt to instill order. Early industrial cities mixed high population densities, muddy and congested streets, jerry-built housing for the burgeoning worker population, and the polluting engines of the factory and the train. City leaders and gadflies alike began to see that planning could be used as a way to create a more pleasing city, to help uplift the atrocious conditions of the urban poor, and to help protect the property values of the urban rich. From this diverse set of motivations emerged some of the basic rationales of planning, which have led directly to today's planning practices.

Aesthetics

Cities are made up of areas owned by the public, such as streets, parks, government buildings, and schools, and areas owned by private individuals. Although most individual landowners look after their own property, they lack the power to fit individual pieces of property together into a more pleasing whole. As any observer of modern urban landscapes can tell you, this lack of centralized planning can result in a lot of ugliness. For example, in the inner city, property is left unkempt and is sometimes abandoned. Once-viable neighborhoods deteriorate into wastelands of boarded-up buildings, weed-strewn lots, and generalized decay. In the more prosperous parts of the city, the human landscape is overwhelmed by the jumble of parking lots, oversized signs, treeless housing developments, and the like—all connected by strip highways.

The unsightly result has long led some people to search for a more coordinated city. Such an approach was far easier, of course, when cities could be controlled by one person or by a defined elite. For example, during the Baroque era, prior to industrialization, many cities were designed according to the **Grand Manner**. Planning was used to create a cityscape that was monumental—as a means of glorifying the ruler—as well as beautiful. Aesthetic objectives were key in this approach. The ideals of the Grand Manner included

- A coordinated design for streets and avenues that would help connect various monuments, statues, and other focal points;
- Attention to the topography of the site, as the city was aligned so as to create vistas that could overlook the city or certain urban landmarks; and
- Attention to streetscapes, particularly for the main streets in the city. Broad tree-lined boulevards were the rule.

All of these major design features were then superimposed on the streets and buildings of the working city.

Many European cities were designed according to these principles, often under the aegis of a monarch. In France, the city of Versailles was clearly designed at the behest of Louis XIV in the middle seventeenth

Figure 13.1 This aerial view of Washington, D.C., demonstrates the broad lines, vistas, and overall organization that typify the Grand Manner of planning.

century. The best American example of the Grand Manner is Washington, D.C. Here, Pierre-Charles L'Enfant, a planner steeped in Baroque design, was commissioned to create a city from scratch. He designed a layout that departed significantly from either the hodgepodge of streets or the simple grid (Figure 13.1). L'Enfant's original plan was not truly fulfilled during the course of the nineteenth century. However, at the beginning of the twentieth century it was completed under the **McMillan Plan**, which led to the establishment of the Washington Mall, the set of adjoining parks and pools, and the monuments and public buildings within and surrounding it.

The McMillan Plan was part of a larger movement that swept urban planning around the turn of the twentieth century. The **City Beautiful movement** emphasized the creation of an aesthetically pleasing public city. During the Chicago Exposition

of 1893, a prototype city was built with broad, tree-lined avenues, white buildings of uniform height, uniform neoclassical facades, and numerous examples of civic art: monuments, fountains, and reflecting pools.

This demonstration was the brainchild of architect Daniel Burnham, who lived by the credo to "make no small plans." In 1905, Burnham assembled a massive proposal known as the Chicago Plan. This plan created a series of radial and ring roads, stretching out from the center of the city for 60 miles. It also demonstrated how to implement various elements of the City Beautiful movement. Among these elements were an attention to aesthetics; an appreciation for the facts of city expansion; the notion of creating an integrated design; the construction of large, monumental, and coordinated buildings; and the use of natural amenities.

The City Beautiful Movement never achieved the influence that its proponents desired. It was considered too elitist, too expensive, and simply not practical enough. The countermovement to the City Beautiful is sometimes termed the City Practical. However, this movement should be seen less in opposition to the City Beautiful and more in terms of evolution. The **City Practical movement** heralded the rise of professional planning, greater planning specialization, and larger municipal bureaucracies. It incorporated many of the ideals of creating an aesthetically pleasing city, including (1) the design of broad and coordinated urban spaces, (2) the implementation of large-scale plans in many downtown areas, (3) renewed attention to waterfronts and other urban amenities, and (4) an emphasis on historical preservation, which seeks to retain many of the older structures that give individual cities their unique character.

Efficiency

Planning also was motivated by efforts to create a city that could operate more efficiently. This emphasis on efficiency stems from the well-known notion that development projects that make economic sense from the point of view of private developers may impose large public costs borne by everybody.

As cities grew in the nineteenth and early twentieth centuries, much of this concern with inefficiency was tied into problems of congestion. Cities were growing so fast that more and more people were being packed into existing urban space. Densities skyrocketed, with many city blocks containing more than 1,000 people. Encroachment of properties onto street right of ways, a lack of adequate ventilation, and buildings built up so far as to intrude on sunlight—all of these generated momentum to find some way of controlling congestion.

This was true in both European and American cities. In Paris, one solution was initiated by Baron von Haussmann, who in the 1840s was given broad authority to "regularize" Paris by demolishing congested properties in the inner city and creating a series of long, regular streets lined with imposing apartment buildings, with stores and offices located on the first floor. This process of clearing and redesigning existing cities—with little regard given to those who inhabited the soon-to-be demolished buildings—was termed **Haussmannization** and became a code word for massive urban renewal.

In the United States, concerns about congestion reached a fever pitch in the first decade of the twentieth century. They even led to a well-attended Exhibition of Population Congestion that detailed the horrors of too many people in too small a space. The main solutions to congestion consisted of demolishing existing structures and moving residents of the inner city further out. This was difficult to put into practice at this time, however, because many people did not have the transportation and financial means to move out. Therefore, these ideas were not fully acted on until the 1950s and 1960s when the **urban renewal** movement, backed by billions of federal dollars, cleared and redeveloped about 1,000 square miles of urban land and in the process demolished 600,000 housing units that housed about 2 million people (Figure 13.2).

In the latter part of the twentieth century, at least in affluent countries, worries over congestion eased as many residents did indeed disperse. Ironically, this has generated another set of concerns, framed by the problems of urban sprawl (see Chapter 9). Sprawl is often criticized for creating an enormous array of public costs associated with having to provide

Figure 13.2 Paris in 1870 shows the dramatic effects of Haussmannization.

services to residential and commercial developments in far-flung districts. Costs associated with maintaining roadways for automobiles, extending sewer and water lines to reach those new developments (or suffer the environmental risks of septic tanks), ensuring adequate police and fire protection, and building enough schools are all priorities of the public sector. Table 13.1 enumerates the costs of these community services. For different towns, this indicates that each dollar in revenue generated by residential development costs a community between $1.06 and a $1.67 in services. Commercial and industrial development yields more revenue than expenses, and leaving land open is also economical. There is some dispute regarding these figures, as developers often argue that new homeowners generate more income for the community than these figures acknowledge. How communities choose to deal with this issue has become a major concern of many planners and government officials. We discuss some of these growth management strategies in a later section.

Social Equity Planning

Private urban development helps to create vibrant, bustling cities that can accommodate the needs and desires of many segments of the population. Yet, the poorest members of the society are often left out.

Land-use decisions are rarely made with their interests in mind. The poor are either neglected—given no housing choices, few shopping opportunities, and no greenspace—or they are exploited by predatory lenders, high-interest "money shops," and slumlords.

Historically, urban development left the poor on the fringes away from the city's services and the city's protection. The phenomenon of squatter settlements (discussed in Chapter 15) shows how this occurs in modern cities in the developing world. With industrialization, the location of the poor within the city shifted. Many poor people found their way to the inner city, as the more affluent population moved away from the noise and pollution. In London, Manchester, New York, Chicago, and other industrial cities, people lived in some truly horrible housing that was badly constructed, poorly ventilated, and lacked adequate sewage facilities. People were stuffed into tenements, and it was not uncommon to find more than four people sharing a room.

Concerns became more pronounced in the mid-nineteenth century. A health inspector at that time, Dr. John Griscom, wrote about the burgeoning tenements of New York:

> You must descend to them, you must feel the blast of foul air as it meets your face on opening the door; you must grope in the dark, or

Table 13.1 Cost of Community Services

	Residential	Commercial/ Industrial	Open Land
Connecticut			
Hebron	1.00:1.06	1.00:0.42	1.00:0.36
Massachusetts			
Agawam	1.00:1.05	1.00:0.41	1.00:0.30
Deerfield	1.00:1.16	1.00:0.37	1.00:0.29
Gill	1.00:1.15	1.00:0.34	1.00:0.29
New York			
Beekman	1.00:1.12	1.00:0.18	1.00:0.48
North East	1.00:1.36	1.00:0.29	1.00:0.21
Ohio			
Madison Village	1.00:1.67	1.00:0.20	1.00:0.38
Madison Township	1.00:1.40	1.00:0.25	1.00:0.30
Median ratio	1.00:1.16	1.00:0.31	1.00:0.30

hesitate until your eye becomes accustomed to the gloomy place, to enable you to find your way through the entry, over a broken floor, the boards of which are protected from your tread by a half inch of hard dirt; you must inhale the suffocating vapor of the sitting and sleeping rooms; and in the dark, damp recess, endeavor to find the inmates by the sound of their voices, or chance to see their figures moving between you and the flickering blaze of a shaving burning on the hearth. (quoted in Foglesong, 1986, p. 64)

Such conditions led to high rates of mortality, caused by the combined deprivations suffered by the residents of such hovels. Advocates for better health led the charge to improve conditions, but so did advocates of social health. The main worry among the "respectable" members of society was that these conditions would threaten the social peace, breeding moral depravity, discontent, and socialism. Such events as the draft riots in 1863, in which opposition to conscription during the Civil War sparked widespread violence in New York City that resulted in 1,000 deaths, and the anarchist movement made apparent the need to do something.

Most of the resulting efforts were in the area of housing reform, especially the late nineteenth and early twentieth centuries. New York City, as the largest and most congested American city, played a prominent role in the reform movement, but other cities also attempted to regulate housing. Reforms such as building codes, which allowed only a certain percentage of the lot to be occupied by a tenement building and established minimum requirements for bathrooms, fire escapes, and windows, were spurred by the desire to improve housing conditions for the poor (Figure 13.3). Collectively, these reforms are referred to as **social equity planning**. In addition, European cities ventured into building public housing, but the United States largely eschewed this approach until the 1930s.

Today, the need for social equity planning is still apparent. The decisions of the private marketplace are generally not as good for the poor as they are for the wealthier classes. Previous chapters have shown

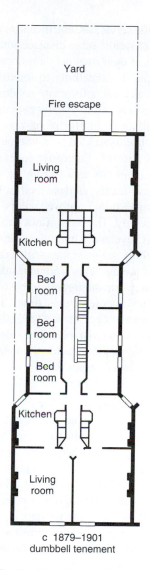

c 1879–1901
dumbbell tenement

Figure 13.3 In the late nineteenth century, population pressures led to new urban designs. The dumbbell tenement design was the winner of a contest, but quickly became notorious as an example of bad, unhealthy housing. (*Source:* Wright, 1981.)

how the city has decentralized, leading stores and jobs to move out to the suburbs and stranding the poor in the inner city. Metropolitan fragmentation, discussed in Chapter 12, often burdens poorer residents of cities with higher taxes but inferior schools and other public services. Gentrification, which leads to urban revitalization, often displaces the poor, who are priced out of their own neighborhoods.

Planners can do something to improve the conditions of the city's less fortunate residents. Corrections are complicated and usually expensive. Public housing is still an option for many poor people, although it has been shackled by numerous problems, as we saw in Chapter 9. Enterprise zones attract businesses to the inner city by offering tax abatements. And housing vouchers, as described in Chapter 10, have also worked to improve access to housing throughout the city. The risks of not doing anything, according to Cleveland's longtime planner Norman Krumholz (1996), are that cities will become either a "sandbox," where the "kids" (urban residents) are put out of the way while the important business of society is conducted in other arenas, or an "Indian reservation" or island of dependency (p. 360). Only with a stronger, more activist planning role, Krumholz argues, can cities begin to tackle the major problems of poverty and racial segregation.

Maintaining Property Values

Early cities were functionally integrated. Residential, commercial, and industrial uses were located in proximity to one another. They were also more socially integrated in that rich and poor shared many of the same neighborhoods. The explosive growth of cities and the increased concentration led to a desire for the government to step in and regulate building and property uses as a means of minimizing **negative externalities** and maintaining property values.

The issue of property values is closely tied to a **property owner's dilemma** and the nature of landed property as a commodity. If a property owner renovates her property but others do not renovate theirs, she will not realize much in the way of increased property values. Conversely, if the neighbors renovate their property but she does not renovate hers, her property value will still increase. Thus, there are no individual incentives for people to maintain or improve their property. Moreover, if everybody follows this principle, then the

neighborhood and all of the property values will suffer. Clearly, then, your neighbors help determine your property value. This becomes especially apparent when your neighbor can put a factory or a sleazy strip club right next to an expensive apartment building. The value of the apartment building invariably goes down.

Zoning came about as a way to control these negative externalities by regulating exactly what could be placed where. **Zoning** is simply the establishment of districts that permit only specified types of land use. Comprehensive zoning was first introduced in German cities such as Frankfurt in the late nineteenth century. Different sections of the city were zoned for different uses, and restrictions on building height and building bulk were introduced (Figure 13.4). American observers admired this system and sought to introduce it to the United States.

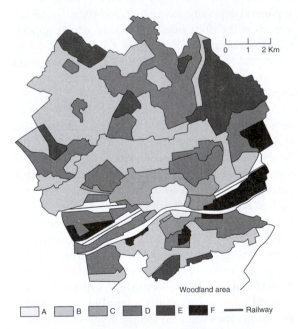

☐ A ☐ B ☐ C ☐ D ■ E ■ F ▬▬ Railway

Figure 13.4 This zoning map of Frankfurt, Germany, was produced in 1910. The inner city (a) is zoned industrial and residential. The (c) zones are high-density residential, the (b) zones are lower density residential, and the (e) zones are designated for large detached houses. Industrial uses are permitted in both (d) and (f) zones. (*Source:* Sutcliffe, 1981.)

By the twentieth century, zoning had become the premier method of urban planning. Enabled by federal and state governments and deemed constitutional by the courts, zoning became a fundamental policy of most municipal governments. Zoning was not an aesthetic movement—it did not constitute a grand vision of the city. Rather, it was adopted as a strategy to minimize the problems incurred by private development. Zoning became the best, most politically attractive way to control nuisances and to maintain property values, and as such it found favor with business leaders, property owners, and civil servants.

Environmental Protection

Although we may think of the environmental movement as dating to the 1960s or early 1970s, concerns about creating a more healthful environment were apparent as early as the nineteenth century. The solutions, such as draining nearby marshes to reduce disease, may run counter to current views, but they indicated a desire to improve the urban environment. Some of the issues discussed earlier, like congestion, also included an environmental dimension. Public health became a major concern because so many cities expanded well beyond their capacity to provide water or remove wastes.

One movement that was clearly tied into the environment was the development of parks. Many European cities had royal preserves that were gradually opened up to the public. There was nothing comparable in U.S. cities. There *was* a great deal of cheap land on the periphery, but this land was often locked up by land speculators waiting to cash in on urban growth. City leaders began to recognize that parks were important and that urban residents needed access to green space. Parks were described as the "lungs" of a city, and by the late nineteenth century many cities had embarked on an extensive program of park acquisition and park design.

Frederick Law Olmstead was the best known park designer in the United States. Olmstead helped to develop Central Park in 1850s New York—then right on the edge of the city's expansion. He also was responsible for other parks in Boston, Brooklyn,

Chicago, Montreal, and Detroit. During the late nineteenth century, he and his students created parks in most U.S. cities. Olmstead believed that parks helped to release workers from the drudgery of city life and were an antidote to the evil influences of the slum.

Some urban elites denounced parks as a "free" benefit to the poor. In fact, the parks that were developed were often too far away for workers who had to labor until nightfall and could not afford the time to take a long walk or a streetcar to the nearest park. Instead, parks were patronized by the wealthy. Many of them became fashionable for equestrians who could ride horses in a natural setting (this at a time when most urban travel was conducted on horseback or with a horse and carriage). Moreover, park development greatly increased values for adjoining properties, a pattern that holds true today. Luxury apartments would be built right next to parks in order to capitalize on this new amenity. Later, Olmstead and his students developed parkways and parklike suburbs that sought to create residential communities in the park (Figure 13.5). These communities were a break from the traditional grid

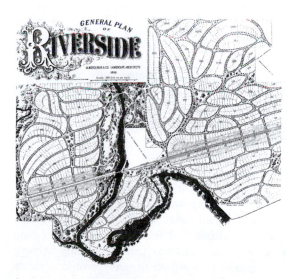

Figure 13.5 Olmstead also designed communities, with houses nestled in a parklike landscape. This is the plan for Riverside, a suburb of Chicago, designed in 1869. (*Source:* Kostof, 1991.)

that dominated most cities, and they were popular among the affluent. In many ways, they presaged some of the modern master plan and golf course communities.

The development of parks also had an institutional effect: It led to the creation of parks commissions. Many of these, like the Cleveland Metropolitan Parks District established in 1917, were metropolitan in scope, covering both the central city and early suburbs. As a result, they foreshadowed some of the other metropolitan-wide agencies that sought to put planning into a larger perspective.

Today, environmental issues are associated with much more than parks. There are concerns with many different types of pollution: groundwater, surface water, air pollution, and so forth. Such problems tend to stretch far beyond the limits of any single municipality. For this reason, the authority to deal with them must go beyond the purview of any given city. Nevertheless, they are still dealt with by planning agencies. The requirements for environmental impact assessments permeate the day-to-day workings of many city, county, and township planners and are the focus of federal and state agencies.

DEVELOPMENT OF MODERN PLANNING

As the rationales for planning came into sharper focus in the late nineteenth and early twentieth centuries, planning remained the province of a few concerned individuals. These individuals were instrumental in creating visions of what the city should be—visions that, although diluted, were still copied in actual designs of cities and neighborhoods. Over the course of the twentieth century, however, planning authority was gradually transferred to a professional cadre that worked within appropriate legal and institutional frameworks. The evolution of these frameworks has helped planning achieve more authority in regard to many everyday facets of land development, but it has perhaps also led to a lack of an overarching vision. Modern planning often focuses on such narrowly defined issues as ensuring adequate parking and requiring urban areas

to adhere to strict separation of functions. This in turn has spawned a counterreaction that reexamines the basic concepts of cities and neighborhoods and considers how they can be improved.

Visionaries and the Urban Ideal

In the early twentieth century, advocates offered up a number of visions of what the modern city should be like. We have already discussed the plans of Daniel Burnham and the City Beautiful movement. The utopian visions were even larger in scope and required the building of cities from the ground up. Like Burnham, the visionaries were private individuals with little public institutional authority. Most were also architects. Nevertheless, they had a great deal of moral authority, and, as a result, their visions influenced the development of cities.

Ebenezer Howard and the Garden City Movement
The first successful effort at realizing a particular urban vision in the twentieth century began as the **Garden City movement**, associated with a mild-mannered British stenographer named Ebenezer Howard. Howard's ideal city was intended to be established away from the main population centers, especially London—the world's biggest city at that time. Garden cities were also meant to be self-contained, with a balance of jobs, housing, and retail. Most significantly, the ideals of the garden city were predicated on the public control of land. People would lease their property rather than buy it outright. The land itself could be held by some sort of corporation, trust, or the government. This would allow for land-use decisions to be made in the public interest.

Some of the specific tenets of the Garden City movement were as follows (Figure 13.6):

• There was to be a maximum population of 58,000. Later Howard conceded the necessity of creating a larger urban system, composed of the larger central city, surrounded by satellite cities, each with a population of about 32,000. These satellites were meant to help siphon off any excess population from the center.
• The general layout of the city was in a series of concentric zones, with plenty of parks and gardens. The

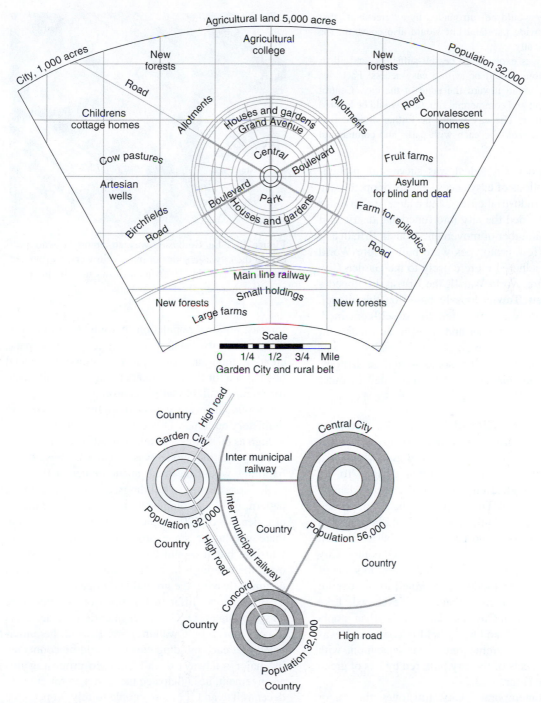

Figure 13.6 Ebenezer Howard's plan for Garden City, proposed as a self-contained community, with a balance of jobs, housing, and retail. (*Source:* Levy, 2000.)

entire city would be surrounded by a "greenbelt" that would provide parkland but would also constrain the city physically.

- The city was expected to be self-sufficient, and all of the functions would be within easy access. Factories would be found toward the edge of the city. Central government and commercial functions would be located in the center. The city would be further divided into internal *superblocks,* each with parks and commercial functions.

The Garden City ideal was successful, particularly the notions of easy access, plenty of open space (a rarity in industrial cities), and a large-scale master plan that divided the city into functional districts. It spawned a number of movements both in Britain and abroad. A few prototypes were built before World War I that adhered more closely to the Garden City design. After World War II, the British developed a host of **New Towns** loosely based on this model. These towns were expected to be self-contained, with a balance of jobs and housing and plenty of parkland. By 1995 some 34 of these New Towns had been built, housing some 4 million Britons. Variations on this theme were attempted in other countries, particularly France.

Le Corbusier's City of Towers

Le Corbusier was a French architect who came up with urban plans that, although never realized as a whole, had an enormous influence on urban design. To Le Corbusier the ideal city combined extreme density with spaciousness. This could only be accomplished through high-rise buildings that would be scattered across a parklike landscape. Le Corbusier created two major urban models: the Contemporary City and the Radiant City. Although different in some of the details, these models conformed to his overall vision of how a city should be developed. Like Howard's Garden City, Le Corbusier's urban utopia was based on all land being held in common. It was also based on extreme functional separation, with different aspects of the city buffered by lots of green open space (Figure 13.7).

The Contemporary City illustrates the major principles of Le Corbusier's vision. Le Corbusier's ideal city was enormous in population and area. He

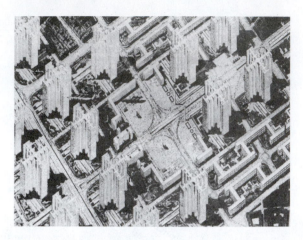

Figure 13.7 Le Corbusier was an architect who perceived the city as a series of massive towers, surrounded by open space. This 1920s plan shows how he intended to redesign a neighborhood in Paris.

forecast an ideal population of some 3 million residents. The city itself was laid out in a vast park, creating thousands of acres of commonly owned open space for the inhabitants to enjoy and allowing for ample sunlight and vegetation.

Individuals were expected to live and work in multistory buildings. Office buildings were to be built as high as 60 stories—as tall as most structures in the 1920s, when this model was proposed. These office buildings would be found at the center of the city. Eight-story apartment buildings, arranged in a zigzag pattern, would accommodate most of the population at a density of 120 people per acre. In this vision, there was to be some provision for single-family housing, but it would be limited in scope. Moreover, the buildings themselves were to be placed on columns, leaving the ground level open.

Because the different functions of the city were so spread apart, Le Corbusier intentionally designed his city not to be a walking city. Instead, he anticipated that each building cluster would be connected by major roadways or rail lines. In proposing this arrangement, he anticipated the tendency for cities to decentralize and for more people to rely on personal transportation. At the same time, parking lots do not seem to have figured prominently in his scheme.

Although neither of Le Corbusier's utopian cities was ever built, he was able to influence the development of a few cities in total and much modern urban design. For example, Brasilia—the new capital of Brazil—was designed to be both spacious and monumental, with plenty of open space. Chandigarh, India—the new capital of the Punjab—was designed by Le Corbusier himself. Both cities are far more spacious than is the norm for their countries, although poverty has led to a large influx of poor people who tend to set up shacks beyond the main streets.

Le Corbusier also had a significant influence on the establishment of urban renewal districts and public housing. In both instances, the ideal of tall buildings surrounded by open land became something of a signature. Unfortunately, in the case of public housing, it has led to many more negative perceptions than positive ones. Le Corbusier's vision of skyscrapers surrounded by verdant parkland has transmuted into blighted concrete blocks engirdled by sinister wasteland (see Chapter 9).

Frank Lloyd Wright's Broadacre City

U.S. architect Frank Lloyd Wright is best known for innovative buildings like Taliesin, Falling Water, and the Guggenheim Museum. But Wright also advanced a utopian vision that is in many respects closer to what the modern suburbanized city has become. Wright's vision was quintessentially suburban. He abhorred large concentrated cities; in fact, he described New York as a "fibrous tumor." He was most interested in liberating people from mass agglomerations and allowing them to live as free individuals. He also believed that the best course of action was to merge town with country, an ideal espoused more than a century earlier by Thomas Jefferson.

Wright referred to his utopia as Broadacre City because it was to be made up of large, privately owned plots. In this regard especially, Wright's plan ran counter to the public ownership assumed in Howard's and Le Corbusier's visions. His plan was for a dispersed settlement of people, linked by spacious, well-landscaped highways traversed in private automobiles. In his city, all residents would own a large lot of land (one or more acres) on which they would grow food and recreate. They would commute by car to their jobs in another section of the city (Figure 13.8).

Of course, with all of this private land ownership, the city would need to be large in area. Nevertheless, it was Wright's contention that each individual should be able to find what she or he needed within 10 to 20 miles of home through the planned arrangement of shopping and factory districts. In many respects, Wright's plan is very close to the modern suburb. You can see this at work in the exclusive districts, the development of edge cities, the automobile dependency, and the dispersal of residences on big lots. Where Wright's vision differed from modern suburban reality was in the expectation that people would work as part-time farmers. However, with the explosion of interest in gardening, even this may not be too far off.

Legal Basis for Planning

The visions of what a city could be were important milestones. They furnished the ideas that helped guide urban design and helped the nascent field of urban planning to see the city as a whole. But the weakness in these visions was precisely that they assumed everything could be controlled by a central authority. Le Corbusier, for one, was contemptuous of politics and the political process. In democratic countries, such high-handedness was not possible, and ideals of urban design were forced to confront the realities of law.

In all capitalist countries, planning must contend with the rights of property owners. Land is something that people work on, extract from, play on, build on, and live on. The different "values" of land—use value, exchange value, and the commodification of land and housing—have been discussed in Chapter 9. For our discussion here, it bears noting that the value of land as a commodity depends on its ownership. If land is publicly owned, it has no exchange value. Land may be leased, with certain rights given to individuals residing on it or otherwise using it. It may even be possible for individuals to own the structures built on the land. The land itself, however, cannot

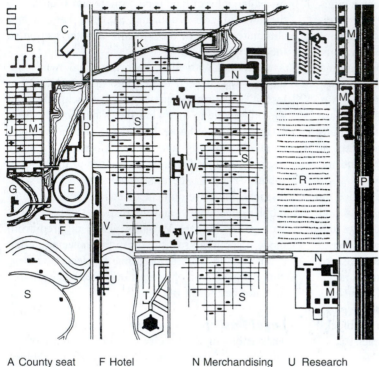

A County seat
  administration
B Airport
C Sports
D Professional
  offices
E Stadium

F Hotel
G Sanitarium
H Small industry
J Small farms
K Park
L Motor inn
M Industry

N Merchandising
P Railroad
R Orchards
S Homes and
  apartments
T Temple and
  cemetery

U Research
V Zoo
W Schools

Figure 13.8 Frank Lloyd Wright created this plan for Broadacre City. He envisioned a dispersed settlement of people, linked by spacious, well-landscaped highways traversed in private automobiles. (*Source:* Gallion and Eisner, 1983.)

be bought and sold. In contrast, if land is privately owned, it is property that can be bought and sold just like anything else. This gives property owners many more rights and the presumptive ability to do what they wish with the land they own.

In the United States, the right to private property is written into the Fifth Amendment of the Constitution, which states "nor shall private property be taken for public use, without just compensation." This is called the **takings clause** of the Constitution, and it is affirmed by the Fourteenth Amendment, which states that no person shall be deprived of life, liberty, or property without due process. In contrast, other countries, although recognizing the sanctity of

private property, do not have the same levels of protection enshrined in their constitutional framework (Box 13.1).

Land is different from other forms of property, for two reasons. First, land may be required for common projects such as highways, ports, airports, and new facilities. Second, land is directly affected by what is around it. As we have seen, what you do with your land can have a major effect on your neighbors' lands. How the government has been able to get around these premises informs the legal history of planning.

In some cases the government purchases land outright through eminent domain, discussed earlier in Chapter 9. The Constitution clearly states that you cannot be summarily deprived of real property just because it is needed for something else. At the same time, the law recognizes that a necessary project cannot be stalled or stopped because one property owner refuses to sell her or his land. Eminent domain allows the government to take land from private owners as long as it offers "just compensation," as written in the Fifth Amendment. When the government acquires land through eminent domain, it pays the landowner for the land, but it also determines the price. The constitutional basis for eminent domain was established in the 1950s. Most recently, in 2005, the Supreme Court ruled (in Kelo vs. New London) that a municipal government could condemn privately owned land by eminent domain in order to benefit a private business project as part of a comprehensive development plan.

In other cases the government simply seeks to regulate the use of land. These situations are generally more complex than outright purchases. Most modern planning involves some restriction on how a parcel may be used. For instance, let's say that a landowner wishes to build a 10-story apartment building, but height limitations require her to settle for a 5-story building. The "loss" of these five stories could translate into the loss of that much potential rent. The property owner might claim that the height restrictions constitute a "taking" unless she is compensated for the potential loss. Excluding certain functions operates in a similar manner. If a property owner wishes to build a factory in land that is zoned residential, then he might claim that the government is "taking" a portion of his property rights and his potential income.

The early twentieth century witnessed a number of court cases that dealt with the issue of takings. These involved a brewery closing under a Kansas prohibition law, height limits in Boston, and zoning in Euclid, Ohio, which prevented a commercial building from being placed in a residential zone. In these cases, the plaintiffs—those who sought to overturn existing property restrictions—lost and the government was granted the authority to restrict what could be built where. However, there was

also an understanding in all of these rulings that planning restrictions could not be arbitrary. Rather, they must involve a means of safeguarding public health, public safety, or public welfare. Planning restrictions were also required to fit within a larger community plan, so that a government could not prohibit the owner of an individual parcel from building a particular structure unless it first had implemented a comprehensive plan that covered all parcels within the community.

As many of the tools of planning became a part of settled law, communities rushed to develop comprehensive plans and zoning regulations. But there has always been a tug of war between the forces of property regulation and the forces of private property protection. Recently, property rights advocates—those who feel that many restrictions are unconstitutional and should be curtailed—have been aggressive in challenging land-use restrictions. They have been successful in some court rulings. In one case, a property owner was told that he would have to provide public access to the beach in return for being allowed to enlarge his house. The Supreme Court decided that the two actions were unrelated and that the property owner could not be compelled to provide access. A case brought by a South Carolina property owner claimed that he was financially harmed by a decision that he could not build on his beachfront property. The Supreme Court ruled that, because these restrictions were imposed after the property was bought and because they rendered the property financially worthless, the owner would have to be compensated. In 2001, the Supreme Court went even further, arguing that a Rhode Islander who bought property in a wetland still deserved compensation for the lost value of development even though restrictions were in place before the property was acquired.

By the late twentieth century, takings issues involved more than just zoning. Environmental laws like the Endangered Species Act have given the government broad powers to limit development in areas that encroach on natural habitats. This has infuriated property rights advocates, and there has been a movement in Congress to enact takings legislation

BOX 13.1   PLANNING RIGHTS IN OTHER COUNTRIES

The U.S. Constitution is very protective of private property, and many people point to this as a reason for long-term U.S. prosperity. At the same time, however, many constitutional and legal provisions have created difficulties for planners. In fact, planning is often easier in other societies. Underlying property rights are not quite as strong, and individual planning boards have greater degrees of discretion. Even when we compare the United States to those societies that are arguably the closest to us in culture—the United Kingdom and Canada—we can see differences (Figures B13.1 and B13.2).

Figure B13.1 Aerial view of suburban development, Las Vegas.

With regard to the view of property rights and especially of takings, the United Kingdom after World War II effectively nationalized development rights. In other words, there exists no basis for British landowners to argue that their development rights have been taken and they therefore deserve compensation. Moreover, if landowners benefit from a permission to develop, they then must pay a charge. The issue of takings is simply not in the picture. In Canada, the Constitution does not explicitly protect property rights as does the U.S. Constitution, so the issue of takings does not apply there as well.

The other difference has to do with the discretion of planning boards. In the United States, planning boards are hamstrung by the need to treat all parties equally, developers and residents alike. This has been the basis for many of the successful court challenges to planning decisions. Zoning has been permitted only when it is applied uniformly. So, a developer who wants to build something that is considered undesirable can still proceed as long as he or she is not violating zoning ordinances. In contrast, planning boards in both Canada and the United Kingdom have a much greater degree of control. In Britain, all new development is at a planning board's discretion. A general plan is prepared, but

that would require the government to compensate landowners when environmental laws reduce the value of their property by a certain percentage. There have also been motions to curtail the reach of the Endangered Species Act or to gut it altogether.

Growth of Planning as a Profession in the United States

In Chapter 12 we discussed how local authority was widely dispersed to municipalities, counties, townships, school districts, special districts, and metropolitan-level planning agencies. Each of these

governments has different powers, and many of them rely on planners of some sort or another. Some may decide to outsource their planning needs to a consulting company, but many prefer to hire in-house planners. There is clearly a huge difference in the number of planners employed, with big cities containing large departments of planning, whereas many townships may hire one person to oversee development or even contract out planning. The Bureau of Labor Statistics reports that in 2004 there were 32,000 planners, up from 13,000 in 1980. This probably does not include large numbers of people local authorities do not have to allow development even if it is in accord with the plan. They may consider other things, and if they decide to prohibit a development, there is little legal recourse. Canada has a more mixed system, which varies by province. But generally, Canadians abide by discretionary planning controls within the context of a zoning bylaw. An application can thus be rejected for a use that, although according with the zoning code, is still considered inappropriate for the neighborhood.

Further differences arise in other countries. For example, France and the Netherlands, like Britain, have very centralized planning. This means that planning decisions for localities are made at the national level in accordance with certain goals to preserve open space, promote social equity, share resources, and so forth. Sweden and Germany have much greater traditions of local control, but they still allow for an enormous government role in the design and guidance of future growth.

Figure B13.2 Suburban Housing in Montreal Quebec.

who engage in planning activities, such as individuals who work within transportation agencies, environmental agencies, and private companies.

Planning is still mainly a public-sector activity. Seventy percent of planners work for local governments, primarily municipalities and counties. Nevertheless, private firms employ planners as well, a bit less than 20 percent of the total number of planners. These firms include both private consulting firms that specialize in a facet of planning (such as historic preservation) and larger companies that wish to have some planners on their staff. A fair number

of the planners employed are certified planners—a special designation that requires an individual to obtain certain credentials and pass a test—but most are simply practicing planning even if they do not have the same credentials as certified planners.

The development of planning as a profession is tied in with the expansion and bureaucratization of state and local government. In addition, planning as a profession emerged as the tools of planning, particularly zoning, were found to be legally based. In 1917 the American Institute of Planners was established; this later became the

American Planning Association (APA), which was instrumental in developing the certification process for planners. Then, in the 1920s, the U.S. Commerce Department introduced the *Standard State Zoning Enabling* (SSZE) Act, which was passed by Congress in 1926.

The SSZE Act was significant for three reasons. First, it underlined the growing desire to inject rationalism into the planning process. The secretary of commerce—Herbert Hoover—was an advocate of a well-ordered society. He believed that the government should not interfere with the market but it should help to facilitate efficiency, standardization, and greater investment safety. That he was echoing a larger social impulse is evidenced by the fact that the text of the SSZE Act itself became something of a best-seller. Thousands of copies were sold around the country. Second, the SSZE Act delegated much of the state authority for planning to municipalities. This was important because states possessed many constitutional prerogatives, whereas localities possessed almost none. The Commerce Department also wrote up a model zoning code that was legally defensible and could be copied by municipalities across the country. By 1926, some 43 states had enabled zoning and 420 localities had zoning ordinances, most of which were closely based on the model code put out by the Commerce Department. By 1929, after it was clear that the Supreme Court considered zoning to be constitutional, 754 localities containing three-fifths of the nation's urban population practiced zoning, and most had adopted the model ordinances. Third, with the publication of the SSZE Act, zoning emerged as the principal activity for planning. The sweeping ideals of the City Beautiful movement and the visionaries discussed earlier were cast in the more prosaic concerns of planning a city that was standard and efficient.

After the 1920s planning became entrenched as an institution at several geographic scales. Localities were on the frontlines of writing and enforcing the new ordinances. States were encouraged to establish planning agencies, and all but one had established these by 1936. These were not exclusively or even predominantly oriented to urban issues, but they did attempt to gather as much information as possible about the physical environment, social characteristics, economic activity, and the building stock. Regional authorities were also established. The most famous of these was the Tennessee Valley Authority, a New Deal program created in 1933 to oversee a man-made system of dams, lakes, and hydroelectric generators across several states. At the federal level, the New Deal ushered in a host of agencies and boards that were charged with building housing, highways, and public works.

Planning as a profession also became more diversified. Although zoning and subdivision approval continue to be a principal activity of many municipal planning agencies, planners as a group have specialized in tasks spread among different public agencies and the private sector. A recent survey of planning activity indicated that nearly all planners are involved with "regulation" to some degree, but, beyond this, there is considerable divergence. Many planners continue to be hired by local governors, charged with developing comprehensive plans, zoning codes, subdivision regulations, and other procedures intended to guide urban development. Other planners become involved in urban renewal efforts and in providing housing to people who cannot afford private market housing.

Still other planners and planning agencies are involved in planning for regional transportation needs. The establishment of the interstate highway system in 1956, a massive undertaking designed to blanket the United States in a network of limited-access highways, as well as the creation of publicly financed mass transit, contributed to the growth of metropolitan agencies that made choices over where best to place the new transportation infrastructure. Environmental planning arose out of (1) the awareness that governments need to regulate private activity in order to minimize harm to the natural environment and (2) a series of laws passed in the 1960s and 1970s that set out the institutional procedures to do this.

Governments also have become more involved in economic development and have sought to increase private business activity in a region as a way to promote overall economic growth and to alleviate poverty in specific neighborhoods. Downtown redevelopment has emerged as a popular specialty among planners who look to revitalize languishing central business districts.

Political Nature of Planning

Regardless of the particular activities in which planners are involved, it is important to note that planning is a highly political activity. We can look at this reality in regard to (1) the different scales of planning concern and (2) the many different stakeholders involved in the planning process.

Planning takes place at several spatial scales. In most cases, local governments are on the frontlines of planning. They are most immediately affected by what takes place in a city, town, or township. County governments may also become involved; in many instances, counties are charged with developing the appropriate zoning and regulatory mechanisms for unincorporated jurisdictions within them. They also sometimes have more regional planning duties such as coordinating the planning objectives of local governments within the county.

Beyond the local level, state and federal governments have long played a large role in planning. State governments are involved in several ways. First, they are property owners in their own right. States own highways, airports, government buildings, universities, and state lands. State actions regarding the use of their property can have a tremendous effect on development. Deciding where to locate a highway, for instance, affects the future for urban and rural areas alike. States may also promote certain areas through their activities. In the 1970s, for example, the state of Massachusetts attempted to locate all state government buildings in the inner cities to spur economic development. Second, states are grantors of a locality's legal rights. Cities and towns must conform to state guidelines as to what they can and cannot do. For instance, some states require that municipalities file a comprehensive plan. Other states may exempt properties under a certain threshold size from planning oversight, meaning that they do not have to follow the guidelines imposed on larger properties. Third, states are the originators of various land-use regulations. States may set out a broad land-use plan for municipalities to follow (e.g., requiring a certain lot size along a lakeshore). They may provide certain guidelines (e.g., stipulating that development be located in already urban areas), or they may modify or revoke a local action. Fourth, states are a funding source for local planning initiatives. Much of the money—even federal dollars—comes to the states, and the states decide where the money should go.

The federal government also has a role to play in planning. In the United States, the federal government has tended to shy away from any sort of national land-use planning (providing a clear contrast with many European countries). Nevertheless, its influence on planning is still profound. This was true as far back as the 1920s, with the passage of the SSZE Act and with several significant Supreme Court decisions. It is still true today, for many reasons. First, like the states, the federal government is a big property owner. It owns military bases, post offices, arsenals, hospitals, government buildings, and huge tracts of land. What the government decides to do with these properties can play a major role in how communities fare. During the 1990s, for example, the government initiated a round of military base closings. This was a sensitive issue, not primarily because of its impact on military readiness, but because shutting a base would lead to the loss of a major employment source, which in turn could cripple a local economy that had come to depend on these jobs.

Second, the federal government has adopted many regulations and issued many laws that affect land-use choices. Among these are the Clean Water Act, the Clean Air Act, the Americans with Disabilities Act (requiring that buildings, streets, and sidewalks make accommodations for people with disabilities), and the Endangered Species Act. The federal government has also passed laws requiring that mortgage lenders locate in underserved neighborhoods. And, of course, the mortgage interest deduction and the establishment of federal protections for mortgages that were discussed in Chapter 9 have played a huge role in homeownership and suburban development. This is only a fraction of the impacts with which local planning officials and private developers must contend. Third, the federal government is a source of funding. It offers money to states and localities. It can also withhold money if certain rules are not followed.

At any scale, planners have to be politically astute. Perhaps in large planning agencies, some planners may be shielded from some of the politics. They may conduct some of the more technical aspects of planning: gathering information, running some analyses, making maps, and so forth. But most planners are thrust in the middle of a very political process. They must consider the interests of myriad stakeholders who would be affected by the plans. **Stakeholders** is an umbrella term that includes all of the interests involved: government, private developers, financiers, and residents.

Figure 13.9 provides some idea of just how elaborate any planning decision can be. At the center of the figure are the professional planners themselves, charged with drawing up the plans and making recommendations. They must answer directly to public officials—city councilors, mayors, county commissioners—and also to "citizen planners"—those who have agreed to serve on planning boards, boards of appeal, environmental commissions, and other oversight bodies. Planners are further motivated by regulations and funding provided by state and federal governments. Beyond this center are a legion of interested and affected parties. The planning group is after all generally regulating a property that is being developed by a private property owner and that will be inhabited by, or located next to, some residents. Developers must get their funding from banks. The residents may decide to organize themselves into a formal organization, garner the attention of the new media, or pressure the politicians. And everybody in a highly charged case will retain the services of attorneys.

To note how this web of stakeholders plays itself out in any planning decision, consider the case of a proposed low-income housing development. On one hand, state and federal governments often require that low-income housing be spread to different communities, although their approach is more carrot than stick. The federal government releases community

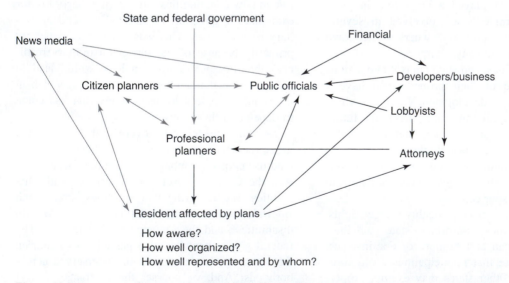

Figure 13.9 Any type of community planning affects a large group of people and entities, the *stakeholders*. This diagram shows the relationship between the different stakeholders in the planning process. Professional planners are in the middle and must take into account a great diversity of interests.

BOX 13.2   THE SEARCH FOR FAIR SHARE HOUSING IN NEW JERSEY

Fair share housing refers to the goal that every community should pick up its "fair share" of moderate- and low-income housing. In practice, provisions regarding fair share housing are difficult to come by. Although society recognizes the need to build housing that is available to the poor, many communities are loathe to allow such housing to be built within their jurisdiction, prohibiting small lots, mobile homes, and multifamily housing. As a result, much of the public housing or publicly assisted housing has been located within the inner cities. Even though housing discrimination per se is illegal, there are few rulings that prohibit a community from designing zoning codes that are exclusionary.

New Jersey is the most densely populated state in the United States and, along with California, the most urban state. It has also been at the forefront of creating the legal background for fair share housing. In the early 1970s, the New Jersey Supreme Court ruled that a township could not designate minimum lot sizes if regional housing needs dictated otherwise. The most famous set of legal cases involved the New Jersey township of Mount Laurel. The New Jersey Supreme Court in 1975 held that a municipality had to "provide a realistic opportunity for the construction of its fair share of . . . low- and moderate-income housing" (from Cullingworth, 1993, p. 67). In other words, communities were prohibited from instituting exclusionary zoning. The second Mount Laurel decision, in 1980, reaffirmed these principles and further argued for inclusionary zoning regulations that would be designed to encourage low-income housing. These regulations might consist of incentives to developers, such as higher zoning densities, or some stipulations. One stipulation that came out of the Mt. Laurel decisions was that a developer should build one lower income housing unit for every four market-rate units (Figure B13.3).

The Mount Laurel decisions were partially successful in putting fair share housing on the radar screen and in proclaiming a need for each municipality to provide for low-income housing. However, resistance to the court's decision among New Jersey state politicians and municipal leaders led to a watering down of the original intent. The New Jersey Fair Housing Act, passed in the 1980s, weakened any oversight over exclusionary zoning while loosely satisfying the court's ruling. As a result, few low-income housing units were actually constructed. After 2003, there were further complaints that the Council on Affordable Housing, established to oversee and execute New Jersey's fair housing obligations, effectively reduced the requirement to one affordable housing unit for every ten new units. In fact, California, with its own fair share housing requirements and incentives for developers, has taken the lead in this area.

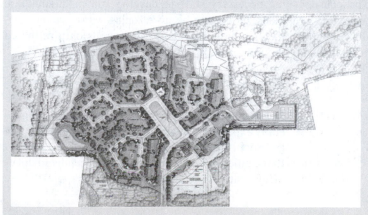

Figure B13.3 Mount Laurel, New Jersey.

development block grants to those municipalities willing to do this. And the idea of **fair share housing**—that all communities in a region should participate in providing low-income housing—still affects policies in many metropolitan areas. Some states, such as New Jersey, have even made this a requirement (Box 13.2). In addition, there will often be a developer interested in providing such housing. She or he may be motivated by the prospect of securing low-income housing tax credits or by some other encouragement, but whatever the reason, the private will is there. There may also be advocacy groups for the poor that are looking to promote affordable housing wherever it can be built.

On the other hand, residents who live next to the proposed development may have no desire to live near low-income housing. They may acknowledge the general need for such housing, but they clearly do not want it close by (see Box 9.2). Planners label this attitude "not in my backyard," or NIMBY. The types of land uses that are often found objectionable are termed "locally unwanted land uses," or LULUs. Low-income housing is a LULU that provokes a NIMBY reaction among nearby residents. These residents make their wishes known to local government officials and to members of citizen planning boards. The news media may also hear of the issue and start reporting on it, which widens the circle of potential conflicts. All sides in this dispute are likely to hire lawyers to present their side of the argument, and they may appeal to the planning boards or to the courts, or both. As a rule, it is the professional planner who must bear the burden of mediating among all of these interests. The planner becomes a flashpoint for the general irritation. However, he or she can do little to adjudicate the controversy. This is left to the elected officials and often to the courts.

COMPREHENSIVE PLANS AND TOOLS OF MODERN PLANNING

Modern planning begins with a document known as the comprehensive plan. The **comprehensive plan** is a plan that is intended first to catalog the existing land uses, population, and an economic profile within a community and then to guide community development well into the future. From a political point of view, the comprehensive plan becomes a critical document that helps to lay out the goals for a community, institutionalize the planning process, create a legal foundation for specific regulations, and bring together all of the different stakeholders within a community.

The historic roots of comprehensive plans can be traced to the City Beautiful movement and the widespread development of parks in the late nineteenth and early twentieth centuries. Frederick Law Olmsted, the influential park developer, argued the merits of comprehensive planning in a 1911 address. Much of the legal and political action during the 1920s also paved the way for the widespread adoption of comprehensive plans. Secretary of Commerce Herbert Hoover championed zoning, but he broadened his focus to include planning in general. The Standard City Planning Enabling Act, passed in 1928—2 years after the SSZE Act—recommended that plans be developed that take into account all of a community's infrastructure, public buildings, and possible zoning plans for locating new buildings and infrastructure. The court decisions at that time indicated that zoning decisions, for instance, needed to be incorporated as part of a larger plan. A comprehensive plan became the vehicle to accomplish that objective. The Housing Act of 1954 helped to make comprehensive plans a reality for thousands of communities. It provided funding to develop master plans, and it allowed for these communities to hire the necessary staff to develop and maintain these plans. Of course, because zoning was a primary element of any plan, these suggestions only furthered the influence of this particular planning tool.

Elements and Steps in Comprehensive Plan Development

Although most communities of a certain size are generally expected to have a comprehensive plan, the size and sophistication of such plans vary tremendously. Large cities often provide beautifully rendered documents, with lots of color pictures and graphics. These are also quintessentially political documents, having been produced by large planning staffs but also with the input of thousands of community residents. Smaller community plans are often simpler, but they still contain many of the key elements.

The basic elements of any comprehensive plan are as follows:

- A long-range vision for the community that usually is presented as a series of goals for the community.
- A snapshot of the physical and human geography of the city. This is an inventory of the current terrain; infrastructure such as streets, utilities, bridges, and ports; publicly owned land, including park land; environmental aspects of the land; historic buildings and other cultural resources; population characteristics of all sorts; economic characteristics; and more.

This aspect of the plan can be a useful compendium of facts that allows planners and other city officials to see exactly what they have to work with. For instance, an important feature may be an inventory of land that is open for more intensive development. Communities with much developable land are in a different position than those that are built out, with little available land remaining.

- An overview of historical and projected trends; for instance, projections of population growth and land-use patterns and how this may all translate into community needs.
- Methods on how to handle these various trends and fit them within the overall and specific community goals. This is the implementation portion of the community plan and, from a planning point of view, it is the most important part of the document.
- Review procedures that show how the community administration will handle changes and implement any new proposals and how community citizens will be able to participate.

The comprehensive plan will present many of these facts for the community as a whole, but it will also subdivide the city into planning districts or zones. This allows for a more detailed breakdown of exactly what may happen to particular sites (Figure 13.10).

A comprehensive plan is an enormous undertaking, and, for that reason, a new one is produced only once every several years. Four steps are involved in creating a plan: collecting data, formulating community goals, creating the plan, and implementing the plan.

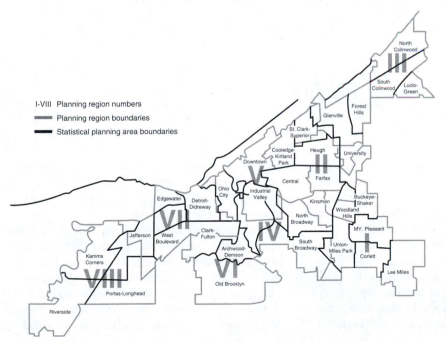

Figure 13.10 Map of a planning district in Cleveland, Ohio. This map comes from Cleveland's own comprehensive plan. Planning districts or zones allow for a more detailed analysis of what may occur in particular neighborhoods.

BOX 13.3 TECHNOLOGY AND URBAN GEOGRAPHY

GIS AND URBAN PLANNING

In recent years, the practice of planning has been transformed by the increased sophistication of Geographic Information Systems and related computer models (Figure B13.4). This makes a great deal of sense considering the urban planning involves the synthesis of a great deal of locational data. Consider a decision on where to place a new municipal building such as a fire station. Several potential parcels are spread throughout the city, and the planner may be called upon to choose the site that 1) will provide the greatest degree of access, thus lessening response times, 2) minimize noise and disruption to potential neighbors, 3) be suited to the particular site characteristics, and 4) be the most cost effective. These and similar variables would be important for any planner to consider, but the analysis is perfectly suited for a geographic database. Pieces of information can be layered and the particular benefits and drawbacks for each potential parcel can be easily

disclosed. Should circumstances change—say with the projected development of a new street or new residential construction in a part of the city—the database can be rapidly updated.

The use of geographic information systems software has permeated planning agencies around the world. It can be used to track the existing geographic trajectories of urban growth and note how well these accord with available infrastructure and may encroach on environmentally sensitive lands. It can enable the planner to create so-called "build out scenarios" that integrates the land available for development with current zoning maps in order to envision possible future patterns of growth. It can be used to assemble and alter property maps, zoning maps, land use maps, and infrastructure maps. Because the material in a GIS is digital, the information can be made available to the wider community over the Internet. Users may be able to access information and immediately note the essential characteristics of a particular property.

The first step involves the *acquisition and analysis of data*. This is the most technical aspect of the plan preparation and is conducted by planners. Planners collect baseline data regarding the physical site, existing development by type, infrastructure, public land, facilities, population, and whatever else would be useful. The emphasis is on those items that the planner needs to know in order to guide future projects, so trends are crucial. We already mentioned one item—developable land—but other items also matter. For example, age distribution is

important, because planning for 100 new senior citizens will have requirements that are different from preparing for 100 new kindergartners. Likewise, planners need to know which parts of the community are growing and which are remaining stable or declining. The data the planner uses can come from a variety of sources, such as the U.S. Census, the Bureau of Labor Statistics, state agencies, and private companies that provide updated and specialty data. In addition, planners gather some data themselves. Today, data analysis is aided by

Figure B13.4 Picture of a GIS application, from ESRI's *GIS Solutions for Urban and Regional Planning*. (*Source*: Da-Wei Liou, GISP, Delaware County Regional Planning Commission.)

computer applications: databases, spreadsheets, statistical packages, computer-aided design programs, and geographic information systems (GIS). The use of GIS in particular has made the analysis of spatial information—which planners use all of the time—much more powerful and efficient (Box 13.3).

The information-gathering step of developing a comprehensive plan does not involve a lot of politics, but the second step, the *formulation of goals for the community*, does. Comprehensive plans usually begin with a vision and a statement of goals for the community. There is generally some consensus on what people wish for their community: continued growth (so that the tax and employment bases increase), preservation of natural and cultural features (so that the community treasures are not lost and the community's character can be maintained), and provision of strong community services (so that civic government can be seen as doing its job). There are a few differences—one community may worry about excessive growth while another struggles to reverse years of blight—but the goals of different communities tend to sound alike.

Although the resulting language can be boilerplate, that is, essentially the same for each plan, the process of determining these goals is time consuming. The planner needs to elicit input from a wide spectrum of community citizens. She may use surveys, public meetings, focus groups, and other techniques to get a grasp on how residents define a livable city; what they believe needs to be improved; what sorts of structures and facilities need to be updated, improved, or replaced; and how they perceive their community. The number of people who have input should be limited only by the number of people who are willing to take the time to give their views. In some cases, this process can generate many perspectives. The formulation of the Portland, Oregon, Metro Plan, for instance, resulted from the input of 17,000 people.

The third step involves the actual *creation of the plan*. This is another point where the professional planners come in and attach a comprehensive plan to maps and language describing the conditions, goals, and means of implementation. Maps are a critical component here because they enable policy makers and citizens to visualize both the past and the projected future geography of a region. Legally, any subsequent actions by the community will have to be based on the comprehensive plan, and the city will have to adhere to these precepts for the foreseeable future. The Florida statutes, for example, state that:

A land development regulation shall be consistent with the comprehensive plan if the land uses, densities or intensities, capacity or size, timing, and other aspects of development by such . . . regulation are compatible with and further the objectives, policies, and uses, and densities or intensities in the comprehensive plan. (from Meck et al., 2000, p. 347; Florida Statutes sec. 163.3194(3)(a) (1996))

The plan itself does not usually get into details—it is not the same thing as a zoning ordinance—but it does lay the groundwork for future development. For example, it may contain broad language to the effect that an area should continue to develop single-family houses or that an area will be earmarked for future industrial development. This is where the basic elements of the land-use plan, discussed above, are laid out.

The fourth and final step of developing a comprehensive plan involves the *implementation of the proposed objectives*. Because the plan is broad, the set of implementation strategies must likewise be broad. These strategies are likely not contained in the plan itself—this would make it too cumbersome—but are instead developed in accordance with the plan. Some of the strategies that are spun off include

- A zoning code,
- Subdivision regulations,
- Growth management strategies,
- Capital improvement requests,
- Earmarking of special zones (e.g., an industrial park), and
- Resource protections.

The hope is that various projects will not collide with one another, for example, where an industrial park harms a key natural resource. There is also a budgetary aspect to implementing a plan, because most of what the community wants to do costs money. How to pay for all of these items is a large issue, and certain projects might have to be delayed.

Zoning

Zoning is a way to regulate the use of land. Land is divided into zones in which the number, types, and features of buildings are restricted, prohibited, or permitted. Zoning developed as a means of excluding incompatible uses. The early zoning laws were promulgated as a way to keep out commercial buildings, breweries, and overly tall buildings. New York City has the distinction of developing the first truly complete zoning ordinances in 1916. These ordinances were developed because of the accelerating problems of congestion, lack of sunlight, incompatible uses, encroachment, and loss of open space. What made New York's ordinances special was that (1) they covered the entire city, (2) they divided the city into four use zones, and (3) they further created five building height zones (Figure 13.11). Moreover,

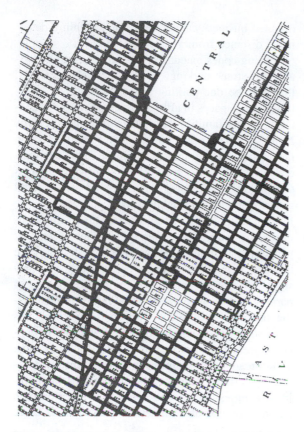

Figure 13.11 New York City zoning map of 1916. The map shows streets (in bold black) zoned for residences and businesses; streets in white are only residential; streets with dots are unrestricted. (*Source:* Barnet and Hack, 2000.)

the zoning maps that were developed considered the preexisting land uses, reinforcing these patterns rather than trying to impose an overarching plan for the city. This was not a visionary document, but rather a truly practical response to a bustling and growing metropolis.

The success of New York's zoning ordinances later encouraged the federal government in drafting the 1920s state and city planning and zoning acts discussed earlier. Zoning became the primary means of implementing land-use controls, but it was generally set up in such a way as to follow what was already in place. Since zoning has been established, the general presumption has been made that

a property owner can develop his or her property in accordance with what is allowed in the zoning district. Any deviations or **variances** from allowed uses are required to go before a special board, sometimes called a *board of appeals*.

Today, zoning entails the determination, location, and detailed description of **use zones**, districts that are based around one or more specific land uses. The most common categories are commercial, industrial, and residential. These may be subdivided, however. For example, single-family residential is often set apart from multifamily residential (duplexes and apartments). Heavy industrial is often distinct from light industrial, with the "heavy" category referring to industries that are especially intrusive, polluting, noisy, and perhaps dealing with toxic substances. Similar distinctions may be found with commercial districts as well. These use zones may be combined with **density zones**. These are especially applicable to residential land, and they determine the ratio of lot acreage to dwelling. For instance, some zoning districts allow one dwelling on every quarter acre, whereas others may allow one dwelling for every five acres. These are minimum lot sizes, and property owners are free to exceed the stipulated lot size. Another type of zoning district is a **height district**, which mandates that a building not exceed a particular height. Height districts are common within large cities.

Many communities also permit **planned development districts** (or planned-use districts), which are intended to create more flexibility within a particular part of the community and may lend themselves to more mixed uses. These districts may allow for a greater variety of uses than standard districts, and are often customized to a particular neighborhood in the city. Planned development districts may come under the heading of **special districts**, which can include university districts, downtown districts, government districts, flood-plain districts, mobile home districts, and others. Zoning ordinances include a lot of requirements, for parking, how a building is situated on the property, and permissible uses. Thus, the creation of special districts can be helpful in promoting more flexible development.

Several issues are involved in zoning. The earliest zoning districts were **cumulative**. The use zone indicated the "most intense" uses allowable. Thus, an industrial zone could include single-family houses, but a residential zone could not include factories. Cumulative zones continued to promote more functional integration in areas where residential uses were proximate to other uses, for instance, apartments located over storefronts. By the 1950s, however, cumulative uses had given way to **exclusive uses**, in which no other use is permitted in a zone. Exclusive zoning regulations have created functionally segregated districts such as industrial parks, shopping centers, apartment districts, and the like.

Another issue involves defining some key terms such as **family**. Most zoning refers to family units and restricts the number of unrelated people who may live in the same dwelling unit. This is, of course, a big issue for college students who often live with several roommates for financial reasons. It can also be an issue in nontraditional family situations. For example, codes can be written in such a way that a grandparent could not take care of a daughter's stepson.

Zoning can often be **exclusionary**. A zoning ordinance can mandate a large minimum lot size in order to retain a community's rural character or to encourage low-density residential patterns. Such **large-lot zoning** is a favored strategy of both rural townships and affluent communities and is discussed in more detail later in this chapter.

Communities are often forced to grapple with how to handle truly objectionable uses. Some districts, for instance, may be designated as "dry," meaning that they prohibit the sale of alcohol. Such restrictions can become a problem for restaurants that seek to move into a commercially zoned but alcohol-free area. More troublesome is the regulation of sexually oriented businesses like strip clubs. Zoning codes must be specific as to how these businesses are defined and how they can be regulated. For example, the Akron, Ohio, code is quite precise on what constitutes a sexually oriented business and where these businesses are prohibited. A sexually oriented business cannot be located within a designated distance from a school.

Zoning codes mandate a certain amount of available off-street parking. For residential dwellings, this may be one parking space per unit, or sometimes more spaces in affluent areas where the expectation is that families own two, three, or more cars. Nonresidential establishments also require parking, depending on the intensity of use. For commercial establishments, requirements are measured as one parking space for so many square feet of retail space. Commercial establishments may also require loading facilities. In these situations the zoning ordinances for parking are often quite generous and are generally based on saturation shopping periods (like the day before Christmas). For this reason, new stores tend to be surrounded by vast expanses of parking that is only partly used (Figure 13.12). Zoning parking requirements can create big problems for inner-city neighborhoods. Many inner-city properties were built before automobile traffic became widespread and so cannot possibly conform to parking regulations. Adjustments, such as sharing parking among establishments, greater reliance on curb parking, or use of commercial parking decks, are necessary in these cases.

Figure 13.12 Zoning today requires a great deal of parking for offices and stores. This often results in a landscape like Houston's, where buildings are surrounded by acres of parking lots.

In addition to zoning codes, planners are also responsible for drawing up and administering subdivision regulations. Most new housing units built in the United States are part of **subdivisions**, in which a tract is divided into two or more parcels. In practice, subdivisions contain dozens of parcels on which a developer builds new houses, townhouses, or apartments. The developer is also responsible for all of the other elements of the tract: streets, sidewalks, drainage, signage, and utilities. There may even be a requirement that enough room be left over for a neighborhood park. This makes a subdivision a work of collaboration between the developer and the planner. The developer normally must adhere to a community's subdivision regulations and cannot develop the property until his or her plans are approved. Modern developments owe their uniform look to fairly standard subdivision regulations.

Problems with Zoning and Responses

Zoning has had a dramatic effect on the development of cities and towns. Certainly, it alters the impact of land value and the land value curve discussed in Chapter 6. By prohibiting certain uses, zoning regulations may prevent a property owner from developing his or her property to its most lucrative use. A parcel in a neighborhood zoned for single-family residential, may be worth much less than if the property were zoned for apartments. Behind the more technical aspects of zoning swirl an array of local interests who stand to gain or lose depending on the delineation of zoning lines and the precise wording of zoning definitions. Zoning has also been criticized because it appears at times to obscure an overarching vision of the community and to promote social inequities.

Effect of Zoning on Community
Zoning tends to engender a great deal of inflexibility. It creates a system that is standardized and, to some eyes, boring. The best known critic of zoning (and planning in general) is Jane Jacobs, who described its pitfalls in a book entitled *The Death and Life of Great American Cities*. Here Jacobs (1961) wrote that:

If it appears that the rebuilt portions of cities and the endless new developments spreading beyond cities are reducing city and countryside alike to a monotonous, unnourishing gruel, this is not strange. It all comes...out of the same intellectual dish of mush, a mush in which the qualities, necessities, advantages, and behavior of great cities have been utterly confused with the qualities, necessities, advantages and behavior of other and more inert types of settlements. (pp. 6–7)

Jacobs' critique of planning in large cities also could have applied to zoning in small towns. A pungent critic, James Howard Kunstler (1996), wrote that:

If you want to make your communities better, begin at once by throwing out your zoning laws. Get rid of them. Throw them away. Don't revise them. Set them on fire and make a public ceremony of it. (p. 110)

Among some of the problems that Jacobs, Kunstler, and other critics have noted are the following:

- The exclusive land uses mandated by most zoning create functionally segregated districts that divorce where people work and shop from where they live. Modern zoning does not allow for the neighborhood shop that people walk to, and instead encourages large shopping centers that people have to drive to.
- The parking requirements of zoning ordinances have led to stores surrounded by huge parking lots that limit walkability.
- Street requirements mandate very wide streets in residential areas—sometimes wide enough for parking on both sides and for two garbage trucks to get past each other without either having to yield. These encourage faster automobile traffic while discouraging pedestrian movement. Moreover, most new subdivisions are created without tree-lined terraces between sidewalk and street, because traffic engineers worry about cars running into the trees.
- Setback requirements mean that houses and stores need to be placed far behind the lot line. This discourages neighborliness and often encourages houses with garages in the front.

- Much of the plot design requires every parcel to have a certain amount of acreage and a certain geometric regularity. The result is that it becomes more difficult to accommodate natural features such as wetlands, woodlands, and stream sheds into the patchwork of subdivisions.
- Minimum lot sizes have also led to more socioeconomic and life-cycle segregation. Housing developments tend to offer housing within a particular price range and with similar configurations. This means that neighborhoods are fairly homogeneous.
- Although zoning encourages uniformity within a subdivision or a community, the zoning plans of one community may not correspond with the zoning plans of a neighboring community. This creates a patchwork zoning that may not work well for a larger region.

These shortcomings can be tied into a larger set of concerns regarding walkability, neighborliness, social segregation, and unnecessary destruction of the natural environment. They have spurred an interest in creating communities that do not share these problems, which is called the *New Urbanism*, first introduced in Chapter 8. Ironically, these "new" communities hearken back to the past—often in a period before zoning codes were as prevalent. For this reason, they are sometimes referred to as *neotraditional communities*. The tenets of neotraditional communities promote (1) walkability, (2) smaller lots clustered together, (3) houses close to the lot line, (4) narrower streets that are often laid out in a grid pattern, (5) functional integration, and (6) more socioeconomic and life-cycle integration. The overriding goal of these designs is to promote a sense of place.

Developers have spearheaded this New Urbanist movement and have constructed some communities based on their principles. Such communities have become a part of the planner's lexicon and have diffused in some form or another to just about every state. Proponents of the New Urbanism, including Andres Duany, Elizabeth Plater-Zyberk, Peter Calthorpe, and Todd Bressi, have encouraged the development of communities where automobile dependence is reduced. They have also borrowed freely from the ideas of Kevin Lynch (1960), who has written about **urban imageability**—"that quality in a physical object which gives it a high probability of evoking a strong image in any given observer" (p. 9)—and the elements of urban design.

In their book *Suburban Nation*, Duany et al. (2000) offer a few ideas about how to make a better town or suburb. One idea, **functional integration** or **mixed-use development**, is an anchor of new town building. Duany et al. advise developers to build corner stores within every new neighborhood. This can lead to even more retail development that is well connected to the rest of the neighborhood. In addition to functional integration, Duany et al. promote more socioeconomic and life-cycle integration, by encouraging the mixture of income levels and generations in their neighborhoods. Another idea is **connectivity**, which states that neighborhoods should be constructed so that each new subdivision is connected with existing neighborhoods. Modern development practices rely heavily on a system of collector roads; the New Urbanism favors the grid pattern (Figure 13.13).

Duany et al. (2000) also advocate everything that will increase walkability as opposed to auto dependence. For this reason, they propose the construction of **pedestrian sheds**, where the elements of each neighborhood are located within a 5-minute walk. Building pedestrian sheds correctly requires smaller lot sizes, clustered together. Pedestrian sheds can also prove beneficial for mass transportation, and Peter Calthorpe has advanced the notion of **transit-oriented developments** surrounding a transit stop.

Finally, Duany et al. (2000) promote a greater definition of the streetscape, accomplished by a number of methods. First, they propose building houses close to the lot line so that people can easily interact with individuals walking on the sidewalk. Moreover, they advocate narrower streets than is the conventional practice, creating a slower traffic pattern and more neighborly interaction across the street. Finally, parking requirements should be reduced, and parking should be visually de-emphasized. This means that parking should be placed behind, instead of in front of, buildings and houses.

The ideas of new urbanism have found favor in most parts of the country. Even the Walt Disney

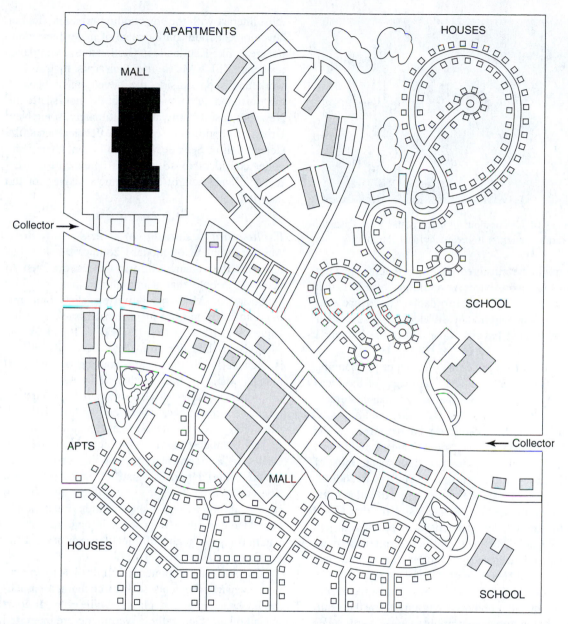

Figure 13.13 Illustration of collector roads and functional segregation within many suburban communities. (*Source:* Levy, 2000.)

Corporation has jumped on board, building a neotraditional town near Orlando, Florida (Figure 13.14). Certain elements of new urbanism have become especially common. **Cluster zoning**, for example, provides a way to develop only part of a lot. Rather than building one house on 2 acres, the idea is to take the lot as a whole and develop only part of it. So, a 40-acre lot could accommodate 20 houses, but

Figure 13.14 Celebration, Florida, is the Walt Disney Corporation's attempt to create an ideal community.

these might be clustered on only 10 acres, leaving 30 acres for open space. An additional benefit is that the houses may be more affordable. **Mixed-use zoning** can also accommodate different land uses. Other forms of zoning have become part of the planner's tool kit.

At the same time, many developers, planning officials, and local politicians are leery of the ideas of New Urbanism. Developers worry that customers will not purchase houses that have smaller lots, are built near the lot line, or have garages in the back rather than in the front. Planners are forced to alter their zoning codes to accommodate most of these ideas. Traffic engineers are unlikely to endorse narrower streets. Cluster zoning in particular often provokes some anxiety. Residents worry that it will lead to denser development and perhaps a less exclusive neighborhood. Politicians often respond to organized resistance to cluster zoning and may try to prohibit this type of development.

Overall, the ideals of New Urbanism confront many practical problems stemming from the realities of contemporary metropolitan areas. Large-scale housing developments in the New Urbanist vein must deal with the economics of housing provision (see a more detailed discussion of housing markets in Chapter 9), such as attracting home buyers and bringing in developers for the needed retail and transportation-related functions. A second major issue is that even a large New Urbanist development

must interact with the surrounding urban fabric. For developments built on the edge of major metropolitan areas, like Kentlands in Gaithersburg, Maryland, residents will have to use their cars to travel to work and shop outside the development because the surrounding suburbs often do not share the New Urbanist design values. Ultimately, some New Urban neighborhoods (especially developments like Celebration or Seaside, both in Florida) have come under considerable criticism as being elitist, overplanned, and socially constricting enclaves for the neo-rich.

Exclusionary Zoning of Class and Race

Another problem of modern zoning is that it has been used to create uniform places designed to keep out people that a community may consider "undesirable." Modern subdivisions slice communities into fairly narrow income categories. Housing valued at $100,000 to $150,000 is found in one subdivision, housing from $200,000 to $300,000 is located in another, elite housing at $450,000 plus is found in yet another. This segmentation of property classes differs in degree from previous class separations, where neighborhood wealth was more broadly defined and it was common to see a modest home built near by a wealthy estate. In a fragmented metropolis, communities include only a narrow band of housing classes. The entrance fee to live in an affluent suburb may be the ability to buy a half-million-dollar house. Gated communities impose their own restrictions and thus represent an additional layer of politics and exclusion.

The political component of all this has to do with how local governments seek to encourage particular housing types and classes while they discourage all others. Generally, governments are interested in maximizing their property tax base, minimizing the need for certain services (especially those for low-income people), and promoting higher property values. The mechanisms for accomplishing this are fairly simple. The easiest way is through the use of zoning. Communities may designate a large minimum lot size—1, 3, or 5 acres—and they can also

Figure 13.15 Large-lot zoning. Mandating large lots of more than an acre makes land and housing prohibitively expensive to many potential residents.

require such amenities as a two-car garage, a minimum square footage, a minimum number of bedrooms, or a required number of bathrooms. Zoning may also exclude all multifamily housing; this tends to minimize rentals. Such zoning decisions may be made for a number of reasons. Large lots are often touted as a method to retain the rural character of a community or to preserve local property values (Figure 13.15).

In addition, modern zoning shuns functional integration, in which commercial, industrial, and all types of residential uses are placed together. James Kunstler points out in *Home from Nowhere* (1996) that this separation of land uses largely eliminated the new building of apartments located over the shop, one of the main types of affordable housing before World War II. Whatever the rationale, such restrictions operate as exclusionary zoning, zoning that inhibits the development of affordable housing.

Exclusion need not always be economic. Zoning has an ignominious history of keeping minority groups out of neighborhoods. Some rudimentary zoning laws were clearly designed for this purpose. For example, in the 1880s San Francisco passed a law that restricted Chinese laundries to certain parts of the city, while New York City zoning laws restricted the spread of immigrant garment districts onto Fifth Avenue.

Although overt tactics of racial exclusion are now illegal, zoning brought about by local governments can have very real racial consequences even today. To understand this process, consider that much of the recent suburban growth resulted from "white flight" out of central cities and that most metropolitan suburbs contain a disproportionately small number of minority groups. Moreover, research indicates that only a fraction of the central-city/suburban racial imbalance can be accounted for by differential ability to pay for housing or by differences in housing preferences. What is left is the legacy of past and present discriminatory practices in the housing market that has kept so many of the independent communities ringing the central city nearly all white. The uses of laws and regulations to bar African Americans and other groups from living where they choose are dealt with in substantial detail in Chapter 10.

It can be quite difficult for governments on a larger scale—whether they are metropolitan, state, or federal—to overrule the zoning decisions made by local communities. The idea that cities are considered to be "creatures of the states," with little constitutional protection, is counteracted by the value that Americans place on local control. Legislatures, which are increasingly made up of people who represent suburban districts, and the courts have been reluctant to abridge this authority. Some attempts have been made, however. For example, in 1969 Massachusetts passed an Anti-Snob Zoning Act that authorized the state to override local zoning in communities with less than 10 percent moderate-income housing. In the 1970s a set of court rulings first found that local zoning could be invalidated if it had a racially discriminatory, though not economically discriminatory, effect. Later, this was narrowed to invalidate only those zoning codes with racist intent. Intent is harder to prove than effect, and that has made the overriding of local zoning statutes extraordinarily difficult. And when it comes to economic exclusion, communities are given a fairly free rein to do as they please (see box 13.2 earlier in this chapter).

The best way to foster racial integration in the suburbs is through the concerted efforts of those communities. Studies have shown that municipalities that are unconcerned about promoting integration or that actively seek to avoid it can often be successful. They can use their powers to block particular types of housing and thus develop a reputation as minority-unfriendly communities. Conversely, some communities have shown remarkable success in fostering integration. A study of two Cleveland area cities—Shaker Heights and Cleveland Heights—demonstrates the power of local authorities to promote racial integration. Beginning in the early 1960s, when a great deal of racial transition was taking place, officials in these communities developed policies designed to encourage racial integration and to discourage white flight. Among these policies were

- Banning "for sale" signs as a way to prevent panic selling.
- Encouraging real estate agents to steer clients into integrated neighborhoods.
- Making low-interest mortgage loans available to people who move into neighborhoods where their race is underrepresented.
- Emphasizing community maintenance in order to allay fears about blight in changing neighborhoods.
- Adopting an aggressive marketing strategy that highlights community amenities and the quality of schools and other services.

Above all, the experience of these two suburbs shows that integration efforts require a sustained effort and whole-hearted community participation. Some municipalities are compelled by court order to open themselves up to more minorities; others may seek to stem the tide of segregation late in the game. In such cases, integration strategies rarely work.

Growth Management

Growth management has become a major aspect of planning, particularly in fast-growing suburban areas. Early planners paid little attention to growth management; their main concern was to expedite growth. This is still the case in many communities, particularly in declining inner cities and inner-ring suburbs. Within newer suburbs, however, residents often express concern that their way of life is disappearing

in the onslaught of new housing development, new shopping centers, and more traffic. In many cases, the issue is focused on the loss of farmland, as farmers sell off their acreage to real estate developers, hoping to capitalize on the higher residential land values. Much open space is lost in the process. Controlling growth in the United States is a very difficult task, however, and attempts to do so have aroused furious opposition from the development industry and a great deal of litigation. Farmers also may feel that restrictions curtail the economic value of their land. Several techniques are used for growth management, with varying effectiveness and political viability:

- *Agricultural zoning.* The simplest growth management strategy would be to zone land so that there can be only one house per 40 or more acres. Generally, there is no requirement that land be used only for agricultural purposes. Agricultural zoning can alleviate the problem of farmland being converted to denser housing lots by not allowing small, suburban-style plots. This might also be done as a quarter zoning system, where a farmer can put down four houses per 160 acres. The problem is that the pressure to overturn low-intensity zoning can be overwhelming. The result is that agricultural zoning may end up being altered. One innovative system, promoted by some developers, has been to design new subdivisions so that they conform with nature, where the impact of the new housing is lessened.
- *Building restrictions.* Communities may try to limit the number of permits they issue a year. This may be a fixed number, a percentage of current housing, or some way to keep permits in line with available infrastructure. The idea of limits has been tried in Hudson, Ohio, where only 100 new units are permitted each year. Boulder, Colorado, tries to limit growth to 2 percent a year, also making sure that 15 percent of housing is affordable to people on a moderate income. Another approach, implemented in Ramapo, New York, was the development of a point system, where different criterion were assigned different point values to ensure that development was limited to places where the necessary infrastructure already existed. All of these approaches were challenged in court, but they were all upheld.
- *Growth boundaries.* This is a situation in which a metropolitan area draws a line beyond which growth is limited. Development outside of the boundary may not be banned, but is limited by a lack of government

investment in infrastructural improvements. Urban growth boundaries, then, are really urban service boundaries. Investments in infrastructure, especially roads, are powerful determinants of growth. If these facilities are limited, then growth is slower. Growth boundaries are very common in European cities but are less common in the United States.

- *Impact fees.* This is a strategy in which a community charges the developer extra money to cover the costs of public improvements. Traditionally most developers have paid for some road improvements and water/sewer lines in the development itself. However, services such as fire stations, schools, and so forth tend to show up later, for example, in school levies. Thus, the costs of the development emerge after the development is completed and are imposed on all property owners in the tax district. In contrast, impact fees impose these costs on the developers themselves. Many states (like Ohio) do not allow impact fees, but other states have used them. Their effect is to increase the cost for housing, because the impact fees are passed on to the consumer.

- *Open space preservation.* Several techniques are used to accomplish this goal. Land can be bought outright for parks or open space. One popular approach has been the purchase of development rights where the farmer is paid the difference between what the land is worth as urban land and what it is worth as agricultural land. The payment of the difference then requires that the land be kept as farmland in perpetuity. Although this is not very controversial because it does not involve any takings, it can be expensive, especially for land that has risen in value.

All of these growth management methods have been tried and are likely to become more popular as communities develop and as people seek to preserve their way of life. They are also likely to be controversial. Developers do not like them, nor do many farmers who resent being cheated out of the full value of their land. Community leaders are also wary of limiting their tax base.

WRAPPING UP

As long as there have been cities, there has been planning. However, it was with the growth of the industrial city in the nineteenth century that the need for planning became more urgent. Planning became a tool by which cities could be made more aesthetically pleasing, more efficient, more equitable, more conducive to maintaining property values, and more environmentally healthful. The seeds of modern planning were established in fits and starts. In the modern era, urban planning was characterized by a tension between the visionaries of planning—those who long viewed the city as a model, an arena for "big" plans—and the machinists of planning—those who viewed the city as a place that needed to be tinkered with and improved in some places but should otherwise be left alone. Over the course of the twentieth century, the practical planners won. Planning today is a professional endeavor, with planners found at all levels of government and in the private sector as well. Moreover, many of the tools used by professional planners, especially zoning codes, have been found to be constitutional and have been implemented by governments at all levels. Planners have also been placed in the midst of a very complex and sometimes contentious political process involving politicians, residents, developers, financiers, political action groups, and lawyers.

In the United States, much of the scope of modern planning involves efforts to guide private-sector development. In this chapter, we discussed how the comprehensive plan has become the principal means by which communities perform this task. The comprehensive plan provides an outline of where the community is in the present, where it expects to be in the future, and what sorts of projects and regulations may be used to help steer it. There are several ways in which this plan is implemented. Chief among these are zoning ordinances that mandate property uses, the density of dwellings and buildings, building heights, and several other specifications. Although zoning has led to greater control of land use, critics have derided it for creating communities that are unappealing and sterile. The response has been the formulation of a new type of urbanism that seeks to reintegrate communities. The visionary planners of the turn of the last century have been joined by a cadre of new urban idealists at the beginning of the twenty-first century who are seeking to alter the nature of modern planning.

READINGS

American Farmland Trust. 1997. "The Cost of Community Services in Madison Village and Township, Lake County, Ohio." Special Report.

Barnet, Jonathan, and Gary Hack. 2000. "Urban Design." In *The Practice of Local Government Planning*, 3rd ed. Washington, D.C.: International City/County Management Association.

Baum, Howell. 2000. "Communities, Organizations, Politics, and Ethics." In *The Practice of Local Government Planning*, 3rd ed. Washington, D.C.: International City/County Management Association.

Benevolo, Leonardo. 1985. *The Origins of Modern Town Planning*. Cambridge, MA: MIT Press.

Cullingworth, J. Barry. 1993. *The Political Culture of Planning*. New York: Routledge.

Duany, Andre, Elizabeth Plater-Zyberk, and Jeff Speck. 2000. *Suburban Nation*. New York: North Point Press.

ESRI. 2006. *GIS Solutions for Urban and Regional Planning*.

Fishman, Robert. 1996. "Urban Utopias: Ebenezer Howard and Le Corbusier." In S. Campbell and S. Fainstein, eds., *Readings in Planning Theory*. Oxford: Blackwell Publishers.

Foglesong, Richard. 1986. *Planning the Capitalist City*. Princeton, NJ: Princeton University Press.

Gallion, Arthur, and Simon Eisner. 1983. *The Urban Pattern: City Planning and Design*. New York: Van Nostrand Reinhold Co.

Garreau, Joel. 1991. *Edge City: Life on the New Frontier*. New York: Anchor Books.

Hall, Peter. 1996. *Cities of Tomorrow*. Oxford: Blackwell Publishers.

Jacobs, Jane, 1961. *The Death and Life of Great American Cities*. NY: A Vintage Book.

Johnson, William C. 1997. *Urban Planning and Politics*. Chicago: American Planning Association.

Kelly, Eric, and Barbara Beckler. 2000. *Community Planning: Introduction to the Comprehensive Plan*. Washington, D.C.: Island Press.

Klosterman, Richard, 2000. Planning in the Information Age. In *The Practice of Local Government Planning*, 3rd ed. Washington, D.C.: International City/County Management Association.

Kostof, Spiro, 1992. *The City Assembled*. Boston: Bulfinch Press.

Kostof, Spiro, 1991. *The City Shaped*. Boston: Bulfinch Press.

Krumholz, Norman. 1996. "A Retrospective View of Equity Planning: Cleveland, 1969–1979." In S. Campbell and S. Fainstein, eds., *Readings in Planning Theory*. Oxford: Blackwell Publishers.

Kunstler, James Howard. 1996. *Home from Nowhere*. New York: Simon and Schuster.

Levy, John M. 2000. *Contemporary Urban Planning*, 5th ed. Upper Saddle River, NJ: Prentice Hall.

Lynch, Kevin. 1960. *The Image of the City*. Cambridge, MA: MIT Press.

Mallach, Alan. 2004. "The Betrayal of Mount Laurel." National Housing Institute, *Shelterforce Online,* 134, March/April.

Meck, Stuart, Paul Wack, and Michelle Zimet. 2000. "Zoning and Subdivision Regulations." In *The Practice of Local Government Planning*, 3rd ed. Washington, D.C.: International City/County Management Association.

Nelson, Arthur. 2000. "Growth Management." In *The Practice of Local Government Planning*, 3rd ed. Washington, D.C.: International City/County Management Association.

Peterson, Jon. 1983. "The Impact of Sanitary Reform upon American Urban Planning, 1840–1890." In Donald Krueckeberg, ed., *Introduction to Planning History in the United States*. New Brunswick, NJ: Rutgers University Press.

Sutcliffe, Anthony. 1981. *Towards the Planned City*. New York: St. Martin's Press.

Wilson, William H. 1996. "The Glory, Destruction, and Meaning of the City Beautiful Movement." In S. Campbell and S. Fainstein, eds., *Readings in Planning Theory*. Oxford: Blackwell Publishers.

Wright, Gwendolyn, 1981. *Building the Dream: A Social History of Housing in America*. Cambridge, MA: MIT Press.

CHAPTER 14

CITIES IN THE DEVELOPED WORLD

From city to city and from class to class, cultural differences appear which have a pronounced effect on the rhythms of daily life, on the bustle or quiet of the streets, and on the security or violence in public spaces. In the long run, they are expressed in morphological arrangements.

—PAUL CLAVAL, 1984, p. 33

Up until now, we have mainly examined cities in the United States and Canada. These are the cities with which we are most familiar and that best illustrate many of the processes and features of urban geography. North American cities also afford a model of urban development less fettered by history, with development going back 450 years at most and in many cases only a few decades. Yet this model also represents a limited typology. What French geographer Paul Claval describes as the "morphological arrangements" or the form of North American cities is shaped by a particular set of cultural practices and historical traditions. If we venture beyond North America, we find cities that have been influenced by separate sets of factors.

In this section, we want to look beyond the North American city and introduce a more global perspective into our study of cities. In this chapter, we examine cities in the developed world, focusing primarily on cities in capitalist Western Europe, post-Communist Eastern Europe, and Japan. Unfortunately, this does not include all developed cities; we are omitting cities in Australia, New Zealand, and East Asia. Also, because of the constraints of space, we must skip lightly over places that are individually distinct. Feel free to consult the recommended readings in the back of this chapter if you wish to explore cities in greater detail.

WESTERN EUROPEAN CITIES

In Chapter 2 we examined the evolution of urban patterns and structure up to and including the Industrial Revolution. Western European cities—those cities now found in the member countries of the European Union plus Switzerland and Norway—lie within a region that was the first to fully urbanize and continues to be one of the most urbanized places in the world. A note: we use the terms Western Europe and Eastern Europe as a matter of convenience, stemming largely from developments since World War II. This division is artificial and considers as "Eastern European" several cities like Prague and Budapest that were capitals of great central European kingdoms and empires. We preserve this categorization, however, because of the powerful role played by Communist political economies in shaping these cities in the latter half of the twentieth century.

It could be argued that, taken as a group, Western European cities are some of the most pleasing cities in the world. They are prosperous and have fewer problems of poverty, crime, and ethnic conflict than other cities. They are also a fascinating blend of ancient, medieval, and early modern history accompanied by bold new building designs and planning innovations. Where else but in France, for example, would the government emphasize the need for each new post office to harmonize with its neighborhood while also making an architectural statement! In contrast to many American centers, Western European cities continue to enjoy vibrant and walkable neighborhoods that are relatively safe. Many also preserve a distinctive mix of stores, with plenty of small independent businesses, open air markets, and outdoor cafes located along tree-lined boulevards and architecturally arresting plazas. It is no surprise then, that a major part of European tourism is based on the simple pleasure of experiencing European cities. Venice, Paris, London, Florence, Innsbruck, and many others derive a large share of their income from their physical beauty and urbane appeal.

At the same time, it is important to see Western European cities as more than an assortment of museums or as some kind of Disneyfied "Main Street." They are living communities beset by the kinds of issues and problems that affect all cities: economic transitions, urban decay, an influx of foreigners, decentralization, increased congestion, and pollution, to name just a few. Many of the issues we discussed in the previous chapters can be readily applied to Western European cities, but with a different twist.

Urbanization and the European City System

Urbanization refers to the proportion of the population that lives in cities. We say that a country is *urbanized* when more than half of its population lives in urban areas. The first country in the world to become urbanized was the United Kingdom, which had become a mostly urban society by 1850. The United Kingdom was followed by a few other European countries, which are listed in Table 14.1. By 1910 a majority of the population in Italy, Belgium, and the Netherlands lived in cities, and Germany was on the verge of becoming mostly urban. No other country in the world had a majority

Table 14.1 Percentage Population Living in Cities, c. 1910

Italy	62.4%
Belgium	56.6
Netherlands	53.0
Germany	48.8
Spain	42.0
France	38.5
Switzerland	36.6
Denmark	35.9
Hungary	30.0
Austria	27.3
Sweden	22.6
Romania	16.0
Portugal	15.6

Source: Pounds, 1990.

urban population, although the United States was close. In Italy, urbanization was concentrated in the northern part of the country—with its long history of urban handicrafts (see Chapter 2)—and also in Naples, which was the capital of a large kingdom and long reigned as one of the five largest cities in Europe.

As the percentage of people living in European cities increased, the size of these cities also increased. In 1700, after European countries had moved into the forefront of overseas colonization and had nearly completed a long transition toward a capitalist economy, London and Paris both had more than a half million people, which placed them among the world's 10 most populous cities. By 1800 Europe had three of the world's 10 most populous cities, and London contained nearly 1 million people. By 1900 London was the largest city in the world, and Paris, Berlin, Vienna, Manchester, and the very westward looking city of St. Petersburg were also among the 10 most populous (Figure 14.1). And the cities continued to grow. By 1925 Europe had about 11 cities with more than 1 million people (four of these in Britain), out of a total of about 31 cities worldwide with 1 million residents.

Why was Europe the first continent to urbanize, and why did it develop so many large cities?

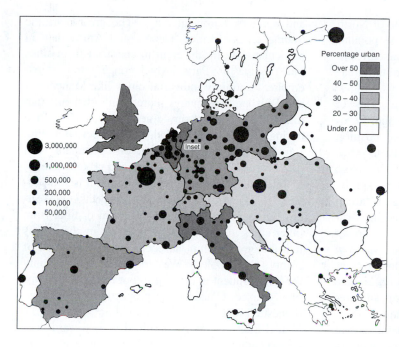

Figure 14.1 Cities in Europe on the eve of World War I. At this point in history, Northwestern Europe was clearly the center of the global economy, was the most urbanized, and contained the world's largest cities.

Two major reasons stand out. First, the European head start resulted from early **industrialization**. The manufacture of textiles, steel, and chemicals in midlands Britain, in the coalfields of Belgium and France, and in the Ruhr and Rhine valleys of Germany encouraged rural people to move into urban areas to work in factories. This could not have happened before the nineteenth century, when industrialization created a new economy. Second, European cities grew because of **imperialism**. Many of the largest cities on the continent were capitals of vast colonial empires. In 1750, for example, Spain, Portugal, Britain, and France laid claim to almost all of North and South America. The bounty that arrived from these territories, plus the overhead required to administer the colonies, caused imperial capitals to swell. By 1900 most of the Western Hemisphere was independent, but the British, French, Dutch, Belgian, German, Danish, and Portuguese still controlled about 35 percent of the entire world's surface outside of Europe, specifically in Africa and Asia. Within Europe were situated the large land empires of Austria-Hungary and Russia. Such holdings required large administrative apparatuses,

and for this reason many European cities grew to tremendous size.

Today, Europe is mostly urbanized, but there are some clear differences among countries. Those countries in the vanguard of the Industrial Revolution, like Britain, Germany, Belgium, and the Netherlands, are strongly urbanized. Other countries are more intermediate. Among these are France, where large segments of the population continue to prefer small-town and rural life, with more than one-third of the population living in communities of less than 10,000 people; Italy, where the urbanized north contrasts markedly with an agrarian south; and Spain and Greece, which may experience greater urbanization as their economies mature. At the low end (for Europe) are many of the Scandinavian countries, Switzerland, Austria, Portugal, and Ireland. Although urbanization rates have leveled off in much of Europe, overall there is a continued influx of people—many now from overseas—into the urban regions. At the same time, the associated problems of congestion, crime, poverty, and housing capacity have become more acute. In addition, cities are increasing in area, as nearby rural land is converted to urban uses. As is true of North America, suburbanization has caused the population of large cities within their official boundaries to decline, while the population of metropolitan areas has gone up.

Although there are now more large cities in Europe than there were 50 or 100 years ago, European cities have lost their **demographic** position among the cities of the world. In contrast to cities in the less developed world, none of the large European metropolitan areas is growing rapidly. As recently as 1950, five of the 25 largest "urban agglomerations" in the world were located in Western Europe, and an additional two were in the Soviet Union. In contrast, by 2005 only Paris and Moscow qualified among the largest urban agglomerations (see Table 1.5). Given these trends, it is conceivable that by 2010 no Western or Eastern European cities will be among the 25 largest cities in the world.

Western European cities continue to maintain their economic and political position, however. Western European cities continue to rank highly on measures of economic and political significance. This is evidenced by the significant number of global cities—cities at the nexus of financial, political, and industrial power—that are located in Europe. (We discuss the notion of world or global cities in Chapter 4.) New York, Tokyo, and London are considered to be in the first tier of such world cities. In Europe, Paris, Berlin, Rome, Milan, Brussels, Amsterdam, Frankfurt, Zurich, Vienna, and Geneva clearly are world centers for a variety of reasons.

Characteristic Features of European Cities

Because European cities differ with regard to size, historical legacy, available building materials, government, role of planning, and recent economic trends, they are difficult to characterize. Certainly, we need to consider political ideological systems, which is why Eastern European cities are normally discussed separately from Western European cities. We might also contrast aspects of cities in the Mediterranean lands of Italy and Spain, which were strongly influenced by the Renaissance and the Catholic Church, with the more subdued middle

and northern European cities. The great maritime trading cities—Venice, Genoa, and Amsterdam in particular—are far different in character from cities like Vienna or Paris, which once administered empires. Certainly industrial cities like Manchester and Duisberg, Germany, share many elements that differentiate them from cities that came of age during the Medieval period, like Bruges, Belgium. Europe is an extraordinarily diverse continent, with disparate histories, geographies, and urban legacies.

Internal variations notwithstanding, it is still possible to point to a number of aspects of Western European cities that render them distinct from other cities in the world. Of greatest importance is that they exist within an economic environment of plenty. The people in Western Europe are not only the most affluent in the world, but they are the most highly taxed. Consider the proportion of the gross domestic product spent by the public sector. In the United States, roughly one-third goes toward public expenditures. In Western Europe it is closer to half. As a result, public coffers have more cash to spend on public projects. There are also differences in the allocation of public spending. In the United States, much government money goes to defense and highway projects. In contrast, European governments spend less in these areas and more on urban development, mass transit, and beautification.

Density and Compactness   European cities are

fairly compact. In the past, most cities were engirdled by a wall. If the population grew, as it did when cities were economically or politically successful, the extra population was crammed inside these fortifications, forcing more intense usage of land. Finally, suburbs (or *faubourgs*) emerged outside the city walls, but these remained close to the walled city proper. Sometimes, walls were based on overly optimistic expectations of growth, as was the case with Siena, Italy, where city leaders constructed a wall that encompassed far more territory than the city ever needed.

Transportation posed another constraint. The reliance of all but the rich on their own two feet for transportation meant that cities could not spread out too much. They were **walking cities**. People needed to travel, and goods had to be transported, using wheeled hand carts, from one place to another in a reasonable period of time. Cities could not grow beyond a couple of miles in diameter, and most were smaller than that. Existing building stock from this preindustrial period ensures that the historical core of European cities is densely populated. There are a few such cities in the United States—Boston and Charlestown come to mind—but these are rare. Except for some planned new towns, nearly all European cities were established as walking cities.

Since the early nineteenth century, European cities have grown tremendously in area. Streetcars, trains, trolleys, and subways all appeared in the late 1800s and into the 1900s. Automobile ownership also became much more common as European societies became more affluent. Today, most households own a car, and excellent mass transportation systems can be found throughout the region. Nevertheless, European cities continue to exhibit much higher densities than American cities, as illustrated in Table 14.2. In the United States, only a few cities have densities in excess of 20 people per acre. More typical are cities like Atlanta where much of the land, even within the city limits, is given over to relatively low density, detached, single-family housing. In European cities by contrast, densities of more than 50 inhabitants per acre are common. This tendency toward greater densities also applies to suburban areas. European suburbs, which contain many high-rise apartment complexes, have greater densities than U.S. suburbs, which are comprised primarily of single-family houses.

Reasons for this high urban density have to do primarily with urban **compactness**, a measure of concentration in the city. It would be wrong to assume that urban compactness is a direct consequence of the overall density, urban and rural, of a country. Although many European countries are more heavily populated per square mile than the United States, several have population densities that are equal to or lower than the United States, yet they still have higher urban densities and urban compactness. Moreover, some countries with a high national density, like England, have lower urban

Table 14.2 Urban Residential Density per Acre

City	Country	Density per Acre
Bucharest	Romania	669
Tiranë	Albania	489
Sofia	Bulgaria	403
Amsterdam	Netherlands	375
Budapest	Hungary	304
Prague	Czech Republic	274
Warsaw	Poland	274
Paris	France	269
Chisinău	Moldova	259
Ljubljana	Slovenia	252
Marseille	France	242
Belgrade	Serbia	237
Athens	Greece	235
Toronto	Canada	227
Talinn	Estonia	180
New York	U.S.	178
Bratislava	Slovakia	175
Cardiff	United Kingdom	133
Stockholm	Sweden	59
Seattle	United States	47
Atlanta	United States	22

Source: World Resources 1998–99: A Guide to the Global Environment. New York: Oxford University Press.

compactness than countries with a lower national density, like Italy.

In Europe, three basic factors contribute to compactness. First, many city dwellers cannot spread out as far as American urbanites. One reason for this is different access costs. The costs of private transportation are much higher in Europe than in the United States. In Europe, two-car families are still in the minority. Gasoline prices are exceptionally high when compared to the United States (Table 14.3). Moreover, European countries are less inclined to build a lot of new roads or to expand the carrying capacity of existing roads. Costs and congestion make a long commute less practical. In many cities, the whine of the gas-efficient, nimble, but madly annoying moped represents one solution to these problems. Another solution is the widespread use of public transportation. Most European urbanites enjoy mass transportation that is far more

Table 14.3 Average Gas Prices: April–May 2006

City or Country	Price per Gallon (in U.S. Dollars)
Hong Kong, China	$6.54
London, UK	$6.36
Rome, Italy	$6.15
Frankfurt, Germany	$6.10
Tokyo, Japan	$4.93
Brazil average	$4.60
Mumbai, India	$4.13
Johannesburg, South Africa	$3.70
United States average	$3.00
Beijing, China	$2.40
Buenos Aires, Argentina	$2.21
Riyadh, Saudi Arabia	$0.91
Kuwait average	$0.78
Caracas, Venezuela	$0.12

Sources: www.CNNMoney.com; Associates for International Research, Inc.

Table 14.4 Mass Transit and Car Ownership

City	Country	Work Trips by Transit %	Cars per 1000 People
Belgrade	Serbia	64	30
Chisinău	Moldova	48	60
Nizhniy Novgorod	Russia	78	69
Riga	Latvia	57	104
Moscow	Russia	85	138
Zagreb	Croatia	52	215
Vilnius	Lithuania	49	215
Copenhagen	Denmark	27	223
New York	United States	51	232
Bratislava	Slovakia	72	282
Budapest	Hungary	66	288
Sofia	Bulgaria	75	310
Cardiff	United Kingdom	13	350
Athens	Greece	34	354
Stockholm	Sweden	37	390
Liepzig	Germany	33	396
Paris	France	40	426
Toronto	Canada	30	430
Atlanta	United States	20	473
Prague	Czech Republic	67	500
Seattle	United States	16	654

Source: World Resources 1998–99: A Guide to the Global Environment. New York: Oxford University Press.

comprehensive and generally cheaper than in the United States, because of greater government subsidies (Table 14.4). At the same time, note that the majority of European urbanites utilize cars, and the proportion is growing.

The second factor is the higher costs of home ownership and home financing. Housing prices are almost always higher in Europe because land prices are higher as a result of its greater scarcity and because European builders tend to use sturdier materials. The cost of even a small house on its own lot is generally within the means of only the upper middle class. A house on a lot of half an acre to an acre, so common in North America, is unaffordable for all but the economic elite. Just as important, the cost of financing a house is higher because most Europeans do not enjoy the 30-year, tax-deductible, amortized mortgage available to Americans. Mortgages are not subsidized by the government, and most mortgage periods are brief. If houses are not inherited or paid for outright, they can be hard to finance. For example, a study of Madrid from the late 1970s showed that an average deposit of 46 percent of the purchase price of a house was required, with the rest to be paid off in five to 10 years.

Not surprisingly, the higher costs of home ownership and financing have led to lower rates of homeownership in Europe. In the United States approximately 65 percent of all households own their own home, a figure that has remained fairly constant during the last several decades. In contrast, European rates of owner occupancy are far lower. For example, in 1970 all Western European countries except for Finland had owner occupancy rates that were lower than 33 percent. In several cities, including Vienna, Geneva, and Amsterdam, only one out of 20 households owned their own house or flat. Of course, most Eastern European cities allowed no home ownership at all before 1989. Because Europeans are less likely to own their own homes, they are more likely to rent apartments within the inner city, which leads to greater compactness. (We discuss apartments later in the chapter.)

Note that places with easier housing financing, like Britain and Belgium, enjoy higher owner-occupation rates. For instance, the Belgian government has provided housing grants to allow families to buy or build their own house. As a result, Brussels is fairly suburbanized with many single-family houses, although it is still more compact than cities in the United States.

The third major factor is that planning is far more stringent across European cities. European governments employ a variety of growth control mechanisms that are intended to contain urban populations within existing built-up areas and that provide for carefully defined outlets for growth beyond city lines (Box 14.1). For example, many cities demarcate explicit boundaries beyond which city-type growth is not allowed to take place. The clear separation between urban and rural uses is especially apparent in densely populated countries like the Netherlands. Here, policy makers have sought to concentrate urban growth in existing centers or in a selected number of "growth towns."

Consequently, cities end abruptly and farm fields begin not too far from the central business districts. Great Britain has developed **greenbelts** around its cities, where suburban land uses are restricted. It has also established about 30 new towns (discussed in Chapter 13) that together contain about 4 million people. These measures have been successful to a certain extent, although the population has sometimes leapfrogged beyond the greenbelts. France has also invested in new towns, which were expected to help relocate some economic activity away from Paris. These types of restrictive urban land-use planning are less common in the Mediterranean countries, many of which do not have a strong national planning strategy. Here, the influence of other factors, especially a tradition of apartment living, promotes a compact urban structure in large and small communities alike.

Historical Legacy Many European cities combine different historical periods, from antiquity to the present day. It is not unusual to see a twelfth-century church tucked beside a Roman theater next to 500-year-old apartment buildings. Such features fascinate because they are still well integrated into the city's contemporary life. Roman amphitheaters are used for rock concerts and bicycle races, while many people still live and work in centuries-old buildings, use medieval streets, and peer over an urban skyline that seems little altered from an earlier time. Of course, this timeless quality is an optical illusion. Beyond the architecture, European cities are in the forefront of change. Certainly, past governments have initiated large urban redevelopments that often caused the loss of older buildings. Nevertheless, part of the way in which many European cities define themselves today is through their embrace of their heritage. The large-scale clearance of older neighborhoods that so typifies American urban development is anathema in much of Europe. **Preservation** is a more common desire than renewal, as the newer demands of society are blended into the older urban fabric. One geographer spoke of an "attitude of anti-progress and anti-innovation" (Holzner, 1970, p. 317). It would be more accurate to say that the attitude is one of great pride in the existing composition of the city and a desire to retain these historical features. The demolition of an historic structure brings about a storm of protest.

The epicenter of all European cities lies in the oldest section of the city. This is termed the **historical core**, and it is the portion of the city within the ancient or medieval walls (Figure 14.2). Most tourists spend all of their time within this section. What distinguishes the European core is that it still functions as the nerve center of the contemporary city. Here one finds the administrative functions of the city, which is very significant in societies where public employment looms so large. Here are financial functions like major banks and brokerage houses. Also, the most important retail functions continue to be found in the core. In this respect, European cores continue to command significant central-place functions lost to many American central business districts. To be sure, there are stores

BOX 14.1   STOCKHOLM'S URBAN PLANNING

Stockholm, Sweden, is often held up as a model of what public planning can accomplish, given public support and a bit of foresight. Stockholm is probably the best example of coordinated urban planning that has created suburbs without sprawl and has allowed rail transportation to flourish in a wealthy society in which most everybody has access to cars.

After World War II, Stockholm began a vigorous effort to plan and direct future growth. At the time it was growing at a rate of about 20,000 people per year. Stockholm was able to renew its central business district, which by the 1930s had fallen into disrepair. The city was developed along an orderly density gradient. It built a comprehensive, workable subway and rail transit system that is still the transportation of choice for many people. It also managed an orderly expansion of suburbs. Each suburb has access, via subway, to the central business district and serves as its own unit, with shopping centers, parks, and cultural facilities right next to the subway station (Figure B14.1). At the same time, these railroad suburbs are not self-contained with regard to employment; rather, a great number of workers commute in and out. Stockholm has also succeeded in keeping housing prices and rents affordable.

The mechanisms that made this planned growth so successful are complex, but three stand out. First, in 1904 Stockholm's assembly bought large areas outside the city, holding them until they would be needed for expansion. The assembly also extended the political limits of the city to these newly purchased areas. Today there is a lot less annexation. However, the city has the power of condemnation, which means that if the government needs land, it can usually acquire it for a fair price. In addition, Sweden established a series of nonprofit housing companies that were entrusted with the responsibility of creating moderately priced housing on this government-purchased land. Finally, since 1971 a metropolitan government for greater Stockholm has been in place that is responsible for mass transit, health, and planning and has its own tax base.

These measures have created a city that is the envy of the world but that still allows for a fair degree of private ownership and suburban living. Of course, there are blemishes in this paradise. The Swedes put up with a higher level of taxation than just about any other country in the world—fully 55 percent of their gross domestic product goes to public administration and public works. Swedish homeowners must also accept the essential blandness and

Figure 14.2 Most European cities, like Todi, Italy, are organized around a historical core. This central location is what gives European cities their character and continues to be valued by tourists and residents alike.

institutional feel of much of the available residential space. In reaction to these problems, the commitment to rigorous planning has worn down in the past 20 years. Beyond the line of planned rail suburbs there now lies a new frontier of automobile-oriented strip corridors and residential developments.

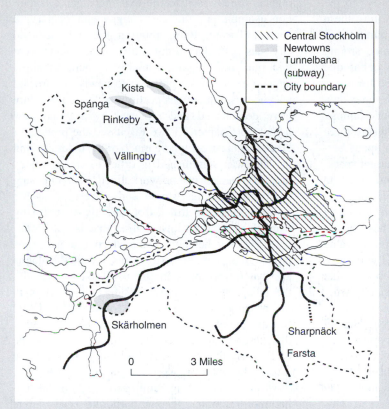

Figure B14.1 The locations of Stockholm's rail suburbs. (*Source:* Cervero, 1995.)

and shopping plazas on the outskirts, but the downtown still retains its position as a place to purchase everyday goods and special items. A study of retail concentration in the 1970s illustrates this point. Long after American retail had suburbanized, cities like Salzburg, Innsbruck, and Klagenfurt in Austria still had between 50 and 70 percent of their retail functions within the city center, and well over 90 percent of their financial functions. Even large cities like Vienna whose centers contained a lower percentage of all metropolitan functions still retained most of the top-level functions in the center.

Another point of distinction is that many people continue to live in the historical core, often on upper floors above the stores and restaurants. This pattern has long typified the European city and is starkly different from the American case, even when downtowns in the United States reigned supreme. In European communities, location in the core area is quite prestigious, and the rent and housing values are very high. Thus, core location is associated with affluence, and the concentration of affluent people further enhances the retail mix in the downtown. Fairly recent data indicate that the population living in the core area is actually increasing in many cities, attesting to the core's attractiveness. This is a reversal of trends from the 1960s and 1970s, when core areas declined with growing suburbanization. This appeal does not extend to districts close by, often those developed during the nineteenth century. Such areas, such as one might find near the train station, are often among the most dilapidated segments of the European city, analogous in some ways to the American **zone of transition**. In many cities, these have become zones for immigrant communities.

The historical core is normally oriented around plazas or squares, legacies of the medieval or baroque eras. These spaces traditionally were used for open-air markets or they surrounded a church; later they were also used to set off a monument. For example, the principal central space in Siena lay where three separate communities merged; the open space between them became the Campo, or communal space, for the town as a whole. Whatever their genesis, urban plazas retain a major orienting function. In the modern European city, they are likely to be surrounded by cafes, restaurants, and shops. In the most heavily visited cities, these open spaces constitute a prime-value intersection. The Campo in Siena is lined with massive open air restaurants and cafes with names like Ristorante al Mangia, catering to the tourist crowd.

An additional attribute of the historical core is the often labyrinthine street pattern, at least among a large number of cities. This reflects the development of cities through the process of accretion, where segments were added at different stages of time, or through *synoecism*, a process in which separate communities grew and eventually merged. This organic pattern of urban development predominated, particularly in cities without a dominant master plan. City form was more likely to be dictated by the contours of topography, be it ridges along a hill, alongside a river bank, or surrounding a natural harbor (Figure 14.3). Even more commonplace are narrow streets. A 1965 study of West German cities indicated that 77 percent of all streets were less than 7.5 meters (or about 25 feet) wide, barely adequate for two-way traffic. By contrast, only 16 percent of U.S. streets at this time were as narrow. Of course, these figures mask enormous variations within the city itself. Street width and parking outside the core area tend to be more substantial, but even newly built roads are comparatively narrow.

As centralized authority and particular design ideals grew more prominent in the seventeenth and eighteenth centuries, existing cities were partially reconfigured with planned extensions, often with regular streets, next to the existing organic layout. For example, in the early eighteenth century, a part of Trieste, Italy, abutting the old medieval city was platted in regular lots, wide streets were laid out, and a grand canal was built to allow large ships to dock right next to newly constructed warehouses. Sometimes portions of the old structure were demolished and replaced by a brand new layout. In Chapter 13, we discussed the process of Haussmannization, where much of the older housing in Paris was demolished in order to create a new, more regular, street network lined with imposing apartment buildings, stores, and offices.

The center of the European city is normally marked by a fairly low skyline that is still dominated by churches and medieval civic monuments. For example, the tallest structures in central Bologna are two towers built in the twelfth century, with the tallest reaching only 322 feet. These remain the primary orienting feature for that city. Other Italian cities feature a prominent *duomo* or cathedral. In Paris, the Eiffel Tower orients the eyescape of the city, but the other buildings are relatively low, prohibited from exceeding a height of 65 feet. Skyscrapers are being built, and they are becoming more common among corporate headquarters and some new apartment complexes. However, this construction is taking place outside the core area (Box 14.2). The result is a profile that resembles a "shallow bowl with a raised rim" (Lichtenburger, 1976, p. 95). The relative scarcity of skyscrapers in Europe means that although Western Europe together contains great concentrations of wealth, only two of the 100 tallest buildings in the world are in Europe: the 981-foot Commerzbank Tower and the 843-foot Messeturm Building in Frankfurt, Germany, which are ranked 91st & 95th in the world. Frankfurt too is interesting as an example of a European city that has adopted a North American-style skyline, replacing many of its older buildings with new office spaces in the downtown. We do not know

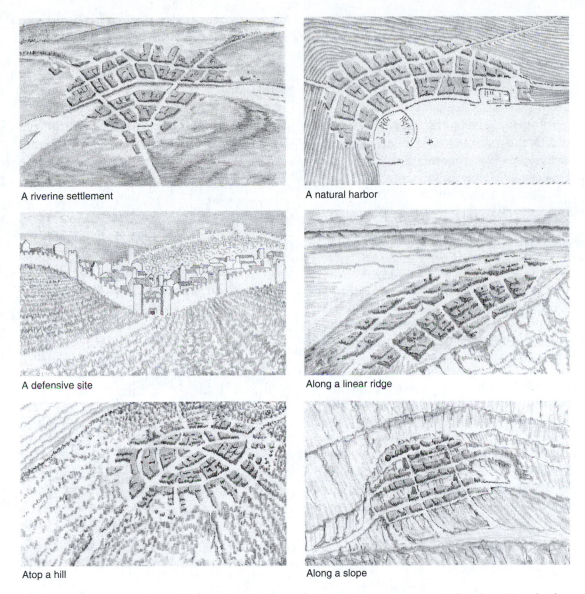

A riverine settlement

A natural harbor

A defensive site

Along a linear ridge

Atop a hill

Along a slope

Figure 14.3 The physical terrain determines the shape of cities and in many cases its function: (a) a riverine settlement, (b) a natural harbor, (c) a defensive site, (d) along a linear ridge, (e) atop a hill, and (f) along a slope. (*Source:* Kostof, 1991.)

yet whether this remains an exception or heralds a new trend.

A final historical element that impacts the morphology and look of many European cities is the city walls. As we saw in Chapter 2, most cities developed a system of walls and other fortifications in order to protect the cities from marauding soldiers but also to serve as a clear demarcation between very separate urban and rural worlds. Over the course of the medieval and Renaissance periods,

BOX 14.2 Postwar Urban Developments: Rome's EUR Center and Paris's La Défense

The process of urban decentralization has altered the morphology of cities throughout the developed world. At the same time that many families and businesses have relocated to the suburbs, new nodes of economic activity have been created beyond the central business district. Many postwar European countries encouraged this trend, fearing too much concentration in the inner city. They fostered the creation of new towns, satellite cities, and growth poles. Their goals were to relieve some of the pressures within the inner city and to promote economic development. Relocating economic activity outside the central city also enabled the construction of new modern districts with little disruption to the historical core.

The EUR district, located 5 miles outside Rome, exemplifies these new development nodes. The EUR district was first envisioned by Mussolini as a paean to Fascist grandeur, and building in the district stopped with his overthrow in 1943. Since the 1960s the district has become a center for government ministries, major conventions and conferences, and business headquarters. Since the 1970s there has also been an expansion of office space, both from new construction and from the conversion of residential space. Housing for the affluent is situated just to the south of these administrative and commercial zones. The EUR district is among the most planned areas in the Roman metropolitan area, maintaining a scrupulous balance between buildings and green space. It is also among the most sterile, with little of the evening activity so beloved by

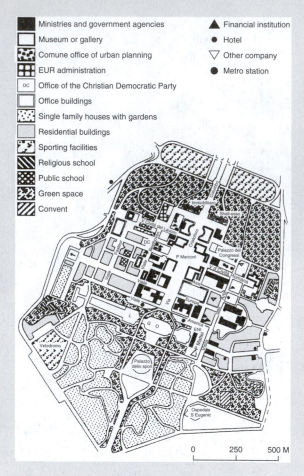

Figure B14.2 Map of the EUR center, on the outskirts of Rome. (*Source:* Agnew, 1995.)

these walls continued to be expanded in order to accommodate larger population growth. They also became more elaborate as a **glacis**—an undeveloped area outside the walls—was built so as to give the city's defenders an uninterrupted line of fire. With the development of strong territorial states and improved artillery techniques, these walls became useless and were gradually demolished. Most of this

occurred during the nineteenth century, when the walls of most of the major European centers were removed (although the walls around Paris remained until the 1920s). The effect of this demolition was to open up an enormous area of land just outside the urban core, and many nineteenth-century redevelopment schemes were able to take advantage of this new space. Probably the most famous example

Italians. Wide streets, office towers, a clear sep-aration of functions—all of these hallmarks of the North American edge city have also gained a foothold in European cities (Figure B14.2).

Another example is La Défense in Paris, situ-ated about 6 kilometers northwest of the downtown, just past the Bois de Boulogne. The district of La Défense was established first in the 1950s as a state development agency, but it took physical form in the 1960s as a venue for substantial office development. The peripheral location of La Défense, combined with its easy access to Paris along rail lines, allowed for the creation of a state-sponsored, but mostly pri-vately owned, skyscraper district. Today, the district is a clear nucleus of employment, providing some 100,000 jobs to the Parisian agglomeration.

Despite its beginnings as a state development project, La Défense is mostly in private hands. Many French and foreign companies house their headquarters in the district, making it primarily an office district. In fact, during the early 1980s La Défense captured more than half of all new office space constructed in the entire metropolitan area. It has also become a major shopping mecca, and there have been efforts to incorporate some residential land into the district.

In appearance, La Défense looks somewhat like the downtown of a modern North American city. In fact, it has been termed the "Parisian Manhattan," with its wide streets, glassed box architecture, and skyscrapers, which are not allowed within Paris itself (Figure B14.3). The district does contain a couple of notable pieces of public architecture: the 108-meter-tall Grand Arche, with its hollow center, and the CNIT exhibition center, which now contains a shopping center and a hotel.

Figure B14.3 Paris's modernistic quarter, named la Défense, contains the Grande Arche.

is the Ringstrasse in Vienna, where the wall and glacis areas were replaced with a circular road that included the city's most important public buildings and housing for the elite (Figure 14.4).

Housing and Social Geography   Compactness and the historical legacy of European cities play major roles in the distribution of housing markets and the resulting social geography. Over the course of centuries, the building materials used within most European cities have proved more durable than the wooden structures favored in the United States. Housing is expected to last for several centuries. The use of stone and brick has even been mandated by some municipal governments. For example, nearly 200 years ago, the government of Helsinki required

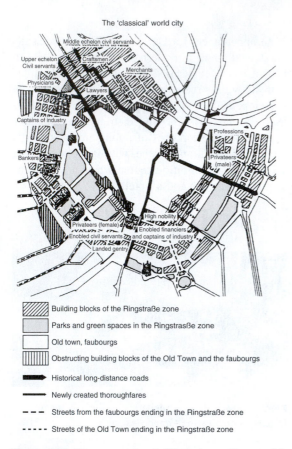

Figure 14.4 The removal of Vienna's wall was followed by the construction of a prominent ring road, the Ringstrasse. This diagram indicates the various urban functions of the Ringstrasse zone, including elegant buildings and parks. (*Source:* Lichtenberger, 1993.)

the use of these construction materials within the central districts. Using these materials raises the costs of building considerably, but it also ensures that housing quality does not deteriorate nearly as rapidly. As a result, older housing built before the twentieth century is considered quite desirable; in fact, there may even be a prejudice against newer housing. As with the United States, older structures are in the center of the city, while newer structures are located toward the periphery. Unlike the United States, however, where most wealthy people choose newer, more spacious housing, many Europeans prefer more centrally located, older housing.

Two other features of European cities are the relatively low rates of owner occupancy (which we discussed earlier) and the much greater tendency toward apartment living. The grand redevelopment schemes in Europe—such as the Haussmannization of Paris or the development of Vienna's Ringstrasse—established grand and luxurious apartment buildings. Each building offered up a microcosm of society, as the most prosperous families occupied spacious second-floor apartments with a panoramic view of the boulevard, while poorer families were pushed into upper-story flats with a courtyard view. Other cities in Continental Europe also exhibit very high rates of apartment living. Overall, in cities with more than 100,000 people, about 80 percent of households live in apartments; in cities with more than 500,000 people, more than 90 percent occupy apartments.

Although all Europeans rely much more on apartments than do Americans—where the lion's share of housing is single-family detached units—there is considerable variation between countries. In Italy, it is not unusual to find apartment buildings in the smallest towns (Figure 14.5). In Great Britain, by contrast, single-family houses are quite common, although at rates still below those of the United States and Canada.

Furthermore, mobility is considerably lower in Europe than in the United States. In the United

Figure 14.5 Apartment living is more common in Europe than in North America. This is especially evident in small-town Italy, such as in this suburb of Rome, where most residents inhabit apartments.

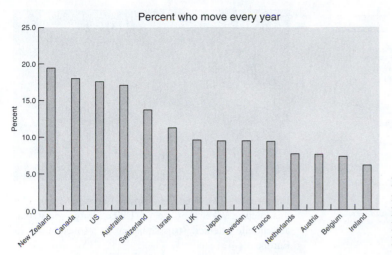

Percent who move every year

Figure 14.6 This chart demonstrates the much greater mobility among residents of North America and Oceania compared to European countries and Israel. (*Source: Long, 1991.*)

States roughly one out of every six people moves every year, the majority of these moves being intra-urban. In most European countries, mobility occurs at about half that rate (Figure 14.6). The reasons behind this differential are complex. The higher costs and more difficult financing of housing may have some bearing, but lower mobility applies in rental housing as well. Lower mobility means that people in rental housing are more likely to maintain their housing and that urban neighborhoods in general are far more stable, with less filtering.

Especially when compared to the North American case, affluent Europeans are more likely to live and stay in the historical core, while many of the poor are found in the city's outskirts. Reinforcing this trend is a greater tradition of providing public housing. In most European contexts such housing extends over a far greater economic range than is true of the United States. Although it is occupied predominantly by low-income households, it very often includes lower-middle-class and even white-collar tenants. In Europe, much of this public housing is placed where land is available, near the city's edge. Paris, for example, is ringed with a series of lower status apartment complexes to the north and south of the city proper, in which are located many of the city's poor, as well as several immigrant populations. Rather than experiencing inner-city blight, Paris suffers from a perceived

crise des banlieues, or crisis of the suburbs, in which suburban public housing is linked in the public mind with social deprivation and minority overrepresentation. Riots in 2005 left little doubt that the existing social and spatial arrangements had created suburban neighborhoods that were desperate and violent.

The social geography of European cities has been studied through techniques drawn from **social area analysis** and **factorial ecology**. Such studies indicated that, like North American cities, European cities are divided by class. Class registers as the principal organizing factor, explaining about one-third of the population distribution in cities. The next significant factors were indicators of density and household type. In European cities as in North America, variations still exist on the basis of household size. However, because mobility rates are lower, Europeans are less likely to move as they go through life's transitions, such as starting families. The main point of difference with North American findings was that ethnic segregation did not emerge as a major dimension of urban morphology. Most studies were done several decades ago, however. In the meantime, cultural diversity and ethnic segregation have become more prominent.

Figure 14.7 presents a schematic of a Western European city. Obviously, a single model of urban social geography cannot account for all of the differences among Western European cities. Nevertheless,

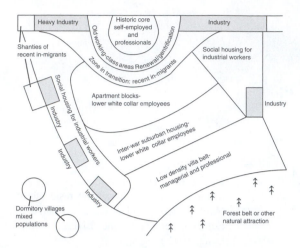

Figure 14.7 Schematic of a Western European city. The figure shows how Western European cities are oriented around a historic core, which also includes a large number of affluent people. Social housing is found along the periphery, near industrial areas. Suburbanization among some of the affluent is also evident.

this schematic illustrates some of the features we have discussed, and it highlights differences with cities in North America. In this, we can see the continued attraction of the historical core, as well as many of the extensions developed in the nineteenth century, which often replaced the wall and glacis. Older industrial zones stretch on one or both sides along the riverbanks or coast.

As with the American city, there is a zone of transition, based in areas where cheaper, pre–World War I housing was constructed. Here are found some immigrant neighborhoods, more transient populations, and working class populations. Very often, this zone extends in an arc from the train station away from the historic core. A broad sector of twentieth-century privately owned or rented housing extends from the inner city toward a natural amenity (like a hill or forest). The edge of this zone contains suburban-style housing for the middle class and affluent, but with far smaller lots than are common in North America. Other sectors often feature public (or social) housing, containing a working-class population. The urban edge is usually marked by a

Figure 14.8 The outskirts of many European cities, like this picture taken outside of Udine, Italy, show that automobile-oriented strip shopping is also common in Europe.

limited-access highway and, in several cases, fast two- or four-lane highways lined with newer shopping and office complexes (Figure 14.8). In several cities, strict growth controls limit this type of retail and commercial sprawl.

Aspects of Change

European cities have confronted several significant changes in the last century, changes that have altered their economic and social structure and that today leave a mark on the urban landscape. The most profound changes occurred as a result of World War II, which physically devastated several cities. Rotterdam and Le Havre, for example, were almost entirely leveled; in the German Ruhr valley, over half of the housing stock in Dortmund and Duisberg was destroyed. In the aftermath, cities were given the opportunity to create themselves anew, though at a tragic loss to their older architecture. Wars continue to ravage the landscape in some parts of Europe, as we sadly witnessed in the former Yugoslavia.

There have also been other, more subtle changes that have transformed the European city. These trends might be categorized into changes in European cities' economic circumstances, changes in the cities' political circumstances, and changes in the cities' social and cultural composition.

Changing Economic Circumstances During the nineteenth and early twentieth centuries, European cities were clearly affected by industrialization. A few places, within England's Midlands and Germany's Ruhr Valley, became cities as a result of the new industrial economy; many others witnessed tremendous growth in their overall size and complexity. Changes in industrial processes influenced urban development. *Fordism*, described in Chapter 4, encouraged concentration, both within particular regions and within clearly defined industrial belts of the city. The last quarter of the century has witnessed a shift toward a post-Fordist economy, marked by more flexible manufacturing processes, a more polarized social structure, and a greater autonomy of business from state intervention. This transition has also accompanied globalization.

Such a shift changes the logic of spatial location. In recent years, many European cities have changed along the same lines as North American cities, albeit in a more modest fashion. The following discussion examines how economic changes have affected the nature and functions of European cities.

Although European cities as a whole continue to retain more of their office functions within a central district, several of these office functions have resituated in the urban periphery. This is true of back-office functions, composed of the necessary clerical support, to front-office administrative functions, which are still overwhelmingly centralized. Clerical workers are being physically separated from the people who administer the companies. The region surrounding Zurich, for instance, has become transformed as steel and concrete towers have proliferated in particular regions. New railroad lines and a new freeway north of Zurich have created a dense corridor of office buildings (Figure 14.9). Like a corporate office complex in the United States, each building is self-contained, and the area shuts down after working hours.

Post-Fordism also entails flexible consumption and living spaces. The major beneficiaries of the new economy are knowledge workers and other highly skilled professionals. Like their American counterparts, many choose to live outside the city,

Figure 14.9 Office buildings in suburban Zurich.

occupying territory that was previously rural. Although this is manifested in familiar housing subdivisions, European exurbanites are also likely to occupy and refurbish centuries-old farmhouses or villas. For example, Keil and Ronnenberger (2000) described the neorural revival in suburban Frankfurt, where a typical sight in front of a remodeled farmhouse is a four-wheel-drive jeep with a surfboard on the roof.

Air traffic ties places together in an increasingly globalized world. With the increased prevalence of air travel, major European airports have emerged as cores of economic activity. At a larger scale, it becomes important for all major services and industries to be situated within an hour or two of a major international airport. Services that depend directly on proximity to the airport—warehousing, courier services, hospitality—require even greater proximity and cluster around airports, where they are joined by other businesses that can benefit from this location. This clustering thus results in the development of a new node of activity. This is particularly true of some of the largest international airports: Heathrow (London), Charles de Gaulle (Paris), Zaventum (Brussels), and Frankfurt's airport, which has become the largest single employer in the entire urban region, providing nearly 80,000 jobs. An additional feature is the introduction of a high-speed rail network, linking existing national systems and creating new systems. Access to this network will become a key facilitator of urban growth, and those cities left behind will likely suffer.

Of course, the interconnection of economic activities across national lines has been an economic mainstay since the Middle Ages, when Genoese bankers set up offices in Flemish and Hanseatic communities. However, some observers suggest that these tendencies have now reached a critical mass where the very character of European cities is being transformed. On the street, the influence of globalization can be witnessed in stores and fast-food restaurants. The large cities contain several McDonald's restaurants; for instance, Milan has six of these within a couple of blocks of its central square. This has led some critics to refer to the "McDonaldization" of the world. European chain stores, like Benetton, are even more evident, as transactions occur freely within the European Union.

It is important to note that, although this homogenization seems a dramatic development to European eyes, compared to most American cities it is still quite restrained. Small independent businesses continue to play a big role in the retail sector. The latest (2005) information from the European Union shows that "micro-firms" with one to nine employees make up 91 percent of all firms and that two-thirds of all jobs are in businesses with less than 50 employees.

Changes in the Political and Cultural Milieu

Although European cities have long been regarded as centers of culture, they have not been considered centers of cultural diversity. The dominant migration patterns in the nineteenth and early twentieth centuries were from the countryside to the city and emigration to overseas destinations such as the United States and Canada. In the last 40 years, this situation has begun to change. Robert Dickinson's text, *The West European City*, published in 1962, had almost nothing to say about immigrants. By contrast, modern studies of European cities cannot avoid the subject. Immigration and cultural diversity have become controversial topics, as can be seen in the emergence of right-wing, anti-immigrant political movements in nearly every European country.

Today's immigrants come mostly from less developed countries, often former colonies. Great Britain draws Jamaicans, Indians, and Pakistanis; France attracts Algerians and West Africans; Italy lures Ethiopians and Somalians; and the Netherlands brings in people from Indonesia and Surinam. Other times, migrants arrive to fill gaps in the labor force. The guest worker program in West Germany brought in a number of workers from Turkey, for example. Initially, many of these workers came without families and rotation back to Turkey was encouraged. However, by the early 1970s labor migration programs in Germany and elsewhere had been greatly liberalized, allowing for longer stays and family reunification. Short-term labor migrants thus became true immigrants in every sense of the word, raising their children and grandchildren in their adopted countries. The increased presence of immigrants is charted in Table 14.5, which shows the immigrant percentages, by country, in Europe. Although this is countrywide data, the vast majority of immigrant groups settle in cities. Over time, immigrants have settled in particular parts of the city. There is no district where a single ethnic group comprises 95 percent or more of the population, as is true among African Americans in almost every large American city. At the same time, most minority populations are distributed unevenly throughout the urban landscape and often cluster in specific neighborhoods. In Paris, for example, North and West African populations are found along the northern outskirts of the city, some in public housing, but many more in private rentals. Conversely, the foreign and foreign-born population in many German cities is more concentrated within the inner city.

The Dutch case is somewhere in the middle. Turks and Moroccans in both Amsterdam and Rotterdam are clustered in older turn-of-the-century and some newer areas, mainly because they require the larger dwellings to accommodate larger families. They are not found in older 19th-century inner-city districts nor in the newest places on the outskirts. The Dutch case also characterizes much of the urban diversity within European cities. There is a concentration to be sure, but it does not exceed 20 percent of a neighborhood for any single group. Segregation levels are modest.

Table 14.5   Foreign Population in Western Europe

| Country | Percent of Population | | Main Population Groups |
	1990	1998	
Austria	5.9	9.1	Not available
Belgium	9.1	8.7	Morocco, France, Netherlands, Yugoslavia, Germany
Denmark	3.7	4.8	Iraq, Somalia, Germany, Turkey, Norway
Finland	0.5	1.6	Russia, Sweden, Estonia, Yugoslavia, Iraq
France	6.3	NA	Morocco, Algeria, Turkey, Tunisia, United States
Germany	8.4	8.9	Yugoslavia, Poland, Turkey, Italy, Russia
Ireland	2.3	3	United Kingdom, United States
Italy	1.4	2.2	Morocco, Albania, Yugoslavia, Romania, China
Luxembourg	29.4	35.6	France, Portugal, Belgium, Germany, United States
Netherlands	4.6	4.2	Morocco, Turkey, Germany, United Kingdom, Belgium
Norway	3.4	3.7	Yugoslavia, Sweden, Iraq, Denmark, Somalia
Portugal	1.1	1.8	Brazil, Spain, Guinea-Bissau, Cape Verde, Angola
Spain	0.7	1.8	Morocco, United Kingdom, Germany, Portugal, France
Sweden	5.6	5.6	Finland, Norway, Iraq, Yugoslavia, Denmark
Switzerland	16.3	19.0	Italy, Yugoslavia, Portugal, Germany, Spain
United Kingdom	3.2	3.8	United States, Australia, South Africa, India, New Zealand
United States	9.4	11.7	

Source: World Development Indicators 2001, http://www1.oecd.org/publications/e-book/8101131E.PDF.

A related aspect of some European cities is the presence of ethnic divisions and even rival nationalisms. These divisions are not related to immigration from less-developed countries. Rather, they occur where cities have become divided by ethnicity. For example, Bolzano, Italy, is divided between the South Tyrolean German-speaking population and the Italian-speaking population. Members of these two groups largely inhabit separate neighborhoods within the city, although they intermingle in various shopping and employment districts. Likewise, Brussels contains both Flemings and Wallonians (French-speaking residents of southern Belgium). Segregation between these two populations in the city mirrors the political partition of Belgium as a whole. Belfast in Northern Ireland has suffered from especially intense religious conflicts.

Finally, the political function of many European cities is changing as Europe changes. Many of these cities achieved their greatest level of growth during the age of imperialism. Paris, London, Vienna, Rome, and Brussels styled themselves capitals of vast overseas and continental empires. Following

World War II, these empires collapsed, and the former imperial powers became small national states. Since that time, these states have joined into a series of associations—the European Common Market, the European Community, and now the European Union—that have promoted greater economic and political integration, including a common currency that debuted in January 1999.

The direct consequences of this increased integration are clear for some cities. For example, Brussels has become the headquarters for most of the European Union's administrative offices, giving it prominence as a diplomatic center and as a headquarters for nongovernmental and intergovernmental organizations. Strasbourg, France—in a borderland that has changed hands with Germany several times—has become the headquarters for the European Parliament, the political arm of the European Union. Other cities have also benefited from increased intergovernmental ties: Geneva, Vienna, Paris, London, and Luxembourg City, to name a few.

Indirectly, the consequences of European integration may be even more profound for certain cities. A common European economy renders many aspects of a peculiarly national economy unnecessary. National borders and separate currencies no longer serve as economic barriers. Cities may be able to serve as central places for markets across national boundaries. Other cities might benefit simply because of their border locations. Increased integration also hurts some cities that are located far away from major transportation corridors.

CITIES IN POST-COMMUNIST EASTERN EUROPE

Cities in Eastern Europe occupy a middle ground between the developed cities of Western Europe, North America, and Japan on the one hand and cities in developing societies on the other. Many Eastern European cities were part of the grand urban traditions of Renaissance, Baroque, and Imperial Europe. Budapest and Prague were two of the major centers of the Austrian Hapsburg Empire and could compete in sophistication and elegance with any European capital. Other cities, like Danzig (Gdansk) and Riga, flourished as key members of medieval Hanseatic trading league. At the same time, however, Eastern Europe generally lagged behind Western Europe in economic development and urbanization. Long after feudalism had ended in Western Europe, it was still going strong in the east. By the turn of the twentieth century, a huge gap in wealth existed between industrialized northwest Europe and the backwaters of Eastern Europe. In addition, much of the urban development in the east was affected by war and imperialism. Wars between the expanding Ottoman Turkish empire and the lands the Ottomans sought to conquer exacted a heavy toll on many of the towns and cities that stood in their path. When the Ottomans finally gained control of the Balkan peninsula, this conquest dampened the growth of many smaller cities and towns. Austrian Hapsburg domination in east-central Europe also siphoned off many of the region's resources to benefit areas further west. In the German areas further north, economic conditions were a bit more advanced; many cities here began to industrialize after 1870. City

growth followed. By World War I, Poland and the eastern portion of Germany were close to 50 percent urbanized.

Any promise of orderly economic and urban development in eastern Europe was disrupted by the world wars and the imposition of Communist ideology. World War I began in the Balkans and involved a number of powers with territory in Eastern Europe: Germany, Austria-Hungary, Russia, and the Ottoman Empire. By the war's end, the empires in the region had been eliminated, replaced by a system of weak national states. World War II was far more destructive. Repeated bombings reduced many Eastern European cities to rubble, genocide lacerated the social fabric of the cities, and the boundary changes after the war found many people separated from places they had previously frequented. In the years immediately following World War II, cities on both sides of the Iron Curtain had to contend with mass migrations of displaced people; perhaps as many as 31 million people had to change their residences.

Countries under Soviet domination were compelled to adopt a Communist ideology that altered the progress of urbanization once again. To be fair, many of the new governments helped regenerate economic activity in devastated communities. Vestiges of the old feudal society were vanquished, industrial production was significantly expanded, and urbanization levels quickly rebounded. The newly installed Communist governments were not interested in repeating capitalist models of urban development. Instead they imposed a particular type of urban development, very different from any attempted before.

Communist Urban Development

Unlike cities in Western Europe and North America, Eastern European cities were not permitted to develop according to market principles. Rather, their growth was directed by the government and was guided by a few simple tenets.

The first tenet was that, with a few exceptions, all land was owned by the state. Property rights as we know them simply did not exist because individual property was not sanctioned. The absence of a bid-rent market meant that the distribution of functions was by government decree. Central business districts existed as a result of government activity and decisions, although it is important to note that many cities contained quite impressive central business districts, in which governments normally chose to build. Similarly, there was less of a density gradient. Many cities were decentralized, with factories, shops, and residences located in equal numbers throughout the urban area. The **egalitarian** premise of socialist society meant that few class divisions were allowed to exist, although the Communist elite generally fared quite well when resources were allocated. This ideology was reflected in an urban landscape that was generally devoid of "good" or "bad" neighborhoods. It also discouraged the construction of distinctive dwellings. Rather, most people lived in apartment blocks, essentially large-scale public housing.

A strong commitment was made to central planning at all levels. Cities were directed by five-year economic plans. Governments attempted to arrange the economic size and specialization of each city within the urban hierarchy. Some cities were established as heavy producers, while others were earmarked as administrative centers or as transportation hubs. Governments also tried to influence the size of cities. For example, they controlled migration into and out of each city. There was also a vision of an optimum city size. Initially, planners wanted to restrict cities to a population of between 50,000 and 100,000. This "optimum" was revised upward until governments finally realized that it was impossible to enforce and the optimum was abandoned. Within the city, planners sought to create neighborhood units that would provide residents with all of their necessities—health care, education, shopping— while they also minimized the journey to work. These **microdistricts** were built, but in reality they did not offer the optimal range of services. Many simply became enormous apartment complexes housing thousands of people rather than integrated communities.

Finally, most Communist cities were perceived as centers of production rather than as centers of consumption. The idea was that these cities would spearhead economic modernization with new socialist factories. As a consequence, the industrial sector was overemphasized, while consumer services were marginalized. Stores and services atrophied from a lack of support and, at least in principle, the absence of private enterprise. A few Communist states, notably Yugoslavia and Hungary, relaxed some of the restrictions against private enterprise and were rewarded with a greater availability of goods.

Figure 14.10 shows the model of the ideal Communist city as embodied by the actual city of Magnitogorsk. The schematic emphasizes the linearity of the ideal city—parallel belts of housing (with services) and industry separated by a green zone. This arrangement produced a more even spread of industry and provided ample green space.

The ideal of a rational ordering of urban functions that would give everybody a healthful surrounding environment and minimize the journey to work was only partly realized. The lack of a market for land often resulted in more confusion rather than less. In the end, workers tended to go all over the city, for shopping and working, rather than to just one specific area. Communist societies thus discovered what capitalist planners found over and over again:

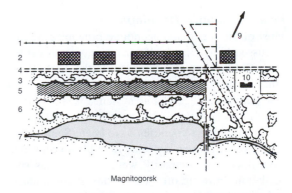

Magnitogorsk

Figure 14.10 The Soviet city of Magnitogorsk demonstrates some of the principles of the Communist city. Functions are laid out in a linear pattern. Nearest the river was a long linear park, followed by a residential area, a green zone, a thoroughfare, a factory zone, and the railway. (*Source:* Bater, 1984.)

It is simply impossible to enforce a jobs/housing balance such that all people live where they work and work where they live. Many governments did make up for this in part through the heavy subsidization of mass transportation. In Moscow, for instance, it was possible to ride the extensive subway system for a few pennies. In addition, the governments found it difficult to provide housing for everybody who needed it. Ideally, every person was supposed to get housing directly from the state. In reality, housing was more flexible. By the end of the socialist era, a majority of housing in Hungary, Poland, and Czechoslovakia was owner occupied, at higher percentages than those that prevailed in many Western European countries.

Ideals of equality were also sidestepped, as cities became socially segregated. For example, a study of Hungary showed that in many cases the best connected members of society, usually members of the Communist Party elite, were able to enjoy a better quality of housing at highly subsidized prices, while poorer, less influential families often paid more for lower quality housing. Similarly, a study of Warsaw discovered that better educated people lived in new, well-equipped cooperative dwellings, whereas the poorly educated lived in old, badly equipped flats or small houses.

Post-Communist Development

Most of the social and economic principles we just discussed were cast aside as countries discarded their Communist governments in the late 1980s. Since that time Eastern Europe has implemented new political and economic systems. It is important to note just how varied the experiences of different Eastern European countries have been. Some countries, like the former Yugoslav Republic of Slovenia, have done extraordinarily well. Slovenia has succeeded in throwing off the shackles of communism and centralized Yugoslav control. In 2005 it enjoyed a per capita gross national income of approximately $22,000, not far below that of neighboring Italy and Austria and greater than Greece. The Czech Republic and Hungary are almost as prosperous. The cities in these places buzz with new development, and

although many people are still underemployed, a greater share of the population has begun to enjoy the fruits of a consumer society (Box 14.3). At the other extreme is Albania, a country that has barely emerged from decades of totalitarian repression and that has yet to undergo a true industrial transition. In between are countries like Bulgaria, Romania, Poland, Slovakia, Croatia, and most of the successor states of the Soviet Union. Despite these variations, we can identify a few basic changes that have turned Eastern European cities in a new direction.

With the introduction of capitalism, cities have moved away from a centrally planned economy and toward a **market economy**. This is particularly evident in the land market, where property is treated as a commodity to be bought and sold. Especially within desirable cities, values of certain properties have risen considerably.

The **sectoral weighting** of the economy has changed. Inefficient industries—previously protected by an absence of imports from the West—have been rapidly abandoned in the wake of capitalist restructuring. Large tracts of industrial land have been left abandoned and the workers in these industries have been laid off. By contrast, the previously neglected service sector has expanded tremendously. Much of this transformation has been instigated by foreign companies, but there has also been an upsurge of small-scale private enterprise in many cities. With changes in the economy, a strong gray- or black-market economy has proliferated as people seek to eke out a living in any way possible.

In addition, evidence suggests that socioeconomic divisions within the cities are increasing and that the housing situation is generally quite unstable. A few individuals—often former government and party officials, entrepreneurs, former scientists, and experts—are wealthy enough to afford newly constructed, high-quality housing in central locations and in new suburbs. Many households whose economic situation has stabilized have opted to move out of some of the Communist-era housing estates, which may yet become zones of urban blight. Gentrification is pushing existing populations

BOX 14.3   THE OLD AND NEW CITY OF PRAGUE

Of all of the Eastern European cities to emerge from Soviet domination in the late 1980s, Prague in the Czech Republic is the most luminous (Figure B14.4). Much of Prague's success is a direct product of its past. Established in the ninth century, Prague grew rapidly during the fourteenth century. The city developed a strongly cohesive central historical core, built along both banks of the Vltava river. Later, Prague became one of the major centers of the Austrian Empire, after Vienna and Budapest, and was further developed with architecture dating from the Hapsburg era. Fortunately, Prague was spared during the world wars. In the post-Communist era, Prague has emerged as the primary city and capital of a fairly prosperous country and as a major tourist destination for Westerners, including a large community of American expatriates, eager to sample its riches.

The structure of Prague mixes the oldest with the newest elements: from the medieval and Hapsburg far past, to the Communist near past, to the capitalist present. The city is laid out as a series of concentric circles. At the center is the historical core, by far the most prominent administrative and commercial part of the city, but containing only 5 percent of the total population. Surrounding this core is a ring of pre–World War II apartment blocks, sprinkled with industrial districts, that still contain about 40 percent of the population. Around this ring is another belt of more luxurious single-family houses and garden towns, inspired by the thinking of Ebenezer Howard (see Chapter 13). This belt is surrounded by an outer periphery that is situated within the municipal boundaries but is still largely rural. Fortunately, the Communist government, which ruled from 1945 until 1989, left much of this urban development alone, focusing instead on the construction of large housing estates. Initial plans called for a balance of housing, jobs, and services, but these ideals were quickly abandoned in favor of quick construction.

Since the collapse of the Communist government in 1989, Prague has been the focus of intense change. The Czech Republic—especially Prague—has emerged as a favored investment region for foreign trading companies and producer services. These companies have occupied much of the historical core and have also built some new structures nearby in the older prewar districts. Residential usage in the center has declined, especially for lower-income people. Gentrification has taken hold in the remaining residential properties; rent in one central district increased five-fold between 1995 and 1998. By the end of the 1990s, the outer city also suburbanized, as single-family houses, new apartments, and especially stores, warehouses, and offices were constructed. Two huge shopping malls have already been built, with two more in preparation. As with other economically promising cities, Prague is beginning to add a ring of development on its outskirts and has also revitalized much of its inner city as well, particularly near the core. However, Prague has also become more divided economically. It now has greater income disparities than Great Britain, and a large segment of the population is shut out of the increasingly expensive housing market.

Figure B14.4 Prague, Czech Republic, has become a popular destination among tourists, largely because it has retained much of its historic charm.

of poor and elderly out of desirable areas. Housing shortages, bad enough during the Communist period, have become acute as property rents have been allowed to escalate and state subsidies have dwindled. Much of the new housing that has been developed has been for the affluent, who still constitute a small segment of society.

The previous totalitarian nature of economic planning has created a distaste for any form of urban planning. Local governments are often weak, and many have to contend with a daunting array of problems. Many local issues, such as historic preservation, may end up taking a backseat to problems of finding jobs and housing for everybody.

Eastern European cities have a long historical legacy dating from before the Communist era, although the region as a whole was not highly urbanized. Many cities, especially small and medium-sized cities, experienced their greatest growth during the Communist era. The imprint on the land, in the form of massive factory works, huge apartment complexes, and triumphalist architecture, is a new legacy with which the post-Communist city must contend.

CITIES IN JAPAN

Outside of Europe and North America, the most populous developed region is Japan. Unlike most other Asian countries, Japan was never victimized by outside colonization. Strong and self-sufficient, Japan maintained a society that was closed to the outside world from the 1600s until 1868, when it opened itself up to Western commerce and diplomacy. During the late nineteenth century, Japan became an imposing military and economic power. Japan defeated China in 1895 and Russia in 1905, becoming one of the most powerful nations in the world. Japanese colonial expansion in the years leading up to World War II created a vast East Asian empire. Japan's defeat led it to renounce imperialism and military aggression but also enabled it to concentrate fully on economic development. Today, Japan is the second largest economy in the

world, after the United States. According to *Fortune* magazine, it is the home of five of the world's fifty largest corporations in 2007, and one of the world's 20 largest banks (a decline from 1990, when it contained 11 out of 20!). Even with its recent spate of bad economic fortune, Japan's economic power extends much farther than its military power ever did.

Japanese cities have a long history, primarily as administrative centers for lords and samurai. Although Japan was a feudal society before 1870, it contained a fairly well-established system of towns. Many of the significant Japanese cities of today were once old "castle towns" controlled by the regional lord. Preindustrial Japan contained three especially important cities—Edo (Tokyo), the political capital; Osaka, the commercial capital; and Kyoto, the sacred center—that were large by world standards.

After 1870 commerce and industry became much more important and significantly affected Japanese urbanization. By 1875, Japan was only about 10 percent urbanized. Tokyo, the nation's capital and primary city, was large, but it had fewer than 1 million inhabitants and was dwarfed by large cities in the United States, Europe, and China. No other Japanese city was among the 30 most populous in the world. By 1925 Japan's cities had begun to assert themselves. Now Tokyo was clearly in the top tier of cities, along with London and New York. It had become a "world city" in terms of its population and would soon become one in terms of its economic influence. Yet urban Japan contained only about one-fourth of the national population. In contrast to North America and Western Europe, Japan remained overwhelmingly rural. It was only after World War II that Japan urbanized rapidly, shooting from 24 percent urban to 72 percent urban between 1945 and 1970, a transformation more dramatic than that of any other country. Japan thus accomplished in 25 years what had taken the United States 100 years. By 1968 Tokyo was the largest city in the world, a position it maintains to this day, and Osaka was the fourth largest.

In addition to overall urban growth, Japan's industrialization also spawned a major redistribution of its population. Peripheral castle towns atrophied as more people moved to the coastal plain along the Pacific coast of the main island of Honshu. A densely woven urban landscape, known as the Tokaido corridor, was created among Tokyo, Nagoya, and Osaka. This section contains some of the densest populations and highest land values in the world. If extended further south, Japan's **megalopolis** also includes Kyoto (the ancient capital and still an important city), Kobe, Hiroshima, and the northern Kyushu island cities of Kitakyushu and Fukuoka (Figure 14.11). This megalopolis contains almost two-thirds of Japan's population on only 3 percent of its land.

Structure of Japanese Cities

The complexity of Japanese cities cannot be fully described in this brief section, and you might wish to consult a couple of useful books listed in the Readings section for more information. However, a few important aspects of Japanese cities are mentioned here. First, the primary factor that must be considered in Japanese urban morphology is that of density. Japan's population density of 876 people per square miles is similar to England, Holland, and Belgium, but Japan has a far more rugged topography. The amount of land available for agriculture or urban development is a small proportion, perhaps one-eighth, of the total. This lack of exploitable land dramatically boosts the physiological density, that is, the number of people divided by the amount of land suitable for most agricultural and urban uses. Therefore, the Japanese have had to devise ways of accommodating urbanism within tiny spaces. Further complicating the picture is Japan's location on some major tectonic fault lines. Earthquakes are quite common, and, until recently, tall buildings were rare.

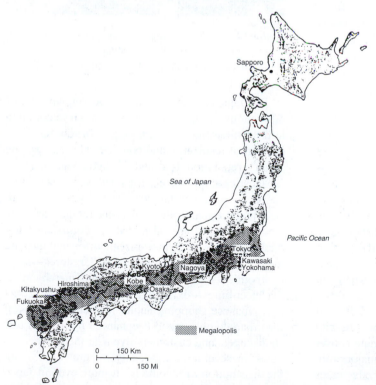

Figure 14.11 The bulk of Japan's population lives in a megalopolis, stretching east to west from Tokyo through Osaka to Fukuoka on Japan's southern island of Kyushu. (*Source:* Karan, 1997.)

Land in Japan is incredibly valuable. Up until the early 1990s, land prices increased rapidly but the collapse of Japan's "bubble economy" brought down property values. When Japanese property was at its peak, the Japanese land price per unit area was 100 times greater than that of the United States and office space in Tokyo cost 10 times more than in New York. In fact, Japanese real estate speculation in the United States was prompted by the relative cheapness of American land. Today, even after the cooling of land prices, Tokyo remains the world's most expensive city, according to a CNN/Money survey, followed by Osaka.

As a result of density and cost, the Japanese use all of the available land in an intensive manner. Within the cities, almost no property is allowed to go idle. If it is being held on speculation, it will be used for something else on an interim basis. The size of housing space is restricted by its cost. The Japanese are a wealthy people, but most cannot afford spacious housing. The average price for a newer condominium in the overall Tokyo region is about $500 per square foot. As a result, the average household crams into a tiny living space, smaller than one finds in Western Europe and downright diminutive by American standards. Most Japanese prefer to entertain outside their homes.

Japanese cities are compact and monocentric. Compactness has long been a feature of the Japanese lifestyle, even when the population was smaller and rural. Streets are narrow, parking lots are rare, shops and residences are small, and inside the home most Japanese utilize space to the fullest. This compactness extends to the city as a whole. As a rule, Japanese cities have decentralized, but they continue to be intensely focused around the central business district. Because land here is so expensive, most residential uses have been pushed out in favor of commercial property. The mass transit system, among the most efficient and most crowded in the world, ferries people into the city (Figure 14.12). The average Tokyo commute is over two hours round trip and congestion is a major problem (see Box 14.4). Even so, polycentric edge cities are rare.

Figure 14.12 Japan's trains are so popular that it often requires the services of professional "crammers" to ensure that everybody can get on board.

The Japanese neighborhood is a complex mix of different uses. The functional separation so common in the United States is replaced by **functional integration** of residential and commercial uses. Despite Japan's reputation as a land of huge conglomerates, Japanese cities are havens for small businesses, especially stores and restaurants. There are proportionately twice as many wholesalers and retailers as in the United States. Mom-and-pop stores flourish because the Japanese prefer to patronize them, even if they are more expensive. Huge category killer stores—large retail outlets specializing in one type of merchandise, like electronics—exist but have yet to fully penetrate into Japanese shopping habits. The cohesiveness of the urban neighborhood is enhanced by the fact that shopkeepers and customers live near their stores.

Japanese cities are socially integrated. Overall, the distribution of income is far more even in Japan than in the United States. Even heads of giant

BOX 14.4 TECHNOLOGY AND URBAN GEOGRAPHY

HIGH TECHNOLOGY INTELLIGENT TRAFFIC SYSTEMS AND CONGESTION RELIEF IN JAPANESE CITIES

As is true throughout the world, automobile usage in Japanese cities is increasing rapidly. High densities and limited space have aggravated traffic congestion. The traditional way to deal with traffic congestion has been to build more highways. The difficulty many Japanese cities experience is that the demand for roads far outstrips any opportunity to increase road capacity. Many Japanese cities were built up well before the automobile era and space is already at an extraordinary premium. Moreover, citizens in Japan have balked at developing more and wider roads, worrying about the effect on the social and natural environment.

Enter the promise of high technology. Intelligent Traffic Systems (ITS). These systems promise to not only reduce traffic congestion but to also enhance traffic safety. Japanese auto companies have been leaders in this field, with Toyota and Nissan particularly active. One of the more promising developments has been proposed by Nissan Motors. They are piloting a system that relies on vehicle-to-infrastructure communication. The information comes from optical beacons along the side of the road (other ITS use sensors planted in the road itself), and information from other vehicles as well. Data from these sources is then sent to a driver's navigation screen where real-time maps exhibit traffic flow. This way, congestion roadblocks can be avoided. Perhaps more valuable is the ability of this system to let drivers know of the approach of other cars and also to warn drivers of speeding in school zones. Toyota is proposing to test a similar system.

Intelligent transportation system technology has become increasingly popular. Global positioning devices on vehicles and sensors on or under roadway combine with fast computers to process and deliver traffic-related information in an intuitive way (Figure B14.5). These tests now taking place in Japan promise to help mitigate the worst effects of increased traffic in cities throughout the world.

Figure B14.5 High technology navigation systems now being tested in Japanese cities promise to alleviate urban traffic congestion while enhancing safety.

corporations are paid relatively modest salaries, and there are far fewer desperately poor people in Japan. This greater economic equality extends to places as well as individuals. Within Osaka's metropolitan area, for example, the wealthiest jurisdiction has a per capita income only 50 percent greater than the poorest town. This contrasts sharply with spatial income gaps in U.S. cities. In the Cleveland metropolitan area, for example, the wealthiest census tract enjoyed a median household income of more than $200,000 in 2000, a number 35 times greater than the poorest tract. Japanese neighborhoods are relatively well integrated in terms of income and occupation, although they certainly contain many different levels of housing quality from expensive condominiums to older wooden, low-income housing. Nevertheless, there is some place-based social separation. Wealthier people prefer to live closer to work, especially in Tokyo, where they tend to occupy more inner-city locations.

Despite the crowding and the jumble of different uses, Japanese cities are exceptionally clean and relatively crime free. Litter is not a problem, although industrial and automobile pollution has become onerous. Rates of both violent and property crimes in Japan are among the lowest in the world. Most women feel safe walking alone at night, and a lost wallet will more often than not be returned. An overwhelming sense of social cohesiveness marks Japanese society.

Changes in Japanese Cities

Japanese cities have changed rapidly in the last half century, and they continue to change. Some of this change has been orchestrated by Japan's powerful government ministries. In the 1980s, for example, the government established a plan to create a series of technological cities, which it called *technopolis cities*, that would operate as high-technology incubators (Figure 14.13). An additional goal was to try to redirect some of the growth away from the major cities. This plan was intended to aid regions that were relatively backward and that continued to suffer from "brain drain" of their best and brightest residents. Its success is hard to measure right now,

⊕ Established in 1986 or before
○ Established in 1987 or after

Figure 14.13 Map showing Japan's technopolis centers as of 1993, after which the program slowed. Technopolis centers were designated by the government to act as incubators of high-technology industries. (*Source: Japan Economic Planning Agency, 1993.*)

because Japan has been in a profound economic slump since the 1990s.

One change not directly orchestrated by the government is the increase in Japan's urban diversity. The Japanese consider themselves unique, and they consider Japan to be a homogeneous society. This is not entirely true, however; about 4 percent of Japanese belong to some minority group. A few people with Chinese ancestry inhabit the southern island of Kyushu, and there are still several Ainu peoples, an indigenous people of Japan, living in the northern island of Hokkaido. There is also an outcaste group, the Burakumin, who are of Japanese descent but have been marked as a distinct caste for 1,000 years. The Korean community, many of whom were forced into Japan after it colonized Korea, are now largely Japanese born but are not citizens. In addition, the 1980s and 1990s witnessed a surge in immigration among Chinese, Brazilians, South Asians, and Filipinos. Most come for employment and take jobs shunned by the Japanese themselves. Unlike class groups, which are largely integrated, distinct ethnic groups, including the Burakumin, are segregated within Japanese cities.

WRAPPING UP

Although all cities share some common characteristics, it is important for urban geographers to recognize some of the major differences among cities, particularly among broad cultural regions. Cities within the developed world share many traits. By and large, they possess adequate infrastructure (utilities, water, sewer, streets, housing) to accommodate most of their population. They are primarily found in countries that have already urbanized and where population growth in general is stable. This means that urban populations are increasing slowly, if at all, and most cities are mature.

Within this broad set of characteristics, however, differences abound. Most of this chapter has focused on Western European cities and has tried to uncover features that distinguish these cities from those of North America. In addition, we have discussed how European cities are changing. What are the new challenges—economic and social—they must confront, and how are they dealing with these challenges? One set of cities experiencing massive changes are those of Eastern Europe. For most of the twentieth century, these cities were organized according to the logic of communism. As a result, particular economic forces that are intrinsic to urban organization elsewhere, such as land value, were of negligible importance. Since the 1990s, these cities have contended with transitions to more of a free-market system. Japanese cities represent something else entirely: they exist within the developed world but fit within an entirely different cultural realm. Within all of these areas, cities display important individual variations, but understanding broad differences is important, too. In Chapters 15 and 16 we will examine the fastest growing cities in the world—those cities that exist within the developing world. We will see how economic constraints and population growth help to create a whole set of different features.

READINGS

Agnew, John. 1995. *Rome*. World Cities Series. New York: John Wiley and Sons.

The Auto Channel 2006. Nissan To Test Intelligent Transportation System in Japan. http://www.theautochannel.com/news/2006/09/20/022453.html (accessed 10/26/2006).

Bater, James. 1984. "The Soviet City: Continuity and Change in Privilege and Place." In J. Agnew, J. Mercer, and D. Sopher, eds., *The City in Cultural Context*. Boston: Allen & Unwin.

Burtenshaw, David, Michael Bateman, and Gregory Ashworth. 1991. *The European City: A Western Perspective*. London: David Fulton.

Cervero, Robert. 1995. "Sustainable New Towns: Stockholm's Rail-Served Satellites," *Cities*, Vol. 12, pp. 41–51.

Chandler, Tertius, and Gerald Fox. 1974. *3000 Years of Urban Growth*. New York: Academic Press.

Claval, Paul. 1984. "Cultural Geography of the European City." In J. Agnew, J. Mercer, and D. Sopher, eds., *The City in Cultural Context*. Boston: Allen & Unwin.

Dangschat, J., and J. Blasius. 1987. "Social and Spatial Disparities in Warsaw in 1978: An Application of Correspondence Analysis to a 'Socialist' City," *Urban Studies*, Vol. 24, pp. 173–191.

Dickinson, Robert E. 1962. *The West European City: A Geographical Interpretation*. London: Routledge and Kegan Paul.

Enyedi, György, ed. 1998. *Social Change and Urban Restructuring in Central Europe*. Budapest: Akadémiai Kiadó.

French, R. A., and F. Hamilton, eds. 1979. *The Socialist City: Spatial Structure and Urban Policy*. New York: John Wiley and Sons.

Fujita, Kumiko, and Richard Child Hill. 1993. *Japanese Cities in the World Economy*. Philadelphia: Temple University Press.

Hitz, Hansruedi, Christian Schmid, and Richard Wolff. 1994. "Urbanization in Zurich: Headquarter Economy and City-Belt," *Environment and Planning D: Society and Space*, Vol. 12, pp. 167–185.

Holzner, Lutz. 1970. "The Role of History and Tradition in the Urban Geography of West Germany," *Annals of the Association of American Geographers*, Vol. 60, pp. 315–339.

Karan, P. P., and Kristin Stapleton, eds. 1997. *The Japanese City*. Lexington: University of Kentucky Press.

Keil, Roger, and Klaus Ronneberger. 2000. "The Globalization of Frankfurt am Main: Core, Periphery and Social Conflict." In Peter Marcuse and Ronald van Kempen, eds., *Globalizing Cities: A New Spatial Order?* Oxford, UK: Blackwell.

Kesteloot, Christian. 2000. "Brussels: Post-Fordist Polarization in a Fordist Spatial Canvas." In Peter Marcuse and Ronald van Kempen, eds., *Globalizing Cities: A New Spatial Order?* Oxford, UK: Blackwell.

Knox, Paul, and Darrick Danta. 1993. "Cities of Europe." In Stanley Brunn and Jack Williams, eds., *Cities of the World: World Regional Urban Development*, 2nd ed. New York: HarperCollins.

Kostof, Spiro. 1991. *The City Shaped: Urban Patterns and Meanings Through History*. London: Bulfinch.

Lichtenberger, Elisabeth. 1970. "The Nature of European Urbanism," *Geoforum*, Vol. 4, pp. 45–62.

Lichtenberger, Elisabeth. 1976. "The Changing Nature of European Urbanization." In Brian J. L. Berry, ed., *Urbanization and Counter-Urbanization*. Beverly Hills, CA: Sage Publications.

Lichtenberger, Elisabeth. 1993. *Vienna: Bridge Between Cultures*. World Cities Series. New York: John Wiley and Sons.

Long, Larry 1991. "Residential Mobility Differences Among Developed Countries," *International Regional Science Review*, Vol. 14, No. 2, 133–147.

Noin, Daniel, and Paul White. 1997. *Paris*. World Cities Series. New York: John Wiley and Sons.

Pounds, Norman. 1990. *An Historical Geography of Europe*. New York: Cambridge University Press.

Rhein, Catherine. 1998. "The Working Class, Minorities and Housing in Paris, the Rise of Fragmentation," *GeoJournal*, Vol. 46, pp. 51–62.

Sailer-Fliege, Ulrike. 1999. "Characteristics of Post-Socialist Urban Transformation in East Central Europe", *GeoJournal*, Vol. 49, pp. 7–16.

Short, John R., and Yeong-Hyun Kim. 1999. *Globalization and the City*. New York: Longman.

Sýkora, Ludek. 1999. "Changes in the Internal Spatial Structure of Post-Communist Prague," *GeoJournal*, Vol. 49, pp. 79–89.

Szelenyi, Ivan. 1983. *Urban Inequities under State Socialism*. Oxford, UK: Oxford University Press.

van Kempen, Ronald, and Jan van Weesep. 1998. "Ethnic Residential Patterns in Dutch Cities: Backgrounds, Shifts, and Consequences," *Urban Studies*, Vol. 35, No. 10, pp. 1813–1833.

White, Paul. 1984. *The West European City: A Social Geography*. London: Longman.

CHAPTER 15

CITIES IN THE LESS DEVELOPED WORLD

'Chicago' [a district in Abidjan, Ivory Coast] is a slum in the bush: a checkerwork of corrugated zinc roofs and walls made of cardboard and black plastic wrap. It is located in a gully teeming with coconut palms and oil palms, and is ravaged by flooding. Few residents have easy access to electricity, a sewage system, or a clean water supply. The crumbly red laterite earth crawls with foot-long lizards both inside and outside the shacks. Children defecate in a stream filled with garbage and pigs, droning with malarial mosquitoes. In this stream women do the washing. Young unemployed men spend their time drinking beer, palm wine and gin while gambling on pinball games constructed out of rotting wood and rusty nails. These are the same youths who rob houses in more prosperous Ivorian neighborhoods at night.

—ROBERT KAPLAN, 1994, PP. 48–49

In 1850, the average urban dweller was likely to be a factory worker in one of the new industrial cities in Great Britain, New England, or the Ruhr Valley. In a world that was still overwhelmingly rural, he or she would have recently come from the countryside, where opportunities had withered, to live and work in one of the great steam-powered mills. By 1960 urban life was more commonplace, and the average urban dweller would likely be an office worker in any number of large or medium-sized cities spread throughout North America and Europe. Several urban dwellers would have come from the country and some may have immigrated from abroad, but many others would have been born and raised in the city.

Today, in contrast, the average urban dweller is likely to live in a third world city, one whose population is 10 times greater than it was in 1960. In this volume, the terms **third world**, **less developed world**, and **developing countries** are used interchangeably. They all refer to the same type of national economy: one that has yet to fully industrialize and where a large portion of the population continues to live in poverty. Inhabitants are likely to be very poor, perhaps living in a jerry-rigged shanty town—without benefit of water, sewers, or electricity—or maybe in slightly better, but still impoverished, accommodations. Like the average urban dweller of 150 years ago, the urbanite of today is probably also a migrant from the countryside, fleeing a rural existence that holds no more promise. Like the urban dweller of 1850, today's urbanite is entering into a city where conditions may be charitably described as unhygienic, uncomfortable, and possibly dangerous. In fact, in many respects, the situation today in many third world cities is worse. But for those who decide to migrate, this city—squalid as it may seem to our eyes—offers hope and the possibility of a better life. So people keep coming.

THE NEW URBAN MAJORITY

The majority of the world's current urban dwellers live in third world cities. Cities in less developed countries have mushroomed while cities in the developed world have remained largely stable, at least in terms of population if not in consumption of land. Looking back at Table 1.5, you can see that third world cities now constitute 21 of the world's 26 largest cities. Yet, you may be unfamiliar with many of them. They do not often make the news, unless they are afflicted by some vast human or natural disaster. They are rarely tourist destinations in their own right, although some are staging points en route to tropical resorts. They are not yet pivotal in the global economy, lacking stock markets, corporate headquarters, and major banks. In fact, most third world cities are made up primarily of very poor people. Nevertheless, these cities will loom larger and larger as the century progresses. They will increasingly enter into our consciousness, both because of the many problems they face and also because of the promise they hold for humanity.

How the Cities Have Grown

As we have discussed in previous chapters, Europe and North America were the first regions to urbanize, primarily as a result of a shift from an agrarian to an industrial economy. Throughout the world, urbanization percentages roughly followed rates of economic development. Thus, cities in the less developed world (as defined by their economic development) remained overwhelmingly rural well into the 20th century.

A map of world urban percentages shows that developed countries, as a whole, have a far greater percentage of their population living in cities than do less developed countries (Figure 15.1). In the more developed countries of Europe, North America, Japan, and Australia, about 72 percent of the population resides in urban places; in the less developed countries that number is only about 35 percent. Several factors, however, complicate this picture.

In terms of urbanization, the differences among less developed countries exceed differences among developed countries. Less developed countries display a tremendous range in the percentage of urban residents. One reason for these differences is income.

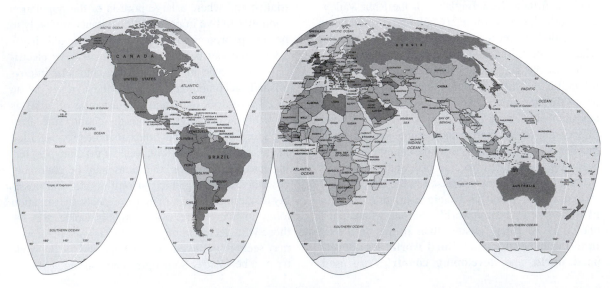

Figure 15.1 Map of world, by percent urban. Great variations exist among the more urbanized countries in the developed world and the less urbanized countries in the developing world.

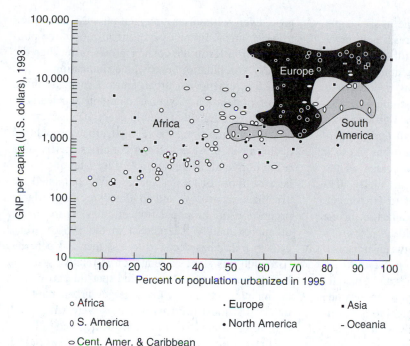

Figure 15.2 The percentage urban is loosely related to the GDP per capita, a measure of relative prosperity. (*Source:* Porter and Sheppard, 1998.)

Figure 15.2 illustrates a strong positive relationship between gross domestic product (GDP) per capita and urban percentages. This is not surprising when you consider that wealthier countries usually possess a more dynamic economy and are more likely to undergo structural transformations that spur rural-to-urban migration. There are several exceptions to this trend, however.

Latin American countries, for example, are highly urbanized. As a whole, about three-quarters of the population in Central and South America live in cities, a proportion similar to that of North America. Uruguay and Argentina—in South America's more prosperous "southern cone"—have reached urban proportions of 90 percent. Another region that is more highly urbanized is North Africa and the Middle East; for example, Libya is about 85 percent urban. In these areas the urban percentage exceeds what would be expected given income levels. Some analysts refer to this phenomenon as **overurbanization**—a level of urbanization exceeding apparent economic development. There are several factors that could account for this phenomenon. In the case

of Libya, it is likely a function of oil money and an overall arid climate inhospitable to many rural pursuits. In contrast, in China and India a relatively small percentage of their population lives in cities. These countries have levels of urbanization that are smaller than what would be expected, a phenomenon known as **underurbanization**. The factors behind this are also complex. Both countries emerge from very old traditions and a long history of rural, village life. In China moreover, there is the legacy of a government that until recently tightly controlled population movements and forced many of its residents to remain in the countryside. However, with national populations of a billion each, both China and India have more people living in cities than anywhere else in the world and China is urbanizing quite rapidly. At the other extreme from South America and the Middle East are the countries in sub-Saharan Africa, with urban proportions of only between 15 and 45 percent, with the exception of South Africa.

These different rates of urbanization notwithstanding, the less developed world is catching up quite rapidly to the developed world in terms of urbanization. In 1950, fewer than one in six people in the third world lived in urban areas; now more than one in three do. And, although the population of developing countries is increasing at a rapid rate, the population of some urban areas is increasing even more rapidly—at a rate approaching 5 percent a year. This rate far exceeds the urban growth rates in developed countries, which are all under 1 percent (Figure 15.3). This fast increase has led to a situation where today just under 50 percent of the world's population can be said to be urban. By 2030 the urban proportion will be closer to 60 percent. This change is due entirely to urbanization in the third world and not in the first world.

It is important to distinguish between urbanization and urban growth. *Urbanization* refers to the percentage of people who live in cities and generally results from a shift in population from countryside to the city. *Urban growth* simply refers to the overall growth in the population that lives in cities. If the national population is increasing overall, cities grow even without any population shift from rural to urban areas. In the case of urbanization, the population of cities in the country grows faster than the country's population as a whole, indicating a shift from the rural to the urban areas. Urbanization on top of population growth is common and leads to urban populations that double every 10 years or so.

At the same time, the rates of urban growth are declining in most developed countries, partly as a result of overall decreases in fertility rates and partly because more of these societies have completed the urbanization process and so already contain a large proportion of the population in cities. From a rate of approximately 5.2 percent in the 1950s, urban growth today has declined to less than 3.4 percent. Although this shows a reduction in relative growth, it is important to keep in mind that this growth is taking place within a much larger urban base. In the 1950s, most third world cities were small—all had fewer than 5 million residents, and all but 20 or so (most of them in China) had fewer than 1 million. Today, a smaller relative growth on top of much larger urban populations results in many new residents every year.

The explosion in the urban population has created a whole new set of megacities, which we defined in Chapter 1 as cities with metropolitan populations of more than 8 million. As discussed in that same chapter, in the past most of these megacities were located in the more developed countries. Today, they are predominantly found within the less developed world. In fact, some geographers have estimated that Mexico City's population will exceed 35 million in 20 or so years. The fact that most of the world's most populous cities are located in less developed countries does not mean that cities in Europe, Japan, and North America are shrinking. In fact, they are not. However, they are not growing as rapidly as cities in Asia, Africa, and Latin America. At the same time, it is important to note that cities like New York, Tokyo, and London grew rapidly during earlier historical periods. There is no reason to think that growth rates in the new megacities will not likewise slow down; in fact, there is some indication that this is happening now.

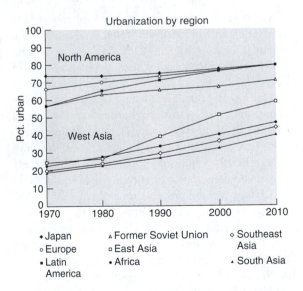

Figure 15.3 Urbanization rates by region. North America, Japan, and Europe are at the saturation stage of urbanization and so are not urbanizing much more. Other Asian regions and Africa, on the other hand, experienced tremendous urbanization during the last three decades of the twentieth century.

Demographic Factors Involved in Urban Growth

In considering why third world cities have grown so large in such a short period of time, we first consider the main demographic factors that lead directly to urban population growth. In the next section, we then discuss the underlying reasons that cause some of these demographic factors, particularly migration. Demographic factors are tied directly to city growth and express this growth as a function of overall population increase and population redistribution. Three demographic processes contribute to urban growth in less developed countries: natural increase, rural-to-urban migration, and the primate city phenomenon.

Natural Increase Nearly all less developed countries are in the midst of a population explosion. Overall, national populations are growing at an annual rate of between 1 and 4 percent. Although immigration and emigration can affect population growth, they are not nearly as important a factor as **natural increase**—the gap between the number of births and the number of deaths. Less developed countries are in the midst of a demographic transition dating to the latter part of the twentieth century during which their death rates have declined rapidly while their birth rates have remained high. Under these circumstances their populations will continue to increase until their birth rates come down. Some countries, notably China, but also many of the newly industrialized countries of East and Southeast Asia, have essentially closed the gap between birth and death rates, whereas in countries in Africa and the Middle East, the gap remains enormous. High rates of natural increase mean that third world cities are growing independent of migration.

Urbanization Curve Most third world cities are now at the acceleration phase of the urbanization curve. As discussed in Chapter 3 (see figure 3.8), the urbanization curve represents an "S" shape moving from a rural society, where less than 20 percent of the population lives in cities, to an urban society, where more than 75 percent lives in cities, a phase

known as **urban saturation**. The acceleration phase links these two phases and represents a period of tremendous rural-to-urban migration, also known as **urban in-migration** (not to be confused with international immigration). Once a society reaches urban saturation, increases in city size are often more a function of urban-to-urban migration, in which people move from one city to another in search of better opportunities or amenities, than of rural-to-urban migration.

The degree to which in-migration accounts for urban growth must be considered alongside the overall rate of urban growth. For all lower- and middle-income countries (what we might consider as less developed countries), the average annual rate of urban growth is 2.7 percent per year. Of this, approximately 44 percent is due to migration with the remainder due to overall population growth. Compare this with countries in the developed world, where the urban population grows at a stately 1 percent a year, with migration contributing only 30 percent of this.

There exists wide variations among countries (Table 15.1). In China, both the degree of in-migration and the overall urbanization rate are high. China's cities are growing at a phenomenal rate, but little of it is due to the overall population growth rate. The same is true of the very populous countriy of Indonesia, where urbanization rates continue to be high. By contrast, Asia's other demographic giant—India—exhibits slightly lower urban growth and a much lower percentage of growth that stems from migration. A highly urbanized country like Uruguay exhibits both small contributions of in-migration toward urban growth and low rates of urban growth in general, indicating low urbanization increases and low natural increases. Brazil lies somewhere in the middle; its urban population grew by little more than a quarter between 1990 and 2003. However, because it has such a large population to begin with, this transformation helped to feed already enormous megacities. In general, you can witness the much higher contrinution of migration among certain fast growing countries (such as in sub-Saharan Africa) and some rapidly developing

Table 15.1 Estimates of Net Migration's Share of Urban Growth, 1990–2003

	Urban Growth %	Migration Share
All Low and Middle Income Countries	2.7	44%
Albania	1.3	123%
Lesotho	4.2	76%
Indonesia	4.2	67%
Bangladesh	4.1	59%
Kenya	5.6	57%
Nepal	5.2	54%
El Salvador	3.8	50%
South Korea	1.8	50%
Thailand	1.5	47%
Iran	2.8	46%
Nigeria	4.9	45%
Phillippines	3.9	44%
Angola	4.9	43%
Tunisia	2.6	42%
Ecuador	3.0	40%
Sri Lanka	2.1	38%
Brazil	2.1	33%
India	2.5	32%
Colombia	2.7	30%
Costa Rica	3.0	30%
Uruguay	1.0	30%
Cuba	0.7	29%
Peru	2.3	22%
Iraq	2.2	−9%

Source: World Bank, *World Development Indicators 2005,* Table 2.1 and 3.10. Calculations of share of urban growth by author.

economies (such as China and South Korea). Interestingly, many countries in Europe also report a very high share of urban growth from migration, but largely because their population growth rates are either stagnant or declining. In general, these figures demonstrate that urban growth in the third world is affected by both urbanization and natural increase, but that the contribution of each component varies.

One additional point to consider is the extent to which urban migration to cities is temporary. In many countries, people (often working-age men) move to the city to find jobs but continue to support a family in the village. They never expect to reside permanently in the city and so are termed **circulators** or **temporary migrants**. Circulators can be substantial in number, reaching 70 percent of the total urban population in China, Indonesia, and the Philippines, and they are a significant presence in nearly all third world cities. As a group, circulators are often not counted in the census, so the actual size of many cities is underestimated (Box 15.1).

Primacy Living in a third world city today has come to mean living in a very large city of more than 1 million inhabitants; more than one-third of urban dwellers now live in such cities. (This, however, is still lower than the situation in the United States, where about one-half of the population lives in metropolitan areas of more than 1 million.) Much of the growth of large cities or megacities relates to the rank-size relationship of cities, discussed in Chapter 4. Intense urbanization focused on a single **primate city** provides the fuel that enables that city to grow into a megacity. Many third world countries contain a single primate city that is disproportionately large. A simple rule of thumb is that this city is significantly greater than twice the size of the next largest city. An example of a primate city is Lagos, Nigeria, which contains about 10 million people, three times larger than the second-largest city of Kano. Similarly, Mexico City contains over 17 million people; Guadalajara, the next largest city, contains only 1.6 million. In Latin America overall, an average of 23 percent of the urban population of each country resides in the primate city, or about 18 percent of each country's overall population.

Not all third world countries, however, are built around primate cities. For example, both China and India contain several large cities but do not have a single primate city. Brazil contains two primate cities, São Paulo and Rio de Janeiro. São Paulo is more populous than Rio, but both cities are much larger than any other Brazilian cities. In India, the four largest cities are primate within their respective macroregional spheres.

There is more to primate cities than their population size. Primacy also indicates a disproportionate

BOX 15.1 MIGRATION AS A HOUSEHOLD PROCESS

Rural-to-urban migration is a key factor that propels third world urbanization. But what propels migration? Much of the migration analysis conducted by social scientists is based on the experiences of people in North America and Europe and has emphasized the importance of economic opportunity and amenities. Migration in the third world is probably also based on these concerns, but it may have additional complications. First, the push factors of village life, economic as well as cultural, are powerful agents in getting people to move to the city. In fact, they may be more important than the pull factors of the city. Men and women flee village constraints and traditions in order to partake of a freer life. Although cities are clearly perceived as places of hope and opportunity, rural residents move to the city not so much because of the great opportunities in the city but because there are no opportunities at home.

Second, different groups move for different reasons. Young men may seek money, young women may seek greater social liberties, and older women may seek to be near their relatives. Third, migration is often part of a larger household strategy that seeks to diversify the income streams by sending some household members into the city to find work. In these instances, urban settlement is simply one stage of **circular migration** whereby migrants move to the city for a few months and then return to the village when they can be most useful there. Fourth, the choice of destinations follows patterns previously set forth by friends and relatives. **Chain migration** occurs as individuals learn about opportunities from people who have already made the move and may help smooth the way. This was also true of migration in countries that are now industrialized.

Refugees are another category altogether, because they are pushed by fear of being persecuted or worse should they remain in their home regions. Political instability spurs massive refugee migrations, and refugees have become a major issue in many third world countries. Refugees sometimes move to cities, but they are often forced into makeshift camps that can grow to be as populous as many cities.

share of economic activity, cultural dominance, and political control. Primate cities tend to overwhelm their countries, becoming the only destination of choice for ambitious people and acting as the primary fulcrum of growth and development. Primate cities also contain the major cultural activities, from movies to publishing houses to the premier universities. Moreover, many primate cities operate as the country's capital, with the mayor of the primate city being a major political force in his or her own right.

Recently, countries have attempted to balance the growth of their primate cities with that of other cities, a process termed decentralization to smaller urban areas. One comparatively straightforward strategy is to move the country's capital to another city or to create a new city altogether. In the 1960s, for example, Brazil's capital was moved from Rio de Janeiro to Brasilia. Brasilia was intended as a showcase for Brazil's aspirations, and it was meant to siphon off population from the overcrowded coast to the sparsely populated interior. It has now become a major city in its own right, with over 2 million people. Moreover, it has affected the relative population of Brazil's two main cities, as Rio has fallen further and further behind São Paulo. More recently, the capital of Nigeria was moved from Lagos to Abuja, and Pakistan's capital was moved from Karachi to Islamabad. Suggestions have even been made that Argentina's capital could be moved from Buenos Aires to a small city in the Patagonia region.

The latest data indicate that, for whatever reason, the growth of primate cities has slowed, at least in comparison with smaller cities. The World Bank (2005) reports that even though the percentage of the population that was urbanized increased between 1990 and 2003, from 44 to 49 percent, the proportion of the urban population living in the largest city declined a little, from 17 percent in 1990 to 16 percent in 2003. As an example from an **advanced developing country** like South Korea—a country that is on the cusp of entering the ranks of the industrialized, wealthy countries—Seoul continues to be a primate city with one-quarter of South Korea's urbanites and one-fifth of the total population. But Seoul's growth, which was 5 percent between 1970 and 1975, and had had dropped to less than 2 percent between 1990 and 1995, is now predicted to actually decline an average of 0.5 percent a year between 2006 and 2020 (from the database CityMayors, UN Habitat.org).

Primate cities are not found only in the less developed world—Vienna, London, and Paris are examples of first world primate cities that once ruled large empires—but they are more common in the third world. Perhaps because third world countries have such high poverty rates, primate cities have come to be viewed in a mainly negative light. In national economies in which scarcity is the rule, large urban centers absorb a highly disproportionate share of limited resources. Most investment funds continue to be focused around the primate city. Several case studies demonstrate that more than half of all manufacturing growth and foreign investment are concentrated in and around the primate city. Moreover, branch headquarters of multinational corporations tend to locate there. This is not necessarily a negative development, however. In poor countries with limited amounts of investment capital, skilled labor, and institutional support, primate cities often provide the necessary agglomeration economies that concentrate capital and highly skilled labor in one place. They are often the locus of tremendous innovation, and they may help propel the entire national economy.

At the same time, however, massive population growth has created serious problems for primate cities. Land costs tend to be high, making it especially difficult for the poor to find decent housing. Pollution and congestion run rampant, and crime is often a severe problem.

Third world cities are growing as a result of a combination of natural increase, in-migration, and primacy. However, there is a wide range of experiences among these cities. For example, most African cities south of the Sahara are growing due to massive rural-to-urban migration. The emancipation of South Africa is the latest reflection of this trend as Africans who were once prohibited from living in cities are now free to move to those areas with the greatest employment opportunities. In many Asian countries, urban growth is more a function of natural increase than of migration. In most Latin American countries, by contrast, urbanization rates are already quite high, and many countries have reached the phase of urban saturation. In Latin America, therefore, the growth of particular cities is more a function of urban-to-urban migration, with the increasing size of select cities largely due to urban primacy.

ORIGINS OF THIRD WORLD URBANIZATION

Demographic factors do not address the deeper reasons behind the massive urbanization that is causing cities in the third world to swell. Certainly, one could argue that it is now the turn for less developed countries to urbanize, and as such they are merely following the path set down by Britain more than 150 years ago. However, British urbanization took place over a much longer period of time. Indeed it could be said that the speed of urbanization among less developed countries is unprecedented, and that the sizes their cities are now reaching exceed anything the world has yet seen, particularly in light of that fact that they often lack the necessary jobs, shelter, and infrastructure to accommodate existing residents, not to mention new arrivals.

Theories abound concerning the causes of third world urbanization. These theories view the causes and prospects for third world urbanization quite differently, and they have real relevance for how basic policies related to urbanization, including investment, housing provision, and debt relief, are formulated. Although there are many specific theories, they can be distilled into two overarching perspectives: modernization and the international political economy.

Modernization Perspective

The modernization perspective derives from neoclassical economics, and it dominated the way we viewed third world cities for many decades following World War II. Essentially, the modernization perspective argues that the less developed countries are, in fact, "developing"; that is, they are in a process of transition from preindustrial to industrial society. This transition influences all aspects of society. Population growth can be attributed to a demographic transition from high rates to low rates of mortality and fertility. Developing societies are also in the midst of a capitalist transformation in which production and markets, including many labor markets, are opening up. This in sharp contrast to the more restrictive labor conditions that marked many colonial societies. The modernization perspective also assumes that cultural changes might replace indigenous values with "Western" values, including rationalism, science, and a strong work ethic. Enfolded within this set of transitions is an economic shift from an agrarian economy, based on subsistence and primary sector activities, to an industrial economy based on manufacturing.

According to the modernization perspective, such interlocking transitions spur the growth of cities in a manner that resembles earlier urban growth in Europe and North America. As the economy becomes more industrialized—as the economic emphasis shifts from the primary to the secondary sector—jobs and investment are increasingly located in urban areas. Cities, and the primate city in particular, serve as catalysts for further development by concentrating capital, infrastructure, and highly skilled labor in a central place. It naturally follows that for a period of time, wide discrepancies will exist between a more modern, developed, westernized sector on the one hand and a traditional, underdeveloped sector on the other hand. These sectors correspond geographically at first with the modern sector characterizing the region surrounding the primate city and the traditional sector characterizing much of the rest of the country. According to the modernization perspective, this **dualistic structure** is also transitional. In time, secondary and then tertiary cities become targeted for investment in a kind of "trickle-down" effect. This process might also be described as **hierarchical diffusion** (Figure 15.4). Over time, modernization will diffuse to the entire country, at which point the country will be developed.

The economic disparities between rural and urban regions within a country are often quite marked. Figure 15.5 demonstrates the level of poverty in the 1990s between rural and urban regions in selected countries. What is notable is that rural poverty exceeds urban poverty in *every single case*. In countries like Rwanda, Bolivia, Peru, and Papua New Guinea, rural poverty is more than three times greater than poverty in the cities. These disparities clearly motivate rural-to-urban migration.

The modernization perspective further proposes that initial disparities in development within a country result in mass internal migration from poorer to wealthier regions, sparks a great deal of movement to a single city, and thus promotes urban primacy. As modernization diffuses, however, the concentration in one main center deflects to several other urban centers. In the optimistic assessment of this perspective, greater wealth allows cities to catch up with the demands for jobs, housing, and services.

Support for the modernization perspective comes primarily from the experiences of the developed world. However, the indications are certainly strong that a number of less developed countries have undergone the same series of transitions, at least as far as more objective information is concerned. For example, figure 15.2 demonstrates the close association between urbanization and economic growth. Countries that show progress in terms of their average income also are more likely to increase the proportion of their population that lives in cities. Likewise, a sectoral shift can be noted as the primary sector share of the economy diminishes and the secondary sector share increases. Other data also point to shifts in demographic trends; for example,

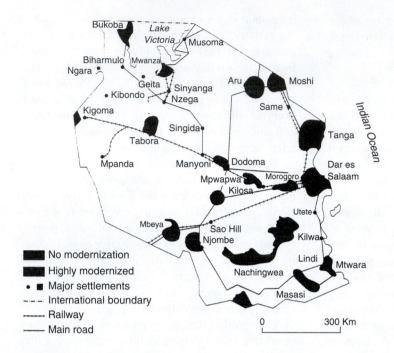

Figure 15.4 Map of the modernization surface in Tanzania. This map was developed by geographer Peter Gould in the 1960s. He saw the distribution of development "islands" linked by transportation lines through underdeveloped countryside. (*Source:* Potter, 1990.)

average fertility in many countries has declined and population growth, although still apparent, has eased.

Not all less developed countries, however, appear to have followed a Western model of modernization. For example, several countries have continued to urbanize in the absence of any economic growth. For instance, the average urban population of countries in Africa increased by 4.6 percent annually between 1990 and 2003, although per capita GDP increased by 2.8 percent during that same period. Other, more subjective attributes may be harder to

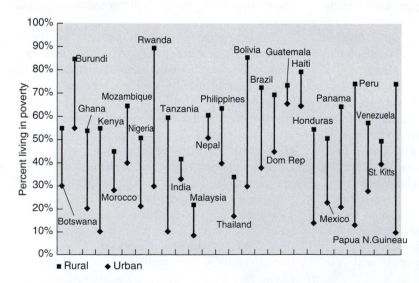

Figure 15.5 Urban and rural poverty for selected developing countries during the 1990s. (*Source:* Potter, 1999.)

BOX 15.2   TECHNOLOGY AND URBAN GEOGRAPHY

BRIDGING THE GLOBAL DIGITAL DIVIDE

Today, modernization is closely aligned with the expansion of various information technologies, espcaily access to computers, email, and the worldwide web. The Internet and the personal computer have become such a pervasive feature for so many of us that we forget that there remain large numbers of people who have sporadic or no access to this important technology. Within the last decade there has been much discussion of a "digital divide" between those who are connected to the Internet and those who are not. This divide is found at several scales, but probably is it nowhere as apparent as between the countries in the developed world compared to countries in the less developed world. The latest data confirms these disparities. According to UN-Habitat (table A-3), in 2002 there were 282 computers per 1000 people in the developed regions, compared with only 66 computers per 1000 in less developed regions. In most African countries, the ratio is less than 10 per thousand.

As for the Internet, the data is equally bleak. According to the International Telecommunications Union (http://www.itu.int/ITU-D/ict/statistics/ict/index.html) the rate of Internet penetration in the less developed world is one-eighth the level of that of the more developed world. Data published by Internet World Stats http://www.internetworldstats.com/stats.htm breaks down Internet usage by broad region and country. The result in Table B15.1 shows that North America and developed countries in Asia have very high rate of Internet usage at least as far as the percentage of the population with some exposure to the Internet. Europe lags behind but the penetration rate among countries in the European

Table B15.1   Internet Usage by Region

World Regions	Internet Usage %	Usage Growth 2000–2006
Developed World		
North America	69.10%	112.00%
Asia MDC[1]	66.41%	86.37%
Oceania/Australia	54.10%	141.00%
Europe	38.20%	193.70%
Less Developed World		
Latin America/Caribbean	15.10%	361.40%
Middle East	10.00%	479.30%
Asia LDC	7.33%	560.17%
Africa	3.60%	625.80%

[1]Asia MDC includes more developed countries in Asia: Japan, South Korea, Taiwan, Singapore, Hong Kong and Macao.

Union is far higher, at over 50 percent. Countries in the less developed world show much lower rates of Internet penetration. However, these are also countries poised to expand most rapidly in the coming years. Data is not available that distinguishes between urban and rural uses, although it is clear that Internet access can bring many of the advantages of the city, especially access to information, to those who live in rural locales.

The challenge of providing Internet access to residents of developing countries has been taken up by several agencies and philanthropists. One notable contributor is Professor Muhammad Yunus who was awarded the 2006 Nobel Prize in Peace for his advocacy of micro-loans through his Grameen Bank. Professor Yunus has also established the Grameen Cybernet. This is currently the largest Internet Service Provider in Bangladesh and has been in the forefront of trying to bring several of Bangladesh's companies and consumers into the online revolution.

discern, including shifts in cultural, economic, and political values. Moreover, people in less developed countries also suffer from less access to the newest internet technologies (see Box 15.2).

International Political Economy Perspective

The international political economy perspective proposes several theories to explain third world urbanization. The primary element these theories have in common is a consensus concerning the inadequacies of the modernization perspective. The main critique is that the modernization perspective tends to view economic development and urbanization as isolated with a particular country. It does not consider the links between the economic development of one country or region and the economic development of other countries. Just as the economic system operates as an integrated global unit—and has done so for more than a century—so explanations of urbanization need to take into account the interdependence of regions. In addition, the historical conditions of countries vary tremendously. Countries have developed during different economic eras and it is impossible to equate industrialization and urbanization in the late twentieth century with processes that occurred during the mid-nineteenth century.

Moreover, the internal structures of countries vary a great deal as well. Given the history of colonialism and continued neocolonialism, the failure of modernization theorists to take this into account constitutes an enormous oversight. Even among developing countries, there are wide variations in whether they were colonized, for what purpose they were colonized, and when they achieved independence. For example, most American countries declared independence well before interior sub-Saharan Africa was ever colonized and even before the British government formally took over the administration of India from the trading companies.

Colonialism One theme of the international political economy perspective specifically examines the conditions of colonization, which shaped the economies, the roles, and the distribution of cities. Most of the largest third world cities began as colonial capitals, including Calcutta, Bombay, Singapore, Lagos, Nairobi, and just about every city in the Americas. Some areas, chiefly in the Middle East, had a strong legacy of precolonial cities. In these areas, the colonial powers tended to occupy the existing cities and turn them into centers of imperial control. In most other areas, the colonial powers built the bulk of the cities themselves, in a manner that best suited their economic and political

needs. Likewise, the urban system was developed in order to serve colonial demands. This is obviously true in those areas where cities either did not exist prior to colonization or were wiped out by the colonizers, as occurred in Latin America. However, it also applies to those places, such as India, that enjoyed a rich urban tradition.

The demands of the colonial economy that drove the establishment of cities and determined the roles of colonial cities were quite clear: Cities were the specific conduits through which European powers extracted raw materials from the hinterland. Most colonial cities were established as ports and were more closely tied to the specific European power, often termed the **metropole**, than to the colony's interior. Geographer James Vance (1970) has created a **mercantilist model**, which is illustrated in Figure 15.6, that describes how colonization operated over time. The stages of this model are exploration, initial extraction on the coast itself, and the establishment of a colonial port tethered to the mother country. From this port, further settlements serve to extend the colonizers' reach into the interior, often along major river routes, in the search of more resources. The initial port, which continues to exercise an overwhelming predominance, bridges the interior of the colony with the colonizing power. Over time, the interior of the colony may begin to develop internally as market centers and internal transportation links help to create a more balanced urban system.

Vance's model of urban development illustrates much of the process whereby today's third world cities were established during the colonial period. Cities were established in order to funnel materials to the colonizers. For example, Robert Potter and Sally Lloyd-Evans (1998) demonstrate this process with regard to Barbados. By the nineteenth century, the main city of Bridgetown had developed primarily to transport sugar from the island's interior plantations to European kitchens. Control of the sugar crop was based outside the island, and the profits from the sugar trade flowed out as well. This economic system created a highly skewed urban pattern with most urban growth occurring along the

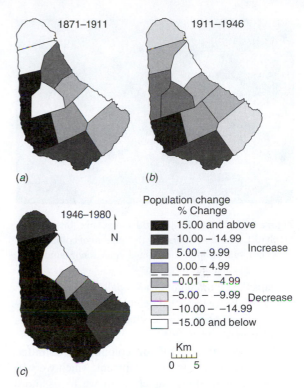

(a)   (b)

(c)

Figure 15.7 Barbados did not develop evenly, as this map indicates. From 1871 until 1946, clearly the higher levels of growth have occurred on the western side of the island, while the eastern side lost population. Since 1946, there has been some growth on the eastern side, but the western side of the island remains dominant. (*Source:* Potter, 1985.)

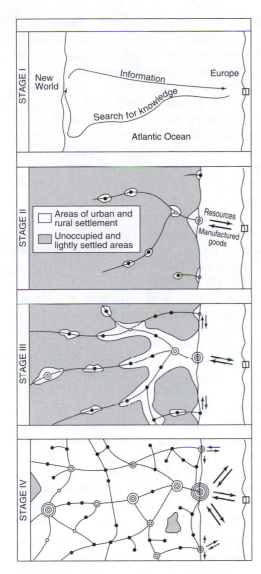

Figure 15.6 Mercantile model as developed by geographer James Vance. These four panels represent stages in the development of an urbanized region. The first, the exploration stage, entails the hunt for information and knowledge. In the second stage, settlement coincides with the creation of settlement pockets near the coast and along river routes. In the third stage, expansion broadens the area of settlement. By stage 4, an urban network, complete with central places, has been developed. (*Source:* Vance, 1970.)

western coast (Figure 15.7). Later, several of these coastal cities emerged as market centers in their own right, primarily for products manufactured in the metropole. Colonial cities were almost never centers of industrial production, a role that they had to develop after independence.

Politically, colonial cities were established as administrative centers that represented imperial power on colonial soil. The nature of the colonial impress varied depending on whether the city was new or had existed prior to colonization. (We discuss this in further detail in Chapter 16.) In any event, large, impressive structures were built, including the main government offices, business headquarters, and

Figure 15.8 Many third world cities, like this photograph of Lagos shows, display the impress of colonialism. Older colonial buildings are found in the foreground here.

perhaps the colonial governor's palace (Figure 15.8). Likewise, European-type neighborhoods were established that generally excluded the indigenous population.

The general patterns of colonialism admitted wide variations in local development, which we will discuss later in this chapter when we focus more on urban development within different regions. The underlying economic principles, however, were remarkably similar throughout the colonial world, and they produced an urban system that was skewed toward the West. As Stella Lowder (1986) remarks, "Settlements were bases from which the extraction of minerals, cash crops, or the railroad conveying them, or the ports exporting them could be overseen; they were promoted strictly in relation to their function in expediting production or in the administration enhancing it" (p. 82). In addition to the main port city (often the administrative capital of the whole colony), secondary cities in the interior were built up where there was a concentration of resources, or at the ends of railroads, or at a strategic fork in the river. For example, the early city of San Luis Potosí in Bolivia was built next to a silver mine, and it reached its apex around 1600. The Indian city of Delhi was enhanced by its position along the Ganges River. In Africa, interior cities like Nairobi, Lusaka, and Elizabethville represented imperial forays into the interior.

Economic Disparity Following national independence, colonialism was replaced by a relationship termed **neocolonialism**, in which the ex-colonial economy continued to provide raw materials to the former metropole. This relationship indicated a continued dependency on the former colonial power. According to some scholars, most notably Andre Gunder Frank (1969), the terms of trade between **satellite** and metropole were such that the satellite country continued to focus on primary products for export. In return they might import manufactured products.

This system worked to the disadvantage of the satellite because manufactured products are far more valuable than primary products in that manufacturing helps to create a dynamic, balanced economy that generates a tremendous amount of profit. In contrast, the production or extraction of primary materials might enrich the few families who own the land or the mine, but it leaves most of the population in abject poverty. The continued concentration of an economy on producing primary materials, termed a **commodity export economy**, also does very little for the satellite country's stability. Rather, the satellite becomes wholly dependent on outside demand for the main export commodity (over which it has no control), and it is forced to import most manufactured products (Figure 15.9). This continued relationship between a third world that produces raw materials and an industrialized first world does nothing to foster economic development in poorer countries. It is what Frank termed the "development of underdevelopment."

Early dependency theories were later recast in terms of a world system composed of core, periphery, and semiperiphery regions. The **core** refers to those areas of the world that control the economic capital essential to economic development. Core countries are characterized by a concentration of economic power, a diversified economic base, relatively high incomes, and greater economic, social, and political stability. The **periphery** refers to areas that are economically dependent on the core. Peripheral countries are characterized by a general lack of economic power, an economic base

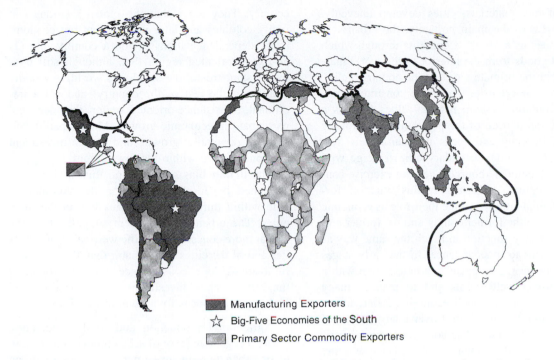

Figure 15.9 Some countries in the developing world have industrialized and export manufactured goods. Among these countries are Mexico, Brazil, India, and China. Other countries continue to export primary sector products—agricultural items, forestry goods, and minerals.

that produces just a few commodities (commodity export economies), incomes that are very low and very unequally distributed, and enormous price fluctuations. Small changes in the core can produce vast changes in the periphery. As a consequence, core countries experience only a tenuous social and political stability.

The **semiperiphery** is an intermediate category that lends a bit more sophistication to later dependency theory. Not every country fits neatly into the categories of core or periphery. Many of the countries we consider "developing," for example, Brazil, Mexico, and India, export primarily manufactured products. Other countries, such as the East Asian "tiger economies" of South Korea, Singapore, Taiwan, and Hong Kong, have achieved fairly high incomes. Thus, many countries lie somewhere between the core and the periphery. The semiperiphery countries are striving to get out of

the dependency trap, and their economic profiles are far more oriented toward manufactured products. These countries have accrued some indigenous economic capital, although many have accumulated deep external debts in their desire to develop. Compared to peripheral countries, they are characterized more by medium incomes, and they have a more developed middle class. Some, but not all semiperipheral countries have employed measures, such as steep import taxes and onerous quotas, to protect their native industries. In contrast, core countries are too powerful and peripheral countries too dependent to resort to these measures, at least not to the same degree, although protectionist impulses are found everywhere.

The processes of colonialism and dependency that we have just discussed clearly have had an impact on the development of cities. In a country with a purely peripheral economy based on the export of raw materials, cities develop unevenly. Beginning with the main port city, the urban system operates as a series of conduits through which to funnel goods from the interior to the world market. Within the primate city live the country's elite, or national bourgeoisie. Under the constraints of a global economic system, national elites (always a minuscule proportion of the population) control the national economy and focus it around their own interests. Over time, secondary cities emerge with their own "regional" bourgeoisie who exercise considerable regional influence. In this situation, formerly colonial cities continue their role as economic links between the former colony and the former colonizer, and they function in much the same way as they did prior to independence. In the early stages of independence, Europeans continue to live within their restricted settlements and to manage many aspects of the neocolonial economy. Later, native elites are able to gain control over a larger share of the nation's resources. The socioeconomic disparities do not alter that much, however, because a tiny group of wealthy elite holds economic sway over an impoverished majority.

With time, political pressure and the desire for greater economic autonomy alter many of the starker neocolonial arrangements. Although several less developed countries continue to be disproportionately involved in primary products and although the urban structure reflects this, what really drives urban growth is the uneven development that persists within the countries themselves.

Urban Bias Urbanization is a consequence of economic development. In the absence of industrialization, there is no motivation for large-scale urban growth. An economy developed solely for the demands of extraction can accommodate only a tiny percentage of its population within cities, and it is for this reason that third world cities remained so small up until the 1960s. When the economies attempted to industrialize, then large-scale urban growth could begin.

Many scholars, however, claim that urban growth tends to reinforce existing divisions within a country. They argue that the global relations that typify colonies and later independent but economically dependent nations divide a country into (1) an export-oriented region that, although still poor by the standards of the developed world, is wealthy relative to the rest of the country; and (2) a traditional, subsistence-oriented region that does not participate in economic growth. Most urban development, population growth, and capital investment are concentrated within the first region.

The **urban bias** goes beyond this, however, as explained by Josef Gugler. The decision-making elite within third world countries live in the main cities. The urban bias argument suggests that they are far more concerned with the well-being of urbanites and of the cities they inhabit than they are with rural areas. As a consequence, the overwhelming majority of capital investment, public spending, and high-quality labor is found within the cities:

> Agricultural production and rural manufacture are foregone in favor of urban production because of urban bias in investment; in favor of urban unemployment and underemployment because urban earnings are high relative to rural; and in favor of services provided to satisfy every whim of an urban-based minority that indulges in the conspicuous consumption of services. (Gugler, 1993, p. 24)

Part of this focus on cities—above and beyond the economic incentives that cities generate on their own—may explain why third world cities tend to have healthier, better educated, and more prosperous populations than do rural areas.

Armstrong and McGee (1985) applied the model of urban bias to Ecuador. For most of its history Ecuador was involved in the production of cocoa, coffee, and bananas. Consequently, the country had a classic export economy that focused around the main port city of Guayaquil. The commercial and financial elites of the country lived there, and the branch offices of foreign companies were located there. Since the 1970s, a great deal of oil has been extracted near the capital of Quito, which has begun to catch up to Guayaquil as a major economic and population center. Within this **binary system**—where the two largest cities overshadow the remainder of the urban structure—the focus of investment is clearly in Quito and Guayaquil. Modernization is focused around these two cities. They attract almost all of the capital investment, and the headquarters of national and foreign banks and most new industrial production are located there.

Regional centers in Ecuador, although smaller and less prosperous, are showing signs of progress. For instance, Cuenca in southern Ecuador is an old colonial city that has begun to acquire some trappings of modern production and has the industrial sectors, the newer suburbs, and the surrounding shanty towns to show for it. By contrast, the rural areas, especially those that do not participate in the cash crop or petroleum extraction economy, are left far behind. The lack of investment in rural areas compared to urban areas can be seen in these statistics from 1974: Nearly 90 percent of housing in rural areas had no electricity or sewer service, whereas in urban areas the figure was closer to 16 percent (Armstrong and McGee, 1985).

The fact that new industrial activity is focused around cities is not by itself evidence of a true urban bias. Cities attract development for several sound economic reasons. There is a long legacy in places like Great Britain and Japan of urban areas being in the vanguard of national economic growth. Greater opportunities in urban areas are what enticed greater capital investment as well as more labor migration to the cities, hastening the process of urbanization. What makes less developed countries different are the political impacts of this urban bias, which may result in diverting public resources away from the countryside and into the cities. Certainly, less developed countries display gaps in the health of urban and rural residents, with rural residents suffering higher infant mortality rates.

Urban bias as such is hard to measure. Any possible bias would be made up of myriad governmental decisions, and it is difficult to know whether budget allocations that seem to favor cities at the expense of rural areas represent impartial policy decisions or blatant favoritism. One index, which measures the imbalance in government allocations between the farming sector and manufacturing and commercial sectors, suggests that the poorest countries in the world tend to have the greatest disparities between these economic sectors. Again, intentionality cannot be measured here, and the emphasis on more advanced economic activity could be viewed as a rational attempt by poor nations to develop.

CHARACTERISTICS OF THIRD WORLD CITIES

The previous sections have examined third world cities in light of their growth and their connection to larger currents of development. But what are the characteristics of the cities themselves? How similar are they to cities in North America, Europe, and Japan? Is it possible to generalize about them, or must we consider each region independently? Of course, each city has developed under a unique set of circumstances, from its indigenous roots, to its colonial roles (if colonialism was present), to its twentieth-century development and position with the modern state. Moreover, what we think of as "third world" or "less developed" cities encompass a range of wealth and per capita purchasing power from about $12,000 a year to less than 50 cents a day. Nonetheless, some challenges are faced by all of these cities that help to set them apart and that create a unique urban character.

Many of the challenges faced by third world cities revolve around the fact that they are unable to accommodate their massive growth. Third world cities suffer from their own popularity, and in this regard they bear some resemblance to the fast growing cities in the developed world. But richer cities usually have enough jobs—rapid population growth is usually spurred by a heightened demand for workers—and they have the wherewithal to build enough housing and to provide adequate services, leading to the expanses of newly constructed subdivisions seen in almost every American boomtown. These options are not available in third world cities. Village dwellers migrate to the big cities in search of opportunity, but they encounter enormous difficulties in finding regular, full-time, paid work. As we discuss later, they must resort to other approaches in order to eke out a living. Likewise, neither the commercial private sector nor the already strapped public sector in such cities can possibly build enough housing for the new arrivals, especially because what we consider established housing is affordable for only a small fraction of the populace. Housing and jobs, therefore, are the chief challenges faced by third world cities, accompanied in some cases by ethnic conflicts and governmental corruption.

Effects of Growth

In his introduction to *In the Cities of the South,* Jeremy Seabrook (1996) points to the paradox of the third world city. On the one hand, we look at such urban explosions with horror. According to Seabrook, " 'population' is a metaphor for uncontainability, the inadequacy of civil services, the breakdown of law and order." Cities are thus metaphorically linked to natural disasters. On the other hand, we can view these cities as places of renewal, "to applaud the courage and endurance of people in the slums, to admire and wonder at their capacity for adapting, for building their own shelters, for creating a life for themselves, for finding a livelihood somewhere in the city economy." As was true of all cities throughout history, third world cities grow for a reason. People are seeking a better life. In the process, they swell the physical and civil infrastructure beyond the breaking point. As a result, third world cities exhibit high levels of problems and pathologies, such as poverty, pollution, crime, and inadequate housing.

Consider the negative effects of rapid growth among some communities in the United States: overcrowded schools, pollution, traffic congestion, inadequate fire protection, and perhaps high crime rates. Cities in the less developed world normally have to deal with far greater growth, with few of the assets available to richer cities. More people come in than scarce resources can accommodate, forcing the city to stretch far beyond its capacity. The density of such cities can be staggering. In Cairo, for example, population densities approach

300,000 people per square mile—four times that of Manhattan but with many fewer high-rise buildings. In such environs, housing is so tight that people actually occupy tombs.

Third world cities must contend with a problem of providing basic services, especially water, sewers, waste collection, and electricity. In North American and European cities, virtually every household, even in slum areas, has some source of electricity and water and some type of sewer system. Unfortunately, as you can see from Table 15.2, this is not true in third world cities. For example, in the large Indian cities of Mumbai (Bombay), Delhi, and Madras, only one-third to a little more than one-half of the households are connected to sewer and water systems, and only three-quarters have access to electricity. In most African cities less than one-third of households have access to sewers, and less than one-half are connected to water and electricity. The situation in Latin America is a bit better, but a

Table 15.2 Service Availability: Urban Households Connected to Utilities

City	Country	Water (%)	Sewer (%)	Electric (%)
Luanda	Angola	41	13	10
Ouagadougou	Burkina Faso	32	0	35
Douala	Cameroon	19	3	42
Kinshasa	Congo	50	3	40
Addis Ababa	Ethiopia	58	0	96
Nairobi	Kenya	78	35	40
Lagos	Nigeria	65	2	100
Dakar	Senegal	41	25	64
San Salvador	El Salvador	86	80	98
Rio de Janeiro	Brazil	95	87	100
Bogotá	Colombia	99	99	99
Santiago	Chile	98	92	94
Lima	Peru	70	69	76
Bombay	India	55	51	90
Delhi	India	57	40	70
Jakarta	Indonesia	15	0	99
Lahore	Pakistan	84	74	97
Manila	Philippines	95	80	86

Source: World Resources 1998–1999: A Guide to the Global Environment. New York: Oxford University Press.

large proportion of the population remains unserviced. Given the geography of service provision, the districts containing informal housing and especially squatter housing are much more likely to go without services. Slim municipal budgets have enough trouble servicing long-standing neighborhoods. They cannot possibly provide newly urbanized districts with water, sewers, electricity, and roads, and they are reluctant to extend services to areas that are illegally occupied to begin with.

Another effect of this tremendous population growth is pollution. The average urban third world resident consumes and wastes far fewer resources than residents of richer nations. For instance, per capita emission of carbon dioxide in the United States was about 20 metric tons in 2003, while Japan and wealthy European countries ranged between 5 and 13 metric tons. By contrast, the average carbon dioxide emission for African countries average under 1 metric ton, and for Asian and South American countries it was generally under 5 metric tons. However, poor cities are unable to employ the new and expensive technologies that can filter emissions in the air and dirty discharges in the water. Other air pollution indicators suggest that industrialization has exacted many atmospheric costs. Delhi, India, for example, reports about five times as much particulate matter as Los Angeles. The sulfur dioxide levels in Teheran, Iran are approximately eight times that of New York City. Mexico City has long been a poster child for problems of smog and air pollution. Here, the effects of smog and pollution have been estimated to be equivalent to the effects of smoking two packs of cigarettes a day, killing some 100,000 people a year.

Compounding the problem of air pollution is the lack of sufficient waste disposal. Only half of the dwellings in the third world are connected to sewers, and the vast majority of these dwellings churn out untreated sludge and human excrement. Cities are a little better (about 74 percent access), but still have problems dealing with all of the excess waste. In Bangkok, for example, human waste is thrown into storm drains, cesspools, and septic tanks. In such cases, groundwater is severely polluted, and rivers and canals are turned into open sewers. The disposal of corpses in the Ganges River in northern India has become such a major hazard to health that the government has resorted to breeding turtles that will eat the bodies. In most third world cities the stench of raw sewage indicates the presence of disease-causing organisms.

Housing

The lack of adequate housing is the first thing that visitors to a poor city notice. The ride from the airport often passes through acres of shanties. Along city streets, makeshift dwellings perch, occupying whatever space is opened to them. The downtown itself is usually occupied by thousands of homeless people, who are called **pavement dwellers** in Indian cities because they sleep on the sidewalks (Figure 15.10). The lack of decent housing affects a huge proportion of the population in poor cities, perhaps as many as 50 percent of all urban dwellers. According to the 2006 World Development Indicators, only 20 percent of city dwellers in Mozambique, 23 percent of urban Ethiopians, and 42 percent of urban Bangladeshis live in "durable dwelling units." In Madras, India, about 6,000 legal housing units are built each year, but at least 30,000 new units are needed. Here as elsewhere, supply is but a fraction of demand. The World Bank (2000) estimated that in the 1980s within third world cities, only one housing unit was constructed for every nine households in need of a dwelling.

In addition to coping with severe housing shortages, third world cities must address the diverse housing needs of different categories of urban migrants. On the one hand, large numbers of families migrate into cities, hoping to reestablish themselves there. These people are looking for permanent housing. On the other hand, many people come to cities on a more temporary basis. Young men frequently come to look for work with the intention of returning home to their village once they have made enough money. They will use their wages to buy housing in their village rather than in the city. Other people come as temporary sojourners, entering and exiting cities on a

(a) Cairo, Egypt

(b) Caracas, Venezuela

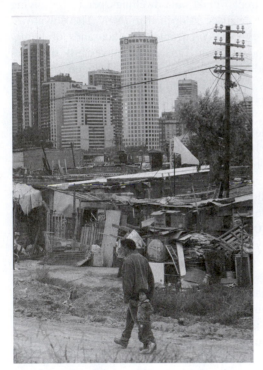

(c) Buenos Aires, Argentina

(d) Bathinda, India

Figure 15.10 Common scenes from cities in less developed countries.

seasonal basis. The housing needs of these various groups will be substantially different.

The provision of housing in third world cities is taken up by several different sectors. These can be loosely categorized as the public sector, the commercial private sector, and self-help housing.

Public-Sector Housing **Public-sector housing** is constructed by the government for its citizens, sometimes at a cost to the resident, but often subsidized. In the former Soviet Union and in Eastern Europe, this sort of housing comprised a large share of the overall market. It has also been tried in several third world cities, although it represents a relatively small proportion of the total housing stock. Up until the early 1970s, much of the public housing conformed to relatively high standards, following design principles (in regard to materials, space, and services) that better suited middle-class incomes. This made these units expensive to build. For instance, one-half of the population in Rabat, Morocco, was unable to afford public housing in the 1970s. Other cities faced similar difficulties, meaning that the public housing had to be generously subsidized. Even then, it was not affordable by the poorest residents.

In constructing public housing, many countries followed the lead of the industrialized world in developing large housing estates, often located far from existing jobs and businesses. This construction has taken various forms. In Hong Kong, massive six- to seven-story "H" blocks were constructed during the 1950s and made cheap by the provision of common facilities, the allocation of minuscule amounts of space, and densities that topped 2,000 people per acre. Construction in the 1960s was more generous, perhaps reflecting Hong Kong's growing wealth. In Caracas, Venezuela, the government destroyed existing slum properties and threw up hastily constructed *superblocks* that contained about 16,000 apartments (Figure 15.11). Although these dwellings were fairly comfortable in comparison to much of the existing housing, they were poorly maintained and offered few social amenities. As a result, the superblock neighborhoods greatly deteriorated. The unsuitability of such housing for poor residents in Rio de Janeiro was demonstrated by the propensity of some beneficiaries to vacate nice, government-built housing because it was too far from job opportunities.

Of course, some countries have tried to build entire communities. One approach practiced by several countries has been to divert some of the population into satellite cities, where population pressures are less severe and land is more available. New town creation emerged as a big component of public housing, often with a mixture of public and private monies (Box 15.3).

Figure 15.11 In the 1970s, the Venezuelan government constructed a set of giant apartment blocks, known as *superblocks*.

Although the efforts are laudable, public housing has generally been able to accommodate only a very small proportion of the population. Cost is an issue of course, as is the fact that the government budget simply is not large enough to subsidize every new housing unit. An additional issue is that, paradoxically, a lot of the new public housing is reserved for relatively well-off people. This began after independence in many countries, as the new administrative elite occupied housing once owned by European colonialists. Even within new public housing, however, governments often offer special deals to wealthier residents. In Lagos, for example, the upper-level bureaucrats live in subsidized public housing even though they are among the minority who could afford housing in the private commercial sector. In others cases, governments use some of their housing budget to try to entice their staff to relocate from the large cities to a new city designated as an administrative center.

One strategy that has succeeded in some cities involves housing established by **work units**. These are categories of people established according to where they work, for instance, a factory, a government bureau, or a store. This type of housing can be considered public or private, depending on the status of the workplace. It has been most widely practiced

BOX 15.3 Cairo's New Towns

Like other developing societies, Egypt has undergone rapid urbanization, much of it focused on the city of Cairo, the largest city in Africa. Egypt experiences special difficulties as well, in that the population is confined to the land bordering the Nile River. The press of people has created huge difficulties for Cairo. People live in graveyards and rooftops, urban services are woefully deficient, and unemployment is high. Cairo's City of the Dead, made up of several million Cairenes who live in the vast cemeteries that ring the eastern side of the city, is evidence of how people have sought housing in the most unlikely places.

One proposed solution to these problems has been the construction of new towns, a program that began in 1969. In implementing this program, the Egyptian government looked to the Garden City program of Britain and also at attempts by many countries to redirect population away from densely populated areas. The decision was made to build several new cities that were distributed throughout Egypt, but were more focused on the greater Cairo area. These cities, 14 in number as of 1996, were intended to support large populations of between 100,000 and 500,000 people. They were also meant to serve different economic roles. Some were intended as centers of industry. Others were supposed to help decentralize agricultural marketing. Still others were supposed to help in the reclamation of agricultural land from the desert. To promote these cities, the government provided a variety of incentives, including tax breaks, free or low-cost land, and the relocating of some governmental functions, especially to Sadat City. All of the new cities were constructed on a massive scale, with a modernistic, concrete-intensive style. Have these cities performed their function? According to geographer Dona Stewart (1996), who studied these cities, the results have been mixed. On the positive side, the cities have succeeded in attracting businesses, thanks to the lower costs of doing land and other necessities. This is especially true of those

new towns located closest to Cairo. However, they have failed to attract the needed residents. People in Egypt simply cannot afford to live that far away from their jobs, because most lack access to private transportation. Egyptian firms have often provided the necessary transportation for the workers themselves, but have not provided it for the families of these workers. For those new towns located close to Cairo, a pattern of reverse commuting has developed, with people continuing to live in overpopulated Cairo and commuting to the underpopulated new cities (Figure B15.1).

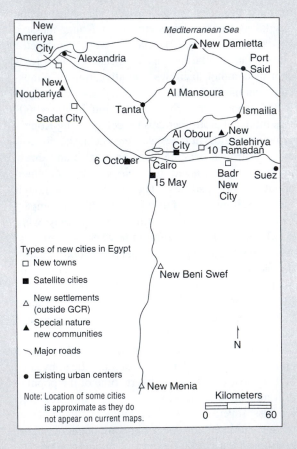

Figure B15.1 The location of Egypt's new towns. (*Source:* Stewart, 1996.)

in China, where until recently all work units were state owned. In Beijing, for example, about 91 million square meters of residential floor area were constructed between 1949 and 1991, increasing the city's housing supply almost eight-fold. Much of that housing was constructed through various work units that involved industries, government bureaus, and universities. An article from the official Chinese press stated that about 18 million square meters of housing were consutructed in 2000. Although much of the housing would be considered cramped by Western standards—in one city (Jinan) per capita living space in 2000 was only 10.5 square meters, or about 110 square feet—it still represents tremendous advances both in the supply and the quality of housing (see Box 16.4 in the next chapter). In fact, it is nearly triple the per capita living space from the 1970s.

Commercial Private-Sector Housing Housing built for profit by a construction company or a private contractor falls under the category of commercial housing. Most of the housing in North America is commercial housing. This is not true in most less developed cities, however, due primarily to the high costs associated with this kind of housing. In less developed countries the **commercial private sector** may have the capacity to build new housing, but few new residents can afford these houses. According to a recent report by the UN-Habitat Programme (2005), while housing prices are four times average incomes in the developed world, they are about six times income in Latin America, seven to ten times income in Asia, and over ten times income in Africa.

There are four principal reasons why commercial housing is so expensive in these countries. First, land costs are quite high. The land market is complicated and often uncertain, because ownership rights are often unclear and even harder to establish on paper. The supply of land may be limited, especially when land is held publicly or must be assembled from numerous smallholdings. All of these factors contribute to the high price of land. Many families must work several years just to afford the land itself,

helping to explain why so many people must either rent or build shelter on land they do not own.

Second, building costs are high. Most housing construction in third world cities still mandates the use of expensive durable materials (cement, brick, steel, and concrete) that may be in short supply locally. The difficulty in procuring these supplies adds to their cost. Third, access to credit can be difficult. Consider how few houses or even apartments would be built even in developed countries if there were no established lending institutions. This is the situation in many third world cities, which find themselves bereft of the financial infrastructure needed to provide loans to builders and potential customers. An estimate from the 1980s indicated that fewer than 10 percent of all housing transactions involved mortgages, and the tightness of credit all around squeezed the housing market. More recent estimates suggest much the same thing—mortgage finance is difficult to acquire in many cities in the less developed world. To give one example from Peru, only 1.3 percent of all title deeds were obtained with the help of mortgage loans (UN-Habitat 2005). Ironically, some developing countries have experimented in offering low-interest loans—below market rates. But like the public housing mentioned above, many of these loans went to the most privileged groups. Thus, even when financing becomes available, it often comes loaded with restrictions and stipulations that place it out of reach for all but the elite. The age of mass-market, middle-class housing has yet to dawn in less developed countries.

Fourth, most construction is driven by the elite. It is intended for the wealthiest classes—either residents of the city or visitors. Many third world cities have witnessed an explosion in "big ticket" construction. For example, Kuala Lumpur, in Malaysia, now boasts the two tallest buildings in the world, and other cities have rushed to build up their skylines. Expensive hotels and luxury apartments have also become commonplace in the largest cities. These projects tend to tilt the construction sector away from the housing demands of middle- and low-income families.

Self-Help Housing Because assistance from the private and public sectors is inadequate, the need for housing must be met in other ways. Outright homelessness is a common phenomenon, but most urban residents attempt to better their lives through **self-help housing**. The term refers to housing that is constructed informally by the residents themselves, rather than through private contractors or by the government. It is also referred to as **self-built housing**. This term cannot be compared to the custom housing built by many middle-class and affluent consumers in the United States. In third world cities, self-help housing is a strategy of the very poor, who seek to provide themselves with some shelter. Consequently, it constitutes a huge percentage of the total housing in these places. In India, for instance, between one-third and one-half of all urban residents live in housing constructed by themselves and their friends.

The primary advantage of self-help housing is its lower cost. According to one estimate, it costs at most one-fourth as much to build this type of housing as it would to construct a comparable unit in the public sector. Why does self-help housing cost so little? One reason is that the residents undertake all of the labor themselves and therefore do not have to use relatively highly paid professionals (architects, engineers, and contractors) or even skilled laborers. In addition, there is no formal design. But the most important reason may be the use of inexpensive building materials that are available locally. Many of these materials in fact are waste products from other construction projects.

A second advantage of self-help housing is upgradeability. Many units are constructed fairly simply but allow for a gradual improvement in the quality of building materials over time. In addition, they can be expanded if there is enough land.

The major disadvantage of self-help housing, beyond its possible inadequacies, is its uncertain legal status. Most self-help or self-built housing can also be considered unauthorized housing. The term **squatter settlement** has become widely used to describe the third world urban condition. Squatter settlements are built by residents who occupy land

Figure 15.12 Squatter housing in northern Jakarta along some of the canals. Refuse fills the canals, but the land is not privately owned and, therefore, is available for settlement.

to which they have no legal claim. Most cities have nearby areas in which the vacant land is occupied by squatters. Sometimes this land is useless for almost anything. Land situated along river banks or railroad lines or right next to dumps, although undesirable to commercial builders, can be enormously useful to potential residents (Figure 15.12). Likewise, unused plots of land in the inner city may be held for speculative reasons or because they are subject to some kind of property or inheritance dispute. These lands become very desirable to squatters.

Many of the enormous squatter settlements found in so many third world cities occupy peripheral land that belongs to the government. This type of land seizure results quite often in permanent settlements. The quantity of such land allows for the gradual development of real communities. The names of such settlements vary by city: *favelas* in Brazil, *shanty towns* in English-speaking Africa, *bidonvilles* in French West Africa, *colonias populares* in Mexico City, *kampungs* in Indonesia, *barriadas* in Peru. Government ownership of this land also makes it more likely that the squatter population will not be evicted. This is especially true when the squatters are organized and when they occupy the area quickly in a coordinated fashion.

Actual illegal squatting, although widespread, is less common than other forms of unauthorized housing. Many times, the owners of the land that is occupied by residents are aware of the settlements and see them as a way to collect rental income from lands that would otherwise be left idle. Much of the time, these settlements are unauthorized because they violate various zoning codes; they violate lot lines, they are not built with stable materials, they promote fire hazards, and they are not supplied with water and sewer. The landowner and the residents often have a mutual interest in flouting the laws.

The quality of self-help housing varies tremendously. Most of the initial housing constructed is abysmal, with a life span of less than five years. But given time, many such settlements can show tremendous improvement. This process is sometimes referred to as **autodevelopment**, in which individuals work to improve their own housing conditions. A study by Richard Ulack (1978) demonstrated how the quality of the squatter settlement was tied largely to its tenure. Those settlements that had been allowed to remain for several years—and thus had transformed into established neighborhoods—were able to autodevelop into stable, working class communities. New settlements, or settlements that were under constant threat of demolition, remained at a very low level of livability.

Increasingly, governments in less developed countries have come to realize that self-help housing is here to stay and that it can offer at least a partial solution to the housing crisis. In many cities, with the assistance of the United Nations and the World Bank, there has been a general shift away from government-sponsored public housing to assisted self-help housing, denoting a change from a *top-down policy* to an *enabling policy*. The enabling approach exists to funnel housing assistance through community-based organizations, groups that are operated for and by members of the community. In this manner, residents are given a greater stake in their housing and more control over the best means of providing housing. The enabling approach is thus a variant of self-help housing, but one that involves the larger community. The money need not come from the government; in fact, it is often financed by outside organizations or governments.

Many city and national governments have embraced two approaches related to self-help housing. One approach has been to promote the upgrading of existing housing, largely by focusing on providing water, sewers, electricity, and roads. For example, in Jakarta, Indonesia, the Kampung Improvement Program improves the infrastructure of roads and utilities and builds up some of the social welfare facilities. A second approach is to establish sites ahead of time and provide them with necessary services and perhaps the rudiments of a shelter. This approach, known as the *sites-and-services approach*—has met with some success. For example, in Nairobi, Kenya, the city government provided 6,000 small lots connected to water sources, sewers, roads, and lighting utilities. Each lot contained at least a toilet or so-called "wet core." In these endeavors, the government is viewed as an enabler of self-help housing. The government made these lots available at no or low cost to people who then built their own housing.

Employment Opportunities and the Informal Sector

Despite conditions that are appalling to Western eyes, the reason why many cities in the less developed world are growing so rapidly is the perception among migrants that cities are places of hope, of opportunity. Significantly, rural migrants have been falsely portrayed as desperate villagers who come to the city after having failed miserably in the countryside. In fact, the opposite is true. Those who migrate to the cities are among the best off of the peasantry. They tend to come from wealthier parts of the country, to be better educated, and to have had some experience in nonagricultural occupations. These are the sorts of people who would have some knowledge of jobs in the cities and some extra money to finance their journey.

In a balanced urban hierarchy, many of these people would migrate to smaller cities. That is the hope and expectation of many urban planners. As we have seen, however, it is the huge primate cities that exert the greatest magnetic pull. Unfortunately, although many jobs have been created in both the public and private sectors, most third world cities have not generated the necessary agglomeration economies to absorb anywhere near all of the newcomers. For example, in the 1980s, some researchers estimated that 1 billion new jobs would have to be created worldwide between 1985 and 2000—primarily in less developed countries—to bring about full employment. This has not happened.

The disparity between the growth of good jobs and the population influx has had several consequences. One consequence is that many third world countries have a very small middle class. As a result several such countries suffer from a high degree of income inequality. The World Bank (2000) has compiled data on the ratio of the incomes of the wealthiest 20 percent to the poorest 20 percent in each country. In each industrialized country, the ratio is less than 10:1. In contrast, in the industrializing middle-income countries, especially in Latin America, ratios are higher, with most exceeding 10:1 and with several exceeding 15:1 ratios. Brazil is the global champion of inequality, with a ratio of about 32:1. The results can be witnessed in some of its biggest cities. In Rio de Janeiro, for instance, income inequality is manifested spatially, with almost one-half the population living in peripheral areas and earning less than $1.50 a day per capita (Figure 15.13). Indeed, during the 1980s the poorest half of the population in Rio saw their share of overall income diminish. In both Rio de Janeiro and São Paulo, inequality further increased between 1990 and 2000 according to data complied by Portes and Roberts (2004).

This income inequality is reflected in the labor market. Simply put, there are not enough regular jobs for all of the people who want them. This means that many cities in less developed countries are split into two sectors: (1) a more formal sector, where the regular, wage-earning jobs are found; and (2) an informal sector, where self-employment in a variety of peripheral occupations is often the rule.

Formal Sector   The **formal sector** is made up of those jobs, either in government or private concerns, that provide a reasonably steady wage. The formal sector consists of the large industries, services, and the government, which employ those workers privileged enough to find a steady, permanent job. It also includes firms that employ people on a more temporary basis.

The number of people who actually find reasonable paying jobs in these new industries is a small proportion of the total adult working population (sometimes no more than one-third). For example, Portes and Roberts (2004) report that Latin American cities suffer from formal unemployment rates of up to 20 percent but that the overall level of labor vulnerability—constituting unskilled self-employed workers, unemployed workers, and workers without any government or legal protection—is as high as 50 percent. Workers in the formal sector usually started

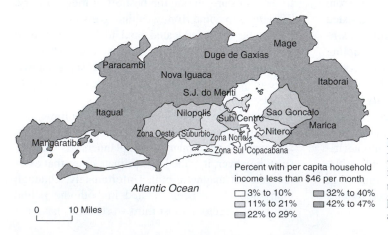

Figure 15.13 Poverty in Rio de Janeiro, Brazil, 1990. This map indicates that poverty in Rio de Janeiro is found further away from the coast and central city and out in the more peripheral neighborhoods. (*Source:* Ribeiro and Telles, 2000.)

off with some advantages, such as academic credentials, greater wealth, or the good luck of knowing somebody with influence. Or they got their jobs through political patronage. Besides the elite, they are the only people who earn any significant income. This restricts the demand for the products they produce because not enough people can afford them.

Formal sector employment in poor countries today is likely to be a consequence of corporate shifting and the outsourcing of labor-intensive jobs from countries like the United States, where wages and benefits are high, to countries like Thailand and China, where these costs are quite low. The sweatshops have moved from the first to the third world, and it is in these factories that people may earn only a few dollars a day for unskilled or semiskilled work. But it is important to keep in mind that although such conditions seem horrific to our point of view, they represent opportunity to those doing the work.

Informal Sector Because the industrial labor market is never in a position to employ more than a fraction of the urban workforce and the government cannot fill the gap, people are forced to eke out a living in some other way. For some people, returning to the village is an option, but most do not choose this path. They opt instead to find work within the **informal sector**.

The informal sector is hard to define. According to Potter and Lloyd-Evans (1998), the informal sector "refers to unaccountable and unregistered activities" (p. 172). The informal sector also means different things. It "encompasses wealth and poverty, productivity and inefficiency, exploitation and liberation" (p. 177). Informal sector jobs exist on the margins, but they make up much if not most of the employment in third world cities and therefore are very visible. (Although informal sector activities also are found in industrial cities, particularly in the inner city, they affect a very small percentage of people and so are not nearly as visible.)

A large variety of jobs fall into the informal sector (Table 15.3). Activities include retail distribution, particularly food, fresh water, newspapers,

Table 15.3 Variety of Informal Sector Jobs

Agricultural Activities
 Market gardening
 Urban farming

Manufacturing and Construction Activities
 Food processing and home production
  of hot food
 Garments
 Crafts
 Jewelry and trinkets
 Shoes
 Household goods
 Electrical and mechanical items
 Alcohol production
 Construction

Trading Activities
 Street corner sales
 Vending
 Newspaper hawking

Services
 Laundry
 Domestic services
 Hardware repair
 Driving
 Odd jobs
 Maintenance and gardening

Other Activities
 Begging
 Protection
 Illegal activities (e.g., drugs)

Source: Derived in part from Potter and Evans, 1998, p. 173.

and jewelry; artisans who produce small items for household use; small garden farming; personal services such as laundries, repair shops, and gambling services; and, of course, scavenging and begging. In Havana, Cuba, some people clean and refurbish automotive spark plugs—an important task in a country in which every mechanical item is carefully preserved. What unites these diverse occupations? They do not require any special credentials to gain access, and these jobs can be conducted without a large capital investment.

The biggest advantage of the informal sector is that entrance is not restricted on the basis of education or skill qualifications, in contrast to the formal sector, where entry can be quite difficult. Another advantage is that the informal sector relies on family resources and self-enterprise; in fact, it makes use of all members of the household to generate an income. Informal enterprises usually work "under the table" and are unregulated. They are also conducted on a small scale and make intensive use of labor as opposed to formal sector work, which tends to be more capital intensive.

We must be careful with these broad distinctions, however. Although the informal sector represents an option for those who cannot enter the formal sector, barriers do sometimes exist that restrict employment. For instance, retail hawkers may wish to keep their territory to themselves and will not look kindly on newcomers. Rather than perceiving the formal and informal sectors as being separated by a rigid divide, it probably makes more sense to view them as existing along a continuum.

The biggest disadvantage of informal sector work is that it is often very low paying and unsafe. Moreover, informal sector jobs provide no stability, and workers possess no legal rights or access to private or government benefits. Although recognition and even encouragement of the informal economy is probably a good idea, given current realities, there is a thin line between an economic sector that operates as a means of escaping poverty and one that maintains a reserve force of cheap, exploited labor.

What percentage of the working population is employed in the informal sector? Although it is impossible to know this for certain, Table 15.4 presents data from the United Nations that estimate the size of the informal sector in some major cities. Unfortunately, several of these figures may be inaccurate.

Attitudes toward the informal sector have changed quite a bit in recent years. At first, the informal sector was seen as a marker of backwardness that would be eradicated once the economy progressed. Workers in this sector were actually seen as failures. More recently, the idea of the informal sector has become more elaborately articulated. Rather than being viewed as an undifferentiated mass of unskilled workers, informal sector labor

Table 15.4 Size of the Informal Sector in Some Major Cities

City	Country	Percent
Luanda	Angola	36
Ouagadougou	Burkina Faso	60
Douala	Cameroon	66
Kinshasa	Congo	80
Addis Ababa	Ethiopia	61
Nairobi	Kenya	52
Lagos	Nigeria	69
Dakar	Senegal	47
San Salvador	El Salvador	38
Rio de Janeiro	Brazil	34
Bogotá	Colombia	54
Santiago	Chile	23
Lima	Peru	49
Bombay	India	68
Delhi	India	67
Jakarta	Indonesia	33
Lahore	Pakistan	60
Manila	Philippines	20

Source: World Resources 1998–1999: A Guide to the Global Environment. New York: Oxford University Press.

is increasingly being perceived as filling a niche in societies without adequate formal employment. Government policy has shifted toward helping people help themselves in small-scale enterprises. It is too early to tell whether such attempts will be successful.

WRAPPING UP

Urbanization in the coming century is going to be focused in the less developed world. The big cities of the past—London, Tokyo, New York, Paris—are no longer growing very much. Demographically, the twenty-first century will belong to cities like Mexico City, São Paulo, Lagos, and Delhi. These cities continue to expand and, more importantly, they are located within countries where the urban population as a whole is still growing. We are already at a stage where the average urban dweller lives in the third world. This trend will become truer in the current century. It also raises a paradox, because cities in the less developed world are unable to sufficiently accommodate their burgeoning populations.

This chapter has focused on some of the common issues that affect cities in the less developed world. First, it examined the phenomenon of rapid urbanization, often resulting from rapid population growth in general, rural-to-urban migration, and primate cities. Second, it examined how third world urbanization has developed as a result of overall economic development but also because of the impacts of colonialism and uneven development. Third, it noted some general characteristics of third world cities, especially with regard to the inadequacy of housing and employment opportunities. In this respect, we have also considered some possible solutions. Because the problems are so vast and the solutions sometimes elusive, it is easy to despair about the future of these cities. But it is also important to remember that periods of rapid urban growth within all societies have been remarkably unsettling and often chaotic. In these cases, the cities have remained as beacons of hope. Over time, they have matured to become more stable and more pleasant places to live.

READINGS

Armstrong, Warwick, and T. G. McGee. 1985. *Theatres of Accumulation: Studies in Asian and Latin American Urbanization*. London: Methuen.

Brennan, Eileen. 1999. "Urban Land and Housing Issues Facing the Third World." In J. Kasarda and A. Parnell, eds., *Third World Cities: Problems, Policies, and Prospects*. Newbury Park, CA: Sage Publications.

Fik, Timothy. 2000. *The Geography of Economic Development: Regional Changes, Global Challenges*. New York: McGraw-Hill.

Frank, Andre Gunder. 1969. *Capitalism and Underdevelopment in Latin America*. New York: Modern Reader.

Gugler, Josef. 1993. "Third World Urbanization Reexamined," *International Journal of Contemporary Sociology*, Vol. 30, No. 1, 21–38.

Gugler, Josef, ed. 1996. *The Urban Transformation of the Developing World*. Oxford: Oxford University Press.

Kaplan, Robert D. 1994. "The Coming Anarchy," *Atlantic Monthly*, Vol. 273, No. 2, pp. 44–76.

Kasarda, John, and Allan Parnell, eds. 1993. *Third World Cities: Problems, Policies, and Prospects*. Newbury Park, CA: Sage Publications.

Keivani, Ramin, and Edmoundo Werna. 2001. "Modes of Housing Provision in Developing Countries," *Progress in Planning*, Vol. 55, pp. 65–118.

Linn, Johannes. 1983. *Cities in the Developing World: Policies for Their Equitable and Efficient Growth*. Oxford: Oxford University Press.

Lowder, Stella. 1986. *The Geography of Third World Cities*. Totowa, NJ: Barnes and Noble Books.

Mohan, Rakesh. 1996. "Urbanization in India: Patterns and Emerging Policy Issues." In J. Gugler, ed., *The Urban Transformation of the Developing World*. Oxford: Oxford University Press.

Porter, Philip, and Eric Sheppard. 1998. *A World of Difference: Society, Nature, Development*. New York: The Guilford Press.

Portes, Alejandro and Bryan R. Roberts. 2004. "The Free Market City: Latin American Urbanization in the Years of Neoliberal Adjustment" URL www.prc.utexas.edu/urbancenter/documents/Free%20Market%20City%20text.pdf (accessed October 23, 2007)

Potter, Robert B. 1985. Urbanisation and Planning in the 3rd World: Spatial Perceptions and Public Participation. New York: St. Martin's Press.

Potter, Robert B. 1990. Cities and Development in the Third World. Commonwealth Geographical Bureau.

Potter, Robert B. 1999. *Geographies of Development*. Harlow, UK: Longman.

Potter, Robert, and Sally Lloyd-Evans. 1998. *The City in the Developing World*. Harlow, UK: Addison-Wesley Longman.

Pugh, Cedric. 1995. "Urbanization in Developing Countries: An Overview of the Economic and Policy Issues in the 1990s," *Cities*, Vol. 12, No. 6, pp. 388–398.

Ribeiro, L. C. Q., and Edward Telles. 2000. "Rio de Janeiro: Emerging Dualization in a Historically Unequal City." In P. Marcuse and R. van Kempen, eds., *Globalizing Cities: A New Spatial Order?* Oxford, UK: Blackwell Publishers.

Seabrook, Jeremy. 1996. *In the Cities of the South*. New York: Verso.

Short, John, and Yeong-Hyun Kim. 1999. *Globalization and the City*. New York: Longman.

Sit, V. 1995. *Beijing: The Nature and Planning of a Chinese Capital City*. New York: Wiley.

Smith, David D. 2000. *Third World Cities*. London: Routledge.

Stewart, Dona J. 1996. "Cities in the Desert: The Egyptian New-Town Program," *Annals of the Association of American Geographers,* Vol. 86, No. 3, pp. 459–480.

The World Bank. 2000. *World Development Report 1999/2000*.

Ulack, Richard. 1978. "The Role of Urban Squatter Settlements," *Annals of the Association of American Geographers,* Vol. 68, No. 4, pp. 535–50.

United Nations Human Settlements Programme. 2005. *Financing Urban Shelter: Global Report on Human Settlements 2005*. Earthscan.

Vance, James. 1970. *The Merchants' World,* Englewood Cliffs, NJ: Prentice Hall.

REGIONAL VARIATIONS IN URBAN STRUCTURE AND FORM IN THE LESS DEVELOPED WORLD

[The] city is a mosaic of cultural and racial worlds each invoking the memory of other lands and people; the tree-lined avenues of Phnom-Penh and Saigon reminiscent of Paris; the canals and stuffy buildings of old Batavia, replicas of the medieval Dutch town; and towering skyscrapers of downtown Singapore are part of the universal Western central business district.

—T. G. McGee, 1967, p. 25

What geographer T. G. McGee (1967) attributes to certain Southeast Asian cities could be extended to include most cities in the less developed world. As we saw in Chapter 15, most third world cities jumble together many cultural and racial worlds. In part, these cities are legacies of a colonial past. European imperialism and colonialism throughout the nineteenth and early twentieth centuries pervaded all but a few societies, and most of the important third world cities today can trace their dominance to this period. The McGee passage quoted above goes on to describe the magnificent cultural variety that is found within Southeast Asian cities and that is likewise true of so many cities. At the same time, however, it also focuses on the divisions among the very wealthy, the middle class, and the many, many poor: "Here the contrasts are not those of the cultural diversity of the racial worlds of the inner city, but the contrasts of wealth and squalor" (p. 25). It is this economic divide that looms largest in most third world cities.

Many models exist of North American cities (see Chapter 8). But what of cities in the less developed world? Although we must acknowledge the tremendous variation among cities, it can still be useful to point to some general economic, social, and spatial characteristics at least for cities within larger regions. The previous chapter outlined some of the general factors that affect the growth and development of third world cities, as well as the issues of housing and employment, which define the living conditions within these cities. However, numerous other factors must be considered.

First, ethnicity helps to structure every city. Like their counterparts in Europe and North America, Asian, African, and Latin American cities are kaleidoscopes of diverse religions, languages, races, nationalities, and castes that vie with one another for salience and space. In fact, it might be argued that in lands where resources are scarce, ethnicity takes on an even more important role in allocating goods, services, housing, and jobs to families. The factors causing such diversity are not the same as those applied in the West, where immigration from other countries plays the major role. Rather, these major cities often reflect the incredible diversity of the countries. India, for instance, contains almost 50 languages, a half-dozen strongly held religions, numerous nationalities, and a potent caste system. These groups come together in India's major cities.

Second, the legacy of colonialism is still powerful. Initial decisions regarding the layout of third world cities that were made during the colonial era have helped shape these cities to this day. The legal and political structures guiding these cities were often established at this time as well. The imprint of the colonial era is also found in the examples of architecture, in open spaces, and certainly in the location of elite neighborhoods. In addition, most third world cities (whether they wish to acknowledge it or not) are still tied to the former colonial powers through trade, banking, tourism, the direction of migration, and language.

Third, economic development varies within countries, but even more so among countries and regions. The idea of the third world as an undifferentiated mass of poverty and despair has given way to a perception that there are several "worlds" at different stages of development. Some cities have experienced fairly robust growth and industrial development. These cities are undergoing far different trajectories than the cities where urban population growth has not been accompanied by economic growth. Likewise, different countries have followed strikingly different ideological paths. Countries like the Dominican Republic, which have fostered inequality, are strikingly different from countries like Cuba, which have been guided by socialist principles.

This chapter presents several generalized discussions of cities within various less developed regions, drawing on features that help us to characterize the general urban experience within these regions. At the same time, it provides examples from actual cities within these regions. Because these are regionally based examples, please keep in mind that a great deal of diversity is found among cities within regions, just as Las Vegas differs from Boston. Some of this diversity has to do with city size, some with differences in regional economies, and some with different political systems. Whenever possible, we will try to comment on some of these intraregional distinctions.

THE LATIN AMERICAN CITY

The phrase *Latin America* is convenient shorthand for those countries in South America, Central America, and the Caribbean. Most of these countries are Spanish speaking, although the largest country, Brazil, is Portuguese speaking. There is also some use of English, French, and other languages as well. Compared with the rest of the third world, Latin America is by far the most urbanized region, and we can safely say that most of the countries in the region have gone through the urbanization process. Most of the region's urban growth took place between 1940 and 1980 and resulted largely from rural-to-urban migration. At this time, cities in six large Latin American countries increased an average of 4.1 percent a year, while the rural population stagnated. The huge metropolises (major cities within the region) gained substantially from this migration, but the intermediate cities between 100,000 and 2 million gained even more. According to the Population Reference Bureau (2006), 76 percent of Latin Americans lived in cities as of 2000, the same proportion as the developed countries. Four out of five citizens of South American countries live within cities. Expectations are that the percentages will not increase that much in the next century, so we can consider the urbanization process largely completed in this area.

Most of the countries in Latin America can be considered middle-income countries. With the exception of three small and very poor countries (Haiti, Honduras, and Nicaragua), gross national product (GNP) per capita ranges from $1,000 to $10,000. This range begins at about the global median and extends into the ranks of the global upper middle class. This reflects the fact that Latin America has undergone a great deal of industrialization. Between the 1930s and 1960s, much of the impetus for economic change came from policies that tried to reduce dependence on imported manufactured goods. New domestic industries were fostered in everything from textiles to shoes to automobiles. Many countries established state-owned companies, relying partly on socialist models to spur development. More recently, industrial development has been spurred by multinational corporations that have established important branch plants in urban areas. These large corporations often bypass the biggest cities for intermediate-sized, lower-cost urban areas. Places like Mexico's urbanized northern border zone and parts of Brazil's Amazon region have benefited from these locational decisions. Several Latin American countries have been able to realize incipient advantages based on their resource bases—for example, Mexico and Venezuela are both major exporters of oil—and on their tremendous human capital.

At the same time, urbanization, overall income growth, and industrial development have perpetuated tremendous inequality. As a whole, Latin America suffers the greatest degree of income disparities of any region (although sub-Saharan Africa appears a close second). The expansion of jobs in public administration, the growth of the professional class, and the rise of large industrial complexes have enabled large numbers of people to get decent jobs with some benefits, and they have even enabled a small elite to become quite wealthy. According to official statistics, the percentage of the urban employed population working in a professional or managerial capacity increased from about 7 percent in 1940 to 16 percent in 1980. Between 1980 and 1998, the professional and technical workforce continued to increase in Brazil, doubling in Mexico and Uruguay, tripling in Costa Rica, but remaining flat in Venezuela and Columbia. But these figures, which suggest that a huge formally employed labor force has emerged, are probably optimistic. Much of the growth occurred during the 1980s. The 1990s witnessed considerably stagnation. At this point in time, the United Nations estimates that three out of four Latin Americans can be considered "lower income." Many of these people are nonpermanent and only tenuously employed.

Colonial Legacies

Virtually all of Latin America's important cities were established within the 100 years of the Spanish and Portuguese conquests. A geographically vast urban network was created for the express purpose of subduing and controlling the countryside. Even at

this early period, the colonial society was intensely urban. All political authority was vested in the cities, which controlled the surrounding countryside. In Spanish America, the main capitals were headed by a *viceroy* (or representative of the king), while other cities were given administrative control over smaller districts. The bulk of wealth came from the countryside, and the majority of people still lived there, but cities were clearly the focal points of the South American colonies.

The Spanish and Portuguese do not appear to have made any real attempts to develop the countryside. The main purpose of development was to extract the countryside's mineral and agricultural wealth. Many settlers intended to make their money and then return to Europe. Leading citizens (usually the first to come over) were granted vast tracts of land called *encomiendas*, as well as Indians to work these lands. Despite their possessions, most huge landowners chose to live in the cities.

This colonial society was highly stratified, and only landowners held any power. The founding families monopolized most of the available wealth. They were followed by later colonists of high rank. Next came the Spaniards of lower rank, foreigners, *mestizos* (people of mixed European and Indian ancestry), Indians, and finally black slaves. The cities swelled as indigenous groups whose livelihoods had been destroyed were forced to come looking for work.

Latin American cities had a distinctive form that still can be seen today (Figure 16.1). Where they could, the Spanish set up a grid pattern oriented around a plaza. This was primarily an empty block used for periodic markets, public gatherings, or military possessions. Around this plaza were located the main public buildings, the mansion of the viceroy, and the cathedral. This area and adjacent blocks marked the first zone, which was generally the only part of the city that was paved and well lit. Surrounding the first zone was a second zone inhabited by a rudimentary middle class consisting of artisans, clerks, and small proprietors. This zone was not nearly as well serviced. Beyond this zone were settlements inhabited by unskilled workers.

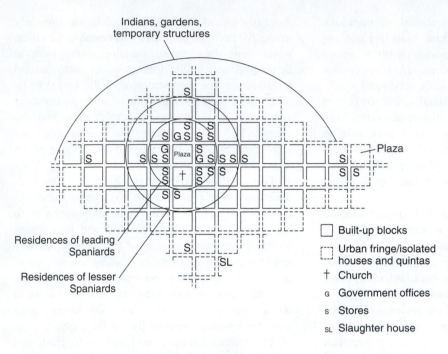

Figure 16.1 Model of a colonial city in Latin America. This displays the focus of the Spanish colonial city around a plaza, with status declining with distance from the central plaza. (*Source:* Sargent, 1993.)

Independence and the onset of industrialization in the nineteenth century largely accentuated these trends. Some of the biggest cities, like Mexico City and Lima, grew much bigger than the others as they became centers for administration and export. Demand from Europe and North America for new products enriched a few people, who spent money on ever larger mansions in pleasant surroundings, but it did not do much to improve the conditions of the majority of the population.

Modern Latin American Cities

The modern Latin American city is at once a center of hope for people within the region and a cumulation of social and economic ills. Latin Americans love their cities; they see themselves as an urban people. This is represented in the café culture, lively streets, extraordinarily vital downtown districts, and numerous public activities that take place within the city. The magnetism of the city, along with dwindling opportunities in the countryside, has long pulled people away from the countryside in search of a better life. Yet Latin American cities—some of them among the biggest in the world—are hard pressed to

deal with this influx. Many urban residents want the basic comforts of life but find themselves scrounging for whatever income they can find.

Themes of City Life Three themes that help us to characterize the modern Latin American city are (1) urban primacy, (2) spatial polarization, and (3) uneven economies. We begin with *urban primacy*. Rural-to-urban migration was concentrated on a few centers and occurred in explosive bursts during the 1950s and 1960s. This migration generated high overall levels of urbanization, with extreme concentrations in just a handful of primate cities. Import substitution models of economic development—in which Latin American countries attempted to substitute home-produced items for manufactured imports—tended to focus economic energy on these centers even more. In the 1980s, this trend was partly altered. Smaller cities began to grow more quickly as the economy shifted more toward exports. A good example is the development of industries known as ***maquiladoras*** on Mexico's border with the United States. These are often concentrated in labor-intensive industries such as textiles, clothing, furniture, and electronic goods. The growth of industry here, spurred by the desire of American companies for cheap labor and good location, has prompted the growth of several smaller cities. Figure 16.2 shows the growth in the major Mexican border cities between 1900 and 2005.

The second theme is *spatial polarization*. Many Latin American countries have a highly unequal income distribution, with a large gap between rich and poor. In the 1960s and 1970s, the wealthy chose to remove themselves from the problems of poverty by establishing fortified citadels. There was also a movement toward the urban periphery. This trend followed the North American model in some ways, but it differed in two important aspects. First, many of the wealthy chose to remain near the downtown. Most Latin American cities exhibit something of a Western European model, where wealth and income decline with distance from the center city. Second, the number of people able to afford such a move was small, and the elite sector was generally contained in one or two directions only. Figure 16.3 shows both of these patterns, with elite districts found at the core stretched along two wedges. Urban services followed this wedge or corridor. Many of the poorest residents likewise moved to peripheral locations, but they came to reside in massive squatter settlements that were removed from the affluent suburbs.

In recent years, continued urban growth and the legacies of the Latin American debt crisis have forced more middle-income people to establish neighborhoods in formerly impoverished areas and have led some squatters to infiltrate neighborhoods that were the preserves of the rich. Spatial separation in Latin American cities is in no manner "pure." São Paulo, to give one example, was transformed from a city where different socioeconomic groups lived at some distance from one another to a place where the wealthy and the poor live much closer together. Note that the fact that the rich and poor no longer live far apart does not mean that income disparities have diminished. In addition, their proximity to poor populations has encouraged wealthy residents to create social distances and physical barriers and to ensure that their habitats, often luxury apartments, are heavily fortified and have tight security.

The third theme has to do with the *uneven economies* that forced many rural residents off the land because they could no longer be sustained by traditional agriculture. Lands were taken over by modern agribusinesses, and the "outplaced" residents left for the cities. But the city economy did not have enough formal employment opportunities to absorb these newcomers. At the same time, without welfare protection and no real chance to go back to the villages, the new residents were forced to make do. The informal economy swelled, absorbing more than

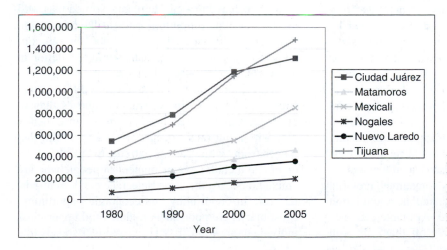

Figure 16.2 Mexican communities bordering the United States have grown from small towns to big cities. Of the six cities shown here, all but Nogales has a population over 300,000 as of 2005.

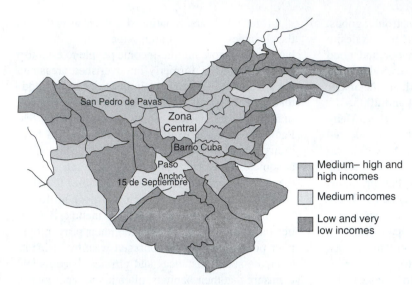

Figure 16.3 San Jose, Costa Rica, exhibits the tendency among Latin America's affluent to live in the central city (*zona central*) or along a defined corridor or wedge stretching outward to North American style suburban dwellings. (*Source:* Lungo, 1997.)

one-half of the urban labor force in the 1970s. For a time the informal economy was perceived as a compensating mechanism for the limitations of the formal economy. However, current indications are that it is too limited to absorb all of the workers who cannot find jobs in the formal economy. Moreover, economic downturns can create situations in which residents can find nothing in either economic sphere.

In addition to these three themes, some other peculiarities are seen in the Latin American city. One of these is the nature of race, discussed more fully in Chapter 10. Latin American cities, like the American and Canadian cities to the north, are products of immigration. Voluntary immigrants from Europe, and to some extent Asia, were joined by involuntary immigrants brought over by the slave trade. These groups then mixed with the indigenous Indian populations, which in some cases continue to comprise a sizable proportion of the population (Figure 16.4). These indigenous groups tend to be poorer than the average individual within each country. Although urbanization rates among the various indigenous groups are lower than average, recent years have witnessed a movement of Indians to the major cities—sometimes crossing international borders. Poverty and new migration merge to produce disadvantage. Available evidence indicates that Indians are worse off than others in

all areas of urban life, including income, housing, education, and health. In addition, they are looked down upon by the urban ethnic majority.

Likewise, the proportion of people of African descent is high in many Latin American countries, although the percentages vary. In total, nearly 10 million slaves were forced into the Americas between 1450 and 1870, less than 4 percent of whom were brought to North America. Of the remainder, the largest numbers came to the West Indies (about 4.5 million) and Brazil (more than 3.6 million). As a result of this massive slave trade, African-origin residents now constitute a majority within Caribbean nations such as Jamaica, Haiti, and Trinidad, as well as an enormous proportion of Brazil's population. According to Ribeiro and Telles (2006), Brazil contains the second highest African-origin population in the world, second only to Nigeria.

Significantly, race is constructed far differently in Brazil and other Latin American countries than in the United States. It is not considered an either-or proposition but rather occurs along a spectrum that ranges from "white" at one extreme to "black" at the other and includes a large number of people who are "mixed race." At the same time, race plays an important role in opportunity and economic opportunity. Most blacks are poor; most middle- and upper-class individuals are white. Even in an all-black society like

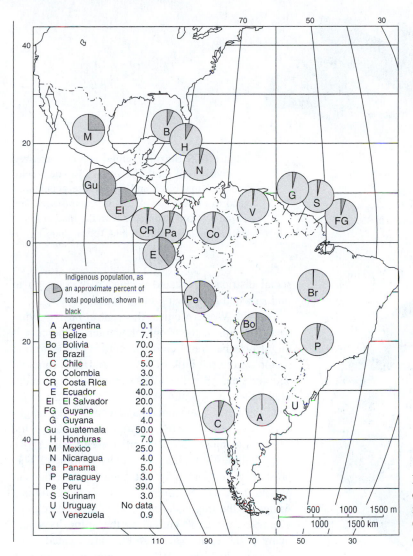

Figure 16.4 Map indicating the percentage of the population that is indigenous. Many countries, such as Bolivia, Guatemala, Ecuador, Peru, and Mexico, contain a significant number of Indians.

Haiti, gradations in skin color are generally linked to economic status, with lighter-skinned blacks comprising the Haitian elite. Race also is a significant predictor of residential location (Figure 16.5). Segregation levels are not quite as pronounced in Rio de Janeiro as in most American cities, but they are still pronounced, even among those households that are considered comfortable.

Spatial Layout In many respects, the spatial layout of Latin American cities reflects their colonial legacy, the presence of a wealthy elite, a substantial middle and working class, and the large population of desperately poor people who have migrated in search of a better life. It also reflects the fact that municipal services can expand only so much. Sewers, water, electricity, paved roads, and other services are limited and tend to be found near the center and in more established areas. Figure 16.6 provides one model for the Latin American city. It is important to keep in mind, when examining this model, that considerable overlap exists between

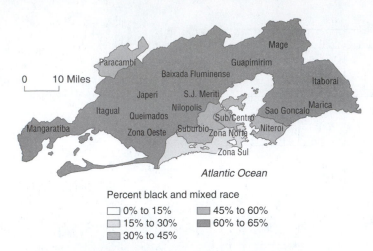

Percent black and mixed race

☐ 0% to 15%   ■ 45% to 60%
☐ 15% to 30%   ■ 60% to 65%
▨ 30% to 45%

Figure 16.5 Brazilian cities are characterized by divisions of race. This map of Rio de Janeiro indicates that black and mixed-race populations tend to cluster outside of the central zone and in the outskirts. Compare with the map in figure 15.13. (*Source:* Ribeiro and Telles, 2006.)

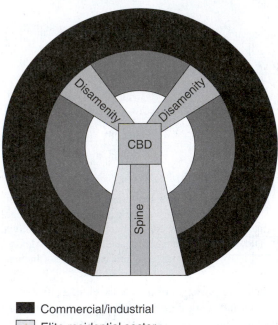

■ Commercial/industrial
☐ Elite residential sector
☐ Zone of maturity
■ Zone of in situ accretion
▨ Zone of peripheral squatter settlements

Figure 16.6 Model of Latin American city. Although this model has been criticized for being overly general, it remains a useful way to understand the spatial logic of Latin American cities. (*Source:* Griffin and Ford, 1980.)

social districts. As stated earlier, it is common to find rich and poor living close together.

As with Western cities, the central business district (CBD) is at the economic center of the city. It might also be considered the center of the formal sector, where the bulk of investment and economic activity goes. But the CBD serves an even more vital function in Latin American cities. Locations near the CBD are valued, and central-city neighborhoods are considered prestigious, similar to the situation in most European cities (see Chapter 14). The wealthiest members of society live there. This prestige is reinforced by the pattern of settlement around the CBD. Stemming out from the CBD is a wedge of the city focused on the most prestigious avenues. This area, known as the **spine**, is where many of the Latin American elite are located.

Surrounding the CBD are zones of decreasing residential quality. A **zone of maturity** generally contains completed houses, paved roads, and other services and is home to those who have enough money to rent or own houses. These are often the more privileged workers employed by the formal sector, perhaps corresponding to between one-third and one-half of the workforce. Beyond this zone is a **zone of mixed settlement** that contains some completed houses but also a large number of slums. This zone is often converted into more settled neighborhoods as the working class expands and as municipal services are extended. Often, newer public housing is located here.

Beyond this zone are the squatter settlements. The outer fringes of the city are composed of the poorest people. Sewers, running water, and garbage pick up are practically nonexistent. In Mexico City, for example, 3 million people lack these basic services and the number is growing all the time. Many of the people forced to live in these squatter settlements, known as *colonias popolares*, work in the informal sector. Often these areas are growing most rapidly because many new migrants must settle there.

Most Latin American cities have at least some squatter settlements. Buenos Aires may be the wealthiest large Latin American city, but even here massive squatter settlements have begun to appear along the outskirts. In addition, different squatter settlements are sometimes segregated by ethnic group and place of origin, mainly because people live near people they know. For instance, vast numbers of Andean Indians have settled in the eastern fringes of Lima, Peru.

In the Latin American city, proximity to the center determines an individual's position in society. This pattern bears some similarity to the traditional city discussed in Chapter 2, and it is the reverse of the concentric zone model discussed in Chapter 8. Geographical divisions in residential locations correspond with economic divisions between the formal and informal sectors. The inner sections of the city represent the formal sector where industrial and economic growth is most prominent and where the elites and the permanent workforce are likely to locate. The outer sections of the city represent the informal sector where all of the migrants come to live without adequate housing or stable employment.

SUB-SAHARAN AFRICAN CITIES

As a broad region, sub-Saharan Africa experiences the lowest proportion of residents living within cities: approximately 34 percent for the region as a whole, although individual countries range from 9 to 89 percent. Nevertheless, urban growth today in this region is quite rapid. Sub-Saharan African cities were almost all small colonial outposts before the 1950s; only Johannesburg in South Africa contained more than 1 million inhabitants. Since independence, however, these cities have begun to balloon in size, such that today about 25 cities boast populations in excess of 1 million, and a few (for example, Lagos in Nigeria and Kinshasa in Congo) have more than 5 million inhabitants.

What accounts for this growth? To begin with, the region is growing rapidly through natural increase. Births far exceed deaths, to the point where the overall population is expected to double in about 20 to 25 years. But the urban population is increasing even more rapidly, by close to 5 percent per year. This is the highest urban growth rate of any region in the world, and it means that the urban population will triple within the next 20 years. These numbers indicate that more than just population growth is responsible. In addition, as in Latin America, people in the countryside are moving to the cities. Where will these newcomers settle? Why are they moving to the cities? The growth of African cities, as with all cities, must be viewed through the prism of rural push and urban pull.

What has made African urbanization more difficult, perhaps, is that the push factors of rural landlessness and poverty are more significant than any opportunities present in the cities. Put another way, there is less of a correspondence between urban growth and overall economic growth. To an even greater degree than in other less developed regions, migrants arriving in African cities face uncertain employment and housing. Sub-Saharan Africa's marginal position within the global economy means that it suffers from woefully inadequate private investment and a retarded industrial base. Sub-Saharan Africa is the one region of the world that has experienced a net decline in economic growth during the past 25 years. While the urban population grew by 4.7 percent annually between 1970 and 1995, the per capita GDP declined by 0.7 percent per year. In a 2000 report, the World Bank stated that:

> Cities in Africa are not serving as engines of growth and structural transformation. Instead they are part of the cause and a major symptom

of the economic and social crises that have enveloped the continent. (p. 130)

The problem was blamed on "distorted incentives" such as food subsidies to urban inhabitants, as well as a growing fear for personal safety in the countryside. The legacy of colonialism, which superimposed provincial and then country boundaries with no regard to nations or ethnic groups, means that most countries suffer from ethnic antagonisms, political instability, and rule by *coup d'état* and strongmen. These economic and political difficulties culminate in flawed policies, a climate of fear, and cities that grow without any economic rationale.

Is there hope? Well, between 2003 and 2004, the per capita GDP in sub-Saharan Africa actually increased by 2.6 percent, led by Nigeria, South

Africa, and Ethiopia. The burden of debt was slowly going down and merchandise exports were all on the rise. Still, there is a long way to go.

Indigenous Influences

Until recently, sub-Saharan Africa was considered a region without a legacy of cities. Indeed, compared to many other world regions, the size and number of cities were modest. Nevertheless, cities did exist throughout the continent (Figure 16.7). Historically, much of sub-Saharan Africa participated in a farming economy and showed early indications of central authority—prerequisites for the formation of cities. In several instances, cities emerged as entrepôts at the end of **extended trading routes**. Timbuktu, in present-day Mali, was a key outpost for cross-Saharan

Figure 16.7 Historical centers of urbanization in Africa. Prior to European colonization, Africa contained a number of important urban centers. Many of these were placed along major caravan routes, or on ports, or as centers of kingdoms. (*Source:* Mehretu, 1993.)

caravan trade. Mogadishu, in present-day Somalia, and Mombasa, in present-day Kenya, were significant centers for trade along the Indian Ocean. As merchant posts, these cities were likely to be quite sophisticated and culturally diverse, blending Arabic, Berber, Persian, and native African elements. In other cases, cities developed as centers of administration for ancient African kingdoms: Ghana and Songhai in the north, Zimbabwe in the south, and Luba and Lunda in the Congo basin.

Among the most elaborate of precolonial African societies were the *Hausa* societies in western Africa. These were patriarchal, slave-owning societies, most of which had converted to Islam. They were also isolated from main centers of power, including several African empires. The Hausa cultural region included several warring city-states, ranging from 300 to 13,000 square miles, that flourished between 1450 and 1804. In the center of each state was the **birane,** or principal city. The situation, as defined in Chapter 1, of the *birane* was significant. The city had to be located near constant water supplies, ironstone deposits, and certain "nature spirits." In addition, the *birane* was always located in areas of rich agricultural potential, and high office in Hausa societies was identified with farming.

Kano, in present-day Nigeria, is a great example of a *birane* (Figure 16.8). Kano was surrounded by an enormous earthen wall, some 15 miles around in an irregular oval and about 30 feet tall with ditches on either end. It had about 15 gates made of iron-clad wood. Within this wall were the built-up town, some villages, and ironstone hills. All told, this *birane* was about 12 to 15 square miles in area and contained approximately 50,000 people. The "city" portion constituted about one-third of the walled-in land. It was dominated by a mosque, aligned toward Mecca, with a tower to call the faithful to prayer. There was also a marketplace filled with sheltered stalls and often surrounded by specialized workshop areas for crafts. The residential lands within Kano were divided into several compounds, known as *gida,* of which the most important belonged to the ruler. Each compound was made out of mud brick and contained open areas and sequences of huts. Socially, the *gida* included a

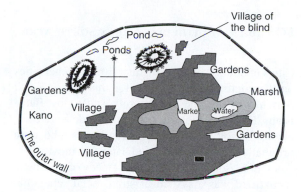

Figure 16.8 Kano, in present-day Nigeria, was an important Hausa city-state in the period between 1450 and 1804. A large outer wall encircled the built-up area or *birane,* agricultural fields, villages, and iron resources. (*Source:* Griffeth, 1981.)

large extended family, headed by a patriarch, with unmarried sons, wives, and slaves. Hausa governments treated the compound as a single unit for tax and census purposes. Outside of the town but within the wall were villages, including villages for lepers and the blind. There was also plenty of cultivated land within the walls.

European Intervention

Cities in colonial Africa were established historically late. Most early European settlements were established on the coasts to facilitate shipping. Thus, these ports served primarily as service areas. For instance, Cape Town, located at the southern tip of Africa, was established to provide water and provisions to Portuguese sailors rounding the Cape of Good Hope. Most nefarious were the settlements established as funnels for the trans-Atlantic slave trade. For example, Lagos developed in part because of its role in the slave trade. Slaves captured from the north were imprisoned on Lagos Island before being shipped to the Americas.

During the "scramble for Africa" in the late nineteenth century, European colonizers developed most cities to serve the economic role of siphoning goods from the coast and the political role of governing the native populations. The same cities

BOX 16.1   Apartheid in Urban South Africa

Cities in South Africa are distinct from all other cities on the continent. One reason for this is that South Africa was the one region truly settled by Europeans. Both the cities and the countryside were colonized, first by Afrikaans-speaking Boers who were originally from Holland, and later by the British. Another reason is South Africa's legacy of apartheid. **Apartheid** was a system of strict racial separation that allowed the minority white population to exercise complete political and economic control over the majority black African and mixed-race populations. Apartheid was legally abolished in the 1990s, but the legacy remains in the cities.

Throughout the twentieth century, South Africa developed an impressive system of cities, most notably Johannesburg, Cape Town, and Pretoria. Ultimately, these cities were intended to be the exclusive preserves of the white population. Black Africans were expected to live in one of a dozen designated "homelands," with the eventual goal that these should become independent countries. As a result, most black Africans were not officially allowed to inhabit the cities unless they were granted work permits, and even then they were not allowed to bring their families. The black population was divided into a minority who were considered to be more or less permanent urban residents of white South Africa, the so-called "townsmen," and the vast majority who were considered temporary residents of white South Africa, known as "tribesmen." Tribesmen were subject to resettlement at

any time, and resettlement programs resulted in the forced removal of about 4 million blacks, often from South African cities. Black Africans were often separated out into the very outskirts of cities, where they tended to form large, sprawling "townships," of which the most famous was Soweto, a suburb of Johannesburg (Figure B16.1). Complicating this racial picture was the presence of mixed-race or "colored" populations, as well as Asian Indians. The colored and Asian populations tended to live within the cities.

The Group Areas Act, passed in 1950, codified apartheid at the urban scale. It mandated that

Figure B16.1 The legacy of racial segregation in South Africa led to vast disparities of wealth. This photo shows township houses in Kwa-Mashu, a poor township outside Durban, South Africa.

often served both functions. To quote Ed Soja and Clyde Weaver (1993), cities:

> were designed to distribute scarce resources in such a way as to promote an exploitative emphasis on economic relations, to facilitate control and domination by a nonindigenous colonial elite, and to solidify a condition of dependency within the international market system. (p. 240)

African cities either created or developed during this period served the interests of Europeans and were meant mainly as places to house and employ European overseers or colonists. The extent to which these cities accommodated the native African population varied significantly from place to place. It is possible to construct a rough typology of sub-Saharan African cities.

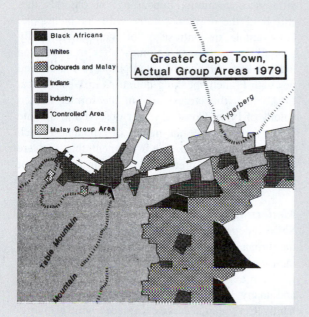

Figure B16.2 South Africa's apartheid regime mandated the separation of races within cities. This map for Capetown, South Africa demonstrates this type of racial zoning. (*Source:* Western, 1996.)

neighborhoods be uniformly of a single race. Consequently, by 1976 nearly 500,000 colored and Asian Indians had been forcibly removed from their homes and moved into designated neighborhoods. Figure B16.2 shows the establishment of Group Areas within Cape Town. Each race was granted a territory within which its members were legally required to reside. Space was manipulated at the

urban level to minimize the chances that the different races would come into contact with one another. Thus, the territories were usually arranged sectorally, with industries, rivers, and major roads acting as boundaries. Because segregation was legally enforced, neighborhoods were almost entirely segregated, except for some live-in servants in the white neighborhoods. Boundaries separating Group Areas were so rigid that no member of one race could enter into the neighborhood of another race without a pass or permit. This was not a major problem for whites, but for other races it imposed a hardship because they often needed to work in "white" areas.

Domination by the white population was reflected in the quantity and quality of allocated lands. There was a rough rule of thumb that whites should receive four times as much land as black Africans and three times as much land as Asians and coloreds. Moreover, whites were always given the most desired land in the city.

Since the abolition of apartheid, *de jure* **segregation** (as legally required by the government) is no longer in place. Members of each race are ostensibly free to live in any portion of the city. At the same time, however, *de facto* **segregation**—where racial separation persists as a phenomenon—is a major issue in South African cities. *De facto* segregation is caused in part by the economics of housing, more specifically, the inability of nonwhites to afford housing in white neighborhoods. Some of the factors present in U.S. housing markets and discussed in Chapter 9, such as discrimination and steering, undoubtedly continue to play a role.

A few cities were truly indigenous in that they developed with little European intervention. Addis Ababa, Ethiopia, is the best example. The city was established in 1886 as the administrative capital by the Ethiopian emperor Menelik II, and it grew to a population of about 60,000 by 1910. Because Ethiopia was never under European control, with the exception of Italian occupation in the late 1930s,

Addis Ababa was allowed to develop in accordance with its hinterland and as a true administrative center for Ethiopians, although merchant activity was discouraged. In contrast, settler cities were intended for the exclusive use of Europeans and made no provision for African inhabitants, except as servants. The cities in South Africa clearly exemplify this pattern (Box 16.1).

Colonial cities were inhabited by Europeans, Africans, and often migrant laborers from South Asia. These cities served principally as administrative capitals, whose purpose was to serve the European colonists. Many African cities fell into this category. These cities were clearly marked by racial and occupational divisions (Figure 16.9). Europeans occupied the best lands—high ground with extensive infrastructure. Although their residences were located close to the downtown, they often resembled a leafy suburb. In contrast, the Africans often were wedged into dense pockets in segregated neighborhoods. Asian Indians were located in their own suburbs, but they were also present throughout the city—within the CBD and in the African areas—as small-scale business owners and traders.

Although it is true that only a small minority of cities are "exclusively" colonial (Mehretu, 1997, suggests only 28 of the 146 biggest cities), the colonial influence throughout sub-Saharan Africa is still tremendous because (1) the area was not colonized until the late nineteenth century, (2) the region was not highly urbanized prior to the arrival of Europeans, and (3) most cities were set up to serve the interests and comforts of the colonists. Consequently, the nature of many African cities is related to their colonial origins: French cities vary significantly from British cities, which vary from Portuguese cities. Many of these colonial-era differences continue, depending on the ties that still bind the former colony with its metropole. For example, in contrast to Portugal, which rapidly fled all of its former colonies after they became independent, France has scrupulously maintained ties with French-speaking countries in West Africa. In Abidjan, the largest city in the former French colony of Ivory Coast, a writer observed in the late 1970s that "you see the names of reputable French firms, and may think for a moment that you are driving through a pretty little town in the south of France." This would not be the case today.

Modern African Cities

Since independence, the population and especially the urban population of sub-Saharan Africa has increased tremendously. Consequently, African cities have experienced an unprecedented expansion, and many have been transformed from predominantly European reserves to places with primarily African populations. The differences among these cities are large, which makes it difficult to develop a coherent model of the sub-Saharan African city, but we can identify a few elements that help to characterize these cities.

One attribute is the fact that cities are made up almost entirely of newcomers. Only a tiny minority of the urban population is made up of people who were born there, generally less than 10 percent.

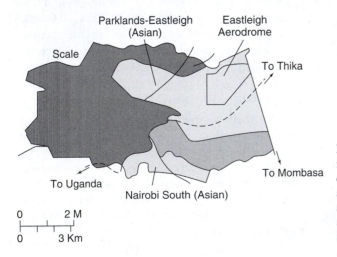

Figure 16.9 Nairobi, Kenya, was the capital of an important British colony. As with many African colonial cities, land was rigidly divided into European, African, and Indian areas. These also corresponded with wealth and housing quality. After decolonization, the European area continued to be occupied by European expatriates and more affluent Africans. (*Source:* Mehretu, 1993.)

Consequently, high-ranking government officials and those fortunate enough to enjoy good jobs in business have been able to occupy neighborhoods formerly reserved for Europeans. In contrast, the majority of people, faced with bleaker prospects, have been forced to scramble for whatever jobs and housing are available. In most cities the proportion of people employed in the informal economy exceeds 60 percent. In addition, squatter settlements on the periphery of the cities have grown tremendously.

Another characteristic of African cities is the continued salience of **tribalism** or ethnic affiliation. New arrivals coming to the city identify primarily with their tribe, which helps them to navigate through this new and unusual society. More so than in Western cities, African cities may help to promote tribal identification, because it is through tribal connections that people find jobs and housing. Likewise, family ties exert an extraordinary importance, affording food and shelter to the new arrivals. Moreover, many urbanites continue to maintain ties to the village, to the extent that they feel it is important to retain land, family, and position there. They might still consider the city to be a temporary way station rather than a permanent residence.

Finally, the role of women, although still deficient by Western standards, is more positive in the cities than in the countryside. Men who come to the city may leave their families behind but continue to plan for a return. Single women who move to the city cannot be assured of continued contacts. Rather, many end up severing their village ties. Although women are still occupationally restricted in cities compared to men, cities are clearly viewed as more liberating places. For instance, married women are far more likely to divorce their husbands in the city than in the village, testifying to their greater economic and social independence.

SOUTH ASIAN CITIES

Asia contains the oldest cities in the world. At a time when most Europeans were dispersed throughout a rude wilderness and North America was a land of fields, forests, and villages, empires in India, Persia, and China boasted the preeminent cities, by far the grandest on the planet. Today huge disparities exist in urban places and urbanization within Asia. Japan, discussed in Chapter 14, is a fully developed country that is highly urbanized. In addition, "tiger" economies like those of Korea, Taiwan, Singapore, and other Southeast Asian countries are urbanizing very rapidly. Many of these countries have become urban only since the 1990s. In contrast, the countries of South Asia (primarily India, Pakistan, Bangladesh, and Sri Lanka) contain some of the largest cities in the world, but at the same time they have one of the lowest levels of urbanization. These levels range from 23 percent in Bangladesh to 29 percent in India to 34 percent in Pakistan.

Nevertheless, large numbers of urban dwellers live within South Asia. India, for example, has more urban dwellers (220 million) than does the highly urbanized United States. Moreover, the numbers are increasing rapidly. Soon the urban population of India will surpass the entire population—both urban and rural—of all of North America. As with other less developed countries, the two factors fueling the growth of Indian cities are the continued high rates of natural increase (around 2 percent) and rural-to-urban migration, with natural increase having a greater effect. As a whole the levels of urbanization in India may increase in the coming decades (Figure 16.10), but urban growth there is still lower than in many parts of the world. Moreover, recent evidence indicates that the rate of urbanization has slowed. Although urban growth continues, it is not accelerating as quickly as we might expect, and it is far lower than the rates of urbanization in Africa and Southeast Asia. Although Indian cities are growing, and the proportion of people who live in the cities is slowly increasing as well, India does not seem to be following the general rule of urban acceleration. We discuss why a bit later.

The effects of in-migration vary depending on the city. For example, within India, Mumbai (formerly Bombay) is seen as a dynamic place with plenty of opportunity. An estimated 10,000 people move into Bombay every day. In contrast, Kolkata

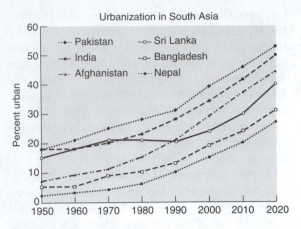

Figure 16.10 Urbanization rates for South Asian countries. Although it contains many enormous cities, South Asia is one region with low levels of urbanization. Urbanization rates are increasing for each country, however, as this figure shows. (*Source:* Dutt, 1993.)

(formerly Calcutta) does not enjoy this level of popularity because it is accurately viewed as being a less economically dynamic city. Overall, India's best educated workers, as well as many of its downtrodden, eschew Calcutta in favor of other urban centers.

A Typology of South Asian Cities

Historically, South Asian cities have had very different origins. The Indus Valley civilization was the second-oldest urban civilization in the world and probably the best planned. Since that time, South Asia has hosted an array of large established kingdoms, each organized and prosperous enough to host large, impressive capitals. Moreover, South Asian civilizations continued to flourish well into the modern era as empires dominated by Islam came into direct contact with those dominated by Hinduism. The influence of these historical cities continues in the modern urban landscape. For instance, India's capital city of Delhi had its origins as an imperial capital of the same Mughal emperor who built the Taj Mahal. The city was named Shah Jahanabad, after the emperor, and was oriented around a massive red fort, where the emperor and his entourage lived, and the main mosque of the city.

Adjoining these planned elements was the largely organic city, filled with winding streets, shops, and markets. Indeed, all along the "Mother Ganges" is a procession of ancient cities that grew to importance prior to European conquest. Dacca, now the capital of Bangladesh, was also developed prior to colonialism and retains some of its older elements.

The legacy of these older cities influences much of the so-called **bazaar** city (Figure 16.11). The

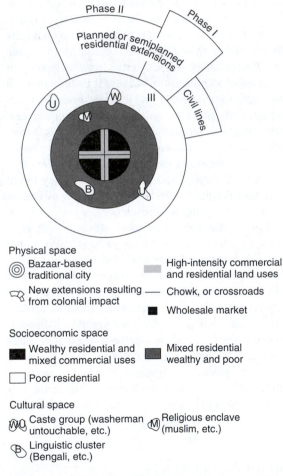

Figure 16.11 Plan of a bazaar city. The South Asian bazaar city is built around a trading center. Merchants often live above or in back of their shops. Wealthier families are, in general, found near this central area as well. (*Source:* Dutt, 1993.)

one element that marks these bazaar cities is the presence of a traditional crossroads, bazaar, or *chowk* at the center of the city. Within this *chowk* are crowded numerous small retail shops that sell everything from food and hardware to clothing and jewelry. Competing shops, selling the same items, tend to cluster together, creating small bazaars for each good. This central area also contains a variety of other functions: hotels/inns, theaters, restaurants, and pawnshops. There may also be a separate enclave composed of wholesale shops.

The center also contains the dwellings of the wealthier merchants, who often live in the same building where their shops are located. This center is surrounded by a ring that includes wealthier residences mixed with the poor dwellings of servants. The ring beyond that primarily includes the poor. In analyzing the patterns of South Asian cities, particularly within Hindu India, it is important to keep in mind the continuing significance of caste. Although discrimination based on caste is illegal, caste continues to orient daily life. Certainly, different neighborhoods around the *chowk* are delimited by caste—even lending the name of the caste to the neighborhood. The bazaar city is also one where functional separation among residence, business, and workshop does not exist. Rather, these functions cluster together.

Colonial influence in South Asia began with many European powers, but in the final analysis, the British clearly played the dominant role. The British imposition in South Asia was directed first through the British East India Company, which was chartered by the Crown for trade with Asia. It acquired unequaled trade privileges from the Mogul emperors in India, and reaped large profits by exporting textiles and tea. As Mogul power declined, the company intervened in Indian political affairs and led eventually to direct colonization of India.

Many cities arose from British colonialism. Chief among these are the so-called **presidency cities**. On colonization, the British established capitals for the three large provinces, or presidencies. These capitals were Bombay, Madras, and Calcutta. The influence of this decision was profound, as each city

continues to dominate its respective region. Beyond their administrative functions, these cities operated primarily as export enclaves to funnel materials from the interior and then ship them to England. The sites chosen were all intended to facilitate access to sea lanes and to the interior. They were also easily defended from attack. All but Bombay had poor natural harbors. For instance, Calcutta's site, established on the east bank of the Hughli River, was beset by shifting sandy shoals and tidal bores. Because the three presidency cities were built by the British, they demonstrate a much greater colonial imprint than other cities in South Asia do.

The model of the South Asian colonial city is still an appropriate way to view these cities (Figure 16.12). Because the primary function was

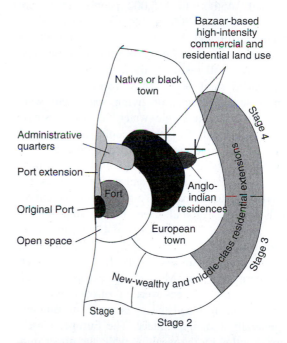

Figure 16.12 The South Asian colonial city is built around a fort, constructed by the European colonists. Surrounding this fort is a *maidan* or open-space area, and outside of this is the contemporary CBD and legacies of the rigid division of the residential landscape between European, native, and mixed races. (*Source:* Dutt, 1993.)

trade, the port facility was the crucial element of the city. Located next to the port facility was a walled fort, which in turn was surrounded by an open space, or **maidan**. South Asian colonial cities were split into the European and indigenous districts. The contrasts between the two districts were quite marked. The administrative section and the Western-style CBD acted as the center of the European (mainly British) community and included hotels, stores, and museums. The British areas were laid out in regular fashion. Most British officials lived in large colonnaded bungalows surrounded by parkland or formal gardens.

The indigenous neighborhoods could not be more different. Although a few Indians were quite wealthy, most inhabited extremely congested neighborhoods. Residential densities in some Calcutta wards approached 145,000 to 165,000 people per square kilometer (almost 700 people per acre) in 1941. Officials estimated that more than three-fourths of all residents lived in *bustee* or slum quarters, and two-thirds of all residents lived in buildings made of unbaked mud brick. Most residents had less than 3 square meters of living space and were forced to share a single water tap and a single toilet with about 25 other people. Nevertheless, these places continued to attract people because they offered more economic opportunity than rural areas. Between the British and native quarters, the mixed-race, or so-called Anglo-Indian, neighborhoods could be found. Here the housing was of good quality, although clearly not as grand as in the British area.

After colonialism ended, the legacy of this arrangement persisted. Most of the Europeans gradually left, and all areas were taken over by native peoples. The fort and the open space surrounding it generally remained intact. The European areas were resettled by the wealthy, while the upper middle classes lived close by. New influxes of people continued to expand what had been the native quarters, adding to the overall congestion of the city. Throughout the last half of the twentieth century, South Asian cities struggled to keep up with their steadily rising populations.

Since independence, several cities have been explicitly created as showcases. Islamabad in Pakistan and Chandigarh in the Indian Punjab are good examples of these cities. Planned cities in South Asia share a lot in common with planned cities in the rest of the world, mainly because they follow a Western model of what an orderly city should look like. In the case of Islamabad, the idea was to orient the population away from the more crowded Karachi. Chandigarh was built by Le Corbusier, the noted French architect who believed in creating monumental buildings separated by open spaces (Figure 16.13). The site was a chosen for its beauty, drainage, water, and room for expansion. The street system is set up as a grid, with roads classified by their uses and accepted speeds. The city itself is divided into 29 self-contained sectors within which people can fulfill most of their shopping, education, and social needs. In addition, a number of provisions have acted to preserve open space, including a green belt.

Modern Challenges

These three types of South Asian cities—bazaar cities, colonial cities, and modern showcase cities—help us to understand the predominant spatial layouts of South Asian cities. At the same time, however, it is important to note some of the significant problems that challenge these cities. Chief among these problems is the inability of urban areas to keep up with the demand for jobs and housing. Mumbai is a good case in point. It is clearly among the most dynamic of Indian cities—the center of India's financial, industrial, and mass cultural life—and it accounts for an incredible 30 percent of India's GNP, although it contains less than 2 percent of India's population. As a result, Mumbai has succeeded in attracting a disproportionate share of migrants: 10,000 a day by some estimates. But the city simply cannot keep up. People come looking for jobs, but these jobs are available primarily to skilled or connected workers. Housing is scarce, and land rent prices exceed those of New York. Consequently, many people in Mumbai end up sleeping on the sidewalks.

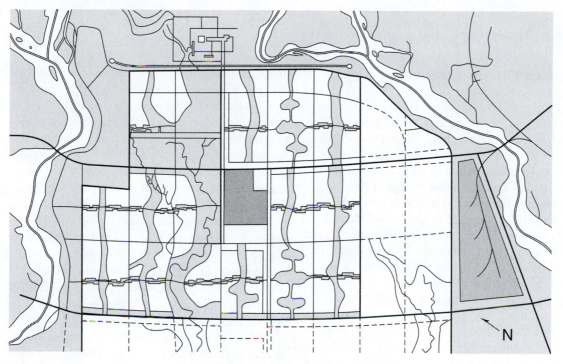

Figure 16.13 Chandigarh, India, is the capital of the Punjab and was designed by Le Corbusier. Although demands for space and poverty have intruded, the city retains much of its original character. (*Source:* Kostof, 1991.) (see Chapter 15)

In fact, all Indian cities, whether dynamic or stagnant, must confront the problem of homelessness. The homeless, called *pavement dwellers* because they actually sleep on the sidewalks, are a common sight throughout the country. Rural migrants come to the city looking for opportunity. Initially they cannot afford housing and in fact prefer to find a job first. Studies indicate that although such conditions are abhorrent to Western eyes, for the pavement dwellers themselves sleeping on the sidewalks is part of a rational decision. Most pavement dwellers are employed in temporary occupations, often as load carriers (e.g., porters, rickshaw pullers, and hand cart pullers). Living on the sidewalks minimizes the distance between where they sleep and the location of possible jobs. Thus, most homeless people live in the CBDs where they cannot afford regular housing, and most sleep out in the

open, jealously guarding their section of sidewalk. Removal of these pavement dwellers would deal a serious blow to their economic prospects.

On the other side of the economic spectrum has been the emergence of the newly affluent in several cities in South Asia. In India, this phenomenon has resulted largely from globalization and the emergence of a well-educated technical class (see Box 16.2). It is important to remember that, although the Indian population is generally quite poor, there are still more than 100 million individuals who enjoy a middle-class lifestyle or better. During the 1990s, programs were initiated to house some of these newly affluent people in neighborhoods that are removed from the problems of urban life. In Kolkata, for example, two new town developments were established just to the east of the city. The older of these developments, Salt Lake,

BOX 16.2 TECHNOLOGY AND URBAN GEOGRAPHY

THE SILICON PLATEAU CITY OF BANGALORE

Mention high technology these days and chances are you will soon be talking about Bangalore, India, recently changed to Bengaluru. Several years ago, Bangalore was a virtual unknown for an average Westerner. To think of Indian cities was to imagine the slums of Calcutta or the exotica of Bombay. Today, though, Bangalore is a city that everybody knows, primarily because of its role in high technology development. In fact, it has been described as the "Silicon Valley" or sometimes "Silicon Plateau" of India. By itself, Bangalore accounted for about a quarter of all of India's information technology activity, but that only hints at Bangalore's significance. From the 1980s, Bangalore has successfully transformed itself from a repository of low wage technicians exploited by multinational information corporations to a production center in its own right that has been able to develop software products for global consumption (Figure B16.3).

What accounts for this growth? Bangalore possesses some natural attractions, among them a pleasant, relatively dust-free climate and a distance away from India's overcrowded Ganges basin. India itself benefits from its high education and greater English language proficiency as well as the fact that they are

about 12 hours' time difference from the main U.S. markets. Bangalore itself was a city aided by aggressive government initiatives. The Indian Institute of Science was established in the early twentieth century and between 1950 and 1980, public sector firms specializing in electronics, aerospace, machine tools, telecommunications, and defense helped to spawn a number of private firms that helped supply the larger public firms. When high technology had become a global phenomenon, Bangalore was particularly well-placed. First of all, the language of high technology is predominately English and Bangalore included a high proportion of individuals who were proficient in that language. Secondly, the city itself was quite cosmopolitan, attracting expatriates who found it to be the best choice for location within India.

This has all made Bangalore very prosperous within the context of India and a place where many Indians come to make their fortune. In this respect, it has come to resemble some of the high tech growth centers of the U.S. There are obstacles to further growth, among which are the still limited size of India's domestic market. Also, further growth depends upon a cadre of people who can make the transition from technical support to business management and development skills.

is expected to contain 250,000 people, while New Calcutta was planned to contain 100,000 housing units in addition to a business district, light industry, and even a golf course. Clearly, New Calcutta was designed for the most privileged segments of Kolkata's population. To underscore this point, there are even plans to build several low-income "service villages" within New Calcutta, perhaps to house the area's servant population.

An additional issue is the continued influence of ethnicity. Distinctions between Muslims and Hindus, among different linguistics groups and nationalities, and among castes continue to play

a tremendous role in the structuring of South Asian cities. A study by Nirmal Bose (1973) of Calcutta is illustrative of many cities in South Asia. During British rule, Calcutta attracted Indians of all nationalities, religious affiliations, and castes, most of whom settled in areas populated by their particular group. These divisions persisted even after India achieved its independence and much of the European population departed. Figure 16.14 illustrates the different segregation patterns within then-Calcutta during the early 1970s. The major division is between the Muslim and the Hindu populations. Kolkata is in the middle

Figure B16.3 International Technology Strip, Bangalore.

of the Bengali cultural region, and the original and largest population consisted of Bengali Hindus. They were initially concentrated in a segregated "native quarter" to the north. The Muslim population is clustered broadly around two landmark palaces given long ago to nobility, but it continues to be differentiated by nationality (Bengalis versus non-Bengalis) and by class (upper-middle class versus lower class). The Hindu neighborhoods are further subdivided into wards inhabited by particular castes. Because castes are essentially occupational groupings, these wards serve as centers for a particular craft. (This layout is similar to that of the bazaar city discussed earlier.) Thus, the banking caste clusters in a quarter distinct from the brass-working caste. The untouchable or scheduled castes are located far from the others, even though they share the same nationality and religion. They are generally restricted to the worst neighborhoods in the floodplains in the city's outskirts. In addition, a number of residents are from outside the Bengali region. These groups have also been identified with particular occupations and, as with the Bengali populations, they have divided along caste lines.

A final issue confronting South Asian cities is the slow rate of urban growth. Despite the fact that

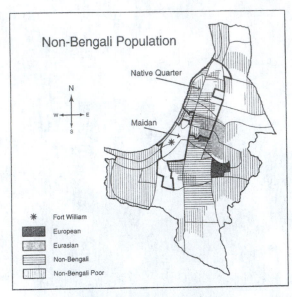

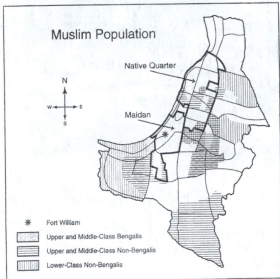

Figure 16.14 Segregation in then-Calcutta demonstrates the continued spatial separation between different groups. (*Source:* Kaplan and Holloway, 1998.)

individuals cities like Kolkata have trouble housing their existing population, the rate of urbanization (in India at least) is lower than we might expect given the rate of industrialization. The technical,

if controversial, term for this is *underurbanization*. During each year of the 1980s and 1990s, the Indian GNP expanded by more than 5 percent in the 1980s and more than 6 percent in the 1990s. But the urban population increased by less than two percent, two-thirds of which could be attributed to natural increase. This slowing down of urbanization could be viewed as a positive element, perhaps a result of enhanced rural development programs. During the 1980s, for instance, hundreds of rural service centers were established, and specific rural areas were targeted for industrial development. Moreover, there appears to have been a moderation in rural poverty, which would reduce the rates of out-migration. The apparent levels of urbanization may be influenced by the fact that, as Indian cities became more saturated, more migrants were forced to reside in villages just outside the city boundaries. On a more negative note, the slowing down of urbanization could be seen as a product of the inadequacies of India's cities, especially their inability to provide adequate employment and infrastructure.

SOUTHEAST ASIAN CITIES

As with South Asia, the broad area known as Southeast Asia blends "indigenous" urban legacies, colonial impacts, and recent attempts to create a new post-independence urban profile. The cities have some common elements, but the visitor is struck by the tremendous cultural and economic diversity among parts of the region. As a region long open to access by land, river, and sea, Southeast Asia has absorbed influences from China to the north and India to the west. Later European powers profoundly affected the development of most cities, creating a system of port-oriented primate cities. With the exception of Thailand, all countries were under the direct political control of European powers, and even Thailand, like China, was under Europe's economic sway. After independence, Southeast Asian countries pursued different economic and political paths, which led to different types of cities. The countries of Indochina embraced Communism and suffered through war, revolution, and genocide. The countries of peninsular and insular Southeast Asia largely embraced capitalism, although with a clear authoritarian and often corrupt bent.

Today, the countries of Southeast Asia continue to differ. Economically, the region includes several very low-income countries (Cambodia, Laos, Burma, and Vietnam), several middle-income countries (the Philippines, Indonesia, Malaysia, and Thailand), and a few high-income microstates (notably Singapore and Brunei). Overall prospects for the region are considered quite good, recent downturns notwithstanding, and this has lent a dynamic, prosperous gloss to many of the cities.

Nevertheless, urbanization rates in Southeast Asia continue to be fairly low. Until the 1970s less than 20 percent of the population of most of these countries lived in cities. Unlike South Asia and much of East Asia, Southeast Asia enjoys lower population densities in much of the land—some places are incredibly remote. More recently, urbanization levels have crept up but are still low, even by standards of less developed countries. The major exception to this pattern is the city-state of Singapore, which is entirely urban. Also, Malaysia and the Philippines contain an urban majority. In contrast, the other countries in Southeast Asia are only between 17 and 38 percent urban. In all of these countries, urban activity is concentrated in one or two primate cities, which absorb almost all of the economic activity. Migration patterns—still skewed toward these primate cities—reinforce this trend.

As one example of urban primacy in Southeast Asia, consider the case of Bangkok, the primate city in Thailand. In the 1970s, Bangkok contained more than 75 percent of Thailand's telephones, consumed more than 82 percent of its electricity, and collected 82 percent of its business taxes and 73 percent of its personal income taxes. Things have really not changed that much in the ensuing decades. Bangkok still accounts for 75 percent of Thailand's GDP and contains 50 percent of its factories. Demographically, Bangkok contains roughly 50 percent of Thailand's urban population, although Thailand itself is still predominantly rural.

Indigenous Influences: Sacred and Market Cities

Despite its low level of present urbanization, Southeast Asia has a long history of cities. During the first millennium A.D., several states and kingdoms emerged in this region. At first, smaller states that claimed Hindu Indian influence appeared in present-day Vietnam, Sumatra, Java, and Borneo. Many of these states later coalesced into the large maritime empire of Sri Vijaya. Within present-day Cambodia, in the Mekong River delta, the Khmer kingdom emerged. In addition, other kingdoms arose in present-day Thailand and Burma.

The presence of such organized political and social power made the creation of substantial cities possible. T. G. McGee (1967) draws a useful distinction between **market cities**, which were oriented toward commerce and were located along the coasts, and **sacred cities**, which embodied the secular and spiritual authority of the state. These two types of cities performed distinct functions and had different patterns, but they often coexisted within the same country.

Because of its central role in the kingdom, the sacred city was usually land based and located within the interior of the kingdom. It was the center of government and the military, and it was also the spiritual center. The location of the city was determined by **geomancy**, a system of locating and aligning the city according to divine principles. The city was a microcosm of heaven, and so its location was critical. In the case of Angkor Thom, capital of the Khmer kingdom, the city was aligned around the *bayon*, a large stone mountain temple. Still, the imperial ruler could move the sacred city at his command, and he often did. For example, the capitals of both Vietnam and Burma were moved in this fashion.

The sacred city was extraordinarily well ordered, with the order determined by distance from the imperial compound. In the middle of the city were the palace and the primary temples. Angkor Thom is an excellent example of such a sacred city (Figure 16.15). A large square wall was constructed around the *bayon* (or main temple) and palace to

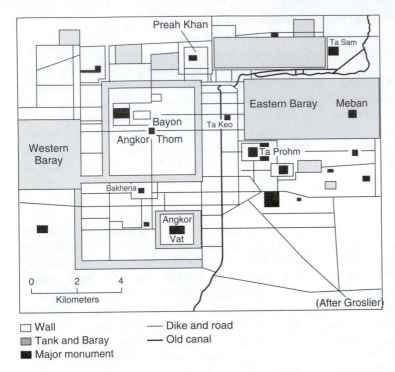

Figure 16.15 Angkor Thom, a site in Cambodia, was an excellent example of a sacred city within Southeast Asia. The major temples in the city are displayed in black. Each temple required the services—in the form of tribute from surrounding villages—from tens of thousands of people. (*Source:* McGee, 1967.)

help frame the city. The *bayon* and palace were surrounded by the elite functionaries, such as priests, warriors, and administrative officials, whose proximity to the center reflected their elite status. The main artisans and merchants were located further from the center. Outside the wall were villages made up of the rural population needed to service the sacred city. McGee (1967) reports that at its peak, Angkor Thom required the service of 306,000 people in 13,500 villages.

Market cities were a different variety altogether, and they were shaped by the fact that Southeast Asia long attracted substantial maritime trade, with merchants coming from distant lands. Unlike sacred cities, market cities were located along the coasts, with the whole of the city hugging close to the shoreline. The trading population could be divided between the indigenous merchants and foreign merchants, who almost always occupied separate quarters of the city. Hoi An, a Vietnamese city located close to Da Nang, was a quintessential market city. It was situated on the coast, next

to the Thu Bon River, which meanders into the interior. In the seventeenth century, both Chinese and Japanese merchants settled in Hoi An and occupied neighborhoods separate from the indigenous population and from each other. So separate were these neighborhoods that they established completely separate administrations. The Chinese and Japanese were later joined by Dutch and Portuguese merchants. Each of these groups has left reminders of their presence in the form of distinct architectural styles.

The Colonial City in Southeast Asia

Colonialism affected every country in Southeast Asia and was responsible for three main geographic legacies: (1) the establishment of major administrative and extractive cities along the coasts, sometimes in places where prior indigenous cities had flourished, but other times in wholly new areas; (2) the development of the dualistic colonial city that separated European and indigenous populations; and (3) the explicit creation of a middleman minority,

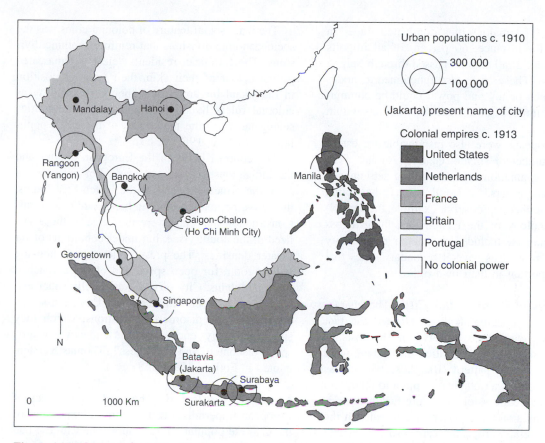

Figure 16.16 In the early 1910s, Southeast Asia was largely controlled by European countries (Thailand being the sole exception). Many of the large cities that continue to dominate the region were boosted by their functions in servicing this colonial economy and as capitals. (*Source:* Forbes, 1996.)

made up of Chinese settlers, who were socially, economically, and spatially situated between the European overlords and the indigenous population.

Locational Aspects Figure 16.16 shows the situation of Southeast Asia as of 1910. Although the Portuguese had been the first European power to truly penetrate this region with the capture of Malacca in 1511, by the nineteenth century their influence had declined. By the early twentieth century, Southeast Asia was divided into French Indochina, the Dutch East Indies (now Indonesia), British Burma and Malaya, the American

Philippines (wrested from Spain in 1898), and an independent Thailand. Europeans initially came to dominate trade, but they remained to exploit the rich bounty of the interior. Nevertheless, they made their primary urban impact on the coast. They established major colonial capital cities on the coasts, usually at the site of some existing indigenous settlement. Among these capitals were Rangoon, Saigon, Bangkok, and Batavia (now Jakarta). This preference for coastal sites reflected the European need for ports, because these cities were principally intended to be "head-links" between the raw materials of the colonial hinterland and the European metropoles. The major cities dominated trade. In Indochina, for instance, 60 percent of all imports and 75 percent of all exports passed through Saigon in the 1930s. These cities also functioned as nodes through which policy and power could be communicated and imposed on the colonial subjects within the interior.

The Europeans were also responsible for establishing a number of smaller centers. Among these were railway junctions towns, mining settlements, district headquarters, and hill towns that often served as summer capitals. For example, the sprawling Dutch colony of the East Indies, flung across 5,000 kilometers, included the major capital city of Batavia as well as several secondary cities that became important in their own right.

The Dualistic Form of the City The characteristics of these colonial cities reflected the fact that they were intended to serve the interests of the European powers. The cities themselves were laid out on a grid pattern (Bangkok, which was never colonized, is a notable exception to this) with an occasional concession to a pre-European element, such as a sultan's palace or a temple. In the preindustrial era, Europeans were also responsible for building walls around several Southeast Asian cities, such as Malacca, Manila, and Batavia. European institutions were concentrated in the cities. These institutions included the colonial governments and the main organizations of a capitalist economy: banks, shipping companies, trading companies, and insurance agencies. These institutions, which were almost all European owned, came to monopolize the essential financial aspects of the economy. In the nineteenth century, as factories were established across Europe and North America, the Southeast Asian urban economy retained its focus as a trading conduit. Much of the manufacturing that was established was either small-scale artisanry (dominated by ethnic middlemen) or shipbuilding and railway repair firms. However, the cities retained an emphasis on tertiary activities, which include trade, as opposed to secondary activities.

The main social feature of colonial cities was the socioeconomic divisions that reinforced ethnic divisions. The European residents "clearly demarcated by the colour of their skin, their superior position in the social hierarchy, and their responsibility as colonial rulers lived in encapsulated communities segregated from the major part of the city's population" (McGee, 1967, p. 63).

The contrast between the European quarter and the indigenous quarter was stark. For example, in Java, the principal island of the Dutch East Indies, the native population lived in haphazard conditions. Construction materials were the same as those utilized in the countryside, but under conditions of far greater densities. The press of jerry-built housing left no room for open space and often encroached into floodplains. City services, especially water and sewers, were absent. In fact, some European scholars decried the disorderly conditions, which they speculated may encourage a "tendency towards social discontent and unruliness" (Thomas Karsten, quoted in Forbes, 1996, p. 8).

Chinese Population The third major legacy of European imperialism came from the expansion of the Chinese population. Of course, the Chinese had long been influential in this region. Vietnam, for instance, was often considered to be a part of the Chinese sphere of influence and was expected to pay tribute to the Chinese emperor. Chinese emigrants settled in trading cities before the rise of European imperialism. But it was during the colonial period that Chinese settlement flourished. Many Chinese were encouraged to move to these regions during the Ming Dynasty (1368–1644) as ambassadors of trade, and they continued to move even when the Manchu Dynasty, which followed the Ming Dynasty, forbade it. Settlement in Southeast Asia afforded a degree of autonomy and prosperity that was not possible within much of China itself. In addition, most Europeans were favorably disposed toward the Chinese minority. They established the Chinese as a classic **middleman minority**, situated between the colonialists and the indigenous population. Most Chinese established

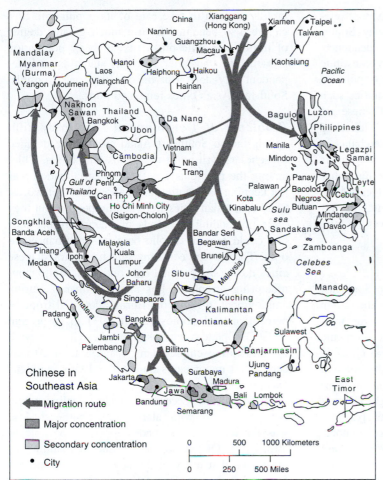

Figure 16.17 Today, Southeast Asia contains more than half the world total of overseas Chinese. This map shows the important flows that took place from southern China to south Vietnam, southern Malay, Java, and other regions. Relations between the Chinese and "host" population have been economically beneficial but sometimes politically and socially volatile. (*Source:* deBlij and Muller, 2003.) Please note that this figure was originally produced in color and was repurposed for use in this book.

themselves as small traders and retailers, serving the native population. A substantial proportion of artisans were also Chinese.

Partly as a legacy and partly because of their continued success in business, the Chinese became a relatively prosperous minority, about twice as affluent as the native population in several colonies. They also came to comprise a substantial proportion of the population of several Southeast Asian countries, and an even larger proportion of the business population. Today, the percentages vary between Singapore, where the Chinese constitute a clear majority, and places like the Philippines where they are a much smaller minority (Figure 16.17). Nevertheless, the Chinese remain a visible presence in almost every society, particularly within the urban areas. They are an even greater business presence.

From the beginning, the Chinese population was separated residentially and commercially into distinct "Chinatowns." These Chinatowns became very significant as commercial centers. They were usually located adjacent to the European CBD, and they were far denser and more populous than the European centers.

The Chinese also became an important element in the political landscape in many Southeast Asian countries, especially after independence. For example, in Singapore, where they constitute a majority of the population, they wield political control. Significantly, in some other countries such as Malaysia and Indonesia, where the Chinese are economically powerful, they are also often used as scapegoats. For instance, Chinese merchants in cities such as Jakarta are often targeted during times of civil unrest. The term "Jews of the East" has been used to describe the Chinese in Southeast Asia, although the Chinese presence is, if anything, far more prominent in Southeast Asia than was the Jewish presence in Europe.

Modern Cities

After World War II and into the 1950s, Southeast Asian countries became independent, although in many cases they were forced to fight for their independence. As we have just seen, the economic and political roles of many of the large cities in this region became established during the colonial period, as did many of the cultural aspects of these cities. Nevertheless, independence brought changes to Southeast Asian cities. Most obviously, after independence there were no longer large numbers of Europeans and European enclaves. Instead, these neighborhoods were taken over by the indigenous elite. The political economy also changed. Each country could choose its own path, although all were shackled by the colonial economy that they inherited.

One dramatic change was rapid urbanization. During the 1950s and 1960s the urban growth rates exceeded 4 percent per year in most cases. In 1940, no city in the region had more than 1 million people. In contrast, by 1970 seven cities did, and by 2000, eight cities had populations in excess of 2 million.

This massive growth had implications for the urban infrastructure. The problems plaguing all third world cities, discussed in Chapter 15, intensified within Southeast Asian cities. The only exception here was Singapore, which was able to modernize

rapidly enough to take care of its population. Singapore also benefited from a much greater degree of initial economic prosperity, a lower population growth rate, and, after 1965, its status as an independent city-state. But beyond this one example, Southeast Asian cities remained poor.

Problems of Development

The many difficulties facing Southeast Asian cities were detailed by scholars writing in the 1960s and 1970s. Chief among the problems was that industrialization was not keeping pace with urbanization. In other words, Southeast Asian cities were adding people, but they were not adding the kinds of manufacturing jobs that could provide a solid base for an urban economy. The service economy that had marked these cities during the colonial era continued, while manufacturing atrophied. For instance, manufacturing employment in Rangoon, Burma, declined from 24 percent of total employment in 1931 to 18 percent in 1953, a pattern witnessed in other cities as well. Manufacturing employment was less than 20 percent in all major cities during the 1950s, with the exception of Manila.

In an advanced economy, such a decline would not be viewed with alarm, but Southeast Asia was far too poor and undeveloped to be able to afford this. Of course, the decline in manufacturing meant that many of the new arrivals could not find adequate jobs. They were compelled to enter the informal sector, and in many cases they entered into illicit occupations. For example, some Southeast cities became well-known centers of the sex trade.

Not only could these cities not provide enough jobs, but they lacked adequate housing for the new arrivals. Consequently, each of the major cities developed a significant number of squatter settlements. McGee (1967) estimated that as of 1961, 25 percent of the populations within the city limits of Jakarta, Kuala Lumpur, Manila, and Singapore lived in some sort of squatter arrangement, sleeping on the street or within an illegally occupied house. The lack of jobs and housing led to social problems that were concentrated in the cities. Income disparities between the few elite and the many impoverished; ethnic tensions, particularly between the indigenous population and the Chinese ethnics; and even crime, which was far higher in the cities than in the countryside, plagued the Southeast Asian cities.

In Southeast Asia, some countries took the socialist path, leading to the long war that involved nearly every country in the region in some form or another as well as France, the United States, China, and the Soviet Union. Socialism had several ramifications for the cities involved. In some cases, socialist governments attempted to reduce the urban population, particularly within the primate cities. The most tragic example occurred after the Khmer Rouge took control of Cambodia in 1975. The city of Phnom Penh, which contained 3 million of the country's 8 million people, was forcibly deurbanized. All residents were forced out under pain of death, and many were massacred outright. In less than a year, the city's population shrank to only 50,000. Less draconian measures were taken in Saigon, after it was conquered by the communist north and renamed Ho Chi Minh City. Rural-to-urban migration was restricted and there were attempts in the late 1970s to move some 1.5 million people out of Ho Chi Minh City, although these plans were never completely fulfilled. Socialist governments also adopted strict guidelines for urban development. For example, Hanoi, the longest lasting socialist city, had virtually no private stores, few automobiles (bicycles ruled the roads), and huge, government-constructed housing projects on the fringe of the city.

Prosperity and Urban Form   The first generalized model of the modern Southeast Asian city (Figure 16.18) was based around the old colonial-era port and included a Western-style CBD. In many ways this model resembled the big city downtowns from the colonial period, with the wide streets, modern hotels, and tall buildings on display. The second CBD was usually a Chinatown, which was far more bustling than the Western CBD. Some cities also had an Indiatown, providing yet another commercial

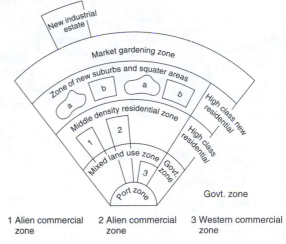

1 Alien commercial zone   2 Alien commercial zone   3 Western commercial zone

a Squatter areas   b Suburbs

Figure 16.18 Model of a Southeast Asian city. Southeast Asian cities share many of the attributes of other ex-colonial, third world cities. Poor squatter areas are found on the periphery and there is the continued legacy of colonialism within the CBD and some of the more affluent neighborhoods. In addition, the Chinese and (to some extent) Indian businesses are found within the "alien commercial" zones shown here. (*Source:* McGee, 1967.)

core. Occupying a distinct sector beside the Western CBD was the elite corridor. This sector began with the government buildings, continued through the high-class residential area formerly occupied by the Europeans, and then terminated in the new suburban estates. Outside of this corridor, residential zones tended to be laid out a bit more haphazardly than in Western cities. The fringe areas included squatter settlements as well as new suburban communities. Beyond these fringe areas was an intensive market garden zone.

The 1980s and 1990s were largely kind to Southeast Asia. War ceased, ideology subsided, and many national economies grew at incredibly rapid rates. Economic growth rates of between 7 and 10 percent every year were common. Manufacturing finally caught up to urban development, and several countries (Singapore, Thailand, Malaysia,

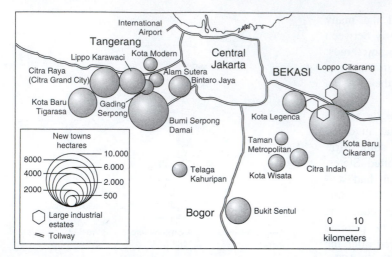

Figure 16.19 As third world cities have mushroomed in size, governments have tried to redistribute some of this population through the creation of "new towns." This map shows the location of new towns within the Jakarta, Indonesia area (see also the box on Egypt's new towns in Chapter 15). (*Source:* Dick and Rimmer, 1998.)

Indonesia, and the Philippines) emerged as major exporting economies. As a result, the cities became more dynamic and prosperous. More and more people came to be considered middle class—perhaps one-third of the total population in several countries. Some planners suggest that the urban pattern should be altered to incorporate certain Westernized elements: gated residential communities, suburban shopping complexes, outlying job opportunities—in short, edge cities. This is a way for newly affluent people to enjoy their wealth and also to escape the continued ills of the poor and the perceived violence of the city. In many cities the rise of large "new towns," which bundle together many of these elements, has become quite visible (Figure 16.19).

WRAPPING UP

Certainly some common attributes are associated with all third world cities. Nevertheless, it would be a mistake to consider only the similarities. To be sure, all third world cities are greatly influenced by less developed economies, substantial urbanization, and the influence of colonialism, but these factors vary by degree. European colonialism affected nearly all third world cities, for example, but each broad region of the world experienced indigenous

urbanization prior to this. The legacy of precolonial cities can be extraordinarily significant, as was true of the South Asian bazaar city, or it can be more of an ancient relic, as is the case with most Latin American cities. The patterns of colonialism are also important. Different European powers attempted to pattern the colonial city after cities in their homeland. There were also very different approaches to how imperial governments handled the indigenous population. Boxes 16.3 and 16.4 give examples of cities that emerged under different conditions.

Cities also differ in regard to culture. In this chapter, we have chosen to categorize cities in their location in broad cultural realms, such as the Southeast Asian city, but, in fact, culture is present at several scales, down to the ethnic characteristics of urban neighborhoods. Great disparities also exist in levels of economic development. Some cities are clearly middle income, even verging on rich. Singapore's per capita income rivals that of the United States. Other cities are desperately poor and are completely overwhelmed by the onrush of people. These social, political, and economic differences generate different urban geographies. There are models of each type of city, and these are useful ways to start thinking about cities, but it is important to remember that each city is a product of a unique set of conditions.

BOX 16.3   THE MIDDLE EASTERN CITY

As discussed in Chapter 2, the first cities in the world appeared in present-day Iraq. This region is part of what we now consider the Middle East, a broad territory extending from Morocco to Iran. From these beginnings, cities diffused throughout the region: into the area that is now northern Iraq, along the Nile River, and throughout the Mediterranean world. Many cities were also founded along the major inland trading routes. But the Middle Eastern city of today owes most of its character to the growth and expansion of Islam during the seventh and eighth centuries.

Islam contributes to what is perhaps the most fundamental aspect of Middle Eastern cities: the blending together at the core of the main mosque and the bazaar. At the very center of the city, the main (or Friday) mosque defines the religious character of the Middle Eastern city and combines many social and spiritual aspects of life (Figure B16.4). Melded in with the mosque is the bazaar, which is both the primary commercial center of the city and the chief public space. The bazaar is composed of numerous stalls located in passages, and it is often covered.

Figure B16.4 Islamic cities contain a central or "Friday" mosque. This scene is from Cairo, Egypt.

It can form a compact nucleus, and it is often linear, snaking from one part of the city to the next.

Janet Abu-Lughod (1987) identifies three themes that help to characterize the Islamic city. One is the relative stability of neighborhoods, which function as truly cohesive communities of socially similar people. There is not a whole lot of population shifting within the city, and many neighborhoods enjoy a long legacy. The neighborhoods have historically functioned as building blocks in the Middle Eastern city, segregating the population on the basis of family groupings, religion, and ethnicity. This segregation was mostly voluntary, although at times it slipped into a means of control as people were compelled to live in certain quarters. These neighborhoods traditionally included dominant, wealthier households and poorer, more subordinate households.

The second theme is gender segregation and the creation of male and female spaces. Urban design was meant to protect visual privacy and included regulations on building heights, window placement, and the layout of houses. These were all intended to shield women from strangers' eyes. Strict gender segregation also has rendered a more clearly defined division among public (male), private (female), and semiprivate spaces. An account recalled by Abu-Lughod (1987) describes a house in Saudi Arabia where there is "a wing for the men, usually on the first floor, with an access to the garden and to the ground floor balconies. . . . The second and third floors belong to the women; one is for daily living and another for receiving guests" (p. 26). The third theme is the relative strength and cohesion of the neighborhood unit. The neighborhood maintains its social integrity even in the face of wider neglect and even chaos. "Neighborhood" in this case becomes a defensible space. The fact is that, although many Middle Eastern cities have a confusing look, they enjoy a tight-knit and logical organization.

BOX 16.4 THE MODERN CHINESE CITY

The modern Chinese city is reflective of all the grandeur of past empires, the oppression of past colonialism, and the dreams of a new socialist reality. Today, cities in China are rapidly entering a new era of global capitalism, with free markets, glass office towers, chic shopping streets, private housing, and social stratification—all balanced against a political regime that is still Communist.

Of course, the Chinese city has a long and illustrious history, some of which we discussed in Chapter 2. However, the nineteenth and early twentieth centuries were not kind to China's economy and to its cities. Although China was never politically colonized, it became an effective economic colony of several European powers, the British foremost among them. Many Chinese cities were forced to provide residences for Europeans, who controlled most aspects of the economy. In many cities, such as Shanghai, the Europeans lived within special Western enclaves that were exempt from Chinese rule. In Beijing, the European influence was much more muted—the city remained the center of government and the home of the emperor—but even there,

hotels, military garrisons, churches, banks, and other Western institutions emerged.

When the Communist Party assumed power in 1949, many Chinese cities were in a state of decay. There was a housing shortage, and most housing that did exist was in a dilapidated condition. Consequently, many people lived in terrible slums. Moreover, cities were filthy, with inadequate sewage facilities, water supplies, and garbage collection. The new communist government dramatically altered the Chinese city. Cities were cleaned up, and the government sought to provide decent housing for everyone. This goal was achieved through the transfer of much of the private housing stock to government ownership and the construction of new housing.

In the process of redeveloping the city, the government also altered the political, social, and economic bases of Chinese cities in several ways. First, all cities were managed from the central government. Second, cities were reoriented toward industrial production, and social areas were reoriented around production sites. The placement of industrial

READINGS

Abu-Lughod, Janet. 1987. "The Islamic City—Historic Myth, Islamic Essence, and Contemporary Relevance," *International Journal of Middle East Studies,* Vol. 19, pp. 155–176.

Bonine, Michael. 1993. "Cities of the Middle East and North Africa." In Stanley Brunn and Jack Williams, eds., *Cities of the World: World Regional Urban Development*, 2nd ed. New York: HarperCollins.

Bose, Nirmal. 1973. "Calcutta: A Premature Metropolis." In *Cities: Their Origins, Growth and Human Impact—Readings from Scientific American*. San Francisco: W. H. Freeman and Company.

Brush, John. 1962. "The Morphology of Indian Cities." In Roy Turner, ed., *India's Urban Future*. Berkeley: University of California Press, pp. 57–70.

Caldeira, Teresa P. R. 2000. *City of Walls: Crime, Segregation, and Citizenship in São Paulo*. Berkeley: University of California Press.

Chakravorty, Sanjoy. 2000. "From Colonial City to Globalizing City? The Far-From-Complete Spatial Transformation of Calcutta." In P. Marcuse and R. van Kempen, eds., *Globalizing Cities: A New Spatial Order?* Oxford, UK: Blackwell Publishers.

De Blij, Harm and Muller, Peter, 2003. *Concepts and Regions in Geography*. New York: John Wiley & Sons.

Dick, H. W., and P. J. Rimmer. 1998. "Beyond the Third World City: The New Urban Geography of South-East Asia," *Urban Studies,* Vol. 35, No. 12, pp. 2303–2321.

Dutt, Ashok. 1993. "Cities of South Asia." In Stanley Brunn and Jack Williams, eds., *Cities of the World: World Regional Urban Development,* 2nd ed. New York: HarperCollins.

sites prefigured the location of new residential areas. Factories and state enterprises developed their own residential communities right next to the workplace, as discussed in Chapter 15. Other functions, such as providing goods and services to the residents, were developed within these workplace units, thus integrating employment, residential, service, and retail functions in one area. Third, with the exception of the Communist Party elite, there was no neighborhood stratification by social class. Because the newly built housing was adjacent to the work units and almost all housing was allocated by the work units, this resulted in a great deal of occupational and social segregation. At the same time, some housing divisions did exist among the different work units and often among the old inner-city areas (often with the worst housing), newer areas inhabited primarily by factory workers, and areas occupied by Communist officials.

More recently, economic reforms have allowed for the quasi-ownership of land, which may now be leased, if not bought outright. The increasing tendency toward a capitalist economy has increased income disparities within Chinese society. Within cities, new social areas have emerged. High-priced commercial market housing has been built in distinct neighborhoods of the city. This housing provides more space and more exclusivity than regular housing (Figure B16.5). It has also led to greater emphasis on consumer goods. Restaurants, health clubs, and dance halls have opened up to accommodate the desires of the newly affluent. These trends are likely to continue as China's economy expands as a whole and as economic disparities among individuals, which are already substantial, deepen.

Figure B16.5 Changes in the Chinese economy and land markets have allowed for the development of affluent residential neighborhoods.

ECLAC. 2000. *Social Panorama of Latin America, 1999–2000*. United Nations Publications.

Esman, Milton. 1986. "The Chinese Diaspora in Southeast Asia." In Gabriel Sheffer, ed., *Modern Diasporas in International Politics*. New York: St. Martin's Press.

Forbes, Dean. 1996. *Asian Metropolis: Urbanisation and the Southeast Asian City*. New York: Oxford University Press.

Griffeth, Robert. 1981. "The Hausa City-States from 1450 to 1804." In R. Griffeth and Thomas, C. eds., *The City-State in Five Cultures*. Santa Barbara, CA: ABC-Clio.

Griffin, Ernst and Larry Ford, 1980. "A Model of Latin American City Structure," *The Geographical Review*, Vol. 70, pp. 397–422.

Hu, Xiuhong, and David Kaplan. 2001. "The Emergence of Affluence in Beijing: Residential Social Stratification in China's Capital City," *Urban Geography*, Vol. 22, No. 1, pp. 54–77.

Kheirabadi, Masoud. 2000. *Iranian Cities: Formation and Development*. Syracuse, NY: Syracuse University Press.

Krishan, Gopal. 1993. "The Slowing Down of Indian Urbanization," *Geography*, Vol. 78, No. 1, pp. 80–84.

Lungo, Mario. 1997. "Costa Rica: Dilemmas of Urbanization in the 1990s." In Alejandro Portes, Carlos Dore-Cabral, and Patricia Landolt, eds., *The Urban Caribbean: Transition to the New Global Economy*. Baltimore: Johns Hopkins University Press.

McGee, T. G. 1967. *The Southeast Asian City*. London: G. Bell and Sons.

Mehretu, Assefa. 1993. "Cities of Sub-Saharan Africa." In Stanley Brunn and Jack Williams, eds., *Cities of the World: World Regional Urban Development,* 2nd ed. New York: HarperCollins.

Mukhopadhyay, Anupa, Ashok Dutt, and Animesh Haldar. 1994. "Sidewalk Dwellers of Calcutta." In A. K. Dutt, ed., *The Asian City: Processes of Development, Characteristics and Planning*. Boston: Kluwer Academic Publishers.

Murphey, Rhoads. 1996. "A History of the City in Monsoon Asia." In J. Gugler, ed., *The Urban Transformation of the Developing World*. Oxford: Oxford University Press.

Neville, Warwick. 1996. "Singapore: Ethnic Diversity in an Interventionist Milieu." In Roseman, Laux, and Thieme, eds., *EthniCity*. Lanham, MD: Rowman & Littlefield.

O'Connor, Anthony M. 1983. *The African City*. New York: Africana Publishing Company.

Oliveira, Orlandina, and Bryan Robert. 1996. "Urban Development and Social Inequality in Latin America." In J. Gugler, ed., *The Urban Transformation of the Developing World*. Oxford: Oxford University Press.

Pan, Lynn. 1994. *Sons of the Yellow Emperor: A History of the Chinese Diaspora*. New York: Kodansha International.

Peil, Margaret. 1991. *Lagos: The City Is the People*. Boston: G. K. Hall.

Portes, Alejandro, Carlos Dore-Cabral, and Patricia Landolt. 1997. *The Urban Caribbean: Transition to the New Global Economy*. Baltimore: Johns Hopkins University Press.

Population Reference Bureau, 2006. *World Population Data Sheet*. Washington D.C.: Population Reference Bureau.

Rakodi, Carole. 1995. *Harare: Inheriting a Settler-Colonial City: Change or Continuity?* New York: John Wiley and Sons.

Ribeiro, Luiz Cesar de Queiroz, and Edward E. Telles. 2000. "Rio de Janeiro: Emerging Dualization in a Historically Unequality." In P. Marcuse and R. van Kempen, eds., *Globalizing Cities: A New Spatial Order?* Oxford, UK: Blackwell Publishers.

Sargent, Charles S. 1993. "The Latin American City." In B. Blouet and O. Blouet, *Latin America and the Caribbean*. New York: Wiley.

Sit, Victor. 1995. *Beijing: The Nature and Planning of a Chinese Capital City*. New York: John Wiley and Sons.

Soja, Edward, and Clyde Weaver. 1976. "Urbanization and Underdevelopment in East Africa." In B. Berry, ed., *Urbanization and Counter-Urbanization*. Beverly Hills, CA: Sage Publications.

Telles, Edward. 1992. "Segregation by Skin Color in Brazil," *American Sociological Review,* Vol. 57, No. 2, pp. 186–197.

Ward, Peter. 1998. *Mexico City*. New York: Wiley.

Western, John. 1996. *Outcast Cape Town*. Berkeley: University of California Press.

World Bank, 2000, *World Development Report, 1999/2000*.

World Bank, 2006. *World Development Indicators*.

Yeung, Henry Wai-Chung. 1999. "The Internationalization of Ethnic Chinese Business Firms from Southeast Asia: Strategies, Processes and Competitive Advantage," *International Journal of Urban and Regional Research,* Vol. 23, No. 1, pp. 103–127.

Yeung, Yue-Man. 1976. "Southeast Asian Cities: Patterns of Growth and Decline." In B. Berry, ed., *Urbanization and Counter-Urbanization*. Beverly Hills, CA: Sage Publications.

INDEX

A

AAG. *See* Association of American Geographers (AAG)

Abie's Irish Rose, 305

Abu-Lughod, Janet, 485

Acropolis, 42

Advanced developing country, 432

Advanced services, 79, 170, 172

Aesthetics, in urban planning, 361–62

Agglomerate, 137

Agglomeration, 146

Agglomeration economies, 170–71
    CBD centrality and, 146–48

Agglomeration linkages
    ancillary linkages, 147
    of CBD, 147–48
    companion linkages, 147–48
    competitive linkages, 147–48
    complementary linkages, 147–48

Agora, 42

Agricultural surplus, 30

Agricultural zoning, 392

Agriculture
    cities and, 28
    seed, 33

Aid to Families with Dependent Children (AFDC), 286

Air conditioning, 161

Air passenger transportation, 68

Albertson's, 112

Albuquerque, New Mexico, 355

Al'Ubaid, 36

Amenities, 82–84, 221
    bundles, 222

American Dream, 245

American Institute of Architects, 252

American Planning Association (APA), 376

Americans with Disabilities Act (ADA), 377

America's New Downtowns (Ford), 155

Ancillary linkages, 147

Angkor Thom, Cambodia, 478

Annexations, 353–56

Anomie, 194

Antipode: A Radical Journal of Geography, 11

Apartheid, in South Africa, 466–67

Archical diffusion, 433

Arterial highways, 161

Asian cities. *See* South Asian cities; Southeast Asian cities

Asian immigration, 320–30
    immigrants, 310
    influences, 328–30
    population, map of, 321
    urban orientation and, 321–23

Asian Indian immigrants, 323–26

Asians, racial residential segregation and, 260–61, 262

Assimilation, 305

Assimilation, zone of, 149–50

Association of American Geographers (AAG), 14

Athens, acropolis in, 42

Atlanta, business/professional service jobs
    employment percentage in, 154
    locational characteristics of, 154

Atlantic Alliance, 71

Autarky, 48

Autodevelopment, 449

Automobiles
    ownership of, 400
    sprawl and, 243, 247–48
    as wireless Internet provider, 140–41

Automobiles/airplane epoch, 72–73

Automobility, 247

B

Baby boomers, 84

Backbone, of networks, 128

Back-office activities, 121

Backward linkages, 169

BANANA (Build Absolutely Nothing Anywhere Near Anything), 223

Bangalore, India, 474–75

Bank of America, 110

Basic *versus* nonbasic activities, economic activities and, 168

Bastide cities, 54–55

Bathtub model, 66, 67

Battery Park City, 206

Batty, Michael, 135

Bazaar city, 470

Bedroom communities, 161

Behavioral urban geography, 11

Berry, Brian, 252

as tourist city, 105
violence in, 365
zoning map, 385
NIMBY (Not In My Back Yard), 223, 380
Nixon, Richard, 286
Nodes, 20
Nonbasic economic activities, 168
North American Free Trade Agreement (NAFTA), 175, 312
Northern China, urban development in, 40

O

Occupational neighborhoods, 39
Office of Management and Budget (OMB), 4
Old wave, of immigrants, 295
Oligopoly, 183
Olmstead, Frederick Law, 367
Open space preservation, 393
Oppositional culture, 284
Orfield, Myron, 345, 347, 349
Organic city, 39, 40
Organic regime, 344
The Other America (Harrington), 285
Outcast ghetto, 272–73, 276
Outsourcing, 166
Overnight information flows
Federal Express, 101–4
Internet and, 128–31
Overstimulation, 191
Overurbanization, 427

P

Paris, France, postwar urban development in, 406–7
Park, Robert, 194
Parkins, Almon, 8
Pavement dwellers, 443, 473
Peak land-value intersection (PLVI), 148, 157
Pedestrian access, 241
Pedestrian sheds, 388
Peer effects, 279–80
Peet, Richard, 12
Penn, William, 337
Periphery, 94, 171, 438
Perishable information, 129
Personal computers, 120–21
Physical geography tradition, 6–7
Planned cities, 39, 40
Planned development districts, 385
Planning. *See* Urban planning
Plater-Zyberk, Elizabeth, 388
Platt, Robert, 9

Plotegy, 110
Pluralist theory, 344
Polarization
metropolitan, 352
processes, 171
social, 204, 275
spatial, 204, 459
Political economy
approaches to, 185–88
basic concepts of, 185–86
circuits of capital, 186–88
Polycentric developments, 148
Polycentrism, 347
Polytheistic religion, 45
Pooled credit, 316
Population
graph, of East Coast cities, 64
New York City, 96
Populist machine, 341
Possibilism, 7
Postmodernism, 13–14, 203–15
The Postmodern Urban Condition (Dear), 13
Postmodern urbanism, 208–10
Postwar institutionalized ghettos, 268–70
Postwar sprawl, 244–48
Potter, Robert, 436
Pounds, Norman, 49
Poverty
city and, 276–84
culture of, 283–84
morality and responsibility and, 283
urban, 276–78
war on, 285–86
Powderhorn Park Neighborhood Association (PPNA), 288
Power, 203
world cities and, 93–100
Prague, Czech Republic, 417
Predatory lending, 232, 233
Pred's model of circular and cumulative causation, 69–70
The Preindustrial City: Past and Present (Sjoberg), 37
Preservation, 401
Presidency cities, 471
Priestly class, 31
Primacy, 430–32
Primary circuits of capital, 186
Primary multipliers, 169
Primate city, 430
Principle of least effort, 75
Producer services, 79
Product cycle model, 182–85
Production, 167–88
built environment for, 187
flexible, 176

CREDITS

Chapter 1

Page 3: Table 1.1 (Source: U.S. Bureau of the Census, 2002.) **Page 7:** Figure 1.5 (Source: Pattison, William, 1964. "The Four Traditions in Geography," *Journal of Geography,* Vol. 63. pp. 211–216.) **Page 8:** Table 1.2 (Source: Complied by J. O. Wheeler.) **Page 9:** Table 1.3 (Source: Complied by J. O. Wheeler.) **Page 11:** Figure 1.6 (Source: Yi-Fu Tuan, 1976. "Humanistic Geography," *Annals of The Association of American Geographers,* Vol. 66, pp. 266–276.) **Page 13:** Table 1.4 (Source: Compiled by J. O. Wheeler.) **Page 15:** Figure B1.1 (Source: Lo, C.P., Yeung, A.K., 2000. *Concepts and Techniques of Geographic Information Systems.* Upper Saddle River, NJ: Prentice Hall.) **Page 17:** Table 1.5 (Source: United Nations, *World Urbanization Prospects*.)

Chapter 2

Page 34: Figure 2.5 (Source: A. J. Rose: Patterns of Cities. Sydney: Thomas Nelson, 1967, p. 21. Based on "The Origin and Evolution of Cities" by Gideon Sjober. Copyright 1965 by Scientific American, Inc. Reprinted with permission. All rights reserved.) **Page 52:** Figure 2.14 (Source: Fritz Rorig, 1967. The Medieval Town. Berkeley: University of California Press.)

Chapter 3

Page 62: Table 3.1 (Source: *Atlas of Early American History: The Revolutionary Era, 1760–1790.*) **Page 63:** Figure 3.1 (Source: U.S. Census of Population.) **Page 64:** Table 3.2 (Source: U.S. Bureau of the Census.) **Page 65:** Figure 3.2 (Source: U.S. Bureau of the Census.); Figure 3.3 (Source: U.S. Bureau of the Census.) **Page 66:** Table 3.3 (Source: U.S. Bureau of the Census.) **Page 67:** Figure 3.4 (Source: Hernie and Plane, 2006, p. 453.) **Page 68:** Table B3.1 (Source: Airports Council International-North America.) **Page 69:** Figure 3.5 (Source: Pred, 1966, p. 25.) **Page 76:** Figure 3.12 (Source: Batten, 1995, p. 319.) **Page 78:** Figure 3.13 (Source: Wyckoff, 1988.) **Page 79:** Table 3.4 (Source: Warf and Wije, 1991, p. 161.) **Pages 80–81:** Tables B3.2–B3.6 (Source: *County and City Extra*, 2006.) **Page 83:** Table B3.7 (Source: Hackworth, 2005, p. 504.) **Page 84:** Table 3.5 (Source: Glaeser, Kolko, and Saiz, 2001.) **Page 85:** Table B3.8 (Source: Warf, 2006, p. 561.)

Chapter 4

Page 90: Table 4.1 (Source: Friedmann, 1986, p. 72.); Figure 4.2 (Source: Friedmann, 1986.) **Page 91:** Table 4.2 (Source: Godfrey and Zhou, 1999, p. 276.) **Page 92:** Figure 4.3 (Source: Godfrey and Zhou, 1999.) **Page 95:** Table 4.3 (Source: Short, 2004, p. 297.); Table 4.4 (Source: Short, 2004, p. 300.) **Page 96:** Table B4.1 (Source: Regina Armstrong, Urbanomics, quoted in *The New York Times,* 2006, February 19, p. 26.) **Page 98:** Table 4.5 (Source: Taylor, Walker, Catalano, and Hoyler, 2001.) **Page 99:** Table 4.6 (Source: Beaverstock et al., 2000, p. 131.) **Page 100:** Figure B4.2 (Source: Beaverstock and Smith, 1996.) **Page 101:** Table B4.2 (Source: Norris, 2006, and U.S. Treasury and Federal Reserve.) **Page 102:** Figure 4.6 (Source: Beaverstock, 2000.); Figure 4.7 (Source: Mitchelson and Wheeler, 1994.) **Page 103:** Table 4.7 (Source: Smith and Timberlake, 2001.) **Page 104:** Table 4.8 (Source: Beaverstock, Smith, and Taylor, 2000.); Figure 4.8 (Source: Mitchelson and Wheeler, 1994, p. 96.) **Page 106:** Figure 4.9 (Source: Johnson, 2003.) **Page 108:** Table 4.9 (Source: *Fortune*, April 17, 2006, p. F-1.) **Page 109:** Table 4.10 (Source: *Fortune*, April 17, 2006, p. F-31.) **Page 110:** Table 4.11 (Source: *Fortune*, April 17, 2006, p. F-25.) **Page 111:** Figure 4.10a-d (Source: Graff and Ashton, 1994); Figure 4.10e,f (Source: Graff, 2002, 2004.) **Page 112:** Figure 4.11 (Source: Graff, 2006, p. 60.) **Page 115:** Table B4.3 (Source: Derudder et al., 2007 p. 84.)

Chapter 5

Page 120: Figure 5.1 (Source: Updated from Lemon, 1996.) **Page 115:** Figure 5.4 (Source: After Ceruzzi, 2000, p. 289.) **Page 127:** Table 5.1 (Source: 2001 TeleGeography, Inc.); Figure 5.7 (Source: Walcott and Wheeler, 2001.) **Page 128:** Table 5.2 (Source: Walcott and Wheeler, 2001.) **Page 129:** Figure 5.8 (Source: Wheeler and Mitchelson, 1989.) **Page 130:** Table 5.3 (Source: Mitchelson and Wheeler, 1994.) **Page 131:** Table 5.4 (Source: Wheeler, 1999.) **Page 133:** Table B5.1 (Source: TeleGeopgraphy, 2006.) **Page 137:** Table 5.5 (Source: Gong and Wheeler, 2002.) **Page 138:** Table 5.6 (Source: Ó hUallacháin and Leslie, 2007, p. 1594.) **Page 139:** Figure 5.9 (Source: *Customer and Business*

Services Locations, Georgia Power, Inc., 1999, and Walcott and Wheeler, 2001.)

Chapter 6
Page 154: Table 6.1 (Source: Calculated by Gong and Wheeler (2002) from U.S. Bureau of Census, 1997.); Table 6.2 (Source: Derived from Gong and Wheeler, 2002.) **Page 158:** Figure 6.10 (Source: Bochert, 1997.) **Page 159:** Figure 6.11 (Source: Erickson, 1983.) **Page 163:** Figure 6.12 (Source: Zeng, et al., 2005, p. 417.)

Chapter 7
Page 173: Table 7.1 (Source: U.S. Bureau of Labor Statistics.); Table 7.2 (Source: Compiled by J. O. Wheeler.) **Page 174:** Figure 7.3 (Source: Wheeler, 1986.) **Page 178:** Table 7.3 (Source: Florida, 2005, p. 54.) **Page 179:** Table B7.1 (Source: Wilson and Wouters, 2003.) **Page 181:** Figure 7.6 (Source: Florida, 2002.); Figure 7.7 (Source: Wheeler and Park, 1981.) **Page 183:** Table B7.2 (Source: Newsome and Comer, 2000, p. 113.) **Page 187:** Figure 7.10 (Source: Harvey, 1983.)

Chapter 8
Page 195: Figure 8.2 (Source: From R. J. Johnston, *Urban Residential Patterns.* London: Bell, 1971, Figure 6.3, p. 253.) **Page 198:** Figure 8.5 (Source: Modified from Ernest W. Burgess, "The Growth of the City: An Introduction to a Research Project," p. 53, in R. Park, E. Burgess, and R. McKenzie, Eds, *The City,* Chicago: University of Chicago Press, 1967/1925, pp. 47–62.) **Page 199:** Figures 8.6–8.7 (Source: Modified from C. D. Harris and E. L. Ullman, "The Nature of Cities," *Annals of the Association of Political and Social Science,* Vol. 242, 1945, pp. 7–17.) **Page 202:** Figure 8.8 (Source: Modified from R. A. Murdie, Factorial Ecology of Metropolitan Toronto, 1951–1961, Research Paper No. 116, Department of Geography, University of Chicago, 1969, p. 8.) **Page 209:** Table 8.1 (Source: Table 6.1 from Knox, 1994, p. 166; lists his sources: After C. Jencks, The Language of Post-Modern Architecture, New York: Rizzoli, 1977; and J. Punter, "Post-Modernism: A Definition," Planning Practice and Research, 4 (1988): 22.) **Page 210:** Figure 8.12 (Source: Modified from M. Dear and S. Flusty, "Postmodern Urbanism," Annals of the Association of American Geographers, Vol. 88, pp. 50–72, Figure 4, p. 66.) **Page 212:** Figure B8.3 (Source: Kwan, Mei-Po, 2002, Fig 1.) **Page 213:** Figure B8.4 (Source: http://geogwww.sbs.ohio-state.edu/faculty/mkwan/Gallery/STPaths.htm.) **Pages 216–217:** Figure B8.5 (Source: Adapted from Brown, M. and Knopp, L., Figure 2, Figure 3, Figure 4, 2006.)

Chapter 9
Page 225: Figure 9.1 (Source: From Short, John R. 1984. *An Introduction to Urban Geography.* London & Boston: Routledge & Kegan Paul, Fig. 7b, p. 128.) **Page 226:** Figure 9.2 (Source: From Johnston, R. J. *Urban Residential Patterns: An Introductory Review,* London: G. Bell (1971), Fig. 3.8, p. 98.) **Page 228:** Figure 9.3 (Source: Adapted from J. Yinger, 1995, Fig. 3.1, p. 32.) **Page 229:** Figure 9.4 (Source: Adapted from Exhibit ES-1, p. iii, Turner, M. A., S. L. Ross, G. C. Galster, and J. Yinger, 2002.) **Page 230:** Table 9.2 (Source: Adapted from Turner et al., 2002.); Table 9.3 (Source: Turner and Ross, 2005, Table 4-1, p. 88.) **Page 233:** Table 9.5 (Source: Immergluck, D. and M. Wiles, 1999, Table 1, p. 8.) **Page 235:** Figure B9.2 (Source: Figure 4 and Figure 5, Immergluck, D. and G. Smith, 2004.) **Page 242:** Figure B9.4 (Source: Figure 1 and Figure 2, Cutsinger, J. and G. Galster, 2006.) **Page 244:** Figure 9.7 (Source: Fig 5.4 in Knox, P., 1994, *Urbanization,* New York: Prentice Hall, [original in T. Baerweld, 1984, "The Geographic Structure of North American Metropolises," paper presented to the 25th International Geographical Congress, Paris.]) **Page 245:** Figure 9.8b (Source: Adapted from http://www.uchs.net/HistoricDistricts/HistDistmap.html.) **Page 248:** Figure 9.10 (Source: Knox, 1994, *Urbanization,* New York: Prentice Hall, Fig. 3.9, p. 49.)

Chapter 10
Page 261: Table 10.1 (Source: Segregation indices calculated by the Mumford Center from U.S. Census data, 1990 and 2000 [http://mumford1.dyndns.org/cen2000/WholePop/WPdownload.html]. Copyright © 2002 by Lewis Mumford Center for Comparative Urban and Regional Research, The University at Albany.) **Page 262:** Tables 10.2–10.3 (Source: Segregation indices calculated by the Mumford Center from U.S. Census data, 1990 and 2000 [http://mumford1.dyndns.org/cen2000/WholePop/WPdownload.html]. Copyright © 2002 by Lewis Mumford Center for Comparative Urban and Regional Research, The University at Albany.) **Page 263:** Figure 10.1 (Source: Modified from: Glaeser and Vigdor, 2001, "Racial Segregation in the 2000 Census: Promising News," Center on Urban and Metropolitan Policy, The Brookings Institution, Washington, D.C.) **Page 264:** Table 10.4 (Source: Massey and Denton, 1989, 1993; Denton, 1994; Wilkes and Iceland, 2004.) **Page 266:** Table 10.5 (Source: Philpott, 1991, Table 5.1, p. 117.) **Page 269:** Figure 10.4 (Source: From Hirsch, 1983, Maps 1–3, pp. 6–8.) **Page 271:** Figure 10.5 (Source: From Jackson 1985 *Crabgrass Frontier: The Suburbanization of the United States,*

New York and Oxford: Oxford University Press, Figure 11.1 as modified in Kaplan and Holloway, 1998.) **Page 278:** Figure 10.7 (Source: Adapted from Mulherin, 2000, Fig. 2 and Fig. 4.) **Page 279:** Figure 10.8 (Source: Adapted from Jargowsky, 2003, Fig. 1.) **Page 282:** Table 10.9 (Source: Rosenbaum and Popkin, 1991, Table I, p. 348; Rosenbaum, 1995, Table 3, p. 237.) **Page 289:** Table B10.2 (Source: Elwood, 2002, Table 1.)

Chapter 11

Page 299: Figure 11.2 (Source: From Ward, 1971, p. 78.) **Page 301:** Figure 11.4 (Source: Oscar Hadlin, 1941/1976, Boston's Immigrants: New York Atheneum, 90.) **Page 302:** Figure 11.5 (Source: Distributions of ethnic groups, U.S. Census Bureau.) **Page 304:** Table 11.1 (Source: Lieberson, 1963.) **Page 306:** Figure 11.6 (Source: Philip Martin and Elizabeth Midgley, 1994. "Immigration to the United States: Journey to an Uncertain Destination," Population Reference Bureau Population Bulletin, Vol. 49, No. 2.) **Page 308:** Figure B11.2 (Source: From Statistics, Canada.) **Page 310:** Figure 11.8 (Source: Riche, 2000.) **Page 311:** Figure 11.9 (Source: Mapping Census, 2000.) **Page 312:** Figure 11.10 (Source: Census 2000, Brief.) **Page 315:** Figure 11.12 (Source: Courtesy of Tom Boswell, 2006.) **Page 318:** Figure B11.4 (Source: Kaplan, 1997.) **Page 319:** Figure 11.13 (Source: Map made by José Díaz-Garayúa.) **Page 320:** Table 11.2 (Source: U.S. Census Bureau, 2002.) **Page 321:** Figure 11.14 (Source: Mapping Census, 2000.) **Page 322:** Table 11.3 (Source: Pollard and O'Hare, 1999, pp. 33, 36.) **Page 323:** Table 11.4 (Source: Census 2000, Summary File 4.) **Page 325:** Figure B11.6 (Source: Adams and Ghose, 2003.) **Page 326:** Figure 11.15 (Source: Airriess and Clawson, 2000. "Mainland Southeast Asian Refugees," in J. McKee, Ed., *Ethnicity in Contemporary America: A Geographical Appraisal.* Lanham, MD: Rowman & Littlefield Publishers.) **Page 328:** Figure 11.16 (Source: Courtesy of Chris Airriess.) **Page 330:** Figure 11.18 (Source: Lee, Dong Ok., 1995. "Koreatown and Korean Small Firms in Los Angeles: Locating in the Ethnic Neighborhoods," Professional Geographer, Vol. 47, No. 2, pp. 184–195.)

Chapter 12

Page 343: Figure 12.3 (Source: Short, 1996.) **Page 346:** Table 12.1 (Source: U.S. Census Bureau, "Census of Governments, Government Organization," series GC(1)-1 (http://www.census.gov/prod/www/abs/govern.html). **Page 351:** Figure 12.7 (Source: Orfield, 1997.) **Page 354:** Table 12.2 (Source: Rusk, David, 1993. Cities without Suburbs. Washington, DC: Woodrow Wilson

Press.) **Page 357:** Figure B12.4 (Source: Germain & Rose, 2000.)

Chapter 13

Page 365: Figure 13.3 (Source: Wright, 1981.) **Page 366:** Figure 13.4 (Source: Sutcliffe, 1981.) **Page 367:** Figure 13.5 (Source: Kostof, 1991.) **Page 369:** Figure 13.6 (Source: Levy, 2000.) **Page 372:** Figure 13.8 (Source: Gallion and Eisner, 1983.) **Page 385:** Figure 13.11 (Source: Barnet and Hack, 2000.) **Page 389:** Figure 13.13 (Source: Levy, 2000.)

Chapter 14

Page 396: Table 14.1 (Source: Pounds, 1990.) **Page 399:** Table 14.2 (Source: World Resources 1998–99: A Guide to the Global Environment. New York: Oxford University Press.) **Page 400:** Table 14.3 (Source: www.CNNMoney.com; Associates for International Research, Inc.); Table 14.4 (Source: World Resources 1998–99: A Guide to the Global Environment. New York: Oxford University Press.) **Page 403:** Figure B14.1 (Source: Cervero, 1995.) **Page 405:** Figure 14.3 (Source: Kostof, 1991.) **Page 406:** Figure B14.2 (Source: Agnew, 1995.) **Page 408:** Figure 14.4 (Source: Lichtenberger, 1993.) **Page 409:** Figure 14.6 (Source: Long, 1991.) **Page 413:** Table 14.5 (Source: World Development Indicators 2001, http://www1.oecd.org/publications/e-book/8101131E.PDF.) **Page 415:** Figure 14.10 (Source: Bater, 1984.) **Page 419:** Figure 14.11 (Source: Karan, 1997.)

Chapter 15

Page 427: Figure 15.2 (Source: Porter, Sheppard, 1998.) **Page 428:** Figure 15.3 (Source: Kasarda, John, and Allan Parnell, Ed., 1993. *Third World Cities: Problems, Policies, and Prospects.* Newbury Park, CA: Sage Publications.) **Page 430:** Table 15.1 (Source: Findley, S. 1993. "The Third World City," in J. Kasarda and A. Parnell, Eds., *Third World Cities: Problems, Policies, and Prospects.* Newbury Park, CA: Sage Publications.) **Page 434:** Figure 15.4 (Source: From Potter, 1990.) **Page 434:** Figure 15.5 (Source: Potter, 1999.) **Page 437:** Figure 15.6 (Source: Vance, 1970.); Figure 15.7 (Source: Potter, 1985.) **Page 442:** Table 15.2 (Source: World Resources 1998–1999: *A Guide to the Global Environment.* New York: Oxford Univ. Press.) **Page 446:** Figure B15.1 (Source: Stewart, 1996.) **Page 450:** Figure 15.13 (Source: Ribeiro and Telles, 2000.) **Page 451:** Table 15.3 (Source: Derived in part from Potter and Evans, 1998, p. 173.) **Page 452:**

Table 15.4 (Source: World Resources 1998–1999: A Guide to the Global Environment. New York: Oxford University Press.)

Chapter 16
Page 458: Figure 16.1 (Source: Sargent, 1993.) **Page 459:** Figure 16.2 (Source: From Sargent data.) **Page 460:** Figure 16.3 (Source: Lungo, 1997.) **Page 461:** Figure 16.4 (Source: Sargent, C. S. 1993. "The Latin American City," in B. Blouet and O. Blouet, *Latin America and the Caribbean.* New York: Wiley.) **Page 462:** Figure 16.5 (Source: Riberio & Telles, 2000.); Figure 16.6 (Source: Griffin and Ford, 1993.) **Page 464:** Figure 16.7 (Source: Mehretu, 1993.) **Page 465:** Figure 16.8 (Source: Griffeth, 1981.) **Page 467:** Figure B16.2 (Source: Western, 1996.) **Page 468:** Figure 16.9 (Source: Mehretu, 1993.) **Page 470:** Figure 16.10 (Source: Dutt, 1993.); Figure 16.11 (Source: Dutt, 1993.) **Page 471:** Figure 16.12 (Source: Dutt, 1993.) **Page 473:** Figure 16.13 (Source: Kostof, 1991.) **Page 476:** Figure 16.14 (Source: Kaplan and Holloway, 1998.) **Page 478:** Figure 16.15 (Source: McGee, 1967.) **Page 479:** Figure 16.16 (Source: Forbes, 1996.) **Page 481:** Figure 16.17 (Source: Adapted from de Blij, H. J. and Muller, P., 2004. *Geography: Realms, Regions, and Concepts,* 11th edition, Hoboken: John Wiley & Sons, Inc. p. 496.) **Page 483:** Figure 16.18 (Source: McGee, 1967.) **Page 484:** Figure 16.19 (Source: Dick & Rimmer, 1998.)

PHOTO CREDITS

Chapter 13
Page 362: Figure 13.1, Mark Segal/Index Stock. *Page 363:* Figure 13.2, Rue des Archives/The Granger Collection, New York. *Page 370:* Figure 13.7, Courtesy Charles W. Steger. *Page 374:* Figure B13.1, James Marshall/The Image Works. *Page 375:* Figure B13.2, Louis Schwartzberg/Getty Images. *Page 383:* Figure B13.4, Da-Wei Liou, GISP, Delaware County Regional Planning Commission. *Page 386:* Figure 13.12, Alex Maclean /Landslides. *Page 390:* Figure 13.14, Robert Harding World Imagery/Alamy Images. *Page 391:* Figure 13.15, Payne Anderson/Index Stock.

Chapter 14
Page 402: Figure 14.2, Courtesy Dave Kaplan. *Page 407:* Figure B14.3, Gavin Hellier/Stone/Getty Images. *Page 408:* Figure 14.5, Courtesy Dave Kaplan. *Page 410:* Figure 14.8, Courtesy Dave Kaplan. *Page 411:* Figure 14.9, Courtesy Glattpark Opfikon. *Page 417:* Figure B14.4, Anthony Cassidy/Stone/Getty Images.

Page 420: Figure 14.12, Underwood & Underwood/Corbis Images. *Page 421:* Figure B14.5, AP Photo/Tsugufumi Matsumoto.

Chapter 15
Page 438: Figure 15.8, Jeremy Horner/Corbis Images. *Page 444:* Figure 15.10, (a) Payne Anderson/The Image Works; (b) ©AP/Wide World Photos; (c) ©AP/Wide World Photos; (d) Robb Kendrick/Aurora Photos. *Page 445:* Figure 15.11, Mark Antman/The Image Works. *Page 448:* Figure 15.12, Edy Purnomo/The Image Works.

Chapter 16
Page 466: Figure B16.1, Getty Images News and Sports Services. *Page 475:* Figure B16.3, Courtesy Rajrani Kalra, Department of Geography, University of Central Arkansas. *Page 485:* Figure B16.4, Christine Osbourne/Worldwide Picture Library/Alamy Images. *Page 487:* Figure B16.5, Courtesy Dave Kaplan.